THE PAPERS OF

WOODROW WILSON

VOLUME 2

1881-1884

SPONSORED BY THE WOODROW WILSON
FOUNDATION
AND PRINCETON UNIVERSITY

THE PAPERS OF

WOODROW WILSON

ARTHUR S. LINK, *EDITOR*

JOHN WELLS DAVIDSON AND DAVID W. HIRST
ASSOCIATE EDITORS

T. H. VAIL MOTTER, *CONSULTING EDITOR*

JOHN E. LITTLE, *ASSISTANT EDITOR*

Volume 2 · 1881-1884

PRINCETON, NEW JERSEY
PRINCETON UNIVERSITY PRESS
1967

INTRODUCTION

THE documents in this volume begin at January 1, 1881, and end at January 31, 1884. They span the period between Woodrow Wilson's withdrawal from the University of Virginia Law School and the completion of his first semester at The Johns Hopkins University. Thanks chiefly to the recovery of the main body of the Wilson Papers for the early period of his life, these materials shed much new light on an interval in Wilson's life heretofore generally obscure. The letters in this volume reveal, to an astonishing degree, the details of Wilson's personal life and development between 1881 and 1884: his love affair with his cousin, Hattie Woodrow, his continuing relationships with members of his family and with Princeton classmates, his life in Atlanta while trying to lay the foundations of a legal practice, his decision to abandon the practice of law for a career in teaching, his courtship of Ellen Louise Axson, and the first stage of his career as a graduate student at the Johns Hopkins. The articles, essays, letters to editors, and other writings now printed also reveal that, intellectually speaking, this was no fallow period for Wilson. These writings show a young man intensely interested in current national politics and in the reconstruction of his native South. They show Wilson also still preoccupied, indeed obsessed, with the problem of effective leadership in the American political system.

The editors have described their methods, guide lines, and objectives in the Introduction to the first volume in this series. There have been few editorial innovations in this second volume. The editors have once again reproduced, insofar as possible, the original text of the documentary record, emending it in square brackets only when absolutely necessary for clarity and changing it silently only to the extent of eliminating obfuscating dashes and, in a few cases, substituting normal punctuation for dashes.

In preparing notes for this volume, the editors have once again been guided by the conviction that they do their job best when they ordinarily follow the rule of editorial reason and restraint. The reader should understand clearly that the editors have made it a rule to re-identify persons, places, subjects, and events in this volume only when the allusion to them is so obscure that the reader cannot easily locate them in the index. For further information on re-identification the reader is referred to the note which precedes the index.

The editors take this opportunity to say a special word about the correspondence between Wilson and Ellen Axson, which begins in this volume. The main body of these letters was for a time in the Wilson Papers when they were in the keeping of Ray Stannard Baker. He printed extracts from them in the first three volumes of his *Woodrow Wilson: Life and Letters*. Mrs. Wilson turned this group over to Eleanor Wilson McAdoo. Mrs. McAdoo later published parts of this correspondence in *The Priceless Gift: The Love Letters of Woodrow Wilson and Ellen Axson Wilson*. She gave most of the letters in her possession to the Princeton University Library in 1962. In addition, about three hundred letters between Woodrow and Ellen were in the body of papers discovered in the Wilson house in Washington in 1963. The editors have been given access to the letters which Mrs. McAdoo retained in her possession when she sent the main body to Princeton. Hence the editors have seen all letters between Woodrow and Ellen known to be extant.

Concerning the period covered by this volume, only a letter from Woodrow to Ellen of September 9, 1883, and a letter or telegram from Ellen to Woodrow of about January 20, 1884, seem to be missing. Fortunately, Wilson wrote and saved a shorthand draft of his letter of September 9, 1883, and a transcript of it is printed herein. Thus, with the exception of Ellen's telegram or letter of about January 20, 1884, the series would seem to be complete through January 31, 1884.

Wilson's letters to his fiancée and wife are among the most important and revealing that he ever wrote. Ellen's letters to Woodrow are equally important, because without them it is not possible to understand his letters, or to know her and the relationship between them. And this is to say nothing about the literary quality and general interest of this correspondence.

Some letters in future volumes are intimate and fully revealing about various aspects of Woodrow's and Ellen's lives. They held nothing back from each other. The editors believe that they would be guilty of grave dereliction of their responsibility if they used their private judgment in deciding what letters to print and what not to print. Hence they will print all of them.

In printing this correspondence, the editors have exercised restraint in identifying the quotations which poured from the pens of the two correspondents. Many, copied from birthday books, calendars, greeting cards, and newspapers, lack significance or a quality that would justify the labor of running them down.

In accordance with their practice regarding documents, the editors have tried to reproduce Woodrow's and Ellen's letters exactly as they were written, using the editorial *sic* and bracketed emendations only when necessary for clarity. However, Ellen's letters present extraordinary problems. She had a tendency to splash a good deal of ink on her papers. Often she edited her letters before mailing them, going back and adding dashes and punctuation, without deleting the punctuation marks that she meant to change. Therefore, the editors have felt obliged to make more silent changes in her letters than they have made in other documents. These consist merely of the elimination of excessive punctuation, the capitalization of words that Ellen obviously meant to be read as capitalized, the substitution of periods for dashes and semicolons when she obviously ended a sentence, etc. Wherever possible, Ellen's text has been reproduced exactly as she wrote it, and silent changes have been made only when absolutely necessary for clarity and at least a minimum ease of reading.

Supplementing what they have already said in the Introduction to Volume 1, the editors take great pleasure in thanking the members of the Editorial Advisory Committee of *The Papers of Woodrow Wilson*, whose names are listed on the inside of the halftitle of this volume, for help in planning this volume; Jean MacLachlan, for editorial assistance; Henry W. Bragdon, for reading the manuscript and making valuable suggestions; Marjorie Putney of Princeton University Press, for patient copyediting; and Mary Krueger, Carole Alsup, Toby Tuckman, and Carol Danks for typing documents and manuscripts.

THE EDITORS

Princeton, New Jersey
September 23, 1966

CONTENTS

CONTENTS xiii

ILLUSTRATIONS

Following page 300

ABBREVIATIONS

ALI	autograph letter(s) initialed
ALS	autograph letter(s) signed
APS	autograph postal(s) signed
att.	attached
D	document
enc.	enclosure, enclosed
env.	envelope
hw	handwritten, handwriting
ELA	Ellen Louise Axson
I	initialed
JRW	Joseph Ruggles Wilson
JWW	Janet Woodrow Wilson
L	letter
P	postal
S	signed
sh	shorthand
shL(S)	shorthand letter(s) (signed)
shP(S)	shorthand postal(s) (signed)
T	typed
WW	Woodrow Wilson
WWhw(S)	Woodrow Wilson handwritten or handwriting (signed)
WWhwL(S)	Woodrow Wilson handwritten letter(s) (signed)
WWsh	Woodrow Wilson shorthand
WWshL(S)	Woodrow Wilson shorthand letter(s) (signed)
WWTD(S)	Woodrow Wilson typed document (signed)
WWTL(S)	Woodrow Wilson typed letter (signed)

ABBREVIATIONS FOR COLLECTIONS
AND LIBRARIES

(Following the National Union Catalogue of the Library of Congress)

DLC	Library of Congress
DNA	National Archives
MdBJ	Library of The Johns Hopkins University
Meyer Coll., DLC	Meyer Collection, Library of Congress
MHi	Massachusetts Historical Society
NjP	Princeton University Library
NNPM	Pierpont Morgan Library, New York
RSB Coll., DLC	Ray Stannard Baker Collection of Wilsoniana, Library of Congress
RSB Papers	Ray Stannard Baker Papers, Princeton University Library
ViU	University of Virginia Library
WC, NjP	Woodrow Wilson Collection, Princeton University Library
WP, DLC	Woodrow Wilson Papers, Library of Congress

[blank]	blanks in the text
[- - - -]	undecipherable words in text, each dash representing one word
[* *]	undecipherable shorthand, each asterisk representing one shorthand outline
[ ]	word or words in original text which Wilson omitted in copying
⟨ ⟩	matter deleted from manuscript by Wilson and restored by editors
[Sept. 8, 1879]	publication date of a published writing; also date of a document supplied by editors when the date is not part of the text
[*Sept. 8, 1879*]	latest composition date of a published writing
[[Sept. 8, 1879]]	delivery date of a speech if publication date differs

THE PAPERS OF

WOODROW WILSON

VOLUME 2

1881-1884

THE PAPERS OF
WOODROW WILSON

Scrapbook

[c. Jan. 1, 1881-c. March 1, 1883]

Inscribed (WWhw) on cover:
"T. Woodrow Wilson 1881"

Contents of Scrap Book

(WP, DLC). A scrapbook of tearsheets and clippings from British and American newspapers and periodicals. WWhw table of contents, printed above, is on loose pages preceding WW's page 9. This scrapbook also includes seven loose pages of WWsh and WWhw notes taken in Professor L. H. Atwater's course on the history of civilization, spring term, 1879.

Private Notebook

[c. Jan. 1, 1881-1884]

Inscribed on front and flyleaf (WWhw):

"Private. Miscellaneous Memoranda etc, and Congressional Government" and "Woodrow Wilson, 1881"

Contents:

(a) "Prolegomena" (WWhw), printed below.

(b) WWhw memorandum on extract from editorial in the New York *Nation*, printed below.

(c) WW's poems, "A River's Course" and "A Song" (WWhw), printed at Dec. 1, 1881, and Dec. 8, 1881.

(d) Notes on "Political Principles" (WWhw).

(e) "Congressional Government Notes" (WWhw).

(f) Extract about Pliny the Younger from a magazine.

Bound notebook (WP, DLC).

Statement of Intention

[c. Jan. 1, 1881]
Prolegomena.

In order to a clear classification of my productions and possessions in the book kind, I would like to give a name to this volume which I now begin to fill; but, truth to say, I know not what name to give it. I intend to scribble in it, from day to day, thoughts and phantasies, compositions grave and gay, scraps of verse and sententious bits of prose, matters autobiographical, facts and observations concerning every variety of topic, anything and everything which may occupy my mind at the moment of writing. I am to manufacture for my own amusement and edification (?) a sort of private periodical literature. This is to be a kind of miscellaneous magazine which will admit to its pages anything which will divert the public to which it is addressed—myself.

WWhw memorandum in private notebook described at Jan. 1, 1881. A glance at the editorial description of the contents of this notebook will reveal that WW did not persevere long in his intention to keep this kind of private record.

A Memorandum

[c. Jan. 1, 1881]
Lord Beaconsfield:—"Lord Beaconsfield will doubtless never hold office again; and considering the stir he has made and the airs of political authority he has assumed, there is something really marvellous in the fact that, though he has been over forty years in public life, he had only held office for six years, at different periods, and had acquired no distinction whatever, except as a novelist and epigrammatic debater, when in 1876 he undertook to regulate the affairs of Europe and redistribute the sovereignty in the British government. His failure in the last stage of his enterprize has been so complete and has taken him so suddenly, that it will probably make the earlier stage seem more absurd, and even ridiculous, than it really was. It would be unfair to throw on him alone the responsibility of his strange, eventful history. He could not have cut the figure he did if the conditions of his success had not existed in Tory society and manners. If Tory culture had not prepared the party for the leadership of a charlatan, a charlatan would never have led it. And whenever the story of Lord Beaconsfield's hold on the Tory imagination is told for a reproach, it must also be told for a still greater reproach that during the period when they were helping this theatrical chief to amuse himself by arranging the great powers of the British Em-

pire in tableaux, the Englishman whose genius had made the most beneficent and striking contributions of the last fifty years to the statute-book, and whose speeches alone (?) maintained the great traditions of English oratory, was the main object of their ridicule and vituperation. There is one feature of the election which may almost be called pathetic. The area of the globe over which the result was looked for with eager anxiety was, of course, very great, and illustrates strikingly the vastness of the Empire. But what gives a touch of splendor to the Liberal victory is that whole races in the East have seen it as a great light. To every Christian still groaning under Turkish rule it means speedy help and deliverance. To the Christians lately emancipated and to the Greeks it means the consolidation and maintenance of their freedom and independence. To the Hindoos it means government for their own sakes and not for the gratification of foreign pride. For the Afghans it means a cessation of pillage and slaughter in aid of a "scientific frontier." To the Turk it means that he must be clean and honest and industrious or die. These things must sweeten their triumph to the English Liberals, and would make it precious even if they did not know that it had probably put an end to the last effort that will ever be made on English soil to set up personal government and restore the mystery of statecraft"– These sentences, which appeared in the New York *Nation* in the latter part of the year 1880–just after the English general election of that year–express with great feeling, though not with uniform elegance, my sentiments concerning Disraeli and my sympathy with the great Liberal party of England. I take exception to the editor at only one point. So long as Jno. Bright lives it cannot be said that Mr. Gladstone *alone* maintains the best traditions of English oratory.

WWhw memorandum, Item (b), in private notebook described at Jan. 1, 1881. The extract was from "The British Elections," New York *Nation*, xxx (April 8, 1880), 264.

Marginal Notes

Thomas Humphry Ward, ed., *The English Poets* (4 vols., London and New York, 1880).

Transcripts of WW Shorthand Comments

Vol. IV, 73:
　[From Wordsworth's "Defile of Gondo"]
Tumult and peace, the darkness
　　and the light–
Were all like workings of one
　　mind, the features

[c. Jan. 1, 1881]

Blossoms! *Such* features are like anything rather than like blossoms

Of the same face, blossoms upon
    one tree;
Characters of the great Apocalypse,
The types and symbols of Eternity,
Of first, and last, and midst, and
    without end.

of any tree the mind can easily conceive of.

John R. Green, *History of the English People* (4 vols., New York, 1878-80).

Vol. IV, 60:

It was common for a King to choose or dismiss a single Minister without any communication with the rest; and so far was even William from aiming at ministerial unity that he had striven to reproduce in the Cabinet itself the balance of parties which prevailed outside it. Sunderland's plan aimed at replacing these independent Ministers by a homogeneous Ministry, chosen from the same party, representing the same sentiments, and bound together for common action by a sense of responsibility and loyalty to the party to which it belonged.

A parallel instance furnished by Washington—a man not altogether unlike William.

Mark Pattison, *Milton* (New York, 1880).
Pp. 51-52:

The Puritan had thrown off chivalry as being parcel of Catholicism, and had replaced it by the Hebrew ideal of the subjection and seclusion of woman. Milton, in whose mind the rigidity of Puritan doctrine was now contending with the freer spirit of culture and romance, shows on the present occasion a like conflict of doctrine with sentiment. While he adopts the Oriental hypothesis of woman for the sake of man, he modifies it by laying more stress upon mutual affection, the charities of home, and the intercommunion of intellectual and moral life, than upon that ministration of woman to the appetite and comforts of man which makes up the whole of her functions in the Puritan apprehension.

What ridiculous slanders!

Leslie Stephen, *Alexander Pope* (New York, 1880).
Pp. 37-38:

The worker in moral aphorisms cannot forget himself even in the full swing of his fervid declamation. I have no doubt that Pope so far exemplified his

This is my impression of all Pope's poetry.

own doctrine that he truly felt whilst he was writing. . . . But it is simply that Pope always resembles an orator whose gestures are studied, and who thinks, while he is speaking, of the fall of his robes and the attitude of his hands. He is throughout academical; and though knowing with admirable nicety how grief should be represented, and what have been the expedients of his best predecessors, he misses the one essential touch of spontaneous impulse.

To Robert Bridges

Dear Bobby,   Wilmington, North Car. Jan 1st 1881

Your letter enclosing the photograph of your "latest annex" has just come to hand. They are good, both of them. The mustache is stronger, altogether more athletic, than were those siders with which you became so enraptured before we left old '79, those that sought so eagerly to skirt your ears; in fact, it compares not unfavorably with my tart side whiskers—for you know I began to cultivate a side crop of some promise before I was introduced to the Law. You would be astonished to see how vigorous they are. I must have them "*taken*" upon the very earliest opportunity.

Well, you see, I'm actually *at home*. I withdrew from the University about a week ago *on account of ill health*. There's nothing serious the matter with me. I just contracted a very severe cold in Virginia which stuck to me and harassed me for almost a month and left me, in the midst of an examination season, unfit for study and unable to afford any loss of time. So, with father's advice, I came home to recuperate. I will not return, but will prosecute my studies here for the rest of the Winter, when I will settle upon a place to practice and plunge immediately into business. I will be able to study very satisfactorily alone, I am quite sure; for I have had enough guidance from skilled and competent guides to set me fairly in the right track and to acquaint me sufficiently with the landmarks of the subject to enable me to travel confidently and explore safely alone.

It was not easy for me to leave the University. Much as it lacks of the charm of old Princeton, it's a fine place. The absence of *class* bonds is partially compensated for by the bonds with which the fraternities bind the fellows together in very intimate & very delightful companionship. Then, too, in leaving the University, I am turning my back on *college life*, which, after all, is the very happiest a man can hope to lead. I shall miss the exercises of the literary societies about as much as anything else. I've fallen fairly in love with speech-making—which *is* a real luxury after one struggles to the *lead* (as I had managed to do, thanks to old Whig's training) of a body of men and begins to realize that he can gain a hearing when others might find difficulty in doing so, and can, by an effort, change a vote while others fail to command their hearers' sympathies. I spoke a great deal at the University and improved very much on my stilted Whig style, I have reason to hope. I know that you will understand the free manner in which I speak of my own accomplishments, Bobby, and that you will not mistake candid confidence for *brag.* I talk to you now just as I used to talk to you in E. W.[1] and on the triangle—just as I would talk to myself. I think that an orator *is* made, in great part, and if there be in me any stuff worth the working, I intend to make as much of an orator out of myself as indefatigable labor can bring out of the materials at hand.

You speak of making a change for something more congenial. What do you mean? In what direction? Will it be a change to some other kind of newspaper work, or will it be an entire change to another employment? Of course I think that you are fitted for something much higher than local work on a daily newspaper whose issues are destroyed and forgotten almost as soon as they are read; and surely the abundant success you have had in reporting would give you reason to hope for very rapid promotion in editorial rank. But then, Bobby, you have not let me entirely into your confidence as to the direction in which you would wish promotion. I know that you want to lead a literary life—and I know that work will bring you all success in such a life; but I want you to let me into your secret hopes, old fellow, as I let you into mine. My path is a very plain one—and the only question is whether I will have the strength to breast the hill and reach the heights to which it leads. My *end* is a commanding influence in the councils (and counsels) of my country—and *means* to be employed are writing and speaking. Hence my desire to perfect myself in both. But as to *your* end and the means? You know that I have already said that I thought that the training of such work as you have now been doing for about a year would be invaluable to you as long as you continued to use it as a means, as long, that is, as you kept yourself above it. But whither, Bobby? To what work next? I ought to understand your aims, and I do, I think. But the means? Reporting is an enemy alike to deliberate thought and to deliberate composition, both of which are essential to such success as I expect for you.

As for the "Christmas-Eve Sketch," I like it very much. You say that I must not criticize its *diction*. Well it is just its diction that I think is least open to criticism. It is simple, direct, and vigorous; and vigor, simplicity, and straightforwardness are, in my opinion, three of the most conspicuous characteristics of a good style. Of course the big-type, *semi-headings*, like all other sensational mechanical tricks, mar a piece of that character by taking away from the air of sincerity which pervades the piece and leaving the impression that it was written merely to catch the eyes of the sentimental. But, aside from the inevitable features of a newspaper column, the fault of the sketch is only *one*, as far as *I* can see—and that one is attributable, no doubt, to the hasty manner of its composition: it is a little *obscure*. That it is so you have yourself, in effect, confessed by telling formally the secret of the spirit in the belfry; thus allowing that the reader could not readily gather it from what had gone before.

I wish that you would send me your newspaper productions more frequently. I always enjoy them—though they always make me *anxious*. For I regard them with as affectionate care as if I had written them myself—am as solicitous of their success as if my own reputation depended upon them. Bobby, I think that we have every reason to be thankful for our friendship for each other. We are bound up in each others welfare, and if we only continue true to ourselves, we need never fear that we will be untrue to one another.

My sickness has thrown me back in my correspondence and I am, consequently, entirely without news of the rest of the boys. Have you heard any particulars of the dinner beyond what the *Princetonian* gave? What would I not have given to have been able to attend!

But I must cut this rambling epistle off right here and say goodnight, old fellow. Next week will see me at work again—when my books arrive from the University.

With all the old love, Your sincere friend,   T. Woodrow Wilson

ALS (Meyer Coll., DLC).
¹ A reference to Bridges' room, 9 East Witherspoon Hall, at Princeton.

From Harold Godwin

My dear Tommy: [New York] Jan 14th 1881.

I received your letter a short time ago. Needless to say I was surprised at hearing of your sudden departure from the Va. U. under such circumstances as you mention, and yet, if you have gathered all you wish there I certainly cannot see why you should have returned anyway. I infer from your letter that your illness has passed, and I am heartily glad of it. . . . So you are going to practice. I am sure it will not take you so long to get your hand well in—but let me know where you shall go. Bridges wrote me this morning that you thought of some northern city.[1] They are I believe more active than are those in the South but whether as Bob says your advantages would be as quickly gained as at your home I should imagine would cause you some hesitancy. . . . I must tell you a piece of good news—viz: we have purchased a controlling interest in the E[vening] Post and hope to change the policy of the paper which has of late been in the hands of a young Yale moralist of very limited capacities as a writer, and still smaller abilities as a man of thought or of the age. . . .[2] I have also wished to ask you for some contributions. We make this new move that everything which goes into the newspaper is worth being paid for. You hold very much my fathers views in politics and sympathize I do not doubt with our traditional free trade policy[.] Any communications from the south, any upon commercial topics showing prosperity or depression in those states, any in fact of social commercial or political interest are especially valuable at this time. If therefore anything comes in your way or enters your head it can do you no harm to send it and will confer a personal favor upon me. Do write me when you get a chance and I shall always find time to answer.

Ever H. G.

ALI (WP, DLC). WWhw notation on env.: "Ans 1/31/81." Also on env.: hw query by Godwin: "Have you a piece of poetry by H. G. pub. in Princetonian in 187[7] or 1878 called 'Funny Folks' should like copy[.] H."
    [1] See WW to R. Bridges, Sept. 18, 1880, Vol. I.
    [2] Godwin's father, Parke Godwin, had apparently purchased enough additional stock from the estate of his father-in-law, William Cullen Bryant, to give himself undisputed control over editorial policies of the New York *Evening Post*. Heretofore, Godwin had been in frequent conflict with the business manager, Isaac Henderson, who was half owner of the paper but who was in debt to both the Bryant family and Godwin. Godwin's control was of short duration, for as the note at Aug. 9, 1881, indicates, he, together with other parties, sold the *Evening Post* to Henry Villard in May 1881. The "young Yale moralist" was Watson R. Sperry, managing editor and son-in-law of Henderson.

To Harriet Augusta Woodrow

Dearest Hattie,   Wilmington, North Carolina, Jan. 15th 1881
    Your letter was a genuine treat. I was fairly hungry for a letter from you, after having had to wait so long for one. Of course I understood your silence perfectly; but still understanding it did not prevent my being very eager to hear from you and to know

all about your vacation doings. That invitation puzzled me considerably. I remembered who Miss Nellie Thomas was; but I did not know that you were visiting in Springfield [Ohio]. If it had not been for the form of the invitation, I would have concluded that Miss Thomas was visiting you. All of your letter was news to me, except the single fact that you had been to the wedding in Cincinnati and had received the slice of the bride's cake containing the ring, whose receipt was of such important meaning. The latter fact I was told by Jessie,[1] who had heard it from one of your correspondents at the Seminary.[2] Have you heard from Jessie yet? When I left she was fully intending to write to you at once. She said that she was almost afraid to write to you now, after having neglected you so long. She is very fond of you, Hattie. I wish for her sake that the Seminary term were ended. She has undertaken entirely too much this year. *All* of every day, Sabbath alone excepted, is taken up by study of one kind or another, and Sabbath afternoon is the only time she has to herself, for her correspondence &c. By the time her two *regular* letters are written (to Mr. Brower[3] and to Aunt Marion[4]) all of her week's leisure is gone and you and I and the rest of her nominal correspondents must go unnoticed. She confessed to me that her engagements were so constant that she had been outside of the Seminary grounds for exercise only twice since the term opened—twice in four months! Fortunately for her this confinement can't continue much longer now, as the term closes early in May. In the meantime I intend writing to her frequently whether my letters are answered or not; for the poor girl seems to feel very much cut off from her relations this year with none but Lottie and Marion Woodrow near her. Yes, Marion is still at the Seminary. I did not mention her because she made less impression upon me than Lottie did, I suppose. She scarcely seems to be present when Lottie is in the room, so entirely does she give way to her pert younger sister.

Though very quiet, my visit to Staunton was an exceedingly pleasant one. Its principal feature was a fine sleigh ride. The rest of the time was spent in-doors, the weather being too disagreeable to allow of much going about, or of any walks such as we used to take last Winter. We used Mr. Hintz's room as our sitting room. Jessie tried to get me to ask Lottie to sing for me—and I suppose that I ought to have done so; but I was stubbornly self-indulgent and stoutly refused to do so. I had the pleasure (?) of calling on Miss Mary Crawford, Miss Janet Woods, and Miss Mary Waddel, the doctor's daughter, as well as upon others of my friends of more advanced age. But perhaps I told you all this before; did I?

Since my return home my health has been improving slowly. Its rapid improvement has been hindered by the miserable weather— a dreary succession of rains and damp mists—by which this section has been burdened ever since my return. I have been at home now for almost three weeks, and during all that time have seen only three days of sunshine. Such weather has furnished me with a capital and a very acceptable excuse for not visiting. Delicate health and wet weather must be enough to satisfy anybody that my stay at home has been compelled by the commonest prudence. The single call I have made was forced upon me. A young lady's mother whom I happened to see one night at prayer-meeting told me that "I must be sure to call on Susie before her return to boarding school." So on Susie I was forced to call. I paid my respects the day before she was to leave for school. I find Wilmington full of new-fledged young ladies, most of whom have emerged from girlhood since the Winter I spent here five years ago, before going to Princeton—the only Winter I ever passed in Wilmington. Most of the girls I knew and visited then are married now. I was just seventeen when we came here, you know, but almost everyone thought that so sedate a youth must be at least twenty-two; so I was invited out with fellows of that age, and got into a set so much older than myself that now I am left without acquaintances of my own age. Mother threatens to make me visit a great deal; and, consequently, I have the delightful prospect of soon having an extended acquaintance among the girls whom I remember only as children. It makes me imagine myself very old when I think that I have been a young man ever since these young ladies were nine or ten years old—whereas the real truth of the matter is that I am only now beginning to visit among those of an age bearing some proper proportion to my own[.] The anticipation of much visiting is not an altogether pleasing one. It bores me very much as long as it is to be begun, though I rather enjoy it after a beginning has been made. The more I visit the more I enjoy visiting, as a general thing—at least when I have interesting and intelligent people to associate with. Since mother's bent on having me make a great many calls this Winter, therefore, there seems to be good reason to believe that I will speedily become quite a "lady's man"—*perhaps*.

A comparatively clear morning allowed me to take a horseback ride before dinner to-day—my first since leaving the University[.] We have a beautiful little mare who serves us both as a buggy horse and as a saddle horse. She is rather frisky during this cold weather, but is all the more pleasant to ride, I think, on that account. I wish that I could have you here to ride with me!

Sister Annie[5] and her little ones—"the menagerie" as father calls them—are still with us. They will leave some time next week. Brother George[5] was over on last Sabbath on a flying visit and may possibly come again next Monday to attend the "musical" mother intends having in the evening. Sister Annie, who has kept up her music wonderfully considering her cares as a housekeeper and mother of a considerable family, is to play one or two pieces; there are to be a few solos, several vocal duets, and two or three choruses. Mother has planned the entertainment rather because she feels that she ought to provide some innocent amusement for the young people of the congregation than because of any hope of fine music. There is an extraordinary lack of musical talent here. But still the best singers and performers in town belong to our congregation and will lend their aid on Monday evening, so that I am looking forward to a considerable musical treat. Certainly our "musical" cannot well be worse than the amateur concert that I had the misfortune to attend at the opera house on last Wednesday evening. Discord seemed to reign supreme, except in some fine orchestral pieces which seemed to have been more thoroughly practiced than the rest.

I was very much amused by your account of your treatment of young Donnan. You *were* pretty hard on the poor fellow; but I think that you were, on the whole, perfectly right. I think that it was very presuming and impertinent in him to venture to do as he did on so short an acquaintance. If your prompt and, in my opinion, merited rebuke came to the knowledge of the rest of the family, as it must have done, the fact that Miss Etta did not in any way resent it only goes to prove that in her opinion too Mr Donnan was served perfectly right—only as he deserved and might have expected.

At last my box of books has come from the University and I am about to begin digging into the law again. I expect to be able to study quite as well here as at the University. I have gone far enough into the subject now to be able to go safely alone. I quite agree with you in thinking that, as far as my professional preparation is concerned, I wont suffer any very considerable inconvenience from breaking off from the completion of my course at the University[.] But it was very hard to leave. The chief regret I had was that I was compelled to end my college days abruptly. I hated to say good-bye to college life, which, after all, is about the happiest, because the freest from care, that one can lead. But, then,

I'm very anxious to get to work and earn a good salary before my thirtieth year comes, you know; so that my hopes for the future prevent my regretting more than is proper that the past *is* the past.

Thursday, Jan. 19th

This stupid letter was interrupted at this point last Saturday, and though it has had to wait until to-day for completion, I am determined to finish it, in spite of my fear that it is scarcely worth continuing.

A rehersal for the musical was the cause of my interruption on Saturday; on Monday preparations for company and practice for the evening busied me all day, and the entertainment of the company filled the evening itself; Tuesday was sister Annie's last day with us; and to-day has been taken up with arranging "my study." So, although you have been almost constantly in my thoughts, I have had to postpone writing until now.

The musical proved quite a success. A large number of our young people came, as well as a goodly number of their elders, and all seemed delighted with the entertainment provided. The music was most of it really excellent. *My* enjoyment was not perfect since it was a house-ful of strangers to me; but still I met some pleasant girls and was, on the whole, well repaid for the effort of entertainment.

I was delighted to find that I had been so fortunate in my choice as to send you the poems of your favorite poet. I have a very slight acquaintance indeed with Longfellow's writings; and I must confess that it was the beauty of the little volume that attracted me rather than its contents.

I suppose that, after the gay Winter you have had, you will be very well content to stay quietly at home next Summer, as you intended doing when last you spoke of the matter. Are you still of the same mind? If you are, I think that I can promise you a short visit as surely as anything can be promised so long beforehand. And now that I have some definite expectation of seeing you and the rest of the family, the time will seem all the longer before it can be realized.

There are all sorts of plans for the coming Spring afloat down in this part of the world. Aunt Marion has promised to make us a visit; Sister Annie has set her heart on having Jessie stop with her in Columbia on her way from school, and on having me join her there &c., &c.; but I expect that it is altogether more probable that I will lead a very hum-drum student's life until Summer is fairly come. But if some of these plans *are* carried out, I will then have something to tell you in my letters, instead of filling up some dozen pages without saying anything: but then you know that it's not my object to write fine letters, but that I simply love you well enough to love to write to you even when I have to write stupidly. Josie[6] wants me to ask you to write to *him*. He promises to answer very faithfully.

Sister Annie left love to be sent to you, and all of our little family here join to [*sic*] sending love to uncle T., Aunt H, Wilson, and the babies[7]—as well as an abundant portion to yourself.

Lovingly Yours   T. W. W.

ALS (WC, NjP).
   [1] Jessie Woodrow Bones.
   [2] The Augusta Female Seminary, Staunton, Va.
   [3] Abraham T. H. Brower of Rome, Ga., engaged to Jessie Bones.
   [4] Marion Woodrow Bones.
   [5] Annie Wilson Howe and her husband, George Howe, Jr., M.D.
   [6] Joseph R. Wilson, Jr.
   [7] Thomas Woodrow, Jr., Helen Sill Woodrow, James Wilson Woodrow, and "the babies," Helen and Herbert H. Woodrow respectively.

To Richard Heath Dabney

Dear Heath,   Wilmington, N. Carolina, Feb. 1st 1881

Though so long and persistently quiet, I am still in the land of the living. Various duties connected with settling down to life here at home have so occupied my time as to preclude extensive or even limited letter-writing. But I had not forgotten you and the other boys—no, not by a large majority—though I *had* entirely forgotten the bundle of clothes that I left with you. I am sorry to have given any cause for trouble or anxiety about them and am a thousand times obliged to you for your care in the matter.

As for my health, I now know that to leave the University was the most prudent step I could have taken. My doctor found my digestive organs seriously out of gear and has confirmed me in the belief that, had I remained at the University and there continued to neglect systematic medical treatment of myself, I might have confirmed myself in dyspepsia and have fixed on myself a very incomfortable future.

But, despite the fact that I am still far from well, and that a wretched spell of weather has prevented my rapid recovery, I am again steadily at work on the law, and am making very satisfactory progress with it. I find that, having gone so far under competent guidance, I now know the land-marks of the subject quite familiarly enough to enable me to explore it with safety and advantage; and I am naturally very much encouraged to find that I can travel so well alone—or, at least, work with so little *travail,* if you'll excuse the pun!

I miss you and the other boys of ΦΨ more than you would believe, Heath; and when Saturday night comes, I find myself wishing that I could drop in at the Jeff.[1] again. Whom have you elected G. P. in my stead?[2] and what was the ultimate fate of the new Constitution in the Jeff?[3] To what fate did the medal question come?[4] Are there any new candidates for any of the honors of the Society in the field? Tell me all you can about the frat. and about the Jeff., when you write—which do as soon as ever you can. I'm fairly hungry for news from you and about you, and about the rest of the boys. Remember me to all my friends by name—and especially to Blackstone,[5] to whom give a special message of love. If my determination to leave had not been so suddenly arrived at and my preparations in consequence necessarily so hasty, I could not easily have forgiven myself for failing to see him to tell him good-bye. Tell Charlie Kent that I shall look eagerly for a letter from him; give my love to George Preston; and assure Joe Blair[6] that, away from him, I would scarcely think that I existed were it not for the reflection, "*cogo, ergo sum.*"

You see, I shall expect all the *news* to come from *you*; from me there's none to come, except that I'm cultivating the acquaintance of some of the Wilmington girls, and am occasionally figuring in private musical entertainments as one just risen in the firmament of *vocal stars*. Altogether, however, I am passing a very hum-drum student's life.

Ask Charlie [Kent] to give my love to Miss Mattie and Miss Susie Minor when next he visits them and to remember me to my other friends among the University young ladies. Don't tell Joe. of my message to Miss Susie! His *cogitations* concerning me might be unkind.

Who secured my room? I hope Charlie and Pendelton[7] did; though I fear my dilatoriness in presenting their names destroyed their chances.

Excuse this rambling budget of messages and believe me, with much love,   Your sincere friend,   T. Woodrow Wilson

P. S. Much love to Sam. Woods.   T. W. W.

ALS (Wilson-Dabney Correspondence, ViU). This was a reply to R. H. Dabney to WW, Jan. 27, 1881, APS (WP, DLC). Charles Wm. Kent to WW, Feb. 23, 1881, ALS (WP, DLC), also replied to WW's letter to Dabney.

[1] The Jefferson Society of the University of Virginia.

[2] General President of Alpha chapter of Phi Kappa Psi. WW had been elected G. P. in the autumn of 1880. His successor was Gray Carroll, University of Virginia, LL.B., '82.

[3] The Jefferson Society adopted its new constitution on Jan. 15, 1881.

[4] The committee, of which WW had been chairman, that had drafted a new constitution for the Jefferson Society had offered three separate plans for

the award of debaters' medals. The Society had chosen the one providing for medals to the best and second-best debaters. C. W. Kent to WW, Feb. 23, 1881, and R. H. Dabney to WW, March 14, 1881, ALS (WP, DLC), make it clear that WW preferred the proposal for only one medal to be awarded to the best debater.

5 John W. G. Blackstone, whom WW had known in the Glee Club.

6 All three were members of Phi Kappa Psi. George J. Preston was at the University for the session 1880-81.

7 John Hunter Pendleton, University of Virginia, '75-'81, M.A., '87; Ph.D., University of Göttingen, '86. The next occupant of Wilson's room at 31 West Range was Richard Brooke Maury, Jr., of Memphis, Tenn., who was at the University for one session only, 1880-81, and took no degree.

Marginal Note

A. H. H. Stuart to the Editor, Jan. 4, 1881, Philadelphia *American*, 1 (Feb. 5, 1881), 266:

It may, then, be asked why are the Southern people so much opposed to negro suffrage? I answer, that the opposition is to *ignorant* suffrage, entirely irrespective of race or color. We do not object to their votes because they are negroes—because their *faces* are dark, —or because they were recently held in bondage. The objection rests on grounds entirely distinct from these. We object to their votes because their *minds* are dark—because they are ignorant, uneducated, and incompetent to form an enlightened opinion on any of the public questions which they may be called on to decide at the polls. . . .

WW Handwritten Comment[1]
[c. Feb. 5, 1881]

Not because the Republican party was dreaded but because the dominance of an ignorant and inferior race was justly dreaded.

1 On clipping of Stuart's letter in the first of two scrapbooks described at c. Jan. 1, 1881.

A Newspaper Article

Stray Thoughts from the South

Wilmington, N. C., February 12, 1881.

Serious and dispassionate examination of the "southern question" might almost lead one to wish that legislation were stopped and legislators stripped of their functions; because it is just the silliness of bringing such a "question" into practical politics that has retarded the natural processes of reforming nature and worse confounded a confusion which was already bewildering and hopeless enough. It was just the folly of those who ignorantly imagine that it was within the power of legislators to change the whole face and constitution of society at a single stroke, to complete a revolution by an act of Congress, that has held the South back from her natural destiny of regeneration. The first thing that it is necessary to realize in attempting to understand the present condition of the South and to forecast her future is that the civil war was the immediate cause of a revolution of almost unparalleled proportions. An entire social system was utterly destroyed, and the South was as absolutely separated from her past as though a period of a hundred years had thrown its length in between. The war found her an agricultural section; and, having stripped her of her slaves, left her with her only industry a total wreck. She had to begin absolutely anew; to adopt agricultural methods to which she was unused; to extend a commerce yet in its infancy, and to organize mechanical industries with which she had hitherto had no practical acquaintance whatever.

The South has, therefore, started upon an entirely new race, and in measuring her success, both in commerce and in industry, it should constantly be borne in mind that her commercial and industrial history covers less than twenty years. We stand at the beginning of the first period in her new progress, and in speaking of her prospects must venture on the uncertain and hazardous ground of prediction with few clear signs to guide us. The doubtful things are, however, principally the things social and political, not the things commercial and industrial. Her commerce is gradually working a regeneration of its own, its chief strength at present being the trade in the natural products of her soil; the great staple, cotton; naval stores from the pine forests of the Atlantic States; the rich fruits of her southern borders, the raw sugars of her warmer bottoms; and the tobacco and peanuts of her sandier regions. There are many unmistakable indications of the steady increase of this trade which is naturally her own. As the schooling in new and economical methods of cultivation goes on of course there is a sure multiplication of products and as sure an enlargement of results. Comparison of statistics shows a steady increase in the cotton crop, that increase being especially large during the few years last past. The crop of the year 1878-79 exceeded that of the previous year by some 300,000 bales; and the crop for 1879-80 is estimated to have been greater still by some 813,000 bales, in spite of weather the most persistently unpropitious. Other crops are increasing by still larger steps—principally because they are cultivated instead of merely fostered. Hitherto southern farmers have known comparatively little of the proper methods of fertilizing and have grown only those things which would spring up almost spontaneously. They have not known what it is to coax nature, but have merely sown and waited for her gifts. Now they are learning better ways. I am told that in South Carolina so great is the demand for fertilizers that certain phosphate companies have found themselves obliged, in order to fill their orders, to supplement the means of rail transportation by chartering vessels to bring for them guano from distant guano mills. Under these new plans of cultivation usual products have found growth in unusual localities. In North Carolina the rice crop, during the war and until very recent years confined almost exclusively to the wet bottoms of the Cape Fear district, has spread to the feet of the mountains which rise upon her western borders; and the receipts of rice in the port of Wilmington alone have increased since the year 1878 from 20,000 to 100,000 bushels, or have been enlarged five-fold in three years, with prospects for the present year of a still further growth of a[t] least fifty per centum. Rice, indeed, seems destined to become one of the staple productions of the state now that it has been found that the low-lying lands of the interior yield it as kindly and bounteously as do the swampy tracts near the coast. Here, too, tobacco finds a natural growth and is every year pushing itself up into a higher place among the principal items of wealth and the chief objects of commerce. Then in Louisiana we hear of whole districts of country reclaimed by art from swampy sterility and devoted to the production of the sugar canes, and in Florida of the careful improvement of her tropical fruits and of their rising value in the fruit markets of the world.

Now the most part of this rapid and hopeful betterment in a system so long stagnant is the spread of a few principles of practical wisdom set forth right plainly the other day in the conversation of a Texas farmer, as plain as his own wisdom, who was heard by a friend of mine to say to a fellow-farmer whom he had met in a neighboring southern state: "The reason we make bigger crops and make more money out of 'em in Texas than you do here isn't because we've got better lands and more capital and more luck and longer good seasons. Some of us ain't got as good land as you have. But we don't hire as many hands to do our own work for us as you do. We can't afford it. We've got small farms and we're bound to work 'em ourselves. And we do; and we make 'em bring all we can; we make every acre tell." Well, there's common sense, conveyed in unconscious rebuke, and much sense which has until lately been very uncommon among our farmers. But the Texas system is spreading. Texas is still a new state. She did not have the slave system of labor long enough or on a large enough scale to give time for the accumulation of the vast half-tilled estates to which that system gave rise, and she was, consequently, able to begin with a system based upon true principles of economy. And now that system which she has tested is finding favor with those states which are beginning anew. Everywhere throughout the South, as far as I can ascertain, the number of small holdings is on the increase; and small farmers, sowing their own seed, following their own ploughs and reaping their own crops, find each year bringing them a more abundant harvest.

Such are some of the surer signs which brighten the future of southern commerce. Then, too, southern merchants are by many successes giving evidence of determined energy and cautious enterprise. Trade in its broader sense, trade beyond the narrow bounds of local exchange and the business of common carriage, is as new a thing to most portions of the South as is free agricultural labor; and, considering the fact that they are establishing a new profession and constructing a new machinery, southern merchants are enriching themselves and their communities much faster and much more surely than could have reasonably been expected. Commerce is, however, merely the handmaid of agriculture and manufacture, and when many men find employment in commercial undertakings it is a sure sign that the agriculturalist and the manufacturer are not idle. Accordingly the increasing activity of southern trade is itself one sign of the growing strength of southern agriculture and manufacture. Other indications are abundantly plentiful. Foremost among the industries of the South naturally and properly stands the manufacture of cotton. One or two of the Southern States had gone timidly and tentatively into this occupation before the war and had met with very encouraging success. Georgia, especially, had found profit in the business, and the Augusta mills, employing several hundred skilled laborers, had an established reputation and a handsome income at the outbreak of the war. Even that struggle did not seriously affect its prosperity; during its progress the resources of the company are said to have been doubled; and since its close to have been quadrupled. Within the twenty years which have elapsed since the war cotton factories have sprung up in every part of the South—notably in the two Carolinas and in Georgia.

And the activity and success of those mills that have been built are little less than astonishing. Examining the present census returns, I find that the five principal cotton-manufacturing states of New England—Maine, Massachusetts, New Hampshire, Connecticut and Rhode Island—are estimated to have in their factories 8,851,329 spindles; and that the five principal cotton-manufacturing states of the South, namely, Virginia, North Carolina,

South Carolina, Georgia and Alabama, have only 495,937: that is, that the New England states employ about seventeen times as many spindles as do the five southern states named. And yet the former consumed, according to these same tables, only about eight times as much cotton as did the latter. The New England states are said to have used 1,132,268 bales; the five southern states mentioned, 154,829. In other words, while the New England factories consumed about one bale of cotton to every eight spindles, the southern factories used about one to every three and a half spindles. Moreover, I am credibly informed that during the last decade the increase in the consumption of cotton for manufacturing purposes in New England was only eighty per centum, while in the South it was one hundred and twenty per centum, and that the actual amount consumed during the same period by New England and southern mills respectively was in about the proportion of five to one. And the profits realized from southern mills seem to have been great in proportion to their activity. The average gross earnings of the Augusta (Ga.) mills are stated to be 12 per centum of its capital; during the last ten years the average profits of the factories at Langley, S. C., have been 8 per centum upon their capital, and in that period there has been an accumulation of a surplus amounting to about one-fourth of the whole capital invested; and last year the Van Cluse mills (of South Carolina) realized 21 per centum profits; those of Greenville, S. C., 25½ per centum.

Another striking indication of the rapid industrial progress of the South is the recent growth of her towns both in wealth and in population. Some instances of this are scarcely less astonishing than the birth of cities which has followed upon mineral discoveries in the West. I learn that ten years ago the present site of the town of Birmingham, Ala., was a cotton field. Now it is a brisk manufacturing town, with a population of six thousand. The town of Wilmington, N. C., has by industrial enterprise almost doubled its population since the war. It now has fine guano mills, connected with the Navassa Guano Company, two large and prosperous cotton presses, six flourishing lumber mills, two rice mills, a busy cotton factory, a tobacco manufactory, and a sash and blind factory which has established a large reputation and drawn liberal patronage from other states. These are the principal manufacturing establishments of a town of only seventeen thousand inhabitants, and it is only following the example set it by numberless other towns of the South, as, notably, by the city of Atlanta, Georgia, which since 1860 has grown from a village into a city. In 1860 the town of Atlanta had a population of about 9,500; in

1870 her population had increased to 21,789; in 1880 she is reckoned in the census returns to have considerably more than thirty thousand. This extraordinary growth is due in part to the fact that she is the centre of an extensive railway system which connects her directly with every quarter of the Union; but it is principally attributable to her activity in trade and manufacture. Its chief manufactures are iron, flour and tobacco, though others are fast assuming a place among the first.

The principal strength alike of southern commerce and of southern manufactures is their naturalness. They are indigenous. Her growing industries are such as a perfectly natural division of labor would from the first have assigned her; such as the unnatural system of slave labor alone kept her from establishing long ago. Nothing could illustrate more strikingly the healthy principles of free trade than this happy extension of her industries which is now taking place. Nature has placed a superabundance of raw materials at her free disposal, and has furnished, in streams that never run dry or grow tired, motive power easy of command and of inexhaustible utility. With these facilities inviting her the South has entered upon a rivalry with northern manufacturers in which she needs and asks no "protection" even for the infancy of her manufactures. That her rivalry with New England in the manufacture of cotton is already successful is proved by the apprehensive arguments of her New England competitors against its possibility; and by such declarations as that of the *Cotton* newspaper of New York, that "we are on the eve of an extensive transfer of this great industry from the North to the South;" and of Mr. Thompson of Rhode Island, that soon "all" coarse cotton goods will be made in the South. Hitherto coarse goods only have been made by most southern mills, because of the want of skilled labor, in which alone they are lacking. But with the influx of capital which is certain to come soon where it can find its most facile, and therefore most profitable, employment, will come skilled laborers as well, and then there need be no limit to the production of cotton goods of all grades. Indeed some southern mills are already producing the finer fabrics. The Wilmington (N. C.) mills make and supply in large quantity the cloth on which calicos are printed; and the Augusta (Ga.) factory has long employed skilled hands in the production of fine goods. Then, too, the South is found rich in an abundance of ores which invite to the building of other manufactories such as have for years flourished in Atlanta.

In short, as I have already said, the doubtful things of the South's future are the things social and political, not the things commercial and industrial. For manufacture she has few artisans, and little material whereof to make them. But with the coming of capital and the immigration of skilled workmen, she has nothing to fear and everything to hope for. Her only serious trouble may be that capital is frightened away and immigration discouraged by influences of which it would be necessary to speak more at length.   T. W. W.

Printed in the New York *Evening Post*, Feb. 16, 1881; editorial heading omitted.

From Robert Bridges

Dear Tommy,   New York City. [c. Feb. 16, 1881]
    Since your letter reached me I have made a change and have been kept very busy. As you will surmise I am on the *Post* with Pete.[1] Today I sent your letter.[2] Our literary critic pronounced it excellent, said it forecast the points of an article in the International[3] which he had seen in the proofs but which has not yet appeared. I read it coming up on the elevated from work. Of course I liked it. It could not be clearer put and the style is fine for a letter. It is an unusual thing for a newspaper letter to have any pronounced style. Yours has—it would not be yours if it did not. There is a an [sic] easy flow, "flexibleness" the critics call it, about the letter which you have certainly acquired since leaving college. Your style was always dignified and exact, but this has the *spring* about it which will give you a hearing among the people. I was thinking to-day how odd it was that we three, who wrote together in college, & had so much in common should all have a hand in the paper which I held. It seemed to me that some of the old dreams were being realized. I hope many more will come out of the future to each one of us. . . .   Your friend   Bob Bridges.

ALS (WP, DLC) with WWhw notation on env.: "Ans 2/24/81."
    [1] Harold Godwin.
    [2] "Stray Thoughts from the South," printed at Feb. 12, 1881.
    [3] Edward Atkinson, "The Solid South?" the *International Review*, x (March 1881), 197-209.

From Harold Godwin

My dear Tommy: New York. [c. Feb. 21, 1881.]
    I can send you but a few words, for I am full of business, to tell you that your letter[1] has been published, but I fear under circumstances not as happy as might have been. As I wrote you there has been a tendency and an intention on our part of raising the price of correspondent matter but this has not yet been done and

your article shares the fate of all others that come here. What you will be paid for it I cannot tell you yet as it has not been measured, but presume not very much as it is 3 cents a line matter as at present correspondence is paid. I know they would be glad to have more from you, but I dont like to invite you to write until I can assure you something better than this.

I will roll up a couple of papers containing the above mentioned and send it to you. . . . Ever   H. G.

ALI (WP, DLC) with WWhw notation on env.: "Ans 2/24/81." Also on env.: miscl. WW figures.
¹ "Stray Thoughts from the South," printed at Feb. 12, 1881.

An Unpublished Article

[c. Feb. 22, 1881]

Stray Thoughts From The South

Upon reading so much as has been published of the Philadelphia *American's* "symposium" on the South,¹ the feeling which predominates is one of decided disappointment. The fact which most obviously takes from the value of the discussion is, that it is made up almost altogether of the contributions of politicians, who, as politicians are wont to do, waste their ink in insisting on party doctrines. Some of the contributors are so pitiably weak as to indulge in coarse abuse of those from whom they ask respectful attention and considerate treatment; many of them are utterly unable to forget that they are members of a party, or to realize that there is any further future than the next presidential campaign; and most of them persistently assume the absolute impeccability of the white people of the South and the unqualified malignity, or the stubborn stupidity, of the Republican population of the North. Now, one of the first things necessary in order to a proper understanding of a question of such "pith and moment" as the state of Southern politics is to rid our minds of any such idea as that wisdom will die either with us or with those who differ from us in opinion. Neither blindness nor clearness of sight is epidemic in either the North or the South: and if any class of Northern people that may be represented by the Philadelphia *American* sincerely desires to bring about a better understanding between the two sections, every Southerner of honorable principle ought to be glad to contribute what he can to this mutual enlightenment without heat or spite.

The purpose which the editors of the *American* wish to accomplish by the discussion which they invite seems itself to be proof that they are themselves far from appreciating the full significance of what they see in Southern politics. They profess a strong desire "to do away with that bar to the highest national political prosperity known as 'the Solid South.' " That desire is, when looked at from their standpoint, a very creditable one; but it is an ignorant desire. The South has not concerned and does not concern herself largely or actively in *national* politics. It is a very vital mistake to suppose that it is upon matters of national policy that the sentiment of the South is unanimous, or her opinions "solid;" and this error it is that has colored and obscured almost every discussion of Southern politics that I have seen or heard. The South is of one mind on matters of supreme consequence in the administration of her local, her home, affairs; upon these principally, upon these only. The present party preferences of the great majority of Southerners are not hard to comprehend. The explanation may all be found in the records of the proceedings of the thirty-ninth Congress, the Congress which decreed reconstruction. They set their faces stedfastly against the Republican party not because of its present but because of its past policy. They uniformly vote with the Democratic party not because they approve of its national policy so much as because it represents the constitutional opposition to a party which has time and again manifested a desire and a purpose rudely to interfere in their local affairs. They are, therefore, simply in opposition to the dominant party.

The enfranchisement of the negro undoubtedly explains everything in the political condition of the South that calls for explanation at all. It is a simple enough matter to understand what choice an English people would make when the alternatives presented to them were, to be ruled by an ignorant and an inferior race, or to band themselves in a political union not to be broken till the danger had past. They determined, as any community of their Northern fellow citizens would have determined under like circumstances, never to suffer themselves to be ruled by another race in every respect unlike themselves; and in that resolve they cannot be, they should not be, shaken. The temporary rule of that race was fatal enough. It, for example, elevated into absolute power the "carpet-bagger," upon whom a national condemnation has fallen. Short as was his sway, the "carpet-bagger" saddled the South with a terrible burden of debt, which must be paid by means of taxation so grinding as to make poverty poorer and to frighten away the thrifty immigrants of whom Southern industries stand in such immediate need, or must be repudiated to the permanent detriment of that credit upon which Southern commercial enterprize is dependent. The determination of the Saxon race of the South that the negro race shall never again rule over them is, then, not unnatural, and it is necessarily unalterable. Keeping this fact always in mind, we have a clue to the solution of other things which, without this fact, might seem hard to be understood. The whole truth of the case is tersely summed up by Hon A. H. H. Stuart, who has written the only valuable, certainly the only instructive, letter yet contributed to the *American*'s "symposium."[2] The Southern people are, he says, opposed "to *ignorant* suffrage, entirely irrespective of race or color." They do not object to the votes of the negroes "because they are negroes—because their *faces* are dark,—or because they were recently held in bondage. The objection rests on grounds entirely distinct from these. We object to their votes because their *minds* are dark—because they are ignorant, uneducated, and incompetent to form an enlightened opinion on any of the public questions which they may be called on to decide at the polls." Southern people, therefore, instinctively combine in opposition to a party which by establishing ignorant suffrage declared to the world, to quote the words of the late Senator Morton,[3] "that the exercise of American suffrage involves no intellectual or moral qualifications; and that there is no difference between an American freeman and an American slave which may not be unmade by a mere act of Congress." They are bound for the preservation of their own liberties and in the interests of self-government to maintain an united resistance to the domination of an ignorant race; and they are, consequently, in conscience bound to remain united against any party which threatens to force that domination upon them. Hitherto the only party that has shown an inclination to do so has been the Republican party—hence the unanimity of the South in opposing the continuance of its rule.

Everything points to this one fact as to the hinge of the whole controversy. That the South cares comparatively little for other subjects of party policy is indicated by the subordinate part her representatives have usually taken in the nominating conventions of the Democratic party. Nor have Southern Congressmen often since the war taken the lead in the deliberation of the Houses. They have no great public measures upon which unitedly to insist. Upon a great many questions regarding the non-partizan administration of the national government there is very far from being universal accord of judgment and conviction among the intelligent classes of the South; but their close agreement upon the one question which is just now more vital than all others beside to them makes them appear to those who do not appreciate their situation to be determinedly combined on every other matter of politics. They are for a time content to subordinate every minor difference of opinion to the paramount necessities of self-defence.

What is the outlook, then? Is the South always to remain "solid." No, not always: only so long as the necessity for defence continues. And that necessity will continue only so long as the negroes remain ignorant and unfitted by education for the most usual and constant duties of citizenship. There is already in many portions of the South a very noticeable and hopeful betterment in the social condition of the race—and social advance is generally, if not always, accompanied by mental and moral improvement. The more energetic among the negroes are slowly acquiring habits of thrifty self-support. In some sections, notably I believe in northern and western Georgia, they are becoming extensive land-holders and industrious farmers of their own lands. There are here and there whole communities of negro proprietors who are the fore-runners, as far as we can judge, of an exceedingly valuable, because steady and hardy, peasantry. These men are many of them intelligent citizens: the possessing of earned property always sharpens and opens the intellect. In this class of the negroes alone are found the men who venture to vote independently both of fear and of prejudice. It is not against them that there is need of political combination, but against their fellows who remain in darkness. There is of course a great deal that is very encouraging in this self-elevation of the race, for it proves them capable of still further progress. But the process of self-betterment is necessarily a slow one. For their elevation they need liberal and powerful aid and systematic encouragement. Those of them who will not or cannot educate themselves must be compulsorily educated and permanently reclaimed from ignorance and indolence

Do not these considerations suggest the means of removing the necessity, or, as some will have it, the menace, of Southern solidity? Whoever will undertake to aid the impoverished South in lifting the negroes from degradation will do everything that can be done in coöperating with natural forces towards the accomplishment of that end. To remove Southern fear and distrust of the Republican party is another matter [.] That will require many unquestionable proofs of the final determination of that party to accept in all good faith the situation of the two races in the South as they find it, and not a few years of honest endeavor on its part to relieve the white population from the imperative necessity of self-defence against the ignorant masses of the negro race, and thus to remedy so far as is possible the mistakes of reconstruction. But if this plain duty to itself were performed by the Republican party, I can see nothing to forbid the expectation of a speedy re-division and healthy readjustment of parties in the South.

Besides this problem of negro citizenship, which is peculiar to herself, the South seems to have fewer political difficulties with which to contend than many of the powerful states of the North. She has no cliques of despotic partizans to dominate over her legis-latures and no masters of corrupt intrigue to fill her state offices with personal adherents and puny puppets. There are here as else-where the caucus to dictate and federal patronage to harrass; but no "machine." Southern representatives in Washington, though for the most part men of mediocre ability, are still, with few ex-ceptions, men of considerable intelligence and generally of un-questionable character, unstained by corruption.

A further corroboration of the view I have taken of the present state of Southern politics is suggested by one of the questions which the Philadelphia *American* has asked its contributors. It inquires, "Are the Northern Democrats a help or a hindrance to Southern political prosperity?" It ought not to require much knowledge to answer that question. Northern Democrats have had scarcely anything whatever to do with Southern political pros-perity either for better or for worse. They have not since the war had it in their power seriously to affect the affairs of the South one way or another. Southern Democrats are a party to them-selves, because, as I have repeatedly stated, their party organiza-tion is based on matters not of national but of local policy. They have little in common with Northern Democrats save that they constitute a part of the same constitutional opposition to Re-publican rule and act under the same name. One does not have to read many of the better newspapers of the South to see into what contempt many of the dealings of the national party calling itself Democratic have brought it in the minds of thoughtful men throughout the Southern states. A great number join with the editor of the Atlanta (Geo) *Constitution*, the chief journal of a city of over thirty thousand inhabitants, in doubting the patri-otism and questioning the statesmanship of "those who assume to lead and control the Democratic party of the North," and in pro-nouncing them "narrow-minded timeservers," who depend upon the South to secure for them the fat things of office; and those who are not prepared to go so far in condemnation, certainly do not go far in love or admiration. Their adherence is merely nomi-nal and at the most temporary and provisional.

The people of the South have, in a word, set their faces sted-fastly and with all the determination that is within them towards the accomplishment of two principal objects: the unobstructed and peaceful development of the wealth which their country is capable of producing and the industries she is capable of maintaining, and the conclusive establishment of their right of self-government within the provisions of the Constitution; resolved the while never again to harbor a threatening thought against the maintenance of the Union, nor ever again to be other than loyal and patriotic citizens of a country they will ever revere: and upon the varying fortunes of these principles will depend her varying party alliances.   T. W. W.

WWhw MS. (WP, DLC) with Parke Godwin's comments (repeated in Harold Godwin to WW, April 10, 1881) on verso of last page. WW sent this second "Stray Thoughts from the South" to the New York *Evening Post* on about Feb. 22, 1881. The *Evening Post* rejected it in April (see Harold Godwin to WW, April 10, 1881). Then WW incorporated it into a longer article, "The Politics and the Industries of the New South" and submitted the new essay to the *International Review* (see WW to the Editor of the *International Review*, April 30, 1881). It was rejected again, and WW laid the manuscript aside. He sent it in a letter to Robert Bridges on March 18, 1882, and the New York *Evening Post* published the second half of the article under the title "New Southern Industries" on April 26, 1882. The first part of this essay is published under its original title and its approximate date of composition, April 30, 1881; the second half, under its new title and its date line in the *Evening Post*, April 20, 1882.
1 The Philadelphia *American*, a weekly magazine, announced in its issue of Jan. 29, 1881 (I, 241), that it would publish the comments of leading Southerners on the "Solid South." It published these statements in its issues between Feb. 5 and April 2, 1881, but WW, at the time he wrote this article, could have read only the thirteen comments published in the issues of Feb. 5, 12, and 19, 1881.
2 A. H. H. Stuart to the Editor, *The American*, I (Feb. 5, 1881), 265-67.
3 Oliver H. P. T. Morton, United States Senator from Indiana, 1867-77.

To Robert Bridges

Dear Bobby,   Wilmington, N. Carolina, February 24th/81
   I was delighted at receiving your letter. I expected of course, after hearing from Pete that Mr. Godwin had secured a controlling interest in the *Post*, that you would before long be in New York. But I was uncertain as to the *when* of your move and the *how* of your employment on the E. P. I was relieved, therefore to know that the change had actually been made, and that you had obtained a satisfactory position. For it does seem from your description of it to be very satisfactory—at once a place of responsibility and not too exacting duties. How splendid it is for you two fellows to be together as you are! I sometimes find myself regretting that I too had not gone into journalism and thus put myself in the way of a chance of being some day associated with you and Pete in editorial work. Would not that be a grand realization of our college dreams! Well, when you get to writing editorials, I shall ex-

pect you to give my political views a hearing and their author, if he ever deserve prominence, a fair amount of credit. And, speaking of my political views, the principal, if not the only, consideration that makes me hesitate in my choice between the North and the South as the place in which to begin my professional work is that in the South I would have more immediate prospects of gaining an influence over political opinion, though the North offers more abundant opportunities of large professional favor— ultimately at least—and of lucrative employment.

I sent a letter on Southern politics through Pete to the Post the other day which I hope will be published as it takes a rather broader view of the matters of which it treats than is given to the vision of the politicians who vainly waste their small strength in endeavoring to establish party positions. I am more than pleased, Bobby, by what you say of my first letter, on commercial affairs. Such matters were rather new to me and I did not anticipate very great success in treating of them. But your comments reassure me. If my style is improved—by being "limbered up"—I don't know how the improvement came about. Probably my mind—my faculties—are less stiff than they were. I wrote a good deal, and, above all, *spoke* much, at the University and *thus* escaped a little from the shackles, may be.

I am still steadily at work on the *elements* of the law. It's a tremendous subject. It seems to grow larger and larger the further you go in endeavoring to see all its sides. But it is exceedingly interesting when properly presented and certainly affords fine occasion for mental drill of the severest and, therefore, most lasting and valuable sort.

I relieve the tasks of study by visiting the girls semi-occasionally. Some of the damsels here are quite talkative and attractive (two characteristics which don't always go together) and I enjoy some of my visits very thoroughly. Have you met any N. Y. City girls yet? or are you living on the picture and remembrance of the Rochester companions of the "Children's table"? You make these latter out to be very charming persons whom one would like to meet.

I have not heard recently from any of the boys except you and Pete, and it makes me feel very *blue* sometimes that I must always be so very far away from you all. I'm glad to know that Charlie [Talcott] has secured so desirable a place. In what capacity is he in Kernan's office?[1] Much love to Pete and plenty for yourself. Do write whenever you can.

Your sincere friend   T. Woodrow Wilson

ALS (Meyer Coll., DLC).
  1 Talcott had just become a clerk in the law office of Francis Kernan, United States Senator from New York, 1875-81.

From Edward Wright Sheldon

My dear Tommy: New York. March fifth, 1881.

The article in *The Nation*[1] sent you by this post vividly brought back the many talks we have had regarding the admission of Cabinet officers to seats in Congress. If the bill of the late Congress on the subject had become law, President Garfield might have favored the country with a little stronger Cabinet. However, the old Ship will sail on.

I have snatched a moment to let you know that the law has not destroyed my interest in constitutional government. As for yourself, the law, I think, will prove but a stepping stone to greater things than a quiet attorney's life.

Very sincerely,   Edward W. Sheldon.

ALS (WP, DLC) with WWhw notation on env.: "Ans 3/14/81." Also on env. WWhw note: "See organization of German government—especially 'Council of the Circle.'"
  1 "The Admission of Cabinet Officers to Seats in Congress," New York *Nation*, XXXII (Feb. 17, 1881), 107-109.

Two Unpublished Letters to the Editor

[c. March 21, 1881]

What Can Be Done for Constitutional Liberty.

Letters from a Southern Young Man to Southern Young Men

I.

It would not be the part either of wisdom or of good-will to encourage young men to do service in the partisan contentions of politics. No one who has ears with which to hear or eyes with which to read can have failed to learn of the crooked dealings which render such contests odious, and of the corruption which is daily bringing our national government into deeper disrepute at the same time that it is diligently robbing not a few of our State governments of their efficiency and their honor. The politician who avoids the stain of depravity or escapes the stigma of dishonesty must expect no better reward than the humiliation of being praised above his fellows for those qualities to lack which would be his shame. Who, then, will be bold enough to approach the rising generation with the advice that they risk their characters and jeopard their fortunes in this poor game, in which the prizes are so small and the hazards so great. Certainly, if office seeking and getting be the whole of politics, or office holding the only means of influential leadership in matters of government and policy, no wise man should do so.

But, happily, all political power does not dwell with the officers of government, nor all political influence with the elected representatives of the people. There are powers independent of the executive and voices of authority outside the halls of legislatures. There are contests for the ear of public opinion, contests of discussion whose proper place of expression is the public platform and the public press: and in these, surely, young men may take an honorable and a useful part. In these days of disgust with politics older men may be falling into the despondent habit of regarding patriotism as little better than a cant term; but it is to be hoped that with most young men it is still a vital principle: and to those upon whom it does act as an incitement and an inspiration there is now, if ever there was, an imperious call to enlist in this service of privately studying and publicly discussing the great political issues of the time.

The greatest issue of the time seems an issue of life and death. If the national administration can be reformed it can endure; if it cannot be, it must end. Robust as its constitution has proved to be, the federal government cannot long continue to live in the poisonous atmosphere of fraud and malfeasance. If the civil service cannot by gentle means be purged of the vicious diseases which fifty years of the partisan spoils system have fixed upon it, heroic remedies must be resorted to: for, undoubtedly, the degradation of the civil service is the gigantic evil beside which all the other dangers that threaten our republican union are dwarfed, and cleansed it must be, whether by power of law or by power of revolution. But it is not the part of a self-reliant, self-governing people to go beyond law even in such straits. An enlightened, determined, and combined public opinion can bring matters to a settlement right quickly when once it makes its sovereign will known and promises to make its sovereign power felt. Since reform cannot originate within party organizations or with the agents of government, it must be compelled from without.

There is wanted, then, for the present treatment and future settlement of this and others of the pressing questions of public administration, not a new party but a new spirit. A new party would but long for the sweets of office from its cradle to its timely grave. A new spirit is wanted—a spirit of enquiry, of study, of discussion, of active determination; and the hope of its birth is in the patriotism, the disinterested ambition, and the courage of the young. There must be a great, combined, aggressive, constitutional agitation of opinion, and its organization, its leadership, and its impulse must be supplied by the strength, the purpose, and the ardor of the young. It must be a movement full of vigorous life and its veins must, therefore, be warm with young blood. The old and more experienced dogs may be able to scent the game with a keener sense, but the young dogs must run down the chase.

It ought not to require many invitations to bring young men into this service. The young men of the South, particularly, ought to feel the zeal of their ancestors renewed within them at such a call. It has become the common topic of regretful remark amongst Southerners who love the South that the old political manhood of their section has given place, since the war, to careless indifference or cynical disregard of public duties; and it is indeed true that such seems to be the case. But it is only a seeming. It is education that is lacking, not manhood. An intelligent nation cannot be led or ruled save by thoroughly-trained and completely-educated men. Only comprehensive information and entire mastery of principles and details can qualify for command. Not every one that speaks, but every one who compels respect and attention by proved ability and by tested competence to speak, with authority, will be hearkened to. He who thinks lightly of learning and cares not for cultivation of mind cannot justify any hopes he may have of winning an orator's laurels or a leader's victories. Necessity—a necessity born of the calamities of war—has constrained Southern young men to forego the benefits of complete education in the higher branches. The struggle for a livlihood has left them no leisure for intellectual pursuits: and lack of education has done more than aught else to keep them in the background of public life. We are only now entering upon the period in which a Southern literature can be built up and Southern eminence in national counsels restored.

To study, then, to study is the imperious necessity which rests upon all young men of ambition. When our college halls are thronged not only by the well-to-do youth of the cities but also by sturdy youth of the country side working their way laboriously through their courses of study without complaint of the heavy necessity of earning at the same time their own support, we can be sure that a generation of leaders is in training. Not that the doors are anywhere shut to all but college-bred men. The college-bred have over their competitors only such an advantage as professional athletes have over amateurs. There is scarcely a young man in any of our Southern towns who is so closely bound by business that neither the hours of the evening nor any of the hours of the day are at his disposal for reading and self cultivation. Has it never occurred to any of those youths who spend their evenings at bars, or in club-rooms, or in constant rounds of visiting, that by setting apart a portion of their leisure hours to reading, to a study of history and of the great topics of the day, they might see opened to them the way of gaining such influence and renown as would some day make them the favorite toast at those bars, the boast of those club-rooms, the talk of those social circles? A great deal of genius is summed up in the capacity for hard and patient work. Those who will not work at all, or who work spasmodically only and are impatient for immediate and great results, only delude themselves when they dream that they are unrecognized geniuses. Let them look to it that their fellows do not set them down for quite the opposite.

When Southern young men learn to reckon intellectual pursuits at their true value, a new and pure fountain of influence will be opened. I sometimes illustrate to my own mind the power of special knowledge, and its importance to those who would lead, by scenes which are often witnessed at sea. When a passenger vessel is tossed by a storm which runs its course so savagely that wreck and death seem imminent and inevitable, to whom does the passenger look most confidingly for aid and protection? Does not the commonest seaman seem to him more able to preserve him from the terrors of the storm than even the bravest and most accomplished of his fellow-passengers whom he knows to be ignorant of the practical arts of the sailor? So it is in all things. We must prove our skill and establish our claim to knowledge before we can hope to be allowed to direct others.

I have written what this letter contains, Mr. Editor, as some sort of introduction to other thoughts and suggestions of a less general and more practical nature which I shall, with your indulgence, take the liberty of offering to the readers of your paper from time to time in the future, as occasion may serve, in letters which will lay claim to attention only because of the desire to do good which will prompt them and the anxiety to arrive at the truth which will direct their discussions of those questions of public policy which will furnish their main topics.

II.

When one comes to speak of the administration of our national government the word that springs first and most naturally to his lips is *corruption*; and when the mind recalls the primitive purity of our institutions and the onetime uprightness of those who stood foremost in our public service, and, in anxiety, seeks to search out the secret of the later decline and to question its presentiments of approaching ruin, the finger of every witness points to that hateful motto: *"To the victor belong the spoils."* The patronage of office has sold us into political bondage. The system which Jackson originated and Grant perfected has stolen away our political virtue. The words uttered by Daniel Webster in 1832, as he stood at the cradle of that system, now strike us like a fulfilled prophesy: "Sir, if this course of things cannot be checked, good men will grow tired of the exercise of political privileges. They will have nothing to do with popular elections. They will see that such elections are but a mere selfish contest for office; and they will abandon the government to the scramble of the bold, the daring, and the desperate."

"This course of things" seems already to have run almost to its fatal end; but it may yet be checked. There still remain open ways of escape. What are the most practicable means of quitting ourselves of this burden of official patronage? We know that there are some who are strong in their advocacy of reform; but to what practical measures in our own behalf do they direct us? Many are uttering very manly calls upon public opinion to assert itself and make exercise of its sovereignty; but do they advise this multitudinous monarch, the people, how it is to act? We all of us admire outspoken denunciation of wrong and applaud exhortations to turn again to virtue and to rectitude; but we cannot go into an undiscovered country unless we be guided. The reform of governments is not an every-day business: we must be taught the out-of-the-way trade. Young men are enjoined to lend their strength to the good work; but they are at a loss to know when and at what point to apply their strength. But no one appears to be ready to enlighten or direct them. It must be, after all, that the means of reform are so obvious that its advocates do not deem it necessary to point them out. The people must make imperative demand to be better governed; and that is the whole of the matter.

But this is not all of the puzzle. This demand actually seems to be daily a-making. There is every reason to believe that the public mind is already made up. So stiffly does the breeze of opinion set towards reform that all the political papers of the country have long since gotten well before it, and none thinks of beating up against it. And those who are seeking with all their breath to blow this wind into fiercer blasts, complaisantly tell us that all who still essay to weather it are losing heart. Or the metaphor may be changed and it may be said that the people has declared its will; that the land is full of heralds whose loud voices proclaim its decrees. The winds seem to be bringing to each community from every quarter the news that upon this great question all the country is agreed. The nation is of one mind. What then? Has the blow been struck? Do the rulers hear the voice of the nation, and is reform already inaugurated; or do we still wait for its coming? "If it were done when 't is done, then 't were well it were done quickly."

The fact is that public opinion seems to have been disappointed of its omnipotence. Those who enjoy the "spoils system" do not readily bend the knee to the people. And those who hope some day to come into the favors of that system cautiously draw rein and will not lead the hunters who would pursue it to destruction. All party platforms, it is true, have Civil Service Reform planks; Congress has a select committee on Civil Service Reform; and the President suggests an appropriation of money to sustain a trial of a better order of things. Possibly the country may some day be startled by learning that the government has experienced a sudden impulse of unselfish purpose and surrendered its patronage. But there is no violent probability that any such thing will soon happen. Public opinion is left to hum and haw in distressing embarrassment over the question, What is to be done? How is the popular will to enforce its authority? What advantage is there in being unanimous?

Much every way. But there is a great length of difference between unanimity of desire and unanimity of purpose. A wish differs from a determination to act as greatly as unconfined vapor differs from applied steam. Boil water in an open pot and its vapors impotently dissolve in the air; confine those vapors in an engine's boiler and they are ready to drive power through the pipes. What needs to be done, therefore, is to condense the vapors of public opinion and find or invent some engine that they can successfully propel. There are models which we may copy. There must be a great organized agitation: and there have been great organized agitations in furtherance of similar causes both in this country and amongst our kinsmen, the English. Who does not know of the great anti-corn-law agitation in England? Who has not heard of the struggles and the victories of the Anti-Corn-Law League, of its immortal leader, Richard Cobden, and his no less distinguished lieutenant, John Bright? For a seemingly hopeless cause, against which all conceivable odds were at first accumulated, that

League won a success than which there could be none more complete. And by what means? By means of association, a combination having a complete central organization which became the parent of branch organizations in every part of the Kingdom; an organization whose treasury was not only filled by subscriptions but also replenished by the receipts at immense fairs and gigantic bazaars, which, planned by the leaders of the League and conducted by ladies whose enthusiastic sympathy was enlisted in its cause, were for weeks together a daily and nightly attraction to innumerable crowds in more than one of the great cities of the Kingdom; an organization whose funds, thus collected, were expended in the publication and free distribution of such literature as would most forcibly and persuasively recommend its objects to every man who could read or intelligently heed what was read to him, and in the support of lecturers sent to every corner of the Kingdom, that there might not be a public hall in England that had not echoed to the proclamation of the gospel of free-trade and rung with the acclamation of its converts. As the years went by and Parliamentary elections recurred, more and more free-trade candidates were successfully pressed upon the choice of the popular constituencies, till in 1846, the seventh year of the League's existence, Parliament, under the leadership of Sir Robert Peel, yielded to the pressure and accepted the doctrines which Cobden and Bright had been eloquently preaching outside of Parliament, in the country, and no less eloquently advocating within Parliament itself, through so many years of seemingly hopeless battle with opposing prejudice.

It is not enough that the people should be agreed to *think* something; they must be agreed to *do* something. Surely there is no lack of high motives for undertaking this disinterested work of inciting the people to such resolve, no lack of an inspiring cause to set before those whom it is sought to induce to league themselves together in a crusade for reform. If love of country have power to impel any, to what more congenial work than the elevation and purification of the country's government can that love direct? If a desire to promote the happiness of others is strong in the breasts of any, how quickly should it prompt them to enter upon that service of reform whose object is to prevent the removal of public servants for mere opinion's or party's sake and assure them of no change but promotion so long as they continue diligent, upright, and faithful in the discharge of their trusts, and thus to release thousands from that most degrading servitude,

slavery of mind, and to revive their self-respect, secure their efficiency, and quicken their zeal by restoring their independence.

Will. Work.

WWhw MS. (WP, DLC). The title and sub-title, repeated by WW at II, have
been omitted. It seems impossible to give a precise date for the composition
of these two articles. WW's reference to the President's request for an appropriation "to sustain a trial of a better order of things" furnishes no certain
clue, because Hayes requested such an appropriation in his Annual Messages
of 1879 and 1880, as did Arthur in 1881. The best clue to the date of composition is WW's call for the formation of a national citizens' league for civil
service reform. Such an organization, the National Civil Service Reform League,
was formed in August 1881, just before the death of President Garfield at the
hand of a disappointed office-seeker. Moreover, the fact that WW was unusually
bent upon writing articles of current political interest in the spring of 1881
supports the assumption that he wrote these articles at about the same time.
The agitation for civil service reform had of course been mounting for several
years.

To Richard Heath Dabney

Dear Heath,   Wilmington, N. C., March 22nd/81
    Your welcome letter[1] came close on the heels of one from Char-
ley,[2] and the double feast furnished proportionate enjoyment. I
think of you fellows very often and very affectionately, and would
give a great deal to be able occasionally to drop in on you. The
more news of the University people and University things you can
manage to retail in your letters the surer will be the welcome of
the same.
    Time is treating me kindly, though I am still far from feeling
complete confidence in my stomach's good behavior. I, having
nothing harder or more disagreeable to do than read law according to my own devices, am much hapier, "I trow," than ye poor
slaves who have the torments of measles and the irritations of
special examinations, postponed to suit others' convenience, to
undergo with what equanimity ye can simulate. I spend some
portions of the leisure I make for myself, by close economy of
time in the matter of study, in the company of fair damsels who,
if they are not always good talkers or often skilled in entertaining,
are at least uniformly good listeners and are generally well enough
disposed to submit themselves to be entertained by a well-meaning
young man who exerts himself to sustain a much larger reputation
for intelligence than he has any right to. I am prevented from
bestowing too much attention upon any one of these interesting
creatures whom I may find a trifle more charming than the rest
by the wholesome fear of my young brother, whose soul is never
more at ease, and whose spirits are never higher than when he has

the opportunity, for which he is constantly and slily in wait, of discoursing on the exhibitions of my supposed preferences.

But, while not neglecting the privileges of society—so to speak —I am the more while a slave to the seductions of literature[.] As I wrote to Charley,[3] I've lately sought a new introduction to Fox. I have just completed Trevelyan's *"Early History of Charles James Fox"* and have been more entirely captivated by it than by anything I have read since Macaulay, his uncle. The book would be more properly entitled an history of the early portion of the reign of Geo. III; but still there runs through its wonderly vivid description of the men and the society and the politics of that dark period of Eng. history a clear and complete enough narrative of the early life of Fox to furnish me, at least, with much new light concerning that remarkable man's career and to supply me with materials for an entirely new estimate of his character.—But I wont tire you with a recital of my crude opinions about a book you may not care to read. If you would follow my advice, however, you will not let another vacation pass without reading it every word. I know it would repay you.

I've spent so much ink in trying to make you envy my good luck in being able to command leisure enough to do something besides breaking my mental neck in a head-long race over several thousands of pages of law, that I come to the end of the sheet and have only a short time left before the closing of the Northern mail. I'll hoard the rest of my empty items till next time. Write me letters full of gossip about yourself and the boys and the Jeff and everything else pertaining to our one-time walk and conversation. With much love to the boys, yourself not excluded,

Yours sincerely   T. W. Wilson

ALS (Wilson-Dabney Correspondence, ViU).
    [1] R. H. Dabney to WW, March 14, 1881, ALS (WP, DLC).
    [2] It was C. W. Kent to WW, March 11, 1881, ALS (WP, DLC), in reply to WW to Kent, Feb. 26, 1881, which is missing.
    [3] WW wrote on the env. of Kent's letter of March 11, 1881: "Ans. March 16/81"; but WW's letter is missing.

From Hiram Woods, Jr.

Dear Tommy,   Baltimore, 3/30/81

Your very welcome letter was duly received[.][1] I was delighted to hear from you again, and to learn of your gradual recovery from your recent sickness. The Stomach is nothing to trifle with. Would that boarding house Madams could learn this! . . .

Your Friend & fellow ΦΨ   Hiram Woods, Jr.

ALS (WP, DLC) with WWhw notation on env.: "Ans April 14th 1881."
1 WW's letter, which is missing, was a reply to H. Woods, Jr., to WW, March
9, 1881, ALS (WP, DLC), on the env. of which WW wrote: "Ans March
11th/81."

From Harold Godwin

My dear Tommy: New York, [c. April 10, 1881]
Your letter[1] had to be set aside for a long time on account of an almost unprecedented pressure in those columns. Mr. Eggleston[2] only looked over it a few days ago. He was afterward in doubt about it because he had been pitched into for expressing the same convictions in regard to the negro of the south as you did and so sent the letter to my father. He thought it injudicious to use it and wrote a note to that effect on the back of it. I translate it for you as the chirography is bad and blurred:

"This article has many good things in it; but I think on the whole that it is injudicious: First, because it directs attention to the discussions of another paper, and second because it makes confessions of southern policy that would be taken advantage of by the stalwarts.

signed P. G. ["]

I am of course very sorry to send you back your letter but think that the explanation above is sufficient to satisfy you respecting the delay etc. I hope Tommy that this will not discourage you from trying your hand at it again. Your first letter was highly complimented in the office and as you see the other elicited admiration from those who read it. I wish I could write you more but I am dreadfully busy and will undertake to write again ere long.   Ever   Harold Godwin

ALS (WP, DLC).
1 WW's second "Stray Thoughts from the South," printed at Feb. 22, 1881.
2 George Cary Eggleston, literary editor of the New York *Evening Post* from 1875 to 1881.

To Richard Heath Dabney

Dear Heath,   Wilmington, N. Carolina, April 20th 1881
Having kept yours of the 3rd lying unanswered on my table long enough to whet your appetite for a reply, I sit down to satisfy (?) you by filling a few lines with such matter as I can find in lieu of news.
Both your letter and Charley Kent's were keenly enjoyed not only because they were from two dear friends, but also because

they were full of University news. I sincerely hope that the result of the medal contests will be as satisfactory as the issue of the race for the presidency. What do you think will be the effect on the minds of the judges of the change of *name* of the medals—of the use of the word *speaker*.[1] Although Lefevre's mind is capable of constructing a fine *argument*, his diction rather clouds his meaning and his delivery is not such as to give it the force it might otherwise possess. I suppose he *is* the first speaker among the contestants; but I have thought that possibly a sudden inspiration coming upon one of his opponents might throw doubt upon that fact.—But all this will possibly be settled by the time my letter reaches you. I shall expect both you and Charley to give me very full accounts of the contests. By-the-way, who is to be president and who are to be medalists of the Wash?[2] What prospect has she for an interesting exhibition at the Finals? And who is the most prominent candidate for the Magazine medal? Has James'[3] star gone as completely down in that contest as in the other? How are the Standing committees of the new Constitution of the Jeff. working? I'm overwhelming you with questions, I know: but I've not asked half the number I would like to have answered by you.

I've turned professor of Latin since my return home. There are no schools here of any worth at all, and, consequently, my younger brother has to be instructed at home. I have charge at present of his classical education and find the exercise of teaching an excellent training for myself. I had an idea that I knew a good deal about Latin until I came to teach it. Of late teaching the grammar has not been my only exercise in Latin, however. I've been reading Trollope's recently issued life of Cicero and have of course made it a point to read most of the passages in Cicero's works to which Mr. T. refers *passim*. Of course Cicero is easy to translate, but I experience the consequences of three years' neglect of Latin even in reading him. My principal trouble is, of course, is [*sic*] a loss of a Latin *vocabulary*. But facility of translation is rapidly coming back to me. As for Trollope's work it is simply charming—as vivid and entertaining and instructive as Trevelyan's *Fox*.[4]

I see by this morning's paper that the schemings of my friend Beaconsfield are at last at an end. His death has not inclined me to any *James*ian snuffles. The old fox could not have lasted much longer and I'm prone to feel only releaf at his departure. From many things I've recently seen afloat in the papers I am apt to think, too, that the regret of the tories at his loss (?) will be only of the lips!

Give much love to Charley, Harry, Pat, Geo. P., Hunter,[5] and my other friends. I think of them much and often.

Do write as often as you can, Heath, to

Your sincere friend and bro in ΦΨ   T. Woodrow Wilson

ALS (Wilson-Dabney Correspondence, ViU).

[1] WW had apparently forgotten that the new constitution of the Jefferson Society referred to contestants for medals as "debaters." Kent and Dabney, in letters to WW just before this letter to Dabney was written, did not refer to contestants as "speakers." These letters are C. W. Kent to WW, March 29, 1881, ALS (WP, DLC) with WWhw figures and notation on env.: "Ans April 11th 1881"; and R. H. Dabney to WW, April 3, 1881, ALS (WP, DLC) with WWhw notation on env.: "Ans April 20th 1880 [sic]."

[2] The Washington Society of the University of Virginia.

[3] Samuel H. James, University of Virginia, Law, '83.

[4] WW's copy of Anthony Trollope, *The Life of Cicero* (2 vols., New York, 1881), is in the Wilson Library, DLC. He did indeed translate numerous Latin passages—but into Graham shorthand!

[5] Kent, Daniel Henry Hughes, Jr., University of Virginia, '81, Archibald Patterson, George J. Preston, and John Hunter Pendleton.

To Harriet Augusta Woodrow

Dearest Hattie,   Wilmington, N. Carolina, April 22nd 1881

Your first letter from your new quarters in Cincinnati reached me quite promptly and of course gave me a great deal of pleasure. I was delighted to learn of your success in finding a boarding place so altogether agreeable and no less gratified to know how entirely your new instructors please you and are pleased with you. That they should be pleased with their new pupil, however, seemed to me very much a matter of course—they could not well be otherwise, at least if they knew her as well as I hope I do. You see I am no longer afraid of a repetition of the old charge of flattery, for a[n] expression of one's *sincere* sentiments can never justly be called flattery—and I would rather that you should doubt anything else about me than that you should doubt my sincerity.

It was very sweet in you to say that my letters are always interesting to you because they are written by me, if for no other reason. I shall write to you with fewer misgivings if that is the case—with fewer misgivings, that is, concerning the reception my letters may meet with. Letter-writing is not always, or often, easy to me. Although I have written letters more or less constantly ever since you and I first corresponded, and have for a number of years had numerous regular correspondents, I still feel when I sit down to write, even to an intimate friend, that I have a hard job before me. Of course it's not always an *unpleasant* task. Sometimes, as when I write to you, it is, as you know, altogether a labor of love. But ordinarily I can compose an equal portion of an essay or a speech with much greater facility. I believe that ladies are the only natural letter-writers. I never yet knew a man who came naturally by the art. Most of them labor and groan over the composition of a letter as if in actual pain, and after all their agonies don't produce much to boast of. In fact, it's only after reading the stuff that other fellows write that I am at all content with what I manage to write myself.

Studying music in Cincinnati must, according to your account, be a delightful occupation. Why, the opportunity of hearing so much fine music is a musical education in itself. Wouldn't I like to be your escort to the evening entertainments? Yes, more than I can tell you—more than you would believe. I am so glad that you are taking lessons in singing from a competent instructor. The ability to sing is a much rarer gift than the ability to play either upon the organ or the piano—that is, the ability to sing *well*—and it oftener gives pleasure to a larger number of persons. What I mean is, that it is a more *sociable* accomplishment. One can more frequently sing in company with others than play in company with others. I sincerely wish that my ability to sing was as great as the pleasure it gives me to do so. But I've never taken any lessons in singing, and of late I've been taking less pains than usual in cultivating my voice in that direction. I've been cultivating it in other directions quite assiduously, however. I practice *elocution* hard and systematically every day. I intend to spare no trouble in gaining complete command of my voice in reading and speaking. We intend having another "musical" soon, though, in which I will be obliged to sing a little. You must be prepared, of course, to teach me something of what you are now learning in order that we may sing together a little next Summer. Our next *musical* will be for Aunt Marion's benefit. She came this (Saturday) morning. We had expected her to come last Thursday morning, but she was delayed by Marion's and Helen's[1] sickness. They were both too unwell to start just when they had expected to start; but they are now looking very well indeed, I think. Dear little Helen isn't fat yet. She is very persistently *lean*; but she seems to me stronger and better than she was last Winter, or last Summer. We were nearly deprived of Aunt Marion's visit altogether by *Jessie's* sickness. She was, Aunt M. says, very unwell indeed for several days. She, as well as several others in the Seminary, had just been vaccinated; and some of the young ladies who had been vaccinated at the same time with Jessie were also sick when she was. Of course they were quick to attribute the mischief to impure vaccine matter and, in consequence, were naturally very much alarmed. Jessie has quite recovered now; but at the first news of her indisposition and the first hint of the supposed cause, Aunt Marion's impulse was to go right on to Staunton.

Do you really practice eight or nine hours every day, Hattie? *Eight or nine hours*! Are you not afraid of injuring your health? I should think that simply the fatigue of sitting so long on so stiff a seat as a piano stool would be injurious to you. I sincerely hope that you wont hurt yourself by too much zeal. I wish that being tired of practice would *always* lead you to write me a letter, as it did in the case of your last. You must often be tired and always to rest yourself in that way would result very delightfully for me. You are as good as you can be now in answering my letters promptly, I think; but, in spite of that fact, the intervals between your letters sometimes seem terribly long to me.

My study has, at my suggestion, been temporarily converted into a bed room for Aunt Marion, and, consequently, I am writing now one story higher than usual. I don't know that my greater elevation of situation, my nearer proximity to the heavens, gives me any special inspiration. I wouldn't like to claim for *this* epistle a special inspiration. Still my third story window here commands quite a pretty view of the town, and quite an extensive one, for our house is placed upon the only elevation in this immediate neighborhood which has any just claim to the name of a *hill*; and I can't help thinking how little is happening in this big place that is worth writing about. There [are] a plenty of pretty girls here, but I can't write about them. Pretty things must be *seen* to be appreciated, and too many of these fair persons have little more than their good looks to recommend them. I've found out one or two both pretty and attractive, and, having succeeded so far, have contented myself and made little further search[.] Don't imagine from all these things I tell you about my stay-at-home habits that I am not fond of society. I am passionately fond of social visiting; but I have too much respect for the claims of my *law* upon me to allow myself the liberties I might otherwise enjoy.

Now, dear Hattie, write to me as soon and as often as you can, wont you? All join me in sending the largest measure of love. Send love to all at home from me when you write. You know that I love you dearly, so that goes—or might go—without the saying.

Lovingly Yours   Woodrow

ALS (WC, NjP).
[1] Marion McGraw Bones and Helen Woodrow Bones, who accompanied their mother, Marion Woodrow Bones, on the visit.

From Harold Godwin

My dear Tommy: Roslyn, L. I. April 24th 1881.

While sitting this evening in my father's library with my sister and brother-in-law lately married, I pulled from my pocket a bunch of letters and found your last among them. It gave me great pleasure to re-read it and I experienced a little pain to think that you should have been discouraged so easily by the *Post*. I fear that you would have a hard time of it in a newspaper office, not because of any refusal to soften or change your sentiments, for this is never asked of an editor, but if you felt that you could not write at all simply because something you happened to say was considered merely injudicious. I do not however wish to bring you to task or anything of the kind. What I say is merely what came into my head on reperusal of your last. . . .

Bob does a little reading but expects to do much more. He wrote a stunning obituary on Beaconsfield and is rapidly getting into the ways of the office and making himself indispensable. . . .

                              Ever   H. G.

ALI (WP, DLC) with WWhw notation on verso of env.: "Ans. April 29th 1881."
On recto of env.: WWsh draft of letter to H. Godwin, April 29, 1881.

Draft of a Letter to Harold Godwin

Dear Pete,   [Wilmington, N. C., April 29, 1881]

Your letter was hugely enjoyed. You had been silent long enough to whet my appetite for a letter to a very fine edge.

I don't think that you altogether understand my position in *opposing* the advice. I jumped at your kind suggestion that I should write something concerning the South for the paper, simply for the enjoyment of expressing some thoughts that had been gathering in my mind for some time. Of course if I had undertaken the functions of a regular correspondent of the paper, the smile you give my withdrawal would have been well deserved. To draw back into my shell under such circumstances would have been ridiculous in the highest degree. But as I was writing only for my own pleasure—and because you had expressed a wish that I should do so—I did not care to modify the careful expression of my opinions simply in order that they might find publication. In short I am entirely selfish in the matter. If I went regularly into journalism—and I sometimes wish that I had done so—I would have done nothing to miss a laugh at my sensitiveness.

Of course I am delighted to hear of Bob's great success in his own position. I knew it would come, but I did not know that it would come so soon. Tell him that he must send me his article on Dizzy [Disraeli], and that he *must* write to me very soon, if he don't want to incur my severest displeasure.

Transcript of WWshL (draft) on recto of env. of H. Godwin to WW, April 24, 1881.

To the Editor of the *International Review*

Dear Sir,[1]   Wilmington, North Carolina [c. April 30, 1881]
  I take the liberty of sending you a short article[2] on the political and industrial questions which the present condition of affairs in the South suggests to every one who casts a thought in that direction. It is a Southerner's view of the "Southern Question." Knowing, as I do, that there exists in the North a genuine desire to understand the sentiment of the South regarding those matters which most nearly concern Southern interests, I have written this article on "The Politics and the Industries of the New South" in the confidence that it would be more than usually interesting to your readers in both sections of the country. I have paid much attention to the subject, and, as I am no more of a politician than it is every conscientious citizen's duty to be, I have, I think, been able to treat it without party bias.
  Permit me to say of myself that I belong to that younger generation of Southern men who are just now coming to years of influence; and I believe that I represent these men of my own age in being full of the progressive spirit, and in being anxious to make a very candid avowal of principles for the purpose of bringing about such a mutual understanding between North and South as will be the only sure foundation for agreement and harmony between the people, or between the parties, of the two sections.
  I will thank you very much for giving my article the benefit of your careful perusal. I leave it to stand on its own merits. In case you should wish any references concerning myself, I shall be glad to give them—either among Northern or among Southern gentlemen whom you may know.
                    Very Respectfully Yours, Woodrow Wilson

P.S. If the paper should not prove acceptable, be kind enough to return it *by Express*, leaving me, of course, to pay the charges.
                              Respty, W. W.

ALS (Henry Cabot Lodge Papers, MHi).
  [1] There were, actually, two editors—Henry Cabot Lodge and John T. Morse, Jr.
  [2] See the note on "Stray Thoughts from the South," printed at Feb. 22, 1881.

Revision of an Unpublished Article

[c. April 30, 1881]

The Politics and the Industries of the New South

Americans are self-reliant in great things as in small, and in nothing more than in politics. This self-reliance often shows itself in a preference for heroic remedies, in a haste to anticipate nature's remedying processes by legislation. This preference for drastic measures, and this haste in their application have nowhere appeared more conspicuously than in the dealings of the country with the "Southern question." Haste was made in applying the extremist measures of reconstruction and in erecting a federal supervision of State elections; and then a pause was made, only because of the perplexity caused by the failure of such remedies to work a cure of the evil, and not because the will to take other bold steps was wanting. But, now that the pause is given, we had best employ it in studying the disease we had thought that we understood from the first.

The proper temper in which to approach the consideration of this subject of the South and its future is one of perfect candor. On the one side there must be perfect straightforwardness in revealing the facts, and on the other, perfect good faith in accepting them. There have already been several more or less well-directed efforts to bring about such a mutual understanding. Some of these endeavors have originated with the press. During the early months of the present year the editors of the *American*, a candid Republic[an] weekly published in Philadelphia, diligently sought an expression of opinion from leading political men in each of the Southern States, propounding to them several clear questions and publishing their answers in full. But, on the whole, the result was decidedly disappointing. One fact most obviously took from the value of the discussion: almost every one of the whole series of letters was the contribution of a politician, and the "symposium" was simply a feast of politicians, who, as politicians are wont to do, only drink many hearty toasts to the doctrines of their party. Some of the contributors were so pitiably weak as to indulge in coarse abuse of those whom they were supposed to be addressing, and from whom they asked respectful attention and considerate treatment; many of them were utterly unable to forget, even for the moment, that they are members of a party, or to realize that there is any further future than the next Presidential campaign; and most of them persistently assumed the absolute impeccability of the white people of the South and the unqualified malignity, or the stubborn stupidity, of the Republican population of the North. Of course this is not the spirit in which to approach a question of such "pith and moment[.]" It is not necessary to assume that wisdom will die with either the one or the other party in the controversy. Neither blindness nor clearness of sight is epidemic in either the North or the South, though much unreasoning prejudice there is in both; and if any class of Northern people that may be represented by the Philadelphia *American* sincerely desires to bring about a better understanding between the two sections, every Southerner of honorable principle ought to be glad to contribute what he can to this mutual enlightenment without heat or spite.

The facts concerning the present political condition of the South are very simple and very plain facts, and may be clearly stated in very few words. The principal fact is the old and now familiar one, that the South is "solid." It is somewhat astonishing that this apparent solidity of Southern political opinion, though so often deplored by some, so often sought to be explained by many, and so often recognized by all, should still be the subject of such universal misapprehension. It would seem that the editors of the Philadelphia *American* misunderstand it no less than do most of their countrymen. In inviting the discussion to which I have referred they declared their purpose to be "to do away with that bar to the highest national political prosperity known as 'the Solid South.' " Their desire, when looked at from their standpoint, was a very creditable one; but it was, none the less, an ignorant desire; for I reckon it a very vital mistake to suppose that it is upon matters of *national* policy that the sentiments of the South are unanimous, or her opinions "solid."

This error it is that has colored and obscured almost every discussion of Southern politics that I have seen or heard. The South has not for some time concerned, and does not now concern, herself largely or actively in national politics. She is of one mind on subjects of supreme consequence in the administration of her local, her home, affairs; upon these principally and upon these only. Upon their concern in these matters which affect the safety of their property, the integrity of their city, county, and State governments, the prosperity of their business, and the comforts of their homes,—upon these almost exclusively depend the choice which the white voters of the South may make between allegiance to the Democratic or allegiance to the Republican party. The enfranchisement of the negro, therefore, undoubtedly explains everything in the political condition of the South that needs any explanation. Since their emancipation the colored people of the

South, governed by what influences it is not now necessary to inquire, have uniformly been compacted, if not in political sentiment or conviction, always in political action; their vote, constituting an immense though not a preponderating proportion of the whole vote of the South, has been united with a solidity which seemingly presents no cleavage line. Under such circumstances the choice of the white voters was quickly and naturally made. The alternatives presented to them were, to be ruled by an ignorant and an inferior race, or to band themselves in a political union not to be broken till the danger had passed. They did what any English people would have done. They determined, as their Northern fellow citizens would have determined under like circumstances, never to suffer themselves to be ruled by another race in every respect so unlike themselves; and in that resolve they cannot be, they should not be, shaken. For they know how fatal was the temporary ascendancy of that race. It, for example, elevated into absolute power the "carpet-bagger," upon whom a national condemnation has fallen. Short as was his sway, the "carpet-bagger" left upon the South a terrible burden of debt, which must be paid by means of taxation so grinding as to make poverty poorer and to frighten away the thrifty immigrants of whom Southern industries will soon stand in such immediate need, or must be repudiated to the permanent detriment of that credit upon which Southern commercial enterprize is dependent. The determination of the Saxon race of the South, that by no division amongst themselves shall the chance for a repetition of such ruinous follies ever again be offered, is necessarily unalterable.

The hostility between the white and the colored citizens of the Southern States is not, therefore, of the nature of a social feud between two hostile races. Of late years the *social* relations between the two have uniformly been characterized by the utmost friendliness. The whole truth of the case could not be more clearly summed up than in the words of the Hon. A. H. H. Stuart, of Virginia, who wrote what seems to me the only valuable, certainly the only truly instructive, letter contributed to the *American's* "symposium." The Southern people are, he says, opposed "to ignorant suffrage, entirely irrespective of race or color." They do not object to the votes of the negroes "because they are negroes—because their *faces* are dark,—or because they were recently held in bondage." "We object to their votes because their *minds* are dark, —because they are ignorant, uneducated, and incompetent to form an enlightened opinion on any of the public questions which they may be called on to decide at the polls." The position is a very intelligible one, then. If these ignorant voters were not combined, there would be no need that the intelligent voters should combine in opposition to their power. Since they are united there is every reason why they should be unitedly opposed.

This is that supreme domestic concern which determines the action of Southern majorities in national politics; and it is to this fact that everything seems to point as to the hinge of the whole controversy. That the South cares comparatively little about other subjects of party policy is indicated by the subordinate part her representatives have, since the war, usually taken in the nominating conventions of the Democratic party. Nor have Southern Congressmen of late years often taken the lead in the deliberations of the Houses. They have had no great national measures upon which unitedly to insist. Not that they have ceased to feel any lively interest in national affairs or that the results of the war have thrown them into a state of sullen indifference. Quite the contrary. They have accepted the verdict of arms with hearty sincerity and are prepared to stand by the Union henceforth with manly loyalty. Their hope is their belief: that this is "an indestructible Union of indestructible States." But there is a crisis in the South, a crisis which affects the whole country, but which does not affect all parts of it alike. It is of great moment in the eyes of the entire Union, but surely of greatest moment in the eyes of Southerners. Their every energy must be bent to the task of bringing them out of their present perplexity and trial in safety and final assurance of strength.

But they cannot be a party to themselves in this work. They must strengthen their influence by national alliances. With which, then, of the two national parties must they act? Assuredly not with the Republicans. The Republican party were the authors of reconstruction. They created this ignorant suffrage which is such a menace, declaring to the world, in the words of the late Senator Morton, that "the exercise of American suffrage involves no intellectual or moral qualifications; and that there is no difference between an American freeman and an American slave which may not be unmade by a mere act of Congress"; and, having created this terrible, unthinking power, they did all that they could to perpetuate its ascendancy. If the Southern people feel themselves in conscience, and in interest, bound to maintain a united resistance to the domination of an ignorant race, surely they must continue to resist any party which manifests even an inclination to force that domination upon them. They must find what constitutional means of opposition to that party they can, and they do find some such means in coöperation with the Democratic party. Their present party preferences are thus easily understood. They have uniformly voted with the Democratic party not because they always approved of its national policy so much as because it represents the constitutional opposition to a party which has time and again manifested a desire and a purpose rudely and without sanction of law to interfere in their local affairs. They are for a time content to subordinate every minor difference of opinion to the paramount necessities of self-defence. Upon a great many questions regarding the non-partisan administration of the federal government there is very far from being universal accord of judgment and conviction among the intelligent classes of the South. It is their close agreement upon the one question which is just now, to them, more vital than all others beside[,] which makes them appear, to those who do not appreciate their situation, to be determinedly combined on every other matter of politics.

This state of facts cannot be too much insisted upon or too constantly presented to the consideration of thoughtful friends of the Union. The adherence of the South to the Democratic party of the North is hardly more than nominal and is certainly at the most temporary and provisional. That party has done nothing that entitles it to command the fealty of the South. They can hardly claim to have exercised any positive influence in the affairs of the South either for better or for worse. And if they have no claims of gratitude on the South, it must be only necessity which binds that section to their organization. Indeed one does not have to read many of the better newspapers of the South to be convinced that many of the recent dealings of the national party calling itself Democratic have brought it into deep contempt in the minds of not a few staunch citizens in the cotton States. Great numbers join with the editor of the Atlanta (Ga.) *Constitution*, the chief journal of a city of over thirty thousand inhabitants, in doubting the patriotism and questioning the Statesmanship of "those who assume to lead and control the Democratic party of the North," and in pronouncing them "narrow-minded timeservers" who depend upon the South to secure for them the fat things of office; and those who are not prepared to go so far in condemnation certainly do not go far in love or admiration.

What is the outlook, then? Is the South always to remain "solid." No, not always: only so long as the necessity for defence continues. And that necessity will continue only so long as the negroes remain ignorant and altogether unfitted by any sort of education—whether the education of the schools or the education

of experience—for the most usual and constant duties of citizenship. In looking for the time of at least partial fitness on their
part we may hope that we are looking to no very remote future.
There is already in many portions of the South a very noticeable
and hopeful betterment in the social condition of the race—and
social advance is generally, if not always, accompanied by mental
and moral improvement. The more energetic among the negroes
are acquiring habits of thrifty self-support. In some sections,
notably, I believe, in northern and western Georgia, they are becoming extensive land holders and industrious farmers of their
own lands. There are here and there whole communities of negro
proprietors who are the forerunners, as far as we can judge, of
an exceedingly valuable, because steady and hardy, peasantry.
These are many of them intelligent citizens: the possession of
earned property always sharpens and tempers the mind. In this
class of the negroes—and in this class only—are found the men
who venture to vote independently both of fear and of prejudice.
It is not against such that there is need of political combination,
but against their fellows who remain in darkness. There is, of
course a great deal that is encouraging in this self-elevation of the
race, for it proves them capable of still further progress. But the
process of self-betterment is necessarily a slow one; they have not
all the ability to raise themselves. They need liberal aid and systematic encouragement: not direct aid in self-support or encouragement in unwarranted aspirations, but aid in removing the obstacles to the highest worldly success and encouragement in
training themselves for greater efforts and substantial achievements. Those of them who will not or cannot educate themselves
must be compulsorily educated and permanently reclaimed from
ignorance and indolence.

Do not these considerations suggest the means of removing the
necessity, or, as some will have it, the menace, of Southern solidity? Whoever will undertake to aid the temporarily impoverished
South in lifting the negroes from degradation will do everything
that can be done in cooperating with natural forces towards the
accomplishment of that end. And whoever will honor themselves
by such an undertaking, and at the same time show to the Southern whites that they do not regard the help they are offering as
an aid to "missions" in a heathen land, will win the lasting gratitude and the warmest love of every true Southerner.

To remove Southern fear and distrust of the Republican party
is another matter. That will require many unquestionable proofs
of the final determination of that party to accept in all good faith

the situation of the two races in the South as they find it, and not a few years of honest endeavor on its part to releive the white population from the imperative necessity of self-defence against a mass of ignorant voters, and thus to remedy so far as is possible the mistakes of reconstruction. But if this plain duty to itself were performed by the Republican party, I can see nothing to forbid the expectation of a speedy redivision and healthy readjustment of parties in the South.

Besides this problem of negro citizenship, which is peculiar to herself, the South seems to have fewer political difficulties with which to contend than have many of the powerful States of the North. She has no cliques of despotic partisans to dominate over her legislatures and no masters of corrupt intrigue to fill her State offices with personal adherents. The administration of government in the Southern States, though not always wise and sometimes inefficient, is generally untainted with corruption. Caucuses there are, of course, to dictate; and federal patronage there is to harrass; but there is no "machine." Southern representatives in Washington, too, though for the most part men of mediocre ability, are still, with few exceptions, men of considerable intelligence and generally of unimpeachable character.

Turning from the political to the industrial prospects of the South, a brighter future offers itself for our contemplation. Whatever doubts may darken the political distance, there are few to forbid the most confident hopes of rapid and termless industrial progress

WWhw MS. (WP, DLC). See note on p. 31 above for identifications and the history of this essay.

Two Essays for a Contest[1]

[c. May 1, 1881]

Congress: Inside the House

It is probable that the average American has as little real insight into the methods by which he is governed as the average Russian has into the secret ways of the autocracy which rules him. Of course an American who does not know that the powers of federal administration are somehow in the hands of the President, that the prerogatives of legislation are in some way exercised by a representative Congress, and that high judicial functions somehow rest with a supreme federal Court, is a notable curiosity. Knowledge of the general exterior construction of our national government is, no doubt, of the common stock of all American school-children. But probably it is equally obvious to every Russian who is sane that absolute power of rule is in the hands of the Czar and his officers and agents; and yet the ways of despotic rule, the inner machinery of monarchical sway, are past finding out by the common man. We all know that our coin comes from the national mints; but how many of us understand the processes of coinage? The green room is in every respect different from the stage.

Its Committee rooms are the green rooms of Congress. Within their privacy legislation is dressed for the public stage. Without the aid of its Committees, Congress would blunder sadly in its public rehersals. No one can understand the workings of Congress who does not comprehend the functions of its Standing Committees.

The House of Representatives has about thirty-five or forty principal committees, of which those on Ways and Means, on Appropriations, on Banking and Currency, on Commerce, on Post Offices and Post Routes, on Rail-Roads and Canals, on Patents, on Foreign, on Military, and on Naval Affairs are probably the most important. The organization of committees such as these was made an imperative necessity by the Federal Constitution itself. The framers of that instrument appear to have adopted absolutely, and without thought of qualification, that theory which Montesquieu believed could be drawn from the constitutional practice of England, namely, that the legislative, executive, and judiciary departments of government must be kept entirely separate and distinct in order to a wise and clement exercise of their powers. Accordingly each department of the federal government was hedged about with very sharply-drawn restrictions; every wall of separation that could anywhere be reared was built, and no gates of communication were cut save such as opened both ways and seemed capable of being easily guarded on either side.

The language of the Constitution did all that language could to prevent any one of the departments from gaining supremacy over the others, but facts were more absolute than constitutional provisions. Holding as it did all the substantial powers of government, the Congress was in reality the regnant department. No practicable distribution of authority between the several branches could have prevented the law-making body from dominating. The Legislature soon realized its own supremacy and soon provided means for exercising effective control over the administration of national affairs. Adopting the usual division of executive departments, the House set in authority over the Treasury a standing Committee of Ways and Means and a standing Committee on Appropriations; over the department of State a similar Committee on Foreign Affairs; over the Interior department like Committees on Indian Affairs, on Commerce, and on Patents; over the War Office and the Navy bureau a Military and a Naval Committee respectively; over the Post Office, a Committee on Post Offices and Post Routes; and over the department of Justice a Committee on the Judiciary. In the Senate a similar distribution of labor was made.

The duties of these committees are plain and simple. They virtually determine the legislation of the House in their respective departments. Every bill introduced by any representative must be without debate referred at once to the Committee within whose province it comes; and no proposition which does not originate with or wear the sanction of one of the Standing Committees can be considered unless two-thirds of the House call for a suspension of the rules. Consequently almost every measure which passes the House—every measure which comes under the consideration of the House—is framed by one or other of these Committees. Their right of initiative within their own spheres can never be questioned. A member who is not one of the Committee on Foreign Affairs cannot reasonably expect to have any influence in determining the international policy of the House; perhaps he has been put on the roll of the Committee on Invalid Pensions and finds himself obliged to expend all his energies within its sphere. No member who has not been appointed one of the Committee on Commerce can have any potential voice in commercial legislation; possibly he is one of a select committee on Epidemic Diseases and finds that it is only in its deliberations that he can wield any positive influence. The most experienced economist in Congress can give no special direction to the action of the House in regard to financial matters unless he have a place on the Committee of Ways and Means; he may be only chairman of a select committee on the Ventilation of the Hall.

And so around the circle. Legislation originates in the Committee rooms. There all the deliberating that means anything is done. The speeches made on the floor of the House are addressed to constituencies. Indeed, if not intended for the ears of constituents, they might as well not be spoken: they are never heard amidst the disorderly noises which assail the ears of all who enter the vast Hall of the House. One's lungs must be made of rubber, and one's throat of sounding brass to overcome the noises of conversation which prevail; and a speaker's eloquence must be powerful, not only in volume of voice, but also in attractiveness of style to arrest the indifferent attention even of his nearest neighbors.

This plan of legislating by means of committees, though its results are not always the best, and though it does not always operate equitably, is a very natural arrangement, and one which is apparently demanded by the necessities of the case. Choice in the matter was necessarily restricted. How, otherwise, could the House ever digest the immense mass of proposals which would be brought before it? How, otherwise, could it ever mature its measures and dispose of its business? Either the House must consent to remain in all the helplessness of a mass-meeting, or it must have these Committees, or it must put itself under the guidance of a Cabinet, as the British Parliament has done, make that Cabinet its standing executive committee and grant it the prerogative of initiative in legislation. The first of course no sane men could think of doing; to do the last would be to violate that sacred theory of Montesquieu's, as it was understood on this side the sea, by uniting the legislative and executive departments in the persons of the Cabinet ministers. These Secretaries would both lead the House and rule the executive—would rule the executive because they led the House. So the Committees must be chosen

True the Committee scheme was not a perfect one. The Speaker of the House must appoint the committees, and thus, instead of being simply the presiding officer chosen because of his impartiality and his knowledge of parliamentary law, must be a party leader selected because of his partiality and knowledge of party management. Then, too, these committees must deliberate away from the eye of the public, in the unapproachable privacy of separate rooms, and the door must thus be left open for corruption to steal in upon committee-men. There must be as many lobbies as there are committee-rooms. Contractors must become close friends of the gentlemen of the Appropriation Committee. The members of the Rail-Road Committee must dream of subsidies. Besides, what dignity remains for Cabinet officers to wear? They are only the chief agents of the committees which determine the policy of their departments. They have no discretion in the exercise of their functions, save when some committee has forgotten to direct them, or where some loosely-drawn law has lengthened their rope a little. The executive is a check on Congress only when Secretaries are stupid or stubborn or self-willed in following or refusing to follow instructions.

This thing of Congress delegating its deliberative duties to Committees of its members does seem to defeat some of the most important purposes of its Constitution—seems, for instance, to preclude such exhaustive public debate of its measures as is necessary to the enlightenment of the country and to the incorrupt and deliberate performance of its principal functions—but what better arrangement could be made? Were it not for that theory concerning the separation of the departments, the officers of the *Cabinet* might be introduced to fulfil the essential offices of the Standing Committees in directing legislation. They would constitute an executive committee of the Houses and a connecting link between the Legislature and the Executive such as would greatly facilitate the operations of government. They could never force Congress beyond its wishes, and they would always be able to acquaint it with the needs of the departments. They would be in a position intelligently to direct legislation without having the power to misdirect it. They would have every means of information without any means of undue concealment. They would have it at heart to protect the Executive against encroachments and would be equally interested in preserving the prerogatives of the Legislature. Instead of being witnesses to inform committees, they would be witnesses to inform and counsellors to guide Congress. Frauds could no longer hide in the records of the departments and corruption could no longer tempt. Who would be worth corrupting except these Secretaries who would daily have to account for themselves and their policy in the trying hours of keen, eager, and searching, public debate? And when these hours came any weak man who might have strayed into the Cabinet would quickly wish himself out of it, so he might escape without disgraceful discomfiture. Only the strong and the competent could bear the brunt of such ordeals and venture to show their faces another day. The country would be pleased to know what laws it was passing and why it was passing them, even if such knowledge were conditioned upon closing the committee rooms.

Of course such a Cabinet-committee must be composed of members of Congress and must always be made up from the ranks of the majority: and the President might sometimes find advisors not of his own party thrust upon him. But the President would scarcely find this more disagreeable than having his Cabinet at the bidding of ill-informed Committees of the opposite party.

This idea of uniting the interests, without in any way uniting the functions, of the legislative and executive departments of government—an idea which has proved a very serviceable one in the practice of more than one of the freest governments of the world —seems an attractive one at first sight in the eyes of practical statesmen; but that stubborn theory concerning the separation of the departments will not hear of it with any degree of allowance.

Some Legal Needs

That State system which is the most characteristic feature of our plan of national government, however admirable in theory and however generally valuable in practice, is not without its serious inconveniences and manifest drawbacks. From the standpoint of the legal practitioner, for instance, it often seems sadly at war with any uniform administration of the laws such as good government seems to demand. State lines are indeed very sharply marked for the lawyer. They indicate the boundaries of different jurisdictions; they limit the domain of differing laws, sometimes of different systems of law; to cross them is to exchange, perhaps, one rule of practice for another; to ignore them is utterly to confuse all knowledge of American law. The degrees of latitude which separate Maine from Louisiana are not more in number nor greater in extent than the degrees of difference which distinguish Maine law from the laws of Louisiana; and even those States which derive their systems of law from the same original have in many cases widely diverged from one another in their later legal policies.

But it is not in the practice of the law only or chiefly that these diversities of legal policy are a cause of embarassment and confusion[.] That every State legislature has practically unrestricted control over almost all the legal relations of the citizens of the commonwealth it represents, and that there in consequence exist within the limits of the Union 48 separate and distinct bodies of law,[2] alike only in their main features, and differing often widely in very many material points, must of course perplex and confound professional practitioners in cases without number; but that is amongst the least of the disadvantages arising from such a state of things. The evil that results to the nation at large from the exercise of this extensive legislative independence on the part of these forty-eight legislatures is a very serious one, and grows to more threatening proportions as the country increases in population and advances in wealth. It begins to become manifest that there are some public affairs, now left to the determination of local legislatures, which are of such vital and universal interest as to demand a uniform and somewhat inflexible policy in their administration.

Unfortunately it needs now only to be stated to be believed that the standard of ability among the members of State legislatures has fallen shamefully low. The emoluments pertaining to the office of State legislator were never at any time considerable, and the dignity which attached to his functions in colonial times seems long since to have departed. It has for many years required an effort of patriotism on the part of any leading citizen to consent to the self-sacrifice involved in the duties of State legislation. It is best plainly to aknowledge that our State lawmakers represent for the most part a very low order of politicians. And of course upon the minds of such men local prejudices and transient passions have the strongest hold; narrow views meet with their readiest acceptance and selfish purposes lead them in a natural bondage. They are most of them men of the hour, swayed by momentary impulses; who if not of limited understanding, are of unlimited inexperience and boundless audacity. However many, however honorable, however brilliant the exceptions, of such a cast are the great majority of State legislators.

With this fact in mind we can readily understand the dangers to which many States are more or less constantly exposed. We can see how it is that State Constitutions are continually tampered with. We can sympathize with Californians who, living under an almost socialistic Constitution,[3] also live in habitual fear of the license which that law gives to the headstrong ignorance of their rulers at Sacramento. We are not at a loss to account for the fact that many States sadly in need of development and with many advantages of soil and climate to freely offer plan and appeal in vain for immigration. We are prepared to admit the almost unanswerable logic of that argument in favor of federal control of railways and telegraphs which founds itself upon the local oppression of tyrannical corporations whose chief power for evil flows from the labors of its agents in the lobbies at State capitals.

Whither these considerations lead us is now plain. There are some subjects of legislation which the present Constitution of the Union leaves to the determination and regulation of State Assemblys, and which are yet affairs of such paramount importance and such universal concern as to make a uniform and fixed policy in their direction of vital necessity to the whole country, or at least to larger sections of it than are included within the boundary of any single State. Prominent amongst these matters is the care of those vast tracts of forest land which stretch along the borders and extend into the interior of many States without any break in their own continuity, and which in some portions of the continent spread their unbroken length and breadth over many parallels of latitude and through many degrees of longitude. As her forests begin to disappear a State may endeavor by provident provisions of law to guard against their total destruction and to provide for their partial restoration, and still, in spite of her wise forethought, be visited with the droughts and harassed by the vicissitudes of climate which she had feared as a consequence of the clearance of her lands because her neighboring States, into whose territories these same forests extend, have been indifferent and improvident. There are now parts of the Union in which wholesale levelling of forests daily proceeds without check or hindrance. We are warned by observant citizens of the States which occupy the central and western regions of the continent that a rapid change of climate and a marked decrease of fertility are being brought upon whole sections of the country because of the wasteful and unforbidden demolition of extensive forests; that districts once densely wooded will oneday soon have to replant its forests to bring back the rains and stave off sterility.

But the superintendence of forests is not the only matter of universal concern which demands a uniformity of policy such as only the federal government would seem to be able to insure. There are others of equal, if not of superior, importance. The determination of what property shall be subject to debt and under what conditions debts are to be contracted and collected, would seem to be one of these; for from the capricious and vacillating policies of the different States upon this supreme commercial matter result the disastrous checks and shiftings of trade from which so many communities suffer ever and again, and industrial embarassments greater even than those which would come from the want of a uniform standard of value or a uniform system of currency.

What are we to say too to such a power as that of abolishing capital punishment for crime being left within the province of State legislatures? Ought any local legislative body to be allowed discretion so unlimited that it may at any time bring upon whole communities an epidemic of crime? Is not the whole country shaken and jeoparded by these local trangressions of the laws of good government?

Look again at the control exercised by State legislatures over that institution which is not less fundamental to society than is the institution of property itself, the institution of marriage, of the family. Are there not States where the privilege of divorce has been so extended that marriage has become an empty mockery and every encouragement given to a licentiousness which threatens the entire organization of society itself with destruction?

WWhw MSS. (WP, DLC).

¹ The text of these two essays is printed from drafts replete with emendations. Wilson submitted copies of them, perhaps with additional changes, to the Philadelphia *American*, a weekly magazine, for its college prize contest in the spring of 1881, probably on about May 1. No announcement of this contest appeared in the regular issues of the *American* during the spring of 1881. But for later references, which make it clear that the contest had been announced then, see the Philadelphia *American*, ii (Aug. 6, 1881), 270, and iii (Oct. 22 and Nov. 19, 1881), 22, 86.

The first essay, "Congress: Inside the House," was selected for the final competition and assigned the number "A.B.25." Wilson, so informed, wrote this number in the upper left-hand corner of the first page of his own copy. His second essay, "Some Legal Needs," apparently did not make the final round in the competition. However, as we shall see, Wilson finally received payment for it as well as for "Congress: Inside the House."

The *American* seems to have abandoned the contest and paid off some or all of the contributors. JRW to WW, August 14, 1882, notes that the magazine was offering $15 for Woodrow's piece, which had been "waiting for the judges' decision," and predicts that the contest would never come off. It was a correct prediction: the *American* published none of the entries. The managing editor, Howard M. Jenkins, wrote to Wilson on May 15, 1883 (printed as an Enclosure in JWW to WW, June 7, 1883), enclosing payment of $30 for "the two essays submitted for the 'College Prize' Contest, in 1881."

² Wilson was obviously referring to the territorial and District of Columbia governments as well as to the thirty-eight state legislatures.

³ Wilson was here referring to the California constitution of 1879, which had been written by a convention dominated by Dennis Kearney's Workingmen's party, allied with rural anticorporation delegates. The constitution of 1879 was notable for its provisions for regulation of railroads, taxation of banks and utilities, and equalization of tax valuations. See John W. Caughey, *California* (New York, 1940), pp. 453-58.

To Harriet Augusta Woodrow

My sweetest Cousin,   Wilmington, N. Carolina, May 10th 1881

Aunt Marion and the two girls left us yesterday and I am again in the second story quietly writing to you as before. The party left yesterday under father's charge. He will accompany them all the way to Staunton, as that lies directly on his route to Maysville. At one time he thought of going around by way of Washington and Cincinnati and thus making an opportunity of stopping a few hours at least in Chillicothe. But he is so pressed for time that he found it necessary to go direct to Maysville. As it is, he will probably be kept away for three Sabbaths, as he has to attend a meeting of an important committee appointed by the Philadelphia Council,¹ as soon as the General Assembly adjourns.²

Of course we have enjoyed Aunt Marion's visit immensely. She seemed to enjoy it very much herself. I think it does us great good in one respect to have visitors with us occasionally: they leave us with a very much higher appreciation of Wilmington.

We are apt to grow tired of it and greatly underrate it ourselves, whilst visitors seem very favorably impressed with it. Marion declared before leaving that the girls she had met here were the nicest she had ever met anywhere. Helen found plenty to occupy her mischievous little hands in mother's big flower garden. The little monkey did one thing which quite took away mother's breath for a minute. She went into the green-house and finding a cigar box full of rich earth in which some seedlings that mother had been carefully nursing were just beginning to sprout nicely, quite innocently emptied it of its contents and appropriated it to her own uses! Mother had a hearty laugh at the unconscious mischief done, in spite of her momentary regret at the loss of her young plants.

On reaching Columbia, on their way hither, Aunt Marion was met at the train by sister Annie, brother George, and their two boys, Wilson and George. As they passed through at night, sister could not take [her] little Jessie down to the depot. She took the boys because Aunt Marion had never seen either of them. She had not seen sister Annie since her marriage—had not seen her since she spent the Summer in Rome, about eight years ago. It has been longer than that since *you* saw her, has'nt it? How delightful it would be if you would come South next Autumn when we expect Jessie [Bones] to visit us, on her way to Columbia! But we will talk about that next Summer during that visit to which *I* am looking forward with so much eagerness. Do you think that I will or can be eloquent enough to persuade you to come?

To-day, the 10th, is "Decoration Day" with us—that is, it is the day on which the ladies of the *"Ladies' Memorial Association"* conduct the now empty ceremony of decorating the graves of the Confederate dead. It is a day of regrets for me; not of the same sort of regrets that are supposed to engage the thoughts of others, however. *My* regret is, that there should be any such ceremonious decoration of these graves. I think that anything that tends to revive or perpetuate the bitter memories of the war is wicked folly. I would, of course, wish to see the graves of the Confederate soldiers kept in order with all loving care. But all the parade and speech-making, and sentimentality of "Decoration Day" are, I think, exceedingly unwise.

The contents of your last letter pained me a good deal. Is'nt it sad to think how little respect is had for the Sabbath, not in Cincinnati only but in *most* of the cities of the country! I was heartily sorry that you had such a bitter disappointment about that grand concert; for it *must* have been a very sore disappointment. I tell you, Hattie dear, the more I see of society the more I am convinced that a girl who is conscientious is shut out from a great many pleasures which seem in themselves very innocent. But there would be very little pleasure in going to a Sabbath concert with an uneasy conscience as a companion; would'nt there? So that, after all one don't miss much *real* enjoyment by being conscientious. I don't think you need care what Mr. Rudolphsen may think of your not using the ticket he was polite enough to give you in so complimentary a manner. If he can't respect and honor your religion, his good opinion is scarcely worth having. Speaking of Mr. Rudolphsen, it is a shame that you should have to submit to the annoyance of his ill-timed compliments and attentions! Of course I can't blame him for admiring you,—since to do so would be to blame *myself*—and I suppose that all German musicians have ungovernable tongues; but it must be very hard to know how to repel such advances, and it must detract something from the value of his instructions that he should be thus inclined to abuse his privileges.

I am glad that you like to write letters, and if the only drawback to your enjoyment is the apprehension of adverse criticism, you need certainly have no such fear in writing to me, as I am sure you know. I would be far too indulgent towards anything that you might write ever to criticise it, even if I were to find anything in what you wrote deserving of criticism.

You did *not* say that you practiced "eight or nine" hours a day. I have looked at your letter again and find that you said "seven or eight" hours. How I got the wrong impression I can't imagine. I read the letter twice and both times read that portion of it incorrectly. You said, "I have a fine upright piano in my room and practice seven or eight hours a day" which left me with the impression that you spent that length of time at the piano every day —and I naturally thought that a great deal.

Next week we are to have the regular annual Sabbath School picnic. The picnic grounds are on the shores of a lovely lake about two hours ride from here on the rail-road to Columbia. Hitherto I have escaped these picnics as I've always been away in May, but this time I must go, I suppose. I am rather afraid of these *promiscuous* picnics. One is never *sure* of having a nice time at them, because one can never be sure of being able to pick one's company for the day. I shall try hard, however, if I go, to get with a pleasant party of girls and *manufacture* a nice time for myself. Certainly the only way to enjoy a picnic is to make up your mind before hand that you will enjoy it at all events.

When does the term close at the College of Music? It can't be very far off now, is it?

Dear Mother and Josie join me in sending a great deal of love. You know how much I send—just as much as you desire.

Lovingly Yours   T. Woodrow Wilson

ALS (WC, NjP).
¹ This was the second General Council of the World Presbyterian Alliance, which met in Philadelphia, Sept. 23-Oct. 3, 1880. JRW had been elected a delegate to the Alliance by the General Assembly of the Presbyterian Church in the United States on May 26, 1876.
² The General Assembly of the southern Presbyterian Church met in the First Presbyterian Church, Staunton, Va., May 19-28, 1881.

From Robert Bridges

Dear Tommy,   New York, May 12th [1881]

. . . I have grown interested in the politics of the day,—also in the political sentiment of the country as expressed in the newspapers of every section. My exchange reading is a daily education in this respect. Most of the Southern papers fall to my lot, and I have been especially interested in noting the tone of their editorial articles. From them many new ideas, as to the spirit of the educated part of the South, have come to me. There is a liberal tone about the Atlanta *Constitution*, New Orleans *Times*, Memphis *Appeal*, and Vicksburg *Herald* which pleases me and shows me some finger-boards which point to your political future. Unless I read blindly I see indications of a growing discontent with the Bourbon Democratic party, but not, as some seem to think, a growing desire to unite with Republicanism. It is an independent spirit which does not find its affinity in either political party, but which I believe will before many years crystallize into a new form. That new form, if I read aright, will accept the principles of national supremacy which the war determined. But its chief end and aim will be the social and industrial improvement of the South, and to that end it will adopt principles of Universal Education and Free Trade. The South's experience of in many cases a corrupt carpet-bag government has pre-disposed them to civil-service reform, and made them anxious for something more than well-sounding talk on the subject.

There are four points, no one of them new it is true, which, however, have not been grouped together before. As the fundamental principles of a party. They have appeared in platforms as mere catch-words, or perhaps as cheap drapery to conceal the debilitated form of a decrepit and dying party

But I don't mean to write about politics, especially as what I have written does not come from real knowledge of the situation, but is only inferred from my reading. . . . It is just a year since I began work in journalism and in that time I have had but a few days of rest. It has been a pretty severe initiation, but has brought with it some degree of success. Ah, Tommy, if we only could remain true to our old dreams, and never mistrust them, how much more we could accomplish. They put life in nerve and muscle, and make what seems tangled and mysterious, plain and straight. . . .   Your Old Friend   Bob Bridges

ALS (WP, DLC) with WWhw notation on env.: "Ans. May 24th 1881." Also on env. WWhw notes: "What the National Republican League and What its platform? What *Scrutin de liste?*" These were questions for WW's letter to Bridges of May 24, 1881.

From Richard Heath Dabney

Dear Tommy,   University of Virginia, May 16th 1881.
   . . . The election for president came off some time ago & the result was that Shepherd[1] was elected–(to my satisfaction) on the first ballot, his opponents being Dick Smith[2] and Repudiator Walker.[3] . . . As for the orators, I avoided them as I would a pestilence, though indeed if I had had time I think I should have gone around just to see what sort of a monkey show it was. Fenn,[4] a thing which wears a long coat that fairly drags the ground, got the medal. He howled, (I am told) on the glory of the Lone Star State. I don't remember whether I have ever told you that "Judge" Wilkerson[5] has been sitting at our table since you left. He is a bully good fellow. . . .
   I am as ever Your friend & bro. in Φ.Ψ.   R. H. Dabney

ALS (WP DLC) with WWhw notations on env.: "Ans. 5/31/81."
   [1] Stonewall J. Shepherd, University of Virginia, Law, '81, had been elected president of the Washington Society. Dabney is responding to the questions in WW's letter of April 20, 1881.
   [2] Richard M. Smith, University of Virginia, M.A., '82.
   [3] Probably Robert J. Walker, University of Virginia, Law, '81. His nickname, "Repudiator," referred to the movement in Virginia to repudiate or scale down the large state debt. There were outright repudiators, and perhaps Walker was one of them. On the other hand, he may have supported the Readjusters (see note 1 at May 24, 1881), who were frequently but inaccurately called repudiators. The other Walker who attended the University of Virginia in 1880-81 was Cyrus Walker, an undergraduate.
   [4] Francis Marion Fenn, University of Virginia, '81.
   [5] William W. Wilkerson, University of Virginia, Law, '81.

To Robert Bridges

Dear Bobby,   Wilmington, N. Carolina, May [24] 1881
   The receipt of your letter gave me a great deal of genuine pleas-

ure. It seemed to me an age since I had heard from you, and I was actually beginning to fear that your engrossing duties were taking at least the edge off of the old friendship. I know that you will forgive the suspicion now that I have frankly confessed it— for the confession evidences the trust I still put in you. The simple fact of the matter is that I value our friendship so very highly that I am made uneasy—perhaps morbidly so—by every interruption of our intercourse.

You need never have any fear of tiring me with politics—at least not with such political topics as your letter contains. Of the unsavory particulars of party intrigues and of *personal* politics; of Garfield; of Blaine; of Conkling; of Garfield vs. Conkling and Conkling vs. Blaine, I have indeed heard enough and more than enough. No one can have been more disgusted than I with the dirty business of which Mahone was the central disfigurement, with the chagrin of the Democrats at the sinister successes of Republican rings and at their own loss of the valuable aid of the Virginia scamps.[1] But in political *principles*, in genuine political opinions honestly held, in political tendenc[i]es, and in the broader phases of party movements I become more and more interested day by day. I like nothing better than to talk of such things and write about them and hear of them from others who do their own thinking.—All of which is *a propos* and introductory to this remark: that I was specially interested in what you said of the tendenc[i]es of opinion shown in the Southern press and that I am gratified beyond measure to hear of the liberal and independent tone taken by leading Southern journals. I seldom see any Southern papers except our own Wilmington *Star*, than which a more puerile and picayune sheet I think it would be hard to find. Its editor is an *exceptional* ass. I have no doubt you are correct in your interpretation of the direction of opinion in the South. Certainly *I* sympathize with all that you deem characteristic of the new sentiment of the South. I am particularly glad that the Atlanta *Constitution* is prominent among the leading advocates of these old principles made new and fitted to a re-forming society. I think it more than probable that I will finally settle upon Atlanta as my place of practice and, therefore, it is satisfactory to know that its leading journal is supported in such opinions—for I don't believe that the Atlanta *Constitution* or any other paper ever freely consents to support any doctrines which are not acceptable to the majority of its subscribers. Atlanta is not in every respect an attractive place, but it is now one of the largest and one of the most thriving places in the South. It has every advantage of situation and seems likely to continue to grow and to prosper; and, since I have at length about come to the same opinion that you pronounced some time ago, namely that I can probably find a more favorable opening and a wider sphere of influence in the South than in the North, I do not know that I could do better than to settle in Atlanta, the capital of one of the most thrifty of our Southern States, provided circumstances are moderately favorable to my going thither.

I suppose you knew of the fate of my second letter to the *Post*, did'nt you?—and perhaps you had a little laugh at my expense, for my sudden and sensitive withdrawal into my shell because of the return of my piece must have seemed strange; but my opinions concerning the political condition and prospects of the South are very clear-cut and definite and fixed and conclusive, and, although it was only the *form* of my article that was seriously objected to, still I could hardly have changed the form without altering the substance: and, as I was writing as much for my own pleasure as for the purpose of getting my opinions into print and before the reading world, I did not think it worth while to amend what I had said by making a second trial at its expression. I can wait for more favorable circumstances: when I can publish and no one will be responsible for what I say but myself.

Give Pete lots of love from me. I have more and more reason, the more I know of him, to value his friendship very highly indeed. The old fellow's made of genuine good stuff, and is bound to succeed, in my opinion, when he finds the work he wants. If you lose him from the office, it will truly be a severe loss to you. His friendship for you is a very sterling article and I'll be exceedingly sorry when you are deprived of his companionship.

And now I've got some questions to ask you, Bobby. Since I've left the region of reading rooms my means of information is somewhat limited and I'm going to draw on your knowledge of the contents of *exchanges*. And first, what is *Scrutin de liste* which is agitating French parties?[2]—or was agitating them before this little Tunis affair that is creating such a stir was undertaken?[3] I take the London *Times* (weekly) and with all that has transpired in English and European politics *since my subscription began* I am pretty familiarly acquainted. But *Scrutin de liste* seems to have been introduced into French discussion in the interval between my leaving the foreign papers of the University reading room and beginning to take the *Times* on my own account, and I am, therefore, somewhat at a loss to understand its exact meaning, though I have gathered from various indirect sources of information a vague idea of what it is. Can you help me to a clearer comprehension of it. Its name certainly suggests nothing very definite.

Then, second, what is the National Republican League and what its recently promulgated "platform" of principles.[4] From hints that I have caught as to its purposes, I suspect that it holds opinions concerning tenure of civil offices and others [sic] matters which are of special interest to me.

And, thirdly, is there any truth in the rumor that Carl Shurtz is to take "editorial charge" of the *Evening Post*?[5]

I wont trouble you with answering any more questions this time. I hope that I have'nt given you too much to answer already!

I read your sketch of Beaconsfield and liked it much, principally because it did not say much in praise of the crafty old fox. I have read everything concerning him that I could lay my hands on ever since my Soph. year in college and the more intimate I have become with his career the less have I liked the man and the smaller has grown my admiration for him, though of course his wonderful success and his many conquering qualities have often created in me a feeling closely akin to admiration. No one could dispute his *brilliancy*, but the brilliant is not always the admirable or the beautiful. He was simply a King among Jews. To *some* that may seem high praise; to me it does not.

Besides studying law daily I don't do much except read the papers and an occasional book, and practice elocution. To the latter I devote about an hour every day, and my voice is, I am sure, fast improving under the treatment. I took some lessons from a very capital instructor some months ago, and now I am my own tutor, with the guidance of a very excellent text-book prepared by an experienced teacher. In addition to the vocal exercises I make frequent extemporaneous addresses to the empty benches of my fathers church in order to get a mastery of easy and correct and elegant expression in preparation for the future. My topics are most of them political and I can sometimes almost see the benches smile at some of my opinions and deliverances.

I have recently finished Trollopes Life of Cicero and have enjoyed it hugely. It is one of the most vividly written biographies I ever read. The first volume is altogether enjoyable because it tells of the brightest and most honorable portion of the great Roman's career. The second volume, after Ceasar comes on the stage is not so enjoyable. Next I am to read Caesar's life, Froude's *Sketch*.

But I must stop. It is time for the evening mail to close and I want to get this off. Do write as often as you can, Bobby; I always look anxiously for your letters. All that you can tell me about yourself and your thoughts interests me entirely. With much love,

Your sincere friend   T. Woodrow Wilson

Love to Wilder

ALS (Meyer Coll., DLC).

¹ The "Virginia scamps" were William Mahone, John H. Massey, and Harrison H. Riddleberger, leaders of the Readjuster movement in Virginia, the objective of which was to scale down or readjust the state's public debt. The movement cut across party lines, but its chief opponents were conservative Democrats who had passed funding laws in 1866 and 1871. The Readjusters captured the legislature in 1879 and the governorship in 1881, and they wrote many Readjuster principles into law in the Riddleberger Act of 1882. Mahone was elected to the United States Senate in 1880 and by voting with the Republicans in the special session of March 1881 gave them control of the upper house. He was rewarded with important committee assignments, and Riddleberger was made sergeant-at-arms. WW was undoubtedly referring to this transaction in his remark about "dirty business."

² A system of voting for members of the Chamber of Deputies, proposed in May 1881 by Louis Gambetta. It gave each elector of a *Département* as many votes as the *Département* had deputies in the Chamber and permitted the elector to distribute his votes or concentrate them on one man. The scheme was offered as a substitute for the *scrutin d'arrondissement* in which the elector voted only for the deputy from his *arrondissement*.

³ Tunisia was made a French protectorate under the terms of the Treaty of Bardo imposed on the Bey of Tunis in May 1881.

⁴ WW's question was probably prompted by an item in the New York *Nation*, XXXII (May 12, 1881), 326, noting the formation in Philadelphia of a National Republican League by Pennsylvanians who had opposed a third nomination for Grant in 1880. The League was led by Wharton Barker and Rotch Wister and aimed to "elevate and purify" the Republican party by a number of reforms, including the introduction of a good-behavior tenure and a pension system into the civil service system.

⁵ See note at Aug. 9, 1881.

To Richard Heath Dabney

My dear Heath,   Wilmington, N. C., May 31st 1881

In pursuance of a sudden resolution to square accounts with all my correspondents, I have for the past week been bravely writing letter after letter until now all my correspondents are in my debt except yourself. Yours was the last letter to come, of those that I have been answering, and I have felt obliged to reply to them in chronological order, lest I should come hopelessly into arrears to some one.

I was astounded, I must confess, at the result of the oratorical contest in the Wash. Her materials must be poor indeed, if Fenn be her best "orator." I remember the fellow well. That is, I remember his appearance—there was little else about him to strike one. He suggested to me a greasy junk-shop Jew who had been partially washed and renovated and oiled that he might appear to less overwhelming disadvantage among decent people. The extravagantly long coat and the tilt of his hat were enough to fix upon him the stamp of vulgarity. The leaders of the Wash. can't feel that they have much ground for congratulating themselves on the result of separating the medals and setting up a false standard by laying down a false distinction. I am glad that Wilkerson won the debater's medal. He used to impress me as one of the very best men in Minor's classes—always familiar with the lesson and always clear-headed,—every way a *solid* man. You are fortunate in having secured him for "our" table.

Instead of growing duller and quieter as the warm weather comes on, times are becoming more lively here. We are having all sorts of excursions and entertainments, the latter chiefly musical—for very few people here seem unduly eager to give "parties" or dinings. The principal *social* events of the season have been *wedding* receptions. Various young couples have recently hazarded union. Meanwhile I go pensively amongst the darlings yet unmarried and wonder how many years of comparative starvation will suffice to bring me enough practice to think of risking my fortunes in like ventures!

How is Sam. Woods getting on now? Give the old fellow lots of love from me when you see him. I would so like to have an afternoon's controversy with him after the manner of old times.

Here's a tidbit from the New York *Sun* that I'm tempted to send you for practice in the "heavy English" style of pronunciation:

"Do you play the guitar?   Who has red auburn he-ah

No. I don't play the guitar;   She plays the guitar
                                                         Quite tra-la-la.

But my sist-ah   Have a cigar?"

Lippitt

I *had* a touching piece after the style of the poem touching the experiment of writing "Agnes, I love thee" in the sand; but it's in a book, and too long for transcription in this epistle, so you'll have to wait for it as best you can. I thought when I read the article on Fraternities in the Magazine that the sentiments were exceeding familiar.[1] I first guessed that Chas. [Kent] was the author. Certainly it expresses my sentiments—and expresses them with considerable force too.

How are the prospects for the degree? Do you still stick to the big ticket. I suppose it don't seem so big now that I'm not near enough to drop in on you in study hours! How I would like to do that same, though! I hope you'll have the very best luck. Much love to all the boys, and regards to all inquiring friends—to Lefevre and Andrews, whether they inquire or no.

Very sincerely Your friend, and bro. in ΦΨ   T. Woodrow Wilson

ALS (Wilson-Dabney Correspondence, ViU).
   [1] This was Philadelphos [R. H. Dabney], "Secret Fraternities," the *Virginia University Magazine*, xx (April 1881), 389-93. This article praised fraternities for their legitimate activities but severely condemned their intrigues in electing the Final Presidents of the literary societies.

From George Howe, Jr.

Dear Tommie   Columbia S. C. June 24/81
   Yours with spectacles turned up all right this morning.

   I am very sorry that the mistake was made about the frames. It is possible that my measurement was not altogether accurate. Be that as it may, the spectacles were sent by to-days mail and you will have them in a few days.

   About the solutions for your nasal aparatus and throat; you are correct as to the strong solution being for the throat, the weaker for the nose. I do not remember which I directed to be put up in greatest quantity[.] It is probable though, that the solution for the nose, the weaker, would be in greatest bulk, since there is most waste.

   You can easily ascertain by consulting the prescription at the drug store. You did not say whether the folks noticed any change in your voice. . . .   Yrs affly   Geo Howe jr

ALS (WP, DLC) with misc. WWhw and WWsh notations on env., including WW's practice signature "Woodrow Wilson."

From Robert Bridges

Dear Tommy: Snug Harbor. Staten Island Aug 9th 1881
   . . . Of course you have read all about the change in proprietorship of the *Post*—of the new and very intellectual Trinity who have taken it in charge.[1] It has been very successful and promises to be even more so in the future. There are both capital and brains behind it and the old paper has a new lease of life. The change does not affect my position and I don't apprehend that it will. Pete will stay for some time yet and may be for another year. Lately he seems rather inclined to stick to it. You know his restless disposition and consequently it is hard to predict what he will do. . . .

   Now Tommy you can't complain of the length of this letter— if you can of its tardiness. Its the same old Bob who writes it and I hope you wont repay his tardiness in like coin. I did not want to write a letter with biliousness all through it—so I waited till I could send one which was like me. I am anxious to hear of your settlement. I hope you have decided for Atlanta. The more I read of it, the more I am impressed that it is the vortex of the new South and pebbles dropped there will make a greater stir than stones in shallower places. Write me soon and please direct hereafter to "Office *Evening Post*."

Your Old friend   Bob Bridges.

ALS (WP, DLC) with WWhw notation on env.: "Ans. 8/22/81." Also on env. misc. WWhw notes on Bridges' letter.

1 The new proprietor of the New York *Evening Post* was Henry Villard, who purchased it in May 1881. The "new and very intellectual Trinity" to whom Villard entrusted the paper were Carl Schurz, editor-in-chief, and Edwin L. Godkin and Horace White, associate editors. Godkin, who had been editor of the New York *Nation* from its founding in 1865, continued the *Nation* as the *Post's* weekly edition. On Schurz's withdrawal in 1883, Godkin became editor-in-chief of the *Post*, serving until 1900.

From Janet Woodrow Wilson

My darling Son,   Wilmington N. C. Aug 20th 1881.

. . . I am glad you found old friends in M[aysville]. It must have been pleasant. Of course I have no news. Dr. Smith of the S. W. Presbyterian,[1] in noticing the Minutes, commends the style in which they are printed, but adds that he wished he could praise the *accuracy* of the volume as well—and speaks very severely of some mistake in the published statistical Report of the N. Orleans Presbytery. I hunted up the original Copy, and found as I expected that if there was any mistake it was to be laid at the door of the Presbyterial Stated Clerk, and I took advantage of your father's absence, and wrote Dr. W.[2] a note to that effect. I wrote very carefully—so that he could not possibly take offence. At the same time I think he will be careful how he criticises the next number of Minutes. . . .   God bless you   Lovingly   Your   Mother

ALS (WP, DLC) with WWhw notation on env.: "Rec'd Aug. 23rd 1881."

1 The Rev. Dr. Henry Martyn Smith, editor, *Southwestern Presbyterian* of New Orleans, 1869-94; Moderator, General Assembly of the southern Presbyterian Church, 1873.

2 The Rev. Dr. John N. Waddel, Chancellor, Southwestern Presbyterian University at Clarksville, Tenn.; Moderator of the General Assembly, 1868.

From Joseph R. Wilson, Jr.

My darling brother,   Wilmington N. C. Aug 20th 81

. . . We went this afternoon to hear *dear* Bro Window-glass preach and we heard him talk about when brothers lose sisters and husbands lose wives &c, when he talked about husbands los-

ing wives he looked very sad and die-away. I expect he was thinking about his wife and *dear* Brother Norpukes, it was a very touching exhibition. Mama says it is a great comfort to her that you dont
have to suffer with us. . . .

The U. S. ship of war "Yosemite" commanded by Rear-Admiral
Joseph R. Wilson is almost ready for sea. I have got 21 men[,]
the 2nd lieut.[,] Boatswain, 2nd Ass. Engineer, one midshipman
and a cabin boy made—so you see I only have to make about 50
more men to make. and then there are a few things on deck to
make, and one or two boats to finish; would you have a commander besides the Admiral? I have determined to have the "Yosemite" the flag ship on the Mediteranian station.

So please make me an Admiral instead of a captain (unless you
want to make both) in full dress unifrom. . . .

Brother dear, please write to *me* very soon because it is such
a treat for me to get a letter.

Mama joins me in piles of love to you all,—from Woodrow Jr
up.   Very lovingly and affly   Your brother J. R. W. U. S. N.
(over)

P. S.   I am looking very anxiously for my Rear Admiral, and a
letter from Mr Thomas Woodrow Wilson, Sect U. S. Navy
                                            J. R. W. U. S. N.
ALS (WP, DLC).

To Robert Bridges

Dear Bobby,   Maysville, Kentucky, August 22nd 1881
Your nice long letter from Snug Harbor was forwarded to me
from home last week. I need not tell you that I enjoyed it. My
appetite for anything from you is always of the keenest kind and
this last epistle of yours was as great a gratification to it as usual.

I am here on a visit to my oldest sister, who is the wife of a
Presbyterian minister, the Rev. A. R. Kennedy. Until about a week
ago, when I arrived here, I had not seen her since the early part
of Soph. year, and, as you may imagine, the pleasure of being once
more with her now is proportionately great. Maysville is, as you
know, may-be, on the Ohio, about 50 miles above Cincinnati. It
is a very flourishing little manufacturing town of about six or
seven thousand inhabitants. Like so many others of the towns
which crowd the shores of this great but unreliable river, it spreads
itself out to great length, being prevented by steep hills from
leaving the river many blocks away even at the broadest point of
the narrow strip of shore. Lying close, as it does, in its narrow

cove, backed by green hills which here leave the river for a space only to return to it almost immediately, its situation is a very attractive and a very picturesque one.—My Georgia cousin, Miss Jessie Wilson [Woodrow] Bones—a very plump and pleasing person despite the *lean* suggestion of her name—is with me. Next week we will go on to Chillicothe, Ohio, to see other relations; and there I will expect another letter from you.

Your letter brought me the first news I had had of old Stouty's[1] death. I was sincerely grieved to hear of it. Do tell me the particulars of his death, if possible, when you write again. As far as Stouty himself is concerned, I doubt if death were a calamity. Unless I've very wrongly estimated his character, he was as well prepared to die as any man in '79. He seemed to me a simple, stedfast Christian. But he was such a sterling man that his death seems to me a great loss to the class—the loss of a hard and intelligent worker.

Jack Davis with German beer blossoms in his nose! The idea! Why the old poller never could boast of much beauty, and the new color in his countenance can scarcely enhance its charms! And how can it comport with the German theology in his eyes?[2]

Your letter contained two bits of information which gave me much satisfaction. One was that you will soon have an opportunity to visit your home and see the little black-eyed girl and the bonnie Nan. You have certainly earned a holiday by this time. The other source of my satisfaction is, that you contemplate preparing an article on the "Spirit of the Advanced Press of the South." I hope that you will not confine yourself to a newspaper article, or series of articles, but will write an extended paper for one of the Reviews. I suppose that's what you intend doing; is'nt it? With such abundant materials as you must have you can undoubtedly produce something well *worth* publishing in any magazine. Whether or not Review editors will give an article by an unknown author due attention, my own experience has proved to be a very different question. But the trial must be gone through, and I don't think that *you* need anticipate anything but ultimate success. Whenever I have leisure sufficient I intend to give the publishers every opportunity to become familiar with my name, *and my desire to publish*.

I think that you may regard it as settled that I will try my fortunes in Atlanta, and that, unless extraordinary obstacles present themselves, I will there set myself to the everywhere arduous task of establishing a practice. So far Atlanta undoubtedly appears to be the centre of the new life of the New South, and some centre of activity is what I eagerly seek. I don't feel that I am yet anything like well equipped for the bar, Bobby, but I know enough of law to be able to *find* whatever information I desire on any particular point, and I console myself with the reflection that every one who enters such a profession as that of law must be content to begin on small accumulations of knowledge—*mastery* in any department being of necessity a thing which only many years of close and ceaseless labor can achieve. I have, therefore, determined to seek admittance early next year; so that you may expect to meet at our reunion at Princeton next June, instead of simple "Tommy," a full-bearded stranger calling himself a lawyer, and thinking much professionally of ancient and modern legal lore.—And yet you may expect to see simple "Tommy" after all; for I don't believe that I've changed a bit in spirit, in essence, in my loves and tastes—in anything but, perchance, in outward form—since I turned my physical back on dear old Princeton.

I have just received a letter from my mother in which she encloses a cutting from the New York *Sun*, headed "Princeton's Treasurer," in which much is told of Harris's crooked ways in the matter of drawbacks, of his criminal mismanagement in connection with the neglected drainage which brought the fever last year, and of other rascalities which we all suspected many years ago, but which have only now, it seems, been brought to the full light. The reporter charges Harris only with such things as I believe him quite capable of and his account of the present state of affairs is, therefore, to me, easy of credence. I hope that the board of trustees will get speedily rid of the Rev. Wm!3 I send you the scrap from the *Sun*, as you may not have seen it. To have a *suspected* Treasurer is almost as damaging to the college as having a truly rascally one could be.

My reading, of late, has been very small in amount and very unusual in kind. I've been looking some into Biblical discussion, thus coming at least to the outskirts of theology. Curious to discover wherein the heresy of the Rev. Prof. W. Robertson Smith consisted, I have been reading his twelve published public lectures on the "Old Testament in the Jewish Church."4 They have interested me very much indeed; but I have been prevented from deriving full profit from their perusal by a very perplexing circumstance: I find that I am not sufficiently familiar with the views of Biblical critics called orthodox to be always quite sure when I've hit upon a heresy! This is a serious inconvenience, as you may imagine; but, as I've been informed that Prof. Smith's errors are of no very vital or faith-damaging sort, I am not alarmed to find that all his conclusions regarding the history of the Old Testament canon greatly recommend themselves to my accept-

ance. I take no pride in being a heretic—I believe that there is nothing more honorable to both the mind and the heart than *faith*—;
but I am compelled to give credit to Prof. Smith's conclusions,
at least until they are overturned by superior scholarship, from
some quarter or other. At any rate my understanding of the objects and meaning of the Old Testament books has been greatly
cleared by W. Robertson's aid.

As an antidote to Biblical criticism, I've been reading aloud to
my sister and cousin a novel by Thomas Hardy, the "Trumpet
Major." I chose Thomas Hardy's work because I've lately seen him
rated by several English Magazines of high authority as first among
living novelists, since George Eliot (alias Marian Cross) has left
the field. I have been fully repaid. His style is fresh and vigorous,
his story graphically told, and his characters admirably sustained.
Another evidence of rare gifts is the variety of his creations. I
have been reading, in Harper's *Magazine*, his "Laodician" and
have found it in almost every respect different from the "Trumpet Major"—different in everything but in diction. Everywhere in
his writings I find originality, though it is not always originality
of the highest kind. It is originality of plot—originality in devising
incidents and conceiving situations—rather than in creating characters. His characters are various, however. He has no stock
types.

I have met many estimable and many cultivated people here.
Even the west enjoys the amenities of civilization. Sometimes I
wonder, Bobby, what would have been the history of this vast
continent of ours if Englishmen and Europeans had found settlement and made homes in it a century or two earlier than they
did. What would the West have been if it could have remained
isolated from the East. Of what sort would its communities have
been had they retained their primitive organizations and known
nothing for whole centuries of the influence of Eastern ideas?
How would the East have fared, for that matter, if men had continued to depend on the variable breezes to bridge the Atlantic
for them and on sailors as their news-carriers? As it has been,
civilization has taken to itself steel wings which never tire and
steam lungs which are never exhausted and voices electric and
telephonic which disregard distance, and man must be smart indeed to escape her influence! Consequently there is hardly a revival of art in Europe before homes on the Pacific slope are decorated as beautifully as any home on the Atlantic side of the continent, and that not by foreign artists imported to do the work,
but by fair inmates of those homes themselves. There is a house

here, at which I have several times visited the family of one of Kentucky's Congressmen, whose walls are decorated with many beautiful paintings by one of the daughter's of the family, and with pen and ink sketches from the same hand which would pass anywhere for steel engravings. Of course this is not any longer "the West," but one can hardly get far enough west to get altogether out of the region of culture or entirely beyond the limits of that community of ideas which facile means of communication have made a bond of union between all parts of this country. "Freedom of the Press" is an expression which carries a very big idea in it now-a-days. It implies the difference between the darkness of Russia and the light of England and America. But I am getting into big topics here, and musn't bore you with these ramblings. You see the temptation to have one of our old "talks" is strong upon me whenever I take up the pen.

Give Pete lots of love. Many regards and congratulations to Roessle. Be sure to send me a letter to Chillicothe.

Your very sincere friend   Woodrow Wilson

P. S.   You see I am no longer "Tommy," *except to my old friends*; but have imitated Charley [Talcott] in taking the liberty of dropping one of my names, as superfluous.   Yours   W. W.

ALS (Meyer Coll., DLC).
¹ William F. Stoughtenburgh, '79, died at sea from consumption on July 17, 1881, on the way home from a teaching post in the Protestant College at Beirut.
² John D. Davis, '79, who had just returned from Germany after attending the Universities of Bonn and Berlin. A "poller" in the Princeton vernacular was a keen student, a "grind."
³ They did not. Harris died in office in 1885 after serving as treasurer for fifteen years.
⁴ William Robertson Smith, *The Old Testament in the Jewish Church, Twelve Lectures on Biblical Criticism* (New York, 1881). Smith, a theologian and Semitic scholar, was elected to the chair of oriental languages and Old Testament exegesis at the Free Church College of Aberdeen in 1870. An exponent of modern methods of biblical scholarship, he wrote several articles for the ninth edition of the *Encyclopaedia Britannica* (1875-89), which brought him under suspicion of the authorities of the Free Church. He demanded a formal trial in 1877. The indictment against him was quashed, but he was dismissed from his chair in June 1881 by a vote of no confidence. The trial became a famous incident in the movement to liberalize the Free Church.

From Joseph Ruggles Wilson

My beloved Woodrow—   Boston Septr. 3, 1881

You will see that we are separated by a great space—but then this is a space which contains *one* element only of separation: the geographical. In cases where affection exists mutually, as in ours, material distance serves to *unite* by causing the separated to think more frequently of and long more ardently, the one for the other. And I do indeed long to see you again—to look into the face which means so much to me.

One of your letters I received (mother writes me there were two sent). It did me a "heap" of good, and I was correspondingly grateful to you.

I am expecting to leave this on Monday—5th—for another week at Saratoga—then, on 12th to go down to New York—and, on 19th to start for home—where I shall expect to find you.

I am glad that you have had—and especially that you enjoyed —the opportunity of visiting Marion & hers. Yr. visit must have been an unspeakable pleasure to her. No doubt you will still more be pleased and please where you now are—if Hattie knows how to give pleasure and receive it. I trust that you will at least find great satisfaction from your stay in C[hillicothe]. Please give my love to *all*, by name—especially though (aside) to dear Hattie and dear Jessie both of whom I love as my own children almost.

I cannot write a long letter—but intend only to convey assurances of my great respect and unalterable affection for the dearest and best of sons.   Your affc   Father

ALS (WP, DLC).

From Marion Wilson Kennedy

My dearest brother:—   Maysville, [Ky.] Sept. 8th 1881.
. . . By the way, nearly everyone thought, it seems, that you and Jessie were engaged to be married, and many have been the comments made on your devotion to your lady-love. A number of persons refrained from calling because they did not like the idea of interfering with your enjoyment of each other's society! Miss Fannie Blattenman was telling me about it yesterday, and at least half-a-dozen others have told me of it. All express themselves as charmed with Jessie's sweet, pretty face, as well they might be, and my friends are all disposed to quarrel with me for not taking *you* about with me more. . . .
          Lovingly your sister,   Marion W. Kennedy

ALS (WP, DLC) with WWhw and WWsh notations on env.: "Received [WWsh] Sept. 11/81"; "Answered [WWsh] [Oct.] 3/81."

To Charles Andrew Talcott

Dear Charlie,   Chillicothe, Ohio, September 22nd/81
    Your letter,[1] sent to Wilmington, has found me here in Ohio.

I have come so far from home on a visit to the family of an uncle —the uncle after whom I am named, Mr. Thomas Woodrow. I have been making this Summer a sort of visiting tour among near relations previous to settling down to legal practice, anticipating that this will perhaps be the last opportunity that I will have for some years to do such visiting

Of course your letter was exceedingly welcome, Charlie, and, equally of course I assure you, your long silence had wrought no offence. I never thought you anything but a dilatory correspond-ent—you can be depended on for any good work but the writing of a letter. But I have always felt sure that, in your case as in mine, the tardiness arose from no lack of friendship. I cannot tell you how often I have wished for a letter from you, or how eagerly I have devoured the few scraps of news of you that have reached me from time to time; but I have never felt actually *hurt* by your neglect. Your letters, when they do come, have all the additional spice of agreeable surprises. I don't say these things to confirm, by justifying, you in your *evil ways*(!), but simply as an assurance that nothing so small can impair my friendship for you one whit.

My correspondence with the rest of the gang, with the exception of Bob., has been almost as spasmodic as ours. While Pete was in Europe, and for some time after his return, the interchange of letters between us was as brisk as possible. Latterly, however, he has fallen to owing me letters for long periods at a time. I think that the restlessness you speak of as having lately taken posses-sion of him may have something to do with this decline in the vigor of his correspondence. Epistles come to me from the "Cow" at long intervals. He has at last fixed upon the practice of medicine as his profession, you know, and now his excuse for not writing is always the necessity of constant attendance upon lectures, or other studious preoccupation. With the dear old Scot[2] my inter-course has been somewhat more regular, though even it has not been unbroken.

Since I last wrote to you I have, of course, been more or less uninterruptedly at work on my law. You know I was not able to complete my course at the University on account of ill health. I left last Christmas. We were exceedingly ill fed there, and I was, in consequence, so troubled with that most usual students' foe, the indigestion, that I gave up the idea of staying the remaining six months of the course for fear of becoming a confirmed dis-peptic. After leaving the University I read quite steadily at home until the beginning of the Summer, when I set out on the trip I am now enjoying.

After innumerable hesitatings as to a place of settlement, I have at length fixed upon Atlanta, Ga. It, more than almost every other Southern city, offers all the advantages of business activity and enterprize. Its growth has during late years been wonderful. Since the war its population has increased from nine to thirty-seven thousand. And then, too, there seem to me to be many strong reasons for my remaining in the South. I am familiar with Southern life and manners, for one thing—and of course a man's mind may be expected to grow most freely in its native air. Besides there is much gained in growing up with the section of country in which one's home is situate, and the South has really just begun to grow industrially. After standing still, under slavery, for half a century, she is now becoming roused to a new work and waking to a new life. There appear to be no limits to the possibilities of her development; and I think that to grow up with a new section is no small advantage to one who seeks to gain position and influence.

Wilmington, N. C., Oct. 1st 1881

Interruptions of various sorts prevented my finishing the letter I was writing you when in Chillicothe, so I must add a few lines by way of conclusion now.

My vacation trip is over and, once more at home, I am about to set myself to the daily perusal of law books again. After a holiday work will go hard with me for a week or so, but I'll soon settle down against the collar just as before I doffed the harness.

In all my Summer wanderings I saw but one Princeton man. Chillicothe is the home of the great Massie of '80,[3] and while I was there he called on me. I used to think him a blatant empty-pate in college; but I think, since meeting him, that I then did him injustice. Certainly in the conversation I had with him a week or two ago, he seemed a *modest*, straightforward sort of fellow with plenty of good sense and a good deal of affability. I am more and more convinced that it is *never* altogether safe to judge a man by his appearance. Massie's appearance—his big mouth and testy, often scowling, manner—was and is all against him; but scarcely more so than was Geo. Johnstons against him or Job. Trotter's[4] against him. These instances remind one of the ugly leaden casket, in the Merchant of Venice, which contained the true portrait within

I had news of another Princeton man, Pete. Hamilton. He has returned from Europe, and this Summer he took the Summer law course at the University of Virginia. On my way home, I was delayed several hours in Charlottesville and availed myself of the opportunity offered to visit my old friends at the University—prominent amongst whom was, of course, Prof. Minor[.] His comment on Pete was as full of accurate discernment as are his comments on the law. He thought that Pete had "a very inquiring mind." His three months' acquaintance with "the young metaphysician from the South" had not led to any further discovery than that, apparently. One could hardly hit upon a more accurate description of Pete's mental characteristics.

I rec'd a letter from the "Cow" some weeks ago in which he told me of the then recent marriage of Denny, '76, to a Miss Lulu Chapman, Hiram's cousin, and a very charming girl, if she is always as she was when I met her in Baltimore.

My vacation roamings have broken in on my observations of recent political events. With us, however, there was not much to observe except Garfield, and his death will have to be some time past before the factions can venture upon an active stir in public matters. In the mean time, rest.

I shall hope very persistently for another letter from you, Charlie. Tell me all about yourself and keep your eye on the *Triennial!*[5] With much affection,

Your sincere friend,   T. Woodrow Wilson

ALS (photostat in RSB Coll., DLC).
  [1] C. A. Talcott to WW, Sept. 17, 1881, ALS (WP, DLC).
  [2] Robert Bridges.
  [3] David M. Massie.
  [4] George W. Johnston, '79, and Edward H. Trotter, '79.
  [5] A reunion of the Princeton Class of '79, scheduled for June 1882.

To Harriet Augusta Woodrow

[Chillicothe, Ohio, Sept. 25, 1881]

Uncle Thomas does not yield at once, as you supposed he would, but promises carefully to consider the subject as regards the propriety of the marriage of cousins—for *there*, he thinks, the *only suspicion* of an objection lies. He is inclined to think that there is no real, substantial objection even there—especially since both mother and father favored the idea of our marrying, without a moment's hesitation.

Now, Hattie, for my sake, *and for your own*, reconsider the dismissal you gave me to-night. I cannot sleep to-night—so give me the consolation of thinking, while waiting for the morning, that there is still one faint hope left to save me from the terror of despair.   Yours, if you would   Woodrow

ALS (WC, NjP).

EDITORIAL NOTE
WILSON'S PROPOSAL TO HATTIE WOODROW

The evidence so far presented of a mildly affectionate relationship between Wilson and the brown-haired, blue-eyed, vivacious cousin who was four years his junior, hardly prepares the reader for a proposal of marriage, a refusal, and the agitated note just printed. It would seem that Hattie was not prepared either, although her articulate cousin had long since convinced himself that what he felt was surely love, and his mother had assured him in her letter of April 13, 1880, that she and his father offered "nothing in the way of *disapprobation* . . . of what you wish in the matter."

The cousins first met as small children, and when Wilson wrote Bridges on March 15, 1882, that he "first met her" at Staunton, he was thinking of the young woman with whom he had begun to correspond during his senior year at Princeton, and not of the child who was the eldest of the five children of his mother's brother, Thomas. His letters through 1881, of which only the three printed in Volume I of this series, and the six in this volume, were preserved by Hattie, warmed under the influence of his occasional sight of Hattie during his visits to his Aunt Marion Bones in Staunton while he was a student at Charlottesville. On these occasions the infatuated "cousin Tommie" (he had so inscribed a volume of Longfellow to Hattie "with the warmest love") was enchanted by her voice. He thought it the equal of world-famed Adelina Patti's, and he was ravished by his "Rosalind's" rendition of "The Last Rose of Summer."

Then, in late summer of 1881, Hattie invited him and their cousin Jessie Bones, her schoolmate at Staunton, to come to Ohio for a visit, and it was there, against a backdrop of picnics and parties, that his downfall came. As he was to write Bridges, the visit confirmed him in "a passion which had for some years" been irresistibly growing upon him.

But Hattie did not love him, and when, on the night of September 25 he took her from the dance floor at a party and ardently proposed, she gave the too close relationship as her reason. The two remaining letters of the love-lorn series fill in what happened: his abrupt departure from the dance and retirement to a local hotel for the night because he thought she wanted him to go; the desperate note scribbled in all too self-conscious lover's anguish on a scrap of torn paper and sent to Hattie's house that night; his call upon her father next morning; and his departure that day for home. Hattie's brother, James Wilson Woodrow, who was later to go to Princeton, went with Wilson to the station and saw him off. But not before that appropriately operatic encounter at the station with "Eddie," Edward Freeman Welles, whom Hattie would soon marry, and the rejected suitor's perturbed observations to Jimmy.

And not, of course, without leaving Hattie to cancel parties and make embarrassed excuses. Yet the friendship endured. Hattie attended both of Wilson's inaugurations and was warmly welcomed to the White House by both of Wilson's wives. And Hattie's grandson,

Donald Wilson Thackwell, married Wilson's granddaughter, Faith Wilson McAdoo.[1]

[1] For some charming recollections, not, however, quite accurate in every detail, see Helen Welles Thackwell, "Woodrow Wilson and My Mother," *The Princeton University Library Chronicle*, XII (Autumn 1950), 6-18.

Two Letters to Harriet Augusta Woodrow

My darling,   Ashland, Ky., Sept. 26th 1881

I find that I will have to wait here in Ashland full six hours, having rushed off from Chillicothe just about that number of hours before the time of departure of the train which makes through connections with the trains on the C. and O. In view of so long a time of waiting, I have taken my favorite pen from my trunk in order to write a few lines to you and a few to dear mother

I found the travelling arrangements on this route much better than I had anticipated. The same train comes all the way to Ashland, coming beyond Ironton to Petersburg on the Ohio side, and being ferried across thence to Ashland on an immense barge. Jessie will, accordingly, have to make only one change between Chillicothe and Staunton, and, by taking the train which leaves Chillicothe at 7:30 in the evening, can come through without delay. This relieves me of considerable anxiety on her account. Oh, that you could change your determination and come on with her! But such a thing is too good to hope for!

I am agreeably surprised in finding the hotel here a very comfortable one—that is, comfortable as way-station hotels go. It is, at least, an hundred per cent. better in every respect than either of the hotels at Huntington. But with my present light spirits no temporary inconvenience could cause me any irritation. I'm content for the present in any quarters.

I suppose that to many my abrupt departure from Chillicothe would seem a little hard to understand under the circumstances. Uncle Thomas—who expressed himself as perfectly satisfied with the state of the case after our interview of this morning—said that he saw no reason for my going immediately. But I saw several reasons for doing so. One was that you seemed to desire it; and another was that I thought, after what you had said, I owed it to you to leave matters for the present as they stand—to trust all to you; and yet I felt that, after the terrible nervous strain I had gone through, I would not be sure of having control enough over myself to leave the subject alone. So, to go away was the kindest service I could do you; and I did it *as such*, notwithstanding the tremendous effort it cost me.

We did not have our group picture taken, did we? Will you do me a *great* favor—and do it on my own terms? I am not going to make any hard request, but one very easily complied with. I want you to go to Simond's gallery, wearing your pink dress, or any other dress similarly cut about the neck,—since the photograph can't reproduce the color—and have a cabinet taken *in profile*. Let the picture include your figure to the waist; let your head be slightly bent forward and your eyes slightly downcast. Jessie can arrange the minute particulars of the pose, of course, and the artist must be made to acquiesce. There are two more conditions: there must be only *one copy* of the photograph, unless you want one for yourself; and I must bear the expense of the work, since it is to be done specially for me. Now, you think me very absurd, don't you? Well, may-be I am; but wont you indulge this whim of mine, please, since it is a very innocent one? It wont cost you much trouble and it will give me an immense deal of pleasure. Oh, I forgot something! Don't wear any hat, but let your hair be dressed as it usually is in the mornings. Now you wont refuse me this, will you? however foolish you may think it.

My ride to-day has not tired me very much. I feel quite fresh to-night, though a little sleepy. I am writing in the hotel office, in the midst of all sorts of noises and confusion. Every one of a crowd of men is apparently trying to talk louder than his neighbors, who, as even he must realize, are talking very lustily indeed. This house seems to be overflowing with transient lodgers, and such lodgers are not always, nor often, of the best class of citizens.

Did Wilson tell you that we saw Eddie at the depot—at the *station*, I mean? He was with a couple of friends, each of whom was remarkable in his way, though the two were remarkable in very different ways. Eddie expressed regret at my departure! Wilson and I concluded that, if the sentiment was not merely formal— as it probably was—it was not genuine. If he has *any* feeling at seeing me go away, it is probably a feeling of relief at getting me out of the way.

You must write me a full account of the whist party that you are to have to-morrow night—about who were there, what the notable incidents of the evening were, who was your partner, what part you took in the entertainment of the guests—as, for instance, by singing or playing—&c., &c. I hope that you will have just the nicest sort of time.

How did the ceremonies pass off to-day? Did Mr. Mayo volunteer an address?

It is a delightful privilege to while away this time of waiting by writing to you, but I must not run on any further for fear of being tedious. About three of the six hours are gone, and, by the time my note to dear mother is written, train time will be comparatively near.

With abundant love to uncle T. aunt H., Wilson, the little ones, and dear Jessie,   Yours, with abiding love,   Woodrow

Wilmington, N. Carolina, October, 3rd 1881

My darling, (may I call you that?)

I am home at last, after one of the most fatiguing journeys I ever undertook. Thanks to two missed connections and a roundabout route, I was on the way from Monday at one o'clock until Thursday at half after six in the morning. Having been so long on the road, and having had so much to think about the while, it seems to me fully a month since I left Chillicothe

As you may imagine, my arrival in Columbia took sister Annie complitely by surprise. She was not expecting me then, and she was not expecting to see me *alone* when I did come. I stayed with her only about three hours, arriving a little before seven and leaving a little before ten. She is looking very bright and well, and the children are as full of life and health as possible. Little Jessie is just the prettiest little creature I ever saw

Since reaching home I have learned that there is much probability of our having sister Marion and her boys with us about Christmas time. If we could get sister Annie with her little ones and sister Marion with hers here at the same time our family would be united again for the first time within more than five years. If such a reunion could be effected this Winter before I leave home for Atlanta it would be a great satisfaction to us all. How father's nerves would stand the *noise* of the united households I would not venture to predict. He bore the racket made by sister Annie's boys when they were here last Christmas very manfully; and I do'nt suppose that five boys would be much worse than two. At any rate it would be only a difference of degree and not one of kind.

I suppose that you will have had "Olivette"[1] by the time this reaches you. I am beginning to think that I am destined never to hear an opera. Whenever I have felt sure of having an opportunity of hearing one, some unforeseen thing has happened to prevent. I am determined to hear one some of these days, even if I have to travel all the way to New York to do so.

I find that my lady friends have not yet returned to town, so

I am at liberty to study as hard as I please—and I please to study *very* hard for the next three months—without any social duties to distract me[.] By-the-way, I have been much worried since leaving Chillicothe by the thought that I left you the unpleasant task of making excuses to the Fullertons and others for my not having called before leaving. I am so sorry to have caused you that annoyance.

The only really noteworthy incident of my homeward journey was my delay in Charlottesville and consequent glimpses of old friends. It made quite a pleasant break in my travel. It is always pleasant, of course, to receive cordial greetings from old acquaintances, and certainly the greetings I received in Charlottesville were cordial enough. I don't know that I would have gone out to the University at all had it not been that I met one of Prof. Minor's daughters at the rail-road station as I was getting off the train. I was tired and just a little inclined to be low-spirited, and so did not feel much like calling; but of course I could not disregard Miss Minor's urgent request that I would not leave without calling. Accordingly I had my trunk taken to the hotel, dressed, and rode out to my old haunts. Afterwards I was very glad that I had gone. The two Minors are both exceedingly agreeable, unaffected girls. Besides, they are quite pretty, and seemed genuinely glad to see me—all which circumstances combined to make the time spent with them seem very well spent. Prof. Minor gave me a very hearty welcome.

Once out at the University, I had to visit my other acquaintances there, so I called on Mrs. Prof. Davis[2] and her daughter. They gave me quite as cordial a reception as did the Minors, and managed, during the few minutes I remained with them, to make themselves very entertaining. Mrs. Davis talks specially well. She is quite cultivated and converses with the oiliest of tongues. The only thing that ever mars my enjoyment of her conversation is her inclination to *flatter*. I have never once met her that she has not managed in some way to express her admiration of my speaking. This is, as you may suppose, a little embarrassing.

It still lacked some days of the time for the opening of the session, and I, consequently, saw only two old student acquaintances.

I find that, although this section has not escaped drought altogether, it has been much more favored in the matter of rains than have most other sections. Mother's garden is considerably parched, but she still has an abundance of roses and the grass plots and evergreens look fresh and green. Beyond one or two broken trees there are now no signs left of the work of the two hurricanes.

Now that I am once more fairly settled in my study, school has begun again. I try to occupy my thoughts daily with the law, not yet with much success to boast of, however. My thoughts are not to be so easily and immediately controlled. They find you a much more attractive subject than rules of court.

I did not realize how thoroughly anxiety and broken rest had unhinged my temper and unstrung my nerves until my weary journey had added physical exhaustion. But now several nights of sound and dreamless sleep have made me like myself once more —only to make me realize that my love for you has taken such a hold on me as to have become almost a part of myself, which no influences I can imagine can ever destroy or weaken.[3]

I am waiting anxiously to learn whether or not you have determined to gratify my whim about the picture. I shall be sadly disappointed if you do not have it taken as I requested. It would not be much trouble, would it?

You do'nt know how hungry I have become for a word of news, or of some sort, from you. The past week has been an amazingly long one! I have managed to allay my impatience for a letter *from* Chillicothe by sending several *to* Chillicothe. The answer to my letter to Aunt Helen I am awaiting with fear and trembling —and yet with much confidence in her kindness.

I wont apologize for the stupidity of this letter. I did not write it in the hope of entertaining you, for I had little that is entertaining to relate, but simply to indulge myself in the feeling that I was putting myself into communication with you. Tell dear Jessie that mother has prepared the snuggest room for her (and your!) reception and that we are looking forward very anxiously, because very eagerly, for her coming,

All—all three, father, mother, and Josie—join me in sending a great deal of love to Uncle Thos., Aunt Helen, the little ones, Jessie, and your own precious self—though to the last-named I claim a title to send the largest quantity myself. Please give my regards to Mrs. Sill.[4]   Lovingly Yours,   Woodrow

ALS (WC, NjP).

[1] English version, first produced in London in 1880, of the operetta, *Les Noces d'Olivette* (1879) by Edmond Audran.

[2] Either the wife of John S. Davis, Professor of Anatomy and Materia Medica, or the wife of Noah K. Davis, Professor of Moral Philosophy. Both had daughters.

[3] Possibly alarmed by this passage, Hattie, according to her daughter's recollection, cut off the correspondence. When it was resumed, WW's salad days were over.

[4] Hattie's maternal grandmother.

From Charles William Kent

My dear Wilson,   University of Va Oct 5th 1881
     . . . They told me at Prof. Minors that they had the pleasure of
your company at tea not long since. I *wish* I could have seen you
and I think that, if I had known you were so near, I would have
tried to see you. They all seemed to think you were looking well
though there seems to be diversity of opinion upon the effect of
your beard upon your personal pulchritude. I hope you will allow
me to judge by coming on during the year or if you can not
come[,] by forwarding your photograph. . . .
                         Truly your friend   C. W. Kent

ALS (WP, DLC) with WWhw notations on env.: "Rec'd Oct. 7th 1881" and
"Ans. Oct. 12th 1881."

From Joseph R. Wilson, Jr.[1]

M[ost]. R[evered]. B[rother].   Wilmington N. C. [Nov.] 2nd 81
     I am getting along very well with my latin and other studies.
Papa says, of course pay the freight on the piano[.][2] Mama's piano
has not come yet but we expect it in a day or two. . . .
                    Your loving bro.   J. R. W. Jr.   U. S. N.
ALS (WP, DLC).
     [1] WW was visiting his sister, Annie, in Columbia, S. C., having left Wil-
mington on Oct. 29, 1881.
     [2] JRW and JWW had apparently given Annie a piano, probably their old
one, and it had just arrived.

From Hallet and Davis Company

Dr Sir   Boston, Mass. Nov 7th 1881
     Your card to hand and in reply will say that we feel confident
that the longer you use the Piano the better you will like it. When
you have tried it to your entire satisfaction we would be pleased
to receive a letter from you and we will print it with your permission.   Yours Truly   Hallet & Davis Co

ALS (WP, DLC).

From Lyman Hotchkiss Atwater

My Dear Mr Wilson,   Princeton College Nov. 19. 1881
     I learned today that Mr Sperry,[1] recently of the N. Y. Evening
Post, had purchased a Journal in Wilmington, Del. and desired
to procure an assistant—who would be willing for a time to share

with him the risks of an incipient enterprise by accepting *for a time* low wages.

As I threw out a hint about journalism in my note of yesterday, I inform you of this opening—not knowing at all what your leanings may be—especially in reference to working on a Republican Journal. The assistants on an editorial staff are often entirely relieved of expressing themselves on politics, beyond giving news.

However this may be, if you wish to pursue the subject, please signify it to Prof. Wm. M. Sloane[2] to whom Mr Sperry has written on the subject—and he will put you in communication with Mr S.

Dr. McCosh received an application today for a teacher in some preparatory school of Latin, Greek, French & German, at about $800 a year.

I suppose you would not care for this.

Yours truly   L. H. Atwater

ALS (WP, DLC).
[1] Watson R. Sperry and Isaac Henderson had just purchased the Wilmington (Del.) *News*. See note 2 at Jan. 14, 1881.
[2] Professor of Latin at Princeton at this time; Professor of History, 1883-97.

Two Poems by Wilson

A River's Course.

Dec. [1] 1881

I know a deep river that chafes with its shores
And roars with rage at its bondage,
Surlily turning its quick currents about
When crossed by rocks in its voyage.

With hisses and sighs its dark currents run down
The grim, frowning mountains between,
Leaping fiercely and high o'er hindering crags,
Or skulking in gorges unseen.

When at last it has forced its rough, toilsome way
Past the outmost spurs of the chain,
It quietly steals 'long the edge of the mead,
As if courting good humor again.

Good humor returned with the sunlight and ease,
It speeds briskly over green fields,
Until, cooling itself under green-grown banks,
Into a thick forest it steals.

In the depths of the wood its waters divide,
Encircling a bleak island rock,

From whose towering height a gray castle looms,
Which is dumb to the stranger's knock.

Where a narrow bridge spans the stream to the east
A windowless tower rises,
Its sheer sides built high in embattled strength,
Its one gate barred, 'gainst surprises.

From this frontal tower stretch the winding curves
Of walls that are scarred with traces
Of fierce assaults made with hot, maddened hate
By proud princes of dead races.

Within in the wall's embrace towers marked by time
Rear high their gray, turretted crests,
Draping their sides in clinging ivy, that hides
The wan wrinkles roughing their breasts.

The inner courts and great halls of this castle
Never now hear the tread of men;
Where feasting was regal now screams the eagle
And grow the rank weeds of the fen.

The owls find homes in its vaulted roofs and domes;
The moss grows rank in its chambers;
Its windows are draped with the light silken webs
Which spiders spin 'tween their slumbers.

In dining hall rots the old oaken table;
In bed-room the garniture moulds;
The tapestries stiffen and crack as with pain
When the winds sport amongst their folds.

The alarm bell up in that crumbling turret
In silence has rusted its tongue;
The only sound that e'er rouses its temper
Is the chirp of the sparrows' young.

The winds that oft wander in wild wantonness
Through the desolate corridors
Shriek shrill with delight at the lorn lonliness,
And slam in rough sport the doors.

Where the walls creep down to the swift water's edge
And stand with their feet in the flood,
The tide hastens past the falling ruin aghast
As if fearing some stain of blood.

The streams pass the island with hurrying flow,
With a rush both frightened and fleet,
Till, beyond the forbidding and gloomy pile,
Their currents carressingly meet.

With darkened faces the wedded currents race off
Moaning, as a burden of song,
Notes that now sigh, and anon rise in a cry,
Like mem'ries of unrevenged wrong.

When the river has quit the thick forest shades
And entered a bustling city,
Men do not ween what saddest things it has seen,
What signs of death and of pity.

Running briskly past the noisy town so vast,
The river flows merrily on,
Till its waters meet and unchafingly greet
Banks of green, gently-sloping lawn.

Not with brilliant flowers and trellised bowers
Are these grassy slopes surrounded;
Great oaks stretch their shades over deep, silent glades
Where the velvety turf is bounded.

Beyond the broad stretches of the pleasant lawn
A goodly mansion stately stands,
With windows wide and many a shading porch,
The manor house of ample lands.

On the grass two merrily romping brothers
Are playing in free, childish glee:
A lovely lady they call to as "mother"
Is laughing their gladness to see.

His mistress's laugh, so joyous and cheery,
From his place in the grateful sun
Rouses the great sleeping dog from slothful dreams
And sends him to join in the fun.

Breezes make the great oaks in the groves to nod
In monotonous melody;
Gleeful birds sport and sing in the silvan courts
Many an artless rhapsody.

The river takes up in musical ripples
Echoes of the sweet lady's laugh;

It answers the songs of the leaves and the birds,
And its heart seems lighter by half.

Its journey's now short to the bed of the sea,
But its pace is none the less fleet
Till it peacefully pours its waters, at last,
Out at old Ocean's briny feet.

A Song

Dec. 8th/81

Sing, ye feathered songsters,
Sing in full concert all your quaintest strains,
Each richest note that melody contains,
Each pleasant chord, each harmony sonorous
Join ye in one ringing chorus;
Your voices raise in sweetest praise:
My love is won and joy fills all my days.

WWhw entries, Item (c), in the private notebook described at c. Jan. 1, 1881.

From James McCosh

My Dear Sir   Princeton, N. J., Dec 15 1881
    I am glad to hear from you[.] But you do not say anything about yourself. I am interested in your welfare.
    There will be a Local Examination for entrance to Princeton College at Cincinnati June 22d-23d. The place will be advertised in spring in the Cincinnati papers.
    If your cousin[1] or you write me in April or May I will give you details which are not yet settled   Yours Ever   James McCosh

ALS (WP, DLC).
    [1] James Wilson Woodrow, of Chillicothe, Ohio.

From Charles William Kent

My dear Wilson,   University of Virginia December 20th 1881
    I snatch a little while from my Moral Philosophy studies to answer your most welcome letter,[1] which was duly received and in the first place let me say that I heartily approve of your plan that we make our letters an exchange of ideas on whatever may be at the time interesting. . . .
    In adopting the plan which you propose I feel that I am to be the gainer and I fear that whatever thoughts I may have to offer will have neither the charm of novelty nor any merit of expression.

Time and again I recall with pleasure and profit, conversations with you which prompted me to thought and some study and I often think that if I had you here this session I would be enabled to decide whether or not I should enter the contest for the Jeff. medal. . . . Just here let me ask your opinion on a question, which was brought to my notice by Jno: Jenkins the president of the Wash.

Not long ago that society was adopting a new constitution drawn up by Lewis Coleman, Toy & John Jenkins and John vacated the chair and it was occupied [by] Bailey,[2] who in the absence of the vice president had been called to that position. The society split on the very question which we so fully discussed in the Jeff, viz, the medals. The question came to a vote and John (on the floor) voted and thus brought about a tie. His vote did not at all change the result but it was so close that it made him think and question himself whether he as regular president of the society had a right to vote. I held then as I do now that when he leaves the chair and another member is presiding over the deliberations he is no longer president and has a right to vote. It seems to me that it is not the spirit of parliamentary law to deprive two men of their votes. On the other hand, the principle which I have enunciated might be abused and an unprincipled president might take advantage of it to give one side a vote and thus carry his side. For instance if it was known that the vote would be 15 to 14 against the presidents views[,] by vacating the chair and calling the vice-president, who belonged to the majority to the chair, the vote would be 15 to 14 in favor of the presidents opinion. Another question of entirely different nature and fruitful in points upon which opinions might differ is this, Is the Y. M. C. A. doing a wrong to place in its Reading Room a magazine which permits such articles as The North American Review has published from the pen of [Robert] Ingersoll?

Does some filth destroy the whole magazine or must we hold ourselves responsible, for the evil which may be done by such articles, when infidel works can be easily procured and with little cost? These and other questions arise from thought on the subject and I would like to have your views of the subject. I leave it to you to propose in your next any question upon which you think an exchange of views would be profitable. . . .

Your true friend   C. W. Kent

ALS (WP, DLC) with WWhw notations on env.: "Rec'd Dec. 22/81" and "Ans. Dec. 28/81."
  1 It was WW to C. W. Kent, Nov. 19, 1881, in reply to C. W. Kent to WW,

Oct. 26, 1881, ALS (WP, DLC). JWW sent Kent's letter to WW in Columbia, S. C., in JWW to WW, Oct. 29, 1881, ALS (WP, DLC). On the back of the env. WW wrote: "Kent's letter Ans. Nov. 19th 1881." WW's letter is missing.

[2] Lewis M. Coleman, University of Virginia, M.A., LL.B., attended 1878-82 and 1885-86; Walter D. Toy, University of Virginia, M.A., '82; John B. Jenkins, University of Virginia, M.A., '85; Alfred R. Bailey, University of Virginia, '80.

From Edward Ireland Renick[1]

My dear Sir: Atlanta, Ga. Jan'y 15th 1882

A letter from Faison of Clinton N. C.[2] this morning informs me that you purpose coming to Atlanta to practise Law. I do not know what arrangements you may have made, but if you are coming, as I came, a total stranger, it would give me much pleasure to be of some service to you. I was for more than a month hard at work endeavoring to get an office. Offices even now are hard to get. I have secured a very good one[3] and am occupying it alone at present, though for some time that talented North Carolinian, & I am glad to say, my old & warm friend, Walter Page,[4] was with me. He is now in N. Y. & I am *lonesome*. If you choose, we can office together—share expenses—and quiz out of the "Institutes."[5] At any rate my office is open to you, until you can do better. One likes from the first to have a "down town" place of resort—where he may read, write &c. I hope you will use me: If you like a boarding house where you can have home life, I can recommend mine most warmly. I board with Mrs. J. Reid Boylston 344 Peachtree St. She is a Charlestonian & a grand daughter of old Governor [John] Drayton. Her house is all warmth, light, gayety. She is not a professional boardinghouse keeper. On the contrary she is rich—tolerably so at least. The excellence of the place cannot be exaggerated. Reed of the Law Class at Univ. of Va of 1878[6] (I believe) is located here. J. C. Jenkins of Charlotte N. C. a graduate of Princeton & Columbia Law School—is in my building.[7] Aylett of Richmond, another Univ. B.L. is here—but not as a lawyer.[8]

I should, probably, in offering the above proposition, introduce myself—for tho' we were classmates—I not only was never introduced to you, but, on account of my close confinement, & your short stay—we scarcely saw each other. I may say, therefore, that I am well known by most of the members of the Law Class last session—& especially by the Alpha Taus,[9] one of whom I am; that I succeeded in getting my degree, and have Mr. Minor's endorsement. Excuse this portion about myself—as I consider it due to you & to me, that it should be said.

I shall be glad to furnish you with any information that you may desire relative to Georgia law, to method of admittance to the bar, to Atlanta's attractiveness &c.

Very truly Yours   E. I. Renick

ALS (WP, DLC) with WWhw notations on env.: "Rec'd. 3/20/82" and "Ans. 3/27/82."

[1] Born in Baltimore, 1852. Roanoke College, B.A., 1877; University of Virginia, LL.B., 1881. Practiced law in Atlanta, 1881-84. Clerk and Solicitor, United States Treasury Department, 1884-93; Chief, Bureau of Statistics, Department of State, 1893-94; Chief Clerk, same department, 1894-98. Associate counsel in New York law firm of Coudert Brothers, 1898-1900. Died April 2, 1900.

[2] Walter E. Faison, University of Virginia, LL.B., '80.

[3] It was Room 10 on the second floor of a building at 48 Marietta Street in Atlanta. WW later moved in with Renick.

[4] Walter Hines Page, born Aug. 15, 1855, at Cary, N. C. Attended Trinity College (now Duke University), 1871-72, and Randolph-Macon College, 1873-76. Fellow of The Johns Hopkins University, 1876-78. Reporter for the *St. Joseph* (Mo.) *Gazette*, 1880-81, and New York *World*, 1881-82; literary critic and editorial writer for the *World*, 1882-83. Editor of the Raleigh *State Chronicle*, 1884-85; reporter on the New York *Evening Post*, 1886-87. Business manager of the *Forum*, 1887-91; editor, 1891-95. Associate editor, *Atlantic Monthly*, 1895-98; editor, 1898-99. Partner in Doubleday, Page and Co., 1899-1918. Founded *World's Work* in 1900 and served as editor until 1913. Ambassador to Great Britain, 1913-18. Died at Pinehurst, N. C., Dec. 21, 1918. Author of *The Rebuilding of Old Commonwealths* (1902); *A Publisher's Confession* (1905); and *The Southerner* (1909).

[5] John B. Minor, *Institutes of Common and Statute Law* (4 vols., Richmond, Va., 1876-79).

[6] John P. Reed, who attended the University of Virginia Law School in 1880-81 and was briefly associated with Renick in the practice of law in the early months of 1882.

[7] James Jenkins, University of Virginia, '76; Columbia Law School, LL.B., '81.

[8] Lewis D. Aylett, University of Virginia, Law, '81.

[9] Members of the Alpha Tau Omega Fraternity.

Letter to the Editor: "Anti-Sham" No. 1

[Jan. 25, 1882]

To the Editor of the N. C. Presbyterian:
Dear Sir:—

It is due to the cause of truth to call the attention of your readers to some deliverances recently made by the editor of the Wilmington *Morning Star* upon the occasion of the installation of the newly-appointed Romish bishop of North Carolina.[1] Probably those articles were not very widely read, but wherever they are read they must have misled. The installation of Bishop Northrop was the occasion of two discourses by two prelates of high standing in the Romish connection, Archbishop Gibbons of Baltimore, and Bishop Keane of Richmond.[2] These discourses filled the editor of the *Star* with an enthusiasm which impelled him to declare the day of their delivery "a memorable day for Wilmington," "a notable day in the history of our little city." Had he stopped with these harmless ebullitions of feeling, one could have overlooked them as outbursts of an innocent, though ignorant, admiration. But he was not content with these. With a hardihood such as generally accompanies imperfect knowledge, he proclaims the two Romish orators models of the truest methods of public speech, and incidentally decries the written sermons which are weekly the means of the instruction of thousands from nearly all the Protestant pulpits in the land. Having condemned Protestant preachers in order to point his praise of the Romish, he asserts, with candid ignorance, that Archbishop Gibbons presented "a striking picture of the progress of *Christianity* from its inception until now," showing "in very choice language and by apt illustrations its progress, its persecutions, and its triumphs." That there might be no doubt about his inability to distinguish between a true history of Christianity and a history of Romish organization, the converted editor avers that he believes the address uttered by Bishop Keane, on the evening of the day of installation, to have been "a very grand discussion of what constitutes the religion of Christ," exhibiting "the principles, power, provinces and fruitions of that religion which Christ perfected and deified," and "full of the very marrow of the Gospel."

It ought not to be necessary to warn any Protestant reader—nay, any intelligent reader—against putting any trust in the opinions of one who can write with such disregard of history. Certainly it is not necessary to assure such writers that something more reliable than their judgments will be needed to convince those who know Rome that she has suddenly become the herald of the true faith.

Probably the editor of the *Star* does not realize that, in giving unqualified endorsement to the views of Romish prelates, he is helping on the aggressive advances of an organization whose cardinal tenets are openly antagonistic to the principles of free government—an organization which, whenever and wherever it dares, prefers and enforces obedience to its own laws rather than to those of the state—an organization whose avowed object it is to gain ascendancy over all civil authority. In other words: probably the editor of the *Star* does not *think*, and every one should be warned against the influence of those who speak without sober forethought.   Anti-Sham.

Printed in the Wilmington *North Carolina Presbyterian*, Jan. 25, 1882; also printed, "but not by Request," in the Wilmington *Morning Star*, Jan. 27, 1882. The authorship of the three "Anti-Sham" letters, along with the reason for the choice of the pen name, is revealed in WW to R. Bridges, March 15, 1882.
1 "Installation of a Bishop," Wilmington *Morning Star*, Jan. 17, 1882. The

editor was William H. Bernard, the prelate, the Rt. Rev. H. Pinckney Northrop.
   [2] Archbishop (later Cardinal) James Gibbons of Baltimore and the Rt. Rev.
Joseph Keane, Bishop of Richmond, later Archbishop of Dubuque.

From William Francis Magie

My dear Wilson,   Princeton, Feb. 5, 1882.
    . . . I am sincerely sorry for your ill health that sent you away
from the University. I knew from the College papers how successful you were there & had always hoped to have you graduate
at the top. It would be delightful if you could get your professorship here, but so far as I can see there seems to be no opening
for what you want to be.[1] There is quite a number of young men
here now but the places are all opening in the Natural Sciences
and not in Literature and Philosophy.
    Hoping to hear from you again & to see you at the dinner next
June I am   Yours very sincerely   W. F. Magie

ALS (WP, DLC) with WWhw notation on env.: "Rec'd and Ans. 2/7/82."
   [1] The editors have found no evidence that WW was at this time contemplating a career in teaching.

Letter to the Editor: "Anti-Sham" No. 2

[Feb. 15, 1882]
To the Editor of the N. C. Presbyterian:
Dear Sir: *114951*
    The strange uses to which advertising may be put are illustrated
in an interesting manner by an advertisement of the "Young
Catholic Friends' Society," which recently occupied a prominent
place in the columns of the Wilmington *Morning Star*.[1] In one
respect that advertisement is worthy of all praise. As a public
avowal of the patriotism of the advertisers and a public repudia-
tion on their part of the principles contained in that "Syllabus
[of Errors]" which, issued in 1864, is the latest and most authoritative declaration of the dogmas of the organization to which they
adhere, it must be received with sincere gratification by all their
staunch fellow-citizens. They may rest assured that the communication lately addressed to this paper—the communication against
which they seem to direct their advertisement—was not meant to
convey any imputation of lack of patriotism against them, or
against other individuals of the Church of Rome. Even had such
a doubt of their principles been entertained, that doubt must now,
of course, have been dispelled by this their public declaration.
    But, while the "Young Catholic Friends' Society" may be thus
easily exonerated, they cannot be understood as establishing their

right to represent the entire organization of which they constitute so infinitesimal a part. Fortunately for them, they differ from the leading and gover[n]ing authorities of the Romish hierarchy. Sir A. T. Galt, late Finance Minister of Canada, informs us "that the Roman Catholic Church at Quebec extended its demands to the general assertion of the superiority of ecclesiastical over civil authority, to positive interference with both votes and candidates in the elections, and to the extraordinary proposition that the Divine assistance claimed to be given to the Pope alone, speaking *ex cathedra* on faith and morals, descends with undiminished force to the bishops, priests, and curés." True, this was in Roman Catholic Quebec; but it does not appear that the Romish authorities have hesitated to move in the same direction in Protestant America. In Cambridgeport, Massachusetts, several leading Roman Catholics, men of intelligence, wealth, and position, sent their children to the public schools, in preference to the parochial schools of their own Church, for the excellent reason that better instruction was given in the former and that the parochial schools were not free. They received a peremptory command from the priest of the parish, one Scully, to send their children to the schools under his direction, and when they declined to comply they were refused the sacraments and were publicly preached against as slanderers, scoundrels, and liars. When appeal was made to the Archbishop, Williams,[2] he declined to interfere and declared that "Father Scully's course throughout had met his unqualified approval"; and the *Freeman's Journal and Catholic Register*, of New York, boldly proclaimed "that Father Scully of St. Mary's, Cambridge, is fighting the battle of the Lord against the enemy. He is speaking the language in Massachusetts, where Satan's seat is, that the Vicar of Christ speaks to all the world from his prison in the Vatican." This is the same journal that is reported to have said, in its holy rage, "Let the public school system go from whence it came—to the Devil."

Education seems to be the chosen gate of Romish invasion in this country. Bishop McCloskey,[3] of Kentucky directs that as soon as possible parochial schools be established throughout his diocese, and adds, "Now it is our will and command, that where there is a Catholic school in the parish, parents and guardians in such places should send their children or wards, who are under nine years of age, to such Catholic school: and we hereby direct that this obligation be enforced under the pain of the refusal of absolution in the sacrament and penance." In Louisville, to which the authority of this decree extends, about seven thousand children of Romish parents are said to attend the public schools.

What is taught in Romish schools is not a matter of speculation. Writing to Mr. Dexter A. Hawkins, of New York, Cardinal Antonelli[4] says that he "thought it better that the children should grow up in ignorance than be educated in such a system of schools as the State of Massachusetts supports. That the essential part of education was the catechism; and while arithmetic, geometry, and other similar studies might be useful, they were not essential." Dr. Brownson,[5] a trusted authority amongst Romish teachers, admits that "The cause of the failure of what we term Catholic education, in our judgment, is in the fact that we educate, not for the present or the future, but for the past, which can never be restored," and that that education "aims to restore a past age and order of things, which it is neither possible nor desirable to restore, for it could be restored only, if at all, by a second childhood."

The *Catholic Review* said, in 1871, "We deny, of course, as Roman Catholics, the right of the civil government to educate; for education is a function of the spiritual society as much as preaching." Cardinal Cullen[6] avowed a like opinion. Indeed, wherever its dominion extends the Romish hierarchy adheres with desperate determination to the purpose of absolutely controlling the education of the youth of its communion; and they who control the education of the youth of any community control the social and political destiny of that community. What sufficient reason is there for believing that, when Romish teachers gain amongst us the supremacy they so eagerly seek, we will fare better than does Belgium, where, Mr. Laveleye tells us, "The clergy also begin to use the confessional as a means of obtaining decisions conformable to their own interests from the judges. If the magistrate shrinks from deciding in the sense desired by the Church, absolution is refused to him."

What, then, are the governing principles of this organization— the principles which its chief spokesmen proclaim and it[s] school teachers must diligently instill? Question the author of the paper on the "Catholics of the Nineteenth Century," which appeared in the *Catholic World* of July, 1870, and he, after announcing what modern Romanists intend to do when they control this Republic, will tell you plainly that "The supremacy asserted by the Church in matters of education implies the additional and cognate functions of the censorship of ideas, and the right to examine and approve, or disapprove, all books, publications, writings, and utterances intended for public instruction, enlightenment, or enter-

tainment, and the supervision of places of amusement."[7] Look
to the Syllabus of 1864. It denies that freedom of speech should
be deemed an inherent right of the citizen; it denounces separation of church and state, and demands of civil governments that
they stop not short with punishing those acts which disturb the
public peace, but that they also condemn all acts committed
against "the Catholic religion;" it refuses to admit that the popular
will is supreme; and it rejects the doctrine that accomplished
facts have the force of law. And listen to Archbishop Manning,[8]
speaking in the name of Pius IX.: "I acknowledge no civil superior;
and I claim more than this: I claim to be the Supreme Judge on
earth and director of the consciences of men,—of the peasant who
tills the field and the prince that sits on the throne; of the household that lives in the shade of privacy and *the legislature* that
makes laws for kingdoms. I am the last Supreme Judge on earth
of what is right and wrong."

Having gathered these flowers of belief from some of the many
branches of the tree of Romish doctrine, it is pleasant to know
that their savour is not sweet in the nostrils of the members of
the "Young Catholic Friends' Society." The bouquet might easily
be made much larger without seeking beyond the inner gardens
of Rome. If these are not the principles upon which the Church of
Rome has acted whenever opportunity offered or power was given
it in the past, history must be re-written. Though disallowed here
and there by the candid or the patriotic, these are the principles
of the Papal See, the avowed tenets of arch-hierarchs of the
hierarchy not a few, and the guiding rules of action to every Romish bishop who dares to carry his practice as far as Rome would
have him. In a word, Rome is dominated by the Jesuits, that Society of Jesus which has been justly called "the pretorian guard of
a dangerous ecclesiastical Caesarism."   Anti-Sham.

Printed in the Wilmington *North Carolina Presbyterian*, Feb. 15, 1882.
  1 A "Protest to the People of Wilmington and of North Carolina," two columns in length, appeared in the Wilmington *Morning Star* on Feb. 8, 1882.
Datelined "Rooms of the Young Catholic Friends' Society, February 5, 1882,"
the "Protest" was submitted to the *Morning Star* as an advertisement and was
clearly so labeled. The "Friends" identified themselves as a "beneficial association, formed for the purpose of aiding the needy" and comprising "nearly
all the male Catholics in the city of Wilmington."
  The "Protest" was a reply both to WW's letter to the Editor of the *North
Carolina Presbyterian*, printed at Jan. 25, 1882, and to a similar communication in the *Goldsboro* (N. C.) *Methodist Advance*. The latter had been reprinted in the Wilmington *Morning Star* on Feb. 2, 1882. To the charge that
the Roman Catholic Church sought to assert its authority over civil government wherever and whenever it dared to do so, the "Protest" replied that "Catholics believe, with St. Paul, that there is no power but from God, and therefore
they must obey the constituted authorities, whatever be the form of government." It insisted that Catholics had always and everywhere been loyal citi-

zens under every form of government: "The Catholics of Wilmington and of the State are, and have ever been, as orderly, as obedient to the laws, and as devoted to the interests of city and State as any others. The same holds good not only for North Carolina, not only for America, but for the whole civilized world." In support of this statement, the "Protest" stressed the roles played in the American Revolution, that "great struggle for civil liberty," by such American Catholics as the Carrolls of Maryland and by the King and people of Catholic France. It cited also the impartial conduct of Catholic judges in North Carolina.

The "Protest" declared in conclusion: "We feel that these attacks upon us are futile, but nevertheless they are intolerant, and we therefore protest against them, and assert that the charges contained in them are fallacious. The Church has outlived such charges for many centuries, and as we believe, she will continue to live until the end of time. . . . We protest against the charges which bring into question our loyalty to the government, and against the unchristian liberality which slurringly calls us Romish, or Romanists, or Beasts; and under the constitution of the government which we helped to establish, and which we have ever since helped to support and maintain, we claim the right to worship God according to the tenets of the church of our own choice and adoption. This protest is not put forward in a spirit of controversy, and nothing that can be said will provoke any further notice from this society."

2 Archbishop John Joseph Williams of Boston.
3 The Rt. Rev. William George McCloskey, Bishop of Louisville.
4 Giacomo Cardinal Antonelli, Secretary of State to Pope Pius IX.
5 Orestes A. Brownson, New England author and Roman Catholic convert.
6 Paul Cardinal Cullen, Archbishop of Dublin.
7 "The Catholic of the Nineteenth Century," *The Catholic World*, xi (July 1870), 433-45.
8 Henry Edward Cardinal Manning, Archbishop of Westminster.

From Charles William Kent

My dear Wilson,   University of Virginia, Feby 24th 1882

. . . Your answers to my questions fully satisfied me and I am grateful to you for having so clearly set me right in regard to the parlimentary question. My error is now very evident and arose from my not noticing that the illegality of Jenkins' vote consisted in the fact that Bailey was deprived of his. In other words I overlooked the fact that Jenkins ought not to have been on the floor, when the vote was taken.[1] As to the N. A[.] Review I agree with you and I had come to that conclusion before the receipt of your letter and of course I was glad to have my views substantiated by yours. I was, at first, heartily in favor of continuing that review and for these reasons, because I knew it had been much read, because when I used to read it which was a year or more ago, it was well worth reading and having been uninformed as to its degeneracy I concluded that it was still valuable. . . .

The subject you have proposed for our letters is one in which I am thorough[l]y interested and to which I expect to devote much thought but at present I must confess that I am unable to advance any thoughts that are worthy of your attention. I have not been able to read and think upon this most important subject as it deserves and I have not yet clear, and well defined views in regard to it.

In my humble opinion, true oratory is the greatest power granted unto man. For this broad statement I suppose I should give some reasons but I believe you will agree with me in it. . . .

I do not believe I have said anything, which was not implied in your brief statement of some of the questions connected with this subject and I look forward with pleasure to reading your next, which will no doubt go more fully into these same questions and propose others bearing upon Oratory.

The question of aestheticism seems to be attracting a good deal of attention just now and I am anxious to learn more about it. I want to hear your views on it when you write again and I will give you my opinions then. To say the least I believe that there is more in it, than is generally thought. . . .

Your true friend   C. W. Kent

ALS (WP, DLC) with WWhw notation on env.: "Ans. March 3rd/82." Also on env.: WWhw notes listing points in Kent's letter regarding oratory.
    1 See C. W. Kent to WW, Dec. 20, 1881.

From Richard Heath Dabney

My dear Tommy,   New York Feb. 26th 1882
    . . . I suppose that by this time you are settled in Atlanta, but not being certain, I direct this to Wilmington, whence it may be forwarded to you, if not there. There is a friend of mine, and a Φ.Κ.Ψ. brother of us both, who is in Atlanta, and I think you would like him. His name is Lewis Aylett: I believe you have heard him spoken of quite frequently by Chas Kent, Joe Blair &c. . . .

I sincerely hope, old fellow, that you will rapidly rise in the law; and I haven't a doubt that you will; if you have half a chance. If my wishes could do any good, you would soon have to employ a special policeman to keep the throng of clients from breaking down your office door. . . .

Write soon to your friend—   R. H. Dabney.

ALS (WP, DLC) with WWhw notation on env.: "Ans. March 5th/82."

Marginal Notes

John B. Minor, *Institutes of Common and Statute Law* (4 vols., Richmond, 1876-79).	Transcripts of WW Shorthand Comments
Vol. I, 320:	[c. March 2, 1882]
The wife *cannot* [WW's italics] in like	Geo[rgia]: "No contract

manner convey directly to the husband (except her separate property or by power of appointment), because, save in those cases, no conveyance of a married woman is valid even in equity, unless made in pursuance of the provisions of the statute upon the subject (V. C. 1873, c. 117, § 4, 7), . . .

of sale of a wife as to her separate estate with her husband or her trustee shall be valid unless the same is allowed by order of the superior court of the country [sic] of her domicile." (G. C. '73, 1785)

[John B. Minor] *The Objects of the Common and Statute Law*, pamphlet edition [n.d.] of Vol. III of Minor's *Institutes of Common and Statute Law*, p. 71:

2ᶜ The Wife's interest in the Husband's Chattels, by way of *Paraphernalia.*

The wife takes by the marriage no specific interest whatsoever in the chattels of the husband, save only as respects her *paraphernalia*, a term borrowed from the Roman Law, and derived from the Greek language (παρα ψερνη [sic]), signifying something *over and above her dower.* Our law uses it to signify such apparel and ornaments of the wife, suitable to her position in society, as are given her *by her husband* (for if given by third persons they are commonly supposed to be designed for *separate use*, and are absolutely her's, free from his control). Such *paraphernalia* are the property of the husband, and if he chooses to dispose of them in his life-time, he is at liberty to do so, however unhandsome such exercise of authority may be; but he cannot deprive his wife of them *by will*, . . .

Geo: "The wife's paraphernalia shall not be subject to the debts or contracts of the husband, and shall consist of the apparel of herself and children, her watch and ornaments suitable to her condition in life, and all such articles of personalty as have been given to her for her use and comfort." (G.C. '73, 1773.)

From Robert Bridges

Dear Tommy: New York, March 12th '82

To-night I went to my trunk to look over some letters, and a class *Herald*¹ caught my eye. I got down to leaf it over for a few minutes—and I guess I read almost everything in it before I put it aside. The old days came back upon me with a rush, and with them the remembrance of all my old friends—the Witherspoon crowd—and the man among them all who stood always faithfully near me and was so much to me in all that I did, and hoped to

do. I felt ashamed of myself when I thought how long it had been
since I had written to you. . . .

I suppose you are admitted by this time, and are probably at
work in Atlanta. You are right in the centre of the New South. I
have been following affairs very closely down there—though I put
off writing on it until it was too late. I rather fear that the independent movement is in the wrong hands. I read the *Constitution*
carefully and know it to be a liberal newspaper—and yet I find that
it is opposed to the coalition. I fear that its methods will not lead
the better people of the South into its ranks. I wish you would tell
me something about the reputation which Felton and his crowd
bear among the best people in Georgia.[2] I almost envy you your
political opportunities. I see signs of a new crystallization of politics in your section. These "Mahonizing" movements are sporadic
—but they are the sign of life and activity. They are labor pains,
and the New South and the new Southern party is yet to be born.
I hope you will be on hand at the accouchement. . . .

Your old friend   Bob Bridges

Direct   Care *Evening Post.*

ALS (WP, DLC) with WWhw notation on env.: "Ans 3/16/82."
 1 *The Nassau Herald*, senior yearbook of the Princeton class of 1879.
 2 William H. Felton, physician, Methodist minister, and the stormy petrel
of Georgia politics during this period. An opponent of the rule of Governor
Joseph E. Brown and the New Departure Democrats, Felton was elected to
Congress as an independent in 1874, 1876, and 1878.

Two Letters to Robert Bridges

Dearest Bobby,   Wilmington, N. C., March 15th 1882
    I cannot tell you how much the receipt of your letter gladdened
me! Although I had been brooding over your long silence, I did not
realize how much my spirits had been depressed by it until your
letter came and was read this morning and I felt the bound that
my spirits took, as tho' a burden had been lifted off from them.
You know I had not heard from you since before your last September's visit to your home—nor had I heard from any of the old
gang in all that time. I was just on the point, a few days ago, of
writing to one and all of the crowd, to learn if they had really
forgotten me, when a letter came to me from the Cow[1] which was
full of the old-time spirit of that valuable animal and which contained news of you and Pete from which I knew that you were
both still in your old haunts, at least. And now comes your own
letter with abundant evidence in every line of it that you are your
own self yet—if [George] Shoemaker does think you so changed.

But this letter was not needed to prove that to me. I've never for a moment, even during fits of despondency, doubted your or Pete's friendship; but I did begin to be afraid that something had befallen one or both of you, that you had left New York, were broken in health, or something of that sort.

Since you wrote me the letter which I answered last Summer from Maysville, Kentucky, I have passed through an experience which has had a very deep affect upon me, and which has made me feel all the more eager for the sympathy of my old and dearest friends. You remember that I was then on my way to Chillicothe, Ohio, to visit the family of my mother's brother, Thomas Woodrow, after whom I was named. Well, to make a long, and to me painful, story as short as possible, I was confirmed during my visit there, in a passion which had for some years been irrisistably growing upon me—in love for my cousin, Hattie Woodrow. She went to school in Virginia, in a place a few hours ride from Charlottesville, during my first Winter at the University of Virginia, and it was then and there that I first met her and was first attracted by her. I had seen her when we were both children, but had really never known her before. I never knew a handsomer, more intelligent, noble, or lovable girl than she! After that Winter in Virginia we corresponded regularly until my visit last Summer. I then, as in honor bound, told her of the character of my love for her—and she, with such assurances as led me to believe that she did so only because of our near blood-relationship, refused me.

Now, Bobby, I've related this experience to you in a very bungling, incoherent way, but I know that you will appreciate the embarrassments under which I write. You are the first and only person, outside the circle of my own nearest kin, to whom a word of this matter has been breathed: and I need not tell you that even at this distance of time I am unable to speak of it without such a rush of feeling as makes clear expression next to impossible.

You know me well enough to believe that, although not quickly excited, my love is all the more vehement when once aroused; and you can, therefore, readily understand the suffering I have undergone during the last few months. My disappointment has been the keener and the less endurable because of the conviction that my cousin really loved me as much as I could have desired and rejected me only because of a prejudice which made her regard it as her duty to do so.

Of course I am not such a weakling as to allow myself to be unmanned even by a disappointment such as this, and I have already in great part recovered from the shock; but, naturally,

my work has been considerably broken in upon, and you will not
be surprised to find that I am not yet in Atlanta. For various reasons I have postponed my departure thence until May.

And now let me change the subject, Bobby. It has greatly relieved me to tell you of these things and to assure myself of your
heartiest sympathy.

Since I last wrote to you I have been intellectually busy in the
same desultory manner as of old. I've read all sorts of books besides law books. I've rushed through about half—the best half, I
take it—of the volumes of the English men of letters series so far
issued,[2] and have made other excursions in other, very different,
directions. I've read poetry much and orations more; I've read
encyclopaedias and biographies and novels; but of all the poor
and yet pretentious writing that I've happened upon in my many
expeditions the palm for pure poverty and inexcusable pretention
I would unhesitatingly give to the first volume of John W. Forney's *Anecdotes of Public Men*. Anecdotes! why there is not one
anecdote worthy the name in each fifty pages of the rambling
stuff. It's a mere catalogue of the names of distinguished men
whom Mr. Forney, the most distinguished man of the book, has
known; and to these names he has strung adjectives and epithets
which he hopes may pass as gems of character sketching. The
book is enlivened here and there by quotations from Lincoln and
other men of genius which are worth reading and worth preserving; but which are preserved in much better form, and in
much better company, elsewhere. Oh that I had back the two
dollars wasted on this trash that I might buy *bum wad*,[3] or some
other useful commodity, with it!

I've been writing too—even writing poetry![4] But I have not
published much. I am too busy about other things to have time
for any very elaborate compositions. I have been having, lately,
an amusing passage at arms with my Roman Catholic fellow
citizens here, through the columns of the local press.[5] I found it
a good chance to exercise myself in satire and ridicule, and gloried
in the opportunity of turning my guns against the conceited ig-
noramous who edits our chief daily, the Wilmington *Morning Star*.
Like all men of his ilk he is peculiarly sensitive to ridicule—and I
have reason to believe that he is specially sensitive to it as coming
from *me*. I some time ago wrote a series of editorials for him on
the subject of education, and when they were quoted and lauded
throughout the State he complaisantly appropriated all the credit
to himself.[6] Of course I do'nt care to give the man away; but he
is conscious that I know what a sham he is. He is now making

a figure of himself on the wrong side of the Romish question and I have him in hand. It's poor sport, however, with such small game. Anything legitimate, though, to keep my pen in training.

I quite agree with you, Bobby, in the hope that you will some day conduct a daily in some smaller city—how I wish that that smaller city might be Atlanta—then you might take a hand in that political future which you rightly think will be full of vigorous life and fruitful of glorious opportunities. But, in the mean time, your present position and work are affording you the very best possible training. Your apprenticeship has been hard but it has lasted scarcely two (?) years yet and you are still too young to be impatient of a subordinate position, tho' I know, my dear fellow, how hard it is for one with so strong an individuality as yours to abide being deprived of all power to assert that individuality by being made part of a mere machine. The fact that that machine is a very grand affair does not afford much consolation. But, with health, you can bide your time with confidence. The fact is, I rather envy you, Bobby. I am older than you are—I begin to feel very sedate under the burden of my twenty-five years—and yet you have already gotten a long start of me. I am not even licensed yet —I am not even entered for the race. But I'm very eager to get to work and shall run hard when I'm once fairly on the course.

I am more than gratified to know that you see through the pretences of Mahone and that ilk. There's no truth in them. I am as heartily for independence in politics as any one can be—but not for an independence whose first step is towards the destruction of the public credit, whose first intentions are criminal, and whose main ends are personal. I was in Virginia, you remember, when the readjusters one [won] their first campaign. I heard a speech from Massie [J. H. Massey], an ex-parson, the shrewdest speaker in the Mahone ranks, and the most eager partisan of that party until he saw his main purpose defeated by his being disappointed of the spoils; and I heard Mahone's chief lieutenant, Riddleberger, and what did their speeches amount to? How I wish you could have heard them! Had you been with me, you would now join with me in declaring them productions of the lowest demagoguery—appeals to the basest passions and the most degrading prejudices that ever made the heart of man worthy of distrust. You have a fair type of Mahone and his following near you, in the persons of John Kelly[7] and his party. And I am bound to say that Felton of Georgia is less offensive than Mahone of Virginia only because he has had fewer opportunities of offence

I go all the way with you in thinking that the formation of a new Southern party is a consummation devoutly to be wished, and I will do all in my power to aid in its formation as opportunity offers; but I fervently pray that the South may never be delivered in to the hands of Mahones or Felton's. Give us back the carpet-baggers—the undisguised rascals—rather.—But I can't begin to give you all my views concerning Southern politics in a letter. If I can lay my hands on an unpublished essay of mine on the subject, I will send it to you, and know that you will not think it amiss.[8] Our friendship may be said to have been cemented in *discussion*; so I want you to know my whole mind on this subject as on all others, that we may discuss and agree upon a right solution. I entirely trust your judgment and know that you will trust my observation, knowing that I am not biassed by the love of *either* of the National parties.

You may depend upon it that I will be at the Triennial if it be at all in my power to attend, and if I can visit you in New York I will be only too glad to do it. The fact that my settlement in Atlanta is fixed for May will possibly make it difficult for me to go North in June, but nothing but absolute necessity will hinder me from going. Why a day with the old gang would be worth the cost of any sacrifice to me!

Give lots of love to Pete and beg the dear fellow to write me a line or two at least, just to interchange salutations, if nothing more. Warmest regards to all old friends. Your budget of gossip was a perfect boon to me. With love as warm as ever,

Your sincere friend,   T. W. Wilson.

[1] Hiram Woods, Jr., to WW, March 11, 1882, ALS (WP, DLC), with WWhw notations on env.: "Rec'd 3/14/82" and "Ans. 3/23/82."

[2] The "English Men of Letters" series of brief biographies of British and American literary figures began to appear in 1878 under the general editorship of John Morley. They were published by Macmillan & Co. in London and Harper & Bros. in New York. At least twenty-four volumes had appeared by the end of 1882. Of these, nine are to be found in WW's library: Alfred Ainger, *Charles Lamb*; R. W. Church, *Spenser*; Sidney Colvin, *Landor*; J. C. Morison, *Gibbon*; J. C. Morison, *Macaulay*; F. W. H. Myers, *Wordsworth*; Leslie Stephen, *Pope*; J. A. Symonds, *Shelley*; and A. W. Ward, *Chaucer*. WWhw notations on the flyleaves indicate that he acquired the volumes on Spenser, Pope, and Chaucer in 1881.

[3] Slang for toilet paper.

[4] Two poems, printed at Dec. 1 and 8, 1881.

[5] Printed at Jan. 25 and Feb. 15, 1882. See also at March 22, 1882.

[6] Printed at Aug. 25, 1880, Vol. I.

[7] John Kelly, Democrat, was a congressman from New York, 1855-58, and longtime head of Tammany Hall. In the New York legislature of 1882 he threw the support of Tammany Democrats to the Republicans after the regular Democrats had refused to accept his terms. The Republicans were thus able to organize both houses.

[8] "The Politics and the Industries of the New South," printed at April 30, 1881, and April 20, 1882. For the provenance of this article, see the note at Feb. 22, 1881.

Dear Bobby,　　　　　Wilmington, N. Carolina, March 18th 1882
　　I send you the article I promised in my letter of the other day.
I hope that you will find time and inclination to read it—and I
know that, if you do read it, you will appreciate the spirit of candor and impartiality in which it is written—because you know my
mind as well as I know it myself. With love,
　　　　　　　　　　　Yours in haste,　Tommy

P. S.　Please express the *mss.* back to me when you are through
with it. I enclose enough to defray expenses.　　Yours. T.

ALS (Meyer Coll., DLC).

From James W. Bones

Dear Tommie　　　　　　　　Rome Ga Mar 21st 1882
　　Your letter of 13th was received the day after your father &
mother left & I answer it at the earliest possible moment. I regretted their stay was so brief for every reason but especially because I wanted to have a full talk with them on this subject.[1] They
were with us however so short a time & we were all so taken up
with other matters that it was impossible to enter upon the subject
satisfactorily.
　　You need not have given any reasons for your desire to have the
balance of the Nebraska land divided. As I wrote you in my last
I have no objection to such a step whatever & agree with you that
it would be advisable for every reason. The time has now come
when it can be easily accomplished. During the early years after
your uncle's death the proceeds of land sales exclusive of what
was needed for taxes & other expenses were all turned over by
me to your mother to pay for the Columbia house.[2] My circumstances being easy then I did not need any of the funds. After
my failure it became necessary for your Auntie[3] to draw from the
Estate also & I took steps to effect sales more rapidly. Your mother
& Auntie have now drawn about equal amounts in actual cash
altho the adjustment of interest would show your mother more
largely indebted to the Estate than your Auntie.
　　And now as to the best way of making a division. I hardly think
it would be necessary for you to undergo the expense of a trip to
Nebraska, altho if you desire to do so still, after what I have to
say, I certainly have no objection. Shortly after your Uncle Williams death your mother & Auntie as also your father & I united
in giving your Uncle Thomas power of attorney to manage the
Estate. A copy of the will was sent to Mr Davis for record in each

of the counties. The only debts of the Estate were to your Uncle Thomas who had advanced money to his brother & paid all expenses attending his sickness & death. This indebtedness at first stood on his books as against his brother. It was afterwards divided equally between your mother & Auntie & charged up to them respectively, the old a/c being closed. This indebtedness has been long since discharged. After this your mother & father, as also your Uncle Thomas thought it best for me to attend to the Estate matters & the former gave me a power of attorney to act for them in signing deeds &c. The confidence they then reposed in me they have never so far as I know withdrawn & I have endeavored during these many years to act honestly towards them. The affairs of the Estate have not been left in the hands of agents as you seem to think. I have merely employed them to pay taxes & from time to time find purchasers for the land. Having paid frequent visits to Nebraska I was always able to judge whether the prices offered were reasonable & no sales were made without my approval. When sales were made by them they always sent me the cash proceeds & notes & the latter were collected by me either thru the banks out West or thru the agents. Sometimes the purchasers would remit directly to me. During some of my trips I made sales directly myself & settled with the purchasers without the intervention of our agents. Since the Estate matters have been in my hands I have kept a regular a/c of receipts & expenditures & I am ready at any time to give an account of my stewardship. You will readily perceive that as I have kept the account & not the agents you would not be able to get satisfactory data from them.[4] Nor can I conceive of any necessity for your investigating personally in Nebraska transactions which have extended over many years unless you doubt the correctness of my account. Your entering upon such an investigation would certainly indicate such a doubt to the minds of people out there. If after going over my account you do not feel satisfied of its correctness I would prefer going to Nebraska with you or write to each of the agents for a statement of all monies they have remitted to me. As to a division of the land, I have several times talked with lawyers in Nebraska & the mode they suggest as being most simple & least expensive is this. All lands there are appraised every year or so by the tax assessors & the relative valuation appears on the tax lists. This would serve us as a guide or we could get two or more gentlemen in each county to appraise the different 40 acre lots. Then taking for granted that there is no dispute between the parties in interest we could adjust the a/cs ourselves & divide the land according to location & relative value. Then your mother & Auntie would deed to each other her half interest in the portions assigned to each. This could be all done when you come to Atlanta in May should your mother accompany your father. I hope she will do this any way in order to complete her visit. We can all come together here & arrange matters. I have on hand notes amounting to about $3000. & a few sales are now arranged which will be perfected by 1st of May. Our agents write that there is prospect of a good demand this spring so that we may be able to divide a considerable portion of available means. I think then, my dear Tommy, all that you desire can be accomplished without your taking a trip to Nebraska provided you & your dear parents still have the confidence in me which they have manifested these many years. I will only add that the Patents are still in the care of your Uncle Thomas. As they are recorded I have had no occasion to take them out of his hands. Your Uncle Williams will was probated in Chillicothe. It is in my hands. Your mother has doubtless ere this told you all about the marriage.[5] We have had several letters from the young people & they are of course very happy.

With fondest love from us all to you all

Your affc Uncle   James.

I write in great haste amidst many interruptions.

ALS (WP, DLC) with WWhw notation on env.: "Ans. 3/27/82." Also on env. WWhw and WWsh notes about law.

[1] The "subject" was the Estate of William Woodrow, brother of Janet Woodrow Wilson, Marion Woodrow Bones, and Thomas Woodrow, Jr. Thomas had taken his share earlier. Janet and Marion left their portions together under James Bones's management. Janet, growing dissatisfied, sought a division and placed the entire matter in WW's hands, giving him power of attorney on June 13, 1882. The details of the settlement of this complicated affair will unfold in the forthcoming letters and other documents exchanged among WW, JWW, and James Bones.

[2] This was the house that WW's parents built at the corner of Hampton and Henderson streets in Columbia, S. C., 1872. The house is now a museum.

[3] Marion Woodrow Bones.

[4] WW copied, probably in the spring of 1883, Bones's record into an account book (WP, DLC), inscribed (WWhw) on first two pages: "*Estate of William Woodrow.*" The entries between Sept. 28, 1871, and Feb. 6, 1883, are presumably the ones that WW copied from Bones' book into his own. The entries between July 5, 1883, and Aug. 25, 1884, are WW's original entries made while he was managing his mother's affairs.

[5] Of Jessie Bones and Abraham T. H. Brower, which JRW and JWW attended.

Letter to the Editor: "Anti-Sham No. 3"

[March 22, 1882]

To the Editor of the N. C. Presbyterian:

Dear Sir,—

If the truth were a matter of indifference, some of the recent members of your *most Catholic* contemporary, the *Morning Star,* would afford to a casual reader a rich fund of amusement. Some weeks ago, you remember, an "advertisement" of great length, and—what is less common than length in advertisements—of great vehemence, appeared in the most prominent columns of that paper, purporting to come from the "Rooms of the Young Catholic Friends' Society," and proving, upon perusal, to be a rather excited defence of the Roman Catholic church from certain strictures upon its policy which one or two fellow-citizens of the Young Friends' had ventured publicly to print. Now the style of that "advertisement" was open to criticism, but every one knows that considerable freedom of style is not only allowed but expected in advertisements; and besides, no one could read this particular "advertisement" without having his sympathy for its authors aroused, and his criticicism [sic] of all its minor defects thereby silenced. The Young Friends' declared that they were compelled to adopt this method of answering their adversaries by advertisement, because no paper in this section cared or dared to open its spaces to contributions in defence of Romish institutions. Some might have been tempted to receive this declaration with incredulity; for had not the *Morning Star*, but a few days before, editorially endorsed the doctrines and praised the ceremonials of the Romish church with an overflowing enthusiasm, when the doctrines were preached and these ceremonials were exhibited in our midst with special demonstration, pomp, and circumstance? But, after all, that may have been done by the editors of the *Star* under a sudden impulse of generosity, only in order to please certain Roman Catholic citizens whom they respected, and whom all their fellow-citizens know to be worthy of respect. If so, we must give full credence to the complaint of the advertisers. The generosity of the editors of the *Star* did not extend to the admission of Romish matter which was not editorial.

But, then, advertisers have assuredly enjoyed, since the publication of their manifesto, a most extraordinary privilege, such as is not accorded to all inserters of long advertisements! From the date of their utterance until now, the *Star* has continued to print advertisements of Rome in her most seductive aspects, and to print them in such form and place as to make it evident that they were inserted free of charge![1] Doubtless the editors of the *Star* are thus endeavoring to hush the reproaches of their own consciences and to make amends to the advertisers, and all whom the advertisers may chance to represent, for their selfish exclusiveness in restricting them to advertisements.

Certainly "Religious Toleration" Here, There, and Everywhere is a whimsical heading for an advertisement; but if those short and incomplete extracts introduced under such titles were not advertisements, what were they? If they were meant as expressions of editorial opinion they would, of course, appear in the writing editor's own diction, for it is not his custom to hide himself behind extracts from other papers. If he had meant to put Protestant opinion at defiance, he would certainly have done it openly and not thus covertly. He is not afraid to show his opinions in open day-light. Those must have been advertisements.

But no! there is another supposition which may be regarded as tenable. The captions of these articles speak of *toleration*. Perchance the editors are desirous of making theirs the organ of toleration in this section so noted for intolerance. The appeal of the Young Catholic Friends for the mercies of toleration may have suggested to the editors, a fitting first text wherein to build their opening pleas for freedom of thought and opinion. This seems a plausible theory. The only thing that throws doubt upon it is, that the editors of the *Star* are men of sense and would see that they are making a false start. For their good judgments must have told them that when one combats error, he does not thereby prove himself guilty of the ugly offence of intolerance. They have, of course, read and laid to heart the teachings and precepts of Thomas Jefferson, the immortal apostle of tolerance, and must remember that he says, that there is no danger in error so long as reason is left free to combat it, and that it is upon this wise saying, principally, that he founds his plea for tolerance. It is probable, too, that they inform themselves as to the current questions of the day, and are, therefore, not aware that apprehension of danger from the aggressive policy of the Roman hierarchy is not everywhere, even in this land of secure freedom esteemed mere childish timidity. Possibly they know, as everybody else does, on the authority of men of full information and acknowledged title to speak, that wherever the Romish church is strong, its strength is used to exalt its power above the civil power, and its influence to unfit its adherents for intelligent or patriotic citizenship. Indeed they must know that these pretentions and evil tendencies of the Papal power can be, and have been abundantly proved and illustrated out of the mouths of that power's highest and most trusted representatives.

There is still doubt, then, as to what the editors of the *Star* may have thought themselves to be doing this short time past. They cannot have intended to appear to join in with the cry of some who have been fighting the air by attacking that which does not exist. When they seemed to be endorsing error, persons were found in this community who were quick to challenge their utterances; but their sober editorial minds are above the silliness of thinking that those challengers smacked of anything like religious intolerance. Argal, those pieces with "Religious Toleration in" &c., captions must have been advertisements of somebody or something, after all.

But, if advertisements, they must have been free advertisements. Romanists are indeed shrewd calculators of the main chance, and would not have been likely to put their cause in peril of damage by publishing extracts from the writings of persons on whose sympathy and good-will they could not altogether rely. The editors of the *Star*, with a carelessness which, as gratuitous advertisers, they should have been vigilant to avoid, have in one conspicuous instance, extracted, from an article which appeared in another paper a passage which totally misrepresented the author quoted, and was in an entirely different tone from the rest of his article. Of course they did not want to garble the piece found in the *New York Evangelist*.[2] Probably their eye was caught by this single passage, and they were only negligent in not reading what preceded and followed it; or, mayhap, they found the extract made ready to their hands by some one else, and did not see the rest of the letter. However that may be, they have doubtless by this time discovered their mistake, and will not only excuse but even expect this bit of advice: Print advertisements in advertising columns. Never, through inadvertence, lay yourselves open to the damaging suspicion of seeking to overthrow a neighbors' reputation for fair-mindedness under color of quoting generous sentiments from others. Do not, above all things, fight against the right, even if you can, while so doing, escape detection by wearing other mens' garments. Words, these, to the wise.   Anti-Sham.

Printed in the Wilmington *North Carolina Presbyterian*, March 22, 1882.
[1] Three items appeared in the Wilmington *Morning Star* during the controversy stirred up by "Anti-Sham." (1) "Religious Toleration in Charleston," reprinted Feb. 18, 1882, from the *Southern Christian Advocate*, a Methodist organ, praised a Roman Catholic sermon, delivered in Charleston, S. C., on the agelessness and indestructibility of the Roman Catholic Church. (2) "Religious Toleration in Egypt," reprinted Feb. 26, 1882, from the *Southern Presbyterian*, was an interview with the Khedive of Egypt. It reported that the Khedive was attempting to encourage religious toleration and, although a Moslem, had given land for Protestant missions and hospitals. (3) "Religious Toleration in New York," about which see the next note, was reprinted March 12, 1882. All three items appeared in the *Morning Star's* news columns and looked like other news stories. The editor of the *Morning Star* probably printed them on his own initiative as replies to "Anti-Sham." There is no indication that they were advertisements, paid or unpaid, submitted by the Young Catholic Friends' Society or anyone else.
[2] This was the Rev. Dr. H. M. Field, "Letters of Dr. Field—No. XIII. Roman-

ism at Rome. The Poetry and Prose of the Roman Catholic Church," *The New-York Evangelist*, LIII (Feb. 23, 1882), 1. A reading of this letter does not confirm WW's statement that "the editors," i.e., Bernard, garbled or printed extracts out of context. Field did write in his first paragraph: "The Roman Catholic Church is a study to me. I look at it with the utmost interest, and with a mind predisposed to a favorable judgment. And I see a great deal that I truly admire. But no sooner does this feeling begin to take possession of me, than I receive such a shock from other things which I see that I am driven back into an attitude of disgust and almost of hatred." However, the author went on to mix condemnation with warm praise of many aspects of the ministry and organization of the Roman Catholic Church, and one can hardly say that the general tone is hostile.

From Robert Bridges

Dear Tommy: New York. Mar 30th [1882]

Your essay came all right about a week ago. I read it carefully and was so much pleased with it that I showed it to our managing editor, telling him I thought it would be a good thing to publish. He was pleased with it and would like to print the latter part of it about the "Industries of the South."[1] Of course the *American* Symposium is now out of date and it would not do for a newspaper. If you don't object to seeing your mangled child in print, please let me know soon, and I will superintend the surgical operation —preserve the limbs for you and send you several printed copies of the victim.

The copy is piling in and I must stop.

Yours in haste   Bob Bridges

ALS (WP, DLC) with WWhw notations on env.: "Rec'd 4/1/82" and "Ans 4/1/82."

[1] Printed at April 20, 1882 as "New Southern Industries."

To Robert Bridges

Dear Bobby,   Wilmington, N. C., April 1st 1882

Your kind note of the 30th reached me this morning. Certainly you may use the essay in the way you propose. It was like you to think of such a kindness. I had not meant to seek publication for the piece (or even a *piece of the piece*); but since publication seeks it, I acquiesce with pleasure. I shall expect a letter from you very soon containing your views upon the *political* doctrines of the article. I am anxious to have you agree with me as nearly as you can.

With your note came a letter from Billy Wilder written *ex officio* with reference to the Triennial.[1] I will not reply to it to-day, however, not wishing to answer the questions on so *foolish* a date.

The other day brought Talcott's semi-annual epistle.[2] I will punish him by giving it a prompt answer. How supremely refreshing it will be to see the dear fellow again, if we meet at the reunion! I wonder if he has encouraged his "siders" into growth yet. A portion of his letter will bear transcription. Here it is:

"Hiram [Woods], I see, has blossomed into a doctor. Nervous diseases will at last be cured. If Hiram ever comes near my sick bed I will shoot him. He will cut quite a figure in death bed scenes. But he is in dead earnest, I suppose, and this will make him all the more destructive."

Is'nt that Talcottian? When we come to edit Talcott's life and letters, you and I, that will be a choice tid-bit for *Talcottiana*! Of course we will outlive the dear rascal—especially if he get into New York politics.

With much love to Pete, and much for yourself,
                    Your very sincere friend,   Wood. Wilson

P.S. You see I am gradually cutting my name down to portable size. I'll soon have to have a "shingle" painted, you see, and the shorter the name the shorter the painter's bill.
                                        Yours   W. W.

ALS (Meyer Coll., DLC).
  [1] William R. Wilder to WW, March 30, 1882, ALS (WP, DLC) with WWhw notations on env.: "Rec'd 4/1/82" and "Ans. 4/6/82." Enc.: A. W. Halsey, W. R. Wilder, and W. F. Magie, Committee of '79, printed form letter, n.d., requesting information for the "Triennial Record," with WWhw notation: "Ans. 4/6/82."
  [2] Charles A. Talcott to WW, March 28, 1882, ALS (WP, DLC) with WWhw notations on env.: "Rec'd 3/30/82" and "Ans 4/3/82."

From James W. Bones

Dear Tommy   Rome, Ga. April 5th 1882
    Your last letter was received & I am glad my suggestions as to the mode of making a division strike you favorably. I inclose a petition sent to me from Nebraska for a road, which is to pass thro' a portion of our lands. It will be an advantage to have the road & Marion has signed it. Please ask your mother to affix her signature & then inclose the paper to G W E Dorsey[1] Fremont Nebraska. Please attend to it at once. We incur no expense, only give right of way. . . .   Your affec Uncle James

ALS (WP, DLC).
  [1] Agent for the Estate of William Woodrow.

From Hiram Woods, Jr.

Dear Tommy,   Baltimore, 4/6/82.
    Your very welcome letter was duly received. Many thanks for

your prompt reply. I was somewhat surprised to hear that you were indulging in Poetry. What was the cause of this departure? Possibly the nature of the production might shed some light on the matter. I should greatly like to see it, anyhow, and I trust you will favor some of your friends with a copy. . . .

I am up set by your intimating that you may not be at the Triennial in June. Why, Tommy, you *must* be there. The gang would be lost without the dignified presence of the "Managing Editor."[1] So let your numerous clients know that you are "retained" for a week in the middle of June. . . .

Yours as Ever,   Hiram Woods Jr

ALS (WP, DLC) with WWhw notations on env.: "Recd April 8th" and "Ans. April 19th 1882."
[1] WW was managing editor of *The Princetonian*, 1878-79.

From Edward Hough Trotter

My dear Tommy,   [Philadelphia] April 14th 1882
I feel pretty well worn out & sleepy but feel that I must send you a line or two before putting the shutters up for the night, as this will probably be the last chance I will have during my bachelorhood.

Your letter did me lots of good, old fellow, & I thank you from my heart for all the good wishes and opinions therein expressed. I am about to take the most serious step of my moderately eventful career—& at such a moment a man values the remembrances of old & cherished friends more than during almost any other time.

As far as I myself am concerned the world has prospered with me mainly since our graduation—and as for the young lady who is so soon to do me the great honor of becoming my wife, I feel that no words of mine can do justice to her virtues & to the estimation in which I hold her.

I hope, however, to have the pleasure of presenting you to her at our triennial, when you can tell her all the good & the bad you know of me—but I promise you she will believe only the former.

With best wishes for your success through life, believe me
Your friend always   Edwd H. Trotter
ALS (WP, DLC).

Newspaper Article
New Southern Industries.

Wilmington, N. C., April 20, 1882.
Since the abolition of slavery the South has entered upon a life

as entirely different from her life before the war as the present life of England is distinct from her life in the days of feudal institutions. In being rid by war of those social conditions which bound her previous to secession she exchanged, in one sudden revolution, such as has no parallel in history, institutions essentially feudal for the extremest usages of modern democracy. The analogy is by no means a fanciful one. Vassals and bondmen became freemen and citizens; were raised by one supreme act of national authority to a power and influence in public affairs capable of becoming as great as any that their one-time lords and masters ever exercised. Before the war the great landowners of the South, living in the midst of their vast estates, surrounded by numberless slaves and retainers, dispensing a liberal, sometimes an almost royal, hospitality, the magnates of the counties in which their spacious and luxurious residences spread their many gables —these men were not unlike in their circumstances, in their accomplishments, in their virtues, and in their vices, those lords of England who, in the latest days of feudal institutions, represented in the pride and circumstance of their lives the spirit of the earlier days of their race. Of course Southern gentlemen, eagerly following literature, as they generally did, as the most elevated of pastimes, caught many of the nineteenth-century modes of thought and tints of principle and peculiarities of belief; and they were brought constantly into contact with latter-day methods of life also, and made to feel the outside pressure of the great industrial and social movements which were changing the rest of the civilized world from old to new. But they lived in a society in which not many of these outer impulses were sympathetically felt. Save in foreign cities, and a few of the capitals of the North, they saw little of city life. The Southerner of that day lived for the most part in rural communities, which were not compact enough to serve as good conducting media for new ideas. There were not many towns to serve as nurseries of democratic or any other changeful principles, and until society seemed to have become fixed in its unprogressive habits, there were no railways to make less the distances which separated its isolated parts, and no telegraph to bring them closer in sympathy.

The building up of the new South was left first in the hands of men who, however much of the political opinions and social sentiments of their fathers they had imbibed, were quickly, if not easily, turned to new ways of living; who, while still retaining some of the pride of blood which had been a prominent characteristic

of the slave-holding aristocracy, were not averse from aggrandiz-
ing that pride by seeking success in employments with which their
fathers would probably not have been willing to associate their
family names; who showed the high breeding of their youth in
nothing more admirably than their honest endeavors to redress
their fortunes by any honorable labor their hands could find to do.
They were men, in a word, whose sentiments indeed were of the
past, but whose energies were bent willingly to the present task,
and whose store was laid by the future.

To those who remember the life to which the sons of rich plant-
ers were used before the war the rapid recovery of wealth and
prosperity in the South which the years since the war have witnessed is a subject of profound astonishment, and in all such it
must excite much genuine admiration of the character of the
Southern people. The life of most Southern young men was not
generally such as to justify any very high expectations of their
future usefulness. After their college years were over—and they
were generally over by the time they had reached full manhood—
they returned to their parents' estate to spend the early evening
in the company of the guests of which their hospitable homes were
generally full, the late evening and the small hours of the night
in reading novels, or any other light literature that might for the
time satisfy their fancies or their whims, their mornings in bed,
where heavy sleep failed to refresh them, and their afternoons
astride fine horses, which carried them right bravely on tours of
neighborly visiting. Their lives were one grand holiday. Their
heaviest care was to please themselves. And yet these men, thus
nurtured, were first among the most gallant soldiers of the Confederate armies, and when defeated, were the first to bare their
muscles to any honorable labor that might help them to support
themselves and those dependent on them.

Realizing, by the aid of such a retrospect, the traits of the new
generation of Southerners who are now become the pioneers in a
new development, one may forecast the future with the greater
certainty. The lines of this new development are already set. The
South, until the war an almost exclusively agricultural region,
possessing in partial operation generally only those departments
of trade and those crafts which were the necessary ministers to
the housekeeper or simply handmaidens of agriculture, she will
now turn her attention to the rearing of manufactures and the extension of her internal and foreign commerce, confining all her
agricultural operations which have regard to the supplying of
foreign markets to those staple products, such as cotton, tobacco,

rice, and the sugar canes, in whose cultivation she need fear little successful competition.

Of course, for some time to come her main industrial projects will concern the manufacture of cotton fabrics. In this direction some steps had been taken even before the war. Several flourishing cotton mills had been for many years previous to that time successfully—with large profit, indeed—employing free labor in the production of excellent cotton goods, both in Georgia and South Carolina. Since that time, as is well known, very many similar mills have been erected in various parts of the South. And in every instance, so far as is ascertained, have such investments proved profitable even beyond sanguine expectation. The danger, of course, is that the large dividends which investments in this industry seem to assure will lead in many cases to ruinous speculation. There will soon, no doubt, be more mills than the demand for cotton goods is at all likely to warrant, and then there will be a collapse in many quarters. There seem to be many sure indications of a financial crisis similar, in kind if not in extent, to that of 1873. The main causes of that disastrous prostration of business are now easily enough discernible. The years which preceded it witnessed immense investments in fixed capital. Unprecedented activity in the construction of railways in every portion of the Union, for example, gave a new and powerful impetus to all those industries which are accessory to such enterprises. Vast amounts of money were expended in the construction of iron and steel foundries. Everywhere there were extensive transfers of capital from other employments to this, which seemed for the time to offer greater promise of quick remuneration. Thousands of furnaces blazed to supply material for the railroad builders. But the time came when this wholesale construction of roads had reached its natural term; and then the machinery which had been constructed in its aid was stopped, and the furnaces which had been hot in its service cooled in idleness. Many capitalists, small and great, discovered too late that machinery without work and furnaces without fires constituted fixed capital which was singularly unproductive, and that they were bankrupt. Here, then, was one large contribution to the crisis. Here was one symptom of the reaction from that universal spirit of speculation in which was summed up all the causes of the crisis.

It is not improbable that similar things will be witnessed in the South. So soon as there is too large a transfer of capital from other interests, which now yield small and tardy profits to the cotton manufacture, which at present offers such fair promise of big and prompt returns; so soon as moneyed men in every State and every district feel justified in building their own mills and setting up their own machinery and making their own shirts and sheets, failure will come and workmen will be idle. The likelihood that such a time is near at hand is diminished by the fact that as yet there has been little accumulation of wealth and capital in the South; and, of course, when there is little available money there will be small investments. But, on the other hand, there are already indications that there will be a large influx of capital from the North for the purpose of building up this new industry. These are all signs that the anticipated crisis will be hastened. That it must come sooner or later appears to be indisputable, and the necessity of its coming is greatly to be deplored. But such trials seem to be natural to the youth of all such enterprises, and the conclusion is justified that, like the diseases of children, they are needed to clear the system for healthy life in maturity.

Perhaps, before the critical period arrives in the South, some of the weaker foundations of the cotton-manufacturing interests of New England will have given way. The first shock may be felt there. For it may be reckoned upon as a very grave mistake to suppose that the rivalry between the two sections will be confined to the production of the coarser fabrics. The competition will be restricted to no one department of the work; it will be sharp and eager in all departments. It is already extending itself. Many Southern mills are now manufacturing calico-cloths and sheetings of the best qualities. The main reason relied upon to show the inability of Southern manufactories to make any but the coarser goods is their lack of skilled labor. Undoubtedly this lack does exist, but it is not likely long to continue. There is a large laboring class in the South—composed of men and their families who before the war were known among the negroes as the "poor whites"—which is now furnishing excellent material out of which to make skilful operatives. Few of the negroes have yet proved themselves capable of acquiring any considerable amount of proficiency in any of the mechanical arts save carpentering, bricklaying, and the like. This may be due to their never having been tried in any other of the employments which call for expertness and dexterity—for they are a race peculiarly quick in imitation; but the fact remains and suggests the necessity of looking elsewhere for additions to the force of skilled employees; and by looking elsewhere for the supply is meant, of course, looking to immigration, either from the North or from beyond sea.

It is not in the manufacture of cotton alone, however, that the help of the better class of immigrants is wanted. It is demanded in the development of those ample stores of mineral wealth which are hidden beneath Southern soil, and which, when taken from their dark storehouse, will furnish abundant material for manufacturing establishments no less extensive and no less profitable than those which ring with the busy racket of the loom. For all these trained artisans will be needed; and immigration must be looked to to supply the need, in part at least.

What are the prospects of the reinforcement of Southern labor by immigration? They are as good as could be expected. Much misapprehension exists concerning this matter. Seeing that very few of the many thousands of immigrants who yearly reach our coasts ever turn their faces southward, men, learned and unlearned, have set themselves to explain the fact. Some have confidently attributed it to a state of things which has no existence except in their own fancies. They have pretended to believe that fear of homicide kept these strangers away from the South. Others, with more soberness but with equal ignorance, have cast the whole blame upon land speculators. It is safe to say that the great majority of the immigrants who come to this country from across the Atlantic are either artisans or agricultural laborers. By far the greater number are agricultural laborers. Now, what present attraction has the South for either of these classes? Certainly very little for those who seek labor in the field. If they know anything of the South, they know that in agriculture it is already an old country—as much so as is New England; that it already has field hands in seeming abundance, who by their race and their training are better fitted for work under a Southern sun than any of their European competitors would be likely to be. They look upon Southern agricultural labor, moreover, as confined to the production of cotton; and of the culture of cotton they know nothing. They seek a new country, where the crops they are familiar with are grown, where wages are high, and where their chances of employment and gain seem best; and such a country they find in the West. The truth is, that the South has but small inducements to offer the common farm laborer. The immigration she is most eager to welcome at present is the immigration of capital—not capital in large masses, consolidated in the hands of a few, but capital in small quantities, the aggregate savings of a great many. In spite of the wasting methods of slave labor, land both rich and cheap is abundant in the South. The vast estates which existed before the war must be broken up, and the agricultural future must rest with the small farmer. Any man who will go South with

money enough to buy a few rich acres, and energy enough to cultivate them himself, will prosper beyond his hopes with very little
capital to aid him. Such men the South needs, and such she will
see coming to her markets in yearly increasing numbers.

What is there to draw the artisan, the mechanic southward?
He thinks of the South as an almost exclusively agricultural region, as an old agricultural region. Such she was until within a
very few years past. The great manufactories are in Pennsylvania
and in New England, and they attract him. The fame of the rising
industries of the South has not yet reached him. In the few years
of their existence Southern mills have been abundantly supplied
with employees from their own immediate neighborhood. When
new mills shall have been built; when iron furnaces and foundries
shall have been set burning and driving; when mines shall have
been opened, and the ore is smelted where it is mined—when, in
short, skilled mechanics are wanted, and know that they are
wanted, the South will not lack for workmen; immigrants will
no longer fear homicide. It is a simple question of supply and demand. Immigrants will go whithersoever profitable employment
and a home are obtainable. Labor will flow to the best market as
surely as will molasses or any other marketable commodity.

With reference both to the politics and the industries of the
South, this is the whole truth: the Southern people have set their
faces steadfastly, and with all the determination that is within
them, toward the accomplishment of two principal objects—namely, the unobstructed and peaceful development of the wealth
which their country is capable of producing and the industries she
is capable of maintaining, and the conclusive establishment of
their right of self-government within the provisions of the Constitution, resolved, the while, never again to harbor a threatening
thought against the maintenance of the Union, nor ever again to
be other than loyal and patriotic citizens of a country they will
always revere; and upon the varying fortunes of these principles
will depend their varying party alliances.   W. W.

Printed in the New York *Evening Post*, April 26, 1882; editorial heading omitted. For an account of the composition of this article, which WW actually wrote
a year before, see the note on the article printed at Feb. 22, 1881. This article reveals most clearly WW's identification and support of the basic objectives
of the so-called New South Movement, the most eloquent spokesman of which
was Henry W. Grady, editor of the *Atlanta Constitution*.

From Little, Brown & Company

Dear Sir: Boston, April 24 1882
     Your favor of the 21st rec'd. We expect to have ready the new

edition of Angell & Ames Corporations in the course of a fortnight and will send it post paid for $5.50, that is, $3.50 in addition to the amount now to your credit.[1]

Yours truly   Little, Brown & Co. C. W. D.

APS (WP, DLC).

[1] There is a statement from Little, Brown & Co. dated May 8, 1882, in WP, DLC, informing WW of the shipment of "1 Story Partnership" and "1 Angell & A. Corporations."

From Edward Ireland Renick

Dear Sir: Atlanta, Ga., Apl 25 1882

I was much pleased to hear that you would shortly be with us, & that it was your wish to board at Mrs. Boylston's. I am in a condition to say with increased emphasis all that I have hitherto said commendatory of her, her family, & her table. You will permit me to assure you that as soon as your intention was known to me, the expected enjoyment & improvement consequent upon the intimate association such co-habitation with you would insure me, sent me at once to Mrs. Boylston.

To my disappointment she, with much sincere regret, was constrained to decline. Her family—increased by visiting relatives—will fill her small house this summer. On this account she was compelled recently to beg all her boarders to seek other places, & I only remain. If you will allow me I will take great pleasure in securing you a home in the vicinity—the pleasantest part of town —but remote. Buy all old Ga. Reports you can, they are very scarce. Hoping soon to welcome you to this busy little city I am

Most truly Yours   E. I. Renick

ALS (WP, DLC) with WWhw notations on env.: "Rec'd April 28th 1882" and "Ans April 28th 1882."

From W. Walker Brookes

Dear Sir—   Attorney at Law, Rome, Ga., Apl 25th 1882

Your father sometime ago requested me to write to you & enclose you the address of the publishing house in Atlanta who are preparing our new Code. I have been very busy in court here for a month or more & have failed to comply with my promise to write you—but as there is ample time yet for you to secure a Code I trust you will pardon my delay in the matter. I have written the publisher & enclosed send you one of their blanks which I received by mail to day. You can just sign the card & fill the blank with your name & the post office where you wish the Code delivered—then mail the card to Mess[rs] Harrison & Co & all will be right. The Code will be out about 15th June.

I will write to Harrison & Co about you. I am happy to learn from your father that you are to be a member of our Georgia Bar so soon & hope to meet you at some early day in Atlanta.

Wishing you much success in your profession I am

Very truly yours   W. W. Brookes

ALS (WP, DLC) with WWhw notations on env.: "Rec'd April 30th 1882" and "Ans. May 2nd do. [ditto]."

From William Royal Wilder

Dear Tommy;   N.Y. 4/27/82

My warmest congratulations on your article in last night's *Post*. It is capital & has the solid ring. No one is more anxious than I to see the South resume its importance. Your letter rec'd & many thanks. Will send particulars in 6 weeks. Meanwhile

Fervently   Will R. Wilder

APS (WP, DLC) with WWhw notation on verso: "Ans May 2nd 1882."

Two Letters from Edward Ireland Renick

My dear Sir: Atlanta, Ga. Apl 29th 1882

Since our correspondence began I have been able in a small way to be of some service to you—the service was very slight because of the small demands made upon me, rather than on account of my readiness to serve. But because I have served you, I somewhat shrink from proposing a relationship as office-mates, for fear that a gratitude, which I have done nothing to awaken, might prevent you from exercising your coolest judgment.

Mr. Reed, with whom I have most pleasantly associated for two months, has effected a partnership with an old friend, & I am alone again. I would be pleased to have you as his successor. This wish is natural because I know much of you; it may be improper to express as you may know little of me. I do not mean for you to act hastily or upon scanty information even if the proposition strikes you favorably. So a word as to the office. It is a much coveted one, opposite the Supreme Court-State Capitol (containing State library) & Post Office. Room large—papered—freshly painted. Contains chandelier—grate—desk, table, chairs, book shelf &c. Fronts on a street, two large windows with hoods.

If you care to share this with me—it will cost you but $4.50 pr month. We can get a servant for .50 or .75 pr month in addition.

Please let me hear from you relative to this as I cannot very well afford to pay $9 or $10. & would wish to get some one else if you desire to make other arrangements.

Yours very truly   E. I. Renick

ALS (WP, DLC) with WWhw notations on env.: "Recd May 2nd 1882" and "Ans. same date."

Dear Sir: Atlanta May 2/82

I learn from Mrs. B[oylston] to-day that accommodation can be had for you at her house. Some company for a short time this summer may require some temporary inconveniences, which I ventured to assure her would not meet with serious objection from you. I am glad this place has been secured, & you will be glad, I am sure, after trial.   Yours &c   Renick

APS (WP, DLC) with WWhw notation on verso: "Ans. May 4th/82."

To Robert Bridges

Dear Bobby,   Wilmington [N.C.], May 2 [1882]

Thank you very much for your kindness. The copies of the *Post* and the mss. came all right—but where's your letter? I would rather see it than see any number of my own words in print.—though I confess to liking to see the latter very much indeed.

I am within two weeks of my Atlanta move now and am naturally feeling some anxiety about the immediate future—but am more hopeful and confident than anxious. June's enjoyments will give me a new start after tedious study, study.

Sincerely Yours,   W. Wilson

APS (Meyer Coll., DLC).

From James W. Bones

Dear Tommy   Rome Ga May 12/82

. . . Of course you have seen the accounts of small pox in Atlanta & consequent change in place of meeting of the Assembly to Columbus.[1] There is quite a panic in Atlanta about the dread disease. Will this state of things make any change in your plans? It seems to me it would be best for you to postpone your location there for a month or so at any rate. . . .   Your affc   Uncle James

P.S. omitted. ALS (WP, DLC).
    [1] There was a last-minute change, and the General Assembly of the southern Presbyterian Church met in the First Presbyterian Church in Atlanta, May 18-29, 1882, in spite of the smallpox epidemic in that city.

From Edward Ireland Renick

Dr Sir: Atlanta May 12/82
    Yours just to hand. Room will be waiting for you. Let me know
on what train you will arrive.   Very truly   Renick.

APS (WP, DLC).

From Joseph R. Wilson, Jr.

My darling brother,   Wilmington N C May 15th 1882.
    . . . Stephen was very much pleased with the suit of clothes
you left for him and told me that he wished that you were here
to thank you, but I told him that I would thank you for him, and
he told me to tell you that he was *more* than obliged to you and
for me to give you his love, he seems to like you *very* much.
Father dont seem to trust him very much, after what he said, but
I think he is sincere, dont you? Mary says she did not know that
you were going away last night, and that mama told her that you
were going tonight; I suppose that mama told her so before it
was desided when you would go.
    I dont know what I will do without my *darling* latin teacher[.]
I did not study any lesson this morning, because mama said I did
not have-to, but I am going to try and be as regular as I was when
my dear teacher was here. . . .   Your loving brother   Josie.

ALS (WP, DLC).

An Account of Personal Expenditures

[c. May 16-c. June 15, 1882]

May and June	80.00	
Ink	.35	
" -stand	.25	
Freight and carriage		
(books)	.60	
" " "	2.45	
Car tickets	.50	
Shaving soap	.15	
Closet paper	.50	
Car fare	.20	
Stamp and Stamped		
Envelope	.07	
Paper and pens	.75	
Washerwoman	.50	
"	.50	
Paper-fasteners	.35	
Medicine	.25	
Pkg. Stamped envelopes	.82	
Cravat	.75	
Telegram (Bridges)	.50	
Pkg. Postal Cards	.25	
Shave and Hair-cut	.45	
Car	.10	
Drayage (furniture)	.15	
Soda water	.05	
	10.49	
Brought forward	10.49	
Board	25.00	
Office Rent	6.75	
Washing (2 weeks)	1.00	

June 13—

Travelling[1]	100.00	Breakfast (14th)		.75
Discount on check	.50	Dinner	"	.75
Luggage	.25	Supper	"	.50
Ticket to N. Y.	24.00	Sleeper		2.00
Car	.05	Porter (15th)		.25
Fruit	.10	Elevated Car		.
Supper (13th)	.40	'Bus (2)		.10
Sleeper	2.00	Shave		.15
Telegrams	.90	Breakfast		.20
Porter (14th)	.25	Luggage		

WWhw entries in pocket notebook inscribed (WWhw) "Thomas W. Wilson
[sh outlines for Thomas Woodrow Wilson] his mark" (WP, DLC). This notebook was described at July 1, 1877, Vol. I.
  [1] WW's trip to his class triennial reunion.

From Janet Woodrow Wilson

Wilmington [N. C.] Thursday afternoon [May 18, 1882]
My darling Son,

I hoped that we might have heard from you by this morning's
mail—but I suppose it was impossible. I am anxious to hear all
sorts of particulars—with reference to your boarding house and
office—and the persons with whom you will have to associate more
or less intimately every day—and upon whom so much of your
comfort will depend. And I am anxious to hear how your dear
father fared at the hotel—in the important matter of a room. . . .

Tell papa I don't know how I am ever to get the tobacco odor
out of his study & closet, sufficiently to venture to put any of *my*
clothing there! People will think that I have taken to smoking,
privately! There is no telling what perseverance may accomplish,
however. We have put your desk & book-case in your little dress-
ing-room where they await orders. . . .

I hope you are with your father a great deal, dear—and that he
finds time to introduce you all round. Everybody I see here speaks
so cordially about you. The one sentiment with regard to your future is, "I *have not the shadow of a doubt of his success*!["]

Please kiss your dear father for me & for Josie—and ask him to
do the same to you. I do hope the Assembly is satisfactory. . . .

Yours lovingly   Mother.

ALS (WP, DLC). Enc.: Hiram Woods, Jr. to WW, APS, May 16, 1882.

From Richard Heath Dabney

Dear Tommy,   New York May 28th 1882.
  . . . I have lately been most painfully impressed with a sense of

my own ignorance, and also with an eager desire to learn, by reading Buckle's "History of Civilization in England." If you have not
yet read it, I advise you not to lose another minute. Beg, borrow,
buy, or steal it—no matter which—but read it. If it strikes you in
the same light as myself, it will stir up your soul like the blast of
a trumpet, or the mighty snort of the war-horse.

Truly your friend—   R. H. Dabney.

ALS (WP, DLC).

From Marion Wilson Kennedy

My dearest brother: Maysville, [Ky.] May 29th 1882.

As I judge, from Annie's last letter, you are quite settled in your
new quarters, I will hasten to indulge my strong inclination to
write to you once more. . . .

How did mother stand giving you up, Woodrow? Is she right
well still? Is father quite well now? Tell us what plans father and
mother have for Josie's further education, now they have not you
at home to teach him. . . .

Lovingly your sister,   Marion.

ALS (WP, DLC) with WWhw notation on env.: "Ans. 6/8/82."

From George Howe, Jr.

Dear Woodrow,   Columbia, S. C., May 31 1882

I am sorry to learn by your letter of yesterday that you are so
much under the weather. I am disposed to think that your symptoms indicate too much bile aboard, rather than indigestion proper.
With this view I enclose a prescription for some pills to relieve the
liver torpor, and indirectly the piles. Take two pills each night
until the bowels are fully relaxed, the tongue becomes clean and
the bad taste in the mouth is gone. If two pills prove too active
take one, and if not sufficiently so, take three at night. I write the
prescription in two forms, they are one and the same, but "no.
x" is more elegant than an extemporaneous preparation will be.
In case "no x" is not to be found have the other prepared. If your
improvement after four or five days is not evident, let me hear
again.[1] . . .

We are disappointed that you did not post us as to your father's
movements. We looked for him, *somewhat*, today. What has become of Girardeau's paralysis over the grave of the Confederacy?
I have not followed the discussion, but I would suppose that he
felt rather cheap.[2]

Annie unites with me in love to you and the paternal ancestor.

Yrs affly George

ALS (WP, DLC) with WWhw note about a riddle on env.
    [1] There is an even more clinical diagnosis of WW's trouble and elaborate treatment prescribed in G. Howe, Jr., to WW, c. March 5, 1882, ALS (WP, DLC) with WWhw notation on env.: "Ans 3/6/82."
    [2] A reference to the debate in the General Assembly of the southern Presbyterian Church on May 23, 1882, over a resolution to establish fraternal relations with the northern Presbyterian Church. The Rev. Dr. John L. Girardeau, Professor of Theology at the Columbia Theological Seminary, said in a speech opposing the resolution: "We have been constrained by brute force to give up the institution of slavery, but are we to give up the doctrine because of that. They pronounced us traitors who deserved to be hanged. Dead our confederacy may be, but are we prepared to stand upon the graves of our dead boys and admit that they were traitors." *Atlanta Constitution*, May 24, 1882. The resolution was adopted on May 24. *Minutes of the General Assembly of the Presbyterian Church in the United States* (5 vols. in one, Wilmington, N. C., 1879-82), p. 531.

From James W. Bones

Dear Tommy   Rome Ga June 6/82

I received a letter from your dear mother yesterday in which she tells me of Mr C S Arnal having presented your father while in Augusta recently with an a/c claiming a balance due by him of about $1200. There is no foundation for this claim & I am surprised at Mr. Arnals course. As you doubtless know Bones Brown & Co. several years ago advanced your father funds for building the Columbia house the money to be refunded by sales of Western lands. The whole amount of the principal was paid back but as the a/c ran for several years there was interest. After the firms failure Mr Dougherty handed me statement of a/c showing bal still due by your father of about $1200. On looking into the matter I discovered that he had compounded interest that is he added interest to bal principal each year & charged interest upon interest. As this was an error I made out a correct statement of the account & sent it to him showing that a/c was about balanced & that he must make proper corrections. Since then I have heard nothing further from him or Arnall on the subject until now. I wrote your mother that she must not give herself any trouble on the subject. Your father did right in refusing to settle the a/c[.] I hardly think these rascals will resort to a law suit but if they do there will be no difficulty in making a successful defence. I want you to write Mr C S Arnall & ask of him a full statement of this a/c as also of the Woodrow Estate a/c. & then submit it to me, conferring fully with me before taking any steps whatever. Sometime next month I will be ready to arrange the Estate matters &

will let you know when we had best have a meeting for that purpose.

I need not tell you how glad we will all be to have you run up
& see us at any time.

With love from us all.   Your affec Uncle James

Dear Tommy This letter was mailed to you on the 6th inst but
for some reason has been returned by the P. O.

Some days since I sent you check for $300. but have as yet had
no acknowledgement of its receipt. With love from us all
                              your affec Uncle James.

ALS (WP, DLC).

From Janet Woodrow Wilson

My precious Son,   Wilmington N. C, June 13th '82.

Your note of the 10th inst. and also the Power of Atty. document, came to hand this morning. We went down to Mr. Van
Amringe's office very shortly after their receipt—and enclosed you
will find the result. One question I want to ask, dear—viz. Will this
do away with your Uncle James' power of Attorney? I hope so,
certainly. Now, my darling, just do the best you can with the
property. I am so glad to leave it entirely in your hands.

Have you received your desk & b-case yet? And if so were they
in good condition? Did you find your shirts a good fit? We have
not sent your Album yet—for we feared you would be absent—on
your trip to Princeton—by the time it could reach Atlanta. Is there
anything else you would like to have sent? such as pictures—elocution chart, &c.

Please let us know, darling, when you expect to leave for
Princeton. Do *take* [care] *of yourself*. I hope you will enjoy your
trip, dear, even more than you anticipate.

I cannot tell how glad I am that you continue to find your surroundings so pleasant. I think the one thing I am *most* glad of, is,
that you have found Mr. Renick to be just what he is. It is far
more than I had any hope of. He must be a sure "fellow"—and I
am so thankful.

I write in haste, dear. We love you so dearly—and miss you so
terribly. God bless you, darling boy. You have never been anything but a comfort to me all your life!

Papa & Josie join in fondest love to you
                        Most lovingly   Your Mother

ALS (WP, DLC). Enc.: WWhw power of attorney naming WW as JWW's
legal agent in the partition of the Estate of William Woodrow, and statement

of notarization dated June 13, 1882, and signed by S. Van Amringe, Clerk of Superior Court and Judge Probate, New Hanover County, N. C.

From William Francis Magie

My dear Wilson,   Princeton June 15, '82

Will you please oblige us by responding to the toast to "Politics" at the dinner?[1] Your room matter attended to.[2] I have Mr. Woodrow's name down for the best of the rooms in Edwards, but so arranged that you can give it up if it does not suit. In haste

                    Yours sincerely   W. F. Magie

ALS (WP, DLC).

[1] The '79 reunion dinner. The record is silent about this entire affair, even in the pamphlet, *Record of the Class of '79 of Princeton College. Triennial, 1879-1882* (New York, 1882), issued by the committee named at April 1, 1882, note 1. The pamphlet listed the activities since graduation of class members, and published a "Triennial Re-Union Song" by R. Bridges.

[2] A reference to WW's request commented on in the omitted portion of W. F. Magie to WW, Feb. 5, 1882, that Magie find a good room for James Wilson Woodrow, who would enter Princeton in the autumn of 1882.

Draft of a Letter to John D. Green

Dear Sir: Atlanta, Geo., Aug. 5th, 1882

Miss Isabelle Pratt having consulted me concerning certain premises which she lately rented from Mrs. Kirby, I feel bound to write to you to ask that you will no longer delay to fulfill the engagements into which you entered with Miss Pratt.[1] Of course Mrs. Kirby's distressing illness must be accepted as sufficient excuse for some delay; but longer delay than has already occurred would be both unbusinesslike and unjust to Miss Pratt.

You are doubtless aware that the document drawn up on July 10th by yourself and signed by Miss Pratt is not a lease, but merely a memorandum of a verbal lease. Miss Pratt has a right to require that the surplus furniture which encumbers the porches, and other effects which she did not agree to keep and which are very much in her way, be at once removed, and that the premises be put in the condition in which she was assured that they would [be] when she took them: that is, that they be thoroughly fitted up and equipped as a boarding house.

Miss Pratt is very seriously inconvenienced by your delay in fulfilling your part of the contract entered into, and I am sure that you will not wait longer to remedy the damage already done.

Hoping to hear from you at once.

              Yours very respectfully   Woodrow Wilson

Transcript of WWshLS (draft), Item (h) in notebook described at Sept. 7, 1875, Vol. 1. The letter was addressed to Newnan, Ga.

¹ This was probably WW's first legal business from which he derived a fee. See JRW to WW, Aug. 14, 1882.

Two Letters from Joseph Ruggles Wilson

My darling Son—   Wilmington, [N. C.] Aug. 14, 1882
. . . You will find enclosed draft on N. Y. for $50.

How did you feel when yr. first fee was placed in yr hands. Were said hands "nip'n neager"?

I have read yr recent letters to dear Mother with some concern. My beloved boy you have only one thing to do:—to stick to the law and its prospects be they ever so depressing or disgusting. "Totus in illo" is the uppermost motto when success is resolved upon.

I know yr aspirations, and I know yr. abilities. Your highest ambition can be crowned only when your highest talents are devoted to some one thing which is worthy of them. And surely all things must have changed beyond recognition, if the law does not still afford an atmosphere for the loftiest flight of ambition and scope for the utmost efforts of trained and concentrated thought. Conquer depression therefore as you would overwhelm yr worst enemy, and fight the future with a *brave* front not only but also with a smiling:—trusting to God as to one who is wiser and greater than yourself.

Be sure of our love here at home. It is simply boundless as towards our dearest absentee.   Your devoted   Father.
P.S. You have not said whether you received the Phila American proposition as to your piece that has been waiting for the judges' decision. I would were I you accept the offer of $15.00 for it, and give up (as is proposed to all the contestants) a contest which seems to be destined never to come off.¹

ALS (WP, DLC) with WWhw notations: "Ans. 8/16/82" and "Recd do. [ditto]."
¹ For background about WW's article, "Congress: Inside the House," see the note at May 1, 1881.

My precious Son:—   Maysville, [Ky.] Aug. 20th 1882.
Your two letters, addressed to me here, have been as cool water to a parched throat. I thank you for thus remembering me so affectionately. To have your love is an immeasurable gladness to my heart—especially as it goes out to meet what you largely give with an even larger reciprocation.

It is a source of anxiety to me:—your law-distaste:—an anxiety somewhat relieved, however, by the candor with which you acknowledge the state of your feelings, and by the manly purpose you express to conquer what might otherwise conquer you. *All* beginnings are hard, whatever occupation is chosen:—but surely a fair beginning must be made before the real character of the thing begun can be determined[.] As it is your future is in the land of imagination, and imagination is used to color. Get your feet fully upon the ladder of actual practise—and then, sh'd the ascent prove intolerable, it will not be too late to see what other hill may be attempted. It is hardly like you, my brave boy, to show a white feather before the battle is well joined. Ask help of God, your better and nobler Father, and, in His name, advance your banner. . . .

All send love to him of whom we are all proud:—but none of them sends such a love as that of your unalterable Father.

ALS (WP, DLC) with WWhw notations on env.: "Rec'd Aug. 23/82" and "Ans. Aug. 24/82."

From Robert Bridges

Dear Tommy: New York Aug 22 '82
. . . . If you have any spare time for journalistic work, I think a short letter on politics in Georgia would land a place in the *Post*— I mean a specific letter about the coming campaign with as many *facts* in it as possible. Of course our news columns have covered the general facts—but something more specific in regard to public sentiment on the Stephens[1] nomination—its full significance—and the composition and character of the Gartrell party[2] or parties. Also something about Pledger[3] the negro leader—and his party. Good night   Your friend   Bob Bridges.

ALS (WP, DLC) with WWhw notations on env.: "Rec'd 8/25/82" and "Ans. 8/25/82."
  [1] A reference to the nomination of Alexander H. Stephens for Governor by the Democratic state convention of Georgia on July 20, 1882.
  [2] General Lucius J. Gartrell was an independent, anti-machine Democrat, nominated for Governor by the Georgia Republican state convention on Aug. 3, 1882.
  [3] W. A. Pledger, chairman of the Republican State Central Committee of Georgia, Collector of the Port of Atlanta, and leader of the Negro faction in the state G. O. P.

To Robert Bridges

Dear Bobby,   48 Marietta Street,[1] Atlanta, Geo., 8/25/82
Your letter just rec'd. It would be hard to tell you why I have not written before this. After my return, to tell the truth, I had not the *heart* to write. The reunion—that, at least, which *was* a reunion at first—was very much like a second breaking up of the class, and left me as blue as—well, as the Mediterranean[.] I felt rebellious

against the fortune wh. had separated me so far from all my most loved and most valued friends.

Your letter was "as cool water to a parched throat." Your marvellous old handwriting looks absolutely pretty in my eyes now as it lies here on the desk before me. Just at this present moment I would rather see it than any other *fist* I am acquainted with.

I think that I can promise you, for the *Post*, a short letter such as you wish on the present state of Georgia politics. Not that they have any particular state: for they do'nt *stand* but fluctuate at a terrible rate. Of this you may be sure, that "your uncle Alex." will not have a walk-over

Do you expect your work on the *Nation* to continue. I have always thought that a good position on *such* a weekly paper would be of all journalistic positions the most desirable, giving a man a chance to do careful work, and at the same time affording him leisure to engage in some independent work of his own. I could wish to be a journalist myself if such a place were open to me; but I do'nt know that it would be what you want[.] Is the staff of the *Nation* a permanent one?

I hope that you will have a chance to speak in old Pennsylvania. The political movements now taking place there are amongst the most notable signs of the times, and I would like you to make your first political record just where you wish to make it, on the independent side in that contest. I could wish to be making some speeches myself in our campaign down here, but I am not well enough known yet to care to offer myself for the service. I must bide my time, trusting to my pen and my speeches at the bar to bring me gradually into notice.

I expect to argue a tax case at the next term of our Superior Court, in Oct., which will give me a good subject for a strong speech. It will be in resistance to a license tax sought to be levied by the city and will win much capital for the firm of Renick and Wilson if they can gain it—may bring them into prominence even if they do'nt gain it.[2]

Did I tell you about Renick, first my office-mate and now my partner? He is a capital fellow who studied law with me at the University of Virginia. He is a little older than I, and came to Atlanta about a year ago; is one of the best informed and most cultivated men of my acquaintance, and a perfect enthusiast in his profession. Our division of labor will probably be to assign him the duties of attorney and me those of barrister, since he prefers "office work" and I like most the duties connected with the conduct and argument of cases in court. We are thoroughly congenial and our association will, I am sure, be entirely satisfactory to both of us. Already some practice is coming to us and we are determined that hard work shall make it more and more.

Do write soon again, Bobby. Give my love to all the boys. Yes, I remember quite well Chang's Margerum lecture on the "indifinable *quid*." He quite roused Pete's enthusiasm.

Yours affectionately,   Tommy.

ALS (Meyer Coll., DLC).
    ¹ The address of the fledgling firm of Renick & Wilson. The street address in headings of WW's letters from Atlanta will be omitted hereafter unless it varies from 48 Marietta Street.
    ² It is almost certain that Wilson did not argue this case. See the Editorial Note, "Wilson's Practice of Law."

From Joseph Ruggles Wilson

My precious Son—   Chillicothe, [Ohio] Aug 28 1882
    Your sweet letter was received on Saturday, and, if I could write as good a one, you would have four or five pages to read instead of what is in yr. hand.

My stay here has been pleasant[.] All, at yr. uncle's, have provd themselves even tenderly kind, and I certainly did my best to reciprocate every demonstration of affection:—thinking of you, my darling, the whole time; and doing what I have done almost exclusively for your dear sake. But,—please forgive me for saying it —you have no *large* reason for grieving over yr disappointment— indeed you have not. I honestly and firmly believe that the marriage you desired would have made you happy only for a very little while. I would not have presumed to touch the sore in yr heart— even thus lightly were it not a sore in my own heart, too: but *now* a sore pretty much cured. All the same I admire your unselfishness in still loving where you cannot secure, and in wishing for her happiness even though she may not care for yours in the way you desired. All the family, including H[attie]., speak of you in terms of most flattering admiration. Jimmie [Woodrow] seems fairly to idolize you; and your letters which may be written him when in Princeton, will do him a lot of good—for he will take your advice sooner than that of any other person. . . .

Jimmie expects to leave home on the 8th. I will try to meet him at the Everett House in N. York, and accompany him to Princeton: —for your dear sake, again!

Good bye, dearest boy. I love you more than I can tell.

Affy yr   Father

ALS (WP, DLC) with WWhw notation on env.: "Ans. Sept. 4th/82."

Notes for a Speech Opposing the Protective Tariff

[c. Sept. 23, 1882]

Analysis of Speech before the Tariff Commission sitting in Atlanta.[1]

—Importance of this question felt by me as a young man respecting the future of the South—a question now slumbering, but to wake.

—Indifference and ignorance because tariff tax not felt—no sheriff's receipts.

—Gladstone's "2 Sisters."

—Necessity of convincing United States to endure taxes.

—Ignorance (misapprehension) shown by advocates of protection.

(1) "Dependence on foreign countries"—public policy.

(2) Wages—agriculture, mining, cotton manufacture—equalized by immigration.

—Reasons for *revenue tariff*:

(1) Protection, once admitted, cannot be controlled—removal hurt some of course. Coaches etc.

(2) An income tax whose weight falls upon the poor.

(3) Regulations directed not by commercial principles but by political influences—blessed under official guidance. Our object should be to encourage *both* manufacture and commerce. Object of protection to restrain rather than to encourage latter, because latter cannot be one-sided.

(4) Prevents competition of skill

Because (a) it puts manufactures on an artificial basis.

(5) Creates a false idea as to the proper province of government. Destroys independence (government ought never to do for a citizen what he can as well or better do for himself) Discourages enterprise, and corrupts government.

(6) Made absurd by free trade within the borders of this vast country.

(7) Retards civilization by injuring other nations, preserving barriers between nations and jeopardizing business.

Transcript of WWsh notes (WP, DLC). This document is the earliest extant illustration of a method that WW would later use very extensively, that of preparing and using shorthand notes for a speech without going through the intermediate stage of writing out the text.

[1] The Tariff Commission, created by Congress in 1882 to investigate and recommend, held brief hearings in the Kimball House in Atlanta on Sept. 22-23, 1882.

Testimony Before the Tariff Commission

[*Sept. 23, 1882*]

Mr. Woodrow Wilson, of Atlanta, said:[1]

It is not my purpose to represent or advocate any particular interest, but only to say a few words upon the general issues before you on the subject of protection or free trade. This question of the tariff is one which has been under consideration in Congress for 90 odd years. Early in the century protection was introduced for the purpose of fostering new manufactures in this country. That system was continued down to the time of the war; but since the war it has been upheld professedly for the purpose of raising revenue, and to enable the government to recover from the indebtedness caused by the war. Free trade, therefore, has been a slumbering question, but it will soon become one of the leading questions in all political discussions, because, now that peace has come, the people of the South will insist upon having the fruits of peace, and not being kept down under the burdens of war.

As you have already been told, there is a great deal of ignorance and indifference in regard to these questions in the South. The people here have been content to let things remain as they were. Probably this has resulted from the fact that the tariff is an indirect way of placing taxes upon the people, and they do not feel the immediate effects of it. But when the farmers and others begin to investigate these matters, they soon discover that they are, after all, paying these duties for the benefit of a few manufacturing classes. When a farmer discovers that he can buy a jack-knife of English manufacture for $1.30, while he has to pay $2 for a knife of American manufacture of the same quality, in order that the American manufacturer of cutlery may compete on equal terms with the British, then he feels that he has a personal interest in these subjects.

In thinking of this matter of indirect taxation, I am reminded of one of the few playful passages which illumine the utterances of Mr. Gladstone. In introducing his "budget" in 1861, he referred to direct and indirect taxation, and called them two sisters, the daughters of necessity and invention, one indeed more open and direct than the other, her sister more shy and insinuating; but he said that, as chancellor of the exchequer, he felt bound to pay his addresses to both. We have these two charming sisters in America, but they cannot be said to be the daughters of necessity and invention; they are rather the daughters of invention and monopoly. The necessities of our government are the necessities of the revenue; and it is well known that our government is not embarrassed from any necessities of revenue; on the contrary, it has an immense surplus. It is undoubtedly a part of true wisdom that the taxes laid by the general government should be indirect taxes. The province of direct taxation should be left to the States, and in order that the two systems may not clash and overburden the people, it is a part of wise policy that the national government shall make the most of its taxation indirect.

No man with his senses about him would recommend perfect freedom of trade in the sense that there should be no duties whatever laid on imports. The only thing that free traders contend for is, that there shall be only so much duty laid as will be necessary to defray the expenses of the government, reduce the public debt, and leave a small surplus for accumulation. But that surplus should be so small that it will not lead to jobbery and corruption of the worst sort.

We often hear the question asked by the advocates of protection whether it is a wise and consistent public policy for us to be dependent for supplies upon foreign governments. That was asked in reference to cotton-ties. It was said that the cotton-tie was manufactured almost wholly in England, and the question was put to the witness, "Is it a part of wise policy that we should be dependent on England for our cotton-ties?" In other words, we fear dependence on foreign manufacturers. Now, gentlemen, what does that mean? There is no danger in time of peace in being dependent on foreign manufacturers, because, if they raise their prices, the inevitable result will be that Americans will go into the manufacture and undersell them, and their prices must come down again. Therefore we are in no danger in time of peace. So that the argument of the protectionist must be a war argument. Of course, if a war should occur between this country and Great Britain, it would be greatly to the disadvantage of our southern cotton-balers to be dependent entirely on the English manufacturer for their cotton-ties. So that the protectionist advocates a system which prepares for war, while it has not any consideration for the requirements of the country in time of peace. I ask, is it worth while during fifty years of peace to provide by taxation for one year of war? Is it wise and just to tax the people for a contingency so that millions may be accumulated in the Treasury from the tax on these cotton-ties in order that war at some distant period, which no man sees, may be provided for? War will cost a great deal when it comes; let it not be costing us in the mean time.

Another stronghold of the protectionists is the question of

wages. They say, "How can we compete with the foreigners when the remuneration of labor is so much lower in foreign countries than in our own country?" Well, we can compete with them just as we do in regard to agricultural products. Of course every gentleman knows that our principal agricultural products have no duty imposed upon them. English wheat and other produce may come into our markets free of duty, and there is a freedom of trade in that regard, so far as the farmer is concerned.

By Commissioner Garland:

Question. Do I understand you to say that there is no duty on wheat?

—Answer. So I understand by looking at the last returns.

Commissioner Garland. Such is not my understanding.

Commissioner Oliver. Wheat pays 20 cents a bushel, and the farmers have been asking us to keep that duty on, because they say otherwise it would be imported from Manitoba.

The Witness. Then I was misinformed. But it is a well-known fact that there is a greater disparity in the wages paid for agricultural labor in this country and in England than there is between wages paid in other industries, and although the duties on these agricultural products are lower, our competition with foreigners in this regard is more successful. In other words, we make up for the high price of our wages by the fertility of our land. There is no land in the world that can compare in fertility with the land of the West, and the consequence is, we have an immense advantage in that regard. We have advantages also in other industries, such as in mining and in cotton productions. These are compensations which are provided, and which no human laws can take away.

There are positive grounds, however, upon which protection can be objected to. It is understood that the protective tariff policy was adopted in this country in the beginning on the idea advocated by John Stuart Mill and one or two other eminent writers on the subject in England, who said that a new country might with advantage protect its infant industries, provided the tariff which was laid for that purpose was merely a temporary expedient for building up those industries. It was upon that idea that America first established this protective system. What has been the result? These infant industries at first were protected by very small duties, but, instead of growing into manhood and strength, they have gone into weaker decrepitude. They have needed more and more protection as years have gone on, until the climax has been reached at the present time. That ought to overthrow the whole doctrine in itself. But the danger in imposing protective duties is, that when the policy is once embarked upon, it cannot be easily receded from. Protection is nothing more than a bounty, and when we offer bounties to manufacturers they will enter into industries and build up interests, and when at a later day we seek to overthrow this protective tariff, we must hurt somebody, and of course there is objection. They will say, "Thousands of men will be thrown out of employment, and hundreds of people will lose their capital." This seems very plausible; but I maintain that manufacturers are made better manufacturers whenever they are thrown upon their own resources and left to the natural competition of trade rather than when they are told, "You shall be held in the lap of the government, and you need not stand upon your feet." Such theories discourage skill, because it puts all industries upon an artificial basis. The basis that they rest upon is not that of the skill of the manufacturer; it is because the bounty of the government is put on his trade which enables him to get more for an inferior article than a foreigner could get for a better article.

Protection also hinders commerce immensely. The English people do not send as many goods to this country as they would if the duties were not so much, and in that way there is a restriction of commerce, and we are building up manufactories here at the expense of commerce. We are holding ourselves aloof from foreign countries in effect, and saying, "We are sufficient to ourselves; we wish to trade, not with England, but with each other." I maintain that it is not only a pernicious system, but a corrupt system.

By Commissioner Garland:

Q. Are you advocating the repeal of all tariff laws?—A. Of all protective tariff laws; of establishing a tariff for revenue merely. It seems to me very absurd to maintain that we shall have free trade between different portions of this country, and at the same time shut ourselves out from free communication with other producing countries of the world. If it is necessary to impose restrictive duties on goods brought from abroad, it would seem to me, as a matter of logic, necessary to impose similar restrictions on goods taken from one State of this Union to another. That follows as a necessary consequence; there is no escape from it.

Printed in U. S. House of Representatives, *Report of the Tariff Commission: Testimony Taken by the Tariff Commission.* 47th Cong., 2d sess., Misc. Doc. 6, Part 3 (Washington, 1882), pp. 1294-97.

1 WW testified on Sept. 23, 1882. There is a brief report of his appearance, referring to him as "Mr. Goodrow Wilson," in the *Atlanta Constitution*, Sept. 24, 1882. For WW's own account, see his letters to R. Bridges, Oct. 28, 1882, and to R. H. Dabney, Jan. 11, 1883.

A Legal Handbook

[c. Oct. 1, 1882]

Inscribed on cover:

(WWhw) "*Hand Book of Georgia Courts and Georgia Practice. Renick and Wilson*" and on front flyleaf: (WWhw) "Renick and Wilson *Atlanta, Georgia 1882*"

Contents:

(a) (WWhw) Extracts from and digests of the Georgia Code, including sections on militia districts; justices of the peace: their elections, duties, and fees; justices' courts: their jurisdiction, powers, and proceedings; and garnishment.

(b) (Hw of Edward I. Renick) Extracts from "Attachment Laws of Georgia."

MS. (WP, DLC).

EDITORIAL NOTE
WILSON'S PRACTICE OF LAW

Wilson was examined for admission to the bar in the Superior Court of Fulton County on October 18, 1882. Judge George Hillyer presided, and four veteran lawyers conducted the examination. Hillyer later told Ray Stannard Baker that Wilson's performance had been "not short of brilliant." Wilson also qualified for practice in the federal courts on March 23, 1883.[1]

The letters in this volume reveal that the firm of Renick & Wilson, while not flourishing, was not wholly idle. Wilson's first fee apparently came from the work that he did for Miss Isabelle Pratt.[2] He apparently did not argue the important tax case in October 1882 to which he referred in his letter to Robert Bridges of August 25, 1882. In any event, the case was not listed in the Superior Court docket printed in the *Atlanta Constitution*.[3] But in this same letter to Bridges, Wilson said that work was already coming to Renick & Wilson, and he wrote to Bridges on October 28, 1882, that he had just enough work to keep him in spirits. Meanwhile, he was already engaged in the business of the William Woodrow Estate, and this developed into a fairly important transaction.

We find Wilson writing to Bridges on January 4, 1883, that most of his work involved the effort to collect "numberless desperate claims," and to Dabney on January 11, 1883, that Renick & Wilson

[1] "Petition of Woodrow Wilson for admission to practice Law," Minute Book Q, Superior Court, Fulton County, Ga., Fall Term, 1882, p. 529; WW's petition to practice law in the United States Circuit Court for the Northern District of Georgia, dated March 23, 1883 (Record Group No. 21, DNA); R. S. Baker, *Woodrow Wilson*, I, 148-49.
Reproductions of WW's certificates of admission to practice in these courts are printed in the photographic section of this volume.
[2] WW to John D. Green, Aug. 5, 1882; JRW to WW, Aug. 14, 1882.
[3] P. C. McDuffie, "Woodrow Wilson—A Georgia Lawyer," *Report of the Thirty-First Annual Session of the Georgia Bar Association* (Macon, Ga., 1914), pp. 197-205, an excellent supplement to this Editorial Note, says that the firm of Renick & Wilson filed no cases in either the city court of Atlanta or the Superior Court of Fulton County.

were doing little but hoping much. "Of course," he went on, "we have something to do, something which is developing into *more* by slow degrees." At about this time he became involved in a libel suit on behalf of his cousin-in-law, Abraham T. H. Brower of Rome, Georgia. This involvement, incidentally, was the reason for Wilson's qualification for practice in the federal courts. But he did not remain in Atlanta long enough to help argue the case.

One is entitled, in light of the new evidence in this volume, to question the tradition that Wilson failed as a lawyer, and that this failure drove him into a new vocation. His experience during his first year of practice could hardly have been unique. To be sure, he did not make a living, and his father continued to send him a monthly allowance of $50. But it is doubtful if many fledgling lawyers in Wilson's day in Atlanta and elsewhere made a living or expected to.

As the note at February 13, 1883, points out and Wilson's letters reveal over and over, the main reasons why he abandoned the practice of law were that he began the vocation with grave reservations, was unwilling to do the things that a young lawyer had to do to get ahead, and, most important, felt himself increasingly attracted to a literary and academic career. The biography of one of Wilson's successful contemporaries, Hoke Smith, shows that the chief legal business in Atlanta in the 1880's consisted of damage suits.[4] This was precisely the kind of practice that Wilson found most abhorrent, for one reason because it was highly competitive, and "ambulance-chasing" was by no means unknown.

Another reason often given for Wilson's alleged failure as a lawyer —that there were simply too many lawyers in Atlanta—does not seem very convincing. The Atlanta city directory for 1883 shows 143 lawyers for a population of 38,000—not a large number for a thriving center of business and a state capital.

[4] Dewey G. Grantham, *Hoke Smith and the Politics of the New South* (Baton Rouge, La., 1958), pp. 14-24.

From Joseph Ruggles Wilson

My dearest Son—   Wilmington [N. C.], Oct 21, 1882.

Thanks for your good letter and for the postal, as also for the telegram of Wednesday [Oct. 18]. I have not, as yet, heard direct from yr Mother—i.e., no one at Rome has assured me of her safe arrival there.[1] I infer however that her journey was completed in due time or I would have heard to the contrary. Yes—if only *you* were with me, what a blessing I would enjoy—for I cannot express the loving confidence you continue to inspire in my heart; nor can I be too grateful for the certainty that this feeling is reciprocated by a corresponding sentiment on yr. part.

You write as cheerfully as I could have expected you would under the circumstances—some of them trying enough—of your situation. I do not, however, quite understand why it is that you are appalled by the prospect of so much study of the law. I had supposed that the law comprised a subject wide enough for all the ends both of mental discipline and of mental satisfaction.—It touches upon all philosophy, upon all history, upon all science even, upon all morality, too:—and its practise necessitates the higher gifts of composition and of oratory:—so that, it has occurred to me, a successful mastery of it all around will fit a man for any station in life. Perhaps, however, you refer to *technical* law merely, which I presume is sufficiently jejune. Yet need you be confined to case-study exclusively? At any rate I am sure you will wrestle with whatsoever difficulties that emerge and threaten, like the brave soul you are, like the gifted man you are—and that if you fail it will not be because you have shrunk from hard work or been scared by what frightens ordinary men. Not that I refuse, darling one, to sympathise with you in all those anxieties which you are so kind as to suppose I am able to appreciate the breadth and number of. You have my entire sympathy. Your heart cannot throb, either with joy or grief, without meeting with a corresponding throb in mine. Still, I know, from much sad experience of my own, that it never does to nurse a spirit of depression, or to be other than hopeful:—and hope may be cultivated like any other principle or passion of the soul. *Think as highly of yourself as possible*. Be sure of the correctness of this rule, where the person who acts upon it is not an egoistic fool. My life has been too-much one of self-depreciations, and I deeply regret that it has been so. Both my usefulness and my happiness would have been furthered and augmented by an opposite course of feeling. Hence it is that I so much insist upon your being objectve rather than subjective. The latter has been—and is—the leading fault of my character. Let me not have the misery of thinking that I have transmitted the same to you. A cheerful trust in God as the best & greatest of Helpers and an equally cheerful trust in yourself as your own helper, will carry you through to a triumphant issue.

The fact that you are at last fully "admitted to the bar," and the further fact that business is already coming to your hands, even though it is as yet coming in drops, afford me matter for gratulation as I write.

You have written nothing with reference to an appearance that some of the papers have reputed you to have made before the Congressional Tariff Commission. Or was it somebody else? Tell me about it, please.

What is the First Church [of Atlanta] about to do for a pastor. I wish it would call me—for I don't see how I can much longer remain where I am. My work here seems to be done, and I think I see evidences amongst the people that some of them think so, too. Yet I never preached so well; I never had such a facility for preparing to preach. The fault they find with me is as to visiting. They want a gad-about gossip.

Write soon again I entreat you. Meanwhile give my regards to Mr. Renick, and accept for yourself assurances both of esteem and affection.   Yours, as always, Father.

ALS (WP, DLC) with WWhw notation on env.: "Ans. Oct. 23rd/82."
 1 JWW was visiting in Rome following the death of Marion Woodrow Bones on Sept. 24, 1882. JWW had been unable to go to the funeral, as Thomas Woodrow, Jr., to JWW, Oct. 4, 1882, ALS (WP, DLC), makes clear. WW had represented his family.

To Robert Bridges

Dear Bobby,   Atlanta, Geo., Oct. 28th/82
I guess you thought it very strange that, having promised a letter to the *Post* on the gubernatorial campaign in Georgia, I should have let that campaign pass away without fulfilling that promise. The truth of the matter is, that I should not have made the promise. I made it hastily and on the impulse of the moment: and on that same impulse I actually began the letter. But I did not *know* enough to complete it. I could get no reliable information as to the state of public feeling—the newspapers being written in the brightest partisan colours—and I was too unfamiliar as yet with Georgia to form for myself any fair estimate of state sentiment. I could have written a great deal, but it would have been nothing better than a collection of shrewd guesses and individual opinions.

Since you say nothing of having made any speeches in Pennsylvania during your vacation,[1] I conclude that you did not do the stumping you had planned. I am sorry. I wanted you to make that speech; but, after all, you probably made more capital by your letter than you would have made by your speech.

I made a small beginning towards establishing a local reputation by making a half-hour speech before the Tariff Commission when it sat here. I did not have time for much preparation.[2] I did not know that that notable and farcical body was to sit in Atlanta until it was actually in town, and had not had the most remote idea, of course, of going before it. But along with the Commission came that smart fellow Walter Page, the *World's* correspondent, a great friend of my partner's, and he it was who induced me to speak, promising a good notice in his letter to the *World*,[3] and arguing that whilst I could not expect to make any impression on the asses of the Commission, I would be sure of having the stenographic report of my remarks embodied in the report to Congress, *there*, possibly, to attract some attention.

I am at last fully admitted to the bar, and have just enough business to do to keep me in spirits. I fully sympathize with the Hen.[4] in his impatience of the dreadful drudgery which attends the initiation into our profession. But a stout heart will pull us both through right bravely, I hope. I keep myself in good humor, besides, by indulging in my favourite recreation, composition. I allow myself my afternoons for writing[5]—and for reading on my old and loved topics, history and political science; devouring Houghton, Mifflin, and Co's *American Statesmen* series,[6] and Macmillans' *English Citizen* series[7]—both altogether to my taste. Possibly, if I can find on the continent some specially kind and specially venturesome publisher, what I write may some day see the light, and masquerade in print. But I am no longer confident of finding such a publisher.

I so love to write that I sometimes imagine that I would be happy and useful on the staff of some such paper as the *Nation*; but, may-be, I'm better where and what I am. I'll *make* time and opportunity to write, anyhow, wherever I am. By-the-way, Renick and I want to subscribe for the *Nation*, but do'nt know the present rates. Will you be kind enough to have it sent to us, with the bill? We are anxious to have it sent without delay.

Give much love to Pete from me when you see or write to him—and also much to Chang. You do'nt know how often I think of you in your ninth story office. With much love

Your sincere friend,   Woodrow Wilson

ALS (Meyer Coll., DLC).

   [1] WW refers to R. Bridges to WW, Oct. 7, 1882, ALS (WP, DLC).

   [2] He did, however, make brief shorthand notes for his testimony. A transcript of them is printed at Sept. 23, 1882.

   [3] Page's unsigned dispatch appeared in the New York *World* on Sept. 24, 1882. Page deplored the scornful reception accorded the Tariff Commission in Atlanta and wrote, "No argument of dignity was made to-day except by Mr. Woodrow Wilson. . . . [His] was the only statement made here that in any way showed the sentiment of the people."

   [4] Robert R. Henderson.

   [5] WW was referring to his work on "Government by Debate," about which see the Editorial Note, "Government by Debate."

   [6] A series of brief political biographies edited by John T. Morse, Jr., and published by Houghton Mifflin. WW's library includes copies of all the titles in this series published through 1882: Henry Adams, *John Randolph*; Hermann E. von Holst, *John C. Calhoun*; Henry C. Lodge, *Alexander Hamilton*; John T. Morse, Jr., *John Quincy Adams*; and William Graham Sumner, *Andrew Jackson as a Public Man*. WWhw inscriptions on the flyleaves indicate that he acquired the volumes on Randolph, Hamilton, and Jackson in 1882.

   [7] Macmillan and Company's series, "The English Citizen: His Rights and Responsibilities," began to appear in London in 1881. Seven titles had been

published by the end of 1882. Four of these are in WW's library: Spencer Walpole, *Foreign Relations* and *The Electorate and the Legislature*; H. D. Traill, *Central Government*; and A. J. Wilson, *The National Budget: The National Debt, Taxes, and Rates*. WWhw inscriptions indicate that WW purchased the first one of these in 1883 and the others in 1882.

Marginal Notes

Hermann E. von Holst, *John C. Calhoun* (Boston, 1882).

P. 79: The Articles of Confederation had been supplanted by the Constitution in order to render the Union "more perfect." *If this purpose was to be fulfilled, the Union must continue to grow more perfect, for where life is there is also development.* [WW's italics]

Pp. 81-82: Suppose—and the case might certainly very easily happen—that the federal government exercises a power which has been actually granted to it by the Constitution, and that a State sees fit to veto the law, that the question, as must be the case, is submitted to all the States, and the objecting State is supported by one fourth of the whole number. Is any dialectician sharp enough to disprove the fact that, in such a case, the Constitution, though not a single letter is either added or erased, has been actually changed by one fourth of the States, though that instrument expressly requires the consent of at least three fourths to effect the slightest change? Working in defence of the peculiar interests of the slave-holders with the lever of the state sovereignty, Calhoun thus begins to subvert the foundation of the whole fabric of the Constitution.

Henry Cabot Lodge, *Alexander Hamilton* (Boston, 1882).

Pp. 67-68: This remarkable series of essays, famous as "The Federalist," is still the best exposition of the constitution apart from judicial interpretation. . . . The countless pamphlets, essays, disquisitions, and letters which saw the light at the same time have disappeared. They have been consigned to the dust-heaps of history, and the waters of oblivion have rolled over them. . . .

Transcripts of WW Shorthand Comments
[c. Oct. 28, 1882]
This, however, was to be a growth of *influence*: a change in national sentiment effecting a change in the character of government.

Calhoun of course never contemplated the possibility of questioning an act of Congress passed in pursuance of explicit grant of power. None but doubtful inference could be disputed by the processes proposed.

! A slight confusion of metaphors.

P. 91: Hamilton's scheme [set forth in his first report on the public credit] went farther, seeking to create a strong, and, so far as was possible and judicious, a permanent *class* all over the country, without regard to existing political affiliations, but bound to the government as a government by the strongest of all ties, immediate and personal pecuniary interest. The wisdom of this was obvious, when the object was to sustain a great experiment; yet at the same time Hamilton's purpose was not simply by the spread of a popular loan to unite a numerous body of men in the support of the government, but chiefly and mainly to bring to his side a class already in existence, that which controlled the capital of the country. The full intent of the policy was *to array property on the side of the government.* [WW's italics]

It was to the prejudice and force of this interest that Roscoe Conkling applied, and applied with such signal success, in the campaign of '80, in a speech in which Garfield was directly exhibited as the representative of order in finance and stability in government, and Democrats paraded in the ugly *role* of innovators and experimenters in commercial and financial legislation.

Mr. Hamilton [in his report on manufactures] approves the sevenfold advantage arising from the establishment of varied industries—a many-sided blessing which everyone he thinks must recognize—and then bases his advocacy of protection on the following proposition: manufacturers will grow in a new country under no other system because (1) of the influence of habit, the fear of want of success in untried enterprises, and intrinsic difficulty of the first essays; (2) of the bounties[,] premiums etc. with which foreign nations second the reactions of their own citizens; (3) perfect liberty to industry is not the prevailing system of nations and the United States cannot be dependent upon the combinations of foreign policy.

This proposition cannot stand before the facts and arguments furnished in Professor H. Fawcett's admirable little essay on "Free Trade and Protection" (1878) nor experience nor reason supports the opinion that manufacturers will never grow to strength in a new country unless first fostered by protection. On the contrary, a new country, growing rich on the abundant gifts of its soil, will attract immigration until, by increase of supply, labor is first cheapened and then driven into other natural employments, the handmaidens of agriculture and the mothers of strengthened and vigorous manufacturing industries. Besides, protection cannot be adopted as a temporary

expedient. Once equipped it will be always on a war footing. A famine rid England of protection; but there cannot
be a famine in irons, in silks, or in woolen-stuffs as in
breadstuffs. Protection once given can hardly be taken
away. By weakening the feeling of self reliance, it becomes, apparently, more needful, and by establishing
vested interests which cry out against molestation, and
corrupt influences which enter and command legislatures,
becomes an almost invincible power. "The state decides
what industries are to be called into existence by protection" and the entire industrial economy of the country is
regulated by *political influence* rather than by commercial considerations. As for the commercial policy of other
countries, it can affect only those industries which have
been unnaturally fostered in the hot-house of protection
and cannot bear the influences of the open air.[1]

[1] This comment is on a loose page.

P. 112: To the objection that protection tends to create monopolies and
benefit a class at the expense of the rest
of the community, he [Hamilton] replies
first, that the increase of the price of
commodities, even at the outset, is
much exaggerated, and does not always
occur; and second, that in the end the
establishment of manufactures is a
benefit and profit to all. The same reasoning applies to the objection, that one
section of the country is aided at the
expense of a loss to the other. In the
aggregate and ultimately, all must *benefit*, and agriculture will probably be
directly stimulated, as in the case of
cotton, for which manufactories in the
North will at once open a market. [WW's
italics]

Delightfully begging the question.

Pp. 113: At the present day, . . .
[Hamilton] would probably be foremost
in urging a revision of the tariff and a
gradual reduction of duties wherever it
could be safely done. In other words,
he would now be a *moderate protectionist*, as he was when he sent in his
report. . . . [WW's italics]

Impossible!

P. 156: Whatever inconsistencies
England may have been guilty of, she
has never swerved in civility and respect for success, strength, and wealth,
and this Hamilton well knew. But he

A sort of retaliation
which told more against
the United States than
against England.

did not reckon on this alone. In his report on manufactures a cardinal principle was that of retaliation, and the hand he meant thus to force was the hand of England.

Alpheus Todd, *Parliamentary Government in the British Colonies* (Boston, 1880).

Pp. 472-73: Under parliamentary government, an upper chamber derives special *efficacy* and *importance* from the fact that, being unable to determine the fate of a ministry, it is much less influenced by party combinations and intrigues than the lower house. [WW's italics]

The House of Lords of course [is] weakened by the fact that it represents both a class *and party*.

Henry Adams, *John Randolph* (Boston, 1882).

[c. Nov. 14, 1882]

P. 33: The republican party, which assumed control of the government in 1801, had taken great pains to express its ideas so clearly that no man could misconceive them. At the bottom of its theories lay, as a foundation, the historical fact that political power had, in all experience, tended to grow at the expense of human liberty. Every government tended towards despotism; contained somewhere a supreme, irresponsible, self-defined power called sovereignty, which held human rights, if human rights there were, at its mercy. Americans believed that the liberties of this continent depended on fixing a barrier against this supreme central power called national sovereignty, which, if left to grow unresisted, would repeat here all the miserable experiences of Europe, and, falling into the grasp of some group of men, would be the centre of a military tyranny; that, to resist the growth of this power, it was necessary to withhold authority from the government, and to administer it with the utmost economy. . . .

Strange that the best interpretation of state rights should come from an Adams!

EDITORIAL NOTE
"GOVERNMENT BY DEBATE"

"Government by Debate," Woodrow Wilson's first book-length essay, was the fruit of an obsession for the reconstruction of the machinery of the American national government along the lines of

the British Cabinet system. This obsession, in turn, was the out-
growth of Wilson's early admiration of British politics and political
institutions, various contemporary proposals for reform of the presidential-congressional system, and particularly of Wilson's reading of
Walter Bagehot's encomium of the Cabinet system and scathing indictment of congressional irresponsibility in his classic, *The English
Constitution*.[1]

Wilson launched his proposal for reform through adaptation of
the Cabinet system in "Cabinet Government in the United States,"
published in the *International Review* in August 1879.[2] The acclaim
that greeted its publication was a spur to further effort. Wilson, encouraged by the rising tide of sentiment for civil service reform,
seems actually to have believed that he might organize and lead a
comparable movement for reform of the presidential-congressional
system. That he also believed passionately that the cause deserved
the dedication of all patriotic Americans is abundantly revealed by
his letters and other writings between 1879 and 1882.

Wilson permitted himself one digression in the summer of 1879
to write the long historical essay, "Self-Government in France,"[3] but
he revealed his still consuming passion for the Cabinet system in his
marginal notes on the third volume of J. R. Green's *History of the
English People* in early September of that same year. That Cabinet
government was still a burning concern was evidenced by his reactions to Albert Stickney's *A True Republic* in early October.[4] Wilson
had gone to the University of Virginia to study law. But he found
Stickney's radical proposals for reconstruction of the national government so offensive—and such a challenge to his own plan—that
he spent what must have been many days if not weeks during the
autumn term writing "Congressional Government"—an unpublished
essay, not his later book with the same title—in reply.[5]

Wilson meanwhile was also discovering that law is not an easy
taskmaster. He kicked hard against the pricks, as his father's letters
during 1879-80 reveal, but he sublimated his urge to write on national politics and grudgingly submitted to the discipline of tedious
study. He does not seem to have revised the article, "Congressional
Government," or tried to get it published at this time. However, his
marginal notes on *The Federalist* in the early months of 1880 show
that he still had Cabinet government much in mind. Moreover, he
revised and recopied "Congressional Government" in the late summer of 1880 and submitted it, unsuccessfully, to several reviews.

Course work and increasing participation in student affairs seem
to have absorbed all of Wilson's energies and time during the autumn term of 1880 at the University of Virginia. However, his passion for writing revived quickly once he returned to Wilmington in
late December to continue on his own the study of law. The suggestion by Harold Godwin, son of the publisher of the New York

[1] As the Editorial Note, "Cabinet Government in the United States," Vol. I,
has said in greater detail.
[2] Printed at Aug. 1, 1879, Vol. I.
[3] Printed at Sept. 4, 1879, Vol. I.
[4] See WW's marginal notes on *A True Republic*, printed at Oct. 1, 1879, Vol. I.
[5] Printed at Oct. 1, 1879, Vol. I.

Evening Post, that Wilson contribute articles on current affairs in the South diverted Wilson's interest momentarily from Cabinet government. But an announcement in the spring of 1881 by the Philadelphia *American*, a weekly magazine, of a college prize contest turned Wilson back to his main interest, and he submitted two brief pieces entitled "Congress: Inside the House" and "Some Legal Needs" on about May 1.[6]

Among all of Wilson's writings during the first quarter of 1881, only "Stray Thoughts from the South," a report on southern economic progress,[7] found publication. Bitter disappointment at such a meager reward, and the knowledge that he must soon strike out on his own as a lawyer, turned Wilson back to systematic legal study. He worked with some faithfulness on his law books until about January of 1882. Then, after settling upon Atlanta as the place where he would practice, and concluding that his legal preparation was more or less complete, he broke into print once more with his three "Anti-Sham" letters to the *North Carolina Presbyterian*[8] and "New Southern Industries," a second newspaper article.[9]

He also decided—precisely when we do not know—to write "Government by Debate." His long letter to Robert Bridges of March 15, 1882, mentions recent general reading but contains no hint of plans to write a book. His briefer letter to Bridges of April 1 also yields no clue.

He took his first steps presumably at some time in March 1882, by writing an outline that he set down in the notebook described at September 7, 1875, Volume I. This outline gives us a clear picture of what he then had in mind—a well-integrated, tightly knit description of the federal political system and national political institutions and practices. His chapter headings follow:

Part One: The Revolution Which Must Come
I. The Organization and Workings of Congress
II. The Separation of the Legislative, Executive, and Judicial Departments of Government
III. Committee Government an Isolation of the Departments of Government
IV. The Caucus
V. The Inevitable Conditions of Representative Government
VI. Legislative Administration
VII. Executive Administration

Part Two: Our Future Government
VIII. Political Parties: Can They or Should They Be Destroyed?
IX. Cabinet Government
X. [Blank]

He began by writing each chapter title on a separate page in this notebook. Following the chapter titles, he wrote, on some pages, a brief outline; on a few other pages, he wrote extracts from speeches,

6 Printed at May 1, 1881.
7 Printed at Feb. 12, 1881.
8 Printed at Jan. 25, Feb. 15, and March 22, 1882.
9 Printed at April 20, 1882.

articles, and books. After the page set aside for the still unnamed tenth chapter, he wrote out a memorandum entitled "General Hints," as follows:

"Why have we no great *statesmen*? Because there is no opportunity for personal leadership and predominant influence

"Why have we no great political *orators*? Because there is no in-spiration—there are no *themes* to inspire—no *causes* to incite. Before the war there were *constitutional* themes of the greatest magnitude —hence the orators of whom Webster was the greatest. Same applies to the statesmen-giants of the preceding generation. *Now* what call for giants? Not needed to throw pebbles or *pelt mud. Wend. Phil*[lips] once a great orator because he possessed a great theme—now he seems worn out along with his subject. When fine metal is put into our po-litical furnace *now* it is *debased*, not refined. Witness *Ros. Conkling.* What *cause* have the Democrats. What *principle* have the Republican around which to rally spirited men in proud allegiance? *Principle* —informing and inspiring principle—has left politics. Hence the only orators who have themes are the ministers of the great gospel and the ministers of single ideas—the Cooks and the Goughs. Many spe-cial pleaders. Oratory not possible without *moral elevation* in its sub-jects, not powerful if *aimless*; unless directly aimed at something *possible* and *definite*. To inspire[,] its noise must be the noise of *battle* not the enthusiasms of a *holiday.*

"This no empty question. Oratory essential in a country governed by public opinion. Why? Because the opinions of the orator carry with them the weight of his character. To be a great orator one must have a great character. Essential that the people, besides the anoni-mous press should have leaders whom they have seen tried, whom they know. The Press is *anonimous.*

"*Clear* minds needed for oratory—clear minds make good adminis-trative instruments

"Why subordinate the President to his Cabinet? Why not make the *President* responsible—somewhat as *Stickney* suggests? Because no one man can be equal to all the responsibilities of all the offices of executive government. His supervision can at best be but very super-ficial.

"Notice Macaulays estimate of the defects of the Parliamentary system of government—Anecdotal History of Parl. pp. 284-5."

At the very end of this series, all written, incidentally, in longhand, Wilson wrote on separate pages lists of "*Advantages enumerated*" and "*Objections met.*"

Wilson must have begun writing "Government by Debate" around April 1, 1882, for he completed the first chapter on April 17, as his notation on the last page indicates. The documents are strangely silent about Wilson's progress on the book during the balance of the year. We know only that he had completed and revised the first four chapters by about December 1, 1882, for he sent them to Harper and Brothers three days later. He completed the first draft of the fifth and final chapter on December 22 and the revision of this chapter on about January 3, 1883.

Meanwhile, he had abandoned his outline for a highly integrated book, with chapters devoted to particular subjects, and had decided to write a polemical essay with—as it turned out—five chapters making more or less the same argument. The extant documentary record yields no clue as to why Wilson made this decision. One is tempted to say that it was because he soon discovered that such a comprehensive treatment as he had originally envisaged was beyond his somewhat limited resources for research. But Wilson covered all the subjects in his outline; indeed, markings on the pages of the notebook containing his outline, "General Hints," and so forth, indicate how frequently he used it while writing "Government by Debate." Perhaps he changed his plan because he could more easily cannibalize his earlier writings if he wrote a series of essays with a common theme and a common argument. But such an imputation is speculative if not gratuitous. The simple and probably correct conclusion is that Wilson changed his objective soon after beginning "Government by Debate" and, as he later said several times in letters to Bridges, wrote exactly the kind of book that he wanted to write.

A cursory review of Wilson's writings between 1879 and 1882 makes it clear how Wilson refined and expanded them in "Government by Debate." The cornerstone of the edifice was "Cabinet Government in the United States." It was "Government by Debate" in embryo; indeed, it might be said that "Government by Debate" was "Cabinet Government in the United States" in five separate versions. Chapter Three of "Government by Debate" was a more or less considerable revision of "Congressional Government." On two of the pages of the manuscript of the latter Wilson made interlinear changes before transferring the text to "Government by Debate." In the second paragraph of Chapter Two he used a fragment of the second of the "Letters from a Southern Young Man to Southern Young Men"; in the first paragraph of Chapter Four he incorporated a part of the first of these letters.[10] He relied heavily upon his researches for "Self-Government in France" in his description of the French Assembly in Chapter One. Wilson also absorbed "Congress: Inside the House" into the first chapter.

Wilson of course did much more than recast earlier writings. He added much new historical depth, particularly in the section in the first chapter on the origins of the presidential-congressional system based upon the records of the Constitutional Convention and *The Federalist*. As his footnotes partially reveal, he also relied heavily upon newspapers for new materials on current political developments. The fifth chapter was brand new and was based upon Wilson's very recent reading of the fourth volume of Green's *History of the English People*, Henry C. Lodge's *Alexander Hamilton*, Henry Adams' *John Randolph*, William Graham Sumner's *Andrew Jackson*, and the New York *Nation* and other periodicals.

The most important thing to be said about "Government by Debate" is that it was a tract for the times—a passionate plea to rally thoughtful Americans for reform of the national government. As a polemical work, it reveals much better than its more famous and more academic successor, *Congressional Government*, Wilson's opin-

[10] Printed at March 21, 1881.

ions on hotly debated political issues of the day. But the very fact that "Government by Debate" was a tract for the times was one of its chief impediments to publication. As Wilson soon learned, it was not easy for an unknown young man to find a publisher willing to take the risks of issuing such a book. The major weakness of the work was its lack of structure, development, and order. It was a single essay written five times, with a single argument repeated five times. Such a method led inevitably to repetition and verbosity, and it was another impediment to publication.

Letters printed subsequently in this volume chart fully the wanderings of the manuscript from one publishing house to another between December 1882 and April 1883, and there is no need to repeat this story here. Wilson profited immensely from criticism of "Government by Debate." Moreover, he salvaged part of the manuscript for an article, "Committee or Cabinet Government?," in *Overland Monthly*,[11] and used large portions of "Government by Debate" in *Congressional Government*.

There are two handwritten copies of "Government by Debate" in the Wilson Papers. One, Wilson's first draft, bears the marks of heavy editing and revision exclusively by its author. The other is the copy that Wilson submitted to various publishers. It contains some minor stylistic changes by Wilson, many if not most of which he probably made in the copy before sending it off. It also contains a few emendations by Robert Bridges and additions concerning the progress of civil service reform legislation and administration added by Bridges at Wilson's instructions.[12] Finally, Wilson edited this copy in order to extract from it his article, "Committee or Cabinet Government?" This copy of "Government by Debate" contains a number of changes and additions (mainly transitional paragraphs) that he made before copying out the draft of the article that he sent to *Overland Monthly*. The editors have tried to reproduce insofar as possible the text of "Government by Debate" as it stood when Wilson first submitted it to Harper's. His uncorrected mistakes in copying have been retained.

[11] Printed at Jan. 1, 1884.
[12] WW to R. Bridges, Feb. 5, 1883.

To Harper and Brothers

Dear Sirs,   Atlanta, Geo., Dec. 4th/82

I send you by express to-day the *ms.* of a somewhat extended essay which I have just written upon a subject which is likely to occupy the attention of the country during the present Winter and the coming years only less than those other questions of governmental reform which are now so largely engaging the energies of our best citizens, and which are, apparently, for the time the most pressing.

I have entitled my essay "Government by Debate." I need not detail its contents. They are summarized as much as possible in the *ms*. itself. I will only call to your attention the fact that I have divided my work into five *parts* (the fifth being yet in hand in course of composition), considering it not so complete a treatise as to be entitled to a division into chapters, after the formal manner of a *book*.

Part fifth of the essay, which I am now engaged in writing, will sum up and round out the discussion by the addition of germane matter of interest and suggestiveness.

I beg that you will give my *ms*. a careful perusal—and that you will read the *whole* of it before passing final judgment; for, allow me to say, the interest and strength of my treatment of the subject do not appear from a reading of any portion of the piece so well as from a reading of the whole of it.

The terms of publication I leave, of course, to you, as I am too new an author to think of dictating terms of my own.

It has occurred to me that, as coming from a Southern man—a Southern *young* man—this essay of mine might prove all the more acceptable to the reading public. The sentiments it contains are, as you will see, free from the cant which has marred the writings of Southern men since the war; and display, moreover, an unsectional interest in the affairs of the national government such as has been thought not to exist in the South.

But, aside from any interest of this kind that you may find it to possess, it is a suggestion of a great subject which has been too little considered, if considered at all, by the country, and which, when considered, cannot fail to excite attention and discussion which will be productive of much good. Allow me to suggest that, being of a somewhat similar character, it will possibly receive as favourable notice as did Mr. Albert Stickney's *True Republic* which a year or two ago came from your presses. An article of mine upon the same subject which appeared in the *International Review* about the time of the publication of Mr. S's book attracted a great deal of notice from the press of the country—notice which was partly instrumental in inducing me to undertake this more extended treatment of the theme.

Again begging your careful perusal of my essay, I am
Very Respectfully Yours   Woodrow Wilson

ALS (NNPM). There is a pencil draft of this letter in WP, DLC.

An Unpublished Essay

[c. Dec. 4, 1882]

Government by Debate: Being a Short View of Our National
Government As It Is and As It Might Be.
An Essay in Five Parts. By Woodrow Wilson

Preface

It has not been my object in writing the following pages to give
an exact and exhaustive account of the government of the Union
in all the particulars of its organization and in all the details of
its administration. I have wished to fix attention only upon those
broad and general facts which lie at the basis of its structure and
which are necessary to be presented in a discussion whose object
it is to effect a simplification and improvement of our methods of
legislation and of the practices of our system of executive agency.
If these facts are set forth with sufficient fulness and clearness to
serve the purposes of the argument which they are meant to sustain, the scope of this essay, so far as it was intended to be an
exposition of our system of federal government, is filled, and all
has been said of the actual operations of that system that the
reader was wished to expect. I have meant what I have said to
be "suggestive of principles rather than exhaustive of detail."
Atlanta, Geo.,   W.W.

I

Inside the House of Representatives

"No more vital truth was ever uttered than that freedom
and free institutions cannot long be maintained by any people who do not understand the nature of their government."

The House of Representatives is a superlatively noisy assembly.
Other legislative bodies are noisy, but they are not noisy as the
House of Representatives is noisy. We are told that the slightest
cause of excitement will set the French National Assembly frantically agog; that the English House of Commons is often loud-
voiced in its disorderly demonstrations; and that even our stolid
cousins, the Germans, do not always refrain from guttural clamour
when in Reichstag assembled. Our own House of Representatives,
however, indulges in a confusion peculiar to itself. Probably the
Representatives themselves soon become accustomed to the turmoil in which they are daily constrained to live and are seldom
heedful of the extreme disorder which prevails about them; but a

visitor to the House experiences, upon entering its galleries for the first time, sensations which it is not easy to define or to describe.

The Hall of the House is large beyond the expectation of the visitor. For each of the three hundred and twenty-five Representatives there is provided a roomy desk and an easy revolving chair —a chair about which there is space ample enough for the stretching of tired legislative legs in any position of restful extension that may suit the comfort of the moment. The desks and seats stand around the Speaker's chair in a great semi-circle, ranged in rows which radiate from that seat of authority as a centre. Here and there a broad aisle runs between two rows of seats, from the circumference of the semi-circle to the roomy spaces about the clerks' and Speaker's desks. Outside the seats and beyond the bar which surrounds them are other broad soft-carpeted spaces; and still there is room, beyond these again, for deep galleries to extend on every side their tiers of benches before the limiting walls of the vast hall are reached. Overhead, framed by the polished beams which support them, are great squares of ground-glass, through which a strong light falls on the voting and vociferating magnates below.

One would suppose that it would require a great deal of noise to fill that great room. Filled it is, however during the sittings of the House. It is not the noises of debate but the incessant and full-volumed hum of conversation and the sharp clapping of hands that strike the ear. The clapping of hands is not sustained and concerted but desultory, like the dropping fire of musketry; for these gentlemen in their easy chairs are not applauding any one —they are only striking their palms together as a signal-call to the young pages who act as messengers and errand boys, and who add the confusion of movement to the confusion of sound as they run hither and thither about the hall. Members, too, stroll about, making friendly visits to the desks of acquaintances or holding informal consultations with friends and colleagues. When in their seats, they seem engrossed in assorting documents, in writing letters or in reading newspapers whose stiff rattle adds variety to the prevailing disorder.

Some business is evidently going on the while, though the onlooker in the gallery must needs give his closest attention in order to ascertain just what is being done. Now and again a member arises and addresses the chair, but his loudest tones scarcely reach the galleries in the form of articulate speech; and the responsive rulings of the Speaker are not so distinctly audible as are the ineffectual raps of his restless gavel. Naturally, therefore, very few members try to speak. They do not covet an opportunity to do so in a hall which none but the clearest and strongest voice could fill even if the silence of attention were vouchsafed. However frequent one's visits to the capitol, he will seldom find the House engaged in debate. When some member, more daring, more determined, more hardy, or more confident than the rest, does essay to address the House, he generally finds that it will not listen, and that he must content himself with such audience as is given him by those in his immediate neighborhood, who are so near him that they cannot easily escape listening. His most strenuous efforts will not avail to make members in distant seats conscious that he is on the floor. They are either indifferent to what he is saying, or prefer to read it in the "Record" to-morrow.

This, then, is seemingly a most singular assembly. It seldom engages in lengthy debate, being apparently content to leave that dignified and generally unexciting exercise to the Senate, whose hall is, because of its smaller size, better suited for such employments, and where greater decorum prevails. It would be a mistake, however, to conclude that the careless manners of the House betoken idleness. Its sessions are, on the contrary, generally quite busy. It has been known to pass thirty-seven pension bills at one sitting; thus emulating the Senate which once passed, within the space of ten minutes, seven bills appropriating in the aggregate one million two hundred thousand dollars for the erection of public buildings in several States. The rules of the House ensure expedition and make such wholesale legislation not only possible but usual; for the House does not have to digest its schemes of legislation. It has Standing Committees which do its investigating and digesting for it, and its chief business is to act on the reports of these Committees. It deliberates in fragments, through small sections of its membership, and when it votes upon the bills laid before it by these authoritative Committees it sees little occasion for debate.

It is this plan of entrusting itself to the guidance of various small bodies of its members that distinguishes our House of Representatives from the other great legislative bodies of the world. The English House of Commons is able to follow a much simpler method of procedure. It has authoritative leaders of another sort. The Cabinet, the council of executive ministers, are also its executive committee. The chief officers of the several executive departments are chosen by the Crown from amongst the leaders of the party dominant in the House, and being thus constituted at once the administrators of the government and the leaders of their party in Parliament, the conduct of legislative business under their direction becomes easy enough. The principal measures of each session originate with the ministers and are always submitted by them to the fullest test of unrestricted discussion in the House before a vote is asked. If any of their proposals are negatived by Parliament, the ministers are bound to accept their defeat as an intimation that their administration is no longer acceptable to the party they represent, and are expected to resign or to appeal, if they prefer, to the constituencies for their verdict by advising the sovereign to issue writs for a new election. They have not, of course, all the time of the House at their disposal. Certain days of each week of a session are set apart for the introduction and debate of bills brought in by private members, who draw lots to decide the precedence of their bills or motions on the orders of the day. If many draw, those who get last choice of time generally find the session at an end before their opportunity has come, and must content themselves with hoping for better fortune next year; but time is generally found for a very fair and full consideration of a large number of private-members' bills, and no member is denied a chance to air his favorite opinions in the House or to try the patience of his fellow members by annual repetitions of the same propositions. The attention of Parliament is, however, very properly directed, during the greater part of each session, to a careful investigation and debate of the plans of "the government"— as the Cabinet-committee is called—and private members find by experience that frequently they can exert a more powerful influence on legislation by pressing amendments to government schemes, and can effect more immediate and satisfactory results by keeping a ministry constantly in mind of certain phases of public opinion than they could hope to exert or effect by themselves introducing measures upon which their party might hesitate to unite.

England has thus adopted the simplest and most straight-forward method of party government. The chiefs of the party which has secured the largest representation in the Commons are intrusted with the administration of the government and with the direction of legislation. That party majority would in any case control the policy of the government, and the most honest way for it to rule is that which it has chosen, of putting itself under the leadership of those men of its own ranks who have proved their ability to lead, and entrusting to those leaders the responsible duties of rule. At the same time, ample scope is given for independent thought and action, and every member, whether he be of the majority or of the minority, is allowed his full share of opportunity. If he have a bill to bring in, he has an equal chance with every other unofficial member of having an early day set for its consideration. He can take as prominent a part in the proceedings of the House as his abilities give him title to take. If he have anything which is not merely frivolous to say, concerning any pending measure, he will have repeated opportunities to speak and will be patiently heard to the end. During certain appointed hours of certain days of each week of the session he may call on the ministers for full and explicit answers to every proper question it may occur to him to ask concerning the administration of the public business. He lives under rules which combine in wonderful perfection individual independence with party supremacy.

As might be expected, the task of leading the House is not an easy one for the ministers. Their plans are every day being attacked by their opponents of the minority. They are plied, by friend and antagonist alike, with questions great and small, direct and indirect, pertinent and impertinent, concerning every detail of government and every tendency of policy. The battles which surge about the chief points of their ministry are fierce and protracted. Each measure is discussed until every item and clause of it has passed the ordeal of criticism, until the speakers of all parties have taken their turns at stricture or entered their pleas in vindication, sometimes until the debate has spun itself out to tedious lengths, but always until the whole subject under consideration has been exhibited in its every phase to the constituencies throughout the country, until a blaze of publicity has been thrown upon it and an indisputable meaning attached to the action of Parliament upon it, until every newspaper in London and in the provinces has either spread the debate forth in full in its columns or, at least, extracted its essential points for editorial comment in its most prominent spaces, until newsboys recommend their wares by shrill proclamation of the leading points of yesterday's Parliamentary tilt and every breakfast table in the land knows echoes of the strife at St. Stephens. Each session of Lords and Commons is a grand inquest into the affairs of the empire. They are the nation sitting in committee on the management of public affairs—a committee sitting with open doors and sparing itself no fatigue to secure for every interest represented a full, fair, and impartial hearing.

The Commons in session present an interesting picture. The hall in which they sit is not large. It seems a place meet for hand to hand combats. The cushioned benches on which the members are crowded rise in close series on either side of a wide central aisle which they face. At one end of this aisle is raised the Speaker's chair, below and in front of which are the desks of the wigged and gowned clerks. On the front benches nearest the Speaker and to his right sit the Cabinet Ministers, the leaders of the government; on the front benches to the Speaker's left, sit the leaders of the Opposition. Behind and to the right of the ministers sit the majority; behind and to the left of the leaders of the Opposition, the minority. Above the rear benches and over the outer aisles of the House, beyond "the bar," hang deep galleries, from which the outside world may look down upon the sharp passages of arms which are ever and again taking place between the leaders of the two parties which thus sit face to face with only the aisle between them, charging the atmosphere with an excitement which repeatedly manifests itself in cheers and counter cheers which wake the echoes of St. Stephens and are often the first sounds of voices which will reach every ear in the kingdom as the war of parties proceeds.

The organization of the French Assembly is similar to that of the British Commons. Its leaders are the executive officers of the government and are chosen from the ranks of the legislative majority by the President of the Republic, as English Cabinets are chosen by English sovereigns. They, too, are responsible for their administration and their policy to the Chambers which they lead. They are the Executive-committee of the Assembly and upon its will their tenure of office depends.

It cannot be said, however, that the proceedings of the French Assembly very closely resemble those of the British Commons. In the hall of the Deputies there are no close benches which face each other and no two homogeneous parties to strive for the mastery. There are parties and parties, factions and factions, coteries and coteries. There are Bonapartists and Legitimatists, Republicans and Clericals, the stubborn reactionist and the headlong radical, the stolid conservative and the rash reformer. One hears of the Centre, the Right Centre and the Left Centre, the Right, the Left, the Extreme Right, and the Extreme Left. Some of these factions are mere groups composed of a few irreconcilables; but others of them are numerous and powerful and upon their mutual attractions or repulsions depend the formation, the authority, and the duration of Cabinets.

Of course in a body thus made up there is much combustible material which the slightest circumstances often suffice to kindle into a sudden blaze. The Assembly would not be French if it were not often uproarious. Members do not speak from their seats, as do members of Congress and of Parliament, but from the *tribune*. The *tribune* is a conspicuous structure erected near the desks of the President and Secretaries—a high, box-like stand not unlike those tall, narrow, quaintly-fashioned pulpits which are still to be seen in some of the oldest of our churches. Deputies must gain its commanding top before they may speak, and the race for this place of vantage is often exciting enough. Not infrequently very unseemly scenes take place when several deputies, each equally eager to mount the coveted stand, reach its narrow steps at the same moment. None will give way, so the strongest wins right of precedence by main force. In seasons of unusual excitement, when the passions of the factions run highest, the friends of rival orators sometimes rally to their aid, and there the strongest party takes the *tribune* by storm.

But the French Assembly, turbulent as it is, though often brought screaming to its feet by impetuous words from some eloquent and excited speaker, though again and again betrayed into stormy disquiet and always blown about by every wind of passion, is nevertheless capable of wise deliberation, is generally steady in its political purpose, and, above all, has so far been able somewhat triumphantly to maintain a new and untried Republican system in vigorous and healthy life. It has, moreover, kept the rather delicate machinery of Cabinet-Committee government in smooth operation. Government by an executive ministry representing the majority in the Chambers would seem to stand in jeopardy of a fatal instability, for there are no homogeneous parties on whom ministries can count. But the French system is very far from being unstable. How much stability must that system have which has passed without wreck through such an ordeal of storm as it endured under McMahon's unrepublican presidency! In spite of dictatorial Presidents and reactionist Cabinets, it has stablished itself in republican principles and built itself up in republican practices.

These two great representative bodies, then, the British House of Commons and the French Assembly, so unlike in the elements which compose them, so dissimilar in their habits of procedure, are made kin by that principle of Cabinet government which they both recognize and both apply in its fullest efficacy. In both England and France the Cabinet, a ministry composed of the chief officers of the executive departments, are constituted at once the leaders of legislation and the directors of administration—a binding link between the Legislative and Executive branches of the government. This partial union of branches has been effected

directly in the face of the honored opinion of the great Montesquieu, if the later interpretations of that opinion are to be accepted.
For Montesquieu affirmed, it is to be remembered,—and affirmed
with the surest support of reason and of proof—that liberty could
not long exist if the legislative, executive, and judicial powers
of government were once lodged in the hands of any one man or
any one body of men; and all subsequent political writers have
added their emphatic amen to the principle, that those powers
should always be kept separate and distinct. It becomes interesting, therefore, to enquire just what these discerning and learned
gentlemen meant and what they thought Montesquieu to mean.
When Montesquieu said "there can be no liberty where the legislative and executive powers are united in the same person or body
of magistrates," he manifestly could not have meant that those
powers should be set apart from each other in absolute isolation,
because he drew his deductions from an examination of the political institutions of England where no such isolation was known,
and found in those institutions his only illustrations of secure liberty. The lesson those institutions taught was plain enough. They
were admirable examples of the harmonious coöperation of departments of government so independent from each other as to be
secure in the power to act with perfect freedom of will, and yet so
united as to have a common will in the service of the people. The
law-maker strengthened the hand of the judge and facilitated the
duties of the Executive, though subject to the controlling influence of neither; the executive magistrate lent the aid of his power
to the judge and bent his best energies to the administration of
government without apprehension of hostile interference from
either judge or law-maker; and the judge discharged his exalted
functions without fear of displeasure or hope of reward from executive or legislator; but the judge was the nominee of the sovereign and the sovereign acted through the servants of Parliament.
There was union without identity. Coöperative departments constituted one government and were able to do a work for good government which they could not have done in isolation, inefficient
fragments of a disjointed machine. Such was the model which
Montesquieu set before men as containing all that was best and
wisest in human government; and such was the model after which
Montesquieu's countrymen were one day to pattern their own institutions.

There was another reason why France should adopt Cabinet
government. In establishing popular government she was establishing party government, and Cabinet government is the simplest

and safest form of party government. By making the leaders of a dominant party also the executive agents of government a way is found of binding that party to a definite policy. The legislature is put into immediate communication and close sympathy with the executive departments without being given undue power of coërcion. Legislation is both facilitated and restrained by being put under the direction of a ministry who are more familiar than all others with the condition and needs of the government and who are more interested than all others in building up the efficiency of the legislature and in preserving the prestige and the prerogatives of the executive.

Why, then, it may be asked, was not Cabinet government set up in America also? Why was not the greatest of all popular governments cast in that most perfect of popular forms? For several reasons. First and most evidently because the framers of our Constitution were unwilling to go farther than was absolutely unavoidable in their imitation of the institutions of the mother country. Very far they did go. But the bitter spirit of the war was still abroad among the people and the temper of the country was decidedly averse from copying anything English that could be dispensed with. Besides, such a device as the Cabinet-committee was probably thought impracticable in this country. Indeed, when the government of the United States was organized the place, duties, and responsibilities of the Cabinet ministry in the English system were not so thoroughly determined and understood nor so clearly defined as they have since become, and the framers of our Constitution may have regarded the British Cabinet as an institution peculiar to monarchical government, not seeing in it all the possibilities of its later development as a safe and effective instrument of popular party government.

The debates of the Constitutional Convention upon the proper constitution of the executive are very instructive. The questions involved were of a very delicate nature, and all the members of the Convention seem to have realized the difficulties of the task set before them. Some of them saw from the first that it would be virtually impossible to erect an executive which could maintain any real independence in the presence of the vast prerogatives of the legislature. Roger Sherman, of Connecticut, perceived very clearly the omnipotence which must inevitably belong to the national Congress and frankly declared that "he considered the executive magistracy as nothing more than an institution for carrying the will of the legislature into effect; that the person or persons who should constitute the executive ought to be appointed by, and accountable to, the legislature only, which was the depository of the supreme will of the society." The executive was in his view so entirely the servant of the legislative will that he saw good reason to think that the legislature should judge of the number of persons of which the executive should be composed; and others there were in the Convention who in these matters went far in substantial agreement with him. But the leading purpose of the majority was to establish in the executive an independent department of government, a department coördinate with the legislature and as autocratic as the judiciary, whose independence should be a check upon the powers of Congress, and whose will should be an originating and guiding force in the conduct of national affairs. They preferred a singular to a plural executive and clothed a single man with the authority of rule.

Except by Roger Sherman not a finger in the Convention was pointed directly towards the principle of Cabinet government. An executive consisting of several persons named by the legislature would have been, in principle, much like a Cabinet government: and it was to the formation of such an executive that Sherman looked as the most natural organization of the government. But the Convention was of another mind. Its ideal was a government consisting of three coordinate and coëqual branches, departments dissociated yet constituting a governmental unit. Its hope was that the single and isolated executive which they should create would restrain at the same time that it served the purposes of the legislature. Accordingly it fortified that executive with the power of the *veto* and vested it with a qualified privilege of appointment to the offices of the civil service.

But when now-a-days we speak of "the Executive" we generally mean not only this single chief magistrate, not the President alone, though he is the head and front of the executive organization, but the heads of the several Departments as well. Executive duties are now exceedingly multifarious, and cannot all, of course, be performed by the President alone. The greater part of them is not performed even under his immediate supervision. They keep busy many officials in many offices. They run from things great down to things small. They include the administration of the national finances, the regulation of foreign affairs, the maintenance and discipline of the military and naval forces of the Union, the carrying and delivery of the mails, the prosecution of offenders against the laws of the federal government, the issuing of patents, the payment of pensions, the charge of the public lands, the care of the Indians, the superintendence of education, and the compilation of census statistics. When, therefore, the Constitution speaks of the Executive it means the President, and the President only; but in ordinary use "the Executive" is taken to mean the President and the chief officers of the Departments, the President and his Cabinet—the "Secretaries" of State, of the Treasury, of the Interior, of War, and of the Navy, the Attorney-General and the Post-Master-General. These Cabinet officers are, as everybody knows, appointed by the President, with and by the consent and advice of the Senate, and in them is vested authority to direct all the ordinary business of the Departments.

But above "the Executive" in undisputed supremacy, stands Congress. Roger Sherman was right: the executive is "nothing more than an institution for carrying the will of the legislature into effect," and no contrivance of law can make it anything else. In the United States, as in England, as in France, as in every country which has popular government and representative institutions, the legislature is supreme. Within the sphere of the powers granted under the Constitution to the authorities of the Union Congress is omnipotent. Though in some measure independent of Congress, the President and his Cabinet are in every important affair, merely the servants. They must carry out its financial policy; they must collect and expend the public revenues as it directs; they must observe its will in all dealings with foreign states; they are dependent upon it for means to support both army and navy, nay even for means to maintain the Departments themselves; they are led by it in all the main paths of their policies; and they obey its biddings even in many of the minor concerns of every-day business. Wherever it chooses to interfere it is powerful to command.

Being altogether dissociated from the Executive in its organization, however, Congress is often embarrassed in the exercise of its omnipotence. It cannot deal directly with its agents. The Secretary of the Treasury, for instance, is the financial agent of Congress; but he has no place on the floor of either house from which he may advise their action in financial matters, or give information as to the needs and capabilities of his department, or render an account of the acts of his stewardship. He cannot ask counsel when he is in doubt or indulgence when he is surrounded by difficulties. His real position as the executive financial officer of Congress is in no way openly recognized, and the houses have, in consequence, no easy means of observing the inner workings of the Treasury and are frequently forced to deplore their inability to exercise a minute and careful supervision of the disbursements of the national revenues. And so, likewise, of the other departments. Over all Congress is overlord; but over none is its control satisfactory and complete. In very few cases can it *prevent* executive mischief. The Secretaries, when once appointed, hold their offices for four years and no amount of inefficiency on their part will meantime put them within reach of dismissal by Congress. True, after they have misbehaved and all the harm is done, Congress may set the slow and cumbersome machinery of *impeachment* in operation. But impeachments generally break down, and are at best but inadequate means of punishment. An ounce of prevention would be worth many pounds of that sort of cure.

The immediate agents of the houses in their dealings with the executive departments are their Standing Committees. Constrained to provide for itself leaders of some sort or other, Congress has found them in certain small and select bodies of men to whom it has entrusted the preparation of legislation. Any one who has attended a mass meeting can readily appreciate the necessity which Congress has obeyed—the necessity of facilitating the transaction of business by calling in the aid of committees. Such meetings accomplish very little business, and they are enabled to accomplish that little by one means only, namely by placing some one in the chair and requesting him to appoint a committee of his own choice to draft some resolutions for immediate consideration. The committee is named, retires, and soon returns with written preamble and resolutions which serve as the text or the occasion for the speeches of the appointed speakers. After the speeches comes the confused *viva voce* vote and the meeting breaks rapidly up. Something like this Congress was constrained to do. It could not undertake to consider separately each of the numberless bills which might be brought in by its members. If it were to undertake to do so, its docket would become crowded beyond all hope of clearance and its business fall appallingly into arrears. It must give to Committees the task of digesting this various matter and confine itself to the consideration of business submitted by them.

Accordingly, it constituted several Standing Committees whose duty it should be to prepare legislation for its action and to act as its immediate agents in all its dealings with the executive departments. The Secretary of the Treasury must heed the commands of the Finance Committee of the Senate and the Ways and Means Committee of the House; the Secretary of State must regard the will of the Foreign Affairs Committees of both houses; the Secretary of the Interior must suffer himself to be bidden, now by the Committees on Indian Affairs, now by those on the Public Lands, and again by those on Patents; the Secretary of War must assiduously do service to the Committees on Military Affairs; to other Committees the Post-Master General must render homage; the Secretary of the Navy must wear the livery of the Committees on Naval Affairs; and the Attorney General must not forget that one or more of these eyes of the houses is upon him. There are, besides, Committees on Appropriations, Committees on the Judiciary, Committees on Banking and Currency, Committees on Manufactures, Committees on Railways and Canals, Committees on Pensions and on Claims, Committees on Expenditures in the several Departments and Expenditures on Public Buildings, Committees on This and Committees on That, Committees on every conceivable subject of legislation.

Now, these Standing Committees are very selfish. Congress has made them exacting by spoiling them. It indulges their every whim. The Rules of the House of Representatives provide for the expedition of business by securing beyond a peradventure the supremacy of its committees; and these same rules are, in consequence, a besetting snare to many a new member. Because of their existence his first session generally has in store for him many trials and humiliations—trying experiences which often sadly discomfit him, however diverting they may be to others. A correspondent of the New York *Nation* recently spread before the readers of that admirable journal a very vivid and amusing sketch of the usual adventures of a new member which might be made the basis of a highly instructive commentary on the procedure of the national legislature. There is much that is serious in the comedy. To the new member himself it is all, no doubt, serious enough. His first entrance upon the society of the capital is apt to have a chilling effect on him. He is, of course, unknown to his fellow members, being set down in their minds simply as belonging to this party or to that. Any reputation for ability or eloquence that he may have established in his district counts for little in Washington. Nothing is known of it there. Soon a deep sense of insignificance creeps over him and he actually comes to be gratified at finding that one at least of his new-made acquaintances succeeds in remembering what State he is from. Even in his place in Congress he is made to feel uncomfortably small. When the House organizes for business and is divided by the Speaker into Committees, he hears his name read last on the roll of the Committee on the Militia, perhaps, or of the Committee on Mileage, and catches himself vaguely wondering what his duties as member of such a Committee will chance to be. Mayhap his constituents elected him as an advanced free trader or a determined protectionist, and he had hoped, nay, even ventured to expect to be assigned to the Committee of Ways and Means; but if he confide his disappointment to some friend who sits near him he will surely be very heartily laughed at, unless that friend happen to be himself a new-comer to the House and can in return open his heart on the score of a similar blow to his hopes and plans.

It will never do, however, for the new member to be disheartened because he is unknown to the Speaker and is relegated by that high functionary to work on a Committee of whose duties he knows nothing and does not much care to know anything. He will not allow his ardour for tariff revision to be cooled because he is shut out from a place on the Committee of Ways and Means. He therefore prepares, with conscientious care, a bill whose provisions meet his own convictions and are sure to gain the enthusiastic approval of his constituents, and then, some day taking advantage of a pause in the business of the House, he rises to move the adoption of his measure. But he is at once caught in the toils of the inexorable Rules. The Speaker curtly informs him that his bill can be introduced at that time only by unanimous consent, several voices are raised in loud and decided dissent, and he is compelled to sit down in surprise, mortification, and perplexity.

Moved to respect for the Rules by this first experience of their power of stern rebuff, the new member begins to examine them, to find, if possible, what privileges, if any, they vouchsafe him. He discovers that the roll of the States will be called on Monday and that he can bring in his bill when his State is called. Thus encouraged and instructed, he rises in his place at the proper time on Monday and, sure now of being in order, sends his bill up to be read by the Clerk and prepares to enforce its principles by a speech which may possibly be heard above the noises of the House, or, if not heard by many of the members, will certainly be caught by the reporters and published to the country. But again the Rules entrap him. No sooner does he begin to utter the first words of his much-pondered and long-delayed speech than he is once more called shortly to order by the Speaker, who declares that no debate is in order; his propositions can only be referred to the proper committee. Other States are immediately called, other members propose measures and resolutions which are in their turn sent with equal scantness of ceremony to the appropriate committees, and the new member realizes that, after all his trouble and patient waiting, his precious tariff measure is to have judgment passed upon it not by the House but by the Committee of Ways and Means.

A further study of these repressive Rules and a closer observation of the proceedings of the House soon convince him that, despite all their puzzling intricacies and complicated checks, the Rules are in their main principles simple enough. Their object is the expediting of business, and this object they accomplish by the utmost possible limitation of debate. Of course a great many bills, sometimes several thousand, are introduced by individual members during each session, and there is not time to discuss or even to vote upon them all. Accordingly, the right of individual representatives to have their proposals separately considered must be sacrificed to the common convenience. The bills which are sent by scores to the Clerk's desk on Mondays are all sent to the Standing Committees. Those affecting the Navy go to the Committee on Naval Affairs; those enquiring into the treatment of American citizens abroad fall to the Committee on Foreign Affairs; those asking money for internal improvements are ordered to the Appropriations Committee; those relating to taxation or imposts are claimed by the Committee of Ways and Means; scarcely a topic can be touched which does not fall within the province of one or another of the committees, and so no bill escapes commitment.

A bill committed is rarely heard of more. A bill committed is a bill doomed. How can each bill be separately reported upon? Suppose, for example, that the Appropriations Committee has fifty or a hundred bills referred to it,—and that would doubtless be much fewer than usual—manifestly they cannot report upon each one of them separately. Time would not serve them for such an undertaking. They must do as all of the other principal committees do: they must utterly reject the greater portion of them, and, having from the remainder culled what provisions they like, frame for submission to the House a scheme of their own. Certainly this practice of the Committee must be a source of much chagrin to those members whose propositions are thus immediately upon their introduction buried out of sight; but the necessity for some such system of committee digestion must be evident even to the most disappointed member; at least in the cases of the hundreds of bills brought in by others, if not in the case of the few moved by himself.

The debates of the House of Representatives are, therefore, by an apparent necessity, confined, except on rare occasions, to the reports of the committees. As a rule committee bills and committee bills only are discussed. Even when other bills, gotten in by private members under a suspension of the Rules, do claim brief attention, they are subordinated to the committee bills which are the chief measures and the leading topics of the session. The official leadership of the committees is considered essential to orderly and expeditious procedure. Further expedition of business is ensured, moreover, by brevity of debate. Upon no subject is discussion often long protracted; for even upon these reports of the Standing Committees the House does not care to spend much time. Consequently, its debates upon their contents cannot with strict accuracy be called "debates of the House." They are in the House, but not of it. The period of debate and the number of speakers are usually limited by rule. So long a time is devoted to each discussion and the members of the reporting committee are accorded right of precedence for the presentation of their views upon the subject in hand. Such an arrangement seems to secure thorough enough discussion in most cases. Each committee is composed of members of both of the national parties, and if the question under consideration have two sides, partisanly speaking, those two sides are pretty sure to be exhibited by the committeemen themselves. Besides, the principal committees are usually composed of the older and more prominent members of the House, men whose long legislative experience may reasonably be supposed to have made them better debaters than their fellows, men who have, too, in the deliberations of their committee probably mastered the details of the measure which has been reported by their chairman and are, in consequence, generally able to throw more light upon its provisions than could be thrown by those who had no part in framing them. The plan is evidently a natural and apparently an expedient one. There would seem to be not only manifest convenience but strict propriety in rules which restrict debate to the subject-matter of committee reports and give the floor first and almost exclusively to the members of the reporting committee in order that they shall be at all events the principal speakers. Especially since it is understood that other members are not always or altogether shut off from speech-making. By previous arrangement with some member of the Committee whose proposals are about to be considered, one can, if he has apprised the Speaker of the arrangement, gain the floor when the discussion comes on and crowd his remarks, if he has a knack of condensation, into the space of time resigned to him by his friend, the committeeman. Occassionally, moreover, when there are a great many who are anxious to speak on a pending issue, the House appoints a time, frequently a whole sitting, for general debate in which all that choose may participate.

Why any one should crave an opportunity to speak in a House

whose noises must inevitably overwhelm his voice must seem a great mystery to one who has not known what it is to have constituents to satisfy and gratify. The *Nation's* contributor has said that to try to address the House of Representatives is "very like trying to address the people in the omnibuses from the curbstone in front of the Astor House" in New York city. Provincial gentlemen who read the Associated Press despatches in their morning papers as they sit over their coffee at breakfast have doubtless often been puzzled by items such as sometimes appear in the brief telegraphic notes of the proceedings of the House, to the effect that while Mr. A. was speaking, on the Democratic side of the chamber, so great was the interest manifested in his speech that Republican members crowded over to the Democratic side in great numbers to hear him; or, that while Mr. B. was replying, seats on the Republican side were in great demand; or, that Mr. C's eloquence brought around him from both sides groups of eager listeners. If the readers of the despatches had ever looked in upon a session of the House, however, these items would easily yield up their meaning to them. It is simply that the chamber is so wide that from one side of it to the other is, as Mark Twain would say, a Sabbath-day's journey; and since there is never silence under its roof while the House is sitting one must get near a speaker to hear anything that he says. A speech can no more be heard from the opposite side of the hall than it could be from the opposite side of a water-fall.

When a session is set apart for general debate, there is comparative quiet; but it is the quiet of desertion. The attendance is small. Few besides those who expect to speak care to be present. Those who speak must be content to face a discouraging array of empty chairs and deserted desks. No wonder that they often weary of the delivery of their speeches and either monotonously read them or gladly take advantage of the readily-granted leave to have them printed in the Record, without delivery, as a part of the proceedings. After all, the speeches were intended for the ear of the country or of the constituencies and not for the ear of the House; why then bore the House by compelling it to endure the reading or recitation of what it does not care to hear and is not expected to heed?

The House makes its nearest approach to business debate when in Committee of the Whole. Then something like free and effective discussion takes place. Even then, however, members are not given unlimited scope. They must not talk longer than five minutes at a time. Though the House be no longer the House and has put on the free habits of committee work, it still retains its predilections and still binds itself by rules which are stingy of time to those who would speak. Five-minute speeches, moreover, gain little more attention than is vouchsafed to the one-hour speeches of committeemen during a regular session, for the Committee of the Whole is no better listener than the House. Members are almost as noisy and inattentive as when the Speaker is in his seat.

The conclusion of the whole matter, then, is that legislation is altogether in the hands of the Standing Committees. In matters of Finance the Committee of Ways and Means is, to all intents and purposes, the whole House; on questions affecting the national Judiciary the Judiciary Committee practically dictates the decision of the whole House; when expenditures have received the approval of the Appropriations Committee they have virtually received the sanction of the whole House; the recommendations of the Committee on Naval Affairs are as a matter of course the will of the whole House; and so on, from the beginning to the end of every chapter of legislation. However many exceptions may arise under unusual circumstances, however often party excitement, or factional intrigue, or personal influence may throw the Rules from their ordinary balance, it is a long-sanctioned and seldom-broken custom to allow all legislation to originate with the Committees and be by them conducted to completion. The House's work is done in the Committee rooms. When measures issue thence, only a formal vote in regular session—a vote often given without debate —is needed to erect them into bills, acts of the House of Representatives.

An inquiry into the composition, privileges, and proceedings of the Standing Committees becomes, therefore, a matter of supreme importance and interest to every citizen of the Union. Upon them hangs the whole scheme of our government. By whom are they named, and what is the rule of their organization? The appointment and constitution of the committees of the lower house make up the chief prerogative of the Speaker. The Senate nominates its own Standing Committees by ballot; but the House is too numerous a body to trust itself to do likewise. It is very properly desirous to escape being divided against itself by those selfish, intriguing, factional influences which an attempt at such elections would undoubtedly let loose to the confusion and corruption of its members. The severe and often discreditable scramble for the Speakership which is now every two years regretfully witnessed by the nation would be changed into a bitter and always disgraceful scramble for the chairmanships of the principal committees and for places of prominence and power upon their rolls. It is best not to risk such dangers. It is better to delegate the duty of appointment to an officer who is himself the choice of the House. He can act with greater promptitude and with equal fairness. The power given him is, indeed, immense and practically irresponsible. It constitutes Mr. Speaker the most powerful functionary in the government of the United States. But such power is more safely lodged in the hands of a single person than in the hands of a numerous and wrangling body.

Necessary as they are, however, the prerogatives of the Speaker of the House of Representatives are alarmingly great. He may, of course, discharge his high trust with honour and integrity; but consider the temptations which must overcome him if he be not made of the staunchest moral stuff. Is the public treasury full, and is he bent by conviction or by personal interest or by political connection toward certain great schemes of public expenditure? With how strong a hand must he restrain his inclinations, his dominant purposes if he would deny himself the privilege, which no one else has authority to deny him, of constituting men of like mind with himself a controlling majority of the Appropriations Committee! Has he determined opinions upon questions of revenue and taxation which he fears may not be the opinions which are likely to prevail in the House? Who, if he do not prevent himself, will prevent him from naming those of the same opinion a ruling number on the Committee of Ways and Means? Has he friends whose influence was powerful in bringing about his elevation to the chair? Who will be surprised if he give those friends the most coveted chairmanships? Does one of his friends feel a special interest in building up the Navy? He will consider Mr. Speaker shamelessly ungrateful if he be not given a voice in the determinations of both the Naval and the Appropriations Committees. Does another friend come from the State that Mr. Speaker represents, and does he come from a protectionist constituency? He will have thoughts of Mr. Speaker too hard to cast into articulate speech if the doors of the Committee of Ways and Means be not opened wide to him. The Speaker may, and doubtless often does, reason thus with himself: 'My party has put me into a position in which I can control legislation through my committee appointments and binds me by no rules of choice save that not-too-exacting custom of the House which puts its oldest and most experienced members as first and favoured claimants of the chairmanships of the leading committees; am I not justified, therefore, in exercising the authority of leadership, which has been thus unreservedly given me, to the fullest extent of the discretion it allows? I believe such and such courses of legislation to be in keeping with the principles of my party, or at least conducive to its interests, and that party has given me the power I possess, therefore the committees shall be organized for the promotion of those interests.'

As a matter of fact—unless many outrageous calumnies are allowed to run abroad unchallenged—very few Speakers forbid their own personal preferences and predilections a voice in the appointment of the committees. Many Speakers are men of strong individuality and resolute purpose who have won their position by dominant force of will, and such men are sure to make themselves seen and felt in the composition of the Committees. They are acknowledged autocrats. Other Speakers are mere puppets, obscure men who have been raised to the chair by accidents such as sometimes foist third-rate politicians into the Presidency—men whom caucuses have hit upon simply because they could not agree upon any one else. They appoint committees as others suggest. They go as they are led. In their appointments only those are favoured who have established a claim upon their gratitude or an influence over their irresponsible wills, or those who are nominated to his favour by an irresistible custom of the House.

The magnitude of the influence which the Speaker wields through his power of appointment appears when it is considered whom he appoints. He appoints all the Standing Committees, and the Standing Committees are supreme. He controls the composition of the Committees, and the Committees control legislation with an almost absolute sway. It will be interesting to explore a little further these sources of power by looking more closely into the workings of the committee system. How and where are the proceedings of the committees conducted? They sit in rooms set apart and fitted up for their use. They are provided, at the public expense, with secretaries or clerks who are generally the nominees of the chairmen. With this simple organization of chairman and clerk, a committee's sessions are usually held in comparative privacy, no one who is not on its roll being expected to be present uninvited. To assist it in its determinations it may invite the presence of any executive officer of the government—though it does not appear that it has the power to compel his attendance—and it often allows the advocates of certain measures to present their arguments at length before it. It is thus that legislation is discussed—in the committee rooms rather than upon the floor of Congress. It is by the courtesy of the committees that members of the House who are denied a chance of speaking in the debates of that body are afforded an occasional opportunity of expressing their views. The Associated Press despatches frequently contain such items as this: "The House Committee on Commerce to-day heard arguments from the Congressional delegations"—that is, the members of Congress—from such and such States "in advocacy of appropriations for river and harbour improvements which the members desire incorporated in the River and Harbour appropriations bill." But any committee that pleases may shut its doors against all comers and sit in absolute secrecy. And, even when it admits advocates, no full report of their arguments is taken and no account of the committee's own discussions is published. On what grounds a committee acted is seldom clearly known to the public. Why this or that bill, which was introduced by some member and referred without debate to the committee, was rejected by it, no one can easily tell. The minutes of the committee, if any were kept, are not accessible, and all that appears from the minutes of the House is that the committee in its report made no allusion to the bill in question. The public, in short, can know little or nothing about the motives or the methods of the Standing Committees; and yet all legislation may be said to originate with them and pass through all its stages under their direction.

Now, there are several noteworthy things about this organization of the House and its committees. Very worthy of remark, in the first place, is the *privacy* which characterizes Congressional legislation. If a reference of all matters to appropriate committees be a necessity from which there is no escape, surely it is feasible and beyond all doubt desirable to give as much publicity as possible to the deliberations of the committees, and to subject their reports, when submitted to Congress, to a searching canvass. In the Senate there is generally, perhaps, enough liberty of debate upon the reports of Standing Committees; but in the House of Representatives, which most directly represents the people, the debates upon committee measures are restricted within the narrowest possible limits, and all talking (except conversation) is treated with imperative disfavour. The result is one which greatly affects the character of legislation. The House, content to do without much question what its committees advise, hurries ill-considered and immature bills through all their courses—only occasionally stopping to make a few hasty criticisms, when Committee of the Whole is reached—and sends them post-haste to the Senate, which in like manner, except when in a specially talkative mood, often accepts with small pause of deliberation the decisions of its committees. In a word, the House is a deliberative body which seldom deliberates. It delegates its deliberative duties to committees which are not of its own choosing.

Equally worthy of remark is the effect upon the public mind of this want of publicity in legislation. The nation hears so little of the progress of measures that, however long they may have been under the consideration of committees and however often they may have been actually reported on, they come, when finally passed, as a surprise to the knowledge of the people. A pointed illustration of this was afforded in connection with press discussions of the so-called "Bland Silver Bill." The Resumption Act of 1875 had been considered, as fully as any bill ever is, by two Congresses: that is, it had been recommended by more than one Congressional committee, had been printed, and had been widely circulated throughout the country. It did not become an Act until after as long a probation as could be desired. But when, a few years afterwards, the "Bland Bill" was brought in and had caught the attention of the press of the country, what was said by Mr. Bland's Chicago supporters? Mr. Bland's proposition, it will be remembered, was virtually to repeal the Resumption Act, and the plea which the Chicago papers urged in behalf of his bill was, in effect, that it was really the measure called for by the country, and that the Resumption Act, which it was meant to supercede, was not worthy of consideration because it had been sprung suddenly on Congress and passed by that body both hastily and secretly. They seem honestly to have thought that that Act which had in reality been to all intents and purposes before the country for almost four years before it was passed, had been suddenly introduced and as suddenly enacted, under some spur of hasty determination. And so with other measures. Who, but the politicians and the lawyers, knows what Congress did ten years ago? Legislation is done in a corner—that is, in committee rooms—and the people are constantly ignorant of what is being done and surprised at what has been done. No wonder the Chicago editors forgot even the long-considered Resumption Act.

Most worthy of remark is the irresponsibility of the Standing Committees. Although they control legislation, they are not responsible when legislation limps or even when it runs altogether away from legitimate methods and honest purposes. Of course they are in a sense morally responsible. The blame should properly fall upon them. But blame can do little to restrain or regulate individuals even; and when it is shared by many it is practically felt by none. Liability to blame not only but to punishment as well is the responsibility which spurs to diligence and binds to good faith in the discharge of duty. This is what responsibility always means in the ordinary concerns of private business. Neglect of duty is visited with loss of place. Misperformance of duty brings quick and peremptory dismissal. Such, too, is the only responsibility worth talking about in the conduct of the affairs of a nation. Public, official station should be irrecoverably forfeited by every conscious or wilful departure from the strictest faithfulness or the straitest rectitude. Especially in the discharge of legislative trusts should such responsibility be rigidly insisted on; for to neglect such trusts is to ensure widespread injury of the swiftest fatality. In our system, however, no such responsibility can be fixed upon the Standing Committees of Congress. Their supremacy is nowhere directly acknowledged by written law. It is prescriptive, not statutory, and Congress cannot charge them with culpability because it has accepted their suggestions. If any obnoxious or injurious measure be passed by the Houses, the committee with which that measure originated is of course to blame for its recommendation; but it may hide itself behind the larger blame which must be cast upon Congress for passing the bill, and upon the President for signing it. Who is punishable? Theoretically speaking, Congress and the President; practically speaking, no one. How is the country to go about punishing the President or the Houses? Representatives, mayhap, have such hold upon their districts that they can brave their record, or easily atone for it; and Senators doubtless have too many pledged or dependent friends in the Legislatures at home to stand much in dread of being ousted from their seats.

Besides, Congressmen may one and all plead the coercion of the party whip. Probably a caucus was held by the members who were their fellow-partisans and in that caucus it was decided how the party should vote upon the ill-starred bill, just as often before it had been determined how it should cast its suffrages upon other measures which had never had the misfortune to come under the public wrath. How could they refuse to abide by the decision of the caucus? Were they to break the party because they did not agree with it? Caucus votes are secret, and each erring Representative can make it appear to his constituents that his voice was against the caucus majority, and can claim that it was at fault, not he individually. He can hide behind the party, and no one can punish the party. So it is that legislation may get violently out of joint every session and no one be held responsible or reached by any whip of retribution.

II

Committee Government

"For if such actions may have passage free
Bond-slaves and pagans shall our statesmen be."

It has been proposed to abolish political parties. So hot is the blood brewed by them, so ugly are the passions which are abroad in their contests, that patriotic outcry is often made against them and sanguine men go about to destroy them. When, therefore, a crusade is preached against them the preachers are sure of much sympathy; for right-minded men everywhere see and deplore the degrading and corrupting influence of the spirit of faction which so often rules in political controversies; and, if it were possible that it should do so, they would rejoice to see it pass away. But, even while they cheer the crusade, very few men expect to see party spirit loose its hold on human frailties in their own day, or in any day before the millennium shall have risen and men's minds shall have been softened and broadened into amity and harmony by its beneficent influences. Most men of sober, practical thought, men of affairs who are not given to sentiment of any kind, are prone to believe, though often very much against their wills, that party strife is inseparably incident to free representative institutions. If they are mistaken, it is because they cannot see the future, not because they are ignorant of the past. History furnishes no example of popular government without parties; and if we are to get rid of parties we must accomplish the riddance without the aid of experience.

The present condition of parties in this country is such as to make the wish to be rid of them a very natural one, and such as very properly to quicken the anxiety of patriotic citizens. The spirit of faction seems to be running maddest riot. There is daily justification of the statement, now everywhere made and believed, that parties are organized merely to carry elections, not to carry measures of policy—banded together for plunder, their appetites sharp for the good things of the treasury. When one comes now-a-days to speak of the administration of our national government, the word that springs first to his lips is the word *corruption* and when the mind, recalling the primitive purity of our institutions and the one-time uprightness of those who stood foremost in our public service, begins to question the widespread presentiment of approaching trouble and to search out the secret of the later decline, the finger of every witness points full at that hateful motto:

"To the victor belong the spoils." The system which Jackson originated and Grant perfected has stolen away our political virtue and
sold us into political bondage. Said Daniel Webster in 1832, as he
stood by the cradle of this patronage of office which now has grown
so great, *"Sir, if this course of things cannot be checked, good men
will grow tired of the exercise of political privileges. They will have
nothing to do with popular elections. They will see that such elections are but a mere selfish contest for office, and they will abandon the government to the scramble of the bold, the daring, and
the desperate."*

Mr. Webster, indeed saw clearly the times that were to come.
But he saw more. He saw how and why they were to come. He saw,
as he said, that

> The unlimited power to grant office, and to take it away, gives
> a command over the hopes and fears of a vast multitude of men.
> It is generally true, that he who controls another man's means of
> living controls his will. Where there are favours to be granted,
> there are usually enough to solicit for them; and when favours
> once granted may be withdrawn at pleasure, there is ordinarily
> little security for personal independence of character. The power
> of giving office thus affects the fears of all who are in, and the
> hopes of all who are out. Those who are *out* endeavour to distin-
> guish themselves by active political friendship, by warm personal
> devotion, by clamorous support of men in whose hands is the
> power of reward; while those who are *in* ordinarily take care that
> others shall not surpass them in such qualities or such conduct as
> are most likely to secure favour. They resolve not to be outdone
> in any of the works of partisanship. The consequence of all this
> is obvious. A competition ensues, not of patriotic labours; not of
> rough and severe toils for the public good; not of manliness, inde-
> pendence, and public spirit; but of complaisance, of indiscrimi-
> nate support of executive measures, of pliant subserviency, and
> gross adulation. All throng and rush together to the alter [*sic*] of
> man-worship; and there they offer sacrifices, and pour out liba-
> tions, till the thick fumes of their incense turn their own heads,
> and turn, also, the head of him who is the object of their idolatry.
> The existence of parties in a popular government is not to be
> avoided; and if they are formed on constitutional questions, or in
> regard to great measures of public policy, and do not run to ex-
> cessive length, it may be admitted that, on the whole, they do no
> great harm. But the patronage of office, the power of bestowing
> place and emoluments, creates parties, not upon any principle or
> any measure, but upon the single ground of personal interest. Un-
> der the direct influence of this motive, they form round a leader,
> and they go for "the spoils of victory." And if the party chieftain
> becomes the national chieftain, he is still but too apt to consider
> all who have opposed him as enemies to be punished, and all who
> have supported him as friends to be rewarded. Blind devotion to

party, and to the head of a party, thus takes the place of the sentiment of generous patriotism and a high and exalted sense of public duty.

For a complete picture of the present state of parties in this country we need not go beyond these notable words of Webster's. His prophecy is fulfilled. The administration of the national government has, for the very reasons that he pointed out, fallen into great dishonour; the public service, already corrupt beyond any precedent of its own history, is daily growing more corrupt; and all men know that to enter politics is to hazard character. This is the universal verdict; and one may assert these things now without thought of hearing voices of dissent from any save those whose honesty is directly impeached. The "nay, nay" will come only from the office-holders—or, perhaps, feebly and good-humouredly, from representatives of that dull and comfortable class of people to whom this world and everything in it seem the best and most desirable, and who think to be charitable by being blind.

This is a very dark picture, but it certainly affords no reasonable suggestion of despair. Shadows there are in every life-like picture; and when we perceive the corruption which pervades, as with a prevailing darkness, the high places of the land, it is well to reflect that the fact that this darkness is discerned is itself proof that there is somewhere light with which it stands in contrast, and worth while to resolve so to light up the truth by every lawful endeavour as to make it illumine the darkest places of corruption and make sweet by its influence the darkest spots of intrigue and covert dishonesty. It would be neither brave nor sensible to relinquish hope and cry out that the evil is without remedy. We ought not to run from the danger, but to face it and turn it away. Mr. Webster set us the example. He knew that "the existence of parties in a popular government is not to be avoided," and would have had the country set about cleansing, purifying, and controlling its parties.

The danger consists not in the existence of parties, but in the existence of corrupt parties; and the salvation of the government depends, not upon the abolition of parties, but upon their proper control. If our parties were so open in their operations that the nation could see what they do and why they do it, their purity would be ensured, because their responsibility would be complete. Dishonesty cannot long walk with impunity in open day. It is only in secret and covered places, under the veil of night or within barred and shuttered privacy, that conscious rogues dare to conceive or execute their plans. Where they are seen of men they must wear

cloak's of decency, con smooth words of honesty, and profess fair
purposes of integrity. Public opinion is overwhelmingly on the side
of christian principle, and such principle is a force even in politics. Wherever public opinion can get leave to come, there must
uprightness rule. Whenever the nation is thoroughly informed, its
prevailing voice is the voice of truth. Often and again often—in
times and at seasons without calculable number—popular clamour
has been even outrageously unreasonable; but it has erred only in
moments of sudden passion, or upon questions the whole truth
concerning which it had not stopped to learn, and about which, in
cooler moments, it has afterwards come to think very different
things. Its final, calm conclusion is always squared by the truth.

Anyone who will look the history of party excesses in this country straight in the face must come to the conclusion that those excesses have grown great and are growing greater because those
who preside over them are not within reach of public opinion. The
country seldom knows clearly what Congress is doing, and, when
it does know, has no satisfactory, adequate, or effective means of
holding anybody responsible for what was done. Let us see how this
is: Is not the reading public much more conversant with the particulars of every principal crime that startles any portion of the
Union than it is with the most important transactions of our national policy? Crimes are paraded; legislation is ignored. In connection with no subject of legislation is popular ignorance greater
or more conspicuous than in connection with that which is the
most important of all, the federal finances. Unquestionably the
subject of revenue and expenditure is one of those paramount
subjects of governmental administration which it behooves every
citizen to observe with constant and careful heed. The expenses
of the nation are to the tax-paying citizen only less important than
his own private outlays; but the tax-payer does not realize this
with reference to all taxes. He is conscious that he is pestered with
direct taxes; but he is not sensible of any feeling of enmity towards
indirect taxes; he is, apparently, not aware that he is daily contributing to swell the revenues which pour into the custom-house
coffers. If the government openly claim but a quarter of a cent of
every dollar of his income, he puts his hand very tardily and pro-
testingly into his pocket, and thinks government altogether too
costly a luxury anyhow. If he must pay so much upon the value
of his land, so much upon his horse, so much upon his stocks and
bonds, so much for the privilege of displaying jewelry upon his
person, and so much for the water which fills his bath-tub, he does
so only because there is a *must* attached to it, and is sure that the

sheriff's receipt for the paltry sums is complete and irrefraga-
ble documentary proof of the extortionate overtaxation which he
burns to see mitigated. But not so of the indirect taxation which
swells every item of the expenses of his household and his trade.
Of that he seldom makes complaint. These indirect taxes are in
reality much harder masters than are their brothers, the direct
taxes; but he does not feel their mastery. They are cunning. They
conceal their overlordship. They do not render their authority offensive by sending the blunt sheriff to levy their revenues. They
collect their subsidies through suaver agents, through manufacturers and shop-keepers, through mechanics and tradesmen. When
one buys some sugar, or a suit of clothes, or a hammer and some
nails, or a new plow, he does not realize that he is paying taxes.
But paying taxes he is, "for a' that." He is paying without complaint taxes ten-fold greater than he ever grumblingly paid to the
sheriff. He is paying them because it is thought necessary by the
government to have a custom-house at every sea-port of entry. He
is paying them not so much because the national treasury stands
in need of money as because certain citizens who are engaged in
manufacture stand in need of wealth. When he pays thirty dollars
for a suit of clothes which he might get from Canada or from
England for (say) twenty dollars, he does so because the tailors of
the Union say they need the extra ten dollars to enable them to
carry on their trade. In order that prices may be kept at comforta-
bly profitable figures for our tailors, the Canadian importer must
pay, to the agents whom the government keeps at every point of
usual crossing on the border, thirty *per cent.* of the value of his
goods for the privilege of bringing them accross the line; and for
like privilege of importation the English importer must pay a like
percentage to similar officers at the ports. The farmer pays two
dollars for his indispensable jack-knife because the equally good
knife which is sold in England by the Sheffield manufacturer for
one dollar and thirty cents cannot be brought into this country
unless the custom-house officers be paid one half its value. This is
evidence of the interest taken by Congress in the business affairs
of the knife-makers of the country. And thus it is with everything
of daily use. The fatherly instincts of Congress are large. Every
manufacturer is thus "protected" against foreign competition: so
that it would seem that, after all that has been said about the
generous wages paid in this country, the mechanic who receives
two dollars a day here is really no better paid than the English
mechanic who receives only four shillings, or one dollar, for the
same time; because all the articles of common use which the

American artizan is constrained to buy carry the burden of an average duty of almost fifty *per cent.*, and two dollars go little farther here than four shillings will go in England.

These, then, are the indirect taxes which are so grievous, and yet so subtle that none realizes how grievous they are. They are the principal sources of national revenue. By their side the direct taxes are absolutely puny. The national government, indeed, levies very few direct taxes. It leaves those unloved claims to be made by the States, reserving to itself the pleasanter paths of customs revenue. Surely, then, it is in these paths that Congress needs to be looked after, lest it go at too headlong a pace. One can ill afford to be either ignorant or disregardful of these tremendous indirect taxes which so easily eat up half of his income. It will do small good to grumble at the vexations of direct taxes, if one is to allow his purse to be opened wide by these cunning customs. Manifestly this public income which draws upon every man's private income, and this public expenditure which limits every man's private expenditure are matters of the most vital importance; and the control which the people exercise over both income and expenditure can reasonably be taken as a just criterion of the safety and efficiency of government.

No better test of the excellence of our methods of government can, therefore, be devised than this: the ascertainment of the extent to which the people are enabled by those methods to superintend the financial policy of Congress. This can be made to appear in the course of answers to the following questions: How does Congress regulate receipts and expenditures? Who is responsible for the handling of the vast sums of the national revenues? and, How much control have the taxed over the amounts they are to pay, directly to federal tax-collectors or indirectly to custom-house officials, for the blessings of government and the maintenance of manufactures? The answers to these questions can be most conveniently approached by means of answers to these other inquiries: Who are the beneficiaries of the system of indirect taxation, called the protective system? and, Are the moneys derived from these taxes really needed to defray the current expenses of the government, or are they in large part what they seem to be, subsidies granted to private citizens for the advancement of private enterprises?

Some of these highly interesting questions can be quickly and easily answered. It is plain to see who the beneficiaries of the protective system are. That the revenues collected at the sea-ports and on the Canadian borders are not needed to defray the expenses of government is demonstrated by the fact that, not with-standing lavish outlays upon all the branches of the public service, an annual surplus of many millions usually invites Congress to indulge in every whim and excess of extravagance. Were the raising of revenue the chief object of this protective system, it is quite evident that more might be raised by the imposition of low than by the charge of high duties on imported goods. Foreign steel manufacturers who now are forced to pay seventy-six cents on every dollar's worth of steel that they send to American markets might be counted on to ship many million tons more to their "Yankee cousins" than they now do, if the duty were reduced by one half or two thirds. So might the makers of other things one half of whose value has to be paid for the privilege of displaying them on American counters or retailing them in American shops. The principle is a very simple, every-day principle. A man who covets a certain privilege will take advantage of it much oftener if it is accorded to him on easy terms than if it is yielded him on ex-tortionate conditions. A cheap show pays much better, in the long run, than a dear one. The man who is content to make small profits will amass a fortune much more surely, and generally much more quickly, than the man who is always grasping after big dividends. And when it is considered that, if only so much duty were charged as the necessities of revenue might from time to time demand, the temptation to smuggle would be in great part taken away and the Treasury relieved of the expense of maintaining those revenue cut-ters which lie in and prowl about the sea-ports like so many un-easy watchdogs, it becomes evident that high duties are themselves a source of great outlay on the part of the government and not a fountain of income only.

Obviously the government does not profit by the protective sys-tem. On the contrary, it may safely be said that the government's efficiency is considerably impaired by that system. For, by collect-ing millions more than is required to meet the expenditures of ad-ministration such a temptation to indulge in heedless extrava-gance, covert peculation, open jobbery, and shameless fraud is offered to Congress and to the not-too-scrupulous officers of the executive departments as they cannot—at least, as they *do* not—often resist. Fat millions of surplus would jeopard the honesty of any body of men within whose easy reach they might come.

The protective system, then, has been brought into being by the necessities of the manufacturers, not by the necessities of the gov-ernment. The farmers of the West and the South pay for every im-plement they use prices which are arbitrarily and artificially raised in order that those who manufacture those implements on this side the Atlantic may be secure in a driving trade; and the manufacturers must in their turn consent that the price of their bread may be somewhat advanced in order that foreign wheat may be put at a disadvantage. It is easy, therefore, to answer the two preliminary questions propounded: Private enterprises are the beneficiaries of the protective system, and that system is what it seems to be, a system of subsidies offered to them, and to them alone. It is founded upon the *paternal* idea of government. It exists because the opinion has taken root in this country that it is a proper function of government to offer pecuniary aid to private endeavour. The old and safe doctrine, that government should never do for its citizens that which they can as well or better do for themselves, has been abandoned, and factories are now built and supported by the hand of government. Revenue is made incidental to "protection."

Now, whether protection be wise or foolish, necessary or burdensome, effective or obstructive, it is at least a policy of potent influences and far-reaching results, carrying in its pouch a vast scheme of taxation which stretches out a hand toward every man's pocket; and if the people have no voice in its management they have lost control of taxation and are little better off than if they were not self-governed. Much interest attaches, therefore, to the question which now comes in its turn to be answered: *How does Congress regulate taxation and expenditure?*

When one comes to answer this supremely interesting and important question he is constrained to make a somewhat extensive tour of explanation and illustration before venturing upon a categorical statement. Of course, as everybody familiarly knows, there are annual appropriations for the running expenses of the government. Congress every year votes supplies to cover what are expected to be the necessary outlays of the several Departments. Estimates of the amounts called for are made by the officers of the Departments and by them submitted to the proper committees of Congress. Take, for example, the usual course of appropriation for some one of the Departments. Suppose that it is the season for the submission of estimates in the Navy Department. By the aid of his subordinates, the Secretary of the Navy prepares a statement of the amount needed in each branch of his Department for the current year, and this statement is submitted by the House to its Appropriations Committee. When considered and approved by this Committee, it is returned to the House in the form of a general Appropriation Bill for the Navy—a bill which the rules of the House command the Committee to report within thirty days* after the opening of each annual session of Congress. Having received the approval of the House, the Appropriation Bill is sent in due course to the Senate, is considered by the Senate's Committee on Appropriations, and, under its sanction, receives the approving vote of the upper House and is ready for the signature of the President. As soon as the President's name is officially added to it, it becomes a[n] Act of Congress and is law.

Appropriations for the Navy may from time to time be swelled at the recommendation of the Committee on Naval Affairs, to which are referred "all matters which concern the naval establishment," and which is generally father to such schemes as the enlargement or rehabilitation of Navy. The disbursements of moneys appropriated for the use of the department are under the superintendence of the Committee on Expenditures in the Navy Department, whose duty it is to take care that such disbursements are according to law, and that the accounts of the department are free from mistake, irregularity, or fraud.

But committees on appropriations, it will be observed, advise only what moneys are to be spent, and have no suggestions to offer as to how the moneys needed are to be raised. These suggestions must come from the House Committee on Ways and Means and must pass under the eyes of the Senate's Committee on Finance. These two committees are charged with the weighty duty of advising the bodies they respectively represent as to the methods of taxation most proper or convenient for producing the revenue demanded by the recommendations of the spending committees. It is these committees, therefore, which are the foster-fathers of our manufactures. They do not, in the exercise of their sovereign discretion, see fit to confine themselves to the hum-drum duty of scraping together just revenue enough to meet the running expenses of the government. They find and delight in a much wider sphere of activity in dispensing government favours to the industries of the country.

The long course of committee scrutiny through which departmental estimates have to go before they become embodied in a[n] act of appropriation would seem to offer every possible bar to extravagant expenditure. Quite sufficient opportunity to control taxation would seem to be within reach of Congress through its Committees of Ways and Means and Finance. Certainly the various committees concerned have powers and privileges enough in

* The word "days" was inserted in pencil, and probably was not in the text submitted to the publisher. The sentence is phrased differently in WW's earlier draft. [Eds.' note.]

connection with the duties assigned them. They are the governing
bodies in these matters and unquestionably they have as much authority as can safely be entrusted to governors. Virtually they wield
the whole power of Congress. But then it is a fact worth writing
on the oftest-turned page of the memory, that the action of the
Standing Committees is no more the action of Congress, in reality,
than the votes of Congress are the declarations of the people. In
fact Congress is not as free to debate the recommendations of its
Committees as are the people, through the press, to discuss the
doings of Congress. Sometimes, indeed, the report of some committee touches upon a question which Congressmen on both sides
of the House and at both ends of the capitol have scented out as
a leading issue in an approaching campaign, and upon that question they are content to sit for days together, sending to the constituencies speeches which may serve as personal and party "record" in the days when the policies of individuals and of parties
come to be questioned at the polls. But most committee reports
are hurried through the House after a few speeches by the members of the reporting committee, or altogether without debate.

Now, it is safe to say that *publicity* is more to be valued in the
administration of government than wisdom which works in secret
or prudence which rules in private inner chambers which the
ruled are not permitted to approach. Especially is this true in the
delicate and invidious matter of taxation. A people watchful to
preserve their liberties would much rather have all their treaties
broken and all their relations with the rest of the world thrown
into the veriest hurly-burly of confusion than have their commerce
fettered and embarrassed or their pockets exorbitantly levied on.
They would rather know why and how they are taxed and how
their money is spent than anything else about the conduct of their
government; and evidently their solicitude in this matter is a very
proper one. Taxation is the principal joint of government. Upon
that its efficiency depends. About that all its functions turn. If that
be unhinged, the machine is useless. Hence the paramount importance of those Committees of Ways and Means and of Finance,
and of those spendthrift Appropriations Committees. It behooves
the public to keep an eye upon them rather than upon any others
of the Committees which make up the working force of Congress.
They hold the fortunes of the government in their hands, and if
they are irresponsible the government may go far away from legitimate paths before the country is aware that anything is amiss.

Unfortunately, however, the committees are not easily watched.
As has already been said, they generally sit with closed doors, in

unapproachable privacy. Often they meet in absolute secrecy. Their conclusions, of course, are known; but how and why they concluded thus and so remains too often a secret. A committee sits very much as does a jury, and if anything more than its verdict become known, it is discovered through the talkativeness of some too-indiscreet committee-man, or by the unabashed inquisitiveness of some wily and indefatigable reporter. Occasionally, indeed, a committee rejoices in the excitement of an open investigation of the conduct of some government official. When instructed to inquire into executive transactions or election frauds, it sometimes relishes opening its doors to the public. Especially does it feel constrained to do so when the witnesses summoned or volunteering are persons of conspicuous station or notorious character, concerning whose testimony the country may, for some reason, manifest an interest or a curiosity. On such occasions, it seldom refuses to accommodate itself to the wishes of the newspapers by admitting such reporters as can best cater to the public appetite for scandal. But committees will not always do even this. Nothing that will damage the party of the majority will be allowed to see the light, however clamorous the country may be for the truth of the matter. And, even after publicly taking testimony, a committee generally prefers to resume its natural character of inscrutable jury, and frame its verdict in safe and shielding privacy. It is under no compulsion to deliberate in public. It may follow its own preferences, confessing or hiding its methods and its motives as suits and pleases it best.

Now, the public would much prefer to be present at the deliberations of these omnipotent legislating committees, and especially at the sittings of the taxing and disbursing committees. Since they transact the nation's most important business, it is very desirable that the doors and windows of their rooms should be open, so that the nation might come in and see, or at least stand without and hear, how they direct matters of such pith and moment. Or, if that cannot be, if, perchance, the doors and windows are narrow or not easily accessible, it would be gratifying to hear Congress debate the reports which come from the committee rooms until all possible light was shed upon them, until Congressmen themselves, if not the public, were enabled to understand quite thoroughly the foundation of policy on which every Act was based and all the considerations, whether of expediency or of principle, which spoke either for or against each measure of the session.

But that Congress should actually discuss at length every matter of its business that is not merely trivial or of routine is a very outrageously absurd and impracticable suggestion in the opinion of some people—even of some very sensible people. There are, for instance, in Congress and out of it, men whose long experience in legislative bodies has made them familiar with all the vexatious delays to which legislation is subject when strict and restrictive rules of procedure are lacking; and familiarity with such delays breeds intolerance of them. Such men dread freedom of debate because they know that it is liable to great abuse. They regard it as a convenient tool for the garrulous and the obstructive. 'Why,' they exclaim, 'if Congress were to set itself no limit in the discussion of committee reports, the result would be intolerable. Congress would become a mere talking machine. Don't cant about freedom of discussion: Congress must get through its business, and that is the end of the matter. Give members leave to talk and the business of legislation would be at a stand-still. Absolute freedom of discussion can be used for purposes of vexatious delay. It is a power in the hands of a discontented minority by means of which they can always harass the majority and often altogether defeat its will. All progress can be clogged by the wagging of tongues that love to wag. No, no! If you want freedom of discussion, you must content yourself with the newspapers, the lecture platform, the stump—the pulpit, if you like. Congress is no place for endless talk. If it were not protected against the talkers, its noisy, fruitless, and endless sessions would become a nuisance against which the country would have a right to cry out.'

But, then, it ought to be remembered that these vexations of tedious debate and obstructive tactics are not without their compensating, their overbalancing advantages—advantages against which no mere inconveniences ought ever to be weighed. Little legislation, slow and much talked about, is a thousand times to be preferred to much legislation, prompt and not talked about at all. Legislation would be much freer from stain and folly were Congress to confine itself to passing but half a dozen well-considered bills a year—bills which it had examined piece by piece, had long rolled under its tongue, and had thoroughly digested—than it is now when Congress yearly swallows by the score, whole and undigested, measures equally without number and without merit. Happily there are in this country no hosts of great topics of vital concern and pressing importance importuning quick legislative action for their settlement. There are no iron-bound land-laws fettering our agricultural interests, such as baffle statesmen and puzzle legislators in England. We have no Ireland crying out to us to right her wrongs and mitigate her miseries. We have no established church hanging on to the skirts of our government, a pestering ward. We are not troubled by vast Indian provinces yearly threatening to become desperately bankrupt. We are not confronted with the problem of a House of Lords which we scarcely dare to abolish, yet which we are very loath to keep in authority. We have no re-adjustment of the franchise to set about from time to time. We started free from all these trammels and anxieties and perplexities. What flock of questions that will not wait is beseiging the doors of Congress? What matters warrant helter-skelter haste? None. Absolutely none. The more deliberately Congress proceeds the more acceptably to the people will its action be. The more it talks about what it is doing and what it intends to do, the greater will its usefulness be. The country wants debates that will instruct it, debates that will keep alive its interest in all the affairs of government, debates that will give fullest play to every sentiment and fullest weight to every opinion that may find voice in Congress. It wants its legislative concerns talked about not only till all Washington shall ring and resound with the voices of the contest, till visiting foreigners shall throng the galleries of House and Senate to be witnesses of the gallant passages at arms, but till the entire country shall have been roused to attention and to interest, till the Pacific slope shall have felt the impulses which have crossed the continent from Washington, and Texas shall have heard and cheered the contestants

In short, it is imperatively necessary that Congress should itself master the details of legislation, instead of leaving that duty to its committees, and that it should exhibit in the eyes of the country the utmost diligence and thoroughness in canvassing the details of every piece of work it undertakes to do. At present it falls very far short of doing this, as is abundantly illustrated by the usual course of financial legislation. For when we come, after our long tour of explanation and illustration of the ways of Congress and its committees—ways often so obscure and so hard to find out—to frame an answer to the postponed question, *How does Congress regulate taxation and expenditure?* it becomes clear that we must say that, practically, *Congress* does not regulate these things at all, but that they are regulated by several fragments or fractions of Congress called Standing Committees, and that these much-trusted Standing Committees execute their trusts quite privately, away from the public eye and the public ear.

It is only by very clumsy and roundabout methods that the people can be informed as to the way in which their money is spent. The estimates submitted by the departments are not discussed or examined in public; they are not scrutinized in Congress, where by free criticism they could be made clear and intelligible to the taxpayers, but are conned and passed upon in the privacy of committee rooms. There are no adequate means of public audit. Nay, there is no public audit at all. When appropriations are made, in compliance with the demands of the departmental estimate, Congress has no ready means of ascertaining whether or not the moneys granted have been used as ordered, whether or not they have actually been employed for the purposes for which they were said to be needed. If doubts be entertained concerning the spending methods of any one of the departments, the appropriate committee must be authorized to examine the accounts and question the employés of the department, to learn, if possible, in what way the large sums incautiously and improvidently voted for "contingent expenses" have been expended. Scandalous revelations of peculation and fraud are often made in the course of such investigations; but little comes of them. The investigating committee seldom shows any strong disposition to enlighten the public. Perhaps the chief officials of the mistrusted department are of the same political party as are the majority of the committee, and the report of the latter therefore reveals nothing more censurable than carelessness on the part of the heads of the department, visiting the condemnation of malfeasance and embezzlement upon some poor devil of a subordinate who could have been nothing more than a tool in stronger hands. Or, if the testimony is irresistably damaging to all concerned, it is offered to Congress and the public in a report so voluminous that none but the leisurely, the curious, and the indefatigable, the enterprising searcher for news or the hungry for scandal, can extract aught of information from its unwieldy volumes. Besides, the whole matter generally stops short with the investigation. No one is ever punished, beyond the punishment of the disclosure.

Thus it is that Congress does not and cannot regulate expenditure. Nor does it often exercise any more vigilant supervision over receipts, that is over taxation. It seldom troubles itself to get at the merits of the policies from session to session advocated by the Committees of Ways and Means and of Finance. Not that this matter of receipts is less influential in filling or emptying the public purse than are the items of expenditure. However the revenue may be raised, whether by what is known—and known to be disliked—as direct taxation or by what is easily, because ignorantly, endured under the name of indirect taxation, it is equally and always a burden laid upon the governed and should be carefully kept within bounds by governors. But in all these things Congress defers to its committees.

These taxing committees may do infinite mischief if they be not watched. They are handling edged tools when handling the taxes. Mr. Gladstone, the greatest of English financiers, in the masterly speech by which, as Chancellor of the Exchequer, he introduced to Parliament his financial statement for the year 1861, playfully described direct and indirect taxes as two sisters—daughters of Necessity and Invention—"differing only as sisters may differ, . . . the one being more free and open, the other somewhat more shy, retiring, and insinuating," and frankly owned that, whether from "a lax sense of moral obligation or not," he, as a Chancellor of the Exchequer, "thought it not only allowable, but even an act of duty, to pay his addresses to them both." Two such sisters, of similar charms and like characters, have made a home amongst us also here in America, and to them the chairmen of our Standing Committees of Ways and Means and Finance, our two acting Chancellors of the Exchequer, are eager to pay assiduous court. The parentage of these two seductive American sisters is not, however, the same as that ascribed by Mr. Gladstone to the English sisters. Our friends were fathered by Monopoly rather than by Necessity, though Invention was their mother also. Necessity cannot pretend to be the father of *surpluses,* at any rate. Being confessedly meant as taxes for the support of certain manufactories of the country, the surpluses which flow in such abundant streams into our national treasury can claim none other than Monopoly for father. By whomsoever begotten, they are, at best very mischievous offspring. They tempt the spending committees of Congress to spendthrift habits. They call cormorant pension-seekers from every quarter of the Union. They crowd the lobbies of the capitol with importunate petitioners for subsidies—subsidies for steamship lines and subsidies for rail-road construction, subsidies for every considerable private enterprize. They warrant the Senate in voting millions for public buildings within ten minutes, and the House in pensioning hundreds of unhonored claimants at one vote.*

* "It is a mistake to suppose that Congress acts on few bills. The other day the House passed thirty-seven pension bills at one sitting. The Senate, on its part, by unanimous consent, took up and passed in about ten minutes seven bills providing for public buildings in different States, appropriating an aggregate of $1,200,000 in this short time. A recent House feat was one in which a bill allowing 1,300 war claims in a lump was passed. It contained 119 pages full of little claims, amounting in all to $291,000; and a member, in deprecating criticism on this disposition of them, said that the committee had received ten huge bags full of such claims, which had been adjudicated by the Treasury officials, and it was a physical impossibility to examine them. Such is the existing system of legislation"—N. Y. *Sun,* 1881. [WW's note.]

But these are not the worst things that can be charged against those who fill coffers already over-full. However insinuating and retiring these sly indirect taxes may be, they are taxes "for a' that"; and they are taxes of the most burdensome sort withal, for their weight falls most directly and most heavily on the poor and is least felt by the rich. The charges on imports, by raising the prices of all the most ordinary articles of use and consumption, empty the pockets of the poor, in order that no lowering of prices by foreign competition may empty the pockets of the rich whose trades such competition would affect. If these subtle, masked, stealthy indirect taxes were all the children of honest old Necessity, their claims upon us would be and should be acknowledged without grudge or grumble; but one would like to have some means of humbling the pride and repudiating the claims of these arrogant surpluses; and the public are justified in feeling very uneasy so long as two only half-watched committees may multiply these surpluses or reduce them, nurse or dismiss them, at pleasure.

If, when it is discovered that the "contingent fund" of a department has been spent in repairs on the Secretary's private residence, for expensive suppers spread before the Secretary's political friends, for lemonade for the delectation of the Secretary's private palate, for bouquets for the gratification of the Secretary's busiest allies, for carpets never delivered, "ice" never used, and services never rendered,* any citizen is led to regret that Congress never subjects the estimates and expenditures of the departments to the cleansing test of long and particular and public discussion, much more must he deplore its omission to put the methods and results of taxation to a similar test of repeated debate. Is it not a crying abuse that such matters are so habitually determined in the half-secrecy of committee rooms?

And now this question stands up to be answered: *Who is responsible for the handling of the vast revenues of the national government and for the handling of the coveted surpluses?* The officials of the Treasury Department and the disbursing committees, the several committees on Expenditures, are responsible—but principally the Treasury officials. Responsible to whom? Theoretically to the President, whose servants they are: for the Constitution knows no executive officer save the President. In the eye of the fundamental law, the Treasury is but a department of the Presidency. But, extra-constitutionally, these officials are, indirectly and in an essentially cloudy manner, answerable to Congress, that is to its committees, and their doings are, therefore, known only

* See report of Mr. Windom's committee, 47th Congress. [WW's note.]

to those who have industrious enough courage to wade through the thousand-paged reports of these many-headed masters of theirs: for these things may be learned by the grace of the committees, and in no other way in ordinary times.

The last question is this: *What control, then, have the taxed over taxation.* It can now be quickly and tersely answered. They have just as much control over taxation as they have over the committees which tax. How much that is explanations already made will enable any one to estimate who is quick at the calculation of minus quantities.

Sufficient illustration of the usual methods of Congressional work has now been given to afford ample ground for a consideration of the merits and demerits of committee government. Its merits may, possibly, be most readily estimated by means of a negative process: that is, by reckoning first its defects, and thus leaving its excellencies as a sort of remainder. If, after subtracting its faults, anything of its substance be left, that remnant may be regarded as representing its virtues.

Well, its heaviest condemnation must result from the fact, already so often made prominent in this discussion, that it smothers Congressional debate. Beyond controversy is it true that in every effective system of representative institutions *debate* should be the chiefest duty of the representative body. It ought to be a mere truism, that the essential and characteristic duty of a deliberative assembly is deliberation. And what is deliberation? Not slowness, but a careful weighing of every reason which may tend this way and every reason that may tend that way when thought of action is entertained. It is consultation. It is argument for and against. It is bringing every view of a question into the light, in order that the decision sought may be conformed to knowledge and grounded on wisdom. It is a balancing of *yes* against *no*. It is a measuring of the merits of every mooted question. It is a search after the wisest plans. It is a means of giving consideration and authority to the voices of prudence and sound sense, of discretion and experience. It is thoughtful action.

That Congress, as a body, rarely deliberates is, therefore, evident enough,—as evident as that it is its duty to deliberate. And is this its duty because long and free debates represent the democratic principle of giving every member of Congress the same chance to be heard, of allowing each his turn? By no means. If it were practicable, a scheme of procedure founded on principles of natural selection such as would shut out bores and empty-pates from the privileges of the floor would be much to be preferred to all others. But, even though such rules are impossible, and long and free debates do involve much waste of precious time and do give much-to-be-regretted license to the members from Buncombe, they are indispensable and always instructive. As for the bores and spouters, the assembly that cannot protect itself against such presumers upon its patience and such squanderers of its time, except by restrictive rules which shut out also the wise and the eloquent, is little to be pitied. Long and free debates, let it be repeated, are always instructive. When they are the rule legislation is open and candid; and what is done openly is apt to be done honestly. What is done in a closet is, on the other hand, apt often to run in crooked ways, to be sneaking and dishonest. Measures matured in half-secrecy are as sure to spring from hidden motives and from purposes which will not bear to be looked into as men are sure to stumble in the dark or to be careless of their manners where they are not known; whereas with reference to measures discussed in open publicity there is sure to be a full discovery of motives and a clear avowal of purposes. Commend me to that open system under which all legislation is canvassed with no uncertain voice within the easy hearing of the whole people. If such a system were once to be established in this Union and its merits were once to become thoroughly appreciated amongst us, the bill that was withheld from debate, the party that shrunk from discussion, the policy that lurked in a corner would inevitably and speedily fall under a condemnation that would blast it. The trumpet that gave out an uncertain sound would be known as the trumpet of aliens or of enemies. 'If I am to be served by representatives, I want to be served openly,' is the sentiment of every man that sets any store by constitutional liberty. 'If I am to choose my own government, let me be governed openly and above-board; otherwise, representative government is a snare and a cheat. If I can learn what my representatives are doing, I can regulate my conduct as a citizen with intelligence and can set safe-guards about my civil rights and privileges; but if representatives will not avow their motives and their principles, I might as well give myself into the hands of a secret oligarchy: indeed, as one who prefers straightforward dealings, I would rather do so.'

Free and open debates, again, are valuable not only because they force upon Congress habits of frankness and outspokenness but also because they are one of the most effective means of educating public opinion. Committee government informs the public as to nothing; whereas everything can be known concerning legislation which passes through the ordeal of debate. Even prying, scheming, irreprovable and irrepressible newspaper reporters cannot always unearth the secrets of committees; but with free and full debates to lay bare to public inspection the springs and processes of legislation no man that glances down the news-columns of a country paper can fail to comprehend the main drift of the public business and to become familiar with some at least of the principal issues of every public question. What an education to the voter such news items would be! How much cleared the political atmosphere would become! How much health and purity sun-light would infuse into the action of parties!

Curtailment and discouragement of debate, then, seem to be—nay, do not seem to be, but *are*—the vices of committee government which make its condemnation certain. It is a system which can stand neither the test of philosophy nor the test of common-sense. Whether measured by the standards set up by those who have written with most learning and discrimination upon the philosophy of government, or by that knowledge of life and experience of affairs which are given to every man who has eyes to see or ears to hear, it is inadequate to accomplish the legitimate objects of representative government. The lack of openness alone is sufficient to damn it. If, after this greatest fault be subtracted from the worth of the system, anything of excellence remain under the name of speed, or facility, or convenience, that remainder cannot with reason be esteemed of much value. For it should be noted what a host of ugly mischiefs are covered by this cloak of privacy, and that no facile expedition of business can compensate for the license of deceit it gives.

The theory of our government is, that the laws of the Union are made by the concurrent voice and the coöperative wisdom of the Senate and the House of Representatives. The practice of our government is, that the laws of the Union are made by the concurrent voice and coöperating wisdom of fragments of the Senate and the House of Representatives. Committees make the laws and Congress votes them into currency and potency. Because, truth to tell, voting for laws is not making them. Those who frame measures, who fill them with their pith of policy, are the makers of the laws these measures embody when they have become Acts. The President does not make a law by signing it, nor Congress by voting for it. It is made by its originators. The committees are the law-makers.

Of course the committees are not to be blamed for the abuses of the system which they represent. They have not usurped the powers of the House by violence or stratagem. The House has of its own free will and accord resigned to them its privileges of debate, deliberation, and law-making. The Representatives have voluntarily vacated their functions. The rules which invest the Speaker with the much-inclusive prerogative of appointing the Standing Committees and his nominees with the potent privilege of initiative in legislation and debate, are of the House's own making. The overlordship of the committees depends entirely upon the will of the body they represent. The divinity that doth hedge them is of purely human manufacture. It is the command of the representatives of the people that in the business of legislation publicity and open dealing be sacrificed to dispatch. They cannot stay to talk. Let the committees demand a vote as soon as they please and they shall be obeyed.

III

Cabinet Government

"The only conceivable basis for government in the New World is the national will; and the political problem of the New World is how to build a strong, stable, enlightened and impartial government on that foundation"—Goldwin Smith.

"A humourist of our own day has laughed at Parliaments as 'talking shops,' and the laugh has been echoed by some who have taken humour for argument. But talk is persuasion, and persuasion is force, the one force which can sway freemen to deeds such as those which have made England what she is."—Green.

Committee government is too clumsy and too clandestine a system to last. Other methods of government must sooner or later be sought and a different economy established. First or last Congress must be organized in conformity with what is now the prevailing legislative practice of the world. English precedent and the world's fashion must be followed in the institution of Cabinet government in the United States.

Cabinet government is government by means of an executive ministry chosen by the chief magistrate of the nation from the ranks of the legislative majority—a ministry sitting in the legislature and acting as its executive committee, directing its business and leading its debates, representing the same party and the same principles, "bound together by a sense of responsibility and loyalty to the party to which it belongs," and subject to removal whenever it forfeits the confidence and loses the support of the body it represents. Its establishment in the United States would involve, of course, several considerable changes in our present system. It would necessitate, in the first place, one or two alterations of the Constitution. The second clause of section six, Article One, of the Constitution runs thus: "No Senator or Representative shall, during the time for which he was elected, be appointed to any civil office under the authority of the United States, which shall have been created, or the emoluments whereof shall have been increased, during such time; and no person holding any office under the United States shall be a member of either House during his continuance in office." Let the latter part of this clause read, "and no person holding any *other than a Cabinet* office under the United States shall be a member of either House during his continuance in office," and the addition of four words will have removed the chief constitutional obstacle to the erection of Cabinet government in this country. The way will have been cleared, in great part at least, for the development of a constitutional practice which, founded upon the great charter we already possess, might grow into a governmental system at once strong, stable, and flexible. Those four words being added to the Constitution, the President might be authorized and directed to choose for his Cabinet the leaders of the ruling majority in Congress; that Cabinet might, on condition of acknowledging its tenure of office dependent upon the favour of the Houses, be allowed to assume those privileges of initiative in legislation and leadership in debate which are now given, by almost equal distribution, to the Standing Committees; and Cabinet government would have been instituted.

To insure the efficiency of the new system, however, additional amendments of the Constitution would doubtless be necessary. Unless the President's tenure of office were made more permanent than it now is, he could not fairly be expected to exercise that impartiality in the choice of ministers, his legislative advisers and executive colleagues, which would be indispensable to good government under such a system; and no executive Cabinet which was dependent on the will of a body subject to biennial change— and which, because it is elected for only two years, is the more apt to be ruled by the spirit of faction and caught by every cunningly devised fable—could have that sense of security without which there can be neither steadiness of policy nor strength of statesmanship. It must become necessary to lengthen both Presidential and Congressional terms. If the President must expect his authority to end within the short space of four years, he must be excused for caprice in the choice of his Secretaries. If no faithfulness and diligence of his can lengthen the period of his official

authority by even so much as a single week, it cannot be reasonable to expect him to sacrifice his will to the will of others or to
subordinate his wishes to the public good during the short season
of that brief authority's secure enjoyment. And, if Cabinets be
vouchsafed but two years in which to mature the policies they may
undertake, they cannot justly be blamed for haste and improvidence. They could not safely be appointed, or safely trusted to rule
after appointment, under a system of quadrennial presidencies
and biennial legislatures. Unless both Presidential and Congressional terms were extended, government would be both capricious
and unstable. And they could be the more easily extended because
to lengthen them would be to change no *principle* of the Constitution. The admission of members of Congress to seats in the Cabinet would be the only change of principle called for.

Cabinet government has in it everything to recommend it. Especially to Americans should it commend itself. It is, first of all, the
simplest and most straightforward system of party government. It
gives explicit authority to that party majority which in any event
will exercise its implicit powers to the top of its bent, which will
snatch control if control be not given it. It is a legalization of fact;
for we are not free to choose between party government and government without party. Our choice must be between a party that
rules by authority and a party that, where it has not a grant of the
right to rule, will make itself supreme by stratagem. Party government in one form or another is inevitable; and, if it can be
legitimated and controlled, is unquestionably desirable. It is not
parties in open and legitimate organization that are to be feared,
but those which are secretly banded together, begetters of hidden
schemes and ugly stratagems. In political action, as in all other
action, men must join hand and purpose. Parties are necessary,
though not ill-favoured and illegitimate parties. "Burke admitted
that when he saw a man acting a desultory and disconnected part
in public life with detriment to his fortune, he was ready to believe such a man to be in earnest, though not ready to believe him
to be right. In any case he lamented to see rare and valuable qualities squandered away without any public utility. He admitted,
moreover, on the other hand, that people frequently acquired in
party confederacies a narrow, bigoted, and proscriptive spirit. 'But
where duty renders a critical situation a necessary one, it is our
business to keep free from the evils attendant upon it, and not to
fly from the situation itself. It is surely no very rational account
of a man that he has always acted right, but has taken special care
to act in such a manner that his endeavours could not possibly be

productive of any consequence. . . . When men are not acquainted with each other's principles, nor experienced in each other's talents, nor at all practiced in their mutual habitudes and dispositions by joint efforts of business; no personal confidence, no friendship, no common interest subsisting among them; it is evidently impossible that they can act a public part with uniformity, perseverance, and efficacy.' " "He pointed out to emulation the Whig junto who held so close together in the reign of Anne—Sunderland, Godolphin, Somers, and Marlborough—who believed 'that no men could act with effect who did not act in concert; that no men could act in concert who did not act with confidence; that no men could act with confidence who were not bound together by common opinions, common affections, and common interests.' "* There can be no doubt that that government is freest and best which makes the wisest use of parties, instead of fighting them; which gives to majorities an open authority for whose exercise they may be held responsible; which gives to party principles a salutary prominence and dignity that raise them into respect.

Parties we have now, and professions of party principle in abundance; but party responsibility we lack. American parties are seldom called to account for any breach of their engagements, how solemnly soever those engagements may have been entered into. They thrive as well on dead issues as on living principles. Are not campaigns still yearly won with the voice of war-cries which represent only by-gone feuds, and which all true men wish were as silent as the lips that first gave them utterance? "Platforms" are built only for conventions to sit upon, and fall into decay, as of course, when conventions adjourn. Such parties as we have, parties with worn-out principles and without definite policies, are unmitigated nuisances. They are savoury with decay and rank with rottenness. They are ready for no service but to be served. Their natural vocation is to debauch the public morals, to corrupt and use the people; and the people's only remedy is to be found in a stern and prompt exercise of their sovereign right. These parties must be roughly shaken out of their insolence and made to realize that they are only servants, and, being servants, will be expected and required to act with trustworthiness, with all honesty and all fidelity.

It is only by making parties responsible for what they do and advise that they can be made safe servants. But to discover the best and readiest means of making them responsible, there's the

---

* Morley's *Burke* (*Eng. Men of Letters* series) pp. 52, 53. [WW's note.]

rub! One means there is, and that perhaps the best. Let the leaders of the party be made responsible. Let there be set apart from
the party in power certain representatives who, leading their party
and representing its policy, may be made to suffer a punishment
which shall be at once personal and vicarious when their party
goes astray or their policy either misleads or miscarries. This can
be done by making the leaders of the dominant party in Congress
the executive officers of the legislative will; by making them members of the President's Cabinet, and thus at once the executive
chiefs of the departments of State and the leaders of their party
on the floor of Congress; in a word, by having done with the Standing Committees and constituting the Cabinet advisors both of
the President and of Congress.

Conservative people—and what people are, in all but outward
seeming, more conservative than Americans?—will doubtless object to the change proposed on the ground that it is too extremely
radical; and prejudiced, case-hardened patriots will, of course, cry
out against it as an attempt to introduce English institutions into
our government, to the ousting of institutions peculiarly and dearly American. A short answer will suffice for the latter. Supposing
England to be very hateful and all things English worthy of suspicion, we still should not hesitate to take even from England anything that we know to be excellent and suitable for our purposes.
We may learn even from inferiors. Besides, it happens that we are
most of us of English blood, and are, therefore, apt to have decided aptitudes for English institutions; and—oddly enough, as it
may seem to those who look upon English ideas as alien to this
commonwealth,—to borrow from England now would be only to
follow a time-honoured American example. Alexander Hamilton
has in these latter days been "severely reproached with having
said that the British government was the 'best model in existence.'
In 1787 this was a mere truism. However much the men of that
day differed they were all agreed in despising and distrusting *a
priori* constitutions and ideally perfect governments, fresh from
the brains of visionary enthusiasts, such as sprang up rankly in
the soil of the French revolution. The convention of 1787 was
composed of very able public men of the English speaking race.
They took the system of free government with which they had
been familiar, improved it, adapted it to the circumstances with
which they had to deal, and put it into successful operation. Hamilton's plan, then, like the others, was on the British model, and it
did not differ essentially in details from that finally adopted."* The

* Lodge's *Hamilton* (*American Statesmen* series), pp. 60-61. [WW's note.]

English, indeed, is as perfect a type of representative government as our own. From England we could borrow nothing unrepublican, except primogeniture, titular nobility, and hereditary kingship. Make her sovereign's office elective and her titles uninheritable life titles, and her government would be no less republican than ours. We are not likely to copy her throne or her House of Lords, and we can find nothing else to copy that would not be altogether of a piece with our own most valued methods of government. In our own system we have in some particulars improved upon the British constitution; but we have improved upon it not by adding to it so much as by not taking all of it; and so long as we continue to use only the best of it, we will be quite safe from the perils of unwise imitation.

There is some reason to believe that we do not understand representative government as well as our English cousins understand it; for is it not common in this country to hear intelligent men denounce "the tyranny of partisan majorities," and at the same time, nay almost in the same breath, speak the praises of "true representative government," without at all perceiving the laughable inconsistency of what they are saying? Representative government is only another name for government by partisan majorities; and if such government be in fact nothing better than a tyranny, this at least can be said in its behalf: that it is a form of government which we, in common with all the more enlightened peoples of the world, have deliberately chosen to live under; which has enabled us to live in secure peace and happiness through almost all the years of a century of unexampled prosperity; and which our own race proudly boasts to have established. Party majorities reign over us in municipal, in State, and in national affairs alike. Representative government is party government; and party government is partisan government. This is the only known means of self-government. This is that habit of popular rule which is surrounded by so great traditions and hallowed by so glorious memories.

Not, indeed, that Americans are altogether without excuse for their fear and hatred of the "tyranny of partisan majorities." Their error lies in thinking that there can be representative government without partisan majorities; and that error arises from confounding the government of factions with the government of parties. We have not used the forms of representative government to the best advantage, but have abused them; and it is because we have abused them, and have set up false gods in the stead of the true, that di[s]gust for our system speaks from the lips of citizens respectable both on account of their numbers and their talents. Every day we hear men speak with bitter despondency of the decadence of our institutions, of the incompetence of our legislators, of the corruption of our public officials, even of the insecurity of our liberties. These are not the notes of a tocsin which peals in the ears of only a few panic-struck brains. The whole nation seems at times to be vaguely and inarticulately alarmed, restlessly apprehensive of some impending danger. Not many years ago it required considerable courage to publicly question the principles of the Constitution; now, whenever the veriest scribbler turns his small batteries against that great charter, many wise heads are nodded in acquiescent approval. It is too late to laugh at these things. When grave, thoughtful, perspicacious, and trusted men all around us agree in deriding those "Fourth of July sentiments" which were once thought to hallow the lips of our greatest orators and to approve the patriotism of our greatest statesmen, it will not do for us, personifying the American eagle, to flap wing and scream out incoherent disapproval. If we are to hold to the old faith we must be ready with stout reasons wherewith to withstand its assailants. It will not suffice to say, 'these are the glorious works of our revered ancestors, let not profane voices be lifted up against them, nor profane hands seek to compass their destruction.' Men whose patriotism is as undoubted as our own are flinging their taunts lightly and freely at these sacred institutions of ours, and it must be that they represent a large body of our countrymen who believe that corruption and personal ambition are converting the public service into a money-making trade.

The mischief and pity of it all is that there are unquestionable facts to sustain such charges. The national Legislature which sits in authority over us wears under its guise of constitutionality the hard and hateful features of unrestrained prerogative. We are governed by a narrow oligarchy of party managers. Legislation is a continuing scheme of party aggrandizement. Our commerce is painfully hampered, and every wind of party intrigue plays fast and loose with our finances; and still we seem without recourse of remedy. Matters of public business are given into the impotent hands of men who are notoriously unworthy of trust; and still the people fail to choose any better fitted. Government is become a game of which the governed are only spectators.

These things are so because we have not "true representative government," but not because we have partisan majorities. Majorities do not rule with us. Factions are supreme, factions manipulating caucuses and managing conventions; factions sneaking in committee rooms and pulling the wires that move Mr. Speaker; factions in the President's closet and at governors' ears. There are no great harmonious party majorities. Cliques combine, and "bosses" manage. We have not party but personal government; and we have this because we have no means of keeping politicians to a strict accountability. Our parties are not drilled and marshalled in great combinations because they have no controlling common interest. They run around men in high office and combine to keep irresponsible power—a power which they use to foist favourites into office, not to perfect schemes of statesmanship.

These facts bring much of shame, much of sorrow, and much of discouragement home to us; but to the brave they suggest no cause for dispair. We are undoubtedly fallen upon times of grave crisis in our national affairs; but what is wrong will be righted and what is corrupt cleansed as surely as every day's sun rises and passes on to its setting. Ours is not a race that will tamely allow its liberties to be overthrown. Already discussion of the evils that beset and distress us is assuming a definite shape and uttering a determined voice. Incoherent grumblings and passionate appeals are giving place to calm suggestions of remedy and distinct plans of reform. Echoes of these discussions have been caught even beyond sea, and foreigners are pricking up their ears to hear what it is that we are about to do. They realize that great changes are a-making.

Prominent amongst the most recent and most significant propositions of reform is an incisive essay entitled "A True Republic," from the pen of Mr. Albert Stickney of New York.* This is a book which is easily understood. Mr. Stickney's style is very clear, very pointed, and very manly. He speaks in a manner at once so direct and so candid that it would require some ingenuity to misconstrue what he says. Speaking broadly, his subject may be said to be the present prostitution of our government and the capital needs of our situation. This subject he handles with great fearlessness and considerable skill, brushing away with right vigorous contempt the patent inconveniences of hereditary monarchy; pointing out with discriminating care the defects of parliamentary government; demonstrating with distinctness and strength most of the weaknesses of our own system; exposing with justice and without passion the core-rottenness of American parties; examining with quiet common-sense and sober sagacity the simple business principles on which he conceives true government to rest; and naming

---

* "A True Republic," by Albert Stickney; New York, Harper Bros., 1879. [WW's note.]

with unhesitating frankness and inviolable consistency the radical remedies which he advocates.

As Mr. Stickney himself confesses, however, the changes which he urges are not such as are likely to meet with ready acceptance. The palm-tree is not less native to the poles that is his scheme to our political temper and habits. He throws his doctrines right in the teeth of all the traditions of our race. He would have *permanence in office during good behaviour for all public servants*. His plan would include a President elected by the people through an Electoral College which should meet and "be the judge of the elections and qualifications of its members, as either House of Congress is"—a President holding office for life, or until "removed for misconduct or inefficiency" by the Legislature; a Legislature whose members should retain their seats during good behaviour and have it within their power to remove the President or any other government official "for any misconduct or for any failure on his part to give good and satisfactory results"—a Legislature which should have "absolute control of the money" and "absolute power, in its supreme discretion, of making *all necessary laws*," and of regulating the duties of all public officials; and an Executive organization officered by Secretaries, appointed by the President, and subordinates, appointed by the Secretaries,—an organization in which all should hold office during good behaviour and each official should be responsible to his immediate superiors for the discharge of his duties and dependent upon his diligence for promotion. The Supreme Judiciary Mr. Stickney would leave as it is.

Stated thus baldly and without explanation, Mr. Stickney's plan of reform may seem so radical as to be utterly absurd and altogether unworthy of consideration. But Mr. Stickney cannot be guilty of an absurdity. He is evidently a man of too much sterling common-sense to deal in anything simply extravagant. He is an eminently practical man and enough a man of the world to possess much of that sagacity which only long experience in affairs or keen and close observation of men can give. His book, consequently, must inevitably nettle and exasperate every reader who has resolutely nursed the opinion that our present institutions are the most perfect work of man; for he has a very rigourous logical method, and if one starts with him one must go as far as he goes. Above its foundations the superstructure of his argument seems to stand perfect and indestructible. Admit his premises to your confidence and his conclusions are sure to steal in and take possession of your convictions. It is simply impracticable to laugh his arguments down. He will come very near silencing you if you cannot successfully impeach his foundamental doctrines with a weight of reason superior to that which he unquestionably has on his side. It behooves one, therefore, to note critically upon what ground Mr. Stickney builds.

His grand fundamental assumptions are, that party government is essentially subversive of liberty and utterly incompatible with efficient administration, that it can be uprooted, and that it ought to be uprooted. Now, of course, if it be true that party government can never be anything better than what he describes it to be—the organized rule of men banded together for personal gain, for securing, by fair means or by foul, the spoils of office—every one must subscribe to his opinion, that it is and always will be an unmitigated and intolerable evil, and must heartily join with him in the hope that it may speedily be so thoroughly torn from its rootage as never again to have a chance of life. But Mr. Stickney is undoubtedly in error at each point of his position. He is wrong when he says that parties can be abolished from representative governments, and he is wrong when he pronounces parties irredeemably corrupt: therefore he is wrong when he says that they ought to be abolished. So long as we have representative government[,] party neither can be nor ought to be destroyed. It is sadly true—let it be admitted—that in this country party government has of late years sunk into a degradation at once pitiable and disastrous. But there are ways of raising and redeeming it. There are methods of exalting it to a position of salutary authority. Its rule may be rendered benignant and its power beneficent. And the way of so elevating it is plain. It may be made the best of servants by being kept constantly under the eye and authority of its master, public opinion. This can readily be made evident by a few words upon the present conditions of party government in this country.

The caucus system is now the core of that government. There are caucuses and caucuses, separating themselves into two principal kinds, *nominating* and *legislative*. Of the first sort are those small bodies, too often bands of schemers and office-holders, of idlers and small "bosses," which meet in every election district, however little, to nominate gentlemen for local offices; those larger bodies which generally work themselves into a heat of vexation and intrigue in naming insignificant men for State offices; and those great stormy conventions whose frenzy gives birth to a "ticket" for President and Vice-President of the Union. All office-holders, from town clerks through Congressmen to Presidents, are the children of caucuses of this pattern. Then there is the caucus legislative, the deliberative party committee. Representatives of the same party, assembled in Congress or in State legislature, feel bound to do whatever they do in most inviolate concert: so they whip themselves together into deliberative caucus. If any doubt at any time arise as to the proper course to be taken in regard to any pending measure, there must be secret consultation in supreme party caucus, in order that each partisan's conscience may be relieved of all suspicion of individual responsibility and the forces of the party be concentrated against the time for actual voting. The Congressional caucus rooms are the central chambers of our Constitution.

The caucus was a natural and legitimate, if not healthy, off-spring of our peculiar institutions. Legislative caucuses, and even nominating caucuses, were necessitated by the complete separa-tion of the legislative and executive departments of our govern-ment. By reason of that separation Congress is made supreme within the sphere of the federal authority. There is none to com-pete with it. To it belongs the hand of power—the power of the purse and of the law—and it has naturally stretched forth that hand to brush away all obstacles to the free exercise of its sov-ereignty. But, being master, it was at first embarrassed to find efficient means of exercising its mastery. It was from the begin-ning a rather numerous body and in order to rule with vigour it was necessary that it should itself be ruled. It was, however, so organized, and so isolated from the other branches of the federal system, as to render any authoritative personal leadership im-practicable. There could scarcely be in either House any man or body of men able from sheer supremacy of genius or influence of will to guide its actions and command its deliberations. Some man of brilliant argumentative gifts and conspicuous sagacity might gain temporary sway by reason of his eloquence or a transient au-thority by virtue of his wisdom; but, however transcendent his talents, however indisputable his fitness for the post, he could never constitute himself the *official* leader of the Legislature; nor could his fellow members ever invest him with the rights of com-mand. Manifestly, however, the Houses must have leadership of some kind. If no one man could receive the office of command, it must be given to sub-committees—to bodies small enough to be efficient and too numerous to put all power within the reach of any one of them. In such bodies, accordingly, it was vested, and so birth was given to that government by committees which now ex-ists in such supreme vigour.

That very feature of committee government which makes it seem to many persons the best conceivable legislative mechanism is the principal cause of its clumsiness and is that which makes the Congressional caucus apparently an absolute necessity. It is, that the committees are too numerous to combine for purposes of rule. They cannot act in concert. There is and can be no coöperation amongst them. Instead of acting together they most frequently work at cross purposes. There can be no unity or consistency in their policy. They are disintegrate particles of an inharmonious whole. It is in the existence of these facts that the deliberative party caucus finds its chance. If either of the national parties is to follow any distinct line of action, it must make its determinations independently of its representatives on the committees, who cannot act with that oneness of purpose which is made possible only by prevised combination. The party itself must come together in committee whenever, in critical seasons of doubt, it is necessary to assure itself of its own unity of purpose. It does so come together, and its deliberations are known as the sittings of a caucus. Such, therefore, was the natural generation of the caucus legislative.

The nominating caucus was no less naturally born. It is customary and popular, as every one knows, to denounce the whole caucus system without a single "but" or even a "peradventure." It is known as the favourite machine of "bosses" and others of that ilk, and is bluntly called an outright fraud. As a matter of fact, however, it seems to have originated with very wise and very honest men. It was devised as a fair, natural, and convenient means of deciding between the claims of rival aspirants for office. What more innocent or more proper than that voters of like sentiments should meet and determine by ballot which of several candidates of their own party should be nominated for a coveted place? It were surely better so than to witness party division and to see a party's cause defeated because of the rivalrous scramble of its members for office. Indeed, in the earliest years of the nominating caucus, so long as the citizens of the electoral districts, having the time, had the inclination to attend "primaries," the practices of the system were both incorrupt and efficient. It was in later days, when population had thickened and business competition had begun to confine men to their trades to the almost entire exclusion of everything else, that its disease and feebleness came on. Cities driven by trade do not find room for politics in their crowded marts. The bustle of busy days is apt to banish from men's minds all interests but those of bread-earning and money-massing. The village shopman may spare an evening to the caucus, but the city merchant cannot. As the steps of commerce quicken the political ardour of the trader is prone to slacken.

Besides, it must be admitted that the system had in it from the first the seeds of corruption. Scheming publicans often found it easy enough to combine to thrust unwelcome candidates on electors who were unprepared to meet, and too unskilful to thwart, parliamentary trickery. Shrewd men with no scruples could quickly turn the helplessness of mass-meetings to their own advantage. A caucus could with very little management be packed with subsidized henchmen; and facility for fraud and management of course opened up chances for playing for tempting political stakes —chances which were very attractive to all who were greedy for government salaries. To the feast flocked all the lean and hungry birds of prey, to whose nostrils the scent of the spoils was sweet, and days came in the which men were constrained to exclaim, 'Whence will deliverance come; are not these birds knawing at our very vitals?'

The caucus has thus grown, in the course of time, to be one of [the] greatest political evils that statesmen were ever called upon to deal with. Mr. Stickney justly regards it as one of the chief pillars of misgovernment. He believes that the English in adopting it, as they are beginning to do, "are just entering on that blessed era in the progress toward free government, the era of party tyranny." What remedy, then, is there for the evil? Mr. Stickney proposes one, and thereby exhibits exceptional bravery and independence of thought; for very few even of our most esteemed publicists have aught to suggest on this head. True, there is much talk afloat about the duty of good citizens to go to the "primaries" and withstand in force the iniquities of the mercenaries of machine government. Many voices are uttering very manly calls upon public opinion to assert itself and make exercise of its sovereignty; but they do not advise this multitudinous monarch, the people, how it is to act. Everybody admires outspoken denunciations of wrong and applauds exhortations to turn again to virtue and to rectitude; but very few care to go into an undiscovered country unless they be guided. The reform of governments is not an everyday business, and one would like to be taught the out-of-the-way trade. We are enjoined to the work, but no one will lead or direct. One would suppose that it must be, after all, that the means of reform are so obvious that its advocates do not deem it necessary to point them out. The people must make imperative demand to be better governed, that is all.

But there's the trouble, and the puzzle. This demand actually seems to be daily a-making. There is every reason to believe that the public mind is already quite made up. So stif[f]ly does the breeze of opinion set towards reform that nearly all the political papers of the country have long since gotten well before it, even the one-time open pirates of the spoils system busily trimming their sails, and none so bold as to beat up against it. Besides, those who are striving with all their breath to blow this wind into fiercer blasts complaisantly tell us that all who are still essaying to weather it are fast losing heart. Or, the metaphor changed, it may be said that the people has declared its will; that the land is full of heralds whose loud voices proclaim its decree. The winds seem to be bringing to each community from every quarter of the land the news that upon this great question the whole country is agreed. The nation is of one mind. What, then? Has the blow been struck? Do the rulers hear the voice of the nation, and is reform already inaugurated; or do we still wait for its coming? "If it were done when 't is done, then 't were well it were done quickly."

The fact is that in this matter, as in so many others, public opinion seems to be in danger of being disappointed of its omnipotence. Those who enjoy the "spoils system" love the caucus and do not readily bend the knee to the people; and those who hope some day to come in for the favours of that system, themselves equally in love with the caucus, cautiously draw rein and will not lead the hunters who would pursue it to its destruction. All party platforms, indeed, have civil service reform "planks"; Congress has a select committee on Civil Service Reform; and the President suggests an appropriation of money to sustain a better order of things. Possibly the country may some day be startled by learning that the government has experienced a sudden impulse of unselfish purpose and voluntarily surrendered its patronage. But there is no violent probability that any such thing will happen. Public opinion, meanwhile, is left to hum and haw in distressing embarrassment over the question, What is to be done? How is the popular will to enforce its authority? What advantage is there in being unanimous?

The truth of the matter is plain to see. This caucus on which the "spoils system" rides is a very ugly and a very unmanageable beast. He cannot be driven with a chirp, nor commanded with a word. He will obey only the strong hand and mind only the whip. To rail at him is of no good. He must be taken sternly in hand and be harnessed, whether he will or no, in our service. Our search must be for the bit that will curb and subdue him—*and that bit is Cabinet government.*

Mr. Stickney offers to do away with parties, and thereby remove altogether the caucus; but if it be impossible and undesirable that parties should pass away, we must look to the precedents of our own race for the suggestion of a remedy. Cabinet government would reduce the caucus to its proper service because it would secure open-doored government. It would not suffer legislation to skulk in committee closets and caucus conferences. Light is the only thing that can sweeten our political atmosphere—light thrown upon every detail of administration in the departments; light diffused through every passage of policy; light blazed full upon every feature of legislation; light that can penetrate every recess or corner in which any intrigue might hide; light that will open to view the innermost chambers of government, drive away all darkness from the Treasury vaults, illuminate foreign correspondence, explore national dockyards, search out the obscurities of Indian affairs, display the workings of Justice, exhibit the management of the army, play upon the sails of the Navy, and follow the distribution of the mails:—and of such light Cabinet government would be a constant and plentiful source. For consider the conditions of its existence. Debate would be the very breath of its nostrils; for the ministers' tenure of office would be dependent on the vindication of their policy. No member of a Cabinet who had identified himself with any pending measure could with self-respect continue in office after the majority, whose representative he would be, had rejected that measure by a formal and deliberate vote. If, under such circumstances, he did not at once resign, he would forfeit all claim to manly independence. For him, to remain in office would be to consent to aid in administering a policy of which he was known to disapprove, and thus to lose the respect of all honourable opponents and the support of all conscientious friends. It would be sacrificing principle to an unworthy love of office, preferring mere place to integrity, openly professing willingness to do the bidding of opponents rather than forego the empty honours of conspicuous station held without conspicuous worth. A man who held an office thus would soon be shamed into retirement; or, were no place left for shame, would be driven from his place by a scorn-laden vote.

Moreover, the members of a Cabinet would always be *united* in their responsibility. They would stand or fall together in the event of the acceptance or rejection of any measure to which they had given their joint support. Otherwise they would be no better leaders than the present Standing Committees. The differences, the disputes, and the antagonisms of the council-board would be renewed and reheated in the debates on the floor of Congress. The country would be much scandalized at seeing ministers cross swords in such contests. Personal spites would flame out in public between uncongenial ministers. There would be unseemly contests for the leadership. An ununited Cabinet could offer neither effectual guidance to the Houses nor intelligible advice to the Executive. They would be worthless altogether. Besides, without united responsibility Cabinet government would lack its most admirable and valuable feature: *responsible leadership.* Congress should have an accepted and responsible leader in the person of the chief minister of the Cabinet, the Secretary of State. He, or some one of his colleagues whom custom should nominate, must be the acknowledged head of the Cabinet, or else legislation will drift as helplessly and as car[e]lessly as it does now, for want of some one man to guide it by the authority of his position or the power of his abilities.

Manifestly, therefore, under the rule of a ministry recognizing such and so united a responsibility, there must be the utmost encouragement of debate. What incentive, what inducement, would be wanting? The power and success of a responsible ministry would depend on the ascendency of their policy, and the ascendency of their policy would depend on the suffrages of the Houses. That policy must be vindicated in the eyes of Representatives and people alike. Defeat on a measure of importance would bring the necessity of resignation, and resignation would mean the incoming of the opposition leaders to power and authority. Debate, therefore, would be sought by ministry and opposition both—by the one that the triumph of their party might be approved a righteous triumph; by the other, that that triumph might be changed into defeat and they themselves snatch victory and command. What greater earnest of party sincerity and fidelity could there be than such a system as this? No minister could afford to ignore his party's pledges. Abandoned party platforms would furnish fine material for stout party coffins, and the ranks of the opposition would supply hosts of eager undertakers. How could a Cabinet face the ordeal of debate after ignoring its promises and violating its engagements; and yet how could it escape that trial when the Opposition were demanding debate, and to decline it would be of all confessions the most craven? Always eager to assail the ministers, the champions of the Opposition would have an unquenchable zeal for the fight, and no ministry could afford to refuse them battle.

It becomes every citizen to bethink himself how essential a thing to the preservation of liberty in the republic is free and unrestricted debate in the representative body. It requires the fire of the universal criticism of the press not only but the intenser flame of expert criticism as well, to test the quality and burn away the crudities of measures which have been devised in the seclusion of the study or evolved from the compromises of disagreeing committee-men. The press is irresponsible and often—too often—venally partisan. But Representatives must criticise legislation in their own proper persons and in the presence of the knowledge that constituencies have ears, and that by any blunder of judgment or meanness of sentiment the fairest reputation may be stained and the safest prospects blasted. It is good for these things to be done in the glare of publicity. When legislation consists in the giving of a silent judgment upon the suggestions of committees or of caucuses which meet and conclude in privacy, law-making may easily become a fraud. A great self-governing people should as soon think of entrusting their sovereign powers to a secret council as to a representative assembly which refuses to make debate its principal business. It is only when the whole nation is audience to their deliberations that legislators will give heed to their ways.

Very much good might be done, as has been said, by insisting upon debates upon the reports of the Standing Committees under our present system. But there is no use insisting. No one would care much for such debates. They would mean very little. The rejection of a report would have no other result than to give its subject-matter back to the defeated committee for reconsideration, or, possibly, to postpone the question indefinitely. The committee would not even feel the rebuff, probably. No one committee-man would feel responsible for the result. Neither party would feel rebuked, for each committee is made up of members from both sides of the House. It is because of these inconveniences and these feelings that committees generally have their own way. It is most convenient to let them guide, and little can be gained by opposing them.

There is much object and rare sport, on the other hand, in assailing a responsible Cabinet. They will die game at least. They will not tamely suffer themselves to be ousted of their authority. Then, too, they do represent a party: they represent the very pick and flower of their party. In their defeat or victory the whole army of their co-partisans suffer rout or enjoy success. Between the majority which they represent and the minority to whom they are opposed every debate must become a contest for ascendency, and the introduction of each measure must open up long series of eager and anxious contest.

Here, then, is surely everything that could be desired in the way of a bit for that ugly beast, the caucus. Party interests would constrain the nominating caucus to make choice of men fitted for the work of legislation. In a body whose chief function is debate neither the supporters nor the opponents of a responsible Cabinet can afford to have many weaklings: still less can they afford to have spokesmen whose integrity is under any cloud of suspicion. Thorough debate can unmask the most plausible pretender. The leaders of a great legislative assembly must daily show of what mettle they are. Besides meeting many watchful adversaries in debate, they must prove themselves "able to guide the House in the management of its business, to gain its ear in every emergency, to rule it in its hours of excitement." Rhetorical adroitness, dialectic dexterity, and passionate declamation cannot shield them from the scrutiny to which their movements will be subjected at every turn of the daily proceedings. The air is too open for either stupidity or indirection to thrive. Charlatans cannot long play statesmen successfully when the whole country is sitting as critic. And in Congress itself a single quick and pointed and well-directed question from a keen antagonist may utterly betray any minister who has aught to conceal. Even business routine will tear any thin covering of plausibility from the shams of dishonest policy. There is nothing like having public servants always on public trial.

Since, then, victory must generally rest with those who are vigourous in debate and strong in political principle, it would be imperatively necessary for each party to keep on the floor of Congress the ablest men they could draw into their ranks: and to this imperious necessity beast caucus must yield himself subject. Nominating conventions would hardly dare, under such circumstances, to send to Congress scheming wire-pullers or incompetent and double-dealing tricksters who would damn their party by displays of folly and suspicions of corruption. How could such men lead a minority against a powerful ministry or face the bitter taunts of opponents and the scornful distrust of fellow-partisans?

As every one must know, there are some men, even in America, who do not believe that popular constituencies can ever by any device of government be brought to give chief regard to principles in choosing their representatives. In the opinion of some, the masses cannot exercise an intelligent discretion. Were such opinions unhappily to prevail, they would cut deep at the foundations of republican doctrines. But prevail they cannot, for they are not founded upon truth. "I am not one of those," says Burke, "who think that the people are never wrong. They have been so, frequently and outrageously, both in other countries and in this. But I do say that in all disputes between them and their rulers, the presumption is at least upon a par in favour of the people." "When they go wrong, it is their error, and not their crime." This is the safe middle ground recommended by history. Mr. Stickney is incontestably in the right when he says that, were the shackles of party coercion removed, the choice of the constituencies would in most cases be both deliberate and wise. The early history of our own country abundantly proves that. But, even supposing this were not the fact, the introduction of responsible Cabinet government would compel caucus managers to nominate for Congress the very best men within their election. The party leaders in Washington would not be content with a mere servile majority: they would need men strong of intellect, pure of reputation, exalted in character, and cogent in speech—and such they must have for the tilts of discussion. Corrupt or incompetent men would be an intolerable drag upon them and their party.

And not only so: a new caucus-master would be raised up in the elevation and instruction of public opinion. Free and prolonged Congressional debates, conducted on the one side by men eager and able in attack and on the other by men equally quick and strong in defence, would do more towards informing and instructing public opinion than the press unaided can ever do. Men do not often read newspapers which profess political doctrines or acknowledge party connections different from their own. They read altogether on one side, and they read in colours. No staunch Republican paper will often venture to exhibit the flaws in Republican principles; and the paper which is not stalwartly partisan will surely have a small subscription list. Democratic papers must hold up Democratic dogmas in the lights most favourable to them and in such lights only, else good Democrats will not patronize them. So it is that men read in colours—some in Democratic tints, some in Republican tints, a select few in neutral tints, and none at all in the clear, dry, uncoloured light of truth. It must, however, be different were all political interest to centre in the debates of the legislature. Still men would read their party papers as before—perhaps even more assiduously and loyally than ever—but into whatever paper they might look there must have crept therein at least a skeleton of the great debates at the capital and the whole text of the speeches of the party leaders; and these would, of

course, be carefully scanned by every reader who had any thought
for the government—as diligently read on the one side as on the
other. It would be understood by all that on these debates hung
all the issues of national policy. Each discussion would be a struggle for supremacy on the part of each of the national parties, and
unless these tournaments were watched how could one forecast
anything concerning the political morrow or think anything definitely concerning the next campaign?

Besides, how much more information regarding the questions of
the day can be gained from such debates than from the editorials
and correspondence of the press! Such discussions are led by men
whose chief business it is to study the subjects upon which they
speak; whose chief desire it is to exhibit each topic of discussion
in every phase that it can possibly assume; whose personal authority as men of understanding and of reputation depends on the
mastery of principle and of detail they display in these legislative
contests; whose fame as orators depends on the clearness of statement, the cogency of reason, the elevation of sentiment, and the
ardour of patriotism with which they present their cause and enforce their principles; and whose success as men of affairs, whose
dearest ambition as public men, must be achieved or blasted according as they acquit themselves well or ill in the eyes of the nation. Responsible government would transform Congress into a
grand national inquisition. Under such a system the ministers are
always present to be taxed with questions and no detail of administration can be kept back when any one in either House
chooses to ask about it and insists upon particular information.
Are the Navy estimates before the House? Yonder sits a watchful
member who has a pigeon-hole in his memory—or at least in his
desk—for all the items of every appropriation bill that has been
passed during the last ten years; and he is on his feet every half
hour with several pointed queries to put to the head of the department. 'What, Mr. Secretary, does this item mean? Is not this a
much larger amount than we gave you last year for the same purpose? Does the administration mean to put the Navy on a war
footing, that it asks so much? Why do you come to us again for
money to complete those new frigates? How did it happen that
your original estimates fell so far short? Has there been a sudden
rise in provisions, that you ask more for victualling the fleet this
year than you did a year ago? What is the idea of the Department
in buying less ammunition this year than heretofore, notwithstanding the fact that you are putting more vessels than ever into
service?' What patience of spirit and diligence in business must

Mr. Secretary exhibit to reply to all these vexing interrogations with satisfactory fulness and at the same time with unruffled equanimity!

Public opinion, informed by such proceedings, could easily control, as supreme "boss," the "bosses" of the caucus. Whilst the nominating caucus would be brought into servitude by such a government, the legislative caucus would be killed. Its occupation would be gone. How could there be any necessity for a party often to confer in secret and constantly to marshal itself for the contests of policy when under the recognized leadership of a ministry whose principles are well known and whose course is easily forecast, or even when united and organized in well-understood opposition? The occasion for caucus conferences would no longer exist. Parties could act in concert without them. They could follow distinct lines of policy without resorting to this clumsy and artificial method of manufacturing unanimity. They would have capable and trustworthy leaders under whom to act, and definite, well-recognized principles to advance. They would represent ideas; and would not be bent upon being supreme for mere supremacy's sake.

Of course no interesest [interest] is felt now in the debates which take place at Washington. Nothing depends upon them. No one for a moment imagines that from them will issue changes of policy or transfers of power. The administration of the government is not in the least perceptible degree affected by them. No newspaper cares to print even the chief speeches of a session, because there are no leaders who speak with authority. Politics is regarded as little more than a game, in which the prize is office; and it is significantly true, as an observant Englishman—Mr. Dale, of Birmingham—has remarked, that "the Americans care very little about politics, but a great deal about politicians." This is true simply because there are no ordinary means by which our national parties can be united on grounds of distinct and consistent policy, and because there is nothing in our political contests to excite any lasting interest in the principles involved. How can any one be interested in parties which have no complexion; which are one thing to-day, another to-morrow, taking their colour from the time? Lookers-on can understand, however, the aspirations of this or that politician for office and they are interested in the contest. The rivalry is entertaining. The race is diverting and exciting. Now and then, it is true, great questions engage the public attention. At some crisis, when some overshadowing issue has aroused the sentiment of the constituencies and forces itself forward at the elections, candidates are asked with interest and emphasis what their position is with regard to it. But generally politicians need no creed and can safely rely for success on their personal popularity, or on an indefinite thing called their "record."

But the beneficial effects of Cabinet government would not be confined to the instruction of public opinion and the elevation of Congress into a great deliberative body. It would set up a higher standard of effectiveness in the Executive departments. It is not possible that the Standing Committees of the two Houses should have as full, as intimate, or as exact knowledge of the operations and the needs of the departments as have the chief officers of those departments. Though it is their duty to direct the policy of the departments in all matters, they cannot discern as well as can the Secretaries the lines of administration which are practicable or the means of management which are available. They know little or nothing of the daily perplexities of business in the departments and cannot appreciate the complexity of the executive machinery. They are not in a position to weigh the thousand minor considerations which must sway the determination of administrative officers in the conduct of their official business. They have, in a word, no adequate means of ascertaining those very necessities of the departments which it is their duty to supply by legislation. They are outsiders, and must have a commission from the House they represent before they can even exact any information from the officers of the Executive. The position of a Cabinet-committee would, on the other hand, be infinitely more advantageous. They could act with much greater facility and with much greater intelligence, because with all fulness of knowledge. They would know the needs of the departments as well as the temper of the assembly they were leading and could conform legislation to both the requirements of government and the sentiments of the public, being both prompt and prudent, both liberal and economical.

The union of legislative and executive functions in a single Cabinet-committee would, moreover, raise the standard of legislation and increase the efficiency of the Executive without jeoparding the independence of the one or derogating from the privileges of the other. As chiefs of the administrative bureaux, the ministers would have a personal interest in preserving the prerogatives of the Executive, and as official leaders of their party in Congress, they would be zealous to protect the rights and vindicate the authority of the Houses. They *would* not infringe the powers of the Executive, and they *could* not coërce Congress if they would. They would be simply the intelligent counsellors of the latter, not its masters; its accountable guides and servants, not its autocrats.

This, then, is the picture of Cabinet-committee government. Look upon it and then upon the picture Mr. Stickney has drawn. He suggests, as has been stated, a legislative power vested in a Senate and House of Representatives *whose members shall be elected for life*. He, though a lawyer and a man of business, would like to see one of the plainest and most reasonable principles of law and of business thus violated by the creation of an *irrevocable agency*. The principle of agency is the fundamental principle of representative government. The representatives of the people are the people's agents. Free government is self-government; and any system that would delegate legislative powers to agents whose authority could not be recalled would not be self-government, and would, therefore, be neither free nor tolerable. To denominate such a system representative government would be a patent solecism.

Undoubtedly, as has already been made to appear, the establishment of responsible government in this country would necessitate a lengthening of the legislative term. Biennial elections to the lower House serve well enough under our present form of government. Even the oft-repeated contests for the Speakership and the frequent reconstructions of the committees which are attendant upon the reorganizations of the House, the insecurity of tenure which makes the representative office a station less of usefulness than of profit, and the derangements of business which are incident upon quick-recurring elections, do not altogether condemn the system. It is well enough that Representatives should have a continuing sense of constant dependence on the approving judgment of their constituencies. If there is to be no other feature of responsibility than this in our government, let this by all means be retained. But with Cabinet government biennial elections would prove a source of too great instability. Each election would decide an issue between parties, would determine which should have power and enjoy ascendency, and would not turn, as elections now so often do, upon a mere question of preference in the case of each constituency between this or that representative; and no ministry would care to inaugurate a policy which might be broken down at the end of two years. A Cabinet coming into office at a crisis, or bringing with them many promises of great things to be accomplished, might be ousted at the end of two brief years, before their schemes had fairly matured, by a wave of opposition raised by the natural but transient disappointment of the country that everything promised had not *already* been done. Ministers would not plan for so short a future. They would not have the nerve. They would legislate from hand to mouth. "A mind free from the sense of insecurity is as necessary for great works of statesmanship as for great works of poetry." Biennial elections would ensure a constant sense of insecurity, and, as much would depend upon them, would be too much like biennial convulsions. Their quick recurrence would keep the country in a fever of political excitement which would either warm into riot or waste into exhaustion and indifference.

But there is such a thing as lengthening the legislative term without making it life-long—and a term of six or eight years would serve the purposes of free government much better than a life term.

And what would be gained by Mr. Stickney's plan of allowing the Secretaries of the departments to hold their offices during good behaviour? A Congress of life-seated representatives, such as he wishes to see established, would be obliged to resort to the committee system just as biennial Congresses have been constrained to do: and what would it advantage the government to have the Secretaries who serve the committees commissioned servants during good behaviour? Who would judge of their behaviour whether it was good or bad? In what would good behaviour on their part consist? Congress would judge; and good behaviour would consist in perfect obedience to Congress.

Beyond all question the departments should have permanent organizations. They, no less than great commercial houses, should be organized in strict accordance with recognized business principles. The greater part of their affairs is altogether outside of politics. The collection and ordinary disbursements of the revenue, the general superintendence of the army and navy, the regulation of the mail service, the administration of justice, all the usual and daily functions of the executive departments, what concern have they with party questions? In these things business capacity and honest diligence are all that is wanted. Political belief does not affect an officer's efficiency any more than religious belief might. This is the oft-repeated principle which lies at the source of the great movement towards Civil Service Reform in which all the currents of public opinion are now uniting in a tide against which the stoutest dykes of party custom and party interest cannot much longer stand. It is now universally seen and acknowledged that the public service to be efficient should be non-partisan, and that so far as the nation at large is concerned it can make no possible difference whether the rank and file of its servants entertain this, that, or the other political creed. Not in one office out of five thousand can opinion affect a man's value as a business agent of the government. An organization of the Civil Service in which merit would be the only criterion of appointment and promotion, and neglect of duty the only ground for discharge, is, accordingly, a consummation devoutly to be wished.

But there are executive offices which are political. Those ministers who direct the general policy of the government—if any such there be—must represent the party dominant in the state. The Standing Committees which now stand in the place of such ministers are, as a matter of course, representatives of the ruling majority and, perhaps, under committee government, it would be feasible to have permanent Secretaries set over the departments, since the present quadrennial chiefs have no voice in the counsels by which the policy of the country is determined and might as well be non-partisans as party men. Our choice, however, lies not between biennial Standing Committees ruling quadrennial Secretaries and permanent committees ruling permanent Secretaries, but between government by irresponsible and multitudinous committees and government by some single and responsible body like a Cabinet-committee—a legislative committee composed of the chief members of the Executive Ministry and holding office by a tenure dependent on their political opinions, holding only so long as their policy should be in accord with the views of the majority in Congress.

Mr. Stickney makes much of the objection that ministers acting thus as both executive officers and legislative leaders, absorbed as they would be in the business of the Houses and in the marshalling of their party forces in the daily tilt of debate, could not have the leisure to master properly their duties as heads of the departments and would inevitably fall short of fulfilling their official trusts. This objection is an evident and a weighty one. It must, however, be remembered at every turn of the endeavour to solve this tremendous and perplexing problem of government that we are commanded by the inexorable necessity of compromise. We must take the least imperfect thing we can get; and it seems to be evidently far better to have the affairs of the executive departments controlled by men who know something rather than by men who know nothing of their interests—by men who are in constant, and intimate, and authoritative communication with subordinates who spend their lives in close and exclusive attention to departmental affairs, rather than by men who can command no such means of information; by men whose personal interests, nay whose very ambition, must unite them in behalf of good administration, and who are able, therefore, and willing to agree upon a definite, uniform, and consistent policy, rather than by several scores of men divided into numerous disconnected and inharmonious committees who cannot coöperate and who are only too often indifferent as to the results of measures they ignorantly recommend.

So long as we have representative government the Legislature will remain the imperial and all-overshadowing power of the state: and so long as it does remain such a power it will be impossible to check its encroachments and curb its arrogance, and at the same time preserve the independence and efficiency of the Executive, unless these two great branches of government can be joined by some link, some bond of connection, which, whilst not consolidating them, will at least neutralize their antagonisms, and, possibly, harmonize their interests. A Cabinet-committee would constitute such a bond, for it would be a body which, from its very nature and offices, would be at once jealous of the pretensions of the Houses and responsible for the usurpations of the Executive; interested and therefore determined to yield not a jot of their lawful executive authority, and yet bound to admit every just claim of power on the part of their legislative colleagues.

This is not a matter of theory, but of experience. An Executive having a permanent organization, after the fashion of a great commercial establishment, might possibly be very effective *were it its own master*. But under representative institutions it cannot be its own master. The Legislature is its overlord. Its affairs are completely under the direction of Congress: and it is in view of this indisputable and unavoidable fact that the introduction of a responsible ministry seems the only expedient by which representative institutions can be rendered both beneficent and efficient without prejudice to either the executive or the legislative branch of government.

That must be a policy of wisdom and of prudence which puts the executive and legislative departments of government into intimate sympathy and binds them together in close coöperation. The system which embodies such a policy in its greatest perfection must be admired of all statesmen and coveted of all misgoverned peoples. The object of wise legislation is the establishment of equal rights and liberties amongst the citizens of the state, and its chief business, the best administration of government. Legislatures have it constantly in charge, and specially in charge, to facilitate administration: and that charge can be best fulfilled, of course, when those who make and those who administer the laws are in closest harmony. The executive agents of government should stand at the ear of the legislature with respectful suggestions of the needs of the administration, and the legislature should give heed to them, requiring of them, the while, obedience and diligence in the execution of its designs. An Executive honoured with the confidence of the legislature, and a legislature confiding itself with all fulness of trust yet with all vigilance, to the guidance of an Executive acknowledging full responsibility to the representatives of the people for all their acts and all their counsels: this is a picture good to look upon—a type of effective and beneficent self-government.

The changes in our form of government which the establishment of such a system would involve are surely worth making, if they necessitate no sacrifice of principles. Not least among those changes would be the lengthening of the presidential term, which would be imperative, but which would do no violence to republican principle. The same considerations of policy which point to the President as the proper appointer of Cabinets also suggest that he should hold his office for a long term, if not during good behaviour. He would be entrusted with the appointment of Cabinets, and without a permanent appointing power the whole system would be unstable. It would have no central pillar of support. Then, too, permanence in office would lift the President above the passing caprice of momentary party excitement. He would in a measure become identified with his office. He could afford to name Cabinets with impartiality. Indeed the exalted dignity of his station and his natural regard for his own reputation would make him proudly careful to be impartial. He would, besides, be in a position of great influence. Independent of party, he could throw all the weight of his great office on the side of steady conservatism. Whilst the even course of administration might ever and again be disturbed by changes of Presidential temper or freaks of Presidential whim, such occasional vagaries could never work injury comparable with that which would be wrought by an appointing President holding for a short term as the partisan of this or that political organization, or with the mischief stirred up by the intrigues of Congress, were it clothed with the prerogative of appointment. A permanent President could and would rise above parties, and exercise the high duties of his office with judicial fairness and integrity. A chief-magistracy held by a tenure of honour and fidelity would constitute a proper head-stone for the official structure. The line of non-partisan permanent officials would fitly terminate in a permanent and non-partisan chief.

This, then, is the sum of the whole matter: while Congress remains the supreme power of the state it is idle to talk of steadying or cleansing our politics without in some way linking together the interests of the Executive and the legislature. So long as these too great branches are isolated they must be ineffective. Congress will always be master and will always enforce its commands on the Administration. The only wise plan open to adoption is to make each party, in the persons of its leaders, responsible for those commands and responsible also for the manner in which they are executed. The only hope of wrecking the clumsy misrule of Congress lies in the establishment of responsible Cabinet government. Let the interests of the legislature be indissolubly linked with the interests of the Executive. Let those who have authority to direct the course of legislation be those who have a deep personal concern in building up the executive departments in effectiveness, in strengthening law, and in unifying policies; men whose personal reputation depends upon successful administration, whose public station originates in the triumph of principles, and whose dearest ambition it is to be able to vindicate their wisdom and maintain their integrity.

IV

Government by Debate

"Whatever original energy may be supposed either in force or regulation, the operation of both is in truth merely instrumental. Nations are governed by the same methods, and on the same principles, by which an individual without authority is often able to govern those who are his equals or superiors; by a knowledge of their temper, and by a judicious management of it. . . . The laws reach but a very little way. Constitute Government how you please, infinitely the greater part of it must depend upon the exercise of powers, which are left at large to the prudence and uprightness of ministers of state. Even all the use and potency of the laws depends upon them. Without them your commonwealth is no better than a scheme upon paper; and not a living, active, effective organization"—Burke.

Has America lost her breed of statesmen? Not since the revolution has there gone by an age so poor as this in such fine talents as those which crowned the head of Hamilton, those which sat serene upon the countenance of Washington, or those which were enthroned upon the presiding brow of Webster. At least if such talents exist they have ceased to be exhibited. Public life is even tabooed, for that time seems to have come to which Calhoun looked forward with keen eye: "When it comes to be once understood that politics are a game; that those who are engaged in it but act a part; that they make this or that profession not from honest conviction or an intent to fulfil them, but as the means of deluding the people, and through that delusion to acquire power, —when such professions are to be entirely forgotten, the people will lose all confidence in public men; all will be regarded as mere jugglers,—the honest and the patriotic as well as the cunning and the profligate; and the people will become indifferent and passive to the grossest abuses of power on the ground that those whom they may elevate, under whatever pledges, instead of reforming will but imitate the example of those whom they have expelled." To advise a young man now-a-days to enter public life would be reckoned poor counsel. He had better keep out of politics, say all his friends; for in politics he can win no station without intrigue, can achieve nothing without soiling his hands and clouding his reputation.

Our latest race of political giants came into public service under conditions very different from those which now exist. Webster, Calhoun, and Clay won places of power and preëminence without a suspicion of having prostituted their intellects or compromised their characters. There was no need for Daniel Webster to touch that which was impure in accomplishing his exalted mission; Henry Clay's eloquence had in it no base alloy of insincerity; and John C. Calhoun's character passed through all the tempests of his passion-beaten life without stain or blemish. They were not caucus men; but were leaders because they represented great constitutional causes. Webster and Calhoun each stood at the head of a great school of constitutional interpretation; between the two, on a middle ground of his own, stood the silver-tongued Kentuckian; and the supreme importance of the issues they represented, as well as their conspicuous genius, kept these three always in the forefront of every political movement.

It is an interesting but apparently unobserved fact of American history that almost all the greatest statesmen of the Union have been constitutional lawyers rather than masters of administrative policy. The great battles of our politics have been fought around the Constitution, and the exposition of that splendid instrument has furnished almost every bone of contention. Questions of foreign policy, indeed, gave form and colour to our politics during the first three decades of our national existence; but questions which were solely questions of domestic policy have not often been more than the undercurrents of our politics. Constitutional issues have been the tides, matters of administrative policy only eddies. Even to the present day parties claim to take character from views of the Constitution which have been handed down from party to party from the earliest hours of the Union. Down to the opening of the war of secession constitutional questions over-crowded all others. It was upon opposing grounds of constitutional interpretation that Federalists and Republicans pitched their hos-tile camps; it was concerning the right understanding of the Con-stitution that Whigs and Democrats drew sword; and it is on the lingering shadows of such questions that Democrats and Republi-cans to-day build their uncertain platforms. The leading topics of our political history are such as the implied powers of the Fed-eral government, the admission of new States into the Union, the annexation of territory, the tariff, and all the interests which clustered about the slavery question and the reserved sovereignty of the States. These are the subjects which stand out more con-spicuously than all others, and these all assumed the shape of con-stitutional questions. Very few publicists opposed internal im-provements, for instance, on the ground that they were unwise and uncalled-for. No one who took a statesmanlike view of the matter could fail to see that the opening up of the great water ways of the country, the construction of roads, the cutting of canals, every work which might facilitate inter-State commerce and make intercourse between the various portions of the Union easy and rapid, was a policy recommended by every consideration of wis-dom as a policy national and universal in its benefits. Accordingly no harm was suspected to hide in it and no serious objection made to it until jealousy of Federal power conjured into being the fear that such a policy was extra-constitutional. 'We will not hear of implied powers,' exclaimed its opponents, 'for whither will they lead us? Here, in this writing, are the powers of the Federal gov-ernment set plainly out in the Constitution's distinctest phrase: where amongst them do you find the authority to cut a canal in Ohio, to dig away the bars which shut the mouths of Southern riv-ers or the shoals which hinder seamen in Northern harbours? It is not given you. You are transgressing the bounds which have been set you; and while we have voice it shall not cease to cry out against these usurping implications by which you would stretch your prerogatives beyond the written word of the Constitution.'

What made the tariff leap suddenly to the front as a burning party question in 1833? Was it because a great free-trade movement had been set a-foot and free-traders and protectionists were met in deadly joust? Was this a contest in which Adam Smith might take a hand? Were Cobden and Bright being anticipated in America? Not at all. The Constitution was again invoked. The agricultural States were feeling very painfully the iron heel of that protectionist system which they themselves had consented to have set up, and they fetched their hope of escape from the Constitution. The Constitution conferred upon the general government the right to impose duties on imports, but did that right carry with it the privilege of laying discriminating duties? Could the Constitution have meant that South Carolina might be taxed to maintain the manufactures of New England?

Upon the heels of this controversy came those great contests over the right of secession and the abolition of slavery which tore and convulsed the country for thirty years and which culminated in the supreme catastrophe of civil war. Thus runs the whole story of national politics down to the crisis of 1861. It is a history of two warring principles: on the one side, that principle of nationality which before the appeal to arms was espoused by all the free States of the Union, and, on the other, that principle of States-rights which the slave-holding States of the South stubbornly held to, and which they surrendered only with the surrender of Lee's sword. The contest was indeed irrepressible. However much of a game for gain politics might become, however corrupt and debased the civil service might grow, however supreme and repressive beast caucus might wax, this issue could never be obscured. The people of the two sections were sure to think and sure to act about it. They would send their doughtiest champions to Congress and there in the national legislative halls would proceed that great discussion which no power of party machinery nor trammels of committee rule would or could repress.

While questions thus affecting the very powers and structure of the national government pressed daily for solution there were of necessity great party leaders always in the field. In the presence of these stupendous themes petty partisan disputes and personal interests were dwarfed and made contemptible. What could be compared with that tremendous issue, Is slavery to endure and to extend its dominion, or is it to be forever wiped away from the face of the earth? or with that other still more momentous interrogatory, Is the Union to be torn asunder, or can it be preserved? It was in these contests, involving first the organization and finally the very existence of the Federal government, that great statesmen were raised up whose names will long live in the veneration of their countrymen.

But meantime corruption was growing and extending and thrusting good men out of politics. In spite of these overmastering questions which were strong enough to keep great advocates in the public service, baneful influences were creeping in which were yearly lessening the number of pure and earnest statesmen; and when once the stimulus of those great themes was removed, rapid and universal decadence of the public service quickly set in. Without these supreme issues of constitutional construction to overcome them, corruption and indirection were in their turn strong enough to rule the political realm. And the throne, unhappily, still is theirs. The construction of the Constitution is settled now, settled once for all by the supreme arbitrament of war. Sections no longer stand at deadly variance. North and South are becoming daily more alike and hourly growing into a closer harmony of sentiment. Happily freed from the curse of slavery, the South has entered on a season of prosperity and growth to which no bound or period can be set. Every day her populations are multiplying, her industries extending and strengthening, her commerce quickening its steps, and her civilization expanding, as she strides on towards that position of preëminence to which her boundless resources and unwearied energies give her sure title.

Sectional issues, therefore, are fading rapidly away; and very few constitutional topics now have left in them life enough to divide parties. The questions of the future are to be questions of internal national policy, of federal administration. Whatever foundation of truth the doctrine of the right of peaceable secession may once have had, it is now altogether thrown down, beyond all hope of a rebuilding. Our Constitution has had a great growth. It is now neither in theory nor in fact what its framers are thought to have intended it to be. Like Magna Charta and the Bill of Rights, it is only the centre of a system of government which embodies many principles and wears many features which find no clear recognition in the Constitutional text. The allegiance of each citizen to his State is, in those matters over which the Federal authority extends, subordinate to that allegiance which he owes to the national government. He is citizen of two States, of a national and of a local; and one of these States is no less sovereign and supreme within its sphere than is the other.

One great and grievously-burdensome legacy the war has left. A race question still exists to harass the South. So long as the negro vote of the Southern States is consolidated so long will the white vote of that section continue united. But that cannot now be long. The existing parties in the Union cannot much longer hold together. They are organized, the one to dispense, the other to gain Federal patronage; and if a thorough reform of the Civil Service were to be effected and all promise of illegitimate reward were thus to be denied them, whole battalions of the mercenaries would desert the ranks. Nothing then could save the partisan armies from disorganization. One faction is at present within the fair city and lives in revels on the fat plunder there to be found, and the impudent wassail goes forward loudly; the other, an incongruous horde of the hungry, lays siege without to the coveted treasure, impatiently biding the day when the privilege of pillage may be theirs. Take away the prize that for the one is in possession and for the other in prospect, and the factions must fight amongst themselves. No more alliances can be patched up between antagonistic principles; "green-backers" can no longer lie down in the tents of "hard-money men," neither can protectionists any more stand shoulder to shoulder with blatant free-traders.

Civil Service Reform, then, since it can take away the prize, is the presiding interest of the day. These unnatural and unholy coälitions must be broken up, and they can be broken up by removing the temptations which prompt them. When there are no lucrative offices to be fought for there will be a redivision of parties on lines of principle. But, as has already been regretfully said, it does not seem probable that the Civil Service will be soon reformed under our present form of Congressional rule. It is a significant fact that the reform of the civil service in Great Britain originated not with Parliament but with a responsible ministry. The members of the House of Commons were as loath to give up that control of the national patronage which they were accustomed to exercise by various crooked indirections as are our own Senators and Representatives to surrender that useful influence over the appointments of the Executive which it is their pleasure and their power to possess. The Cabinet of Lord Aberdeen originated in 1853 that reform which has made the civil service of Great Britain the purest and most effective in the world. They knew that it was the "duty of the executive to provide for the efficient and harmonious working of the civil service," and that they could not "transfer that duty to any other body *far less competent to the task than themselves* without infringing a great and important constitutional principle, already too often infringed, to the great detriment of the public service." They therefore determined themselves to inaugurate the merit system, without waiting to first obtain the assent of Parliament, by simply surrendering their powers of appointment to a non-partisan examining board, trusting to the aid of that public opinion which would certainly stand on their side to induce Parliament, after the thing was done, to vote sufficient money to keep the scheme in successful operation.

It will be pertinent to this discussion, as well as eminently interesting and instructive, to inquire how it came about that the ardour of this reform in England originated with the appointing power; how it happened that the ministry were the first to propose a relinquishment of the seductive prerogatives of official patronage. Beyond a doubt they were prompted by a sense of the responsibility of their position. Standing, as they did, at the head of the administration of the government, their fame as statesmen and their ability to perform their executive functions to the satisfaction of the country depending on the purity and effectiveness of the public service, they felt constrained by their regard for the public weal and by every consideration of personal interest, as well as by the very hope of political advantage, to do promptly and well this great act of public justice. It is a striking and suggestive fact, brought clearly to view by Mr. Eaton in his interesting history of the civil service in Great Britain* that those immeasurable improvements which have been made in the public service of the empire since the days of Walpole and Newcastle have gone hand in hand with the perfecting of that system of government by Cabinet-committee which is now the chief beauty of the English constitution. That system was slow in coming to perfection. It was not till long after Walpole's day that unity of responsibility on the part of the Cabinet was a well-recognized principle. "As a consequence of the earlier practice of constructing Cabinets of men of different political views, it followed that the members of such Cabinets did not and could not regard their responsibility to Parliament as one and indivisible. The resignation of an important member, or even of the Prime Minister, was not regarded as necessitating the simultaneous retirement of his colleagues. Even as late as the fall of Sir Robert Walpole, fifty years after the Revolution Settlement (and itself the first instance of resignation in deference to a hostile parliamentary vote) we find the King requesting Walpole's successor, Pulteney, 'not to distress the Government by making too many changes in the midst of a session'; and Pulteney replying that he would be satisfied, provided 'the main forts of the Government,' or, in other words, the principal offices of State,

---

* Dorman B. Eaton, *Civil Service in Great Britain: A History of Abuses and Reforms and their Bearing upon American Politics* (New York, 1880). [Eds.' note.]

were placed in his hands. It was not till the displacement of Lord North's ministry by that of Lord Rockingham in 1782 that a whole administration, with the exception of the Lord Chancellor, was changed by a vote of want of confidence passed in the House of Commons. Thenceforth, however, the resignation of the head of a government in deference to an adverse vote of the popular Chamber has invariably been accompanied by the resignation of all his colleagues."* But it was still a long time before Cabinets were free to follow their own policies without authoritative suggestion from the Sovereign. Until the death of the fourth George they were made to feel that they owed a double allegiance, to the Commons and to the King. Their composition depended largely on the royal whim. Their actions were frequently hampered by the necessity of steering a careful middle course between the displeasure of Parliament and the displeasure of His Majesty. The present century had run far on towards the reign of Victoria before ministries were free to say that they owed service to none but to the Commons of England. When they were so free, however, their position was such as to prompt them to every effort of reform. They were conscious that the entire responsibility of government rested upon their shoulders; and as men regardful of the interests of the party they represented, jealous of their own fair name, and anxious for the promotion of good government, they were naturally and of course the first to advocate a better system of appointment to that service whose chiefs they were recognized to be.

It is this sense of responsibility, this dignifying and elevating sense of being trusted, together with this consciousness of being in such conspicuous station that no breach of trust can go undiscovered and unpunished and no faithful discharge of duty unacknowledged and unrewarded, that spur men on to the highest achievements of statesmanship. The best rulers that a country can have are men to whom great power is entrusted in such a manner as to make them feel that they will be abundantly honoured and recompensed for a just and patriotic use of it, and at the same time to make them know that nothing can save them from full retribution for every abuse of it. *Power and accountability for its use*—these are the two elements which chiefly constitute the essence of good government: and these are the two things which are secured by responsible Cabinet government in a higher degree of perfection than they have ever attained under any other form of government. And not only so. The dignity and power with which

* "Central Government" (*English Citizen Series*), H. D. Traill, Macmillan, 1881. [WW's note.]

the office of Cabinet minister is invested under such a system make that office the highest object of ambition, at the same time that its attainment is made the sure reward of merit. No system breeds statesmen and orators so surely as this, which rewards statesmen and orators with the highest offices in the gift of the nation.

It rears statesmen because it assures to statesmanship a place of authority and leadership in the national councils. The man who proves himself worthy beyond his fellows of a hearing will be certain beyond a peradventure to win a title of leadership in his party; and men who lead their party must constitute its Cabinets: for Cabinets will be party Cabinets, and being composed of members of the Houses, will necessarily be made up of the legislative leaders. Suppose Cabinet government established in the United States: —the President must choose his counsellors from that party which commands a majority in Congress, and must also limit his choice to members of that majority. For of course he could not choose men who were not members of Congress. The Cabinet ministers must have seats in Congress in order to exercise their functions as leaders of legislation, and if the President were to be allowed to nominate for the ministry men outside of Congress, such privilege would be tantamount to an authority to constitute his nominees members of Congress—a prerogative which no sane man would wish to see entrusted to any save a constituency of the people. Pre-eminence in debate and in leadership must, therefore, secure Cabinet office to members of the majority.

The Cabinet, indeed, would, to all intents and purposes, be chosen by Congress. Not, to be sure, by any formal vote; not even by any conscious choice; but by that unspoken homage which assemblies of men always pay to those of their number who prove eloquent and sagacious in counsel: by a tacit suffrage which is no less decisive than actual ballot. This choice the President could not disregard. In naming a Cabinet he must name such men as are willing to act together not only, but such men as can also lead and control their party—such men as the party would follow. Nor would it be hard for him to decide whom to call. Cabinet government is government by debate; and whenever government is conducted by debate, party lines and party leadership are unmistakably defined. The champions of the ministry and the champions of the Opposition are easily recognized. They are the men who are readiest in debate, most practiced in affairs, most astute in counsel, coolest in times of excitement, and supremest in moments of danger. Their position they have won in fair and open competition; and those who are to succeed them are those younger members who are daily establishing their right to be heard by proving their desert to be heard; by showing that they have something to say and can say it with earnestness and power.

There is a danger which seems to some to be inherent in such government, and peculiar to it. They fear that it would be at best but a leadership of artful dialecticians; that those who could most successfully gloss over the defects of a cause with a varnish of rhetoric would be the chiefs of Cabinets; that men who could out-wit the opposition of more thoughtful but less ready men by tricks of phrase, or bear it down by a rush of eloquent declamation, would command seats of authority at the council board; that there would be a reign of sophists rather than of wise men; and that the affairs of the nation would be directed by the wagging of ready tongues rather than by statesmanlike counsel. These ap-prehensions find support in a well known passage of Macaulay's, and have in many minds, no doubt, been suggested by his words. "Parliamentary government," says he, "like every other contrivance of man, has its advantages and its disadvantages. On the ad-vantages there is no need to dilate. The history of England during the one hundred and seventy years which have elapsed since the House of Commons became the most powerful body in the State, her immense and still growing prosperity, her freedom, her tran-quility, her greatness in arts, in sciences, and in arms; her mari-time ascendancy, the marvels of her public credit, her American, her African, her Australian, her Asiatic empires, sufficiently prove the excellence of her institutions. But those institutions, though excellent, are assuredly not perfect. Parliamentary government is government by speaking. In such a government the power of speaking is the most highly prized of all the qualities which a poli-tician can possess; and that power may exist in the highest de-gree without judgment, without fortitude, without skill in reading the characters of men or the signs of the times, without any knowl-edge of the principles of legislation or of political economy, and without any skill in diplomacy or in the administration of war. Nay it may well happen that those very intellectual qualities which give peculiar charm to the speeches of a public man may be incompati-ble with the qualities which would fit him to meet a pressing emer-gency with promptitude and firmness. It was thus with Charles Townshend. It was thus with Windham. It was a privilege to listen to those accomplished and ingenious orators. But in a perilous crisis they would be found far inferior in all the qualities of rulers to such a man as Oliver Cromwell, who talked nonsense, or as William the Silent, who did not talk at all."*

These sentences of the "accomplished and ingenious" essayist, though not his least brilliant, are of the number of his least trustworthy. Parliamentary government is, no doubt, government by speaking; but it is not government by mere speaking. This is well illustrated by one at least of the very examples Macaulay himself adduces. Charles Townshend, indeed, was little more than an orator, and he never rose higher in official position than he was entitled to rise by virtue of such administrative talents as he did possess. His tenure of office was often accidental and generally precarious. He was given place rather because no one better could be had than because he was the best. But William Windham, on the other hand, was something more than a mere orator. He had very considerable executive capacity. During seven trying years of international strife he directed the war department with conspicuous success; and he was always esteemed one of the best ministers of his party. But, granting that Townshend, and even Windham, illustrate the tendency of parliamentary government to exalt talkers above sages, what is to be said of the hundreds of cases which unmistakably exhibit an opposite tendency? Time would fail one to tell of North, of Castlereagh, of Melbourne, of Palmerston, of Russell, of Wellington, and of Northcote. Parliamentary government is government by speaking of a peculiar sort. It is not government by mere dialectics. It does not trust power in the hands of rhetoricians or of declaimers, nor give influence to those who are merely ingenious and entertaining. It grants these to those who have something to say and know when to say it. The speech that wins is the speech which displays sagacity, which convinces of mastery, which is alive with earnest truth, which is spoken as with knowledge, which breathes sincerity, and persuades as with the voice of wisdom.

Consider the great orators of our race. They have been conspicuous no less for their sagacity in the administration of public affairs than for their seductive eloquence. Hampden was a statesman of rare judgment, foresight, and steadfastness of purpose. Walpole excelled all his contemporaries in "skill in reading the characters of men and the signs of the times." Chatham was a master of policy. He won India for England, building a great empire in the East; drove the French from America, preparing thus for the birth of a great republic in the West; and, lending constant and effective aid to Prussia's great Frederick, prepared the des-

* Essay on Pitt. [WW's note.]

tiny of her greater Bismarck. Who could not sit at the feet of
Burke and learn the principles of legislation? Who could teach
Canning skill in diplomacy, or instruct Windham in the administration of war? Was not Fox supreme in enforcing the principles
of righteous government, and Pitt in the guidance of conservative
opinion? Who was ever prompter or firmer to meet a pressing
emergency than was Peel? Gladstone, too, has he not been easily
first in mastery of every branch of political knowledge; and cannot Bright speak unbonneted in the company of the first statesmen
of England?

Our own American orators, too, have many of them won like
preëminence as administrators of government: but they have had
less and less opportunity for displaying such talents as our system
has grown older. It is a common-place of our history that the greatest offices have, as time has advanced, gotten farther and farther
beyond the reach of the greatest men. The "dark horses" win the
presidential stakes. Men of decided opinions and well known record are not considered elegible for popular election. A man like
Daniel Webster would have even less chance of reaching the White
House now than he might have had fifty years ago. Ours is certainly not government by speaking: for the more a man speaks the
more likely is he to publish some opinion which will lose him the
favour of the nominating convention. In Congress speaking is discouraged. That is no place for speech-making, it is said. Let members do their committee work and keep quiet!

This state of things is unnatural and unhealthy. It is natural
that orators should be the leaders of a self-governing people. Men
may, it is true, be forceful and engaging speakers without possessing in their highest perfection any of those qualities which go to
make up a statesman; but they can scarcely be orators without
that force of character, that readiness of resource, that clearness
of vision, that grasp of intellect, that courage of conviction, that
earnestness of purpose, and that instinct and capacity of leadership which are the eight horses that draw the triumphal chariot
of every leader and ruler of men.

Mr. Lowell has called our fashion of government "government
by declamation," and Mr. Lowell is right in this, that our politics
furnish food for declamation and for nothing better. There is no
inspiration for true oratory: for without the inspiration of a cause
no man can be an orator; and there is no great political cause
now that any American can espouse. Once there were such causes.
Patrick Henry had his heart set on fire with the love of liberty and
preached the salvation of his people from the bondage of tyrants.

A like noble inspiration spoke as with the voice of a trumpet from the lips of Otis and Adams and Hamilton, men who spoke as few men ever spoke before; and after them came Webster and Calhoun and Clay, earnest preachers of constitutional doctrine. But why should we expect men to speak now as they spoke then? They could then speak with purpose and with hope. There were great things that could be done. In the early days the colonies could be spurred to throw off the galling yoke of England, to unite themselves under a common government, and by union to raise themselves into a high place among the nations. And later, when the national government had been established in its strength and beauty, there were great constitutional questions to be decided—questions upon which hung the issues of life and death for the Union. Those were days of grand causes which, as of course, raised up strong and valiant champions.

Now, however, all is changed. What common inspiring cause have the Democrats? What standard have the Republicans around which to rally men in proud allegiance? Parties are no longer divided by lines of principle. Republicans hold together only that they may share "the spoils of office"; and what man can number the divers opinions joined under Democratic name? Neither party has any common ground of doctrine. They are not homogeneous but conglomerate—the one representing all who are hoping for office, the other made up of every faction that is opposed to the party which is in power. The Republicans are the "ins," the Democrats the "outs"—and that is the long and short of it. Our political orators, therefore, have no themes. They cannot tell what their parties purpose, for they can but guess how the next caucus will vote, and they know that generally the parties have no purposes worth talking about. They know that their fellow-partisans are often not of the same mind with themselves, and that no definite plan of legislation can be promised or forecast. They cannot establish personal leadership for themselves under our system, which *individualizes* and does not combine. That system affords no channel through which men who are united in a common purpose can exert any considerable influence upon the hap-hazard course of national policy. Almost our only orators, therefore, are apostles of single ideas and ministers of the everlasting Word of God.

Oratory is not possible without moral elevation in its subjects. It is powerless if it be aimless. It is supreme only when employed in the accomplishment of something possible, definite, and laudable. It cannot inspire when inflated with the mere enthusiasm of a holiday. It must be tuned like a call to battle or voiced like a herald of deeds worthy the doing. And without true oratory the politics of such a country as ours are undone. It is fashionable, I know, to say that the best, the palmy, days of oratory are passed; that the press has taken its place; but this is not the truth. The press does fill a large place in our governmental economy; but it cannot have that weight of character, that prestige of personal service, that authority of individual opinion which make the utterances of great orators powerful to the shaking of the nations. The political press is anonymous. It speaks its partisan opinions with no better title to be heard than it derives from the fact that it is likely to be well informed. It is so far from being an independent and self-sufficient power that it is constrained to do homage to the political orator whether it will or no. Look into the English papers. In England the political orator is a power, and Conservative editors must spread before their readers verbatim reports of all the principal speeches of the leading Liberal orators, and Liberal papers must print every syllable of the more formal public addresses of the Conservative leaders. The orator is greater than the greatest newspaper. When he speaks he speaks not only to his immediate auditors, the few hundreds or thousands who run together to stand within sound of his voice, but to the whole country besides. Everybody reads his speech who was not privileged to hear it, and those who heard it read it in order that it may lie fresh in their memories. If the press has usurped his influence, why do men still crowd to hear him? Why do they not wait to read what he said? They can read the speech in tenfold greater comfort, yet they would give all the printed reports for five minutes' audience of the living voice and five minutes sight of the personal presence of the orator. They cannot read without a wish that they had heard.

But we have in America no political orators whom the whole nation insists upon hearing, whose speeches every newspaper must print. Why is this? It is because nothing short of absolute genius can in this country give any man such an unquestionable claim upon the ear of the people. There are only two things that can ever give any man the right to expect that when he speaks the whole country will listen, and those two things are genius and authority. Now, genius is a plant of rare growth; and, as for authority, that is something we are very shy about conferring on anybody in this Union. Not so in England. There integrity and ability are always clothed with authority—albeit that authority is hedged about with a very strict accountability. No one will ever pretend that Sir Stafford Northcote was a genius, or even a good speaker; but being a man of unblemished character and an able and conscientious public servant, he rose, by public and political favour, to be recognized leader of his party in the House of Commons. Therefore it is that he speaks as one having authority. Leadership in the House of Commons is won by competition, and when won it entitles to the highest offices of the State; and Northcote, like many others before him, has gained by simple industry and worth as much right to be heard, as sure audience with the nation, as genius and authority combined have given Gladstone.

Such presiding personal authority our system, as at present administered, will not brook. It gives no man leave to speak for his party. His individual opinion, and that alone, he may give. If he be a genius and by his genius establish his fame as a great orator, he can no doubt so speak his thoughts that they will arrest attention and compel many to give them heed; or, if he be a man of acknowledged learning, of conspicuous virtue, or of great force of character, his word will always carry weight. But nothing short of genius will enable him to hold public opinion in his hand as the potter holds his clay.

Unquestionably this ought to be remedied. What young man who is conscious of fine abilities will choose to enter public life when he knows that no honourable exertion can secure for him any high station of authority in the government of his country? He will prefer other professions in which wealth at least will be the sure reward of diligence and worth. But all men love high place and dote on authority; and if it were once known that these could be won by honourable service, the contestants would be many and eager. We want, therefore, in America a system that will reward merit: and Cabinet government does reward merit. It rewards merit by offering the highest offices of the State as prizes for eloquence, ability, honesty, and faithful service. It constantly draws, as recruits, into the public service the most promising youths of the land, by holding out to them the hope, the confident expectation, that in that service their capabilities will be fully recognized and a position high in proportion to their worth and intelligence readily accorded them. The purifying influences of such elevated and justified ambition cannot easily be overestimated. They would be the regeneration of our public life. They would infuse warm health into our institutions and make the desire for public station again an honourable and exalting passion.

We can contribute to the development of statesmanship by rewarding and honouring it. A survey of the past unmistakably shows that, so far as political affairs are concerned, critical epochs are the man-making epochs of history, revolutionary influences[,] the man-making influences. And the reason is a very plain and evident one. Crises create statesmen because they are peculiarly periods of action, in which executive talents and the gifts of sage counsel find widest scope and most immediate recognition. They are times not only of action but also of unusual opportunities for gaining leadership and commanding influence in public affairs. This chance of establishing such transcendent influence it is that calls into active life a nation's greater minds—minds which might otherwise remain absorbed in the smaller affairs of private business. Here, then, is the principle: Governmental forms will command able minds and strong hearts for the work of administration constantly or infrequently according as they do or do not at all times afford men an opportunity of gaining and retaining an exalted authority and an undisputed leadership.

Now, it goes without the saying that government by supreme Standing Committees, whose members are appointed at the caprice of an irresponsible party chief—by some rule of seniority in legislative service, or because of reputation gained in other and entirely different fields, or because of partisan shrewdness—is not favourable to a full and strong development of statesmanship. Certain it is that statesmanship has been steadily dying out in the United States during the growth of the committee system. In that system there is no place found for personal leadership. The President cannot lead: he is merely the executor of the sovereign legislative will. The Secretaries cannot lead: they are little more than chief clerks, or superintendents, of the departments, with the barren privilege of advising the President as to matters in most of which the President has no power to act independently of the sanction of the Senate. The most ambitious Congressman cannot lead: he can rise no higher than the chairmanship of the Committee of Ways and Means or the Speakership of the House; and what scope for statesmanship has either chairman or Speaker? They are small parts of the machine.

The cardinal feature of Cabinet government, on the other hand, is responsible leadership—the leadership and authority of a small body of men who have won the foremost places in their party by a display of administrative talents and by evidence of high ability given upon the floor of Congress in the stormy play of debate. None but the ablest can become leaders and masters in this keen tournament, in which arguments are the weapons and the people the judges. Clearly defined, definitely directed ministerial policies arouse bold and concerted opposition; and leaders of Oppositions become in their turn leaders of Cabinets. Such recognized leadership is necessary to the development of statesmanship under popular, republican institutions; for only opportunity for such leadership can make politics seem worthy of cultivation to men of high mind and aim.*

It need not be concealed that the introduction of Cabinet government into the United States would be attended with many perplexing difficulties. It would present many questions that must give us pause. It would introduce a new power into our government. The Cabinet would be constituted head and front of the State. But, great as its power would be, that power could not be an object of reasonable jealousy. It would be exercised openly, always under the eye of the people, and subject to the controlling will of their representatives. It could not be abused. The danger is not in that direction; it seems to be in another. Would not the predominant power of the Cabinet dwarf the presidential office? The Cabinet and not the President would be the Executive. The President would become a mere figure-head: the Presidency a mere peg on which to hang the real Executive. Thus it would seem, at least; and would it not so turn out in reality? No; probably not. The Cabinet would take the place of the Standing Committees— would it not?—and not the place of the President. The President would be robbed, no doubt, of much of the semblance of his power; but of how much of its reality? His influence over the policy of the departments is now insignificant. What the Standing Committees do not direct the Secretaries for the most part control. Indeed, were Civil Service reformers to attain the ends they so honourably seek— a consummation devoutly to be wished!—the President would have little to do. Take the appointments away from him, and he might be overburdened with leisure.

The case, then, stands thus: the President now makes appointments and exercises an occasional and general supervision over the departments; under Cabinet government he would be able to exert quite as much control over the conduct of the departments, and some not inconsiderable influence upon legislation besides. The gist of the matter lies here. Under either system the general policy of the departments is decided by legislative, and not by executive, will. It can be no great satisfaction to any man to possess the barren privilege of suggesting the best methods of managing the every-day routine business of the several executive bureaux. If one is commanded to go to this place or to that place, whether he wants to go or not, it is small solace to his reluctant spirit that

* See a discussion of this subject by the same author in *International Rev.*, Aug. 1879. [WW's note.]

he can choose whether he will walk or ride in going the journey. Any change that would give the President access to the legislative ear would be to him a gain, and not a loss, of power; and as president of the Cabinet council he would have such access. He would stand at the elbow of the great Standing Committee into whose hands was entrusted the exalted prerogative of directing legislation.

But what if the President were of one party and his Cabinet of the opposite? Of course this must happen with a President holding office for a long term. He must appoint his Cabinet from the ranks of that party which commands a majority in Congress, and that majority is not likely to remain for many years with the same party. This need be no cause of embarrassment, however. If the President of the French Republic can act with dignity and prudence and tact under such circumstances, surely an American President can perform his duty with no less willingness, discretion, and success. Nothing purges a man so quickly and effectually of partisanship as high responsibility given along with permanency of trust. To make judges fearless and upright, give them their offices during good behaviour. They are lifted above all personal considerations by the greatness of the trust reposed in them. So it would be, also, with a President elected to hold office during good behaviour. He could, and would, rise above partisan feeling. And, if he did not: what then? He still could not escape his duty in the appointment of the Cabinet; and he would be blind indeed if he did not deem it preferable to preside at the deliberations of a ministry representing the power and omnipotence of Congress, rather than at the consultations of Secretaries who, even when of the party of the majority, have no voice in the conduct of legislation. If a man of ability, he might, through the former, exercise great power in public affairs; whilst through the latter, whatever his talents, he could exercise little or none. If weak or a mere partisan, he would in any case be impotent.

But what of the *veto* power? It would fall into disuse. If used, every exercise of it would lead to a governmental crisis. The Cabinet would be the servants, as well as the leaders, of the legislative majority—the chief and foremost representatives of that majority—and they would assuredly never advise the President to refuse to sign a bill which they had themselves introduced or advocated. If, on the other hand, it had passed in the face of their opposition, they could not honourably avoid resignation by procuring a *veto*. Nor would the President care to make use of this prerogative without or against the advice of the ministers. They could hardly continue in office if their policy were frustrated by the President; and, if in the matter of any particular measure they represented the majority, the President could not call upon the minority, to whom his *veto* might be acceptible, to form a Cabinet and oust the true representatives of Congress. The *veto* power, if not abolished by positive law, would undoubtedly fall into disuse. And no one who has watched the course of our government in recent years can think that the disuse of the *veto* would be anything but an advantage. The voice of a *veto* is generally the voice of a mere auctioneer bidding for popular favour. Besides, to preserve it is only to prefer the judgment of a single representative to the judgment of the Senate and House of Representatives. Presidents are not even any longer, in any true sense of the word, representatives of the people. They are mere creatures—or, at least, creations—of national nominating conventions; and this sovereign prerogative consequently sits ill upon them, however well it might sit upon a man chosen by the free and undirected choice of the people.

When all this has been said, it may appear that the Presidential office has been stripped of all its trappings of power and reduced to a mere machine for the nomination of Cabinets. Who would desire the Presidency under this new order of things? As well ask, Who would care to be elected King of England for the term of his natural life? To what station of greater dignity and consideration and power could a citizen aspire? The elective head of a great nation, the central and most honoured figure of a great government! Surely no man could desire to be more! Why is the Presidency considered a prize now? Not because of any great power of governing with which its occupant is invested, but because it is the chief dispensary of favours. The party that wins the Presidency controls all the federal offices—exercising thus a power which is as vast as it is corrupting and illegitimate. If these dirty things prompt ambition, why is it incredible that exalted dignity and honoured station could tempt it also?

The most awkward question that meets the advocates of Cabinet government arises out of the plan of dual representation upon which Congress is made up. Suppose that the Senate and the House of Representatives were of opposite parties, which should the Cabinet represent? In England the powers of the House of Lords have so fallen into disuse that there is no embarrassment on this score to make difficulties for our cousins over the sea. The Cabinet represents the Commons as a matter of course. But our upper House is as high in authority as is our lower. Nay, it is even regarded with higher consideration. It is esteemed in reality the upper House. But, notwithstanding all that, in such a matter as the control of a Cabinet, its claims, like those of the Lords, would necessarily be postponed to the claims of the popular chamber; because the Representatives hold the nation's purse; and they, rather than the Senators, represent that feature of nationality which the Cabinet would represent. To say this is not to say that our form of government is national. It is both national and federal. For certain enumerated purposes it is national; for all others it is federal. In all matters of foreign policy, of finance, of commerce —in all matters in which it is absolutely necessary or manifestly expedient that we should observe a common policy—we act as a nation; in all others the several States pursue their own separate and independent courses. In a very important sense, then, we are a nation: and our national character is typified in the House of Representatives. This nationality the Cabinet, too, should represent: for they would be the leaders of opinion on national topics; they would stand or fall on questions of national policy.

Would the Senate be belittled? Would its authority suffer eclipse? Not at all. Its prestige would not be diminished, because its present claims to respect would in no wise be affected. It is not honoured now because it is the more powerful arm of the legislature, but because it is the more select. Its members are picked men. They are the political leaders of their States. They are generally men who have served long and illustriously in the House and hold on that account strong title to the country's regard. These are the principal grounds for the high consideration in which the Senate is held; and none of these would be taken away by giving the House a controlling voice in the formation of Cabinets.

Besides, it is not to be expected that the political complexion of the two Houses would often be different. It is not often so now, and it would be still less frequently so if the term of tenure of the representative office were made longer. Moreover, there is a quintessential incident of Cabinet government, not yet considered in this discussion, which would render the likelihood of collisions of opinion between the Senate and the House still more remote. That incident is the power of *dissolution*. It would be needful to confer on the President the power of dissolving the House of Representatives and calling for another election, when advised to dissolve it by his ministers.

There would be no danger in bestowing such a prerogative; and there would be no having Cabinet government without it. It would be indispensable to the smooth operation of government. For suppose the Representative chamber elected for a fixed and unalterable period of six years, and in the third year of its term a ministry defeated on some vital point of its programme, so defeated as to feel compelled to resign; how would the government go on? The defeated ministry would and could no longer try to lead a rebellious majority; and that majority would certainly refuse to follow a Cabinet composed of the leaders of the Opposition now temporarily in the ascendent. Any other ministry than the one just resigned could scarcely in ordinary times hold office by any but a very precarious tenure; and the retiring ministers would never be willing to resume the leadership of an assembly which had declined to act with them in regard to an essential measure of their administration. They would care nothing for a nominal or a hampered authority. The only rational recourse in such a quandary would be an appeal to the country. Better dissolve the House and have new elections and a fresh and harmonious majority again than suffer the infliction of three years of crippled, hesitating, vacillating government.

The power of dissolution would be not only indispensable but also without danger. It could be exercised only when its exercise might be advised by the ministry of the day: and for that advice the ministers and their party would be responsible to the country. They would not lightly advise dissolution. They would esteem it much more expedient to let their rivals and opponents essay the formation of a Cabinet and the conduct of the government than to risk on their own behalf an appeal to the country on any frivolous pretext or any impulse of pique. A dissolution would always put a distinct issue before the people. By advising it the ministry would say, in effect, to the constituencies, "In pursuance of our general policy, which was approved by you at the last elections, we laid such and such proposals before your representatives; these proposals they saw fit to reject: we therefore appeal to you, believing that we, and not the majority which condemned our measures, most faithfully represent your opinions upon the questions at issue." It is scarcely conceivable that any ministry, unless they were in truly desperate straits, would risk such an appeal on any matters but such as they esteemed of the highest importance and the gravest import: for to resort to dissolution and new elections without strong claims on the confidence of the country and merely because they were piqued at their defeat would be suicidal. It would certainly bring their opponents into office and cast upon themselves the additional discomfiture and humiliation of an adverse vote on the part of a majority of their countrymen.

The more flexible the forms of popular government, the more perfect are they. It is foolish to regulate them by astronomical periods; to determine that certain representatives shall govern, whether they rule well or ill, for such and such a certain and fixed length of time, and that when that time elapses—not sooner nor later—they shall be replaced by others. Representatives should be replaced only when they have ceased to represent the sentiments of the constituencies. The only practical difficulty, of course, is to fix upon that 'when.' It is prudent and proper, indeed, that legislative terms should have set to them maximum periods—periods beyond which they must not last—; for the trustees of legislative power should be made to render frequent account of their trusteeship; but to put representatives beyond the reach of the people during that maximum period, by providing that in the meantime their actions shall not be subject to question by their constituents, is not demanded by prudence, neither is it consistent with convenience or with good government. It gives governmental forms an inflexibility that makes them breakable. If under Cabinet government the House of Representatives were to be indissoluble for any considerable number of years, serious hitches would occur in the operations of the system. Business would be blocked, if at any time neither the ministry of the day nor the Opposition could command a working majority. The House would have to content itself with makeshift compromises until the tediously delayed moment should come at which it could appeal to the country for its deciding judgment.

The dissolubility of the House would enhance the importance of the indissoluble Senate. Manifestly it would not be feasible to dissolve the Senate. Its constituencies are the State legislatures. The power to dissolve it, therefore, would be equivalent to an authority to call together the legislatures of the States. Then, too, under our present system membership of the Senate is partially renewed every two years and it is thus, perhaps, sufficiently sensitive to changes of public opinion. Moreover, all the purposes of dissolution would be accomplished by the re-election of the representative chamber only. The object of dissolution would be to obtain an expression of opinion by the country; and it is hardly probable that Senators, with all their six-year security, would often care to brave public sentiment by standing in the way of a policy sanctioned by the country. They would offer no factious or unreasonable resistence to the express will of the people as spoken by the newly-elected House. A new election would show them the temper of the country, and they would not be so blind as to ignore or antagonize it. The dissolution of the House would thus answer the purposes of a dissolution of both branches of Congress.

It would not, however, rob the Senate of its independence any more than biennial elections of the House now rob it of that independence. The Senate would become a symbol of the stability of the government. It never dies. Biennially one third of its membership is renewed; but there is no time set at which the entire body ceases to exist and must give place to a successor. It is endowed with the capacity of perpetual existence. Continually rejuvenated, it never grows old. Presidential terms run to an end; Representatives ever and again vacate their powers and give place to new Houses; but for the Senate no flight of years brings a period of death.

Under the rule of the Standing Committees legislation does not halt for lack of the power of dissolution. The harmony of the House seldom suffers an interruption. So far as outsiders can see, legislation flows placidly on, and the majority easily has its own way. Its power is seldom, if ever, broken anywhere but at the polls; partly because there is no freedom of debate in the House, but principally because there is no real concert of action between the committees and no attempt to carry out any definite plans or any consistent policy. The majority does not square its schemes by any clearly-avowed principles; indeed it seldom has any schemes. Each committee obeys its own whims; each member works to establish his own ideas and to satisfy the wishes or vanities of his own constituents; each measure that cannot prevail in its entirety is pruned and stripped of its clauses till it offers the appearance of a fair compromise; each party bids for votes, now by zeal in one direction, again by equal zeal in the opposite; no two schemes pull together; and, after the hurly-burly's done, the composite results of a session stand, in incoherent mass, as the 'Acts of Such and Such a Congress.' If there is a coincidence of principle between several bills of the same session, it is generally accidental. The majority cannot be suspected of having any policy. It is thus that it happens that there is never a transfer of power from one party to the other during a session. The majority remains of one mind so long as the Congress lives, because their purposes are very vague and uncertain and their powers of intelligent coöperation very limited. They represent only a party name, not a political creed; and it is easy to seem to stay on one side when the boundaries of that side are quite indefinite. Of course there is never any necessity to dissolve these short-lived Houses; they always agree with themselves.

But when policies are sharply-defined and boldly avowed, and when legislative terms are of considerable duration, the balance of political power may often turn or be evenly poised in the midst of a session. Party men will do much, will even sacrifice a great deal, to preserve party union and organization and keep their leaders in office. But there are always free lances where there are free combats. Give the House free and frequent discussions and there will spring up scores of independent members, sleepless critics of the movements of their own party as well as of the tactics of their opponents—men who usually coöperate with one of the great parties and who would not altogether renounce party allegiance, but who, keeping party principles always in view and preferring triumphs of principle to mere triumphs of party, would never hesitate to vote against their own leaders whenever they saw, or thought they saw, them departing, were it never so little, from what had been esteemed the true courses of the party, or the true tenets of the party creed. Such men would often be numerous enough to hold the balance of power, and always formidable enough to inspire salutary respect; and whenever their disaffection brought votes to a tie or left ministers in a minority, legislation must either stand still or there must be an appeal to the constituencies, that the country might decide whether of the twain, the ministers or their opponents, were in the right. The people must be the jury. The principle of dissolution is essentially republican. As Jefferson said, the life and strength of republicanism is an absolute acquiescence in the will of the majority; and any mechanism by which the government is rendered sensitive to the will of the majority is in its principle purely republican.

If it be asked, Would not this change of administration with every change of the Congressional majority bring our government under the curse of instability? the answering question must be, How would it make that government any more unstable than it now is? There is now a possibility of a transfer of power from one party to the other every two years; and the history of Cabinet government in Great Britain and in France—and even in the British provinces, where ministries are most frequently changed—does not warrant the conclusion that its introduction here would make a more frequent transfer of power probable. The fact that our Executive remains the same for four years together is of no consequence. The transfer of power that is of effect is the transfer of *legislative* power. Our executive departments are the servants, nay the mere creatures, of Congress; and if the Congressional majority change, it matters little of what party the Secretaries are; they must in any case obey that majority. No, the system would be more in sym-

pathy with republican principles, by being more sensitive to public opinion, and at the same time more stable, with its permanent
head and its indissoluble Senate.

But is it not a scheme of centralization? Would the reserved
rights of the States be safe from infraction by this active and
powerful central authority? Again the answer must be prefaced
with a question: How could the change possibly affect the *nature*
of our government? It would alter the *forms* under which the
federal powers would be exercised; but how would it enlarge those
powers? This would still be that unique and "indissoluble union
of indestructible states" which has stood for the admiration of the
world since first the marvellous Constitution of 1787 received the
sanction of the Confederation. No Cabinet could take to itself any
powers that were not federal; and ministries would be the less
likely to usurp prerogatives not clearly theirs because of the open
system of legislation that would necessarily prevail. The people
could then watch the progress of policies as they cannot now, and
could detect imperialist tendencies in the much-debated plans
of a responsible Cabinet much more readily than in the disjointed and seldom-discussed schemes of inharmonious committees. Everything would be done openly and above board; and, if
the government were centralized, it would be before the eyes and
with the sanction of the country.

It has been well said that "the great fault of political writers is
their too close adherence to the forms of the system of state which
they happen to be expounding or examining. They stop short at
the anatomy of institutions and do not penetrate to the secret of
their functions"; and Burke has declared, in a similar vein, that
in studying the problems that confront us in matters of government we must have regard "not merely to forms of government
and law" but more especially to "whole groups of social facts which
give to law and government the spirit that makes them workable."
It is imperative, therefore, that we should remember, in searching
for truth in this discussion, that the *form* in which our Federal
government is now cast is not essential. Its dual principle, its foundations of State and national sovereignty—these are essential; but
not the formal organization of its departments. That might be altogether changed without infringing a single principle of the Constitution. Certainly an alteration of that organization would not be
an enlargement of the federal powers. The adoption of Cabinet
government would, on the contrary, be a substantial guarantee
that those powers would not be unduly or unwisely extended, since
it would ensure their open exercise and afford an easy means of

controlling the administration of the government by public opinion. "The secret of the functions" of our Federal government, "the spirit that makes it workable," is this, if it be anything, that those institutions which are national should be regulated according to the will of the nation, with all efficiency and with all purity; and that form which most surely effects that end is the form most in accord with the principles of the Constitution. If that form be Cabinet government, then Cabinet government is the form contemplated by the spirit of the Constitution.

Even the changes of form incident to the establishment of Cabinet government in this country would not be great. They would be simply a recognition of existing facts: principally of the fact that Congress is and must inevitably continue to be omnipotent within the federal sphere, and that the committees which rule the House must rule the country. The leading change would be the substitution of a single Cabinet-committee which the country could always control for those committees which now rule without restraint. Cabinet government would be the full perfection of our system.

V.

The Work of Reform

"Law has no force save that which it derives from the consent and respect of those who live under it."

Little now remains to be said in conclusion of this discussion. *Shall the forms of federal administration be altered in accordance with a plan which has been tested and found best by our own ancestors and our own kinsmen, which is now the prevailing system amongst the most advanced nations of the world, and which both reason and our own experience recommend to our acceptance?* That is the single, the plain, the simple issue.

That the country is prepared, or at least preparing, for a change of the instrumentalities of government none but the ignorant and the old can doubt. Some change will soon be indispensable. The future that stands in our face is full of disquieting possibilities. Our populations are growing at such a rate that one's reckonings stagger at counting the possible millions that may have a home and a work on this continent ere fifty more years have filled their short span. The East will not always be the centre of national life. The South is fast accumulating wealth and will faster gather influence. The West has already achieved a greatness which no man can gainsay, and has in future store a power of growth which no man can estimate. These great sections may be antagonistic, or they may not be. Whether they are to be harmonious or dissentient depends almost entirely upon the methods and the policies of government. If monopolies are to thrive in one section at the expense of those who are denied monopolies in another; if government let not alone the industrial pursuits of its citizens, but insist upon hampering them with restrictions, visiting and superintending them through vexatious hosts of prying officials; if government tax, not to support and further its own enterprises, but to feed the enterprises of private persons; if government, in a word, be not careful to keep within its own sphere and square its policy by rules of national welfare, sectional lines must and will be known, citizens of one part of the country will look with jealousy and hatred upon their fellow-citizens of another part, and faction must tear and dissension distract a country which Providence would bless but which man can curse.

If, therefore, there be one need more imperious than another it is that the government of this country be made strong, prompt, wieldy, and efficient. The government of a country so vast and a Union so delicate must be the most honest and the most competent in the world; must be the best informed of governments and the surest and most open and accessible source of political information; must at once guide public opinion and be guided by it. Its strength must consist in the certainty and uniformity of its purposes, in its accord with national sentiment, in its prompt action, and in its honest aims. If, therefore, there be any form of government which combines all these qualities, that form it is which America must have, either now or presently.

That Cabinet government is the form which does combine strength, wieldiness, and efficiency more completely than any other form of government yet devised or known appears not only from the discussions of the foregoing chapters but from the history of the English race and from the modern assent of all enlightened nations. The lesson of English history is very plain to this effect. The British House of Commons, the great prototype of our own Congress, passed, almost two centuries ago, through just such a season of inadequate organization as that in which Congress now languishes. It, too, was once both powerful and clumsy, both omnipotent and awkward, both imperative and incompetent. Here is Mr. Green's version of the story*[:]

* Green's *History of the English People* (Harpers, 1880) Vol. IV, pp. 58-61 *passim* [WW's note.]

In outer seeming the Revolution of 1688 had only transferred the sovereignty over England from James to William and Mary. In actual fact it had given a powerful and decisive impulse to the great constitutional progress which was transferring the sovereignty from the King to the House of Commons. From the moment when its sole right to tax the nation was established by the Bill of Rights, and when its own resolve settled the practice of granting none but annual supplies to the Crown, the House of Commons became the supreme power in the State. . . . But though the constitutional change was complete the machinery of government was far from having adapted itself to the new conditions of political life which such a change brought about. However powerful the will of the Commons might be it had no means of bringing its will directly to bear on the conduct of public affairs. . . . The result was the growth of a temper in the Lower House which drove William and his Ministers to dispair. It became as corrupt, as jealous of power, as fickle in its resolves and factious in spirit *as bodies always become whose consciousness of the possession of power is untempered by a corresponding consciousness of the practical difficulties or the moral responsibilities of the power which they possess.* It grumbled . . . ; and it blamed the Crown and its Ministers for all at which it grumbled. But it was hard to find out what policy or measures it would have preferred. Its mood changed, as William bitterly complained, with every hour. . . . The Houses were in fact *without the guidance of recognized leaders, without adequate information, and destitute of that organization out of which alone a definite policy can come.* Nothing better proves the inborn political capacity of the English mind than that it should at once have found a simple and effective solution of such a difficulty as this. The credit of the solution belongs to a man whose political character was of the lowest type. [The counsel of Robert, Earl of Sunderland,]* was to recognize practically the new power of the Commons by choosing the Ministers of the Crown exclusively from among the members of the party which was strongest in the Lower House. . . . Sunderland's plan aimed at replacing these independent Ministers *by a homogeneous Ministry, chosen from the same party, representing the same sentiments, and bound together for common action by a sense of responsibility and loyalty to the party to which it belonged.* Not only was such a plan likely to secure a unity of administration which had been unknown till then, but it gave an organization to the House of Commons which it had never had before. *The Ministers who were representatives of the majority of its members became the natural leaders of the House.* Small factions were drawn together into the two great parties which supported or opposed the Ministry of the Crown. Above all it brought about in the simplest possible way the solution of the problem which had so long vexed both Kings and Commons. The new Ministers ceased in all but name to be the King's servants. They became *simply an Executive Committee representing the will of the majority of the House of Commons, and capable of being easily set aside by it and replaced by a similar Committee whenever the balance of power shifted from one side of the House to the other.*

* WW's insertion.

Such was the natural generation of Cabinet government in Great Britain. Of course the historian in describing the system which Sunderland thus suggested anticipates steps in its development which were not taken till long after William of Orange was dead. At first, as Mr. Green himself says, it was only slowly and tentatively that William ventured to put Sunderland's suggestion into practice; and, as has already been made clear in this discussion, it was not till the time of George IV that the new system was perfected. It did not spring full-fledged from any brain, but, like all the rest of the great constitution of which it is now the centre, was long a-making. It waited for more than a century for the last threads of its fabric, and is, consequently, no texture of theories, but a stout garment made to wear.

The likeness of our own Congress to the Parliaments which sat just after 1688 is quite notable. It is, like them, supreme; and its supremacy, like theirs, is founded upon its exclusive right of levying certain taxes and granting supplies to the national government. Like them, too, it has felt the need of an organization which would enable it to bring its will directly to bear on the conduct of public affairs and at the same time to keep that will within the lines of a definite policy. Its will is fickle, its policy uncertain, its schemes imperfect. It is "without the guidance of recognized leaders, without adequate information"; and it has not as yet had the sagacity to discover in Sunderland's suggestion the only practicable means by which its power can be made available and its authority salutary. Omnipotent as it is, it can find no satisfaction in the control of the Executive, for it is itself hampered, as the Executive is harassed, by its isolation from the coördinate branches of government. Its committees may command, but they cannot superintend the execution of their commands. The Secretaries of the departments, though not free enough to have any independent policy of their own, are free enough to make very poor servants. When once they are installed in office, their hold upon that office no longer depends on the will of Congress. If they please the President, they need not fear the displeasure of Congress; unless, indeed, by actual crime, they rashly put themselves in the way of impeachment. If their folly be not extravagant or criminal, their authority will be theirs till the earth has four times made its annual journey round the sun. They make daily blunders in administration and repeated mistakes in business, may thwart in a hundred vexatious little ways the plans of Congress, and yet all the while snap their fingers at its dissatisfaction or displeasure. They have not the gratification of power but they have the gratification of a semi-independence which permits them to be tricky and scheming. There are ways and ways of obeying; and if Congress be not pleased, why need they care? Congress did not give them their places, and cannot easily take them away.

The plain truth of the matter is that, if government is to operate smoothly, harmoniously, and efficiently, Congress must consent to the advice of Roger Sherman and choose its own executive servants. There can be no gain in winking facts. Congress will assert its supremacy over the Executive under any circumstances, if not in one way then in another, and it would, beyond a question, be better for it to exercise its authority openly rather than covertly, directly and with strict responsibility rather than indirectly and without any responsibility at all. Why not accept Sunderland's solution? Why not let Congress control that great Executive Committee, the Cabinet; why not let it govern in the face of the nation and, governing thus openly, make itself sure of the nation's intelligent support? Let parties be sobered by being made answerable for the conduct of affairs, elevated by being bound to the support of definite principles, drilled for honourable warfare by being put under a leadership of talent, and for honourable service by being put under the eye of its master, public opinion.

But how bring the country to adopt the new system? There's the rub. It must be confessed at the outset that there is little hope that Congress will lead in the movement. Congress is so organized that it can seldom be counted on to originate any provident or determinate policy; and, greatly as its own power and dignity would be enhanced by the institution of responsible Cabinet government, Congress is not likely to be first in devising plans for its introduction. True, a Committee of the Senate has lately approved a proposal to admit Cabinet officers to seats in Congress, and their admission to seats would be a first step towards the institution of Cabinet government; but the approval of a committee does not always argue success to the scheme approved. Committees often quiet precocious projects by patting them on the back. Congress is not yet even interested in the question, and it is reasonably certain that the impulse and the action, if anything is done, must come from the country.

The country is, indeed, very hard to move. Foreigners who visit the States agree with Mr. Dale, of Manchester, in declaring that there is amongst us "a class including thousands and tens of thousands of the best men in the country who think it possible to enjoy the fruits of good government without working for them"; and of course this class would hardly bestir themselves even in behalf of a reform which entirely recommended itself to their support. But even they can be aroused; and it cannot be that the country at large will ever fail to respond to the calls of a good cause, if those calls be made loud and imperative enough. The chief embarrassment is one which, probably, Mr. Dale did not perceive. It is that even when public opinion has made up its mind in this country it finds great difficulty in carrying its preferences into effect. Even when large numbers of intelligent and influential citizens adhere constantly and with sincere zeal to any great political doctrine which is refused recognition by the Legislature, they can organize no effective campaign for the propagation of their principles. They can force a battle with nobody. Though Congress is generally regardful enough of the temper of the country, and its members quick enough to heed the beck and nod of constituents, its mechanism is such that it is not quickly sensitive to any national sentiment. Local sentiment often finds voice in its halls, national sentiment seldom; because it has no national organization but is disintegrated into independent sections which easily and often take a local colouring. It is, consequently, not often the mouthpiece of the country at large, and public opinion is seriously embarrassed by having in Congress no permanent instrumentality through which to act. Whoever would accomplish anything must devise instrumentalities of their own.

The only available means, therefore, of bringing about such reforms in the methods of our government as are now imperatively needed would seem to be a combined and organized agitation of opinion: an agitation so concerted, so persistent, so powerful as to build up a body of opinion great enough to speak with authority and potent enough to carry its will into action, its action to success; a body of opinion so vast and resistless as to command the aid of legislature and the obedience of all the agencies of government. The press and the platform must be the pulpits from which to preach this new crusade against corrupt, vacillating, irresponsible government. National opinion must be invoked and the people called upon to act. If they can once be brought boldly and unequivocally to declare their will, they must prevail. None can stand against them.

To develop public opinion in regard to this great question may be the work of many years, just because the instrumentalities at command are clumsy and the task is great. The machinery of constitutional amendment is so ponderous and hard to move that none but a truly national sentiment can set it in motion. Besides, the work is without American precedent. There have been so few great constitutional reforms undertaken in this country that Americans are inexperienced in organized agitation. The anti-slavery movement there was, indeed; but it furnishes no proper model for the agitation now proposed. It was a struggle of passion, a mission of philanthropy, rather than a movement of political philosophy; whereas this must be a contest of reason, a mission of statesmanship. This is to be no cause of humanitarians. It cannot supply any vocabulary of cant, any swelling texts about the whip, bondage, and "bartered flesh." It is simply a theme for dispassionate discussion, a cause for the sympathy of all true friends of good government, a work for earnest patriots, and uplifting of the methods of government from awkward inefficiency into quick and healthy energy and efficacy

The key-note of the new movement might well be taken from those noble words of Burke's: "The value, spirit, and essence of a House of Commons consists in its being the express image of the feelings of the nation." Its Senators as well as its Representatives being all men chosen of the people, and none men preferred because of rank, our Congress is our House of Commons; and its "value, spirit, and essence" should consist "in its being the express image of the feelings of the nation." This is the only trustworthy principle of self-government. All other just saws of politics are merely its corollaries; and that must be but a clumsy and indifferent system which does not embody it. It need surprise no one, therefore, that in our own time Congress, when not treated with contemptuous indifference, is regarded with undisguised distrust. It is no more the "express image" of the nation's feelings than were the Commons upon which Burke was used to pass his scornful comment. They were long in open antagonism to the opinions of the nation; and the consequence was speedy and natural. "The results of such a divorce between the government and that general mass of national sentiment on which a government can alone safely ground itself at once made themselves felt. Robbed as it was of all practical power, and thus stripped of the feeling of responsibility which the consciousness of power carries with it, among the mass of Englishmen public opinion became ignorant and indifferent to the general progress of the age, . . . For the first and last time. . . Parliament was unpopular, and its opponents secure of popularity[.]"* How like our own recent and present experiences! Congress is unpopular, and its opponents secure of popularity; and this because there has been declared a divorce between government and the national sentiment; and public opinion,

* Green's *History of the Eng. People*, Vol. IV, p. 203. [WW's note.]

robbed of all practical power and divested of all sense of responsibility, is both ignorant and indifferent.

It is plain to see that there is as much need of Congressional reform in this country now as there was of parliamentary reform in England when parliaments were made up of kings' favourites and representatives of rotten boroughs. Congressmen represent caucuses and conventions, not the people; and, did they represent the unhampered choice of the people, Congress would not bear for any length of time the express image of the national sentiment. For when a session opens there is no determinate policy to look forward to, and when a session is ended no accomplished plans to look back upon. The country can hardly tell whether the works of any particular Congress have been good or bad; and, if it is ascertained that they have been bad, it is well nigh impossible to tell whom to condemn and punish. Plans have been developed helter-skelter under the rule of irresponsible committees; policies have shifted and wandered; both parties have vacillated and gone astray. If the sentiments of the nation have been belied or its feelings disregarded, there can be no surety that if this Congress is ousted and another substituted affairs will go otherwise. Possibly a few stubborn men on one or two committees are at the bottom of all the mischief, and nothing can be gained by punishing them.

But, besides being hasty and unmethodical, Congress is also otherwise incapable. It is still essentially as helpless a body as it was in the earlier days of its experience. Speaking of the first Congress, a recent writer has said, "It is not a little amusing to note how eagerly Congress, which had been ably and honestly struggling with the revenue, with commerce, and with a thousand details, fettered in all things by the awkwardness inherent in a legislative body, turned for relief to the new Secretary. They knew Hamilton's reputation and his perfect familiarity with theories of finance and government, and they seem to have felt instinctively that he was a great minister of state with a well-defined policy for every exigency[.]"* This picture would be "not a little amusing" if we could know whilst looking upon it that it illustrated only the first experiences of the sovereign national body, only the awkwardness of its childhood; that our later Congresses had learned how to guide and control themselves and had by this time established themselves in that well-grounded confidence which is built upon long and successful administration. But we know that such is not the case; that Congress, though not, perhaps, quite so awkward as at first, is quite as ignorant and helpless. Its committees carry it

---

* Lodge's *Hamilton* (*Am. Statesmen* series) pp. 85, 86. [WW's note.]

along through its business smoothly enough, but not intelligently enough; for they have no better means of learning than Congress itself has, and they are, of course, equally in need of guidance and instruction.

In one respect, indeed, Congress is less favourably situated now than it was when Washington and his Cabinet were chiefs of administration. It has not often had a Hamilton to turn to for aid and counsel. Not many years after Washington's administration closed the departments had already fallen into very different hands, and the officers of the Cabinet were almost, if not quite, as indifferently informed in the affairs of the government as were the committees. In 1807 John Randolph was chairman of the Committee on Ways and Means, which at that time was also the committee on appropriations, and he recounts, in an interesting letter to his intimate correspondent, Nicholson, this pitiful experience: "I called some time since at the navy office to ask an explanation of certain items of the estimate for this year. The Secretary called upon his chief clerk, who knew very little more of the business than his master. I propounded a question to the head of the department; he turned to the clerk like a boy who cannot say his lesson, and with imploring countenance beseeches aid; the clerk with much assurance gobbled out some common-place jargon, which I would not take for sterling; an explanation was required, and both were dumb. This pantomime was repeated at every item, until, disgusted, and ashamed for the degraded situation of the principal, I took leave without pursuing the subject, seeing that my object could not be attained. There was not one single question relating to the department that the Secretary could answer[.]"* Probably many other chairmen of Ways and Means have had similar vexatious and discouraging experiences with departmental officials. There have been other ignorant Secretaries of the Navy since Robert Smith, and the chiefs of the other departments have, as every one knows, very often had very confused ideas about more than one item of their estimates.

So it is that the incompetence of the government has been perpetuated. The departments have been ignorant and the committees irresponsible. So low has the reputation of our later Cabinets fallen that writers in the best of our public prints feel at full liberty to speak of their members with open contempt. "When Mr. William E. Chandler was made Secretary of the Navy," laughs the N. Y. *Nation*, "no one doubted that he would treat the department as 'spoils,' and consequently nobody has been disappointed. He is

* Adams' *John Randolph* (*Am. Statesmen series*) pp. 210, 211. [WW's note.]

one of the statesmen who can hardly conceive of a branch of the public Administration having no spoils in it"; and in the laugh we all freely join.

The committees are not yet equally despised, probably because they are not yet equally well-known; but much of their clumsiness is becoming evident to thoughtful observers. Especially in the management of the nation's financial affairs is their blundering noticed.

"So long as the Dr. side of the national account," says a writer in one of our best journals, "is managed by one set of men, and the Cr. side by another set, both sets working separately and in secret, without any public responsibility, and without intervention on the part of the executive official who is nominally responsible; so long as these sets"—these committees, that is—["]being composed largely of new men every two years, give no attention to business except when Congress is in session, and thus *spend in preparing plans the whole time which ought to be spent in public discussion of plans already matured, so that an immense budget is rushed through without discussion in a week or ten days*—just so long the finances will go from bad to worse, no matter by what name you call the party in power. No other nation on earth attempts such a thing, or could attempt it without soon coming to grief, our salvation thus far consisting in an enormous income, with practically no drain for military expenditure.

"The British national financial management is beyond comparison the first in the world, and it is so because the whole matter is placed in the hands of the Chancellor of the Exchequer, Parliament only pronouncing, after full discussion, aye or no in gross—in other words, applying the veto. It is a notable illustration of how with us the veto power is placed at the wrong end of the line.

"The expression for us of the difference between these two systems, of the change from an evil to a sound method, is the admission of the Secretary of the Treasury to a seat in Congress, with the right of defending a policy of unity, system, publicity, and responsibility against secret intrigue, an irresponsible lobby, and chaos. This is the proposition which needs to be forced upon the attention and understanding of the people; and the sooner we give up building our hopes upon any change of parties or of men under the existing system, the sooner we shall get upon the road to some practical result"*

* "G. B." in N. Y. *Nation*, Nov. 30th 1882 [WW's note. He was quoting from G[amaliel] B[radford] to the Editor, Nov. 27, 1882, New York *Nation*, xxv (Nov. 30, 1882), 462-63—Eds.' note.]

It ought to be observed that others besides the financial committees bungle with boldness and facility in their attempts to regulate the affairs of the departments, and that it is not the Treasury alone that suffers from such maladroitness and ignorance. If "unity, system, publicity, and responsibility" are to prevail to the ousting of "secret intrigue, an irresponsible lobby, and chaos," not one only but all of the departments must be represented on the floor of Congress. All the Cabinet ought to be admitted to Congressional seats; and their admission would unquestionably be a step in the right direction, because, once that step was taken, responsible Cabinet government would be near at hand.

We have here in America abundant and daily illustration of Lord Bute's sinister suggestion, that "the forms of a free and the ends of an arbitrary government are things not altogether incompatible." That is an arbitrary government whose methods are secret and irresponsible; and what more secret or irresponsible methods ever existed under the names of free institutions than those which flourish beneath the shelter of committee rule? In our anxiety to escape executive despotism we have thrown ourselves into the arms of legislative tyrants, and now tamely submit to have a many-headed monarch lord it over us.

This, it seems, the people—or, at least, a great many observant citizens—are just now beginning to see, and they naturally turn with expectation of relief to that system which the experience of our own race has approved the best; that system which recognizes without false sentiment or confusion of ideas the true line of separation between those functions which are properly executive and those which are properly legislative,—to Cabinet government, which, bringing the executive of officers of government into the legislature to act under its eye as its Grand Committee, gives into their hands the preparation of all principal measures of administration, and reserves to the legislature an inalienable right to discuss and pass judgment upon such measures with perfect freedom, without cumbering or embarrassing it with such duties of originating schemes as its awkward size and limited facilities for obtaining adequate and exact information would prevent it from fulfilling with anything like wisdom or expedition.

An agitation directed towards the establishment of such new principles and modes of government in this country would, it is fair to presume, be received with instant favour in many quarters, and in all with eventual approbation. It would certainly work a great, nay even a marvellous, change in the character of our public meetings. What are they now but meaningless musters of the curious and the partisan, occasions for empty speech-making and loud-mouthed clamour? If it were not painful, it would be highly diverting to note the course which American political meetings generally take. There is first of all, of course, the assemblage itself to be remarked, sitting, as it always does, entirely at its ease; composed principally of elderly men who loll lazily and even listlessly in their seats, as if altogether too accustomed to gatherings of the kind to be at all roused to expectancy as to anything that may be about to take place, rubbing their bald heads or scant locks with hand or handkerchief in quiet and complacent contemplation, or pouring out in languid accents good-natured gossip concerning those innumerable public meetings which they have attended and at which they remember to have heard 'So-and-So' speak, when 'What's-his-name' was a candidate for the Presidency—days those of eloquence such as one never hears now-a-days, they say—; whilst here and there throughout the crowded room younger men, and even boys, sit or stand, drinking in at their ears the gossip which is afloat about them and pouring out at their lips volumes of smoke which charge the air with the fumes of tobacco and dim the atmosphere almost as with the clouds of battle. All this one can see on such occasions before the speaking begins; and, if one has had experience of such gatherings, seeing all these things makes one feel very much at home.

When the speech-making has set in there is more quiet and a little less smoke. The speaker is probably some well-known local politician whom the audience do not hesitate to address with the utmost freedom and familiarity by the briefest form of his Christian name when they cheer or interrupt him. He is probably listened to, however, with a considerable degree of attention; not so much, one is led to think, because his auditors are interested in his theme as because they like the anecdotes with which he is sure to intersperse his remarks and have a very keen relish for the spicy and vinegared strictures which he is equally sure to pass upon his political opponents, as well as a decided taste for the highly embellished pieces of rhetoric to which he will delight to treat all who hear him. Indeed there is, quite likely, nothing else attractive or noticeable in what he says. These anecdotal, rhetorical, and splenetic passages doubtless constitute the body of the oration. Speeches delivered under such circumstances do not often exhibit any strong attempt at the enunciation of principles or the exposition of policies. Of definite policies the speaker, doubtless, knows as little as his party. His remarks upon the conduct of the government are confined to criticisms of the past, censuring what has been done by his opponents and excusing or extolling what has been done by his friends and co-partisans. His principles are fine generalities which are well-worn, but still glittering. He is likely, one can safely predict, to say a great deal that is laudatory and boastful about the "record" of his own party and a great deal more that is condemnatory and scornful about the "record" of the opposite party, but not at all apt to say anything exact or intelligible about the character of the 'glorious principles' or concerning the nature of the 'grand cause' of which he will not fail to claim to be a proud representative. He will say a great deal that is ingenious and amusing, probably; but not much that is instructive. He will do his best, poor man, to convey a clear and satisfactory idea of the purposes of his party, and though he may not have genius enough to succeed in this desperate endeavour, he will probably do a good deal towards leaving a very favourable impression as to his own good purposes.

It would be easy to imagine meetings of a different kind. It would be easy to picture parties united and organized in the pursuit of special and determinate ends, and in that pursuit putting upon public opinion the tremendous pressure of persistent earnestness of discussion, of agitation in season and out of season; inviting every city and every country-side to public meeting after public meeting, never letting the ears of any community rest long without some potent reminder of the issues that were being pressed or permitting any man's conscience to go long unmindful of the cause that was being advanced. What meetings called by such a body of men would be like it is not hard to surmise. There would be intense listening and earnest, business-like speaking; there would be enthusiasm in audiences and ardour in orators. The business of the hour would be persuasion, the end in view, action.

But whilst it is easy enough to conjure up in the imagination pictures such as this, the organization of such an agitation is hard enough in actual practice. If ever it could be easy, it ought surely to be easiest in the advancement of such a purpose as the establishment of Cabinet government in this country. Cabinet government once set up at the national capital, politics would take a much higher place than they ever can in ordinary times under our present system; and, meantime, public gatherings in its behalf might be made to speak a great deal in its advocacy.

Surely the advocates of no other cause ever had a fuller armoury of arguments. For a people fond of self-government the inducements to its espousal must, when taken all together, seem overwhelming. One consideration there is which would seem to be sufficient of itself to make such a people quick to turn from committees to a Cabinet. In representative governments it is the unquestionable right of every constituency to have, through its representative, a voice in *all* legislation. This right committee government denies and Cabinet government freely accords. Under the former the privilege of exercising this right depends upon accident. If a representative get upon the right committee, he may have a chance in the committee room and on the floor of the House to say something effective to Congress upon the subjects in which his constituents are most deeply interested; but if he get on the wrong committee—he can vote, that is all. Under Cabinet government, on the contrary, every representative has an equal chance of obtaining in the House itself, where all discussion is conducted, a hearing upon every question taken under consideration.

To say this is to say enough for Cabinet government; for without this equality of right a few constituencies win the most coveted committee appointments, and the rest are put at an immeasurable disadvantage. But this is not all. Cabinet government conducted, as it would be, always in a full blaze of discussion, would afford the people unexceptionable advantages for observing the course of administration, for watching carefully and critically the whole plan of government as from time to time framed or developed. Congress would not waste its energies and neglect its proper functions in the prosecution of such committee work as it is now compelled to do. It is not at present equal to the great task which is yearly set it. It is necessary for it to divide itself into numerous committees whose duty it is to mature and throw into shape the measures of each session. The great work is committee work. After that is done there is no time remaining for anything else; certainly no time for the duties of deliberation. To do all its duty, according to the theory of government now received in this country, Congress should first, in its committee rooms, prepare with due care and thought the bills which are to constitute the topics of the session's deliberations, and then, after doing this work thoroughly, give itself ample time to canvass all the measures thus matured, taking nothing upon the mere recommendation of a committee, but submitting everything without reserve to a patient scrutiny of debate in those Houses in which all the committees are gathered together as one supreme Congress. But it cannot do both these things. The years are not long enough. Its only salvation from its present arbitrary and unsatisfactory ways lies in the abandonment of an impossible undertaking, in a resignation to the Executive of those functions which of right and in reason belong to the Executive. Let the executive ministers be brought into Congress as its Grand Committee, and let them prepare legislation and mature policies; and let Congress content itself with those duties of deliberation and investigation, those prerogatives of superintendence, which it is capable of exercising with dignity and success and in which it will unquestionably find its greatest usefulness.

By such an arrangement the regular business of the session will be greatly facilitated and the privileges of private members at the same time greatly enlarged. Congress will be no longer broken up into numberless co-ordinate and practically independent committees, but will devote its time principally to the full consideration of the schemes introduced by the great ministerial committee, which will advise it under a responsibility stricter than any hitherto known in our government, pledging their ministerial seats as security for their wisdom and fidelity. The Houses will have, besides, what they now seldom have, leisure to hear private members in behalf of their own proposals. No member has now any chance of having a bill of his own carefully considered, because every bill must go to a committee and cannot stand before Congress unless a committee be its sponsors. But, if the sessional time now consumed in committee work were spent in the debate of plans prepared by hands more competent and more responsible than those of any committee, by an executive ministry, there would be time enough found for the direct discussion of the measures of individual Congressmen. Ideas now dumb would find voice. Constituencies now silent would become honoured through the untrammelled exertions of earnest and able representatives who can, under the present order of things, find no chance to bring themselves into useful prominence. Criticism of government policies would cease to be sour and would become serious and businesslike, because it would be free and endowed with power. Government would be simplified and legislation purified and reduced to intelligent system.

When such a system prevails the people can govern; but not till then. Then there will be determinate policies, and parties which can be understood and followed; but not till then. Then, too, the finances will take shape. The Secretary of the Treasury will each year submit his budget—his estimate of the revenues of the coming year and his propositions for such adjustments of taxation as will meet the anticipated expenses of government with greatest certainty and least hardship and injustice to the taxpayer—and this budget will be offered to the test of debate. Mr. Secretary will have to answer all questions and satisfy or silence all reasonable objectors; and the country will begin to understand the finances and to come into some control of their management. The people can comprehend matured schemes thus discussed and explained as they cannot the hasty and jumbled proposals of two independent committees whose recommendations are introduced with no attempt at coöperation and passed without much show of serious discussion.

The administration of the other departments also will become plainer and more intelligible. The other Secretaries too will in like manner have to submit well-considered and intelligently-matured departmental schemes to Congress, by it to be examined and judged; and everything will soon fall into definite and reliable system. There will at last be those to whom Congress can safely look for information and guidance, those who are responsible to it for the administration of the government, who represent certain policies and lead rationally organized parties. The Cabinet will be the great Congressional committee; and Congress can devote itself to those duties of debate and superintendence by whose faithful performance it can purify and facilitate government and enlighten the nation.

One of the chief recommendations of the new system will, of course, be the inexorable responsibility which it imposes upon politicians and parties. In an address delivered on a recent occasion,* in the capacity of President of the Birmingham and Midland Institute, Mr. [J. A.]Froude, having in mind, of course, British forms of government, said very happily that "In party government party life becomes like a court of justice. The people are the jury, the politicians, the advocates, who," he adds, rather caustically than justly, "only occasionally and by accident speak their real opinions." Whether or not politicians who speak in the open atmosphere of Cabinet government utter always or ever their real opinions, it is not just here worth while to stop to inquire; but it is reasonably certain that, speaking with the knowledge that the nation is the jury by whom their right and title to rule is to be determined, they at least prefer in their utterances sentiments of justice and wisdom to sentiments of baseness and folly, and that in their administration they prefer methods of uprightness and straightforwardness to methods of fraud and indirection. And these are the things which we wish to constrain our politicians to prefer.

* In the Birmingham Town Hall, Nov. 3rd, 1882 [WW's note.]

We wish above all things to make politics once more an honourable profession, in which our young men may enlist their purest aspirations and to which they may dedicate all their best energies. The government of a great country is not something which can be successfully practiced with study and long preparation. No man can be a statesman who does not spend his life in the study of the great science of government. Knowledge of men and intimate insight into human nature go far towards fitting their possessor to be a ruler of men, but they are not by themselves sufficient equipment. No man who is ignorant of history can read with any certainty the signs of the time which is at hand; temerity itself should blush to attempt to cope with any of the vast problems of national trade and industry without first obtaining a firm grasp of the ruling principles of political economy; and skill in finance, experience in affairs, familiarity with national resources, acquaintance with international relations, and mastery of constitutional practice constitute the indispensable outfit of the statesman. A life time is no more than long enough to acquire the requisite training. Government ought never to be entrusted to amateurs; it should always be controlled by professionals. Any system, accordingly, which elevates politics into the rank of the most honourable professions, and at the same time offers opportunities of long legislative service and assurance of promotion, is a system which ensures competent government. If Cabinet government opens up to young men a career of honourable public service; if its debates promise a chance of distinction to the learned and the eloquent; if its administration affords an opportunity for the display and the reward of all the higher qualities of statesmanship; if it purifies legislation and gives energy to the executive, it is just that form of government of which this country now stands in desperate need. We must have a school of statesmanship and of eloquence.

Mr. Froude, indeed, expresses, in the address already quoted, some distrust of the sagacity of political orators as governors. "The truly great political orators," says he, "are the ornaments of mankind, the most finished examples of noble feeling and perfect expression, but they rarely understand the circumstances of their time. They feel passionately, but for that reason they cannot judge calmly." But even the character that Mr. Froude bears as a licensed literary free-lance and paradoxologist should not warrant him in advancing such opinions without support of just reason, as one who speaks axioms. How often great eloquence and great sagacity in the management of men and the government of states have been united in the same person everyone may know who will read any catalogue of the great orators of our race or peruse the history of self-government amongst other nations. True orators are generally powerful leaders; and no man can be a great, an accepted, leader who does not know the temper, the tastes, the habits, and the sentiments of his fellow men, and especially of his fellow countrymen; who cannot understand the circumstances of his time; who cannot judge calmly as well as feel passionately. The mind of the English orator is not the mind of a mere poet or a mere moral enthusiast; for English audiences will not run after what is merely beautiful or fanciful. They are obedient to reason and to persuasion. The finest passages of the great orations of our language are those which give colour, life, and dignity to reason, which give attractive form to worthy sentiment, which breathe honourable and exalted motives, which appeal to the sense of justice and of unselfishness, which are not mere bursts of feeling, not extravagant but full of good sense, not merely pretty in form but strong in body as well. Inspirations of reason move us more than flights of fancy; and those who can move us most can also rule us; and through us the policies of the country.

At any rate we shall always be ruled by orators as long as we attempt self-government. A vast nation must govern itself by proxy, by delegation, and it will be safe and content under such representative government only so long as that government is conducted openly by the nation's representatives, that is, only so long as it is conducted by candid and unrestricted discussion. Self-government must be managed through the instrumentality of public speech. There is no other safe, no other possible, method. And government by public speech is government by orators—a style of government accepted by all students of history and politics as the freest and best the world has yet seen, and a style with which we may well be content in view of its glorious history and unequalled renown.

A self-governing race presents an interesting and varied picture —a picture somewhat vividly sketched by Professor Seeley of England in a suggestive article which was reprinted not many years ago in the *Eclectic Magazine*: *

A voice in Parliament we all have now, if we consider it; for there must be few of us who cannot command occasionally the space of six lines in the corner of some newspaper, and how many of us have a right to greater prominence than that in the national debate? We have all been admitted to the National Parliament. But

* *Eclectic Magazine*, Vol. XII, pp. 585-'6. [WW's note. He was quoting "The English Revolution of the Nineteenth Century," *Eclectic Magazine*, XII (Nov. 1870), 576-86—Eds.' note.]

there is an inner chamber in which the old House of Commons still sits, revising, resuming, arbitrating, and deciding with responsibility. It is like nothing so much as like Milton's Pandemonium. There, you remember, there was a spacious hall, freely open to the multitude. It was so immensely spacious that it is compared to

"A covered field where champions bold
Wont ride in armed, and at the Soldan's chair
Defied the best of Paynim chivalry
To mortal combat or career with lance."

This is the image of our free and swarming Press. It is 'brusht with the hiss of rustling wings.' It is so crowded that the in-comers have to be miraculously diminished. They are squeezed into small print and mercilessly abridged by the magic wand of an editor, and thus reduced they are 'at large, though without number still, amidst the hall of that infernal court.' But this is not all. There is also an inner chamber of deliberation, where there is more dignity and more ceremony. The old historic Parliament still meets and still preserves its superiority:—

"Far within
And in their own dimensions like themselves,
The great seraphic lords and cherubim
In close recess and secret conclave sat,
A thousand demigods on golden seats,
Frequent and full."

This is a fair suggestion of the chief feature of the political life of a great self-governing nation. Editors may not relish the comparison by which their domain is likened to "that infernal court," and it must occur to those who read Professor Seeley's concluding quotation that "secret conclave" might be applied to a session of one of our secretive committees more fitly than to the open sessions of the British Parliament. But these are simply the unavoidable inaptnesses of quotation. The "national debate" proceeds much as Professor Seeley says, through the great voices of the press and the more authoritative voices of the nation's great central council. Our chief constitutional difficulty is that the freedom of the press is greater than the freedom of Congress. Besides their right to vote, most members of Congress have few privileges which are not also within the reach of those who are not within the "inner chamber." The press is open to them as to others, but the debates of the House are not. The committees have deprived our system of its character as a government by public speech and have converted it into a government by private consultation.

The extinction of the committee system must appear certain to any one who will seriously contemplate the future of the Union. The next twenty years will bring forth great changes—great changes in the commercial and industrial features of the country, and, therefore, great transformations in its political condition. The denser population becomes the more imperatively necessary will it be to have all possible openness and simplicity in the administration of the government, all possible knowledge and sagacity in rulers, and all possible practice to make perfect in statesmanship. A ruling class must be created—not a ruling class of aristocrats or of rich men, not a class boasting itself of hereditary privileges or prescriptive prerogatives, but a class of trained politicians, a profession of statesmen, a race of men schooled and grounded in youth in such learning as opens the mind to a just apprehension of the great questions of state-craft and drilled throughout manhood in the practice-school of national legislation and politics, there learning the practicable methods of government, gaining knowledge of the operation of economic principles, and gathering information as to the resources and the industries of the country.

As the best possible school for the training of such a class, Cabinet government must recommend itself to every thoughtful student of our political history and every intelligent observer of our present political situation. The influence of Cabinet government in England, and in other countries, has been to bring thoroughly-educated young men into public life and into the legislature as recruits to the party ranks, and there to keep the most capable and promising of them in constant train[ing] as leaders and legislators. The tendency of our American system, on the other hand, seems to have been to make shorter and shorter the terms of individual representatives. It is difficult to perceive upon what safe ground of reason are built the opinions of those persons who regard short terms of service as sacredly and peculiarly republican in principle. It would seem natural to regard efficiency as the only just and natural foundation for confidence in a public officer, in republican governments no less than under monarchs, and uniformly short terms, which cut off the efficient as surely and inexorably as the inefficient are apparently as repugnant to republican as to monarchical rules. But such is not American doctrine. A man who has served twenty years in Congress is almost a curiosity; whilst in England a parliamentary service of thirty or forty years is not uncommon, more than one Englishman having, like Mr. Gladstone, stretched his parliamentary career over half a century. A man is considered in his parliamentary prime who has reached the age of fifty and spent twenty-five years in the House of Commons; but a man is here looked upon as being in his Congressional decrepitude who has been twenty years in the House of

Representatives. In England long experience in the work is reckoned necessary to make a man a competent legislator; in the
United States that work is accounted easy enough for any man of
discretion and character.

It ought, of course, to go without the saying that to legislate for
a vast country filled with busy people, crowded with great industries, for a nation representing every grade of social condition
and every variety of commercial enterprise, is no easy task which
can be learned in a legislative session or two. It is a task, as has
been said, which no man can master in less than a life-time of
studious observation and wide experience. Such legislation should
be conducted with method and with careful consistency of policy.
To entrust it to committees composed for the most part of inexperienced amateurs who cannot even coöperate, because hampered and isolated by committee independence, is something worse
than folly. Committee government cannot last, whatever other
system be substituted. The low estimate put by the people—or,
rather, by our constitutional system—upon the work of national
legislation is almost comical. No one imagines that the dry-goods
or the hardware trade, or even the cobbler's craft, can be successfully conducted except by those who have had long experience in
them, who have worked through a labourious and unremunerative
apprenticeship, and who devote their lives to perfecting themselves
as tradesmen and craftsmen; and yet legislation is esteemed a
thing in which the merest amateurs may like enough excel with
ease, which can be taken up with success by any shrewd man of
middle age, which a lawyer may now and then advantageously
combine with his practice, in which a manufacturer may make his
leisure time useful to the country, or of which intelligent youths
may readily catch the knack. This exalted function of government,
which of course requires for its proper exercise more study and
more natural perspicacity than any other human undertaking, is
degraded below the dignity of the humblest handicrafts. All men
are born legislators—says our practice—but no men are born car-
penters or blacksmiths. Trade is something that must be learned;
legislation, something taught by instinct.

As has been time and again reiterated in the course of this essay, in no concern of government are knowledge, skill, and experience more indispensable than in financial management. "The
modern industrial organization, including banks, corporations,
joint-stock companies, financial devices, national debts, paper currency, national systems of taxation, is largely the creation of legislation (not in its historical origin, but in the mode of its existence

and in its authority) and is largely regulated by legislation. Capital is the breath of life to this organization, and every day, as the organization becomes more complex and delicate, the folly of assailing capital or credit becomes greater. At the same time it is evident that the task of the legislator to embrace in his view the whole system, to adjust his rules so that the play of the civil institutions shall not alter the natural play of the economic forces, requires more training and acumen. Furthermore, the greater the complication and delicacy of the industrial system, the greater the chances for cupidity when backed by craft, and the task of the legislator to meet and defeat the attempts of this cupidity is one of constantly increasing difficulty."* There can be no question, therefore, but that, sooner or later, the superintendence of these supreme interests must be put, in this country as in others, in the hands of a responsible ministry of trained publicists. Now, while we are rich beyond all other nations and while nature's lavish gifts make us prodigal of our resources, loose systems of finance, management without method or accountability, may tide us on well enough for a season; but this clumsy and inefficient organization of government must give way to the first severe strain that is put upon it. None but a new country, which feels neither the oppression of taxation nor the perplexities of such entangled social problems as are ever present to embarrass and hinder the policies of old and thickly-settled countries, can put up with committees, can thrive under the government of fragments of a popular assembly. When government is easy and the grossest mistakes favoured with impunity, committees can govern; but the moment government becomes difficult and mistakes fatal, committees must give place to a responsible ministry; government must be steadied by a concentration and responsibility and the institution of recognized party leadership. The guidance of legislation must be entrusted to a few trained men, men of personal and party preëminence, of skill in affairs and experience in controlling men, of knowledge and of character.

The present question is whether it is wise to wait for times of pressure to force a change in the forms and methods of our government; whether it is not better to forestall the crisis by deliberate preparation for its coming, and forestalling prevent it. The inconvenience, slovenliness, and mismanagement of committee government are undoubtedly hastening the critical time; and, whether young and vigourous and rich or not, we cannot in the meantime afford to suffer and support misgovernment. It cannot be the part

* Prof. Sumners *Andrew Jackson* (*Am. Statesmen* series), p. 226. [WW's note.]

of wisdom to squander our treasures and overstrain our institutions. We ought to be wisely and efficiently governed, even if to be ignorantly and improvidently governed be not for the present grievous. The fact that bad government is tolerable does not make it desirable.

The future of this country presents many interesting questions and offers many broad prospects for the contemplation of the publicist. The regulation of its vast trade and its unnumbered industries, the repression of those civil usurpations to which powers like the Romish hierarchy are prone, the perfection of the official organization of the national government and the adjustment of that organization to both federal prerogatives and State rights, the purification and elevation of the suffrage, the assimilation of foreign populations, the aid of education, the restraint of monopolies, the erection of new States—these and scores of other questions of equal magnitude and moment must tax the statesmanship of the generations which immediately succeed our own, and it is the part of prudence to prepare for their ready settlement by perfecting our system of government—by erecting a government strong, flexible, and efficient, open, honest, and informed; a government prompt in action, though deliberate in decision, quick but not hasty, firm but not stubborn, responsible but not servile.

If this discussion—which may fitly be brought here to its close—has established a presumption in favour of Cabinet government as that form which approaches nearest to this ideal, it has furnished at least a foundation for the coming reform; and if it has brought to a considerable number of intelligent readers any new knowledge of the real operation of our federal system and any new light as to the principles which should mould all systems of self-government, it has fulfilled its mission and has contributed all that it was expected to contribute to the political amelioration of that Union which it has cost so much to build and whose wreck or degradation would bring so much of humiliation and disaster to the liberty-loving citizens of its now inseparable States. It should be the prayer of all patriots that this great government be perpetuated in strength, efficiency, and honour; and it should be the endeavour of all patriots to do all in their power to contribute to that perpetuation by opening their minds to dispassionate consideration of every calm and reasonable suggestion of reform, and by bending their strength to the accomplishment of every change that will add any degree of facility, security, or excellence to the instrumentalities of government.

From Janet Woodrow Wilson

My darling Son,   Wilmington. N. C. Dec 6th '82
  I have just put up all the documents I have, with reference to the Nebraska estate. I will send the package through the P. O. & have it registered. Now, darling, please write to James at once, & let him understand that the division *must be made at once*. I *insist* upon this—for I have been made exceedingly uneasy by the discrepancy between his former & his recent statements. It is very certain that the value of the estate cannot have decreased six thousand, eight hundred odd dollars in the last two years[.] And you know I *entreated* him when he sent me the enclosed statement, *not to let it be reduced one dollar more*, that he would send me the bill for taxes. He has utterly neglected my interests—to say the least—almost criminally so.
  Of course he will have to give particulars—in order to enable you to arrange matters. But you know all about it. One thing is certain— I am not going quietly to submit to the reduction of our interest to the amount of $6,800.00 in two years! Dont let yourself be worried, dear. It is to be a *purely business* matter now, you know. I have worried enough about it to serve for the whole family—and it has not done the least good, I am sure. . . .
                         Lovingly your own   Mother.
ALS (WP, DLC).

From Joseph Ruggles Wilson

My most dear son—   Wilmington [N.C.], December 15, 1882.
  I am in receipt of yrs of the 13th, and am pleased with the evidences it furnishes of your good health and fair spirits. Assuming that your professional income does not yet equal your personal outgo, I again take the liberty of enclosing you my check for $50.00.
  Do you not think it possible to spend too much of yr. time in general studies? I mean of course in studies that lie beyond the *drudgery* line of your immediate business? I know well that you cannot widen too greatly the field of study; and I have heretofore advised that you should reap in every fertile spot where literature has a plant which can afford mental nutriment upon being properly prepared and appetizingly digested. It is most pleasing, too, to one who loves and admires you as I do, to know that you prefer (changing the figure) to fish in waters where there are more whales than minnows; and that you are trying to bring to shore,

for examination and even dissection, as also for illuminating oil, certain of those larger denizens of the deep which swim and devour in the great sea of political economy. You will have noticed, however, that I underscored the word "drudgery" on the hither page. I did this in order to invite your more careful notice to that which has occupied my own thoughts not a little: the importance of downright plodding for securing success in the principal undertaking of life: or, to use my first word, the necessity for doing the *drudge* work that stands connected with what we have mainly in hand. . . .

I do not wish, my beloved one, to be understood as implying that you are open to the suspicion of neglecting these essential smallnesses for the sake of reading after unimportant largenesses. But I like to put myself in your place, adding a dream or so from my own broader experiences. Plodding is almost more than genius. Drudgery is almost more than eloquence.

We are all in our usual health, and our spirits are always brightened by your excellent letters. I need not add that we all have for you more love than Uncle Sam can carry

Your affectionate   Father.

ALS (WP, DLC).

From James W. Bones

Dear Tommy   Rome, Georgia, Dec 18 1882
Yours of 14th was reced Saturday morning & would have been answered same day but the close of the week is always an exceedingly busy time. I am rejoiced to hear that your professional prospects are improving so much & trust the day is not far distant when you will feel yourself on the road to great success.

I note what you say as to the early settlement of the Estate matter & will endeavor as soon as possible to give you a clear statement of the whole thing. It would have been done ere this but for your Aunts death. There was some unavoidable delay in the probate of her will as interrogations had to be sent to Staunton. . . .

As to the statement I sent your mother in 1880; it was a correct approximate estimate of her interest at that time, leaving out the question of interest from 1878 to date. Then the additional expenses taxes &c will affect it considerably. But I have no doubt all will be satisfactory & plain when statement is given you. . . .

Your affec Uncle   Jas W Bones

P. S. omitted. ALS (WP, DLC) with WWhw notation on env.: "Ans. 12/22/82."

From Janet Woodrow Wilson

My darling Son,   Wilmington, N. C. Dec. 24th '82.

As Christmas draws near, I feel your absence more than ever—if possible. Your father spoke of sending for you to come home to spend the holiday, but I did not feel justified in encouraging the idea. The truth is the holidays here are *not* a specially cheerful time with us—we feel, more than ever, our isolation. And if you were here, you would feel it too—more than ever after your more pleasant experience in Atlanta. So that I am willing to wait till some more favorable time in the future for your visit.

I wanted to send you a guard of some kind *for your watch*—but have not been able to find anything that I would like to send you—in this delectable place—much to my disappointment. . . .

We are all pretty well—and miss you as much as ever. I think your dear father misses you more, if possible, than I do. Let me hear please as much as you can how you are progressing with your correspondence with James Bones. I am exceedingly anxious to have the settlement completed. I will write at length in a day or two.

God bless you my precious boy. I love you with all my heart. You have been a comfort to me all your sweet life. Papa & Josie join in warmest love.   Your own Mother.

Kindest regards &c to Mr Renick & Mrs Boylston, sister, & families

ALS (WP, DLC).

From Little, Brown & Company

Dear Sir: Boston Jan. 1 1883.

Your favor of the 26th ult. is at hand and by Adams Ex. today we send all the books[1] except Bishop's Stat'y Crimes, new edition of which is nearly ready, and Pomeroy's Eq. Juris, *Vol. 3.* which is not yet published. The former we will forward prepaid @ 5.50 as soon as ready and the latter @ $6. We have made very low prices on this lot, but it is not possible to give a discount of 20% from the "short" prices of our books. Thus the text-books formerly catalogued by us @ $7.50—from which a large discount could be given—are now put at $6. while the trade price remains the same. In addition to the low rates made on this purchase, we also assume the cost of returning the funds, and we trust the arrangement will be satisfactory.   Your's truly Little, Brown & Co.   C.W.C.

ALS (WP, DLC).
    1 Little, Brown's statement dated Jan. 1, 1883 (WP, DLC), shows the ship-
ment of Addison's Contracts, 3 vols.; Bishop's Marriage and Divorce, 2 vols.;
Bishop's Criminal Law, 2 vols.; Bishop's Criminal Practice, 2 vols.; High's In-
junctions; May's Insurance; Morse's Banking, Oliver's Conveyancing; Pomeroy's
Eq. Juris, Vols. I and II; Schenler's Bailments; Washburn's Real Property, 3
vols.; Wharton's Evidence, 2 vols.; and Sedgwick's Damages, 2 vols., for which
WW paid $121.50. A second statement from Little, Brown, dated Jan. 8, 1883
(WP, DLC), shows the shipment of one copy of Cooley's Torts, for which WW
paid $6.50.

Marginal Notes

G. Otto Trevelyan, *The Life and Letters of Lord Macaulay* (2 vols., New York, 1875).

Transcripts of WW Shorthand Comments

[c. Jan. 1, 1883]

Vol. I, 172:
    [The author is quoting from the diary of Margaret Macaulay:] "I said that I was surprised at the great accuracy of his [Macaulay's] information, considering how desultory his reading had been. 'My accuracy as to facts,' he said, 'I owe to a cause which many men would not confess. It is due to my love of castle-building. *The past is, in my mind, soon constructed into a romance.*' [WW's italics.] He then went on to describe the way in which from his childhood his imagination had been filled by the study of history. 'With a person of my turn,' he said, 'the minute touches are of as great interest, and perhaps greater, than the most important events. Spending so much time as I do in solitude, my mind would have rusted by gazing vacantly at the shop-windows. As it is, I am no sooner in the streets than I am in Greece, in Rome, in the midst of the French Revolution. Precision in dates, the day or hour in which a man was born or died, becomes absolutely necessary. A slight fact, a sentence, a word, are of importance in my romance. . . .' "

The germ of his idea of *The History*

Spencer Walpole, *Foreign Relations* (London, 1882).

P. 110:
    The separation of Eastern Roumelia from Bulgaria was the one great achievement which was accomplished at Berlin. Yet Greece was formed into one state. Moldavia and Wallachia were four years after the Congress of Paris united under one ruler; and Eastern Roumelia,

Such artificial divisions, since they can never last, cannot be worthy of accomplishment. Seeing this himself, how can the author by a similar fate, may be drawn into Bulgaria. The tendency of men of the same race and language to draw together is the strongest factor in European politics, and the statesmen who ignore it are likely to witness the discomfiture of their policy.

call the division effect[ed] at Berlin a great achievement?

The Works of the Right Honorable Edmund Burke (Seventh edn., 12 vols., Boston, 1881).

Vol. V, 224-25:

[Lord Keppel] felt that no great commonwealth could by any possibility long subsist without a body of some kind or other of nobility decorated with honor and fortified by privilege. This nobility forms the chain that connects the ages of a nation, which otherwise (with Mr. Paine) would soon be taught that no one generation can bind another. He felt that no political fabric could be well made, without some such order of things as might, through a series of time, afford a rational hope of securing unity, coherence, consistency, and stability to the state.

Does not a written constitution do something of this same sort?

To Robert Bridges

Dear Bobbie,   Atlanta, Geo., Jany 4th 1883

I am going to beg a big service of you. I have recently completed—you must know—an extended essay on my favourite topic, Cabinet government; an essay so extended as to amount in volume to a small book. All but the last part of this essay—which is the result of much reading and the fruit of a great deal of thought—I sent to the no doubt long-suffering Harpers; but, as I expected, they replied that "their reader did not advise them to publish it." Now, to-day I send to *you* part V, and last, of the "work," and what I have to ask of you is this, Please, if you have the time and the inclination, go—or send—to Franklin Square and get my *ms.* (for I have written to Harpers to hold it subject to your order) and read it—passing candid judgment upon it for my sake, and if you like it and think it worth publishing, submit it—can't you, by hook or by crook?—to some one of the *Post's* or *Nation's* staffs who is recognized as a competent critic, and is yet a benevolent fellow who can sympathize with a young author; and if *he* endorse it, advise with me as to what can be done in the way of presenting it thus endorsed to some publisher who is inclined to look favourably upon *ms.* from the South which indicates some revival of literary activity and embodies healthy unsectional sentiment.

I am conscious that I am asking a great deal, Bob, and I ask it with great hesitation; but my hesitation is rendered less by the assurance that you will feel at liberty to decline the trust if any serious obstacle, either of inclination or of policy, stands in the way of your accepting it. I know that you will be perfectly open and outspoken with me. My object, you see, is this, to have my *ms.* go to the publishers recommended by some man whom they know —some one like Mr. Godkin of the *Nation,* say—and to have the negotiations with them carried on by some one who is on the spot and can communicate with them more readily and speedily than I can—for if the essay has any value it is chiefly because it is *timely* and its chance of publication is *now* or never. If I can get nothing more, I would like to have at least the judgment of some thoroughly competent critic upon what I have written, for my guidance. If you get a chance, do find out the reasons of Harpers' reader for rejecting. But I can trust to your discretion in the whole matter. Do what you think best in every respect.

And, now that I have delivered myself of this tremendous request, I proceed to say that I am still following the young lawyer's occupation of *waiting.* One or two minute fees I have earned— nothing more—though I have had business enough of a certain kind, the collection—or the effort to collect—numberless desperate claims.

I think and talk about you a great deal and have long been wishing for a letter from you. Your letters seem to me to contain more than any one else's. This is Atlanta's gay season. I have been to the theatre more this Winter than I ever went in all my life before; and, as the best travelling troupes come here, I have seen many excellent things.

As ever   Your sincere friend   Woodrow Wilson

ALS (Meyer Coll., DLC).

From Robert Bridges

Dear Tommy: N. Y. January 7th 1883
I know that you are anxious to hear about your "baby," so I will write a short note right now to tell you that the vigorous youngster is safe and well in the drawer of this very table, after his long journey—that he has been reunited to his better half—that moreover competent critics have passed upon his merits and declare them considerable—and that there may be several chances yet of

his walking out into the world alone, clad in the latest mode, when I have no doubt that he will make a way for himself or he would not be your offspring.

After receiving your note and the Part V. M.S. yesterday I went to our literary Editor, Mr. Garrison[1] (a son of the abolitionist) and asked him for a note of introduction to somebody in authority at Harpers. He gave me just what I wanted, so that I knew I would be treated with every consideration. After work I went down to Franklin Square. They looked up the MS. for me and it was delivered safely into my hands. Then I suggested that I would like to know the real opinion which led to the rejection of the book. The gentleman got out a register in which are recorded the written opinions of the readers of the firm upon MSS. Two had passed upon your book, and they substantially agreed. Both spoke of its decided merits. One mentioned, as well as I can recollect, that the style was very "clear, pleasing and decidedly literary." If anything his words were stronger on this point. One was impressed with the forcibleness of the argument, the other thought it strong—but he was not convinced thereby. The only positive objection was that, not being on a popular subject it would not meet with a "remunerative sale." That is the gist of the whole matter. Like Schurz, Curtis[2] and Godkin ten years ago in the civil service reform question, you are considered a theorist—ahead of your time. They have just been having their harvest—yours will come—though it may be longer on the road.

Well, I felt on the whole encouraged by the criticisms. It was evidently not a question of the quality of the book—but the quality of the public. Perhaps other publishers may think differently of the public—Putnams for instance. They publish all the good political works that are not pirated nowadays. In fact I have several schemes in my head and I will try them all before I give up. In the meantime I hope you will be patient with me. I have a great many things to do and my plans will probably move slowly, but I am hopeful. It may take me a month or six weeks to accomplish anything and I may fail—but I will treat the youngster as though he were my own—you can be assured of that. This week I expect to read it carefully, and then will begin to storm the mercenary publisher. I have strong hopes of Mr. Garrison's aid—being literary editor of the *Nation* he has many claims on publishers. He has always been very kind to me, and I think he will give me a favorable hearing. I don't like to try Mr. Godkin, directly, for he is a very positive Irishman and a very busy one, and might not give it proper attention. I have other schemes also. So here's hoping.

By the way, I saw a letter the other day from a fellow on the *Constitution* to Mr *Garrison* in which he spoke of the convict system in Ga as being a fruitful field for a good correspondent—of the *Post*. What do you think of it, and is it at all in your line? I have no authority to make an agreement about it—but I thought of you at the time and I believe a good letter would find ready publication. What are your views on the homocide discussion?[3] It has raised some bitter feeling at the South, but some of the strongest newspapers there have approved of the *Nation's* course.

With best wishes and Hope   Your friend   Bob Bridges

ALS (WP, DLC) with WWhw notation on env.: "Ans. Jany 10th 1883
                                              Recd.   "   "   "   "
[1] Wendell Phillips Garrison, literary editor of the New York *Nation*, 1865-1906.
[2] George W. Curtis, author, orator, and editor of *Harper's Weekly*, was chairman of both the New York State and the National Civil Service Reform Associations.
[3] Bridges refers here to editorials in *The Nation* on the causes and excessive extent of southern homicide: "The Influence of Homicide on Southern Progress," xxxv (Oct. 26, 1882), 349-50; "The Rationale of Southern Homicide," *ibid.*, Dec. 7, 1882, pp. 480-81; "Why Capital Does Not Flow into the South," *ibid.*, Dec. 14, 1882, p. 501.

To Robert Bridges

Dear Bobby,   Atlanta, Geo., Jany 10th/83
It was very kind of you to write so promptly. Your letter reached me this morning and brought a great deal of hope and encouragement with it. It gratified me most of all, however, because of the abundant proof it bore of your genuine and generous friendship for me. Not that I needed any further assurances of that; but very few friends would do what you have done, undertake to serve another with all the zest and zeal of one who is labouring altogether in his own behalf. I confidently expected that you would do just as you have done; but it is none the less gratifying to learn that my expectations have been so fully realized.

I hope that *you* will like the contents of my *ms*. I should value your approval as much as, if not more than, that of the professional critics; not only because you know good work when you see it, but also because you can gauge the progress I have made in facility of expression and felicity of treatment, and tell me whether it has been small or considerable—if, indeed, there has been any *improvement* at all. I shall, therefore, await your criticism with great interest.

Your suggestion about a letter on the Georgia convict system is a good one. I will try to inform myself fully on the subject, and, if

I can learn all that I wish to learn within a reasonable time, I will, doubtless, be able to send you something more or less worth reading, and offer it for publication.

In the matter of Southern homicide I am altogether with the *Nation*. I can say *amen* to almost every editorial word it has written on the subject. The letter in the last number (Jany 4th), dated Atlanta and signed "Georgia," was written by my partner, E. I. Renick, and contains about all that can be said in mitigation of the *Nation's* sentence upon Southern civilization.[1] Renick is as entirely in agreement with the *Nation* on this point as I am; and our office has been the scene of many lively discussions upon this head. Almost everyone with whom we have conversed has at first mistaken the issue and insisted upon the fact that, as compared with the North, the South is much happier in the absence of the meaner kinds of crime. When we succeed in pinning them down to *social* and *business* homicides they are, most of them, compelled into substantial agreement with us and with the *Nation*

I hope that you are as well as I am. In spite of the execrable weather we have been suffering, I am in fine health and spirits, having conquered even the catarrh which for the last year or two has persistently possessed me. Besides that, I am rejoicing over a newly-grown mustache which is my present pride and comfort. Christmas here was merry in the extreme. A most wonderful change came over the little city. In ordinary seasons one is impressed with the soberness of our citizens. The bar-rooms are well patronized, of course, but it is a very rare thing to see a drunken man on any of our principal streets. But on Christmas what a transformation! Such another universal drunk is not on record in this part of the country. Our station houses were full to overflowing, and our police-men were crazy with press of business. I, however, spent the day quietly at my boarding house, where a pretty girl[2] helped me nobly to while away the leisure time.

As ever   Yours sincerely and affectionately,   Woodrow Wilson.

ALS (Meyer Coll., DLC)
  [1] "Georgia" to the Editor, Dec. 26, 1882, New York *Nation*, XXXVI (Jan. 4, 1883), 13-14.
  [2] Kate D. Mayrant, Mrs. Boylston's niece from Aiken, S. C.

To Richard Heath Dabney

My dear Heath,   Atlanta, Geo., Jany 11th 1883
The receipt of your letter[1] rejoiced my heart. You great fat Dutchman, you! The idea of your weighing one hundred and sixty-three pounds! How I would like to see you and your beer-wetted

paunch! I should like to be with you for more reasons than one, indeed—not only to renew the pleasures of our old University good-fellowship, but also to share your advantages and delights of study. History and Political Science! why they are of all studies my favourites; and to be allowed to fill all my time with them, instead of, as now, stealing only a chance opportunity or two for hasty perusal of those things which are most delightful to me, would be of all privileges the most valued by yours humbly. I have to be content with a very precarious allowance of such good things. My extra-legal education must proceed by slow and unequal stages. It is, of course, somewhat unsatisfactory to be compelled to master a great science as it were by stealth, at such odd moments as one can snatch from engrossing professional studies; but I am inclined to think that knowledge thus acquired in spite of all obstacles is a possession more valued than it would be had its acquisition been easy and prosperous.

However that may be, I am, at all events, very much interested in even the name of your courses and am impelled to beg that you will give me some particular account of them; that you will tell me just what line the German students pursue—especially in Political Science. To know what they think the best methods of study would be of much advantage to me. I should like, as far as possible, to go along with you in your work.

Yes, I did speak before the tariff commission; and hard work I had of it, too! The whole thing was done almost upon the impulse of the moment. I had temporarily lost sight of the commission in its travels and did not know that it was due in Atlanta—indeed, I had not known that it intended coming here—when there came into our office a friend of Renick's, Walter Page of the N.Y. *World* —who had been traveling about with the commissioners utterly destroying their reputation and overthrowing their adventitious dignity by his smart ridicule—saying that he and the august commission had arrived. We fell into some talk about the commission's work, of course, and before we had gone far Page had discovered my deep interest in and considerable acquaintance with the issues involved and had persuaded me to address the commission the next morning on the general topic of free-trade vs. protection— for, said he, they are much in need of light upon the true principles involved and no one has yet said to them a word upon the general merits of the question. So it was that I hastily prepared a brief and undertook to make a few extemporaneous remarks before this much ridiculed body of incompetencies, influenced by the consideration that my speech would appear in their printed report, rather than by any hope of affecting their conclusions. I found it hard enough work, I can assure you, for the circumstances were most embarrassing. Six commissioners sat around a long table in the breakfast room of the Kimball House and about and behind them sat a few local dignitaries and four or five young men of my acquaintance, besides the reporters usually attendant upon the sittings. Embarrassed by the smallness and the character of the audience, but more especially by the ill-natured and sneering interruptions of the commissioners, I spoke without sufficient self-possession and certainly without much satisfaction to myself; but was compensated for my discomfort by the subsequent compliments of my friends and of the press—especially by the kind words of our Congressman from this district,[2] in whose ability I have great confidence, and who was good enough to say that my speech showed that I both knew what to say and how to say it.

I am to meet several other young men this evening, here in our office, for the purpose of organizing a free trade club, as a branch of the Free Trade Club of N.Y. City.[3] I have for some months past had in my head a scheme for the organization of a "Georgia House of Commons,"[4] as I should like to call it, in imitation of the New York Senate of which you wrote me long ago.[5] But as yet I do'nt know enough suitable fellows here to make such plans feasible, and this free trade club is as near as I can come to anything of the kind at present. I am not sufficiently identified with the place yet to lead in such matters and can, consequently, hasten towards them only slowly.

By the time this reaches you, you will, I suppose, be on the point of delivering your lecture to that organization with unpronounceable name over which Prof. Giesbredt[6] presides. How I should like to be present to hear it, even though I should, probably, understand not a word of it! You must tell me all about it: its title, contents, &c., and its reception

Where have Toy, Lefevre, Jenkins, Dick Smith,[7] *et id omne genus*, gone? Are they still at large or have they settled down somewhere to study? Lefevre must feel somewhat chagrined, I should imagine, at being shut off from taking the same liberties with the foreign languages, which he must be constrained to speak with some modesty and caution, that he was accustomed to take with the English. Toy will, of course, rejoice in the German grind, Jenkins in the German beer, and Dick Smith in German powers of acquisition.

I hear, from friends who have recently returned from a visit to Charleston, S.C., that Kent and Coleman, in spite of that extremely youthful appearance of theirs which is somewhat against them in the eyes of staid and conservative Charleston, are doing excellently well with their school, as we knew they would, and are establishing a fine reputation for themselves, in a place which is said to contain very efficient teachers and very fine schools, small and large.[8] Hurrah for Charley and Louis!

There are some five or six University men practicing law here in Atlanta—some of them doing well and others, like the potentially great firm of Renick and Wilson, doing *very* little, but hoping very *much*. Of course we have something to do, something which is developing into *more* by slow degrees. In the course of about one year we hope to be meeting expenses after some sort; but at present we are not doing so, not by a very large majority. The fact of the matter is that the profession here is in a very disorganized state and young attorneys are unfairly out-bid by unscrupulous elders. The struggle promises to be a long and a hard one, but a fairer one as time advances.

Don't fail to write to me soon again. I enjoy your letters hugely and all details of your experiences abroad, both *studential* and other, are much to my palate.

    With love,   Your sincere friend   Woodrow Wilson.

ALS (Wilson-Dabney Correspondence ViU).

[1] R. H. Dabney to WW, from Munich, Nov. 18, 1882, ALS (WP, DLC).

[2] Nathaniel J. Hammond, of Atlanta, a prominent lawyer whose office was on the same floor as Wilson's and Renick's.

[3] The *Atlanta Constitution* did not report this event. The New York Free Trade Club was organized in May 1877 to study questions in political economy relating to the laws of trade and to promote a public opinion favorable to freedom of commercial intercourse. The documents are silent about the Atlanta branch during the remainder of WW's residence in the city. But see WW to ELA, Dec. 11, 1883, and E. I. Renick to WW, Dec. 13, 1883, for subsequent references.

[4] WW's draft of a constitution for this organization is printed below. There is no evidence that he ever attempted to set up such a group.

[5] R. H. Dabney to WW, April 23, 1882, ALS (WP, DLC).

[6] Wilhelm von Giesebrecht, Professor of History, University of Munich, author of *Geschichte der deutschen Kaiserzeit* (4 vols., Braunschweig, 1873-77), and a specialist in German medieval history.

[7] All friends from the University of Virginia, then studying in Germany, as Dabney had reported in his letter of Nov. 18, 1882.

[8] C. W. Kent to WW, July 28, 1882, ALS (WP, DLC), relates that certain citizens of Charleston, S. C., had persuaded Kent and Coleman to open a boys' school.

Draft of a Constitution for a "Georgia House of Commons"

[c. Jan. 11, 1883]

Constitution of Debating Society

Article I

Name and *Object.*

Sec. I. *Name*: The name of this society shall be *The Georgia House of Commons*.

Sec. II. *Object*: Its object shall be the diffusion of political and historical knowledge amongst the young men of Georgia and the cultivation amongst its members of distinct and intelligent political principles.

Article II.

Organization.

Officers: The officers of this Society shall be a Ministerial Com.[,] a Speaker, a Chairman of Committees, a Clerk, a Deputy Clerk, a Sargeant-at-arms, a Treasurer, and a Librarian.

Article III.

The Speaker:

Sec. I. *Election*: The Speaker shall be elected by ballot at the first regular meeting of the Society in January of each year.

Sec. II. *Duties—ordinary*: It shall be the duty of the Speaker to preside at every meeting of the Society, to keep order and preserve discipline by the judicial administration of the rules and enforcement of the precedents of parliamentary procedure and to exercise all other functions usually devolving upon a presiding officer.

Sec. III. *Duties—Extraordinary*: It shall be the further duty of the Speaker to appoint the Chief of the Ministerial Committee as hereinafter provided, and to call special meetings of the Society when requested in writing to do so by ten members

Article IV.

The Ministerial Committee.

Sec. I. *Composition* and *Appointment*: The Ministerial Committee shall consist of a Prime Minister and four Assistant Ministers. The Prime Minister shall be appointed by the Speaker as hereinafter provided, the Assistant Ministers shall be appointed by the Prime Minister.

Sec. II. *Duties*[,] *Privileges*, and *Responsibilities*:

[1.] It shall be the duty of the Ministerial Committee to prepare political questions, cast in the form of Bills, for the consideration of the Society. In the debates upon these Bills, they shall be deemed the Sponsors of the same, and it shall be their duty to resign their offices when defeated upon any Bill touching any question of American policy.

2. It shall further be the duty of the Ministerial Committee to act as the executive officers of the Society in exercising a careful supervision of the finances of the Society, of the state of which one of their

number, appointed for the duty by the Prime Minister, shall present a semi-annual statement to the Society, presenting at the same time, upon the responsibility of the entire Committee, proposals for the raising and appropriation of the revenue needed for the next sixth [sic] months. Such Financial Minister shall act as Treasurer of the Society.

3. It shall further be the duty of one of the Assistant Ministers, appointed for the service by the Prime Minister, to receive all applications for membership and report them to the Society; to institute and conduct all proceedings under the Disciplinary Rules of the Society; and facilitate in every possible way the business of the Society.

4. It shall, further, be the duty of some one of the Assistant Ministers, appointed for the service by the Prime Minister, to superintend the care of the Society's room (or rooms), and to act as Corresponding Secretary and Librarian of the Society. It shall be the duty of the Secretary to conduct all the correspondence of the Society with outside parties.

5. No member of the Ministerial Committee shall take any important step or adopt any considerable change of policy in performing the duties specially assigned to him without the consent and approval of his colleagues of the Committee.

6. Whenever any important measure proposed by the Ministerial Committee relative to the financial or other administration of the Society is rejected at a regular meeting by the vote of a majority of the members of the Society, it shall be the duty of the Committee to resign.

Sec[.] III. *Replacement of Committee upon its Resignation*:

[I.] Upon the resignation of the Ministerial Committee, it shall be the duty of the Speaker to appoint as Prime Minister the leading member of the opposition by whose vote was accomplished the defeat of the measure upon whose loss the resignation of the Committee was based. Such appointment the Speaker shall make, within one week from the resignation by which the appointment is necessitated, in a written request to the member appointed to form a Committee; which same written request shall be spread upon the Minutes of the next regular meeting of the Society.

2. It shall be the duty of the member so named by the Speaker to appoint, within one week from his nomination, to appoint [sic] from among the members of the opposition party wh. he represents, three Assistant Ministers to occupy the posts of Finance Minister, Judicial Minister and Librarian.

3. A resigning Committee shall in all cases hold their offices until their successors are appointed and organized for office.

Article V.

The Clerk

Sec. I *Election*: The Clerk shall be elected by ballot at the first regular meeting of the Society in January of each year.

Sec. II. *Duties*: It shall be the duty of the Clerk to act as recording and reading Secretary of the Society; keep its Minutes; preserve all its papers and records; and preside over its meetings in the absence of the Speaker.

Article VI

The Deputy Clerk.

Sec. I. *Appointment*: The Deputy Clerk shall be appointed by the clerk and hold office for the same term.

Sec. II. *Duties*: It shall be the duty of the Deputy Clerk to act as Clerk in the absence of his principal, or when his principal is acting as Speaker; and to assist his principal in the discharge of his ordinary duties.

Article VII.

The Chairman of Committees

Sec. I. *Election*: The Chairman of Committees shall be elected by ballot at the first regular meeting of the Society in January of each year.

Sec. II. *Duties*: It shall be the duty of the Chairman of Committees to preside over Committees of the Whole House.

Article VIII.

The Treasurer

Sec. I[.] *Appointment*: The Treasurer shall be appointed by the Prime Minister as provided in Article IV, Sec. II. Subsec. 2.

Sec. II. *Duties*: It shall be the duty of the Treasurer to receive all moneys belonging to the Society and to keep them subject to the orders of the Society, disbursing them as directed by the Society, keeping a full and accurate account of all receipts and expenditures, and enforcing payments of assessments as authorized by the By-Laws of the Society.

Article IX.

The Librarian

Sec. I. *Appointment*: The Librarian shall be appointed by the Prime Minister according to the provisions of Article IV, Sec. II. Subsec[.] 4.

Sec. II. *Duties*: It shall be the duty of the Librarian to keep the Library of the Society as directed by the By-Laws of the Society.

Article X.

The Sargeant-at-Arms.

Sec. I. *Election*: The Sargeant-at-Arms shall be elected by ballot at the first regular meeting of the Society in January of each year.

Sec. II. *Duties*: The Sargeant-at-Arms shall act as ministerial officer of the Society, assisting the Speaker in the preservation of order and in the enforcement of the rules of the Society. He shall assess and report to the Treasurer all fines prescribed by the By-Laws of the Society, and shall have the privilege of appointing, from time to time, when he shall see fit, temporary assistants to aid him in the discharge of his police duties.

Article XI.

Meetings

Sec. I. *Meetings*: The Society shall have at least one regular meeting during each Summer month, and at least two regular meetings during each of the remaining months of the year.

Sec. II. *Quorum*: Fifteen members shall constitute a quorum, when the membership numbers twenty or more than twenty. When there are less than twenty names upon the roll of the Society, one half of the actual membership shall constitute a quorum.

Article XII

Debates and *Proceedings.*

Sec. I. *Questions*: The subjects discussed by this Society in its regular debates shall be political questions of the present century.

Sec. II[.] *Form of Questions*: All questions for regular debate, all amendments to this Constitution, and all proposals affecting the financial administration of the Society shall be presented in the form of legislative bills and go through regular course as such.

Sec. III. *Supply*: All bills affecting the financial administration of the Society shall be considered before their first reading in Committee of the Whole House to be known as *Committee of Supply*; which Committee of Supply shall supercede the Committee of the Whole House usual before a third reading.

Sec. IV. *Ways and Means*: The semi-annual financial statements of the Financial Minister shall be submitted in a Committee of the Whole House to be known as the *Committee of Ways and Means*.

Sec. V. *Bills*: It shall be the duty of the Ministerial Committee and the privilege of any member to propose Bills embodying questions suitable for general debate for the consideration of the Society; but when two or more such Bills at the same stage of their progress are upon the orders of the same day and one of them be a bill proposed by the Min. Com. the latter shall always take precedence. Any member wishing to propose a bill shall give at least one week's notice of his intention to do so; and when such notice is given the Clerk shall at once place the Bill in its proper place upon the orders for General Debates[.]

Sec VI. [blank]

Notes for By-Laws:

—Election of President—particulars
—Request of ten members for the calling of special meeting to be signed by the ten and spread upon the minutes of the meeting called in pursuance thereof
—Method of calling special meeting.

WWhw MS. (WP, DLC).

From W. H. Munger

Dear Sir   Fremont Neb. Jan'y 13th 1883.

Yours of the 10th addressed to the late firm of Marlin & Munger is at hand[.] Mr. Marlin has removed to Denver Colorado and the writer has charge of all the business of the late firm.

It is not possible for me to give you a statement of the exact cost to make a just assessment and division of the real estate without knowing the quantity and how widely separated the various tracts are if at all.

To make such a division as you mention I should want to either go and examine the land in person or send a responsible party to make a personal examination of each tract and report as to the character of soil surface &c and proximity to settlements. The best figures I can give you with present information are as follows. I will send a good trusty and experienced man to personally inspect each tract at an expense of $4 per day and his expenses which will probably be about $3 per day more. If the land is all in Burt County, it can be all examined in an absence of from 3 to 5 days. I will then make the division from his report and see to the recording of the deeds for $25 for the 1st 1/4 section[,] $20 for the 2d 1/4[,] $15 for the 3d 1/4[,] $10 for the 4th and $5 for each remaining quarter section. This is the best I can do. If you will give me a description of the land I can give you the exact figures for which I will make the assessment division &c

Truly yours   W. H. Munger

ALS (WP, DLC).

From James W. Bones

Dear Tommy   Rome, Ga., Jany 13th 1883

Your last letter was received & would have been answered Saturday but I was unusually busy all today. I regret that there must still be some delay in getting the Estate matters arranged. Your Aunts will was probated here in due form & copies sent to Nebraska for record. After some correspondence it was decided that the probate would have to be made there also. The lawyers at Fremont & Tekamah at first differed as to the necessity of this, one contending that a simple record was sufficient, at last however they agreed that the usual form must be observed there. I am daily expecting to be informed that the matter has been finally arranged. I have recd from Mr Dorsey valuation of land in Dodge Co & expect vy soon similar valuation from Burt. Some notes also have been sent on for collection which will be remitted for shortly. I regret these delays but you can depend upon my rendering a satisfactory account of my stewardship at an early day. I cannot see that there is any ground for anxiety on your part. If you need any funds in advance of our settlement let me know.

I had a nice long letter from your dear Mother a few days ago. She said Helen[1] had been sick but was quite better again. I also had a letter from Mami[2] a short time since & was glad to hear they were all well.

Jessie has continued to do remarkably well & also the dear little baby[3]

With love from us all   Your affec Uncle   James W Bones

ALS (WP, DLC) with WWhw notation on env.: "Ans. Jany. 19th/83."
[1] Helen Bones, younger daughter of James Bones, was paying an extended visit to WW's family in Wilmington.
[2] Marion McGraw Bones.
[3] Marion, born to Jessie and Abraham Brower in September 1882.

Marginal Notes

Alexis de Tocqueville, *Democracy in America* (2 vols., London, 1875).

Vol. I, 205-206:

When elections recur at long intervals the State is exposed to violent agitation every time they take place. Parties exert themselves to the utmost in order to gain a prize which is so rarely within their reach; and as the evil is almost irremediable for the candidates who fail, the consequences of their disappointed ambition may prove most disastrous: if, on the other hand, the legal struggle can be repeated within a short space of time, the defeated parties take patience. When elections occur frequently, their recurrence keeps society in a perpetual state of feverish excitement, and imparts a continual instability to public affairs. . . .

Vol. I, 262:

A general law—which bears the name of Justice—has been made and sanctioned, not only by a majority of this or that people, but by a majority of mankind. The rights of every people are consequently confined within the limits of what is just. A nation may be considered in the light of a jury which is empowered to represent society at large, and to apply the great and general law of justice. Ought such a jury, which represents society, to have more power than the society in which the laws it applies originate?

Vol. I, 265:

If, on the other hand, a legislative power could be so constituted as to represent the majority without necessarily

Transcripts of WW Shorthand Comments

[c. Jan. 19, 1883]

It seems to me that it is quite possible to arrive at a happy medium in this matter of frequent elections. They may be made neither too close together nor too far apart—neither so frequent as to threaten with too great mutability, nor so infrequent as to bring revolution. Such medium would seem to have been arrived at in England.

Justice is indeed a great general law; but though sanctioned it is *made* by mankind.

This could be realized under cabinet government

being the slave of its passions; an executive, so as to retain a certain degree of
uncontrolled authority; and a judiciary,
so as to remain independent of the two
other powers; a government would be
formed which would still be democratic
without incurring any risk of tyrannical
abuse.

Vol. I, 382:

The fate of the white population of the
Southern States will, perhaps, be similar
to that of the Moors in Spain. After having occupied the land for centuries, it
will perhaps be forced to retire to the
country whence its ancestors came, and
to abandon to the negroes the possession
of a territory, which Providence seems
to have more peculiarly destined for
them, since they can subsist and labour
in it more easily than the whites.

Vol. I, 396:

The Union was formed by the voluntary agreement of the States; and, in
uniting together, they have not forfeited
their nationality, nor have they been reduced to the condition of one and the
same people. If one of the States chose to
withdraw its name from the contract, it
would be difficult to disprove its right of
doing so; and the Federal Government
would have no means of maintaining its
claims directly, either by force or by
right. In order to enable the Federal Government easily to conquer the resistance
which may be offered to it by any one
of its subjects, it would be necessary that
one or more of them should be specially
interested in the existence of the Union,
as has frequently been the case in the
history of confederations.

Vol. I, 403:

The American of the Northern States
is surrounded by no slaves in his childhood; he is even unattended by free
servants, and is usually obliged to provide for his own wants. No sooner does
he enter the world than the idea of necessity assails him on every side: he soon
learns to know exactly the natural limit
of his authority; *he never expects to subdue those who withstand him, by force*;
and he knows that the surest means of
obtaining the support of his fellow-crea-

such as I have suggested
elsewhere.

! This prediction would
be ridiculous were it not for
the dignity which it may
be said to borrow from the
wonderful esteem and truth
of the author's other
predictions.

This passage is interest-
ing as indicating what was
probably the prevailing
opinion upon this subject
in the United States when
DeT. wrote. Upon this
point as upon others he
probably expresses views
of the Constitution which
he gathered from his intercourse with Americans
during his stay in this
country.

Here is a key to the
South's propen[sity] to
homicide which will unlock
all the mystery of the
problem.

tures, is to win their favour. He therefore becomes patient, reflecting, tolerant,
slow to act, and persevering in his designs. [WW's italics.]

Vol. I. 420:

I have shown in the proper place that
the object of the Federal Constitution was
not to form a league, but to create a na-
tional Government. The Americans of the
United States form a sole and undivided
people, in all the cases which are speci-
fied by that Constitution; and upon these
points the will of the nation is expressed,
as it is in all constitutional nations, by
the voice of the majority. When the majority has pronounced its decision, it is
the duty of the minority to submit. Such
is the *sound legal doctrine,* and the only
one which agrees with the text of the
Constitution, and the known intention
of those who framed it. [WW's italics.]

If this object was at-
tained what becomes of the
right of secession appar-
ently acknowledged on
page 396?

Wilson's Critique of De Tocqueville's
Democracy in America

[c. Jan. 19, 1883]

(1) Was he ever right?

(2) Have these phenomena ceased since?

[3] Quite the best philosophy since Aristotle. Political institutions presuppose a particularly moral and sentimental state of
the community, one of his valuable reflections.

Errors

(1) Ignores the under-riding English elements both in American institutions and in American political character. He did not
quite know England. Overrated the aristocratic character of English government of the time.

(2) Yet underrates the *colonial* character of American history[,] forgets about its contact in colonial times.

(3) He has France too constantly before his eyes, hence not a
pure absolute observer. Always looking at America with a view
to France. Always thinking of the lessons to be learned from
America by his own countrymen. He is apt to think that what is
not French is democratic.

(4) Although he has a very strong practical sense, he is not one
without the tendency which the French have to push the thing
out to its logical consequence, but he has not practical knowledge
of affairs. Perhaps a statesman who understood the difference be-

tween things on paper and things in working, would not have written quite as he writes. Some views may be considered views of mere theorist.

(5) Slightly exaggerated ingenuity. Too often attempted to explain everything—to see farther than others into a millstone. This is what Aristotle would not have done. He had too much moderation, too fine sagaciousness. This is the difference between first and second genius.

Things perhaps doubtful:

(1) Very keen interest in the conduct of smallest local government, the communal government.

(2) Dilates upon the absence of free thought and free speech in America.

(3) Monopoly of the majority.

(4) The rich are discontented.

(5) Changes of the legislature.

(6) Arbitrary authority of the magistrates.

(7) State patriotism in states bound by straight lines.

Power of the Senate tending to increase?

The growth of public opinion, making the leaders of both parties in England resort much more to the stump.

Transcript of WWsh on four small loose notebook pages (WP, DLC). WW indicated that he completed reading the first volume of *Democracy in America* on Jan. 19, 1883. He also read the much briefer second volume, for he marked it heavily but made only one inconsequential marginal note in shorthand. Presumably, he read the second volume soon after the first, hence the date assigned to his critique.

From Robert Bridges

Dear Tommy: New York Feb 2nd '83

I know you have been wanting to hear from me—but I have been holding back for a chance to get Mr. Garrison to read the Essay. I have had it in my desk for about two weeks waiting for the opportunity. He has been very busy, but today told me that he had some spare time. I asked him to read the third part—as I thought it representative. He read it carefully and frankly gave me his opinion, and I will as frankly give it to you. He thinks that the style is too rhetorical—and that it is verbose in parts. Consequently he detected repetitions of idea and argument. He contrasted it with Mr. Stickney's which he says is too condensed. He thinks that you go too far in your argument—and that all the benefits of the cabinet system might be gained by a mere Congressional resolution giving the members of the cabinet seats on the floor of the house, without votes. He also pointed out the fact that the essay predicts a poor prospect for Civil Service Reform legislation—and it has already taken the form of a law.[1] (I also noticed similar allusions in the fourth part.)

Notwithstanding Mr. Garrison's adverse view, I still think that the essay has striking and original merits. I read it very carefully. I think the changes proposed are too radical (as for example—the life tenure for president.), but the general line of the argument for Cabinet Government—seemed to me both clear and forcible. I can get introductions to the Putnams and Holts, and want to push the book on their attention. I think that the references to the Civil Service bill should be changed, and I don't believe that the long allusions to Stickney's book would take with other publishers. Of course these changes rest with your judgment—and I will wait to hear from you before I seek the publishers again. If you decide to make any changes I'll send the MS. by express.

Received a note from Hiram today. I suppose you have heard of his mother's death. He seems very much depressed. Chang Lee will visit me next week, and I expect lots of fun.

I am very tired and have a dull headache—or I would write more—and more clearly.   Your friend   Bob Bridges.

ALS (WP, DLC) with WWhw notation on env.: "Re'd and Ans. 2/5/83."
[1] The Civil Service Reform Act, introduced by Senator George H. Pendleton of Ohio and signed by President Arthur on Jan. 16, 1883.

From James W. Bones

Dear Tommy   Helenhurst[1] [Rome,Ga.] Feby 3/83

The letters I have been expecting from Nebraska have not yet come, so I have drawn off an approximate statement of the present condition of the Estate matters, which I think is nearly correct. It shows your dear mothers interest to be nearly $20,000. A sale has been made which will yield about $1800. cash & it will be consummated in a short time. I have also sent out some notes for collection for which I have not yet reced returns. It will greatly facilitate our division if you will wait a short time for final action until these matters get in. The statement I send you will enable you to give your dear Mother the information she desires in view of their contemplated change of base.[2] I have not mentioned this latter matter to any of the family here as I presume they do not want the thing talked about.

Jessie & her baby are quite well[.] Mami has been suffering from a severe cold but is better. Excuse my writing with pencil. It is late at night & I cannot lay my hand on a pen without disturbing Mami who has gone to bed. Your affec Uncle   James

ALS (WP, DLC).
  [1] Bones' home.
  [2] A reference to the Wilsons' ardent desire to leave Wilmington.

To Robert Bridges

Dear Bobby,   Atlanta, Geo., Feb. 5th/83

Thank you for your candid letter. Of course I am very much disappointed, and somewhat discouraged, by Mr. Garrison's extremely unfavourable opinion of my essay, but I would not have had you withhold it, and it will serve me the good purpose of a guide hereafter. In regard to his criticisms I have only this to say, that the *repetition* was intentional. I wanted to hammer a great deal on the cardinal points of the question and give them constant prominence. I tried to repeat with variety of *form and manner* so as not to tire the reader, but purposely made the substance always the same; the blame for the resulting monotony must fall, therefore, on my defective literary methods rather than upon any defect of treatment.

I admit that you are right in calling the changes proposed *radical*—perhaps they are *too* radical; but if one goes one step with me, he cannot, as it seems to me, escape going all the way. To stop short of the length to which I carry the argument would be simply to be afraid of the legitimate and logical conclusions towards which it inclines with an inevitable tendency. I should be glad to see members of the Cabinet introduced upon the floor of Congress under a plan such as Mr. Garrison, and Mr. Pendleton,[1] favour; but such a plan would, in my opinion, inevitably bring us ultimately to the adoption of every change I advocate. That the changes I advocate are radical does not seem to me to be a fatal objection to my essay, unless they be also visionary and impracticable; and the very boldness of the proposals it contains, and the very fearlessness of the treatment, would seem to me to recommend it to publishers as making it by so much the more saleable. Its boldness may give it an air of originality which it would not otherwise have. At any rate, its conclusions do not stand a single inch beyond my convictions—my *deliberate* convictions.

I appreciate the fact that my extended criticism of Stickney's views may make the essay less acceptable to some publishers, but I do'nt see that I can change it. It is quite usual for writers upon such subjects to review and answer the propositions of others who

have been in the field before them; and in this instance it is particularly natural that a portion of my work should assume the
form of an answer to Mr. S., as he is the only other writer who
has proposed any considerable changes in our forms of govt. Mine
is necessarily a *rival scheme*, and I could not leave him unnoticed.
To fortify my positions I must destroy his.

Of course my statements with reference to civil service reform
must be altered to accord with fact. When I sent my *ms.* off the
Pendleton bill had not passed, and it seemed to me, as it seemed
to the *Nation* to to [sic] most other friends of the bill, that there
was small prospect of its passing now or soon. The changes to be
made are so inconsiderable, however, that I will ask you to make
them yourself. I have a copy of the essay, which is paged somewhat differently from the one you have, but which will serve as
a guide. The first reference to civil service reform occurs about
page 20 of Part III. There, in the paragraph beginning "The fact
is that public opinion &c.," please strike out the sentence "All
party platforms, indeed, &c" as far as, and including the words
"any such thing will happen." Again, on page 35, comes a passage
which should read thus: "This is the oft-established principle
which lies at the source of the great movement towards civil service reform in which all the currents of public opinion are now
united, in a tide before which the stoutest dykes of party custom
and party interest have gone down"; and the sentence "An organization . . . devoutly to be wished" should be stricken out.

On the next page—in order to leave Mr. Stickney out of view as
much as possible—instead of "Mr Stickney makes much" &c., say
"Much might be made of the objection" &c.

Then, passing to Part IV, page 7, tack on to the paragraph ending "shoulder to shoulder with blatent free-traders," the sentence
"Civil service reform, then, became as of course the presiding
issue of the day, and the recent tardy Act was but the natural and
irresistible consummation of the national purpose on that head,"
and substitute in the following paragraph past tenses where you
see they are called for—for instance, "which it *has been* their
pleasure and their power to possess." Strike out also the first part
of this paragraph, down to the words "It is a significant fact &c"

Again on page 10 of same part, after the paragraph ending "recognized to be" insert, as the first sentences of the paragraph
which opens "It is this sense of responsibility," this: "For us these
facts bear this significance, that, however satisfactory may be the
inauguration of that reformed system of civil service now at last

set on foot by legislation in this country, it is to be feared that its administration will not, in the absence of strict ministerial responsibility, be equally satisfactory. In order that it may work well, the public should desire the most complete executive accountability, for without that the public cannot watch its workings." "It is this sense of responsibility &c"

I believe that ends the list of necessary alterations,[2] and I thought it would be easier for you to make these few than to send the *ms.* by express to me. I think that this is about all I can do for the essay. I can't reform its style. The charge of verboseness is a serious one which I shall be careful not to lay myself open to again, but it's too late to reform it in this case. If none of the N.Y. publishers like the piece well enough to publish it, please hold it and I will get you to express it to Boston for me.

I cannot thank you enough, Bobby, for the interest you are taking in my behalf in this matter. I can assure you that I value it at its true worth, and am sincerely grateful. I am exceedingly gratified, too, that you have so high an estimate of the work I have done. I should rather have your admiration than Garrison's, though, of course, your opinion cannot as yet carry as much weight as his in some quarters.

No, I had not heard from or of Hiram in ever so long—not since the Triennial—and, therefore, knew nothing of his mother's death. I am very much shocked by the news. I may say that I knew Mrs. Woods well, and a more amiable woman or more lovable mother I never knew—except my own mother. I am *so* sorry she is gone! I shall write to Hiram at once.[3] My sympathy for him is very genuine.

Well, good-bye for this time, Bobby.

With much love and gratitude,　Your sincere friend

Woodrow Wilson

(ALS, Meyer Coll., DLC).

[1] Senator Pendleton had introduced a bill in 1879 to give Cabinet members seats in either house. Similar proposals had been made in the *Nation* for several years by Wendell Phillips Garrison and by such contributors as Gamaliel Bradford.

[2] All of which Bridges made in his own hand. They are in the second draft of the manuscript.

[3] See at April 25, 1883.

Woodrow Wilson, young Atlanta lawyer,
presented to Hattie Woodrow

Hattie Woodrow, photograph made at
Wilson's request

My sweet Cousin,

Writing in an album is a very delicate task.
Spreading the expression of one's affections on an album leaf
seems like profaning that which should be sacred. In putting
my name among the names of those who love you, however, I
feel that there is no place where it could more properly be. I will
not try here to put in words what I hope has been in the past,
and I trust may be in the future, proved in other ways.

Lovingly Your cousin.
T. Woodrow Wilson

Staunton Va, June 2nd 1880

A page from Hattie Woodrow's album

Joseph R. Wilson, Jr., with his Columbia bicycle

Richard Heath Dabney

Edward Ireland Renick

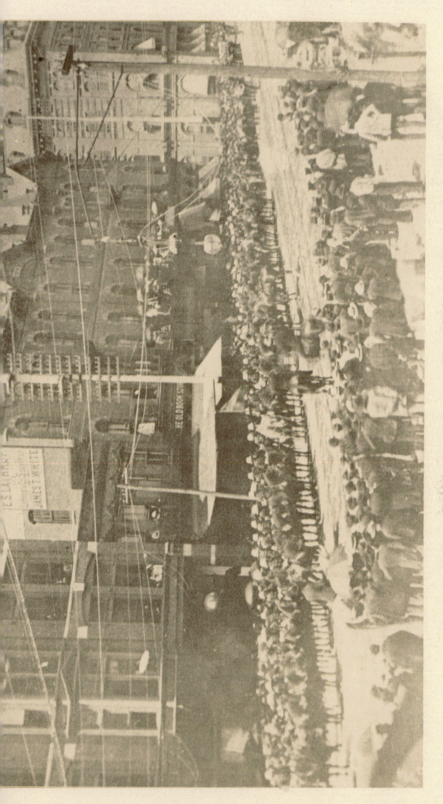

Concordia Hall, 48 Marietta Street, Atlanta, where Wilson and Renick had their office, with funeral procession of Alexander H. Stephens in foreground

STATE OF GEORGIA.

At a Superior Court holden in and for the County of
Fulton, *Fall* Term, 1882.

Know all Men by these Presents, That at the present sitting of this Court
Woodrow Wilson made his application for leave to Plead
and Practice in the several Courts of Law and Equity in this State;

Whereupon, the said *Woodrow Wilson* having produced satisfac-
tory evidence of his good moral character, and having been examined in Open Court, and being found well acquainted with
and skilled in the Laws, he was admitted by the Court to all the privileges of an Attorney, Solicitor and Counsellor, in the
several Courts of Law and Equity in this State, (except the Supreme Court of Georgia.)

In Testimony Whereof, The presiding Judge has hereunto set his hand, with the Seal of
the Court annexed, this *October 19th* 1882.

Geo. Hillyer
J. S. C. A. C.

C. H. Strong Clerk.

Wilson's license to practice law in Georgia courts

The United States of America.

Fifth Circuit Court of the United States,

For the Northern District of Georgia.

Be it Known, That _Woodrow Wilson_ Esquire, has been duly and regularly admitted to practice as an

Attorney and Counselor at Law, Solicitor in Chancery, and as

Proctor and Advocate,

in the Circuit Court of the United States for the Northern District of Georgia, at the _March_ Term of said Court, begun and holden at Atlanta, the _Twelfth_ day of _March_ in the year of our Lord one Thousand Eight Hundred and _Eighty Three_ And he is hereby authorized to appear as such, according to the rules and practice of said Court, and the Laws of the United States.

In Testimony Whereof, I have subscribed my name officially, and affixed the Seal of said Court, at the City of Atlanta, this _Twenty third_ day of _March_ A.D., 188 _3_ , and of the Independence of the United States the One Hundred and _Seventh_ .

R. E. Boyd Clerk.

Wilson's license to practice law in the United States Circuit Court

"Law has no force save that which it derives from the consent and respect of those who live under it."

V   The ~~End~~ Work of Reform

Little now remains to be said in Conclusion of this discussion. Shall the forms of federal administration be altered in accordance with a plan which has been tested and found best by our own ancestors and our own Kinsmen, which is now the prevailing system amongst the most advanced nations of the world, and which both reason and our own experience recommend to our acceptance? That is the single, the plain, the simple issue.

That the Country is prepared, or at least preparing, for a change of the instrumentalities of national government none but the ignorant and the old ~~and old men~~ can doubt. Some change will soon be indispensable. The future that stands in our face is full of disquieting possibilities Our populations are growing at such a rate that one staggers at the reckoning Counting the possible millions that may have a home and a work on this Continent ere fifty more years have filled their short span. The East will not always be the centre of national life. The South is fast accumulating wealth and will faster gather influence. The West has already achieved a greatness which no man can gainsay and has in future store a power of growth which no man can estimate. These great sections may be antagonistic, and they may not. Whether they be harmonious or discontent depends almost entirely upon the methods and the policies of government. If monopolies are to thrive in one at the expense of those who are denied monopolies in another; if government let not alone the industrial pursuits of its citizens, but hamper them with restrictions visit and superintend them with hosts of prying officials; if government tax not to support and further its own enterprises but

Marginal Notes

P. C. Centz [Bernard Janin Sage], *The Republic of Republics* (Boston, 1881).

Pp. 9-15:

[In this, Chapter II, Part I, the author argues that federal and state governments exist in "perfect similarity" and warns against those who would falsely assert the supremacy of federal power.]

Transcripts of WW Shorthand Comments

[c. Feb. 7, 1883]

It seems to me that the author is spinning a web of argument so fine that no practical spider would live in it. Unquestionably there have been great and almost disastrous perversions of federal authority which no statesman and no true constitutionalist could think of trying to defend; but, on the other hand, there are certain stubborn facts and certain inevitable limitations of possibility which cannot be passed by[,] by any practical publicist. Undoubtedly "the people were" and are "the states" and these peoples ordained and established the Constitution; undoubtedly the federal government is for each state but a part of its "machinery of self government" and it therefore holds its powers of the states; undoubtedly its authority is not of its own making but is conferred upon it by the peoples who are the states; but it is not only an integral part of the self-governing machinery of *each* state but also an integral part of the self-governing machinery *of all the states*—it is the servant not only of each of the constituent peoples but also *of all of them*—they have joined in creating this common agent, they have entrusted *to one* set of functionaries certain duties which they found it inexpedient to divide among the many sets of functionaries; they have fused a certain part of each of their several constitutions into a single constitution common to them all, and what is and must be the practical result? An actual union of the peoples for certain purposes. The central government, which they have themselves constituted judge of its own powers and whose decrees they have themselves declared to be the "supreme law of the land," must be obeyed; for they have mutually given their solemn pledge to submit to its authority, and they have deliberately given over their right to recall or anew restrict its privileges except by this regular, this cumbersome and tedious method of amendment upon which they have agreed. If one withdraw, the union is made so far useless for the rest. The danger that the federal power will attempt fatal usurpations does not seem a very formidable peril in times of peace. Its organization is not independently consolidated enough. "Congressmen and Presidential electors are citizens and speak for their respective states" and as they go often to their masters for authority, they come honestly by their opinions of what it is their privilege to do as federal functionaries. The state has practical government, through the patriotism of their federal representatives, and if any one of them is aggrieved by the action of the national government it has much opportunities of constitutional and political reform within its reach, and in the last resort the inalienable right of revolution. The peoples have done this thing, who may complain?

Pp. 16-21:

[In this, Chapter III, Part I, the author attributes to the federal government certain characteristics of absolute monarchy.]

Is not the author firing at a mere figure of speech when he hurls such hot shot at the "government." "The government" is the federal agent of the peoples of the states, and as a matter of fact *it is* supreme within its own sphere. But where is the seat of its supremacy? In the *Congress* which is the head and soul of the whole system—in Congress which is made up altogether of the citizens and subjects of the states, a body which is not very likely to enter upon any very slight schemes of usurpation and state-destruction. The government is not a permanent organization. In times of war—and especially in that time of the Civil War when the whole movement still consisted of states burning with the wish to preserve and maintain the union and when all other powers worked hotly and eagerly in the service of that purpose—legislature and executive may forget their proper functions and run violently beyond their rightful authority; but the time soon returns when the government is again in the hands of the peoples who are the states and they may again control that government which is made up of their own citizens and subjects. The states are bound to render allegiance to the general government just as much as they are bound to render allegiance to the state governments—the one is no less their own creation than the other.

From Joseph Ruggles Wilson

My dearest son—   Wilmington, [N. C.] February 13, 1883.

I cannot conceal from you the truth that your letters have of late given me not a little anxious concern: a concern due not to your lack of visible success in your profession, but to the fact, principally, of your looking towards a succedaneum. Immediate or even speedy success was not expected, at the outset, but *totus in illo* was, and, without the this-or-nothing motto, success is hardly possible and contentment altogether out of the question. Need I beg of you not to think that I am complaining or fault-finding? I am only regretting with no thought of blaming. It is no doubt true, as you say, that the dissatisfaction you sometimes express is not always *felt*—yet it is there as a "background," your own well-chosen word: and needs only a rebellious liver to make it foreground. Now, my darling, will you not have to conquer this enemy —this *mental* liver—this something that leaves you with only one hand instead of two?

But then if, upon a renewed examination of your inward man you shall find a change most desirable—a change say from law to teaching—I will not object to any decision you may come to, and will do my utmost to secure you a position. Yet, "qui fit Maecenas" &c—are you certain, *can* you be certain, that this same enemy will not attack you again?[1]

Meanwhile I would accept the invitation to lecture in the institution to which you refer.[2] It may serve to bring you more into notice; and, if any fool object because the pupils are negroes, just let him object and make the most of it. You have yr defence[.] I am truly sorry that Renick and you are divorced.[3] But—maybe— it is for the better. For now you will stand where every young man ought to stand—alone—or, an opportunity may offer for association with some old practitioner in the law which would be to yr advantage.

With your education, and gifts, and character, and opportunity, you may kick the world before you—*God* helping you as He will for the honest asking.

The love that is in all our hearts for you no paragraphs could express.

Write again soon, and believe me always
Your best friend & affc *father*

ALS (WP, DLC) with WWhw notation: "Ans. Feby 15th/83."

[1] WW was now obviously in process of making the fateful decision to abandon law for a career in teaching. R. Bridges to WW, May 9, 1883, makes it clear that WW, as early as June 1882, was less than enthusiastic about practicing law but had decided to give it a trial. WW to R. Bridges, April 29 and May 13, 1883, are particularly revealing about WW's reasons for changing careers. The Latin is part of a Satire of Horace's which asks why no one is content with his own lot but praises those "who follow other fortunes."

[2] Probably either Clark University or the University of Atlanta, both Negro institutions in Atlanta.

[3] Apparently the "divorce" did not occur until WW left Atlanta. Renick, in his letter to WW of June 23, 1883, still referred to the firm as Renick & Wilson.

From James W. Bones

Dear Tommy　　　　　　　　　　　　　　　[Rome, Ga.] Feby 17/83
I hope you will pardon me for my delay in giving you the in-

formation you desire as to the statement I sent you. This has been an exceedingly busy week with me & I have been far from well, so that I have come home in the evenings quite unfit for any kind of work. Last night I made a pencil memorandum from my book which I now inclose without attempting to put it into anything like proper shape. The item of Expense I distribute under three heads. The $150. sent to Washington had to be paid into the General Land Office in order to secure a missing Patent. One of the land warrants used by your Uncle William proved to be fraudulent & the Patent was never issued to him, only the certificate of entry being among his papers. It took me two or three years to get the matter arranged.

I also give you the calculation of interest on your mothers & aunties a/cs. My reason for adding the interest as one of the amts first & debiting the two a/cs with it was to arrive at the present share of each owner in the Estate. There by deducting the total interest from the aggregate assets, the real assets are shown to be $77,670.68[.] Deducting from this amount the sums drawn by the two owners leaves the present estimated value of the Estate $37,670.29[.] The present actual assets to be divided consist of the notes & land. The notes are land notes secured by mortgage except one for about $500. due to my present firm.

The reason I gave you so condensed a statement was that I supposed you only desired to know your mothers present interest in the Estate & that when we got together you could go over my account fully. I think it very desirable that we should have a preliminary consultation before we make final settlement. There is a great deal of information I can give you which it is impossible to write. If you think it is impossible for you to run up for a day or so, which we would all be exceedingly glad to have you do, I could come down to Atlanta some day soon.

I hope you are feeling better than when you wrote. We are all quite well here & at Jessies.   Your affectionate Uncle James

ALS (WP, DLC).

To Robert Bridges

Dear Bobby,   Atlanta, Geo., Feby. 24/83
    In accordance with your thoughtful suggestion, I have prepared a short piece on Convict Labour in Georgia which I send along with this note, and which may prove acceptable to your managing editor. In case he do'nt think it suitable for publication, never mind sending it back, as it is of very little value. It has been very

difficult for me to get any reliable information about the actual workings of our convict system. The little the article contains was culled chiefly from printed reports and from statute books. Perhaps, after some correspondence with Dr. Felton[1] and others who have interested themselves on the subject, I might gather materials for a second and more interesting letter, in case this one fares well.

I have not been very well recently, but to-day I feel tolerably brisk and at all times I am in the humour to think of you with all affection. No news.

With love,   Yours in haste   Woodrow Wilson

(ALS Meyer Coll., DLC).
[1] William H. Felton was not only a leader of independent Democrats in Georgia but also one of the chief critics of the convict-lease system in the state.

A Newspaper Article

[c. *Feb. 24, 1883*]

Convict Labor in Georgia

Atlanta, Ga., February 26.—It may be said with truth that, although she has known nothing since the war of the old system of penitentiary confinement, Georgia is still experimenting in systems of convict labor. Her policy toward her criminals has vacillated as much as have the purposes and whims of her legislators in regard to all other matters of government. Something like her present plan of convict labor was adopted as early as 1866, but many and differing laws relating to the subject have since been enacted, and even now nobody can be certain that the system will long remain unchanged. An influential minority of Georgians, firm in their convictions, and perhaps growing in numbers, are much dissatisfied with it; every legislature tinkers with it, and nobody seems to regard it as a settled thing.

The history of the system in this State is much like the history of similar systems in neighboring States. It took its rise in that impatience of taxation which is still its main support and strength— an impatience which was like to have emptied the old penitentiary sooner than it did. The last report of Mr. J. W. Nelson, the present Principal Keeper of convicts in Georgia, shows that fifty years ago, under the old penitentiary régime, when the prison roll contained but two hundred names, the expense of maintaining the prisoners after the old fashion was considered by the taxpayers so heavy a burden that by the Act of 24th of December, 1831, the penitentiary was actually abolished. By that act an attempt was made to return to the laws of the imperfect code which had been in force previous to 1816, and, as a supplement to that code, the whipping-post was erected to serve as a terror to those who were prone to commit certain minor crimes. But the laws of 1816 speedily proved inadequate to the needs of 1832. The Legislature of that year was constrained to open again the doors of the State prison, and, in spite of the fact that the taxes collected for the support of the convicts were still always paid with a very bad grace by the people, and that more than one serious attack was made upon the administration of the penitentiary, no further legislative step was taken in the matter until 1866. By an act of that year the General Assembly authorized Governor Jenkins to farm out the convicts to private persons on the best terms possible. But the times were then too troublous for the regular and legal birth of such a system, or indeed of any new policy of peaceful administration, for all law was in suspense; the hand of the Federal Government was on the South, and Governor Jenkins was soon displaced by military rule. General Ruger assumed command of the State, and undertook the executive direction of its affairs in the name of the Federal authorities: and he it was who acted upon the suggestion of the Assembly in the matter of the disposition of the convicts by instituting the present system. He found the prisons of the State crowded and without proper management, and, in May, 1868, thought it convenient and expedient to lease out a number of the convicts. In July of the same year he made a second lease; and in the following November his successor, Rufus B. Bullock, reconstruction Governor of Georgia, contracted with Messrs. Grant and Alexander to lease the entire convict force of the State on easy terms.

Such was the beginning of the present policy of convict leasing. Since 1868 very few legislatures have refrained from meddling with the system. After making trial from 1871 to 1874 of short leases for terms of from one to two years, and after extending the maximum term to five years in 1874, the law now provides for leases for at least twenty years in ordinary cases. The number of lessees is made to depend upon considerations of convenience. The law of 1876 authorized an experiment of which nothing has come. The Governor was instructed to require the principal leasing company, which was constituted a corporation for the purposes of the act, to procure at its own expense a suitable site, either an island off the coast of Georgia or some other place within the limits of the State, of which the Governor should approve, and on that site to erect, at its own expense, under the Governor's direction, "suitable, convenient, safe, healthy, and commodious prisons, barracks, hospitals, guard-houses, and all other dwell-

ings necessary for the safe keeping and comfort of the convicts."
This establishment, entirely under private management, save for
the presence of one or two officers, such as a physician and a
chaplain, appointed by the Governor, was to have been known as
the State Penitentiary, and was to have been convict headquarters
rather than the common criminals' prison, the act contemplating
that certain convicts should be kept within the walls while all the
rest worked without in mines and quarries, or on roads and canals.
But the scheme broke down, and this novel experiment of a private
penitentiary under governmental supervision gave place to the
existing arrangements, which may be very briefly described.

There are at present about 1,200 convicts in the hands of the
several lessees. They are scattered throughout the State in guarded
camps where they can best serve the purposes of the contractors,
some mining coal for Senator Brown, some mining iron ore, some
quarrying granite, others making brick, others constructing tram-
ways, and still others building railroads. A large force has for several years been assigned by the State, without charge, to the proprietors of the Marietta and North Georgia Railroad, by a special
act which contemplated similar contributions of labor on the part
of the State to other railroad companies. For each convict the regular lessees pay the paltry sum of $20 per annum, enabling the
State to realize yearly for the lease of the whole force about
$25,000. The conditions of lease are that the treatment of the con-
victs shall be "in accordance with existing regulations"; in short,
that they are to be well cared for and humanely dealt with; that
they are never to be worked upon Sunday, nor for more than ten
hours on any other day; and that they are never to be corporeally
punished except by some one person in each camp regularly appointed to administer punishment, and by him only when punishment is absolutely necessary for the preservation of discipline. The
lessees further undertake to clothe and lodge the convicts com-
fortably, to be answerable in damages for all escapes, and to release promptly such as may be pardoned or may have served out
their terms, dismissing them with a good suit of citizen's clothes
and money enough to take them to their homes. For the fulfilment
of these conditions the lessees give such bond, with security, as is
deemed sufficient by the Governor; and their diligence and good
faith in the performance of their obligations are sought to be assured by the supervision of the Assistant Keeper, who makes
monthly visits to each of the camps in the name of the State, and
files in the Governor's office frequent reports of the results of his
inspection. Besides the Principal and Assistant Keepers, the State

also employs a physician, to make frequent professional visits to the camps, with a view to securing proper sanitary regulations, as well as for the purpose of rendering his services to the sick.

Such, in brief, is the convict system of Georgia. It is, at least, a consistent one. The State gets altogether rid of the care of all of its criminals[.] It extends its policy of leasing even to cases of misdemeanor, for one section of the law of 1874 provides that persons sentenced to fine, or fine and costs, with alternative imprisonment, may bind themselves, in a sort of penal apprenticeship, for the alternative period of imprisonment, to such persons, approved of by the judge who passed sentence, as shall consent in writing to pay the fine. In such cases the hirer is considered the bailee of the convict and may surrender him to the officers of the court if at any time he grossly misbehaves or attempts to escape.

The criticisms and objections to which this system is open are obvious. In the first place, if intended to operate for the pecuniary advantage of the State, the revenues derived from it are miserably small as compared with the income which might be secured from the system. Both Alabama and South Carolina lease their convicts to private persons, but they get much higher rates than Georgia lessees have ever paid. In Alabama the convicts are divided into three classes, according to their capacity for labor. For those who are capable of the most efficient work the government obtains prices falling very little below the highest market price of labor; for those less efficient good wages are paid, and those least efficient are let out for their maintenance. In South Carolina a somewhat similar plan is adopted, the prices obtained by the State being there proportioned to the kind of labor for which the convicts are engaged. But South Carolina does not lease out all her convicts; she is more thrifty; she retains a number in her well-ordered penitentiary, and there trains them in the handicrafts. The shoes made at the South Carolina Penitentiary are purchased all over that State as the best shoes made for ordinary wear. To a careful and provident system, such as her neighbors have established, Georgia, however, makes no pretence. In her eyes one convict is worth no more than another; and the $25,000 which the leases yearly bring into her coffers fully compensates her as an addition to the pleasure of getting rid of the care of all her criminals.

But this economic objection to the system is the least serious of all. It is not desirable that the chief end of the State in this matter should be to make as much money as possible out of the lease of her criminals. Manifestly, it is a system which is open to gross abuses. The entire care and discipline of the convicts is intrusted to private individuals whose interest it is to get as much gain as possible out of their purchased punitive authority. The friends of the present system insist, that the convicts are treated for the most part without harshness and with a due regard for their health and comfort. But it is known that very disgraceful things have happened in consequence of the fact that the sexes have not always been kept carefully separate in the camps, and it is reasonable to conclude that, in their eagerness to get as much work as possible out of the laborers who are thus put absolutely at their disposal, the lessees do not hesitate to make every hour an hour of toil and drudgery, to the neglect of all those reformatory methods and influences for which government is nowadays always expected to provide.

Indeed, it is evident that the system is quite incompatible with modern ideas of the duty which society owes to the criminal classes. No effort ought to be spared to educate and elevate the inmates of our prisons. No outlay, however great, is wasted which is devoted to the training of convicts in the handicrafts or to their moral and intellectual elevation. No such betterment of the condition of this unhappy class can, however, be accomplished in Georgia convict camps under present circumstances, for the men who people these camps are hired not for their own benefit, but for the gain of their hirers. True, these lessees are bound by the law to observe such plans of reform as may be prescribed by the State; but they are visited only once a month by the public inspector, and they do not pretend to have employed the convict forces for any other purpose than that of profit to themselves. They are restrained from gross abuses of their power by penal statutes and by that salutary authority which has been given to the Governor, to summarily forfeit their lease upon any breach of the law or of their contracts; but they can use their employees without bettering them, and still keep safely within the letter of both contract and law.

If the object of conviction be punishment, it is obviously open to question whether the Georgia system of convict labor at all answers even that end. The majority of the convicts are of the lower class of negroes, who are accustomed to the severest and meanest kinds of manual work, and who are neither punished nor humiliated by being compelled to drudge in chains. The prevailing sentiment of the negroes upon this subject was well illustrated by a conversation between two colored men which I accidentally overheard the other day. The burden of their talk was that if one of their fellows were to rob them of their small savings or of their scanty stores of household wealth, it would neither afford them any satisfaction nor restrain him from committing similar crimes in future if he were sent to work for Mr. Brown in the mines; and they declared their conviction that the whipping-post would be better for all concerned.

But the gravest objections that can be urged against this system rest upon higher grounds even than these. For who can defend a system which makes the punishment of criminals, that high prerogative of government, a source of private gain? Who can justify a policy which delegates sovereign capacities to private individuals? How high an estimate will criminals put upon the dignity and power of government when they see that their own punishment for disobedience of the regulations of that government is made a source of private emolument?   W. W.

Printed in New York *Evening Post*, March 7, 1883; editorial headings omitted.

From Janet Woodrow Wilson

My darling Son,   Wilmington, N. C. Feb 26th 1883.

I received the enclosed letter from your Uncle James this morning. Please give your careful consideration—and let me know what you think as early as possible. I confess I do not know what to think of his proposition. I will write him today & tell him so—but promise to think about it before answering. If you think the proposition worthy of serious consideration, would you like to consult with Mr. Brower with regard to it?—I thought the sort of business your Uncle James is engaged in—a Commission business—required very little capital. If so what does he want with so much capital? You know he has his mother's $4000. already as well as the collections he has made from sales of the land. Has he furnished you with the "particulars" you required? Does he not know that you already have power of Attorney. Another thing—it appears from his letter, does it not, that he is continuing the sale of lands. Can he do that without your knowledge? Is it best that he should do so. But you will know all about it.

Your father received your last very satisfactory letter, with which he was much pleased. He forthwith wrote three letters—in your behalf—and very nice letters they were, I am sure you would think if you could have seen them. One was to Dr. McCosh—another to Dr [Charles] Phillips—& the third to our old friend Dr. Waddell of the S. W. University. On the same day I wrote to your uncle James Woodrow. I hope it will not be long before we hear something encouraging in the way of response. In the mean time what are your plans? Just to go on in the old way where you are? Your father was inclined to advise your coming home—but I objected—for I thought that would seem as if you had made a failure —which is far from the truth. Now when you secure an appointment such as you wish you could come home & spend any interval in preparing to fill your appointment.

Do you know you have not acknowledged the receipt of your last allowance? Is it possible you did not received it? I must stop now[.] I am going to devote Monday to letter writing hereafter— so you may expect to hear regularly again. Has Mr. R. left you? I hope not. Goodbye my darling All send love unbounded

Lovingly Yours   Mother

ALS (WP, DLC). Enc.: James W. Bones to JWW, Feb. 23, 1883, ALS (WP, DLC), proposing that JWW join him in a venture partnership, adding that, as he needed new capital and was limited in funds to money in his wife's estate, it would be advantageous to have also the funds of JWW.

Four Letters from Abraham T. H. Brower

Dear Cousin Woodrow: Oakdene[1] Rome, Ga. 28 Feby 1883

. . . I saw Capt. Featherston[2] last night and after a long talk we concluded that I had better write you and ask you to see Mr. Hammond[3] as soon as he returns from Washington. You could say to Mr. H. that I now had need for counsel in Atlanta, that you being connected with me were representing me, that he wd remember that in the Rome bond matter I had referred Msrs. Jas. H. & Mason Young Trustees to him & that I wished to be well defended in the libel case now pending though the whole thing is an outrage. Mr. Featherston says I may have to pay from $150. to $250. This may be but I can hardly believe it. However we certainly have the privilege of asking these gentlemen at what they value their services.

Capt. F. advised me to ask you what you thought of Mr. Henry Jackson (generally called Harry Jackson). He is not sure whether he wd be of quite the right sort for our case but he thinks you might be considering his name.

Jessie sends love.   Yours very sincerely   A. T. H. Brower

P.S. omitted. WWhw notation on env.: "Ans. 3/5/83."

[1] The Brower home in East Rome.
[2] C. N. Featherston, an attorney in Rome, Ga.
[3] The Congressman.

Dear Cousin Woodrow: Rome, Ga., 3 Mch. 1883

Yours of the 1st inst. reached me over here this morning.

I can hardly say that I am surprised at the business proposition made by Jessie's father to your mother, and of which you write.

Since you so much wish me to candidly express my opinion of the proposition and since it is Jessie's desire that I do so, I will say,

1. That as I have always understood from Mr. Bones that his bus. was a strictly commission bus. I have never known why he should need more than a small working capital.

2. The strictly commission view of Mr. Bones's bus. has been uniformly supported by the tenor of innumerable advertisements in the public prints.

3. Mr. Bones has not to my knowledge given any of the members of his family any information going to show that he was extending credits (& sometimes to irresponsible parties) and speculating in the merchandise in which he deals—all of which I believe are facts.

From the above I draw this conclusion—that as Mr. Bones has allowed his wife & children to continue under the impression that his bus. is solely a com. bus. after its character materially changed, his said wife & children being the only responsible partners in the concern & having contributed the entire (though unknown) capital employed in it, he has shown himself to be altogether too reticent and uncommunicative to suit even the most careless partner.

Now as to my belief. In my opinion all this reticence and procrastination on Mr. Bones's part are due to the fact that his bus., divested of all "ifs" and "buts," is not a profitable or healthy one. I may be all wrong in this; but up to this date I have never had any other opinion.

It is Jessie's and my earnest desire that whatever else your mother may ultimately do, she will, through you, insist on an immediate division of her and mother's interest in the joint trust estate. We wish this because we know mother wd have eagerly sought it and because it seems to us to be the only natural and proper thing to do. If mother's share have been very largely decreased, though Mr. Bones has not said one word to us upon the subject, we feel that the exact condition of affairs should be made known to all three daughters so that expenses may be regulated in accordance with such condition and the remaining principal sum of the trust carefully husbanded.[1]

We are all well. Jessie sends her love.

Very sincerely yours A. T. H. Brower

[1] Marion Woodrow Bones had left her estate in trust to her three daughters and named her husband as executor.

Dear Cousin Woodrow: Rome, Georgia, 10 Mch 1883

I did not promptly answer your letter of the 5th inst. because I was told that a notice in the Atlanta Constitution stated that Col. Hammond had returned on a/c of the Govs. death[1] & possibly (I say) because of unexpected political reasons. Col. H. was my individual first choice after finding that Mesrs. Featherston & Alexander advised my having Atlanta counsel & I hope he will engage in the case. Should he not do so I think I wd prefer ex-Judge [George] Hillyer. We are personally acquainted and so far as I have heard he has weight & influence with the judges & bar of your city.

Capt. Featherston tells me that when he went to argue a case in the U. S. Court some years ago his impression is that in order to do so he had to get a license based upon the fact of his having been in practice at least three years in the State Courts.[2] He and Col. Alexander therefore think that possibly you might have some trouble in filing an answer in your own name. However if we get no Senior Atlanta counsel in proper time you could sign his name or that of Col. A. or both, should we conclude to put in an answer before fixing upon such Senior counsel.

We are all well and are hoping that before long you will drop in to make us a little visit.

Jessie wd join me in love were she here.

Very sincerely yours A. T. H. Brower

[1] Governor Alexander Stephens died on March 3, 1883.
[2] It is interesting that WW qualified for practice in the United States Circuit Court for the Northern District of Georgia in Atlanta on March 23, 1883. See the Editorial Note, "Wilson's Practice of Law."

Dear Cousin Woodrow: Rome, Ga., 12 Mch. 1883

Yours 10th reached me yesterday. I was glad at what you had to say. Yes, tell Col. Hammond that I will retain him at the fee of $200. If agreeable to him I will remit him my N. Y. check for $150. and pay him the balance, viz, $50., after the trial. I do not know whether this is according to the customs of Atlanta or not. If not, I will conform to them whatever they may be. I merely suggest this way as I have never yet paid a fee in full before the service had been performed & so presume the usual custom accords with this practice.

I am sure we could have no better Senior than Col. H. From what you say I see he impressed you as being a *man*. It would be very difficult for me to confer fully with any counsel whom I could not heartily respect and trust.

Please tell me what Co. H's initials are—I forget the middle one as everybody calls him "Nat. Hammond."

Have not as yet heard from Mr. Tom Francis. I think the fact is that having written Burford in a way to give an erroneous impression—thinking that wd be the end of it—he does not now know how to reconcile the facts with his letter.

Very sincerely yours   A. T. H. Brower

ALS (WP, DLC).

Marginal Note

The Works of the Right Honorable Edmund Burke (Sixth edn., 12 vols., Boston, 1880).

Transcript of WW Shorthand Comment

Vol. II, 57:

[From "Speech on American Taxation, April 19, 1774."
[Burke disputes the claim that opposition in Parliament to the Stamp Act encouraged American resistance and continues:] "I am sure there was no protest. In fact, the affair passed with so very, very little noise, that in town they scarcely knew the nature of what you were doing."

[c. March 12, 1883]
A quotable note in discussion of government made by committees

From Robert Bridges

Dear Tommy: New York March 13th 83

Here is some degree of success anyhow but it is not exactly what we were after. I have just received the enclosed note from the Putnams, and it explains itself. I will try and stop there on my way up town tonight and have a talk with a member of the firm. I will then write you immediately as to what would be the probable expense &c. You can then advise me what to do next. I have yet to try the Holts and the Scribners, and, if you think best, I will do so before closing or breaking with the Putnams.

By the way you must not think that I have passed the book off as my own—as you might infer from the note—proud as I would be to be its author. The fact is I talked with one member of the firm and another read the book and probably dictated the letter —having my card as the only address.

In Great Haste   Robert Bridges

ALS (WP, DLC). Enc.: G. P. Putnam's Sons to Bridges, March 12, 1883, ALS (WP, DLC), saying in part: "We should be ready to associate our imprint with the volume, and issue it for the account, and at the expense, of the author, in case such an arrangement seemed to him desirable."

From Joseph Ruggles Wilson

My dearest Woodrow—   Wilmington, [N. C.] March 13, '83.

Please find enclosed draft on N. York for $50.00, and, if perfectly convenient, acknowledge receipt thereof!

The Post came to hand this morning and I have read yr. piece[1] with sincere gratification. I am not sure that I agree with you in all yr. conclusions, but then I am equally not sure that I understand the subject except in a very general way, cursorily not discussively. . . .

As to professorship I have written to various parties, and received answers from two, Drs. Chas Phillips & Waddel (Jno N.) Both would if they could but how can they? &c. The chances are not bright at this moment—but, nil desperandum. . . .

My congregations are very large and apparently enlarging; yet accessions do not multiply, and, on *this* account, Discouragement knocks at my door: and, too often, I let him (if *she* be a *him*) in.

Goodbye with a heartfelt God-bless-you.

Mamma & Josie send a blizzard of love.   Your affc   Father

ALS (WP, DLC) with WWhw misc. notations on env.
    [1] "Convict Labor in Georgia."

From Janet Woodrow Wilson, with Enclosure

My darling Son,   Wilmington, N. C. March 15th '83.

I enclose you three letters. Those of Drs. Phillips & Waddle came a few days ago—they are kind enough—but ar[e] not worth much as regards the matter we have at heart. Your Uncle James' letter is very different—and in our opinion gives the first ray of light—as to anything practical. I confess that I have felt that there was not much chance of getting such a position as you desire—situated as you now are. Now what do you think of your Uncle James' suggestion as to the J[ohns] H[opkins] fellowship? It strikes your father most favorably—that would ensure you what you want, sooner or later—while it would be an honorable position in the mean time—and give you a splendid opportunity for showing your capabilities. I will write to your Uncle James today—and make enquiries as to what steps are necessary to procure such a fellowship.

Please write as soon as you can & let us know your mind in the matter. . . .

Papa & Josie join me in love inexpressible to you.

Lovingly yours   Mother

As to that business affair—I never dreamed that your Uncle James B. proposed to delay the division of the estate! Of course that should be pushed, under any circumstances. And I quite agree with you that such a "partnership" as is proposed, would not be the thing most desirable—under the circumstances. Of course you should at once have full power to act for us. Should you not arrange for it? I dont see how else you can manage the business. Can you make enquiris as to modes of investment? so as to [be] prepared to do the best & safest thing with the money, when we do succeed in getting hold of it.

ALS (WP, DLC) with WWhw notation on env.: "Ans. March 17th 1883." Encs.: John N. Waddel to JRW, Feb. 26, 1883, ALS (WP, DLC); Charles Phillips to JRW, Feb. 24, 1883, ALS (WP, DLC); and letter printed below.

ENCLOSURE

James Woodrow to Janet Woodrow Wilson

My dearest Jeanie: Columbia, S. C., March 14, 1883.

I received your letter just as James was leaving home. . . .

I need not say I will do all I can to help you in carrying out your wishes. I had supposed from my conversation with Tommy in September that he had become fond of the law, and intended to continue in that profession. But if he wishes a change, of course no time should be lost.

I do not at present know of any vacancies; but, as you probably know, there will be at least two vacancies in other chairs at Davidson this summer, and this may lead to a remodelling of all, so that there may be such a vacancy as Tommy (I will learn to say "Woodrow" by degrees) would like to fill.

I think that electing bodies, in choosing Professors, usually look either among successful teachers (academy or other)—or else to special professional schools, like the Johns Hopkins University. I have noticed recently that quite a number of Professors have been chosen from J. H. This suggests that it might be wise, if "Woodrow's" mind is made up to adopt the profession of teacher, to attend that University. And if he should decide on this, would it not be well to try to obtain a fellowship? Attention would thus be directed towards him, as most of the "fellows" and "post-graduate" students at the Johns Hopkins are looking toward Professorships. It is not often the case that a Board is willing to elect one from another profession, except, indeed, in the case of ministers, and then usually those who have been teachers. In very few of our poor Southern Colleges are there Assistant-Professors.

I will keep constantly on the look-out; and if I learn anything, will at once write you. And if you see anything I can do to further your wishes, I beg that you will let me know, and it will delight me to do whatever you suggest. . . .

With much love to Joseph and Josy,

Your most affectionate brother   James.

ALS (WP, DLC).

To Robert Bridges

Dear Bobby,   Atlanta, Geo., March 15/83

Your letter, enclosing Mr. Putnam's note, has just reached me. It does, as you say, bring a slender ray of encouragement; but it is, of course, out of the question for me to assume the expense of publishing my unfortunate essay, or to take upon myself any portion of that expense, for the simple reason that I have not the money, nor the means of obtaining it. I should be quite willing to *give* the *mss.* to the Putnams, or to any other publishing house of similar standing; for it has, of course, never occurred to me as in the least likely that I would realize any pecuniary profit from its publication. But this is the most I can do—glad as I would be, and eager, to pay for the printing of it, if I had the money. You may say, therefore, to the Putnams, if you will, that this is the only proposition I *can* make. They can have the *mss.* upon the consideration of sending me a few copies, when published.

If I had not already felt inclined to upbraid myself for having saddled you with so much trouble in this matter, I should ask that you would try the other New York houses before you give over all further effort. *I* am inclined, of course, though conscious of hoping against hope, to try everything before giving up. But I am beginning to suspect that if the essay really possessed the merits which the publishers ascribe to it in softening their refusal of it, they would readily enough accept it; and I am, consequently, very loath to trouble you with it any more—though I am quite sure that your kindness sufficiently abounds to incline you to do everything for the sake of the affection we bear towards each other. So I conclude with this earnest request, that you will tell me, in fullest candor, what you think best to be done. I will accept whatever you suggest. If you think that there are still chances of success with other publishers, I would, of course, feel better satisfied not to give up until all have been tried. But if you think that I can reasonably look for no better success than I have already had, I

want you to say so without an if or a but, and should wish you
to send me the *mss.* in order that I might recast and remodel it
when I have the leisure and the spirit to do so.

I was ever so much obliged for the copies of my convict letter
you sent me.

Gratefully and affectionately Yrs,   Woodrow Wilson

ALS (Meyer Coll., DLC).

From Janet Woodrow Wilson

My darling Son,   Wilmington N. C. Saturday March 17th [1883]

Your father wrote yesterday to your Uncle James W. for information as to the manner of obtaining a J. H. University scholarship. I am anxious to hear what you think about it. To me, it seems
the brightest look-out we have.

In the meantime, dear, I want to make some enquiries as to
business matters. Your father is anxious to know what is the prospect as to accomplishing a division of the Nebraska estate. He
cannot understand why there should be delay—is extremely
anxious that the division—complete—should be accomplished.
Now, dear, will you write fully as to the matter—stating fully what
is being done—what is to be done—and all about it. I need not entreat you to *push* the matter. I am sure you will do so. Mr. Brower
seemed to think, when he spoke to me of the matter, that a speedy
settlement was our only hope. You know James B. has had all he
asked for—money for the building of his home—and also for the
establishment of his business. Now he has every chance to make
a living for his family. And we on our part must now be assured
that we are released from that mortgage, and must get actual possession of our share of the estate. Of course we have no idea of
spending any portion of our capital—for our future living depends
upon its preservation—but we must get it into our possession in
order to provide for the near future. Our plan is to try and save
enough of our present income, to enable us to purchase a permanent home—as early as possible—where we can live, if our lives are
spared, on what income we can get by investing our capital—
together with what your father can make in his profession. Surely
this is very reasonable. You know, dear, I do not feel that I can
count upon a long life for your precious father. Your grandfather
died in his sixty-third year—five of your uncles died much before
they reached their sixtieth year. I would like, more than I could
tell, to have his mind relieved as to our future. Our great desire

as to the *capital* we may realize, is to preserve it, intact, for our children.

I have not been well lately—or would have written more frequently. I am *so sorry* you are to leave Mrs. B's. Two of Gussy Waltmers sisters are keeping boarders in Atlanta. I will write to Annie to tell you about them. *One* of them is keeping a very desirable boarding house. With unbounded love from us each one

Yours most lovingly   Mother

ALS (WP, DLC) with WWhw notation on env.: "Ans. March 19th 1883."

From Abraham T. H. Brower

Dear Tommy: [New York] March 18th '83

I have been waiting for several days for Putnam's estimate before writing to you. I had a talk with a member of the firm on the day when last I wrote, and yesterday I received the enclosed estimate. The substance of my talk with him is that they will be very glad to print your work with their name on the title page, just as though they had purchased it. They do not give this unqualified endorsement to all works which they print at the author's expense. The book when issued by them would be advertised to the extent ordered by you, the expense to be paid out of the sales made by them. They would also send copies to the reviewers, and distribute them to the trade as you might desire. The plan is to make of it a book which will sell for a dollar—of the style of David A Wells' 'Merchant Marine.' The trade gets such a book for sixty cents— the Putnams would get ten cents for every volume which they handle—thus each volume sold would net you 50 cents. The stereotype plates become your property absolutely.

Now for the estimate. You will see that the great expense is in printing the first 500 copies. These could be printed from the type at about 20% less than from plates—but if the book should sell well then the type must needs be all reset for a new edition at the same expense. You will also notice that the first 1000 copies (netting you 50 cents each) will not come within $75 dollars of making both ends meet. He is now making me an estimate of the same style of type and paper with one lead, instead of two, between the lines. This will bring the cost down so that the first thousand will clear expenses.

You will also notice that any additional demand would be considerable money in your pocket.

The plan would be to start with an edition of 500 copies, as an experiment—and order more as the demand might justify.

I think that I have covered all the points. It is a costly experiment and I don't feel at liberty to advise in the matter. If, however, you decide to try it I will be glad to transact any business for you. It strikes me that it would be inopportune to bring the book out in the Spring or Summer when politics are at a discount. But if it could appear when Pendleton's bill is under discussion it might find a ready way to the public ear. There will be plenty of time to try other publishers before Congress meets, and, if you do not meet with success, you might then try the Putnam's plan in November—bringing the book out after Congress is in session, or about Xmas. . . .

Your friend   Robert Bridges

ALS (WP, DLC) with WWhw notation on env.: "Rec'd and Ans. March 21st 1882." Enc.: G. P. Putnam's Sons to Bridges, March 17, 1883, hw estimate of cost of publishing "Government by Debate": $434.00 for electrotype plates and 500 copies in cloth, plus $141.00 for a second edition of 500 copies.

From Abraham T. H. Brower

Dear Cousin Woodrow: Rome, Ga. 19 Mch 1883

Yours 14th came duly to hand. When one is "down," so to speak, it is particularly gratifying to be treated as though he were in his usual circumstances and not to be plucked & taken advantage of and walked over. I say all this apropos of Col. Hammond simply asking me to pay his usual fee & in the usual manner. I remitted the $100. on Saturday. . . .

Did you know how much confidence and security the kindly interest you take in this case, causes me to feel, you would realize how thankful I am to you for it all.

I have not yet heard from Maj. Francis. I wonder what his silence means.

We are all well & Jessie joins me in love.

Very sincerely yours   A. T. H. Brower

ALS (WP, DLC).

From Annie Wilson Howe

My darling Brother,   Columbia, Mar. 20th/83

You must excuse me for writing in pencil—but I am still so weak that I do not feel equal to sitting up to the table to write with pen and ink. We have had rather a hard time recently. Jessie has been quite sick with typhoid fever, and I have been sick in bed for two weeks myself. . . . I write this hasty note to give you one or two addresses. Mother wrote that you were looking for a boarding house. I am so sorry you have to make a change. The two places I mention are reccomended by Dr. Boggs.[1] One is—Mrs. John Bowie, 120 South Prior St. The other—Mrs. O. F. Simpson, No 1 Capitol Place. Dr. Boggs says you will most certainly lose your heart if you go to Mrs. Bowie's. Her daughter is so lovely. Mrs. Curtis' is another place, but we do not know her address. Mrs. Boggs has boarded there, and says she keeps a very good table. I will try and write again very soon. Please write to us. Thank you for the paper. I need not tell you what I think of your production.[2] I always feel proud of you when I pass the paper around to be read. George unites with me in warmest love to you. Little George is *delighted* with the book you sent. The children also send love to you. Dr. and Mrs. [George] Howe [Sr.] and Mr. Craig always send some message to you when I give them yours, but I always forget them before I write again. In greatest haste and greatest love,

Your devoted sister,   Annie

ALS (WP, DLC) with WWhw notation on env.: "Ans. 3/28/83."
  [1] The Rev. Dr. William E. Boggs, professor at the Columbia Theological Seminary, who had been pastor of the Central Presbyterian Church in Atlanta from 1879 to 1882.
  [2] "Convict Labor in Georgia."

To Robert Bridges

Dear Bobby: Atlanta, Geo., March 21st 1883
    Yours of the 18th, enclosing Putnam's estimate, reached me this morning. The estimate is much less than I had supposed it would be. I should have thought that the plates, even for so small a book, would cost one or two thousand. But, small as the cost would be, it is at a figure which is considerably beyond my means; for I have not a dollar besides what I have to spend for office rent and my own maintenance. If I had the money, I should not hesitate to close with Putnam's offer, which I think a fair one; but, as things now stand, I have no choice. I can only decline the offer and swallow my disappointment.
    Of course I have no means of telling how such a book would sell, but the publishers could easily form a guess as to that; and it seems to inexperienced me that, if Putnam's would accept the *mss.* as a gift, they might reasonably expect to realize from it, if it were opportunely put upon the market, enough to cover expenses at least, if not enough to bring them as much profit as they would receive from my employment of them as mere printers. Their regular sales to the trade throughout the country would, I should suppose, almost meet the expenses of publication.

But, however that may be, I am tied down to this single proposition. I would gladly make the other arrangement, but I *cannot*.

If you carry the *mss.* to other publishers, you may make the same offer to them, since, as I have intimated before, my object is not to make money by the publication of this essay, but simply to get some foot-hold and recognition as an author, so that when I write again I can treat with publishers less as a stranger. I want also to write something which will recommend me as a contributor to the editors of the quarterlies and reviews. In short I want a *start*, and am willing to make it on any terms within my reach.

I should like, by the way, to add a brief preface of about eighteen lines, and a briefer dedication of about as many words, to the essay in case it is accepted.

What did you think of our "little Alex." Stephens, Bobby?—and what did you say of him?—for I suppose of course you wrote the obituary notice for the *Post.* I think, myself, that his death was, after all, no grievous loss to the country. It was a great loss to the State; for just at this moment Georgia is suffering very much for lack of talented leaders. But then, on the other hand, Stephens was so old that his days of usefulness could not have been many more, if indeed they were not already ended. His virtues, his goodness of heart and uprightness of purpose, cannot, it now seems to me, be overestimated; but I did not regard his mind as one of unusual strength, or of unusually fine fibre. He was no genius. His mind was not large nor always clear; but his great sympathies and the intensity of his will power made him use all his faculties in the way in which they would most surely tell, and his frail body, the strange association of bright talents with a wizened visage, made him a conspicuous and interesting figure in our politics. Now it's Bob. Toomb's turn to die; though I should rather assist in burying old Joe. Brown than any other Georgian I know of.

I am quite well and am engaged on the defence of a considerable libel case.

With much love,   Your sincere friend   Woodrow Wilson.

ALS (Meyer Coll., DLC).

From Janet Woodrow Wilson

My darling Son,   Wilmington, N. C. March [c. 26] '83.

I intended answering yours, received last Wednesday morning, before this—but have been prevented in various ways. We are a good deal disturbed as to what you tell us of J. Bs conduct. I cannot help thinking that his idea is, that in case we consent to enter into the proposed partnership, he will be allowed to retain the management of our property—and in that case I am *perfectly sure*—since my conversation with Mr. Brower—that we would never get *one* thousand dollars from it—that the entire thing would be gradually swallowed up—not doing any good to anybody. Not that I for one moment doubt his *honesty*—his uprightness—but I *do doubt* his wisdom—his business capacity. And I think our *regard for him*, even independently of our own interests, should determine us to put it out of his power to make away with our property.

So, my dear, I enclose you money for your necessary trip, or trips, to Rome. You can tell your Uncle J. that it is *not possible* for us to even *consider* any proposition of partnership or otherwise until the division of the estate is accomplished. Besides I wish the entire estate to be in *your keeping*—*no one* else having any power whatever—to dispose of, or arrange for it.

If James B. still has power of Attorney *it must be cancelled.* Now, my darling, it is worth your while to give your first attention to this matter—for, everything depends upon it. You can say to your Uncle, that I cannot determine upon *anything* until this whole thing is settled. It is a [*sic*] not a question as to our confidence in him—as he seems to think. We need the property, and we *must have* it. Sentiment is out of place in such a matter[.] I am glad to know from himself that his business is improving—for he cannot fail to make a good living. You cannot convince either of his younger daughters that he is not a man of unbounded resources—and if he does not summon up enough to [*sic*] courage to control their large ideas, he will have trouble in making enough money to meet their demands. I have *tried* to disabuse Helen's idea that her papa has "just *lots* of money[.]"

Your father wrote your Uncle James W. enquiring as to what is necessary to procure the desired scholarship—or fellowship—in the J. H. Univty we have not heard from him yet. I will let you know immediately when we do hear. He has promised to do all in his power.[1] I will write again in a very few days. I am glad you are comparatively comfortable in your new quarters—especially glad you are not separated from your friends Renick and Gadsden.[2] In haste, with all love love [*sic*] from darling papa, dear Josie & little H.   Most Lovingly Yours   Mother

ALS (WP, DLC) with WWhw notation on env.: "Ans. 3/28/83."
   [1] Dr. Woodrow wrote to President Gilman on about April 1 recommending Wilson for a fellowship in the English Department! There is an undated WWsh copy of Dr. Woodrow's letter in WP, DLC.
   [2] Edward Miles Gadsden was a young lawyer who had roomed with Wilson and Renick at Mrs. Boylston's. The three men had recently moved to a new boarding house run by a widow, Mrs. James S. (Isabel L.) Turpin, formerly mar-

ried to a Mr. Evans, who had died. She had two living children in 1883, an Evans daughter and a Turpin son. She moved to Washington in 1884 and married Renick.

From Robert Bridges

Dear Tommy: New York March 27 '83

I only have a minute in which to write an acknowledgement of your last letter and to enclose another estimate which the Putnam's had already made. I am very busy just at present, but hope soon to be able to see the Holts and Scribners. I now write the *Brief Mention of Books* for the *Post* and the Summary for the *Nation* after April first—making a very considerable addition to my salary (probably about double). If we cant get the essay in book form what do you think of trying the *Princeton, North American* and *International* Reviews for a serial publication in five parts?

Yours in haste   Bob Bridges

ALS (WP, DLC) with WWhw notation on env.: "Ans. 4/3/83." Enc.: G. P. Putnam's Sons to Bridges, March 20, 1883, hw estimate of cost of publishing "Government by Debate": "about 132 pages 12mo long primer type—solid and bound in plain cloth (size of printed page 6 x 3 3/4 inches)," electrotype plates and 500 copies, $330.00; and second edition of 500 copies, $123.00.

From Joseph R. Wilson, Jr.

My darling brother: Wilmington N. C. March 29th 1883.

I am looking forward with a great deal of pleasure to the time I will see you in Atlanta on our way to Rome. I wish so much that you could come and stay with us while you are waiting for your "Fellow-ship."

I am so sorry that Miss Katie [Mayrant] is going to leave for a while, and I am so sorry that you were obliged to change your boarding house. Is Robert Boylston going to stay in Atlanta and work? Please remember me to him. Has Mr Renick left you yet? You have not spoken of him since you told us that he was going to leave you, this is the reason, partly, that we have not been in a hurry about your chair and pictures. We did not know whether he had left you or not. . . .

We are all pretty well and continue to love you *lots* and *gobs*.

Please write to me soon and tell me about debating clubs. Give my regards to Miss Katie.   Very aff your brother   Joseph.

P.S. Do you want your pictures and chair now? J. R. W.

ALS (WP, DLC).

An Unpublished Article

Atlanta, Geo., March 29th 1883.

Culture and Education at the South

No one can now seriously question the material prosperity of the South; for it is everywhere commonly admitted that the renewed South is every year making vast forward strides in commerce and the manufs. True, its financial atmosphere is not quite healthy: business failures are of frequent occurrence and bankruptcy is common; But these may safely be taken to be simply signs of inexperience and of untried strength. They are indeed not without even their features of encouragement; for whilst they no doubt seriously impair the credit of Southern merchants, they also, paradoxical as the statement may seem, indicate the vitality of commercial credit at the South. Vast business enterprises are here built upon very slight foundations of capital, and are so built without much difficulty. Capitalists in many instances seem to be willing to lend thousands upon no other security than the South's prosperity, and Northern and Western wholesale houses extend long credit to Southern merchants, seemingly on the faith of the South's commercial vitality and bright business prospects. Great undertakings, consequently, rise and succeed in the South notwithstanding the fact that the South is as yet, comparatively speaking, without money. Many such enterprises are, of course, soon landed in bankruptcy; but the majority of them are not, and with proper management few of them fail of success.

In short, though Southern business men are poor, their poverty is of a very thrifty sort. What money there is here is in active circulation; it multiplies itself as it runs from hand to hand; it serves a thousand masters and is sure to hurry wherever it may be most wanted to secure credit. As some of the Southern papers have repeatedly pointed out, and as the tenth cencus proves, the Southern people are growing very busy. Atlanta, for instance, the leading manufacturing city of the South, and a city in many respects quite typical of the new South, stands in point of business activity third among the busy cities of the Union. Only Lawrence and Lowell are busier. Forty-six *per cent.* of her population are engaged in gainful occupations and every dollar of her modest capital tells for the full value of every copper that is in it. And this illustrates, in its most favorable light, the energy of the whole South. Retarded though she is by her hot-tempered disposition to condone business and social homicides, and by a certain unmistakable leaning towards the social vices of idleness and extravagance, she is undergoing by rapid stages a permanent revolution and has already left the commercially ruinous past of slave labor far behind her.

Unfortunately, however, her progress in education and culture has by no means kept pace with her progress in commercial enterprise and the mechanic arts. It is a fact unpalateable to Southerners, and disallowed by many of them, that the South has let her eagerness for wealth get ahead of her eagerness for learning, and has permitted her liking for the industrial arts to overcrow her ambition for scholarship. And I am not here alluding to the well-known illiteracy of the South as compared with the other portions of the Union, nor to the fact that, exclusive of the ignorant masses of the negroes, even her white population is distressingly unlettered; but to the fact that the standard of education amongst the best classes is exceedingly low and that even those Southern youths who have the means and the inclination to seek and obtain an education seek it only for a short time and with half a heart, in colleges in which thoroughness of instruction is unknown. The average Southern gentleman, though not illiterate, is at least too often extremely unlearned. Even amongst the best educated classes of the commercial towns, where one might expect to find such information current, literary knowledge is to be found only in scantest quantities. Those who read read, indeed, the best books oftentimes, in addition to the latest novel. They are familiar with the contents of Macaulay and with the name of Burke; they love both the poetry and the prose of Walter Scott; they linger with keen satisfaction over the bright gems of Byron; they recognize the names of some of the older Edinburgh reviewers; they are more or less intimately acquainted with Thackeray and Dickens; but here their familiarity with modern Eng. lit. generally stops. It is hard to find many who know anything of Freeman, or any who have heard even the name of Mathew Arnold. Nor is their ignorance of literature, unhappily, confined to what has been written since the war. Many a conversation with educated Southerners might be recounted which would reveal a much more extraordinary unfamiliarity with the older classics of the lang. Southern lawyers, for ins., like lawyers everywhere else in the English speaking world, are generally amongst the best educated men in the communities in which they live and may, therefore, be taken as intellectually typical of the higher classes: the following anecdote may, therefore be given as significant. In the easy conversation of good fellowship, one day recently, two of the leading practitioners at one of the leading bars of the South were relating to one another some of the many amusing things that had occurred in their varied experiences. Said Mr. A., *a propos* of something just said, "By-the-way, do you know I've long been curious to learn where that famous expression, 'write me down an ass', came from. Well, the other night I stumbled upon the discovery at the opera house. It is said by a laughable old rogue of a justice of the peace in the play in which M'lle Rhea played the last time she was here";—and then, to the infinite amusement of Mr. B., he rehearsed the funny speeches and actions of the old "justice of the peace" who had so much tickled his fancy. He had seen charming M'lle Rhea in "Much Ado About Nothing," and, though he had doubtless heard numberless times of Shakspere's authorship of that pleasing comedy, that had been his first introduction to immortal Dogberry! Mr. B. had not had the good fortune to see the play upon the stage, and so had still only his friend's version of Dogberry's character and humor. And all this was quite of a piece with the ignorance of the Georgian lawyer who sought his bookseller to ascertain whether Guizot had actually written a history of England.

These gentlemen are, it must be confessed, samples of the majority, though not, of course, representatives of a small and choice minority whose pleasure it is to know all the classics of the language. Said one Southern gentleman to another, "Did you ever read 'Noctes Ambrosianae'?" "What?", said the other, "Say that over again, and say it slow!" and then the first, having distinctly repeated the unusual name, proceeded, with not a little show of pedantry, to inform his friend of the great literary fame and achievements of John Wilson. These gentlemen might easily be forgiven for their want of familiarity with the rather tedious "Noctes," but some Southern gentlemen there are who make even that rather neglected work the constant companion of their leisure moments, delighting in its vigorous fancies; and it may be said of many of the young men now growing up at the South that their stock of polite and useful knowledge much exceeds that of their fathers whose education was cut short by the war. Still such young men constitute a small minority even of the educated youth of the better classes; for Southern colleges, from lack of means and consequent lack of competent instructors, are far behind the age. They are still following the old and long-worn—some had hoped worn *out*—collegiate courses. They drill in Latin, Greek, and Mathematics, but they teach adequately neither history, nor political economy, nor political science, nor even English literature, and they are wofully deficient in the sciences

Much of this backwardness is due, no doubt, as I have said, to a lack of means and not to a lack of desire for progress and improvement. Southern colleges have little money and few teachers; their few instructors are generally men who have undergone no special preparation for the work in which they are engaged and who are, moreover, saddled with the duties of more departments than they can possibly conduct with anything like thoroughness. Indeed this last fact constitutes the crowning difficulty in Southern education. The lack of trained teachers runs through the whole system and enervates it. Even where the colleges are well equipped and have faculties made up of men in every way competent for the highest work of instruction, they must neglect the higher branches because of the deficiencies of the preparatory schools. The young men who enter the collegiate halls are not ready to receive instruction in the highest branches. If such instruction were attempted, the students would just have to stagger through their courses under the grievous burden of inadequate preparation. Most Southern children of the better classes attend private schools, and private schools are taught either by excellent and lovable ladies who have been driven by stress of poverty to undertake the duties of teaching, though they have had, of course, only the preparation of an ordinary education, or by gentlemen of decent education who would avoid mercantile pursuits and have not had the means to fit themselves for any other of the learned professions. Southern colleges must, therefore, take up this imperfect education where it was left off by such teachers; what they lack is not the will but the way; though what Southern teachers, outside of the larger cities, lack is, I suspect, something more, for they hardly know enough to be aware that they are behind the age in their knowledge and in their methods of instruction. I believe, however, that the tide is about to turn at the South in educational matters; in some portions of it it has already turned; though in most others it is still ebb, or at best only slack water, and the flood is yet to come.

The less wonder, then, that the South is contributing little or nothing to the permanent literature of the country; it is as yet too early to look for such contributions from her. Not only is education imperfect, but the ravages of the war are too recent; men and youths alike have to cut short their school and college days to enter upon some bread-earning business, and there is no leisured class which can follow literature as a profession and add to its achievements by swelling the number of its successful adherents. The colleges do not carry boys far enough to make real students of them, and after graduation Southern youths have neither the time nor the money to go further. The few recent literary successes of

Southern men have been of a peculiar kind; they have been al-most altogether the fruit of native, self-trained wit. Joel Chandler Harris, the now famous creator of Uncle Remus, never went to college; most of the education he managed to get was picked up in a printing office. So also of Mr. J. A. Macon, the Mississippian whose rising fame is bringing Uncle Gabe Tucker into rivalry with Uncle Remus. Of scant education; tall, lank, sallow, ill clothed, and uncouth in person; eking out a poor living by teaching a coun-try school for a miserable pittance,—a man described by those who have seen him as in appearance and address a "cracker" of "crack-ers"—he seems the genius as little as any man well could. And yet this man, in spite of all disadvantages, has brought his happy faculty with the pen to the notice of the whole nation, and now bids fair to rank first in the new literature which is setting negro character in such humorous forms and is preserving negro dialect in such quaint stories and sayings.

The low state of education in the South is, of course, a fact of serious moment and must cause every lover and every friend of the South many a pang of regret and chagrin; but there are still some hopeful signs of progress and betterment. In this matter, as in so many others, the currents are gradually setting in the right direction, and time will work great changes. It is useless to expect a sudden revolution; probably it would not be the part of wise pol-icy to try to force the pace of the South upon the road towards a better system. Changes of educational plan must run along side of changes of social condition and wait for home accumulations of wealth. As yet parents do not seem to feel the need that is pressing upon their children. The private schools already mentioned, taught by ladies in needy circumstances, by indigent clergymen, or by in-experienced youths fresh from an imperfect college training, are recommended to most parents by small tuition fees. Light as is the cost of tuition at such schools, it is generally as heavy as most par-ents can afford to bear. The number of children seeking an educa-tion is not sufficient, nor the means of their parents considerable enough, to warrant the employment of professional teachers who command high salaries. Besides, this private school system, poor and inadequate as it oftentimes is, is thought by parents to be the best they can afford, and generally it is the best they care to have. In the rural districts, it must be confessed, there is great lethargy with regard to this subject of education—a lethargy which is almost impregnable. The older people of such communities recognize the fact that their children are getting as good a schooling as they themselves received in their own youth, and therewith they are therefore fain to rest content and to require their children to rest content.

The chief consideration which opens the doors to hope, is that it seems to be the natural sequence of history that periods of busy industrial and commercial enterprise, of augmenting wealth, and of expanding prosperity should usher in equally bright periods of intellectual revival. There would seem, accordingly, to be no human prophecy surer or safer than this, that from the loins of the wide-awake Southern merchants, mechanics, and farmers of the present and of the near future will spring a race of orators equal to those of the days before the war, and generations of writers of prose and of song who will employ the powers and music of our unequalled language to spread before their countrymen as rich stores of knowledge and to sing to them in as elevating strains of sentiment as ever regaled or beguiled a nation; for such a prophecy is founded upon the reasonable certainty that, when the mind of an earnest, gifted, versatile, and ambitious people is given free scope for its energies and brought into the light and touched by the invigoration which material progress supplies, it will not fail to apply itself with all success to the highest work within its reach.

But these are things of the future; the task of the present is to bring the South to realize fully its deficiency in point of education; for as yet to the vast majority of the Southern people this want is still in that dispairful category of things which are not seen. The Southern press, indeed, does say a great deal about education and its blessings, but there is some reason to fear that the editors do not in all cases know exactly what they would have. They wish to see education spread and be established; but they are content with a very small amount of it. They often fill their columns with eulogies of colleges which are not worthy of praise and with recommendations of educational schemes which have long ago been abandoned by all sensible instructors; and, what is worse, their columns are not always open to the freest discussion of Southern educational deficiencies, for the only satisfactory comparisons by which those deficiencies can be illustrated are comparisons with the superior educational advantages of the North—comparisons which do not seem to the nostrils of Southern editors to savor of good will toward the South. Consequently that proper agitation of the question which is so much needed is blocked oftentimes by the narrow prejudices of the press; and when the press holds thus aloof one of the greatest and most potent agents of advancement is wanting.

The true motto, therefore, for all wise and politic friends of improvement in Southern educational methods is *Patience*. Nothing can here be done rapidly and at once; it is proper for the present to turn only those stones that can be turned without uncovering rank spots of prejudice: to disclose in entire dispasionateness all the features of the existing system to the view of the Southern people in order that gradually they may come to see its defects; and to reinforce by every possible means that commercial and industrial enterprise which is the parent of activity and the forerunner of intellectual achievement. The Southern people do not easily tolerate the too zealous agitation of any question such as this of education. As regards almost all social institutions they are devotedly attached to the existing order of things and are apt to look upon those who object to that order and attack it as mere grumblers and malcontents who are worthy to be regarded only as nuisances, and heeded only to be put down. We can, therefore, do no more than understand the situation, and patiently work and wait.   W. W.

WWhw (WP, DLC). WW sent this to Bridges on April 3, 1883. R. Bridges to WW, May 9, 1883, and WW to R. Bridges, May 13, 1883, deal with its rejection.

From James W. Bones

Dear Tommy   Rome, Ga. Mar 30 1883
I received your letter yesterday & we will be ever so glad to see you next Friday [April 6]. Make your arrangements to spend several days with us.

The sale I mentioned in my last letter & from which I expected to get $1800. fell thro in consequence of the illness of the purchaser. He is not expected to live & his friends have advised him not to make the purchase. I do not regret this very much as the land is likely to be more valuable ere long.

We are all well except Mami who has been suffering from a severe cold. I had a letter from your dear mother yesterday.
                                              Your affec Uncle James.

ALS (WP, DLC).

From Abraham T. H. Brower

Dear Cousin Woodrow: Rome Ga. 30 Mch 1883
Yours 28th was rec'd yesterday. Inasmuch as Vice Pt. Brown appeared to regret having been so very frank with my brother Ogden and evidently wished to retract somewhat of what he had said, would it be advisable to have my brother act as one of the Commissioners. I had no sooner written the foregoing than I re-

membered that a relative or connection could not act as Com. under our law. I hope Brown wont [alter] any the tone of his testimony to go agst. us.

We are glad you are so soon coming to East Rome. Of course this time you come to us. Let us know when you are coming & by what train.

Jessie joins me in love.

Very sincerely yours   A. T. H. Brower

ALS (WP, DLC).

To Robert Bridges

Dear Bobby,   Atlanta, April 3rd 1883

I am sincerely delighted to hear of your advancement in editorial position and of the consequent increase of your salary: the more so because I conclude from the character of the new departments you have in charge, and from what you once told me of the small amount of time requisite to a preparation of the *Nation's* "*Summary*," that your promotion does not necessarily involve much additional labour.

I should be more than willing to offer the essay to the magazines, in case nobody will give it book form; but I am inclined to look with some disfavour on any scheme which would give you any additional trouble. However, there is plenty of time. It is not as it would be were we anxious to get into print before next winter and the convening of the Forty-eighth Congress.

I send by mail this afternoon, Bobby, a letter which you may offer to the authorities of the *Post*.[1] If sending my letters through you causes you the least inconvenience, or is in any way irregular, I shall count upon you to tell me so, and give me the proper address.

With love,   Your sincere friend,   Woodrow Wilson

ALS (Meyer Coll., DLC).
[1] "Culture and Education at the South."

EDITORIAL NOTE

WILSON'S INTRODUCTION TO ELLEN AXSON

Wilson's negotiations with his uncle, James W. Bones, over the final division of the William Woodrow Estate were nearing completion by the end of March 1883, and Wilson went to Rome on Friday, April 6, for a conference on details. He presumably worked that same day and the next with Bones. On Sunday morning he attended divine service at the First Presbyterian Church with the Bones family. It was a communion Sunday, but Wilson was not so preoccupied that he missed seeing a winsome young lady in a nearby pew. "I remember thinking," he wrote afterward, " 'what a bright, pretty face; what splendid, mischevious, laughing eyes! I'll lay a wager that this demure little lady has lots of life and fun in her!' "[1] Wilson, taking another good look at her when she spoke to James W. Bones' mother, decided that he should seek an introduction.

The young lady, Wilson soon discovered, was Ellen Louise Axson,[2] daughter of the Reverend Samuel Edward Axson,[3] minister of the First Presbyterian Church in Rome and an old friend of his father. Woodrow lost no time in calling upon the pastor. "That dear gentleman," Wilson later wrote, "received me with unsuspecting cordiality and sat down to entertain me under the impression that I had come to see only him. . . . I had not forgotten that face, and I wanted very much to see it again: so I asked rather pointedly after his daughter's health." Axson, somewhat surprised, called Ellen to the parlor. He then opened the conversation by asking Woodrow, "Why have night congregations grown so small?"[4]

The documents are either silent or not very clear about what happened next. Wilson returned to Atlanta about Wednesday, April 11. His letter to Ellen of October 11, 1883, suggests this. It also suggests that he walked, perhaps on Monday or Tuesday, with Ellen and Jessie Bones Brower to Ellen's house as she was returning from a visit to her friends, Arthur W. and Agnes Vaughn Tedcastle. "I remember leaving you that afternoon," Wilson wrote on October 11, "with a feeling that I had found a new and altogether delightful sort of companion. Passion was beginning to enter into the criticism, and had pretty nearly gotten the better of it by the time we had climbed to the top of that hill." That this walk occurred during Wilson's visit to Rome in April 1883 finds some confirmation in his letter to Ellen of January 4, 1884: "And yet I hadn't known you two weeks—it was not two weeks after our walk 'from Agnes'—before I was in love with you."

Whatever the particular circumstances following the meeting in the parlor of the manse,[5] it is clear that Wilson thought much about Ellen after returning to Atlanta. As we shall see, he would go back to Rome in late May not only to resume work on the Woodrow Estate, but also with another objective in mind—and heart.

[1] WW to ELA, Oct. 11, 1883.
[2] Born in Savannah, Ga., on May 15, 1860, the daughter of the Rev. S. E. Axson and Margaret Jane Hoyt Axson, and granddaughter of the Rev. Isaac Stockton Keith Axson, pastor of the Independent Presbyterian Church, Savannah, Ga., 1857-91. For her peregrinations with her family, see the following note on her father. Educated at home and at the Rome, Ga., Female College, from which she was graduated in 1876. She studied art in New York in 1882. Ellen's own letters, printed in this and following volumes, reveal her personality, intimate thoughts, wide reading, and artistic interests.
[3] Born in Liberty County, Ga., Dec. 23, 1833, son of the Rev. I. S. K. Axson and Rebecca Randolph. Married Jane Hoyt, Nov. 1858. Student, Oglethorpe University, 1854-55, and Columbia Theological Seminary, 1855-58; ordained by Charleston Presbytery, autumn 1858; pastor, Beach Island, S. C., Presbyterian Church, 1858-61; pastor, McPhersonville, S. C., Presbyterian Church, 1861-62; Chaplain, Confederate Army, 1862-64; stated supply, Madison, Ga., Presbyterian Church, 1864-65; stated supply, First Presbyterian Church, Rome, Ga., 1865-67, pastor, 1867-83. Died at Milledgeville, Ga., May 28, 1884.
[4] WW to ELA, Oct. 11, 1883.
[5] Eleanor Wilson McAdoo, *The Priceless Gift: The Love Letters of Woodrow Wilson and Ellen Axson Wilson* (New York, 1962), pp. 5-6, is more precise about

the events of this visit to Rome. She writes that Woodrow called at the manse on Monday, April 9, and that Jessie Brower had Ellen to tea with Woodrow on Wednesday, April 11. Perhaps this was a lively tradition in the Wilson family, but it must be pointed out that Mrs. McAdoo's account is based upon an excerpt from WW's letter to ELA of October 11, 1883. The full text of the letter says something very different.

From Janet Woodrow Wilson, with Enclosure

My precious boy—   Wilmington, N. C. Friday April 13–[1883]

The enclosed from your Uncle James came yesterday. I was so engaged, in consequence of the meeting of Presbytery here this week, that it seemed impossible to send it to you yesterday. But you will see there is no time to be lost. *Dont hesitate* dear, *to use your friends*—at this turning point in your life—or you will always regret it. How would it do to send your article[1] on—(in the International)—as a "specimen of work done." In any case you can go "as a graduate student and earn the fellowship by work done under the eye of the teacher." I wont write more now[.] Oh how [I] long for your establishment in life in a way to secure your happiness & usefulness. I do not fear the ultimate result—but the *waiting* is trying —but perhaps all the more useful.

I am in one of my low moods today—these moods are rare with me—but perhaps all the more intense on that account.

Good bye, my darling. Do all you can in the way of securing what you so much desire.

God bless you. We all love you with the tenderest love

Yours lovingly   Mother

ALS (WP, DLC).
[1] "Cabinet Government in the United States."

ENCLOSURE

James Woodrow to Joseph Ruggles Wilson

My dear Joseph: Columbia, S. C., April 11th, 1883.

I have just received a letter from Prof. Gildersleeve[1] in which he says:

"There are no vacancies in the Fellowships just now; but there will be vacancies at the close of the session, and testimonials should be sent to President D. C. Gilman before the middle of May, showing that the candidate is a graduate of a College in good standing, and these testimonials should be accompanied by a specimen of work done in the department to which the applicant desires to devote himself. One fellowship is generally assigned to the Teutonic and English department, and the competition is usually lively.

"The best plan to secure a fellowship is to come here as a graduate student and earn it by work done under the eye of the teacher. That is becoming more and more the rule, and prevents mistakes on both sides."

I hope you will find the above of service.

Please let me know if you can think of anything I can do to further your plans. It will give me very great pleasure to do anything in my power.

With much love to dear Jeanie, the little ones, and yourself,

Your affectionate brother   James Woodrow

ALS (WP, DLC).
1 Basil L. Gildersleeve, Professor of Greek at The Johns Hopkins University. Gilman had handed Dr. Woodrow's letter recommending his nephew for a fellowship to Gildersleeve, whom Dr. Woodrow had mentioned as being an old friend.

Draft of a Letter to James McCosh

Dear Dr. McCosh,   [Atlanta, April 14, 1883]

I take the liberty of writing to ask a favor of you. I am about to apply for a fellowship at Johns Hopkins University and therefore am bold to beg that you will write for my use in making my application something concerning my standing while in college, or more especially concerning my standing in your classes. One of the requirements relative to applications for fellowships at the University is that the applicant shall present a certificate from one or more of his former instructors concerning the character he bore, and reputation for scholarly attainments while under their instruction; and I am sure that a letter from you would clear many difficulties away from my path in my dealing with the University Board in this matter.

I have been practicing law here for the past year and have met with encouraging success; but I find myself in many ways unfit for the practice of such profession; and I have concluded that it would, all things considered, be wise for me to follow my natural bent by pursuing a course of study such as would fit me to become a teacher of political science and history or of English literature. I have, consequently, determined, if I am successful in my application for a fellowship, to spend a year or two in such study with view to secure a professorship in one or other of these my favorite branches of study. I turn to you for assistance in carrying out my plan because I am sure that from you I can get the ready aid of a true friend.

I have written at this particular time because my application must be sent in before the 11th day of May next; if it had not been so I should not have troubled you at so busy a season of the college year.

Hoping that you continue to enjoy sound health, I remain, with sincere regard   Your friend and pupil   Woodrow Wilson '79

Transcript of WWshLS (draft), (WP, DLC).

Draft of a Letter to Lyman Hotchkiss Atwater

Dear Dr. Atwater,   [Atlanta] April 14th 1883.

Again I take the liberty to write asking a favor of you. I am about to apply for a fellowship at Johns Hopkins University and as one of the requirements relative to such application is that the applicant must submit from one of his former instructors a certificate of character and scholarly attainments, I am bold to beg you to say what you can of my standing in the college and in your classes. I would not ask this of you at this busy season of the year were it not that my application must be sent in before the 11th day of May next. It is my wish, if I am successful in obtaining an appointment [to] a fellowship, to devote a year or two to the study of history and political science, remaining at the University, if possible, until I can get a call to a professorship somewhere. I find myself sometimes out of place in the practice of the law. As a study it has been of much profit and source of considerable pleasure to me, but with the conditions of practice, at least as they exist here, I am far from satisfied. I feel therefore that I can do more good and accomplish a larger amount of useful work by following my natural bent and devoting myself to the study and teaching of political science and history of institutions. It is somewhat difficult to conduct at such long chalk a negotiation for the fellowship I desire but I anticipate that that difficulty will be greatly lightened if my application be reenforced by letters from you and from Dr. McCosh.

Hoping that your health continues good, with sincere regard,
                Your friend and pupil   Woodrow Wilson.

Transcript of WWshLS (draft), (WP, DLC).

Draft of a Letter to the Faculty of The Johns Hopkins University

[Atlanta, c. April 14, 1883]

Application for fellowship in Johns Hopkins University

Gentlemen of the faculty of Johns Hopkins University: In making application for appointment to a fellowship which would enable me to prosecute studies in history and political science, I submit, in obedience to your rules:

1. As evidence of liberal education, my diploma from Princeton College, and as testimonials of character and of studious habits, letters from Doctors Atwater and McCosh of that institution.

2. As evidence of a decided proclivity towards the special line of study I have named, an essay, entitled "Cabinet Government in the United States," which I contributed to International Review for August '79, and a sketch of Mr. Gladstone which I wrote for the literary magazine of the University of Virginia in the spring of '80. In explanation of the discrepancy which you may observe between the name of your applicant and the name signed to the article in International Review, allow me to say that I have, since that article was written, shortened my name, in accord with principles of economy and of natural selection, from Thomas Woodrow Wilson to Woodrow Wilson, its essential family components.

The first of these essays is somewhat unsatisfactory because of the necessity, imposed by the limited presses of the magazine, of condensing a large subject within the means of a few pages; and the sketch may not be as acceptable to general readers as it might have been had it not been written for the perusal of a college public; but both articles furnish, I trust, sufficient evidence of my tastes in matters of study, as well as of my aptitudes for literary work.

My record since my graduation from Princeton in 1879 has of course been a very brief one. Much of the time which has elapsed since that date I have devoted to the study of the law, though I have always found time to continue with more or less thoroughness my reading of English history and to pursue what has, ever since the first years of my college course, been my favorite exercise, the study of political science. Not having had the advantage of access to any complete or considerable library my reading in these branches has been necessarily confined to such books as are in my own very limited collection; but of some topics I have been able to obtain a very tolerable knowledge. Following inclination rather than any definite system, I have acquired a thorough knowledge of the English constitution, for instance; and I have gathered from such sources as were accessible a tolerably complete acquaintance with the constitutional history of the United States, as well as with the present actual operation of the federal system. My study of constitutional history, especially of the constitutional history of England, has of course been greatly facilitated by my contemporaneous study of the law, a study to which I was introduced by the distinguished Professor John B. Minor of the University of Virginia and which I pursued for a year and some months under his admirable guidance.

My object in seeking appointment to a fellowship is to prepare myself for a professorship. Even my own limited observation has shown me that the study of history, of political economy, and of political science is sadly neglected in the colleges of the South, and it is a knowledge of this fact and of the new importance which has now come to be attached to these branches,—coupled with a conviction that I can accomplish the most useful results by entering a profession which is entirely in keeping with my most pronounced tastes and by continuing investigations which are unmistakably in the direction of my natural bent, which prompt this application. I have been enough of a student of these branches to have clearly ascertained my decided predilection for them, and I can, therefore, without presumption claim to possess that unfaltering fondness for this special department of study and that serious ambition to devote my best energies to perfecting myself in it which are declared by your regulations to be the chief qualifications required of candidates for fellowships.

Having said this much, I have, I believe, presented all the evidence at my command of my claims upon your consideration. Should I be so fortunate as to secure for this application your favorable attention, and should you deem it of sufficient importance to lead you to wish for further particulars concerning myself or for additional references, I shall be glad to furnish either. In the meantime I may refer you to my father, the Rev. Dr. Joseph R. Wilson, of Wilmington, North Carolina, Stated Clerk of the Southern General Assembly, and to my uncle the Rev. Dr. James Woodrow, Presbyterian Theological Seminary, [who] is also known as [at] South Carolina College, Columbia, South Carolina. I may also venture to refer you to Prof. Orris of the faculty of Princeton, and to Prof. Minor of the University of Virginia.

Very respectfully yours,   Woodrow Wilson.

Transcript of WWshLS (draft), (WP, DLC).

From James McCosh

My dear Sir   Princeton, N. J., April 18 1883
Be so good as inform me what is the issue of your present application[.] I am   Yours truly   James McCosh

ALS (WP, DLC) with WWhw notation on env.: "Ans. 4/23/83."

From Janet Woodrow Wilson

Wilmington, N. C. Saturday A.M. [c. April 21, 1883]
My precious boy—

Your Postal to Josie was received this morning. I have put up
your diploma—and will mail it in good time this afternoon. You
know this is Josie's play day—& as he is busy arranging for one of
his *navy battles*, I feared he might forget the diploma. I hope it
will reach you promptly, & all right. I have done the best I could
in putting it up—but not as well as I wished.

I have not been at all well lately—or you would have received a
reply to your last letter before this. I will not answer fully now—
will only say, that as your father does not seem disposed to pay the
$107.—the tax on the land—you can let the agent retain the neces-
sary sum. I hope by another year we will be able to arrange differently. As to the other matters you write of, I will write more
fully, early next week—but at present I am disposed to think you
can't do better than consult with Mr. Brower—and decide accordingly. Your father thinks we will never realize *anything* from the
estate—says that if it were his, he would *give* it to the first one that
would take it. I tell him I am thankful, then, that it is *not* his. You
know the Spring is his least cheerful season. As to your Uncle
James B's opinion, I think I would not lay too much stress upon
it.

I enclose you your father's cheque for $50.00. I am sorry it
has been so long delayed, dear. I will try not to let this happen
again. You shall certainly read your father's lecture[1]—I am sure
you will enjoy it fully. . . .

My dear boy, do you not know that Dr. Atwater *is dead*? He
died some weeks ago[2]—and I was selfish enough to regret it *on
your account*! But I must stop for the present. With unbounded
love from us each one to our absent darling

Most lovingly   Your   Mother

I think I will send the diploma *by Express*—as it will be safer.

ALS (WP, DLC).
  [1] JRW lectured in the Opera House in Wilmington on April 10, 1883.
  [2] He died on Feb. 17, 1883.

From Richard Heath Dabney

My dear Tommy: Munich, April 22nd 1883.

. . . I received your letter a long time ago, and although, with
my usual procrastination, I have waited so long to answer it, I enjoyed it hugely. . . .

Last semester I heard lectures on German history by Giesebrecht, on the French Revolution by Cornelius,[1] and on the "Culturgeschichte" of the 18th & 19th centuries by Riehl.[2] G. doesn't amount to much, but C. & R. are both very good—especially the latter. He treated the history of all the fine arts, painting, sculpture, architecture, music, &c, philosophy, literature, science, religion, commerce, invention &c &c in the most interesting manner. I am going to hear him this semester on his "System der Staatswissenschaft und Politik"—which I suppose I may freely translate Political Science. He has delivered two lectures now, with which I was much pleased. In his prefatory remarks he said that he would speak not only of the abstract doctrine of government but also of the practical art of governing. Philosophy, Jurisprudence & History must be studied, he says, to understand Polit. Science. He will give, in later lectures, a history of all the theories of government & of the literature of political science. The first main division of his course will be on "Die Lehre vom Volk als den Inhalt des Staatsorganismus"—or, freely translated, the doctrine of the people as the groundwork of the body politic. His first chapter was on "The people as Nation," the second on "People & State." A very rude translation of his definition of the State is: "The State is a popular community founded upon a common system of laws, and for the object of defence against external foes, and the protection of the rights of the individual, and of bringing the well-being of the individual into harmony with the well-being of the Whole." This, he says, is only a provisional definition, which he will alter subsequently. . . .

Good luck & hosts of clients are wished to you by
Your sincere friend   R. H. Dabney.

ALS (WP, DLC) with WWhw notation on env.: "Rec'd May 6th 1883. Ans. May 11th 1883." Att.: WWsh draft of reply.
  [1] Carl Adolf Cornelius, a specialist in German Reformation history.
  [2] Wilhelm Heinrich Riehl, a specialist in German social and cultural history.

To Hiram Woods, Jr.

Dear Hiram,   Atlanta, Geo., April 25/83
    I learned but the other day, through Bob. Bridges, of the sad bereavement you had experienced in the death of your lovely mother. I was inexpressibly shocked by the news. Little as I had seen of your mother, her genuine, full-hearted kindness had inspired me with an almost filial affection for her. No one with any sort of appreciation for womanly character could have failed to esteem her one of the noblest. All the elements which go to make up the character of a lovely wife and a loving and noble mother seemed to me to have been in her combined. I can say

with all sincerity that I esteemed her, amongst all the ladies of my acquaintance, less than my own mother only. I can, therefore, find no adequate expression for my sympathy for you, old fellow. If I so admired your mother, how must you have felt towards her! I wish that you were here within my reach, that I might take you by the hand, and tell you face to face how my heart goes out towards you in this trial.

Your long silence is now explained, and certainly I cannot now take you to task about it. You know you have been owing me a letter all this time, and ever since you slipped away from Princeton last June I have been growing sorer and sorer at heart on the score of our neglected correspondence. I did not like to believe that you thought less of me than you used to think; and now, of course, I don't believe it, and my regret takes the opposite course, of self-blame for not having written to you without standing so stiffly on the selfish etiquette of formal correspondence.

I have nothing special to tell about myself. Time has moved very slowly and very uneventfully since I saw you. I have some practice, just enough to keep me from dispairing of getting more. Practice in Atlanta cannot for some time be satisfactory to any right-minded practitioner. We have, for one thing, no bar association and the most unprofessional tricks consequently go uncorrected and unrebuked. Indeed the town will not for many years afford an opportunity for correcting such abuses. All trades and professions are on their infant legs still; society, half Yankee and half Southern, is made up as largely of unknown adventurers as of gentlemen; boarding-houses are, one would suppose, almost as numerous as homes, and are filled with a floating population of dry-goods clerks, drummers, new-fledged and impecunious lawyers, milliners, seamstresses, *et id omne genus*. Still, everywhere is life and energy, and one has only to be as energetic and pushing as his neighbors, in order to achieve ultimate success. It's rather a vulgar struggle, but an imperative and not altogether demoralizing struggle "for a' that."

I am not sure where this letter can find you, but I shall send it where you were when I last heard from you, Bay View Asylum, whence it can follow you, if you are not there.

With sincerest affection,
Your old friend,   Woodrow Wilson

Give my warmest regards to your father, Miss. Nellie, Frank, and my love to all the children, when you see them   Yrs.   W.W.

ALS (in possession of Arthur W. Machen, Baltimore).

To Robert Bridges

Dear Bobby,   Atlanta, Geo., April 29th 1883

Since I last wrote to you a great change has been wrought in my plans. The ideas embodied in those conversations I had with you last June in Princeton have borne fruit and I am now an applicant for a *fellowship* at Johns Hopkins. I found, what every man finds, that the truth just must be faced; and the truth I have had to face is this, that success at the bar must be very doubtful and at best long delayed, because I am unfit for practice. I have had just enough experience to prove that. In the first place, the atmosphere of the courts has proved very depressing to me. I cannot breathe freely nor smile readily in an atmosphere of broken promises, of wrecked estates, of neglected trusts, of unperformed duties, of crimes and of quarrels. I find myself hardened and made narrow and cynical by seeing only the worst side of human nature. But this is the least part of the argument; here lies the weight of it: my natural, and therefore predominant, tastes every day allure me from my law books; I throw away law reports for histories, and my mind runs after the solution of political, rather than of legal, problems, as if its keenest scent drew it after them by an unalterable instinct. My appetite is for general literature and my ambition is for writing. Small as has been my success in writing, I feel as if, after a thorough and undiscourageable discipline of my faculties, and an ample storing of my mind, I could write something that men might delight to read, and which they would not readily let die. My eager impulse, consequently, is to seek as broad a field of study as possible; and my dread is lest, by any such influences as I now find to surround legal practice, my mind should be made, to use a figure of "Dad's," like a needle, of one eye and a single point. I know that, sooner or later, I could acquire a lucrative practice and earn an honorable support in my present profession; I have not been without encouragement already, and my professional friends increase in number; but you know it was never my wish to be a mere lawyer and I have found this out, that in these struggling times of close population and limited capital a man must become a mere lawyer to succeed at the bar; and must, moreover, acquire a most ignoble shrewdness at overcoming the unprofessional tricks and underhand competition of sneaking pettifoggers.

At any rate, I am perfectly convinced of the wisdom of the step I have taken. I have asked to be made fellow in *history and in political science*. I am not very sanguine of the success of my application, for I have not many evidences of my fitness to submit; but, whether admitted to the privileges of a fellowship or not, I shall, according to my present plan, study a year in Baltimore anyhow—with the purpose of *winning* a fellowship eventually. It has occurred to me, Bobby, that if you, writing as a class mate, were to address a few lines to Prest. Gilman, testifying to my enthusiasm in the study of political science and history, it might affect the fate of my application. Anything reaching Balto. before May 11th would arrive in season to be of service. It would be worth trying, at any rate, would it not, if you have time to write but a note? I wish I could see you to tell you all my plans and all the considerations, as well as all the aspirations, on which they rest. When I get away from the law—from its practice, for I love its study well enough—I shall rejoice like one emancipated. I long to lead the intellectual life and Hamerton speaks only my thoughts in what he says of the relations of the legal profession to the intellectual life (pp. 399-401).[1] Write me candidly what you think of the move. With love, as ever

Your sincere friend   Woodrow Wilson.

ALS (Meyer Coll., DLC).
    [1] Philip G. Hamerton, *The Intellectual Life* (Boston, 1875). WW marked this passage in his own copy, now in the Wilson Library, DLC.

From Hiram Woods, Jr.

My Dear Tommy,   Balto. May 2, 1883.
    Your letter was received last Saturday, and never did a letter receive a more hearty welcome. My long silence is easily explained. Before January I did not write because—strange as it may seem—I did not know your address. In some way my "Class Record" has been lost. I got your address later from Bob Bridges, and a short time after this my dear Mother died. I received a note from Bob Bridges, and I felt sure that he would write the sad news to you. Several times during the past 3 months have I been on the point of writing you, but something has prevented each time. Don't, my dear fellow, ever let yourself for one moment think that I "think less of you than formerly." It has been my fortune to have had during my life a *few* friends—there can never be *many* of this class—in whose love for me I have always had profound confidence: whose friendship it would never occur to me to doubt, and who, I have felt, held the same feelings toward me. You must know that you are one of these few. . . . You have made no mistake when you think of dear Ma's death as a terrible affliction. To me it seems like a great weight which I feel present

all the time. Even when my mind is thoroughly absorbed in work, this deep sense of loss of *something* which was a help & stimulant is always present. . . .

As usual when writing to you, I go way beyond my fixed limit. Do write me soon, and I will give you a prompt reply. Nellie & Pa ask me to thank you for your kind remembrances & to give you their warmest regards.

Yrs as ever Hiram

ALS (WP, DLC) with WWhw notation on env.: "Ans. 5/10/83." Att.: WWsh draft of reply, May 9, 1883.

Marginal Notes

Theodore D. Woolsey, *Political Science or the State* (2 vols., New York, 1878).

Vol. I, 167-68:

Locke has had a wider influence on English political thinking than either the want of originality in his views or the amount of his writings on politics would lead us to expect. In his theory of government he supposes a social compact and a compact between the people and the prince. The breach of this latter engagement on the part of the prince and his line justifies rebellion. In regard to property, as we have already seen, he introduced or made more prominent than before the right derived from labor employed in production. In his theory of the powers of the state he, more than any of the earlier writers, showed the importance of a separation of government functions. The doctrine of a compact between the prince and the people had so much ground for it in the early practice of the Germanic race that history as well as theory could be pressed into its support. It was formally accepted by the English Convention-Parliament, when it was voted that the king had endeavored to

Transcripts of WW Shorthand Comments

[c. May 8, 1883]

The reason for Locke's influence over English public opinion is not hard to see; notwithstanding the introduction of the unnecessary fiction of social compact his opinions tallied more than others with fact and experience as well as that men felt him to be reasonable.

subvert the constitution by breaking the original compact between king and people.

Vol. I, 391-92:

[Woolsey suggests a solution to the problem of how to avoid standing by the nominee of a party regardless of his past conduct or insisting on voting only for men of "thoroughly good character."] We have, then, here two extremes to be avoided, and they can be avoided, unless a rigid principle of political ethics demands that every voter ought to cast his suffrage for the best possible man, whether others will join him in so doing or not. But surely no man is bound to act invariably on this last-mentioned principle. In acting with other men having convictions different from mine, who have a common object to carry with me, there must be of necessity sometimes a yielding of judgement and a compromise. When it is decided, by whatever process— whether that be the miserable expedient of *caucus* or some other—that a man will receive the votes of the party to which I belong, I must decide from a consideration of his abilities and character on the one hand, and from the risk of failure on the other, if I withdraw my vote, whether in the particular case a rebuke of the party for selecting a bad man is on the whole desirable.

"Burke admitted that when he saw a man acting a desultory and disconnected part in public life with detriment to his fortune, he was ready to believe such a man to be in earnest, though not ready to believe him to be right. In any case he lamented to see rare and valuable qualities squandered away without any public utility. He admitted, moreover, on the other hand, that people frequently acquired in party confederacies a narrow, bigoted and proscriptive spirit. 'But where duty renders a critical situation a necessary one, it is our business to keep free from the evils attendant upon it, and not to fly from the situation itself. It is surely no very rational account of a man that he has always acted right; but has taken special care to act in such a manner that his endeavours could not possibly be productive of any consequence. . . . When men are not acquainted with each other's principles, nor experienced in each other's talents, nor at all practised in their mutual habitudes and dispositions by joint efforts of business; no personal confidence, no friendship, no common interest subsist[ing] among them; it is evidently impossible that they can act a public part with uniformity, perseverance or efficacy.' . . . He pointed out to emulation the Whig junto who held so close together in the reign of Anne— Sunderland, Godolphin, Somers and Marlborough—who believed 'that no

men could act with effect who did
not act in concert; that no men could
[act] in concert who did not act
with confidence; and that no men
could act with confidence who were
not bound together by common opinions, common affections, and common interests.' " Morley's *Burke*, pages
52-54. [Last phrase in WWhw.]

From Robert Bridges

Dear Tommy: New York City May 9th 83
. . . As to your plan, I don't believe that I could add anything
to what I said against it when we were at the tri-ennial. I see
many things in its favor the chiefest of which is that you have
reached the conclusion after a mature deliberation, and after a
fair trial of the actual practice of law. I believe in a man following his bent. Still I cannot but see that the material results of the
course you propose to follow will appear even more slowly than
in the law—and a competency in literature and through literary
work will be even farther in the future. There is this great difference, however, that the intellectual life is (or should be) its
own reward. I believe you have the enthusiasm, the faith and the
capacity to make it such—and I bid you God Speed.

I just discover on reading over your letter that it is almost too
late to write the note you requested to Gilman. I will try and
snatch time when I reach the office in the morning to do it—
though I can't see that it will be of any service.

I have been hoping to send you some news of the M.S. It is now
at the Scribner's and I will soon get a verdict.

I have the MS. of your last letter.[1] The Managing Ed. thought
it too much like an essay for the *Post*—though he admired it as
such. If you wish I'll return the MS.

Be sure and come to see me before you settle down to work in
Baltimore. It is only a few hours ride—and I expect it.

Pete sails for Europe on the 19th—may be gone for two years
& may come back in the autumn.

I have written this very hurriedly, after a hard day's work—
but I know you will fill in the dashes.

                        Your friend   Robert Bridges

ALS (WP, DLC) with WWhw notation on env.: "Ans. May 13th 1883." Att.:
WWsh draft of reply.
[1] "Culture and Education at the South," printed at March 29, 1883.

Draft of a Letter to Hiram Woods, Jr.

My dear Hiram   Atlanta, Geo., May 9th [10] 1883

Your letter was mightily enjoyed. It was like cool water to a thirsty man. Until it came I felt utterly in the dark about you. As the address of my letter showed, I did not know that you had left the Bay View Hospital yet. Your account of yourself is extremely satisfactory. You are certainly combining the different kinds of practice in a very practical and sensible way that cannot fail to yield good results. Hospitals furnish facilities to physicians such as lawyers cannot have. There are fees in institutions where one can spend a legal apprenticeship perfecting himself in knowledge and in practice—in asylums for criminals, or for pauper civil clients, where one can gather experience in docket cases. Charity practice is scarcely valuable; so one has just to wait with what patience he can command.

There is some stir in Atlanta today. Our new Governor—did you know that we had one?—is to be installed. My office windows look out upon one of the chief entrances of the big and ugly building which serves new Atlanta for a temporary capitol and whenever I look up from my letter I can see the mixed crowds passing in to the galleries of the House of Representatives to get a view of the inauguration ceremonies. This was a special election you know, to fill the place made vacant by the late Alex Stephens' death; for we are very economical here in Georgia and cannot afford a lieutenant governor. When our Governor is careless enough to die therefore we must have a special election and an extra session of the legislature to count the votes—luxuries which cost something like 10 thousand dollars and make a lieutenant governorship seem inexpensive in comparison. Governor [Henry D.] McDaniel walked in without opposition, receiving consequently a very small vote—only 13 men having voted in one of the counties.[1] He is not remarkable for anything but honesty, which nowadays is remarkable in any politician. His inaugural address will be anything but pleasant to listen to for he stutters most painfully, with so helpless a struggle for utterance as to have led a Tennessee brother to wonder at the scarcity of good candidate material in Georgia. He offered to send over from Tennessee a whole man to serve a state which was about to replace a governor who could not walk with one who could not talk. Georgians are sensible, however, in the opinion that the less a governor talks the better officer he will make.

I have come to a deliberate opinion that North Georgia is altogether a very remarkable quarter of the globe. In southern Georgia, which was settled long before this portion of the state was
reclaimed from the Indians, there is much culture and refinement; there civilization feels somewhat at home, for it is not a
newcomer. But hereabouts culture is very little esteemed, not,
indeed, because it is a drug on the market but because there is
so little of it that its good qualities are not appreciated. Sometimes I am inclined to think that for one who would succeed in
North Georgia anything more than a common school education
is a positive drawback. Here the chief end of man is certainly
to make money, and money cannot be made except by the most
vulgar methods. The studious man is pronounced unpractical and
is suspected as a visionary. All students of specialties—except such
practical specialties as carpentering, for instance—are classed
together as mere ornamental furniture in an intellectual world—
curious and perhaps pretty enough, but of very little use and no
mercantile value. If one had the means and the leisure to be a
philosopher he could learn enough human nature here in Atlanta
to stock two or 3 immortal comedies and several conclusive essays on the middle classes. If any outsider would learn something
about my neighbors, let him read any trustworthy account of the
people of Queen Anne's time; they were North Georgians. In such
a community I suffer, of course, for lack of intellectual companionship, but I am made wise in the ways of the world.

I do not hear often from the boys, but all that I do hear is favorable. Our class seems to me to be doing remarkably well. Do
write soon again to me Hiram; I enjoy your letters hugely I can
tell you. Give my kindest regards to your father and to Miss Nell

Now for a bit of news, Hiram. For reasons which I will tell
you when I see you, or when I can do so without making my letter too long, I have determined to give up law, professionally at
least, and do what is implied by the fact that I have applied for
a fellowship in history and political science at Johns Hopkins.
This I have done since I last wrote you. If it is not too late, and
if you think it of any value, I should be very grateful if you were
to exert with the faculty of the University in my behalf any influence you may have with them, by representing me to be a
splendid fellow, etc. Possibly I will attend the University next
winter whether I get the appointment or not; but of course I am
more than anxious for the fellowship and I know that you will
do everything, if anything can be done. I should have asked you
before had the resolution been taken sooner but it was arrived

at rather tardily. I will write you soon again to let you know my full mind and plans. Until then farewell—

With much love   Your sincere friend   Woodrow Wilson

Transcript of WWshL (draft), (WP, DLC).
¹ McDuffie County.

To Richard Heath Dabney

My dear Heath,   Atlanta, Geo., May 11th 1883

The receipt of your letter was a delightful surprise. I say 'surprise' because it cannot but be a matter of grateful surprise that anyone—even you—away off there in Europe, surrounded by everything that is attractive in the old world, deep in the work of a great university, and looking forward to a Ph.D. in Berlin, should ever think of me, buried in hum-drum life down here in slow, ignorant, uninteresting Georgia. I read this letter of yours with as much envy as I felt when I read the one which preceded it: for who can help envying a man whose [sic] is taking, under the most favourable circumstances imaginable, the very course that one longs to take himself? It is not human nature to do otherwise. I am, however, (let me tell you with rejoicings) about to do what is the next best thing, for a fellow who is confined to the limits of this continent: for I have about made up my mind to study, at Johns Hopkins University, the very subjects which you are now studying in Germany under the great masters with unpronounceable names. In doing this I am, beyond all reasonable doubt, following the natural bent of my mind. I can never be happy unless I am enabled to lead an intellectual life; and who can lead an intellectual life in ignorant Georgia? I have come deliberately into the opinion that northern Georgia is altogether a very remarkable quarter of the globe. In southern Georgia, which was settled long before this portion of the State was reclaimed from the Indians, there is much culture and refinement. There civilization seems to feel somewhat at home, for it is not a newcomer. But hereabouts culture is very little esteemed; not, indeed, at all because it is a drug on the market, but because there is so little of it that its good qualities are not appreciated. Sometimes I am inclined to think that, for one who would succeed in North Georgia, anything more than a common school education is a positive drawback. Here the chief end of man is certainly to make money, and money cannot be made except by the most vulgar methods. The studious man is pronounced unpractical and is suspected as a visionary. All students of specialties—except such

practical specialties as carpentering, for instance—are classed together as mere ornamental furniture in the intellectual world—
curious, perhaps, and pretty enough, but of very little use and
no mercantile value. If one had the means and leisure to be
philosophical he could learn here enough of a certain side of human nature to stock two or three immortal comedies, and several conclusive essays on the characteristics of the middle classes.
If you, or any other outsider would learn something about my
neighbors in Atlanta, and their neighbors throughout northern
Georgia, much can be easily learned in the perusal of any trustworthy account of the English people of Queen Anne's time: they
were North Georgians. It goes, therefore, without the saying
that, though I am by its ways being made wise in worldly craft,
I suffer very much in such a community for lack of intellectual
companionship.

But the greater matter is that the practice of the law, when
conducted for purposes of gain, is antagonistic to the best interests of the intellectual life. One can easily exchange one community for another: he can even live above the deteriorating influences of the community in which his lot is cast, but he cannot
so emancipate himself from the necessary conditions of his profession. The philosophical *study* of the law—which must be a
pleasure to any thoughtful man—is a very different matter from
its scheming and haggling practice. Burke spoke with his usual
clear-sighted wisdom when he spoke of the law as "one of the first
and noblest of human sciences—a science which does more to
quicken and *invigorate* the understanding than all the other
kinds of learning put together; but it is not apt, except in persons
very happily born, to *open* and to *liberalize* the mind in exactly
the same porportion." With equal truth and perspicacity, Hamerton says: "The profession of the law provides ample opportunities for a *critical intellect* with a strong love of *accuracy* and a
robust capacity for hard work, besides which it is the *best of
worldly educations.* Some lawyers love their work as passionately
as artists do theirs, others dislike it very heartily, most of them
seem to take it as a simple business to be done for daily bread.
Lawyers whose heart is in their work are invariably men of superior ability, which proves that there is something in it that affords gratification to the intellectual powers. However, in speaking of lawyers, I feel ignorant and on the outside, because their
profession is one of which the interior feelings can be known to
no one who has not practised. One thing seems clear, they get
the habit of employing the whole strength and energy of their

minds for especial and temporary ends, the purpose being the service of the client, certainly not the revelation of pure truth. Hence, although they become very acute, and keen judges of that side of human nature which they habitually see (not the best side) they are not more disinterested than clergymen. Sometimes they take up some study outside of their profession and follow it disinterestedly, but this is rare. A busy lawyer is much more likely than a clergyman to become entirely absorbed in his professional life, because it requires so much more intellectual exertion" (Hamerton is here speaking, of course, of the *churchmen* of the old world) "I remember," he continues, "asking a very clever lawyer who lived in London, whether he ever visited an exhibition of pictures, and he answered me by the counter-inquiry whether I had read Chitty on Contracts, Collier on Partnerships, Taylor on Evidence, Cruse's Digest, or Smith's Mercantile Law? This seemed to me at the time a good instance of the way a professional habit may narrow ones views of things, for these law-books were written for lawyers alone, whilst the picture exhibitions were intended for the public generally. My friend's answer would have been more to the point if I had inquired whether he had read Linton on Colours, or Burnet on Chiaroscuro.

"There is just one situation in which we all may feel for a short time as lawyers feel habitually. Suppose that two inexperienced players sit down to a game of chess, and that each is backed by a clever person who is constantly giving him hints. The two backers represent the lawyers, and the players represent their clients. There is not much disinterested thought in a situation of this kind, but there is a strong stimulus to acuteness."

I came across this passage with not a little delight a few weeks since, for it embodies thoughts which had long been gathering in my mind, but for which I could never have found such felicitous expression. Now here it is that the whole secret of my new departure lies. You know my passion for original work, you know my love for composition, my keen desire to become a master of philosophical discourse, to become capable and apt in instructing as great a number of persons as possible. My plain necessity, then, is some profession which will afford me a moderate support, favourable conditions for study, and considerable leisure; what better can I be, therefore, than a professor, a lecturer upon subjects whose study most delights me? Therefore it is that I have prayed to be made a fellow of Johns Hopkins; and therefore it is that I am determined, if I fail of that appointment (as I probably shall, since it is not won but given) to go next winter anyhow to Baltimore to attend the University lectures and bury myself for a season in the grand libraries of that beautiful city.

Are you aware that we have a new governor in Georgia? We have just passed through the forms of a special election. We are much too economical in this thrifty State to think of indulging ourselves in a lieutenant governor; so the vacancy caused by the death of "little Alex." Stephens had to be filled by a special election, and the vote counted in a extra session of the Legislature. True, to put all the machinery of a nominating convention, a special election, and an extra session into operation probably cost the people of the State a sum of money in comparison with which a lieutenant-governorship would seem cheap enough; but so long as we think that we are economical our consciences are at peace—and, after all, that's the great matter.

Governor McDaniel was inaugurated yesterday. As I sat here at my desk I could see from my office windows, which look out upon the principal entrance of the big, ugly building which serves new Atlanta as a temporary capitol, the mixed crowds going in to secure seats in the galleries of the House of Representatives at the inauguration ceremonies. They were probably not much entertained, though they may have been considerably diverted, for our new governor cannot talk. He stutters most painfully, making quite astonishing struggles for utterance. A Tennesseean wag expressed great commiseration for Georgia in her poverty of sound candidate material, and offered to send some over from Tenn. for the relief of a State which was about to replace a governor who could not walk with a governor who could not talk. McDaniel is sound enough in other respects, however—not remarkable except for honesty—always remarkable in a latter-day politician—but steady and sensible, all the harder worker, perhaps, because he can't talk.

If my letter were not already too long, I should like to discuss with you Riehl's provisional definition of the State. The definition given somewhere by Woolsey is: "A community of persons living within certain limits of territory, under a permanent organization, which aims to secure the prevalence of justice by self-imposed laws."[1] It is noticeable that the American founds his idea of the State on the authority of the people, conceiving of laws as of course self-imposed, whilst the German does not put the origin of the laws upon the face of his definition. Woolsey's seems to me better in *form*. It is more accurate, at least, to speak of the State as a community of persons living under a common system of laws than as a "popular community founded upon a common system of laws." Woolsey leaves out of his definition, however, the idea of defence against external foes, which Riehl includes. But more of this another time.

Try to write soon again. Your letters afford me the sincerest delight and the greatest entertainment. If you want an appreciative reader, you can't do better than to write to me.

With much love,   Your sincere friend,   Woodrow Wilson

ALS (Wilson-Dabney Correspondence, ViU). There is a WWsh draft of this letter in WP, DLC.
[1] Theodore D. Woolsey, *Introduction to the Study of International Law* (5th edn., New York, c. 1878), p. 34.

To Robert Bridges

Dear Bobby,   Atlanta, Geo., May 13th   1883

Your letter reached me yesterday afternoon. Of course I enjoyed hearing from you: your letters are all the more acceptable because written under such difficulties. As for the *ms.* I sent the *Post*, never mind returning it: it is of no consequence, even in my eyes.[1] I am neither surprised nor chagrined that it was rejected. I wrote it principally for my own amusement and sent it on at a venture, thinking that, if it chanced to serve the editor's purposes in any way, well and good—if not, no harm would be done, and nobody's feelings hurt.

Concerning the other *ms.*—the ill-starred "Government by Debate"—you have already been troubled a great deal too much; with your additional editorial duties, it cannot but be a burden to you; and I have determined to request very earnestly that, if it be rejected by the Scribner's, you return it, *C.O.D.*; I cannot think of giving you any further trouble with it, for I am conscious of having already made entirely too great demands upon your unselfish kindness. I should not conceal, if I could, my disappointment at the dismal failure with which the essay has met, or rather with which I have met; but I am not going to cry over it, or be discouraged by it. I shall simply strive to deserve better at the next trial. I think it would be wise, perhaps, to accept the judgment of the publishers upon the essay; because, though one publisher might make a mistake in rejecting it, and in so doing unwittingly throw away a treasure, a unanimous verdict against it is, most likely, a righteous one, and ought to be acquiesced in. However humiliating, it is, at least, wholesome to acknowledge a failure. It may enable me to do better work than I should otherwise have done.

And now, Bobby, for my plans and their defence. It is a matter of sincere regret to me, of real pain indeed, that those plans don't meet with your approval. Of course I remember our discussion of a year ago on this subject. At the time, as I must confess, (now that I am reintrenched) I was driven from the field by your arguments; and ever since they have been a formidable barrier against the advance of my mind towards that determination which I have now taken—they still, indeed, face me, and dishearten me in my less sanguine moments. Though my present plans have been laid with deliberation, they have been laid in doubt, in hope rather than in assurance. But thus much I can say with confidence, that a year's observation and experience here have by no means reconciled me to remaining in the practice of the law. Perhaps this was not the place for one of my habits and temperament to settle. It would be hard to conceive of a less congenial society than that in which I am compelled to live here. Northern Georgia is altogether a very remarkable quarter of the globe. In Southern Georgia, which was settled long before this portion of the State was reclaimed from the Indians, there is much culture and refinement. There civilization seems to feel somewhat at home, for it is not a newcomer. Here, however, on the other hand, culture is very little esteemed; not, indeed, because it is a drug on the market, but because there is so little of it that its good qualities are not appreciated. So much is this the case that sometimes I am inclined to think that, for one who would succeed in North Georgia in a way that North Georgians could understand and applaud, anything more that [sic] a common school education is a positive disqualification. Here the chief end of man is certainly to make money, and money cannot be made except by the most vulgar methods. The studious man, therefore, is pronounced unpractical, and is suspected and despised as a visionary. All students of specialties— except such practical specialties as plowing or carpentering, for instance—are classed together as mere ornamental furniture— curious, perhaps, and pretty enough, but of very little use and of no mercantile value—; or as mere cranks, to be tolerated on the principle that it takes all sorts of people to make up society, but not to be encouraged under any circumstances. If one had the means and the leisure to be philosophical, he could learn here in this provincial town of Atlanta enough of a certain sort of human nature to stock two or three immortal comedies, and several conclusive essays on the characteristics of the middle classes. If any one should wish to learn anything about the general, broad features of my neighbors' characters, he could easily and pleasantly learn it in the perusal of any trustworthy account of the English people of Queen Anne's time: they were North Georgians. It goes, therefore, without the saying, that, though in its school I am being made wise in the ways of the world, I suffer very much in such a community for lack of intellectual companionship.

But the greater matter is yet to be mentioned: it is that the practice of the law, when conducted for purposes of gain, is entirely antagonistic to the best interests of the true intellectual life. One can easily change his place of residence at my age; he can, by an effort, even live above and aloof from the deteriorating influence of the community in which his lot is cast; but he cannot emancipate himself from the necessary conditions of his profession. The philosophical study of the law—which cannot but be delightful to any vigorous and masculine mind—is a very different matter from its scheming and haggling practices. Burke displayed his usual clear-sighted wisdom when he spoke of the law as "one of the first and noblest of human sciences—a science which does more to quicken and invigorate the understanding than all other kinds of learning put together"; "but it is not apt," he added, "except in persons very happily born, to open and to liberalize the mind in exactly the same proportion." With equal perspicacity, Hamerton says (*Intellectual Life*, pp. 399-401.) "The profession of the law provides ample opportunities for a *critical intellect* with a strong love of *accuracy* and a robust capacity for hard work, besides which it is the best of worldly educations. Some lawyers love their work as passionately as artists do theirs, others dislike it very heartily, most of them seem to take it as a simple business to be done for daily bread. Lawyers whose heart is in their work are invariably men of superior ability, which proves that there is something in it which affords gratification to the intellectual powers. However, in speaking of lawyers, I feel ignorant and on the outside, because their profession is one of which the interior feelings can be known to no one who has not practiced. One thing seems clear, they get the habit of employing the whole strength and energy of their minds for especial and temporary ends, the purpose being the service of the client, certainly not the revelation of pure truth. Hence, although they become very acute, and keen judges of that side of human nature which they habitually see (not the best side), they are not more disinterested than clergymen. Sometimes they take up some study outside of their profession and follow it disinterestedly, but this is rare. A busy lawyer is much more likely than a clergyman to become entirely absorbed in his professional life, because it requires so much more intellectual exertion. I remember asking a very clever lawyer who lived in London, whether he ever visited an exhibition of pictures, and he answered me by the counter-inquiry whether I had read Chitty on Contracts, Collier on Partnerships, Taylor on Evidence, Cruse's Digest, or Smith's Mercantile Law? This seemed to me at the time a good instance of the way a professional habit may narrow one's views of things, for these law-books were written for lawyers alone, whilst the picture exhibitions were intended for the public generally. My friend's answer would have been more to the point if I had inquired whether he had read Linton on Colours, and Burnet on Chiaroscuro." And then follows the illustration of the chess players. You probably recall the rest of the passage, or have the book at hand and can refer to it.

I came across this passage, a few weeks since, with not a little delight, for it embodies thoughts which had long been gathering in my mind, but for which I could never have found such felicitous expression—tho', after all, Hamerton only illustrates Burke's remark. He dont add anything to it.

It is, then, from just these truths that my new determination takes most of its force. You know my passion for original work, you know my love for composition, my keen desire to become a master of philosophical discourse and of the art of public speech, and you know the labour of preparation, the extent of information, the variety of acquisition, necessary for the accomplishment of these ends. I know, on the other hand, the narrowing and materializing influences inseparable from the practice of the law, its power to make a man, as "Dad" once expressed it in a letter to me, like a *needle*, a thing of one eye and one point; I know that no man who expects to gain a livelihood by it can be anything but a mere lawyer; I know its degrading struggles, its denial of philosophical leisure to the studious, its one-sided contests, its jealousy of all other pursuits. Now, put all these things together, my tastes and the limitations of my present profession, and plainly the two sets of fact point to but one conclusion, that my talents, whatever they may be, wont grow freely in the atmosphere of the law. My plain necessity, as a man who seeks to make a living and at the same time to gain opportunities for purely intellectual pursuits, is some profession which will afford me a moderate support, favourable conditions for study, and considerable leisure for travel, may-be, and for observation. What better can I be, then, than a *professor*—to begin with, at least—a lecturer upon those subjects whose study most delights me?

To such considerations it is due that I have prayed to be made a fellow of Johns Hopkins; and therefore it is that I have determined, if I fail of that appointment,—as I probably shall, since it is not won but given—to go next winter anyhow to Baltimore, to attend the University lectures, and bury myself for a season in the grand libraries of that beautiful city. As a lawyer I cannot *hope* to become what I most wish to be—by this other road I may possibly reach the desired goal. That's the whole matter in brief.

What do I wish to become? I want to make myself *an outside force in politics*. No man can safely *enter* political life nowadays who has not an independent fortune, or at least independent means of support: this I have not: therefore the most I can hope to become is a speaker and writer of the highest authority on political subjects. This I *may* become in a chair of political science, with leisure and incentive to study, and with summer vacations for travel and observation; whilst I could never reach such a station by way of a profession in which I should inevitably become engrossed from the very necessities of bread-winning: and by the time a competence was earned my head would be grey and my literary and political ambition smothered, my political knowledge gone.

I have not, as you know, come to my present resolution without mature deliberation: and I most earnestly wish that your judgment could go along with me in the step I am about to take. I doubt my own wisdom, my dear fellow, when I know that you differ with me, and therefore it is that I long to have your approval in this matter. But enough of this subject for the present.

You are, of course, aware that we have a new governor in Georgia. His advent suggests to me the fact that the special election through which we have just passed illustrates one very prominent feature of Georgia policy. We are much too economical in this thrifty State to think of indulging ourselves in the luxury of a lieutenant-governor. True, to put in motion all the ponderous machinery of nominating convention, special election, and extra vote-counting session of the Legislature probably cost the people of the State a sum of money in comparison with which a lieutenant-governorship may seem cheap enough; but, so long as we think that we are economical, what matters it? Our consciences are at ease, and, after all, that's the main thing.

Governor McDaniel is not—so far as I've been able to learn—very remarkable for anything except honesty, but that is a very remarkable trait in any latter-day politician. He cannot lie easily, for he cannot talk easily, and most sagacious men are shy about committing lies to paper. He stutters painfully, making most astonishing struggles for utterance. A Tennesseian wag expressed great commiseration for Georgia's poverty in good candidate material, and offered to send some whole and sound men over from Tenn. to a State which was about to replace a governor who could not walk with a governor who could not talk. However, a man who can't talk will probably do all the better work because of his infirmity. McDaniel is said to be very steady and sensible and is, doubtless, take him all in all, a very comfortable sort of man to have in a place in which no man can do much positive harm to anybody but petty office-seekers and convicts, or to anything but the State's reputation.

But I must stop. I can't in conscience make this letter interminable. It is already, I believe, longer than any other letter I ever wrote. With much love,

Your sincere friend   Woodrow Wilson

P.S. The tin-type is really good. Judging by your face, my dear fellow, you are positively getting *fat*. My love to all friends who inquire.

Yours   W. W.

ALS (WP, DLC). There is a WWsh draft of this letter in WP, DLC.
  [1] "Culture and Education at the South," printed at March 29, 1883.

From Janet Woodrow Wilson

Lexington Kentucky[1]   Sabbath morning [May 20, 1883].
My darling boy,

It is raining this morning, so that it was impossible for me to go out to church—as we have no umbrella. It had ceased raining for a little while—just at church time—and your father & Uncle James went round to the second church to hear Dr. Stratton.[2] The second church belongs to the Northern Assembly.

Your father enjoyed greatly your description of Dr Smoot.[3] What a puppy he is! It is simply disgusting to witness from day to day, the man's plannings to bring himself before the Assembly[.] Of course he is Chairman of the The [*sic*] Com. on Overtures, and thus he has abundant opportunity of making himself conspicuous—legitimately—but that does not satisfy him. You have seen that Dr Pryor—father of Gen. Pryor[4] of N. Y.—is Moderator of the Ass[embly]. He is eighty-two years old—he is *deaf*—and knows very little of parliamentary rules—in addition to this he has been captivated by Smoot—whose stories of his own greatness & distinction, are eagerly *swallowed*. All this is very pitiful. Dr. P. is dependent upon your father for hints as to all points of order—and information as to the names of persons addressing the Moderator. These hints &c are given with great difficulty, owing to the *deafness* of the Moderator, as you will readily imagine.

The Northern delegates were received yesterday morning.[5] It was quite an impressive scene. Your father was *really* master of ceremonies—for nobody else knew what should be done. There were many tears shed. I fear I am hard hearted—for not a tear came to my eyes. Dr. Martin[6] of Atlanta was seated just in front of me and had great difficulty in choking down his emotion. There was much less *gush* than I had feared, however—and I am very thankful that it all passed off so well. As to the money you speak off, dear—I certainly never thought of it as a *loan*—so that you must use it in the way you think will be most to your own advantage—something *permanent*—you alone can decide as to what will be most useful to you. As to the remaining books, I would advise you to retain such as may be useful to you—rather than to part with them at a sacrifice.

Monday morning—Your father was taken quite sick after his return from church yesterday morning. The lime-stone water, together with the very damp weather, have affected him very unfavorably. He has suffered a good deal, & I have been quite anxious —but he is able to be up this morning—and I hope will be all right shortly. Your Uncle James, too, was taken sick about midnight— but is up—though both feel miserable. Many others are suffering more or less in the same way. It is still raining—I will write you again. Be sure you will hear if your father is not better—so dont be anxious. With unbounded love from us both to our precious boy

Your own   Mother.

Make it a point to get home *as soon as you can* dear. God bless you.

ALS (WP, DLC).

[1] The Wilsons were attending the General Assembly of the southern Presbyterian Church, which met in the First Presbyterian Church of Lexington, May 17-31, 1883.

[2] The Rev. Dr. Joseph B. Stratton, pastor, Presbyterian Church, Natchez, Miss.

[3] The Rev. Dr. Richmond K. Smoot, pastor, Free (now First) Presbyterian Church, Austin, Tex., Moderator of the General Assembly, 1882.

[4] "Dr Pryor" was the Rev. Dr. Theodorick Pryor, pastor, Nottaway, Va., Presbyterian Church and Moderator of the General Assembly in 1883. "Gen. Pryor of N. Y." was Roger A. Pryor, a Confederate brigadier, who was practicing law in New York at this time.

[5] "At 10 A.M., the delegates to this Assembly, appointed by the last General Assembly of the Presbyterian Church in the United States of America, were introduced to the General Assembly by the Special Committee, of which the Rev. J. J. Bullock, D.D., was Chairman. The Assembly received them standing, and the Moderator extended a cordial greeting." *Minutes of the General Assembly of the Presbyterian Church in the United States* (3 vols. in one, Wilmington, N. C., and Columbia, S. C., 1883-85), p. 16.

[6] The Rev. Dr. Joseph H. Martin, pastor, First Presbyterian Church, Atlanta, 1873-82; without charge, living in Georgetown, Ky., in 1883.

From Kate Drayton Mayrant

Dear Mr. Wilson   [Aiken, S. C.] May 25th 1883

You can't think how happy your letter made me, why I am just overjoyed at the prospect of seeing you so soon, and yet it is going to seem an eternity to me, I am already counting the days before I can welcome you to our little cottage, be sure to let me know the exact hour you will arrive.[1] I read your letter just before going out to do my usual marketing, and positively I beamed so radiantly on the butchers and bakers that they must have thought I had gotten awfully fond of them suddenly. But how remiss I am not to congratulate you on being able to carry out your cherished plans, and give up a profession which you dislike: I do hope and trust you will succeed in whatever you undertake, and indeed, so strong is my faith, that I have no doubt; you cannot fail.

Mamma sends her love and says she will be delighted to see—your moustache. . . .

I hope no strangers will be here when you come, for it will seem more homelike without them. Give my love to Mr. Renick and "Gaddy" and tell them Mamma and I will be charmed to have them pay us a visit whenever it is convenient, Robert will have been, you are coming, so is Willie, and it would be mean if they slight us. With much love I am

Your affectionate friend   Katie D. Mayrant.

ALS (WP, DLC). Address on env. ("48 Marietta St., Atlanta Ga.") deleted and direction added: "Fowd to—Rome, Ga."

[1] WW must have written Katie about his plan to go to Rome for a final conference on the William Woodrow Estate, and thence to Wilmington by way of Atlanta, Augusta, and Aiken, stopping for a visit with the Mayrants in Aiken.

EDITORIAL NOTE

WILSON'S EARLY COURTSHIP OF ELLEN AXSON

It is now possible to reconstruct the outlines and many of the details of Wilson's courtship of Ellen Axson in May and June of 1883.

If we may believe Wilson's later testimony, he had discovered, soon after his return to Atlanta from his visit to Rome in early April 1883, that he was in love with Ellen.[1] He returned to Rome on about May 27 to resume work with his uncle, James W. Bones, on the William Woodrow Estate.[2] He also lost no time in beginning the courtship, writing from "Oakdene," the Brower home in East Rome, on May 28 to ask

[1] See the Editorial Note, "Wilson's Introduction to Ellen Axson."

[2] A letter from JWW to WW, May 20, 1883, postmarked Lexington, Ky., May 21, arrived in Atlanta on May 22 or 23 and was not forwarded. A letter from Katie D. Mayrant to WW of May 25, 1883, postmarked Aiken, S. C., May 26, arrived in Atlanta no later than May 27 and was forwarded to Rome. Hence WW left for Rome between May 23 and May 27, 1883.

Ellen to ride with him that afternoon. He signed this, the first letter to his future wife, circumspectly, almost timidly: "Very Respty Yours." Ellen accepted. We know nothing about Woodrow's activities during the next few days, but he wrote to his mother on June 1 that he was in love and intended to win Ellen's hand.[3]

Wilson returned to Atlanta on about June 4 to prepare to move.[4] He did not tarry. On June 8 he purchased a Caligraph typewriter for use in preparing documents for division of the Woodrow Estate and other purposes. On the following day he had the firm of A. J. Miller & Company pack and ship his books and odd pieces of furniture to Wilmington.[5] He went back to Rome on June 14 to wind up the Woodrow Estate and, he hoped, to capture Ellen's heart.

Only two hours after he arrived at "Oakdene" he typed out a note asking Ellen to go with him to a concert at the Rome Female College that evening. Ellen declined because of a previous engagement, adding that she would have been glad of the opportunity to welcome him back to Rome.[6]

We have to piece together events of the next two weeks from various sources. Woodrow and Ellen did not correspond again until June 25, obviously because they saw a great deal of each other after June 14. Woodrow was enjoying himself—and Ellen—hugely, for he wrote to his mother on about June 18 that he had decided to stay longer in Rome than he had planned; and he seems to have written also that he meant to ask Ellen to marry him.[7]

Wilson, in letters to Ellen of October 14, 18, and 23, 1883, and of January 1 and April 1, 1884, and Ellen, in letters to Woodrow of November 5 and December 17, 1883, recalled events of Wilson's last week in Rome, when he pressed his suit as ardently as discretion would permit. They referred often to one memorable walk in the late afternoon (what they called evening) along the railroad bed to a rock overlooking the Coosa River. Woodrow, adopting a "very indiscreet plan" in order to test Ellen's reactions, told Ellen about an earlier unhappy love affair and his need for a woman's love. He also talked passionately about his philosophy of life and ambitions and then said that he had no right to ask any girl to marry him. Ellen's reply was brief and noncommittal. She obviously knew what Woodrow meant, but she did not want to encourage him unduly, as she had responsibility for her father's household (her mother had died in 1881), and she had already seen signs of the illness that would soon cause her father's retirement and death.[8] This walk and conversation probably took place on June 25.[9]

There was another meeting that Woodrow and Ellen long remembered. It was the occasion of a picnic at "Oakdene" on Friday, June 29,

[3] JWW to WW, June 7, 1883.
[4] JWW sent one copy of her letter to WW of June 2, 1883, to Atlanta, one to Rome. The one addressed to Rome must have arrived there on June 4. James W. Bones forwarded it to WW in a letter of his own, which WW did not save, noting on the envelope of JWW's letter that it had arrived just after WW left.
[5] Receipted bill for $7.70, WP, DLC.
[6] WW to ELA, June 14, 1883, and ELA to WW, June 14, 1883.
[7] JWW to WW, June 21, 1883.
[8] Particularly WW to ELA, Oct. 23, 1883, and ELA to WW, Nov. 5, 1883.
[9] WW to ELA, June 25, 1883, and ELA to WW, June 25, 1883.

the day before Woodrow left Rome for Wilmington. Jessie Brower first set the date for June 28 and then moved it ahead a day after learning that Ellen could not come on June 28. Woodrow and Ellen went off by themselves. While she sat in a hammock, he asked if he could write to her, adding that Ellen was the only woman he had ever met to whom he felt that he could open all his thoughts. He wanted to confess his love but did not dare to do so.[10] Ellen promised to write. She also must have given clear indication of more than Platonic interest, for Woodrow left Rome on the next day full of high spirits and hope.[11]

[10] WW to ELA, Oct. 14 and 18, 1883.
[11] WW to ELA, April 1, 1884.

To Ellen Louise Axson

Miss Axson,   East Rome, [Ga.] Monday morning   [May 28, 1883]
I write to beg that you will gratify me by taking a drive with me this afternoon. I shall call at 5 o'clock, if that hour will suit your convenience. If you have any previous engagement for this afternoon, I hope that you will vouchsafe me the pleasure of riding with you to-morrow at the same hour
Very Respty Yours,   Woodrow Wilson
ALS (WP, DLC).

From Ellen Louise Axson

Mr. Wilson,   [Rome, Ga.] Monday [May 28, 1883]
I have no engagement for this afternoon, and it will afford me pleasure to take the drive. I will be ready at the appointed hour.
Very sincerely,   Ellen L. Axson.
ALS (WC, NjP).

From Janet Woodrow Wilson

My darling Son,   Wilmington, N. C. June 2nd 1883.
The telegram you sent to Lexington, has been forwarded to us, and was received this morning[.] It is so imperfectly transcribed, that we found difficulty in understanding it—but think we have at last mastered the meaning of it. I am perplexed to know how to answer[.] I sent you all James Bones' letters as to the mortgage upon the 800 acres near Fremont. From those letters you will see that he promises to have the mortgage immediately removed—so that I am distressed that he has not fulfilled his promise. Then I have made a point of repeatedly telling him of my desire that my share in that portion of land, *should be preserved intact*—as it was by far the most valuable—and might be serviceable as a home

under certain emergencies. How it can have come about that the Dodge lands are now of equal value with those of Burt, I cannot understand—for the 800 acres, near Fremont, have *always* been stated as valued at *twenty (20) dollars* per acre—at the least—while the lands in the other county have been stated as worth the average value of *ten (10)* dollars per acre. But, my dear, knowing so little as we really do about this matter—which so nearly concerns us—for we have never been able to get particulars you know—we are not able to give you much help in the way of advice. So we depend upon *you entirely to make the best of it.* I hoped that you might find real help from Mr. Brower—who has had considerable experience—and seems to be so very upright. I told your Uncle T[homas] about the *partnership proposition* & he expressed himself *violently* against it—thought of it just as you did.

We went up to Chillicothe from Lexington, on last Saturday afternoon—arriving at C. about 11 o'clock at night—and were very cordially welcomed. They were all well, and made most affectionate enquiries about you. We left C. on Tuesday morning, and reached home on Wednesday night—after quite a tedious journey—it seemed all the more tedious, as your dear father was quite unwell. He is much better today. The lime-stone water in Lexington deranged people generally.

Good bye my darling. Love inexpressible from us both—Josie will return home from Columbia next Tuesday morning, we hope. We are waiting anxiously to know when you will be able to turn your face homeward

Lovingly   Your own   Mother.

Copy of [this] letter sent to you at Rome.

ALS (WP, DLC) with WWhw notation on env.: "Ans 6/4/83." JWW sent a copy of this letter to WW, care of J. W. Bones, Rome, Ga., which she prefaced with the note: "I will send a copy of this to Atlanta—but you may have left Rome before it can reach you." J. W. Bones sent this letter on to WW in Atlanta with note on env.: "Dear Tom This arrived today just too late for you your Uncle J—"

From James Woodrow

My dear Woodrow: Columbia, S. C., June 2, 1883.

I have not heard of the result of your application at Baltimore, but I hope you have been successful. My chief fear arises from Prof. Gildersleeve's remark that they were more and more selecting Fellows from those who had been in attendance as students.

While at Lexington, Col. Mynatt spoke of a high-school in process of organisation at West End—((?) if this is not the name, it is one of the suburban villages or towns, of which Mr. Howell,

Col. Mynatt's partner, is Mayor)—and from all he said, it seemed to me it presented a favorable opening for one desiring to teach. If you so desire, it would be worth your while to inquire about it. I am sure Col. Mynatt will render you all the aid in his power. He is a good friend of your Father's and of mine.

Your affectionate Uncle,   James Woodrow.

ALS (WP, DLC) with WWhw notation on env.: "Ans. 6/9/83."

From Janet Woodrow Wilson, with Two Enclosures

My darling Son,   Wilmington, N. C. June 7th 83.

[Replying to WW's letter of June 1, JWW complains that James Bones has sold without her consent part of the lands in Dodge County, Nebraska, in which she had an interest. Having agreed reluctantly to an earlier mortgage, she now expresses opposition to another.]

. . . Well, now I have expressed myself, you have not received much help have you. I think anything will be better than having anything *whatever to do with any mortgage.* So I repeat do the best you can. Will the portion turned over to us be really worth the valuation put upon our share of land—viz $10,000? You know that was what James has repeatedly said. Does James B. know that his "Power of Atty" is cancelled? If not he should understand it at once. I am glad you have a safe adviser like Mr. Brower.

As to Miss Ellie Lou—of course I am greatly taken by surprise—not by what you say of her appearance and character—for I have heard all that about her before—& to me, she seemed very attractive and lovely. But I felt distressed that you should be involved in any way just yet. As if you succeed, there will needs be a weary waiting. However I will write you again more fully—when I hear farther. In the mean time your father will add a few lines. Josie joins me in love unbounded.

Yours   most lovingly   Mother.

ALS (WP, DLC) with WWhw notation on env.: "Ans 6/9/83."

E N C L O S U R E   I

From Joseph Ruggles Wilson

Dear Son: [Wilmington, N. C., c. June 7, 1883]

I enclose the within which speaks for itself. The "American" seems to have acted tolerably handsomely after all.

Affy—Father.

ALS (WP, DLC), written on verso of Howard M. Jenkins to WW, May 15, 1883.

7

777777777777

ENCLOSURE II

From Howard M. Jenkins

Dear Sir: THE AMERICAN, Philadelphia, May 15, 1883

Herewith I send check for $30, the price agreed on for the two essays submitted for the "College Prize" Contest, in 1881,[1] and also a receipt for *The American*, to May 11, 1883. The check was drawn several months ago, and its forwarding neglected, until the receipt of the note of Mr. J. R. Wilson brought the matter to mind. Please acknowledge receipt and oblige.

The $3. forwarded has been applied to payment for a new year, as shown by receipt enclosed.

Very Respectfully,   Howard M. Jenkins

ALS (WP, DLC).

[1] For information about WW's participation, see the note at May 1, 1881.

EDITORIAL NOTE
WILSON AND HIS CALIGRAPH

Wilson purchased his first typewriter, a No. 2 Caligraph,[1] from the Atlanta firm of Tewksbury and Cromelin on June 8, 1883, only nine years after the first practical typewriter had been put on the American market. Why he decided to spend $87.00 for such a purpose so soon after he had decided to abandon the practice of law and enter graduate school is not clear. He may have thought that a typewriter would be useful in his graduate work at The Johns Hopkins University, but it is more likely that he thought that it would improve his efficiency as a writer and thus advance his literary career. However that may have been, his use of the Caligraph, and later of the Hammond typewriter, became an important part of his systematic method of work.

By advanced technological standards, the No. 2 Caligraph with its six rows of keys would be considered a monstrosity. Nevertheless, Wilson chose it rather than the then available Remington No. 2, which had a shift for capital letters and was a faster and sturdier machine.[2]

[1] The Caligraph was chiefly designed, under the supervision of George Washington Yost, by Franz X. Wagner, a German mechanic. Its manufacturer, the American Writing Machine Company, first put it on the market in 1881 in two models: No. 1, which had only capital letters, and No. 2, which had separate keys for upper and lower case. The type bars of No. 2 struck the paper on a polygonal platen at a point on the under side of the carriage; this made visible writing impossible. Early advertising claims that it was faster than the Remington because of its double keyboard were erroneous. See Richard N. Current, *The Typewriter and the Men Who Made It* (Urbana, Ill., 1954), pp. 98-105.

[2] The first practical typewriter, designed for the most part by Christopher Latham Scholes, was manufactured and put on the market in 1874 by E. Remington & Sons, for two partners, James Densmore and the same Yost who later was to have a hand in the making of the Caligraph. The first model had only capital letters, but the addition of a shift in 1878 made it possible to type letters in both upper and lower case. For a time it seemed that the Caligraph would outsell the Remington, but the advent of touch typing proved unquestionably that the latter was the faster machine. *ibid*, pp. 50-105.

Perhaps the fact that the Caligraph sold for approximately forty dollars less than the Remington was the decisive factor. In mid-June 1883, when he returned to Rome to resume in earnest his courtship of Ellen Louise Axson, he carried the Caligraph with him, using it only two hours after his arrival to type a note inviting her to a concert.[3] This note is the first extant document from his new machine.

While his Caligraph was still relatively new, Wilson wrote other personal letters on it. One of these brought a tart postscript from his cousin, Jessie Bones Brower: "Be sure you don't write to either Ellie Lou or me on that machine. We dont like it. (I speak for both.)"[4] And good-natured Hiram Woods expressed a decided preference for Wilson's "own hand-writing."[5] Later on Wilson seems to have used the Caligraph less frequently for personal letters. He also put his Caligraph to early use while helping to settle the estate of his mother's brother, William Woodrow. Having received power of attorney from his mother, he worked during the latter part of June 1883 with his uncle, James W. Bones, trustee of the estate, preparing a deed of partition, which was executed at Rome on June 27. Later on he typed other documents relating to this estate.

The first long item to come from Wilson's Caligraph was his article, "Committee or Cabinet Government?", which he sent to Robert Bridges on August 10, 1883, for submission to Jonas Libbey, editor of the *Princeton Review*. "It [the Caligraph]," Wilson wrote, "is an immense convenience; but I prefer to write to my friends *in my own hand*." The task that Wilson set for himself of making typescripts of the essays which eventually became his first major work, *Congressional Government*, was much more arduous. From his literary manuscripts and his letters to Ellen Louise Axson, it is possible to follow step by step the progress that he made on this undertaking. Between December 1883 and the end of March 1884, he drafted the first three chapters of this work in longhand and typed most of them on his Caligraph.[6] On March 30, 1884, when he had almost finished this phase of his work, he wrote to Ellen Louise Axson: "On last Thursday my Caligraph was going all day long, as it was also on Friday and Saturday: for 'essay No. 3' was finished on Wednesday evening and had then to be copied in the fair hand of my machine." The copying of the three essays, he noted, was "by no means a small job" since he estimated they would amount to about 170 pages of "caligraphiscript" by the time he had copied the forty remaining pages.[7] Later, writing from Wilmington, North Carolina, he told of drafting in longhand the last two chapters of this work and of dreading the "tedious drudgery" of copying them on his typewriter: "I have to make *two* copies of Nos. 5 and 6, as I did the others, and that means an almost endless grinding at the caligraph."[8]

[3] WW to Ellen Louise Axson, June 14, 1883.
[4] Jessie Bones Brower to WW, July 15, 1883.
[5] Hiram W. Woods, Jr., to WW, Sept. 10, 1884, Vol. 3.
[6] The WWhw notation, "Dec. 1883 to March 1884," at the front of the first three chapters of his typescript (WP, DLC), indicates that the typing was finished near the end of March 1884.
[7] WW to Ellen Louise Axson, March 30, 1884, Vol. 3.
[8] WW to Ellen Louise Axson, Sept. 6, 1884, Vol. 3.

Wilson typed many more pages on his Caligraph during the next eight years. Among the shorter items extant are such essays as "The Author Himself," "The Character of Democracy in the United States," and "Political Sovereignty," as well as lectures on "Democracy" and "Leaders of Men." It is likely, too, that he used his Caligraph to prepare the printer's copy of his longest book, *The State*, published in 1889, though this cannot be determined for certain because the manuscript is not extant. In addition, he used his Caligraph frequently during the years 1891 and 1892 to type long, detailed outlines for his Princeton and Johns Hopkins lectures on international law, history of law, jurisprudence, and political economy.[9]

Most significantly, he used his Caligraph to type from his first draft (in shorthand) of *Division and Reunion* a second draft, which ran to about 575 pages.[10] This typing of a draft from shorthand notes was a technique that he employed most effectively in the years ahead, especially while he was President of the United States. It was more than a mere copying from the shorthand since he often made changes as he typed.

After using his Caligraph for about eight years, Wilson began to consider a change in machines. "As for typewriters," he wrote Albert Bushnell Hart in 1891, "this is a No. 2 Caligraph which I have been using since 1883 with not a little satisfaction. And yet, having my due share of human nature, I am not satisfied at all. I suspect the Hammond is a better machine for 'literary fellers,' because of its variety of type and visible writing."[11] The worn condition of his Caligraph, particularly of the type, also may have prompted him to consider discarding it.

Wilson made the change near the end of January 1893. One section of his notes on the history of law (dated "Jan. 16, 1893") was typed on his Caligraph, but two weeks later he wrote a letter to Winthrop M. Daniels on a different typewriter—probably a Hammond, the brand of typewriter that he was to use for the rest of his life.[12]

[9] See the large body of WW's academic lecture notes, WP, DLC.
[10] See the Editorial Note, "Wilson's Study and Use of Shorthand," Vol. I.
[11] WW to A. B. Hart, May 22, 1891, to be printed in a later volume.
[12] WW to Winthrop M. Daniels, Jan. 30, 1893, to be printed in a later volume.

From Tewksbury and Cromelin

Atlanta, Ga. June 8, 1883

Received of Mr. Woodrow Wilson eighty seven ($87.) dollars in full payment for one No. 2 M. R. T. Caligraph.

Tewksbury & Cromelin

Typed receipt, signed (WP, DLC).

From Janet Woodrow Wilson

My darling Son—   Wilmington, N. C. June 12th 1883.

I am sorry you were *perplexed* by my last letter. I thought it necessary to let you know all about the matter in question—but certainly had no idea of distressing you. I fear from what you say in yours received today, that you think I still make a point of retaining a portion of the land near Fremont. I want to make it very clear, that I want *nothing* now—except that the *best possible division may be made*. As matters now stand, all *sentiment* is out [of] the question—so, my darling, let the Dodge land go—if you think it to our interest—consider *only* that I want you to be quite sure that whatever decisions you come to, I shall be satisfied that you have acted for the best—done the best that *could* be done. I repeat, that I *do not care* which you decide upon—for I am sure you will do the best that can be done for our interest. Certainly I would not sacrifice one cent in order to retain any part of the Dodge Co. land. I think from what you say that it is possible that the prospects of the other county are quite as good. But *you* must judge—looking at the matter all round. I feel that I am writing very confusedly—but you can make out my meaning.

Dear child, I was distressed only on *your* account. Nothing could give me more happiness than to see you win the sweet girl you speak of for your wife. It was the *weary waiting* that I thought of—and feared *for you*, my precious boy. Whatever *you* wish, *we* will wish for you. But I can bear pain of my own, dear, far better than I can think of your having it to bear—my precious son. Always remember that.

Your father has not been well since our return home. He was quite sick in Lexington—and has not been well since. He wishes to leave sooner than usual this summer—and will go now to Columbia,—before going North—to consult George [Howe] as to his condition. He is very much depressed as to his condition—and longs *for you*, dear. So I beg that you will delay as little as possible on the way. Is it not possible for you to give up your visit to Aiken?—and to delay your visit to Columbia?—or at least shorten it? Please do if you can. I am *very* anxious about your father. I send this to care of Mr. B[rower] that you may get it more promptly. Love unbounded to Jessie & Mr B. Also love to the family at "Helenhurst." Do you know they have not written me a word from there! How is dear little Helen? Love inexpressible from us each one. Most lovingly
Your own   Mother.

ALS (WP, DLC). Addressed to WW care of A. T. H. Brower, Rome, Ga., with note on env.: "Will Mr. B. be kind enough to hand this to W. W. as soon as he reaches R."

To Ellen Louise Axson

Miss Axson,   East Rome, [Ga.] Thursday aft'. [June 14, 1883]

I write in hopes that I am not too late to secure an engagement for to-night. My enjoyment of the concert[1] will be greatly enhanced if I may have the pleasure of your company. I reached town only a couple of hours ago and shall esteem myself very fortunate if it should prove possible for me to hear the concert with you. Had I known long enough before-hand just when I should reach Rome, I should have written from Atlanta to beg this favour.

Very sincerely yours,   Woodrow Wilson.

WWTLS (WP, DLC).
[1] At the Rome Female College that same evening.

From Ellen Louise Axson

Mr Wilson,   [Rome, Ga.,] Thursday [June 14, 1883].

I am sincerely sorry that a previous engagement will deprive me of the pleasure of your company tonight. I would have been glad of the opportunity to welcome you back to Rome.

Sincerely your friend,   Ellen Axson.

ALS (WC, NjP).

From Janet Woodrow Wilson

My darling Son,   Wilmington, N. C. June 21st 83

I have been waiting anxiously, for the news that the *"division"* *has been accomplished*—and for all particulars concerning it. I cannot feel at all at rest while things are as they are. I hope, dear, you will let me have the satisfaction of hearing what I so much desire without delay.

I must confess I was sorely disappointed, when your letter came, to find that you still wished to delay your return home. Your father says he would not have you come on his account, if you are reluctant. I need not assure you that we would not, either of us, wish you to sacrifice *anything* in the way of your own happiness. But *I do not believe that* your present plan is the best way to bring about that happiness. Miss Ellie has seen enough of you to know whether or not she likes you—enough at least to consent to *correspond* with you. And that is your true plan—the *only* plan you can adopt under the circumstances. I do not think it will do you any good to linger longer in Rome than is necessary to accomplish your business. If you were in a condition to marry, then it might be desirable for you to remain & push matters. I need not assure you, my precious boy, that you have our warmest sympathy in this matter. From all I have ever heard of Ellie Lou I feel assured that there does not live a sweeter or purer girl than she. So that if you succeed in winning her, some day, no one will be glad[d]er than I. How is her health now? She used to be very frail. . . .

With warmest love to dearest Jessie & Mr. Brower—& kisses for sweet baby.   Lovingly Yours   Mother.

P.S. omitted. ALS (WP, DLC).

From Edward Ireland Renick

Dear Wilson,   Atlanta 6/23/83

I have been appointed the "Nation's" Agt. & I want to make you a proposition. I consider that I owe you at least $1.00—if I am to be the sole possessor of the papers sent to Renick & Wilson. Allow me to settle the debt in the following manner. Send me $2.00 whenever you choose & receive from me a year's subscription of the "Nation."

Will you be so good as to send me some Rome subscribers? I want the circulation of this paper to increase in the South. So do you. Besides, I want to make some money for my trip. It may be that Mr. Brower's subscription is about to expire. If so, I should like the renewal to be sent me.

Hammond does not think any damages could be recovered from the Pullman Co.

When will you be here? Gaddy goes Monday. All miss you. Remember me to Mr. Brower. I often think of you & that brown eyed lassie "who reads what we read."

                    Yours as ever   Renick

ALS (WP, DLC) with an acrostic in WWhw on env.: "U. R. A. Bu. T. L. N."

To Ellen Louise Axson

Miss Axson,   East Rome [Ga.] Monday morning [June 25, 1883]

I am permitted by Jessie to write, on her behalf and in her stead, to beg that you will go with us on the picnic which we have planned for next Thursday [June 28]. I should—no, not I—I forgot that I was not writing for myself—*Jessie* would be sorely disappointed if you should be again prevented from going with us; and she thinks it safest, therefore, to ask in good season.

I am tempted to add a request of my own—even at the risk of seeming a little selfish and grasping—namely, that you will take a walk with me this afternoon. Since I must leave for home on Friday morning next, I am bent, you see, upon crowding as much pleasure as possible into the remaining days of my stay; and I am the bolder in asking the privilege of this walk because I am sure that, if there be *any* reason why you should wish to decline—even though it should be simply *disinclination*—you will be frank enough, and sensible enough of the spirit in which I make the request—to give it plainly.

Mr. Bones informs me that it was announced at the Shorter College exercises yesterday that the concert will be given on *Wednesday* evening,[1] and not on Thursday, as I had thought.

Very sincerely Yours   Woodrow Wilson

P.S. Jessie bids me add this P.S. to say that the invitation to the picnic extends, off [*sic*] course, to Mr. Axson and Eddie;[2] and I must add that, if you are kind enough to wish to walk with me this afternoon, I will call a few minutes after six o'clock.

Yours,   W. W.

ALS (WP, DLC).
[1] June 27, at Nevin's Opera House. Shorter is a women's college in Rome.
[2] ELA's brother, Edward William Axson, born Rome, Ga., March 1, 1876. A.B., Princeton University, 1897; A.M., 1898. Additional study at Massachusetts Institute of Technology, 1898-99. Married Florence Choate Leach, April 9, 1901. Drowned with wife and young son, Edward Stockton, in Etowah River near Creighton, Ga., April 26, 1905.

From Ellen Louise Axson

Mr. Woodrow,   [Rome, Ga.] Monday morning [June 25, 1883].

Very unwillingly, and with the firm conviction that I am the most unfortunate of mortals, I write to tell Jessie with my best thanks, that I won't be able to go on this picnic either. I last evening made an ill-timed engagement to take a boat-ride on that afternoon, and like Sternes starling "I can't get out" of it. Excuse my keeping Lefoy[1] so long, but all this time I have been trying in vain, to devise ways and means of escape.[2]

There is no reason[,] not even—strange to say—*disinclination*, to prevent my saying most truthfully that I will be happy to walk with you this afternoon. With love to Jessie, I remain

Your sincere friend,   Ellen L. Axson.

ALS (WC, NjP).
[1] Lefoy Brower, A. T. H. Brower's son by an earlier marriage.
[2] The date of the picnic was moved to Friday, June 29, and ELA was able to join the party. WW to ELA, Oct. 18 and Nov. 20, 1883, recall much of their conversation at the picnic.

Legal Papers

Deed of Partition

An indenture of two parts, made and executed by and between Jeanie W. Wilson, of Wilmington, in the county of New Hanover, and the State of North Carolina, of the one part, and James W. Bones, trustee of the estate of the late Marion W. Bones, deceased, of Rome, in the county of Floyd, and the State of Georgia, of the other part, this twenty-seventh day of June A.D., 1883.

Whereas, the said Jeanie W. Wilson, in her own right, and the said James W. Bones, as trustee of the estate of Marion W. Bones, deceased, are seized of, and hold as tenants in common, several tracts or parcels of land situate in Townships 21 and 22 in the county of Burt, and several tracts or parcels of land situate in Township 17 in the county of Dodge, in the State of Nebraska, and the said Jeanie W. Wilson, acting in her own right, and the said James W. Bones, acting by virtue of full powers conferred upon him, as trustee, by the last will and testament of Marion W. Bones, deceased, have mutually agreed to make partition of said land and hold their respective moieties in severalty:

Now it is hereby witnessed, that the said Jeanie W. Wilson and James W. Bones, acting severally as aforesaid, do by these presents make a full, perfect, and absolute partition of the aforesaid tracts or parcels of land between them, the said Jeanie W. Wilson and James W. Bones, into two parts, to be divided in manner and form following, *viz*: That the said Jeanie W. Wilson, her heirs and assigns, shall have and enjoy, to the only use of her, the said Jeanie W. Wilson, her heirs and assigns forever, the moiety as follows: The West half of the N. E. quarter, the West half of the S. E. quarter, the East half of the S. W. quarter, and the South half of the N. W. quarter of Section Four (4), Township Twenty-one (21), Range Eleven (11) in the County of Burt; the West half of the N. E. quarter, the East half of the N. W. quarter, the East half of the S. W. quarter, and the N. W. quarter of the S. E. quarter of Section Nine (9), Township Twenty-one (21), Range Eleven (11), in the County of Burt; the East half of the S. W. quarter of Section Ten (10), Township Twenty-one (21), Range Eleven (11), in the County of Burt; the N. E. quarter of the S. E. quarter, the N. W. quarter of the S. E. quarter, and the S. W. quarter of the S. E. quarter of Section Twenty-two (22), Township Twenty-two (22), Range Eleven (11), in the County of Burt; the N. W. quarter of the N. E. quarter and the S. E. quarter of the N. W. quarter of Section Twenty-seven (27), Township Twenty-two (22), Range

Eleven (11), in the County of Burt; and the N. E. quarter of the N. E. quarter of Section Twenty-six (26), Township Twenty-two (22), Range Eleven (11), in the County of Burt, as and for her full moiety, part, and portion of said tracts or parcels of land: And that the said James W. Bones, as trustee of the estate of Marion W. Bones, deceased, and his successors in office, shall have, for the purposes of the trust vested in him by the aforesaid last will and testament of the said Marion W. Bones, deceased, the moiety as follows:

The N. W. quarter and the West half of the N. E. quarter of Section One (1), Township Seventeen (17), Range Seven (7), in the County of Dodge; the West half of the N. E. quarter of Section Eleven (11), Township Seventeen (17), Range Eight (8), in the County of Dodge; in the Section Twelve (12), Township Seventeen (17), Range Eight (8), in the County of Dodge, the North half of the S. W. quarter and those portions of the S. W. quarter of the S. E. quarter and the N. W. quarter of the S. E. quarter which belong to the aforesaid common estate; and in Section Thirteen (13), Township Seventeen (17), Range Eight (8), in the County of Dodge, the N. E. quarter of the N. W. quarter and that portion of the N. W. quarter of the N. E. quarter which belongs to the aforesid common estate, as and for the full moiety, part, and portion of the aforesaid estate of the said Marion W. Bones, deceased, in said tracts or parcels of land. And the said James W. Bones, acting, as aforesaid, as trustee of the estate of Marion W. Bones, deceased, and under full powers vested in him by the last will and testament of the said Marion W. Bones, deceased, doth, in consideration of the premises, and of one dollar paid him, hereby give, grant, lease, release, and confirm to her, the said Jeanie W. Wilson, her heirs and assigns, the aforesaid moiety, &c., and all the interest, right, and title of him, the said James W. Bones, as trustee &c., as aforesaid, and of all or any persons claiming through him, in said moiety, &c. To have and to hold the same, to the said Jeanie W. Wilson, her heirs and assigns, to her and their use forever. And the said Jeanie W. Wilson, in consideration of the premises, and of one dollar to her paid, doth hereby give, grant, lease, release, and confirm to him, the said James W. Bones, as trustee &c., as aforesaid, the aforesaid moiety, &c., and all the interest, right, and title of her, the said Jeanie W. Wilson, in said moiety, &c. To have and to hold the same, to the said James W. Bones, trustee &c., as aforesaid, for the purposes of the trust as aforesaid. And the said James W. Bones, for himself as trustee, &c., as aforesaid, and for all persons claiming through him, doth covenant with the said Jeanie W. Wilson, her heirs and assigns, that she and they shall and may, forever hereafter, have, hold, and enjoy the aforesaid moiety, &c., free and discharged of all right, title, and interest of him, the said James W. Bones, trustee &c., as aforesaid, and of any and all persons claiming through him, therein or thereto, and of all incumbrances upon the same, done or suffered by him. And the said Jeanie W. Wilson, for herself, her heirs, executors, administrators, and assigns, doth covenant with the said James W. Bones, as trustee &c., as aforesaid, and with his successors in office, that he and they shall and may have, hold, and enjoy, for the purposes of the trust, as aforesaid, the aforesaid moiety, &c., free and discharged of all right, title, and interest of her, the said Jeanie W. Wilson, therein or thereto, and of all incumbrances upon the same, done or suffered by her.

In witness whereof, the said parties have hereunto set their hands and seals, the day and year first above written.
Signed, sealed, and delivered in the presence of

Langdon Bowie	James W. Bones, Trustee.	[L.S.]
W. L. Graves	Jeanie W. Wilson	[L.S.]
	by Woodrow Wilson	atty. in fact.

Georgia—Floyd County,
    Before me, C. O. Stillwell, a Notary Public in and for the State and County aforesaid, personally appeared James W. Bones and Woodrow Wilson and acknowledged the above-written indenture to be their own act and deed.
        Given under my hand and official seal this the 27 day of
        June, 1883.
                    C. O. Stillwell   Notary Public.

WWhw and WWTDS (WP, DLC). Entered in numerical index and filed for record, July 20, 1883, 9:30 a.m., Book I of Deeds, p. 96 (Dodge County, Nebr.); also entered in numerical index and filed for record, Aug. 7, 1883, 2:00 p.m., Book R of Deeds, p. 196, Burt County, Nebr. Att.: quit-claim deed, WWTD, executed by Maria Bones of Augusta, Ga., Sept. 10, 1884; indenture of two parts, WWT, printed below, made and executed between Jeanie W. Wilson and James W. Bones, c. June 27, 1883; WWhw memorandum evaluating worth of notes and lands left in the estate of William Woodrow and setting forth proposed division of this estate between JWW and James W. Bones, trustee.

[c. June 27, 1883]
    An indenture of two parts, made and executed by and between Jeanie W. Wilson, of Wilmington, in the county of New Hanover, and the State of North Carolina, of the one part, and James W. Bones, trustee of the estate of the late Marion W. Bones, deceased, of Rome, in the county of Floyd, and the State of Georgia, of the other part, this [blank] day of June, A.D. 1883.

WHEREAS: The said Jeanie W. Wilson, in her own right, and the said James W. Bones, as trustee of the estate of Marion W. Bones, deceased, are seized and possessed as tenants in common of several tracts or parcels of land situate in Townships 21 and 22 in the county of Burt, in the State of Nebraska, valued at eight thousand nine hundred and eighty dollars ($8,980), and several tracts or parcels of land situate in Township 17 in the county of Dodge, in the State of Nebraska, valued at eight thousand six hundred and fifty dollars and ninety-six cents ($8,650.96); and of certain personal property consisting of one thousand eight hundred and sixty-three dollars and seventeen cents ($1,863.17) in money, and of certain unmatured notes, of the value of sixteen thousand two hundred and seventeen dollars and forty-two cents ($16,217.-42), given for the purchase money of certain other tracts or parcels of land in said counties of Burt and Dodge in said State of Nebraska, said assets and said first-mentioned lands representing a total value of thirty-five thousand seven hundred and eleven dollars and fifty-five cents ($35,711.55);

WHEREAS: By deed indented, made and executed by and between the said Jeanie W. Wilson and the said James W. Bones, and bearing date the twenty-seventh day of June, A.D. 1883, partition was made, in due and legal form, of said tracts and parcels of land first above named; by which said deed indented there was set apart to the Jeanie W. Wilson, in her own right, land of the estimated value of eight thousand nine hundred and eighty dollars ($8,980); and to the said James W. Bones, as trustee of the estate of the said Marion W. Bones, deceased, land of the estimated value of eight thousand six hundred and fifty dollars and ninety-six cents ($8,-650.96);

WHEREAS: It appears from an examination of the accounts of the said common estate of the said Jeanie W. Wilson and the said Marion W. Bones, deceased, that the entire present interest of the said Jeanie W. Wilson in the said common estate is eighteen thousand three hundred and twenty-two dollars and twenty-cents ($18,322.22), and that the entire present interest of the said James W. Bones, as trustee of the estate of the said Marion W. Bones, deceased, is Seventeen thousand three hundred and eighty-four dollars and twenty-nine cents ($17,384.29);

And WHEREAS: It is agreed between the said parties that it is wise, proper, and expedient to make a complete and final division of said joint estate between the parties in interest,

Now It Is Hereby Witnessed, That the said Jeanie W. Wilson, acting in her own right, and the said James W. Bones, acting as trustee of the estate of the said Marion W. Bones, deceased, do by these presents make a full, perfect and absolute division of the aforesaid assets of the said common estate between them, the said Jeanie W. Wilson and the said James W. Bones, into two parts, to be divided as follows, viz; That the said Jeanie W. Wilson shall have, as and for her full part and portion of the said assets, the following notes, to the amount of eight thousand six hundred and thirty-five dollars and seventy-two cents ($8,635.72), namely, the notes (together with their securities) made and executed by Charles W. Sheldon, Charles A. Jack and wife, William T. Munger and Charles H. Pease, for land situate in the counties of Dodge and Burt, in the State of Nebraska, for the total sum of eight thousand six hundred and thirty-five dollars and seventy-two cents ($8,635.-72), and money to the amount of seven hundred and six dollars and fifty cents ($706.50), all right and title to which are hereby renounced by the said James W. Bones, for and in behalf of himself, as trustee of the estate of the said Marion W. Bones, deceased, an[d] of all those whom as trustee he represents; and receipt of which is hereby acknowledged by the said Jeanie W. Wilson, who, in consideration of such receipt, renounces all further claim and title to the other assets of the aforesaid common estate: And that the said James W. Bones, as trustee of the estate of the said Marion W. Bones, deceased, and his successors in office, shall have, for the purposes of the trust vested in him, or them, by the last will and testament of the said Marion W. Bones deceased, as and for the full part and portion of the aforesaid estate of the said Marion W. Bones, deceased, in said assets of the aforesaid common estate, the following notes, to the amount of seven thousand five hundred and eighty-one dollars and seventy cents ($7,581.70), namely, the notes (together with their securities) made and executed by M. S. Cotterell, John Shartell, John Rock, W. B. Newton, John Shartell [sic], D. Kohler, J. H. and S. Tyler, C. W. Sheldon, M. Smith, E. A. Culbertson, and John Black, for land situate in the counties of Burt and Dodge, in the State of Nebraska, for the total sum of seven thousand five hundred and eighty-one dollars and seventy cents ($7,581.70), and money to the amount of one thousand one hundred and fifty-one dollars and sixty-three cents ($1,-151.63), all right and title to which are hereby renounced by the said Jeanie W. Wilson, and receipt of which is hereby acknowledged by the said James W. Bones, who, in consideration of such receipt, renounces, for and in behalf of himself, as trustee of the estate of the said Marion W. Bones, deceased, and of all those whom as trustee he represents, all further claim and title to the other assets of the aforesaid common estate.

In witness whereof, the said parties have hereunto set their hands and seals, the day and year first above mentioned.
Signed, sealed and delivered in the presence of

W. L. Graves	J W Bones Trustee	(L.S)
R. J. Gwattney	Jeanie W. Wilson	(L.S.)
N. P. Floyd l.s.	by Woodrow Wilson,	Atty in fact.

WWTDS (WP, DLC). Att. to deed of Partition between Jeanie W. Wilson and James W. Bones, June 27, 1883.

To Ellen Louise Axson

My dear Miss Axson,   Wilmington, N. Carolina, July 4th 1883

Being much too eager to avail myself of the privilege of writing to you to wait until I reached home to do so, I commenced a letter to you while I was in Aiken; but that letter grew to very considerable proportions as its composition progressed, and there were two things in the way of my finishing it: I felt that to steal so much time for letter-writing from the short two days I was to spend with my kind friends in Aiken was selfish; and I had no pen and ink at command but my "Caligraph." I did not like my letters to you to be machine-written, because I wanted to put into them as much as possible of my natural self, and, as Hamerton says in one of his books, we all of us acquire a personal style in penmanship as we do in the use of language, and the same strong marks of idiosyncrasy exist in handwriting which are to be found in the sketches of artists. So, I gave up writing then, even in face of the fact that by writing early I could the sooner earn the chief reward of the correspondence, namely, hearing from you.

Not having your happy faculty of finding only amusement in all the incidents of a railway journey, the Saturday [June 30] of my departure from Rome dragged along very tediously for me, and it seemed a cruelly long stretch from Rome to Augusta; for what is a man to do whose eyes are good for nothing under such circumstances, and whose eyelids must droop irresistibly into sleep, if they are not kept open by interest in the doings of fellow-passengers, who do not often do anything interesting?

While my train was leaving Rome I stood out on the back platform, to take a last look at "Oakdene," and up–"Maiden Lane," is'nt it?–; not because I thought to see anybody in that street whom I wanted to see (for I knew that there had been a picnic the day

U. R. A Bu; T. L. N.

2nd 1883

The first page of Wilson's shorthand draft
of his letter to Ellen Louise Axson,
July 4, 1883.

before, and that the picnicers would probably be too tired to think of rising betimes in the morning) but because—because the street runs nicely up the hill, and might be expected to look peacefully pretty beneath its generous shade trees in the early morning light! I was, however, very soon past Maiden Lane, very soon past even the big rock that juts out into the river, and I had to settle down into dreary waiting for my journey's end.

During the second half of my ride, after Atlanta had been left behind and Augusta was in prospect, I tried to read. But that was a literally painful failure, and my only remaining resource was to find diversion in watching two fat women who devoted all their energies to the constant gratification of their appetites, except during those periods of unrest which so frequently visited them, in which they were harassed with anxiety as to their possible distance from their stopping-place, and feverishly busy in preparation of their lunches and luggage for immediate disembarkation; the young lady who, though she had been honoured at the station in Atlanta with a good-bye kiss from no less a person than the Governor of the State, was immensely amused, and even a little flattered, by the assiduous professional attentions of the news and fruit boy; and the countryman with voluminously bandaged eye, who kept his one working orb vigilantly alert to spy out every opportunity for gallant service of the two fat women, furnishing them, in his finest manner, with a card containing tables of all the distances, and playing his humble part with a blindness of devotion which prevented his perceiving the ludicrousness of their standing for the last five miles of their journey in instant preparation for departure, only to keep the train waiting beyond its usual time, when their station was finally reached, because in the exigency of that last moment they proved unequal to the weight of their bundles, and femininely unable to cope with the sleekness of their watermelon. But even these interesting people did not much interfere with my sleep.

There is not much pretty scenery on the ride I had to take. The prettiest things I saw were the wild flowers that abound on this side of the Savannah river. These flowers all reminded me of you —though it may be that I should have thought of you without their assistance; for I noticed that some thought of you was connected with every thing else that I saw. There are few things in philosophy more curious than this thing called association of ideas!

I believe that I told you before leaving—did I not?—that I was to stop in Aiken a couple of days on my way home, to visit some Atlanta friends. Well, that is a family that you would like to meet, I think. Mrs. Boylston, with whom I boarded in Atlanta for ten months, and who was the kindest of hostesses, is a prim little person who never for a single moment forgets that she has in her veins the blood of the Draytons of South Carolina. Her love for gossip is as great as her eldest son's love for good eating; her religious principles are as colourless as her skin; and her prejudices are as close-fitting as the body of her plain black gown; but she is kind-hearted and high bred, is stedfast in her friendships, and is anxious to do her duty always—is, in a word, a woman whose faults amuse and whose good qualities win esteem. Mrs. Boylston is staying in Aiken with her sister, Mrs. Mayrant—a person who is all nerves and digestive organs—whom also I knew and liked in Atlanta. But it was Mrs. Mayrant's daughter whom I went to Aiken to see. Miss Katie was in Atlanta with her aunt, Mrs. B. during nine of the ten months of my stay in the house, and of course I got to know her very well indeed. No one who really knows her could fail to be interested in her, though I may say, without even hinting the least abatement of praise, that she is not a woman of the sort most attractive to me. She has a frail beauty which is interesting in itself, and she is intelligent and affectionate; but she could not furnish happiness except for one's leisure hours. Being without strength of body, she lacks hopefulness of disposition. One could only shelter and care for her, as for a delicate flower, which cannot bloom in all weathers. But Miss Katie, though most attractive and companionable in holiday hours, has many sterling qualities which speak the true woman; and she has that keen sense of the subtler forms of humour which is never given to coarse minds. I have spent many pleasant days with her, and I value her friendship very highly indeed, for the friendship of such women means something.

Aiken is an interesting place in which to make a short stay. Its fine wide streets, lined with splendid shade trees, its leisurely ways and pervading silence, make it just the place in which to rest, dismissing all thought of the world's cares, and even of the world's peculiar pleasures. It is pleasanter to visit it at this season, I imagine, than in the winter, for then it is over-run with Northern invalids, its silence invaded by their coughs, and its peace made gloomy and oppressive by daily visions of death.

You may imagine how much shocked and alarmed I was this morning upon reaching home to find that my dear mother had been alarmingly ill with that malarial fever which wastes with its sluggish persistence, seeming to set itself simply to block all the recuperating forces of nature. She is much better now than she was, tho' she is still wan and distressingly unlike her natural self.

I am told that there are now many similar cases of fever here; but one never realizes how ugly these malarial influences are until one's own home is invaded by them.

But I must not weary you with this first letter. When one writes for his own pleasure, he knows not when or where to stop. May I not hope for an early answer? I shall wait for it as a thirsty man longs for cool water. I cannot tell you how much my happiness depends on the continuance and growth of our friendship, which has opened so propitiously, and I feel that the present hope of its growth depends on this correspondence which your sweetly accorded assent has permitted me to open.

With kindest regards to Mr. Axson, and love to Eddie,
Yours most sincerely,   Woodrow Wilson

ALS (WP, DLC). There is a WWsh draft of this letter in WP, DLC, dated July 2, 1883.

From Kate Drayton Mayrant

Dear Mr. Wilson   [Aiken, S.C.] July 6th. 1883.

I received your note yesterday afternoon, and cannot let another day pass without telling you how very, very sorry I am to hear of your Mother's illness, and how deeply I sympathize with you that your return home should be so sad, but I hope and trust that the danger will soon be over, and you will have her quite well again to pet and spoil you. . . .

Oh, I do miss you awfully! the day you left I felt as if some member of the household had died, was in the depths of the blues and did not have even the luxury of crying, for if I wink they want to know the reason why: it does seem so hard that your visit, to which I looked forward so long and with so much pleasure, should have passed away so quickly, almost before I could realize you were here,—but I did enjoy it very much, far more than I dared tell you, for every time I started to speak of it I felt like crying at the thought that you would soon go, that is one of my great faults you know— spoiling today's meeting by thinking of tomorrow's parting—it was very nice of you to come to this dull old place to see us, but we *did* appreciate and enjoy your visit very much. . . .

I cannot write more this morning, but soon will write again. You see when I perceive you have a good reason for writing only a few lines to me I can pass it over and give you a letter in return. Hoping to hear soon of your Mother's improvement I am, with lots of love,
Your affectionate friend   Katie D. Mayrant.

ALS (WP, DLC).

From Ellen Louise Axson

Dear Mr. Wilson,   Rome, [Ga.] July 12, 1883.

As I have always discovered in myself a strange disinclination to "take my pen in hand"—the result of inertia I suppose; and only exceeded by my dislike to ever laying it down again when once "started"—I will "make a break," and utilize the present moment for that purpose, though certain to be shortly interrupted. I have promised that big brother of mine[1] to play chess—so-called, with him as soon as the present amusement, a sparring match with "the young one" begins to weary him. I will venture to say,—"en passant"— that you never saw such parodies on that prince of games as we perpetrate. We are both beginners and likely to remain so, for Stockton says "its an awful bore to think," and a guilty conscience tells me that I take it by no means as seriously as I should. It would drive a devotee mad to see us approach those solemn mysteries in so light and frivolous a spirit.

But one will lay ruthless hands on even the noble game of chess when in extremities like mine, viz. with a brother to be ministered unto, who is in the deplorable predicament of having nothing to do, and all summer to do it in—A condition than which I can imagine nothing more utterly unendurable. Indeed he seems to find it so. It is unfortunate that nature does'nt permit one to hang *all* day on a gymnastic pole with one's head down.

Our wanderer [Edward W. Axson] was restored to us on Monday last, to our great delight; the pleasure of seeing him being enhanced by the pleasure of finding him so much improved. He is a dear boy, and has remarkably "winning ways." It is always interesting to watch children grow and develop, but when they belong to ones-self, and are developing in the right direction, it is far more than merely *interesting*.

I was glad to learn from your very welcome letter, which was duly received on Friday, of your prosperous journey. Methinks you *do* have the faculty for extracting amusement from the incidents of travel, and of communicating it as well. I was much entertained by the account of your "compagnons de voyage"; also by the graphic pen picture of your Aiken friends.

But can it be possible that you have been domiciled for nine months with so charming a young lady as this Miss Katie without serious consequences? Every person of experience will tell you that such a thing is contrary to all precedent, and subversive of all principles. I scarcely know whether to be very credulous, and accept it as a beautiful vindication of my still fondly cherished, though sometimes slightly shaken, faith in "platonics"—or, what?

Though it grows late, I will now try to finish this, the "interruption" having come, and, I am happy to add, finally gone. It came in a form even less desirable than burlesque chess—viz. as one of those wretched beings who "don't take no interest in nothin." Alas, alas, with what blank eyes do some of our fellow-mortals look out on life, and what a totally unmeaning affair they find, or make it! Shakspeare did'nt include, among his seven ages, the "automatic stage," yet not less surely do multitudes travel that way. Perhaps it was not so, in his time; perhaps it is a nineteenth century distemper unknown to the fresh and vigorous young manhood of his "Merry England." But surely in our day it is melancholy to see how large a proportion of the middle-aged there are who appear to have reached that condition, to whom "the world, unutterably fair, is duller than a witlings jest." If I thought it a necessary consequence of growing old I would humbly beg leave to go out and hang myself while I had enough enthusiasm left to accomplish so much—even the enthusiasm of despair. For what is more to be dreaded than life with nothing—real or imaginary—to make it "worth while"? Certainly, no positive sorrow, which may at least be met and borne with faith and courage. But this is more terrible than pain, it is paralysis! Truly "it *is* an uneasy lot to be present at this great spectacle of life, and never to be free from a small, hungry, shivering self, never to be fully possessed by the glory we behold, never to have our consciousness rapturously transformed into the vividness of a thought, the ardour of a passion or the energy of an action!" But what a lengthened tirade is this into which I have been betrayed! I must, after all, have been infected by my friend, tonight, simply grumbling *at* him instead of *with* him. On second thoughts too he *is* right about life; this *is* a weary world, full of manifold trials and tribulations, for example, witness those I am suffering at present with *pens*! This is the fourth I have tried, all equally superannuated.

I am sorry that the pleasure of your home-coming was marred in so sad a manner. We learned with deep regret of the past illness, and present weakness of your mother. But the worse being over, I hope she will now rapidly regain strength, and soon be quite herself again. You should send her here to try the "balmy breezes" of East Rome; which, besides its pure air, possesses another strong attraction, you will agree with me, in the shape of a *baby*.[2] These little creatures grow away from one so fast, that your mother will need to take time by the forelock if she wishes to see her at the truly angelic stage. I stopped there the other day (to return the pamphlet, which I persistantly forgot to give you) and saw the "infant phenomenon." Her cup of happiness, full to the brim before, is now running over; for she is in short dresses, and has made the astonishing discovery that she has a full set of *live toes*, the prettiest playthings in the world!

By the way, Jessie professed to be much concerned for your saf[e]ty, and disturbed at not having heard from you. Perhaps I should have relieved her anxiety, and, especially, have given her the news from your mother, but—I didnt! Very stupid, no doubt. But it is the way of the world to put very astonishing constructions on the simplest facts, and I feared they might not be any wiser in their generation than "tout le monde."

Such a sad thing has happened in our little circle since you left. You remember that Agnes Tedcastle could not go on our picnic because she was busy preparing to receive a friend, who was to arrive on Sat! She failed to come, but wrote that her examinations being just over on Thursday, she was too exhausted to travel then, would reach here on the next Tuesday. On that day they went to the depot, George to Kingston, to meet her, failed to find her, but instead, received a telegram, soon after, that she was *dead*. Literally, killed by commencements. It is *so* sad! She was such a bright, beautiful girl, remarkably lovely both in person and character. She was engaged to George West, a young physician here. Agnes had invited her principally on that account, as it was a long engagement and they were much separated—George being a great friends of hers too. And now he has gone to her funeral! But it is a shame to draw on your sympathy at such length for people you know nothing about. And now as it grows late, and this letter grows long, I will close, with assurances of my sympathy in the task that awaits you, in deciphering this. My poor grandmother has long ago ceased to attempt anything of the sort, adopting the plan of Dr Chalmer's mother, who put his letters on the shelf "till Tammy cooms home to read them himsel."

The special characteristic of my "hand" is that it is hopelessly careless, chaotic, and unintelligible. What mental idiosyncrasies does that denote? I ought to be inspired or shamed into a effort at something better in answering a letter as clear and beautiful as copper-plate or caligraphy (?) but I fear I am past shame.

With kindest regards from all to all, believe me

Your sincere friend,   Ellen L. Axson.

July 18

I wrote this, as you will perceive, several nights ago; and early the next morning heard with deep concern of your mother's serious illness. In the shocked surprise of the moment I could not get my consent to trouble you with this foolish scrawl. But upon second thoughts, hearing only cheering reports from Mr. Bones, have concluded that I will send it after all, late as it is.

I can't tell you how much we sympathize with you in this trouble. Well do I know all that road. We had a case of it just six years ago; and how vividly comes back to me, as I write, those long, still, breathless summer days. The best wish I can make is that all may go as well with you as it did with us, then—ah me! I earnestly trust, and fully believe, that you will have no greater trial than this long suspense, and even that lightened by a strong hope. From Mr. Bones account I should judge it to be one of those low fevers, which carefully watched, are very readily and surely kept under control. How does the temperature run? I remember how, in those days, all the wheels of life seemed to revolve about that little instrument of torture, the thermometer. But I have already taken too much of your time. With assurances of heart-felt sympathy; believe me

Truly your friend,   E. L. Axson.

ALS (WP, DLC).

[1] Stockton Axson, born Rome, Ga., June 6, 1867, was named after his grandfather, Isaac Stockton Keith, but all his adult life used only the name Stockton. Attended Davidson College and the University of Georgia. A.B., Wesleyan University, 1890, A.M., 1892, L.H.D., 1914. Instructor and assistant professor of English, University of Vermont, 1892-94. Staff lecturer, American Society for University Extension, 1894-96; assistant professor and professor of English literature, Adelphi College, 1896-99. Assistant professor of English literature, Princeton University, 1899-1904; professor, 1904-13. Professor of English, Rice Institute, 1913-35. Secretary, American Red Cross, 1917-19. Died Feb. 26, 1935.

[2] Jessie Bones Brower's baby, Marion.

From Jessie Bones Brower

Dear Cousin Woodrow,   East Rome [Ga.] 15 July 1883.

. . . When do you leave for Baltimore next fall? Ellie Lou called on me not long after you left, & I could not refrain from a little guarded teasing, which she took with the prettiest of pretty vivid blushes. She asked while here to see my photograph albums, & evidently with one purpose, as she has looked through them before, if I mistake not. She thought your likeness splendid, & I noticed, although she did not see that I was watching her, that she turned back to the front part of the album a number of times before she got to the end. I think you have every reason to hope for the very best some day. I have not been able to see her again as I have been so very busy, & her Father has been sick too, but I hope to get to see her the last part of this week. . . .

All join in love to you all,

Yours as ever, &c, &c,   Jessie B. B.

P.S. Be sure you don't write to either Ellie Lou or me on that machine. We dont like it. (I speak for both.)

ALS (WP, DLC) with WWhw notation on env.: "Ans. July 25/83."

To Ellen Louise Axson

Miss Ellie Lou,   Wilmington, N.C., July 16th 1883

Will you be amused or glad to receive another letter from me before you have answered my first? If you think that I have written again simply to prove a zeal for the correspondence which needs no encouragement, you will probably be amused; but if you divine the real reason of my writing, you will, I am sure, read with no inclination but one of sympathy. I write for the same reason that has often led me to run, or to sing, or to shout: because I am in high spirits. I am glad and want an outlet for my gladness: I want sympathy, and I write to you because I want your sympathy more than anybody else's.

In a word, my dear mother is very much better, is convalescent, we hope. She has been exceedingly ill—much sicker than I dreamed when I wrote my last letter to you, though then her fever was near its worst. But the doctor had not then pronounced it typhoid—for heaven did not endow him very richly with sense—and we (father, my brother, and I) were too ignorant of the nature of fevers to know at what to be frightened. Imagine the sad plight of the poor lady, left to be nursed through a desperate illness by three awkward, inexperienced, nervous men! And imagine, in pity, your humble servant, later,—now at length thoroughly frightened—sitting up all night in anxious administration of stimulants and medicines! Soon, however, my sister came over from Columbia, an experienced nurse was employed, and the dear patient was brought through. Do you wonder that I am glad, and can you fail to receive with indulgence a letter prompted by such well founded satisfaction?

As soon as mother's recovery is assured and she has gained strength enough for the journey, we must of course be off in search of a change of scene and air; so that, after all, I shall not be in Wilmington all summer, as I expected I should. I shall not be loath to go away, though I must confess that I can ascribe my willingness to get away from Wilmington to none but a very selfish motive. I want to escape the numerous calls I should have to make if I stayed. It will be hard, I am afraid, for you to believe, in view of my repeated and persistent calls at your house while I was in Rome, that I am not fond of visiting; but so it is. I am in a certain sense fond of society—that is, of *some* society—of social gatherings, for example, in which one can find much pleasurable excitement often, and whet his faculties for conversation, at the same time that he learns much from the conversation of others. But it is tremendously irksome to visit most people in their own houses, to have to drive one's mind through long conversations with people with whom one has nothing whatever in common, and for whom one cares not a snap of the finger. So I am secretly glad to give many of my acquaintances here the slip. Visiting young ladies ought, I know, always to be considered by all orthodox persons an improving occupation; but I must say, even at the risk of making you think me abominably conceited, that I find most young ladies exceedingly uninteresting in their own parlours. But let me add right away, as an offset to the conceit of this confession, that I am quite conscious that young ladies generally find me equally tiresome, and often vote me a terrible bore—and that I have not the compensating advantage of being well-favoured and fair to look upon. I do not always, however, I must warn you, wear the decorous manners and cultivate the appearance of serious good sense that I was careful to assume while I was in Rome. On the contrary, I sometimes—shall I confess it?—in some companies, make myself highly popular by making a fool of myself, making any and every diversion rather than be simply dull. I did not want to shock you with the small talk and nonsense in which I often indulge and for which I have a natural propensity; and I would not for the world have expressed to you my liking for the occasional companionship of those girls who love nothing but mischief and fun and frolic. But I can make these disclosures in a letter: for a letter is as convenient as the dark—in either one can make his confessions without too painful a display of embarrassment.

"Which is why I remark," in this connection, that you taught me something about your own sex: namely, that there is, after all, amongst girls a delightful middle class, half-way between those who are cultivated because they can be nothing else and those who charm simply because of their animal spirits, their youth and beauty and attractive feminine ways. I believe you said to me once —did'nt you?—that you never undertook to defend women against disparaging opinions. Well, as far as my own opinions are concerned, women have never stood in need of any defence; but, until I met you, women's charms *did* seem to me to be subject to one very serious limitation. I had longed to meet some woman of my own age who had acquired a genuine love for intellectual pursuits without becoming bookish, without losing her feminine charm; who had taken to the best literature from a natural, spontaneous taste for it, and not because she needed to make any artificial additions to her attractiveness; whose mind had been cultivated without being stiffened or made masculine; who could enter into men's highest pleasures without becoming at all like men in any other respect; and I still thought that "somewhere in the world must be" at least one woman approaching this ideal, though I had about given up expecting to make her acquaintance, and had almost fallen into adopting a low estimate of the young ladies of nowadays. See, therefore, what a delightful lesson you have taught me! If you have not convinced me of the existence of an exceptional class, you have at least convinced me of the existence of an exceptional individual.

I take the liberty of sending you my copy of Hamerton's "*Graphic Arts*,"[1] which I believe you have not read. I know that you will not object to a "second-hand" book, if the *first* hand has been an appreciative one, since books do not deteriorate in the using. This is more presentable than most of my books because it is less scored than most of them with pencil marks and annotations. When I read, in books of my own, on subjects with which I am more or less familiar, I like to mark in various fashions every passage that strikes me either because of its strength or originality of expression, its quaintness, or its sense; besides which marks of emphasis or of critical heed, I often indulge in marginal notes of more or less relevancy. But my pencil was kept out of this book of Hamerton's because I read it with so little previous knowledge of the subject that I had no certain means of judging which of Mr. H's opinions were more just or more original than the others, what information was new and what old. To have preferred one passage to another where everything was new to me would have been like preferring one letter to another in learning my alphabet. I might think x or z much handsomer letters than a, but I should be wofully mistaken in concluding that they were therefore the more useful and notable members of the letter family.

One thing that is constantly forced upon my attention in reading this work is the limited range of the art critic's own peculiar vocabulary. He seems to have so few words of his own, and borrows so freely from the language of other arts. *Scales* of colour are not too hard to imagine, though it is easier to think of scales in music or of scales of weight; but one is somewhat startled by that invasion of musical terms which has overrun the language of the graphic arts, and one's fancy has to be pretty active to follow the art critic when he speaks of light *keys* of colouring, of *notes* of colour, of a *gamut* of degrees, of *tones*, &c., &c. Apparently the eye has fewer words of its own than the ear. It is as if one were to speak of hearing a transparent or iridescent *sound*. May-be the ear, being nearer the tongue than the eye is, has the greater right to use that unruly member and dictate its vocabulary, and so it is not a hardship that the eye has to borrow. Though the eye is the most expressive of the human features, it is silent. It can say much more than the tongue; but the tongue has had pens and pencils made for it, and printing invented for its use, whilst the language of the eye has never been translated into any visible medium. So it is, I may be allowed to suppose, since I am writing nonsense, that no adequate language has been hit upon by the art critic to express the pleasures of the eye, and we have been compelled to ask the ear for the use of its dictionary. It requires, however, a very vigourous effort of the imagination to perceive any affinity between the delicate hues of colour and the high keys of music, though it requires less to appreciate the likeness of unpleasant colours and harsh sounds; and it might be easy to associate sound with a vivid sketch of the planetary systems, if it were drawn with such a clever suggestion of movement as to remind us of the music of the spheres.

But I must really cut this letter short (?) here, lest you should look back upon the day of its receipt as a day of dark visitation. I have written about as much as can be justified by high spirits.

With kindest regards to your father and love to Eddie, and the strongest desire to hear from you,

Yours sincerely,   Woodrow Wilson

ALS (WP, DLC).
    [1] He inscribed it "Woodrow Wilson's compliments to Miss Ellie Lou Axson, July, 1883." The book is now in the possession of Robert R. Cullinane, Washington, D. C.

From Richard Heath Dabney

My dear Tommy: Munich. July 22nd 1883.

It would be difficult for you to imagine how glad I was to hear that you had determined to give up the Law, and turn your attention to more congenial studies. I had often thought that it was a great pity that you had not chosen to become a professor of Political Science instead of a practising attorney. It is my deliberate opinion that one of the principal causes of there being so few Americans of more than local reputation in any of the great fields of Science, is that a very large majority of the ablest young men in the country study law. Law is a subject which by its very nature precludes the possibility of a man's becoming great—a benefactor of the human race as a whole. The greatest lawyer upon earth is still no great man. . . .

If I am glad that you have forsaken the Law and determined to become a professor, still more glad am I that you have selected the very subjects that I have chosen myself. You have considerably the start of me in knowledge of both History and Political Science, but I hope that by industry I may be able to keep enough alongside of you to enable me to feel like your companion on the same great road. It is exceedingly pleasant to me to think, after the joyous college days we have spent together, that our life-paths lead too in the same direction, and that we are both going to strive to come as nearly as possible to the same great goal. . . .

By the way, have you heard that Adams,[1] the assistant professor, (there is no full professor, I believe,) of History at Johns Hopkins, has been elected Prof. of Political Economy at Cornell? He is a free trader, but another man was appointed "lecturer," who is a "protectionist." Unless some one is appointed soon to take Adams' place, I am afraid you won't hear many good lectures at the University next Fall. Comstock, a student of chemistry here, who had a fellowship at Johns Hopkins last year, tells me that Adams is a man of very fine ability. He (Adams) studied under Bluntschli[2] at Heidelberg.

If you don't get the fellowship, why not come to Germany yourself? You would enjoy it exceedingly, and even with the steamer-passage, it would scarcely cost you more than living in Baltimore. . . .   Yours sincerely,   R. H. Dabney.

ALS (WP, DLC) with WWhw notation on env.: "Ans. 2/17/84." Dabney's note on the env. says that this letter has been returned twice across the ocean but that he was sending it again.

[1] Dabney was confusing Herbert Baxter Adams, who would be WW's chief professor at the Johns Hopkins, with Professor Herbert C. Adams of Cornell University.

Herbert Baxter Adams, born Shutesbury, Mass., April 16, 1850. A.B., Amherst College, 1872; student, University of Berlin, 1874-75; Ph.D., University of Heidelberg, 1876. Fellow, The Johns Hopkins University, 1876-78; Associate, 1878-83; Associate Professor, 1883-91; Professor, 1892-1900. One of the founders and secretary of the American Historical Association, 1884-1900. Died July 30, 1901.

Adams was the first great organizer and promoter of historical study in the United States. His reputation as the most influential graduate teacher of American history derived from his emphasis upon original work in the sources and study of history as a science, as well as from the work of his students who, as the first generation of professional historians, laid the foundations of scientific historical work in the United States. WW's relationship to Adams, his reaction to Adams' emphasis upon discovery of the origins of American institutions in their European background, and his changing personal opinion of his professor are revealed clearly in WW's letters.

For biographical information and a list of Adams' writings, see *Herbert B. Adams, Tributes of Friends* (Baltimore, 1902). For Adams' work at the Johns Hopkins, see Hugh Hawkins, *Pioneer: A History of the Johns Hopkins University, 1874-1889* (Ithaca, N.Y., 1960), particularly pp. 169-86, and W. Stull Holt (ed.),

Historical Scholarship in the United States, 1876-1901: As Revealed in the Correspondence of Herbert B. Adams (Baltimore, 1938).

2 Johann Kaspar Bluntschli, born in 1808, was Professor of International Law at the University of Heidelberg until his death in 1881. He was a specialist and prolific author in international law, political science, and history.

To A. A. Thomas[1]

Dear Sir,   Wilmington, N. C., July 23rd., 1883

Mr James W. Bones, of Rome, Georgia, has just forwarded me a postal card sent him by you containing notice of assessments on Burt Co. lands for a certain "Fish Creek Ditch Improvement." This assessment is, I suppose, upon the lands belonging to the estate known as the "Woodrow estate" which has, until within about one month, been jointly owned by Marion W. Bones and Jeanie W. Wilson. The estate has, however, recently been divided, the papers being now on their way to your county to be recorded, if they are not already in the hands of Mr. W. M. [M. R.] Hopewell, the agent of the estate in your city.

You have, under some grave misapprehension, addressed your card to *Maria* Bones. She has no interest whatever in the estate. There is upon record a deed by James W. Bones conveying to *Maria* Bones, his mother, his contingent interest in the estate of his wife Marion W. Bones. But his interest depended on the contingency of his wife's dying *intestate, which she did not do.* Her will, which is on your records, gives her husband no interest whatever, and so the deed to Maria Bones is of no account.

By the division, of which I have spoken, all the lands of the Woodrow estate in Burt Co. are assigned to Jeanie W. Wilson, who has now become sole owner thereof.

We still lack, therefore, official notice of the assessment; and, as it is a matter of some magnitude, involving an expenditure of many hundred dollars, I feel obliged to ask particulars. Be kind enough to give me the assessments *in detail, by land lots,* as I am not at liberty to act in the dark. I should know also the rate per acre of the assessment and upon what basis it is made.

My remittance awaits your answer.

Very Respectfully Yours,   Woodrow Wilson,
Att'y and Agt. for Jeanie W. Wilson

Address me Care Dr. George Howe, *Columbia, South Carolina*

ALS (WC, NjP).

1 Clerk of Burt County, Tekamah, Neb.

To Robert Bridges

Dear Bobby,   Wilmington, N.C., July 26th/83

Atlanta is behind me, the boats are burnt, and all retreat is cut off. The authorities of Johns Hopkins did not honour me with an appointment to a fellowship, but I shall study there next winter "for a' that," and shall, I hope and expect, win a fellowship for the session following: for two years will be none too much for the completion of the course I purpose pursuing, since that course includes an introduction to both history and political science

I left Atlanta more than a month ago—about the middle of June —but did not come immediately home. I spent the latter half of June in Rome, Ga., where I have relatives, and where—you will smile to learn—I forgot my loss of my cousin by falling in love with a charming brown-eyed lassie who is attractive not only because of her unusual beauty, but also because of her unusual accomplishments. She belongs to that class which has contributed so much both to literature and to the pleasures of social life. She is a clergyman's daughter. The conditions of her life and her natural inclination have led her into extensive reading of the best sort, and the dear lassie has become learned without knowing it, and without losing one particle of freshness or natural feminine charm. But I can't describe her. If fortune favours me, you shall know her some day and find her out for yourself: for I've made up my mind to win her if I can.

I reached home on the 4th, to find my dear mother desperately ill with typhoid fever, so that ever since then I've been serving as aid to my sister in nursing, to the best of my untutored ability. The patient is now happily convalescent, however, and we shall soon be off with her to the mountains: so, if you cannot answer this letter within the next two weeks, remember to address me *care Dr. Geo. Howe, Columbia, South Carolina* for we've not yet settled upon a resort, and, the house here will be empty. Therefore I put the duty of forwarding upon my brother-in-law in Columbia.

I must confess to a feeling of deep relief in having escaped from the imprisonment of the bar and having gotten at least within reach of a literary career; and I trust, Bobby, that, before many years have run by, I shall have produced results, by dint of assiduous study and self-cultivation, that will persuade you that I have made no blunder in abandoning the law for a more congenial profession—for to remove your doubts will be as gratifying to me as to succeed in making a name for myself.

The immediate subject of study with me now is the constitutional history of this country, and I am about to go deep into the history of the colonial period; for it is undoubtedly in that period that the key or the keys to all our legal systems, both state and federal, are to be found. Our constitution is a growth, as the Eng. constitution is, and in no sense a manufactured article. At least, so it seems to me now, before I've gotten any very extensive or accurate knowledge of the pre-constitutional period.

Have you thought recently of writing anything of a permanent kind, Bobby? I wish you could find time for such work, because I know of no one more certain of literary success, if you would but seek it; though of course I know how hard it must be to do such work after a day of editorial rush, in the midst of an endless stretch of writing of such a different sort.

With much love,   Yours as ever   Woodrow Wilson

ALS (Meyer Coll., DLC).

To Daniel Coit Gilman

Dear Sir,   Wilmington, N. Carolina, July 26th 1883

It is my purpose to attend the session of Johns Hopkins during the coming winter, for the purpose of pursuing special studies in history and political science; and I should be much obliged if you would send me such of your annual publications as give full information as to the conditions of entrance, the time at which the session opens, the terms of tuition, and the courses of the several departments.   Very Respectfully Yours,   Woodrow Wilson

ALS (WP, DLC).

From Robert Bridges

Dear Tommy: [New York] July 30th 83

You are very kind to write to me when I have been so neglectful of your last letter—but when I have had a pen in my hand all day, and about three evenings in every week—it is almost impossible for me to sit down with any pleasure in my spare time to write a letter—and when I write to you I always want to be in my best mood. . . .

I can appreciate your feelings of relief at escape from the drudgery of law, and your hopes for the future. I do not deny that your argument for the change is strong and in many respects convincing. My only objections to it are as it will affect your material and not your intellectual prosperity. (I am too sleepy to correct that sentence, but you will catch the meaning). I have faith now,

as I always have had, in your ability to conquer the place in literature for which you are striving. And I send you my best wishes
for an early realization of your hopes

Along with them, I can send you some encouraging news. Since
I sent you the letter from the Scribners,[1] I have ventured, notwithstanding your request, to send the M.S. to Jonas Libbey, or
rather to take it to him, and have a little talk on the subject. Today
he returned it to me with the request that I ask you to prepare the
Third (III) Part, together with such parts of the first (explaining
Committee Gov't.) as are needful to make the contrast clear,—for
the *Princeton Review*, the whole not to exceed 20 printed pages.
He thinks that such an article would suit his purpose—and I believe that he will publish it. You know he has the reputation of paying well—and besides the *Review* will give you an introduction to a
fine audience. It seems to me that it would be one of those cases
(which frequently occur in medical practice) where it is justifiable
to sacrifice the child for the good of the parent. So I send the M.S.
to you by express today, hoping that you wont find the operation
very painful. I am sorry that I could not get a publisher for it as a
book, but pecuniarily, at least, I think the new plan will be even
more desirable.

Libbey's instructions were not arbitrary as to what parts he
wished used. He merely gave a general idea of his plan—so that
your own best judgment can be used as to your selection and arrangement of the parts—and the whole construction of the article.
Let me know soon what you think of it.

Truly your friend   Robert Bridges—

I congratulate you on your romance, and hope that the end thereof
will be happiness.

ALS (WP, DLC).
    [1] Not found. Obviously, it was a rejection.

To Ellen Louise Axson

Wilmington, N.C., July 30th 1881 [1883]

My dear Miss Ellie Lou,

Please do'nt be alarmed at the progressive familiarity of the
addresses with which my letters open. ("My dear Miss Axson,"
"Miss Ellie Lou," "My dear Miss Ellie Lou.") I need not assure you
that I do'nt want to seem presuming; but I hate the shackles of
formality. I feel as if at least a hundred miles were added to the
distance between us when I address you by your last name, or with

a formal unadjectived "Miss"; so I venture to take your indulgence for granted and put myself at ease by beginning in my own free way.

Your letter was more than welcome. It was so natural, so like yourself, that I enjoyed every word of it, even one word that I could not make out. It is not necessary to tell you how many times I read the letter: you know I think that anything that is worth reading once is worth reading often. Gentlewomen are your only true letter-writers, after all,—and you seem to me to be before the rest of your sex in the art. It must be that men are too blunt in the expression of their feelings, too self-occupied, too inapt in the art of delicate, *indirect* self-revelation, lacking the grace of conversational ease in their writing, and being incapable, generally, of that "free outpouring of the thoughts in friendly confidence" which constitutes the greatest of all charms in letter-writing. When they write well they are apt to write like Horace Walpole, clever, elaborate, sarcastic, gossipy comments upon the events and personages of society, or, like Macaulay, brilliant descriptions of the society about them, and charming sketches of the persons they have met or of the scenes they have witnessed. May-be men are not good letter-writers because they are wrapped up in themselves, and women are because they can become wrapped up in other people.

But I must not go off into the philosophy of the fact, lest I run with seven-league boots away from what I intended to say, which was simply that, in my humble judgment, you abuse your handwriting without just cause. I cannot claim much better eye-sight than your grandmother's, and possibly I ought not to claim a greater eagerness than hers to appropriate the contents of a letter from you (though I can safely say that her eagerness cannot be greater than mine); so it must be that the writing is very clear. At any rate, *I wish my hand were as desirable as yours is!*

I should like ever so much to take your brother's place in a game of chess with you, though you would probably treat me to a very signal defeat, because I have never become skilled in the great game. I sometimes think that it ought not to be called a game, however: it is too much like work to be called play. I must confess to sharing your brother's emphatic opinion, that "it's an awful bore to think"; at least it's an awful bore to *have* to think when one is playing a game; though of course I have played chess enough to know that it might be made a delightful intellectual diversion.

Since my last letter to you was written I have been engaged in infinitely less dignified occupations than playing chess. For about a week my sister's little daughter Jessie (four years old) the third of mother's four namesakes, has been with us, and I have been altogether her slave. The little beauty is almost as shy as she is pretty; but I had not played horse with her long before she became quite convinced that I was just her own age and, therefore, not in the least an object of suspicion; so she promptly appropriated me to her own uses. You owe this letter to the fact that my young mistress went away, with her mamma, last night: otherwise, I should have had no leisure to think of writing. I am generally accepted by children as their natural play-mate, having never been able to perceive just why I always attract their confidence, except upon the theory that love generates love—a theory which a certain respectable person wishes he could believe in as invariable, but which he has observed to work in practice (as far as he himself is concerned) only in the case of children.

But, whatever may be the truth upon that recondite point, certain it is that I have enjoyed the service of my little niece and have played all sorts of animals, and all sorts of characters with imaginary people, with as great zest as if it had been twenty years ago. You do not know what a gallant steed I am with a young lady on my back, or what interest I take in the fortunes of *pins* when they are supposed to be persons and are involved in the numerous difficulties of an adventurous journey, or are engrossed in the duties of their humble chair homes! I can recommend black pins as excellent servants, though my observation is that white pins are not indulgent masters, tho' courteous enough in their treatment of the conductors of arm-chair sleeping cars.

But there is nothing new to me in the rôle of small peoples' playmate; what I have tried to enjoy since my return home has been the *novel* rôle of *house-keeper*. Of course my sister's time was altogether taken up by the duties of attendance upon my dear mother's sick-bed, so that the supervision of the house-keeping fell upon my inexperienced shoulders; and how much have I learned! I have always held house-keepers in the highest respect; but hereafter I shall regard them as the greatest benefactresses of society. Anybody who can keep house well must have been born with a genius for economy, and must have cultivated, if it was not a natural gift, an infinite patience! Though I have had excellent servants under me, I seem to myself to have passed through a dreary decade of domestic cares. What question of government can compare in importance with the ever-pressing question, what shall be served for dinner? Surely there is no more important institution upon earth than the market, and no more responsible person than the marketer! I never had an adequate conception of the unceasing march of time until I knew the inexorable return of marketing hour, and I never knew what it was to live until I was forced to watch the larder. And then the knowledge I have acquired! What do I not know about the price of eggs, about the succession of vegetables, about the preparation of dishes! House-keeping is indeed a great art, and I am almost ambitious to become a professional in it.

Are you still contemplating a trip to Morganton? If so, when do you expect to start, and how long will you stay? I hope that you will not be disappointed of the beautiful ride through the mountains to which you were looking forward with so much pleasure. Somehow I wish that Morganton were a little higher up and a little cooler, that I might take mother there to recuperate. I also wish that I could think it advisable to take her to East Rome; but the breezes there are scarcely "balmy" enough, as her own experience has proved. The baby is a sufficiently great attraction. If I am to put entire trust in what I am told of myself, I have always been fond of babies; for there is a tradition, recently brought to my knowledge, that when I was a small boy in Augusta I fell very much in love with a certain very sweet baby who was brought on a short visit to our house,[1] but whom you may not remember, as I believe one's recollections of one-self do not often run back as far as infancy.

Does it really require a stretch of credulity on your part to believe that my nine months domicile with Miss Katie Mayrant have resulted in no serious consequences? You do not know how hard to please some unreasonable men are, or how they can steel their hearts against all influences that should conquer them: if you did, you would not wonder at my escape—no, I wont say *escape*, for that is scarcely a complimentary word to use and I will not use it with reference to a young lady whom it would be worth any man's while to win—my *exemption*, rather, from a natural fate. How it happens that I was exempted I will not undertake to say, for to undertake to do so would be undertaking to describe just the sort of woman I want to marry—something I very clearly know but could not very clearly tell. I know her when I see her, but I cannot describe her to other people.

You can judge how much better my dear mother is from the fact that my sister, with her little ones, and her husband, who had come over from Columbia for the day, my brother Josie, and I all went on a family excursion down the river the other day, leaving only father with the convalescent patient; and a jolly trip we had of it! You see we are here within easy reach of the sea, and every day comfortable little steamers go down the river, landing parties of excursionists on the splendid beach at its mouth, and bringing them back to town again in time for tea. Lunching on the sea-shore is a thoroughly enjoyable pastime—and how poor a chance the lustiest lunch stands when it has to face sea-breeze appetites! Knowing your love for the water, I wished I can't tell you how many times during the day—wished *only for your own sake* of course—that you were of our party. In breadth and volume the Cape Fear is really a noble stream from this point to the ocean—about twenty-five miles—and it is splendidly blown about at its mouth by the fine breezes from old ocean. Then, too, if one likes a shaking-up, the captain of the boat is quite willing to go over the bar and let his boat pitch and toss until everybody is ready to cry "enough."

But I am afraid that you are quite ready to cry out enough of this letter, so I will at once put into port, promising not to try your patience so sorely again.

With warmest regards to Mr. Axson and to your brothers, together with some regard, notwithstanding the contrary seeming of the length of this epistle, for yourself,

Very sincerely Yours,   Woodrow Wilson

ALS (WP, DLC). There is a WWsh draft of this letter in WP, DLC.
[1] A reference to a tradition in the Wilson family about WW's first sight of ELA.

From Ellen Louise Axson

Dear Mr. Wilson,   Rome, [Ga.] July 31st, 1883.

Many, *many* thanks for the delightful and valuable book, which together with your letter of the 10th came to hand the day after I had written the supplement to my last weighty epistle. I ought properly to have acknowledged the former at once, but I preferred to read it first. Then too, common humanity demanded that I should allow *some* time to elapse before proceeding to vex you and perplex you with another of my unspeakable scrawls.

I was truly delighted as well as surprised to hear of your mother's speedy convalescence. You have, indeed, reason to be in good spirits; and it is a special cause for happiness that the days have been so shortened. I trust that her restoration to perfect health and strength may continue to progress with equal rapidity.

I assure you I appreciated *very* highly your writing to tell me the good news. Though that motive for writing was certainly not needed by way of apology; for, as I tell my friend Beth,[1] who sometimes does me that most delightful of favours, there is nothing which fills me with such a warm glow of gratitude, as to receive a letter where one is not due. It is, I think, almost the purest and most disinterested expression of friendship. Between it and the regular interchange there is, of course, just the difference between a free gift and the payment of a debt, which *may* be done from a sense of duty, or one knows not what mixed motives.

But I have not as yet thanked you sufficiently for that most invaluable of books, nor told you how much I enjoyed it. How wise and just—how eminently *sensible* is Mr. Hamerton; and how practical and to the point in all he says.

And, oh dear me, what a contrast between his clear luminous style and some of the "Guides" and "Manuals" over which I have struggled, and which seem to have been prepared expressly for the purpose of "darkening counsel." This book has really been of service in restoring me to some slight confidence in my own sanity: for as, in reading, I naturally attribute all lack of comprehension on my part to my own innate stupidity, I have, of late, put down one or two of the aforesaid "Guides" with the firm conviction that I was hopelessly idiotic.

The Graphic Art does seem, as you say, to have borrowed largely from her sister; though in some cases perhaps she might dispute the claim to a word, assert her right to be as ancient as any other, and cite authorities to *speak* on her side. Perhaps being essentially an imitative art, it is more in accordance with its genius to copy its language as well as its forms! Or perhaps, on the contrary, ("since I am talking nonsense") it's imaginative character makes figurative language seem to it more expressive and suggestive than literal, even when the latter is not, or need not be, wanting. For instance, to say that a colour is *loud* implies a little more than merely to say it is too bright, or even "flashy." It suggests the flashiness, and an indefinable something else, a reflex from the ordinary meaning of the word.

But my pen is surely like "Mr. Brook's," a "thinking organ" operating on its own responsibility. I began with the intention of thanking you for the book and giving you my address in Gainsville—and "see what you have."

I must really close now, as I leave the day after tomorrow, and am, of course, very busy. You should see the latest product of my genius; a marvellous Mother Hubbard dress! It is a triumph, I assure you;—"Strange and sweet—All made out of the carver's brains," with the assistance of a few twenty-four-year-old odds and ends of muslin and silk! Oh, if you were a woman, I could by describing it, and the process of it's manufacture, fill you with wonder and despair.

Such wonder and despair, for instance, not to change the subject, as overwhelm my soul, and excite in me a wild desire to tear my hair, when I see people, out of the slightest and most inadequate materials, construct an "exceptional" and unexceptionable individual,—and then proceed to lable her in a wholly arbitrary fashion. Ah, there are some clever men in this queer old world of ours; men almost clever enough to make something out of nothing!

My address in Gainsville is to the care of "Mr. Warren A. Brown."[2] I won't give the Morganton address at present, as my going is still very uncertain; it depends entirely on the reports I get from home during the week in Gainsville. Papa and I have been having a conflict of wills, ending in a compromise. He has been in feverish haste to get me off, imagining that unless I went immediately if not sooner I would follow the example of my cousin, who is just convalescent, and have typhoid fever or something of the sort. He, in the meantime, is really, what he only imagines me to be, very unwell; and I was determined not to leave at all. But as he insists that my presence is such an "aggravation" to him and his nervous complaint, I am forced with a very heavy heart to go as far as Gainsville at least. Of course unless I hear of his decided improvement I will not go farther from home, but will return as soon as I have "built up" to his satisfaction.

I believe that somewhere back in the earlier part of this letter I made a remark about "closing," which I will now try to reduce to practice. With kindest regards to all, believe me

Your sincere friend. Ellen Axson.

Aug. 1.

Yours of the 30th was received this morning and greatly enjoyed. I have only time now for a bare acknowledgment. You will begin to regard the postscript as a regular part of my letters. I write now to say that I won't go tomorrow, after all, and don't know when I shall. My cousin, who was thought much better, has had a sudden and violent relapse. The fever is quite high again, and we fear it is more serious than before.

I have been so disturbed since hearing this, that I forgot to mail my letter today which will explain the various dates.

E. L. A.

ALS (WP, DLC) with WWhw notation on env.: "Ans. 8/12/83"; ditto "9/9/83."

¹ Elizabeth L. Adams, a girlhood friend, was married to Hamilton Erwin, of Morganton, N. C., on January 11, 1882, at Summerhill, S. C. See E. L. Adams to ELA, Jan. 1 and 9, 1882, ALS (WP, DLC).

² Husband of Louisa C. Hoyt Brown, ELA's maternal aunt. He owned a shoe factory near Gainesville, Ga.

An Inventory of Books

[c. Aug. 1, 1883]

A.

American Citizen's Manual, Vol. I.
"   Statesmen, (1) Adams, (2) Calhoun, (3) Jackson, (4) Jefferson, (5) Hamilton, (6) Monroe, (7) Randolph, (8) Webster.

Arnold, Lectures on Modern History.

B.

Bacon, Essays.
Bagehot, English Constitution.
Baird, American College Fraternities.
Boswell, Life of Dr. Johnson.
Bright, Speeches.
Brooke and *Keppel*, Borneo.
Burke, Complete Works.
Butler (Bishop) Analogy.
"   (Sam.) Hudibras.
Byron, Select Poems.

C.

Carlyle, Reminiscences.
"   My Irish Journey.
Carlyle, (Jane Welsh) Letters.
Centz, Republic of Republics.
Chaucer, Prologue &c.
Cicero, de Natura.
Clemens, A Tramp Abroad.
Cobden, Speeches.
"   Political Writings.
Constitution, The
Constitutional Manual and Digest.
Craik, English Literature.

D.

Dana, Geology.

Dante,
De Leon, Egypt under the Khedives.
Demosthenes, De Corona.
Doyle, English Colonies in America.

E.

Eaton, Civil Service Reform in Great Britain.
Encyclopaedia Britannica.
English Citizen Series: (1) Central Govt., (2) Electorate and Legislature, (3) Foreign Relations, (4) National Budget (5) State in its Relations to Trade.
English Men of Letters: (1) Burke, (2) Burns, (3) Chaucer, (4) De Quincey, (5) Dryden, (6) Gibbon, (7) Landor, (8) Milton, (9) Macaulay, (10) Pope, (11) Scott, (12) Shelley, (13) Spenser.

F.

Froude, Life of Carlyle.
"   Sketch of Caesar.

G.

Goldsmith, Complete Works.
Green, Short History of the English People.
"   "   "   "
"   The Making of England, (paper)
Guizot, Meditations on Christianity.

H.

Half-Hours with the Best Authors.

Hallam, Constitutional History of England.
Hamerton, The Intellectual Life.
Hamill, Science of Elocution.
Hughes, Alfred the Great.
" Tom Brown's School-days.
" " " at Oxford.
Hurd, The Theory of Our National Existence.

I.

Interoceanic Canal.

J.

Jennings Anecdotal History of the British Parliament.

K.

Keats.

L.

Lamb, Poems and Essays.
Landor, Imaginary Conversations
Lodge, Short History of the English Colonies in America.

M.

McCarthy, History of Our Own Times.
" (Justin H.) Outlines of Irish History (paper)
McCosh, Intuitions of the Mind.
McMaster, History of the People of the United States.
Metternich, Memoirs of Prince (1773-1829)
Mill, Political Economy.
Miller, First Impressions of England and Its People.
Motley, John of Barneveld.
" United Netherlands.
" Rise of the Dutch Republic.

N.

Nassau Literary Magazine (1877-'79.)
Nicoll, Landmarks of English Literature.

O.

P.

Petrarch,
Princetonian (1877-'79)

Q.

R.

Roscoe, Chemistry.

S.

Scott, History of Constitutional Development in English Colonies in America
Shelley,
Smiles, Self-Help.
Smith (Barnett) Life of John Bright.
" (Dr.) History of Greece.
Stickney, A. True Republic.
Shakespeare, Complete Works with Hudson's Notes
" 's Hamlet, Macbeth, Merchant of V., Julius Caesar, Oth., King Lear (Rolfe.)

T.

Taine, English Literature.
Thackeray, Complete Works.
Thornwell, Discourses on Truth.
Throat and Voice, The
Tocqueville, Democracy in America.
Todd, Parliamentary Government in the British Colonies.
Towle, Certain Men of Mark.
Trevelyan, Life and Letters of Macaulay.
" Early Life of Fox.
Trollope, Life of Cicero.

U.

Ueberweg, History of Philosophy.

V.

Verne, Twenty Thousand Leagues Under the Seas.
Von Holst, Constitutional History of the United States.

W.

Walpole (Chas. G.) A Short History of the Kingdom of Ireland.

Webster, Great Speeches.

Wells, Our Merchant Marine.

White, Every-day English.

"   Words and Their Uses.

Woolsey, Political Science.

Wordsworth, Select Poems.

Wright, Principia and Basis of Social Science.

X.

Y.

Z.

WWhw MS. (WP, DLC). The prime evidence for dating this document is WW's purchase, in late July 1883, of Bagehot's *The English Constitution*, Doyle's *English Colonies in America*, Lodge's *Short History of the English Colonies*, and Scott's *Development of Constitutional Liberty*, for which he received a bill from J. B. Lippincott & Co. of Philadelphia on August 2, 1883. Moreover, there is no book on the list the publication date of which precludes its having been in WW's library as of this date. The document was most probably an inventory of the books which he had just packed for shipment to Baltimore.

For the convenience of the reader, full bibliographical information is supplied below for all cases in which it has been possible to identify the exact title from WW's sometimes rather cryptic citations. These are arranged in the same order as WW's citations. Wherever possible, the references are taken from WW's own copies now extant in the Woodrow Wilson Library in the Library of Congress, in the Wilson house on S Street in Washington, or in the Princeton University Library. If WW inscribed the book, the inscription is printed. Titles not now to be found in one of the above places are starred. Where there are several editions which WW might have owned, this fact is noted, and neither place nor date of publication is given. The fact that a given title is no longer to be found in WW's library is not necessarily significant since he gave many volumes away.

The list follows:

* Worthington C. Ford, ed., *The American Citizen's Manual* (2 vols., New York, 1882-83).

American Statesmen, John T. Morse, Jr., ed.

John T. Morse, Jr., *John Quincy Adams* (Boston, 1882). Inscribed: "Woodrow Wilson 1882."

Hermann E. von Holst, *John C. Calhoun* (Boston, 1882).

William Graham Sumner, *Andrew Jackson as a Public Man* (Boston, 1882). Inscribed: "Woodrow Wilson 1882."

John T. Morse, Jr., *Thomas Jefferson* (Boston, 1883). Inscribed: "Woodrow Wilson 1883."

Henry Cabot Lodge, *Alexander Hamilton* (Boston, 1882). Inscribed: "Woodrow Wilson 1882."

Daniel Coit Gilman, *James Monroe* (Boston, 1883). Inscribed: "Woodrow Wilson, 1883."

Henry Adams, *John Randolph* (Boston, 1882).

Henry Cabot Lodge, *Daniel Webster* (Boston, 1883).

* Thomas Arnold, *Introductory Lectures on Modern History* (London, 1843).

* Francis Bacon, *Essays*. Many editions.

Walter Bagehot, *The English Constitution and other Political Essays*, latest revised edn. (New York, 1882). Inscribed: "Woodrow Wilson 1883."

* William R. Baird, *American College Fraternities*, 2nd rev. edn. (New York, 1883).

* James Boswell, *The Life of Samuel Johnson*. Many editions.

John Bright, *Speeches on Questions of Public Policy*, James E. Thorold Rogers, ed., Vol. 1 (London, 1868). Inscribed: "Thomas W. Wilson, Princeton 1879."

* Sir Henry Keppel, *The Expedition to Borneo of H.M.S. Dido for the Suppression of Piracy: with Extracts from the Journal of James Brooke* (New York, 1846).

Edmund Burke, *The Works of the Right Honorable Edmund Burke*, 6th edn. (12 vols., Boston, 1880). Vol. II is inscribed: "Woodrow Wilson 1883." Also a fifth volume of this same work from the seventh edn. (Boston, 1881), inscribed: "Woodrow Wilson."

* Joseph Butler, *The Analogy of Religion, Natural and Revealed, to the Constitution and Course of Nature.* Many editions.

Samuel Butler, *Hudibras*, with notes and literary memoir by Treadway Russell Nash (New York, 1853). Inscribed: "T.W. Wilson."

* Lord Byron, *Select Poems.* Several editions.

Thomas Carlyle, *Reminiscences*, James A. Froude, ed. (New York, 1881). Inscribed: "T. Woodrow Wilson 1881."

* Thomas Carlyle, *Reminiscences of My Irish Journey in 1849* (New York, 1882).

* Jane Welsh Carlyle, *Letters and Memorials of Jane Welsh Carlyle* (2 vols., New York, 1883).

P. C. Centz (Bernard Janin Sage), *The Republic of Republics*, 4th edn. (Boston, 1881).

* Geoffrey Chaucer, *The Prologue, the Knightes Tale, the Nonne Prestis Tale from the Canterbury Tales; a Revised Text*, Richard Morris, ed. Several editions.

* Marcus Tullius Cicero, *De Natura Deorum.* Many editions.

Samuel L. Clemens, *A Tramp Abroad* (Hartford, Conn., 1880).

Richard Cobden, *Speeches on Questions of Public Policy*, John Bright and James E. Thorold Rogers, eds. (London, 1878). Inscribed: "Thomas W. Wilson, Princeton 1879."

Richard Cobden, *The Political Writings of Richard Cobden* (2 vols., London and New York, 1867). Inscribed: "Thos. W. Wilson 1878."

W[illiam] Hickey, *The Constitution of the United States of America*, 5th edn. (Philadelphia, 1852).

* *Constitutional Manual and Digest.* This title has not been located.

* George L. Craik, *A Compendious History of English Literature, and of the English Language, from the Norman Conquest* (2 vols., New York, 1863).

* James Dwight Dana, *Geology* (Philadelphia, 1849).

Dante Alighieri, *The Vision; or, Hell, Purgatory, and Paradise of Dante Alighieri*, translated by H. F. Cary (New York, 1880).

* Edwin De Leon, *The Khedive's Egypt; or, the Old House of Bondage under New Masters* (New York, 1878).

* Demosthenes, *De Corona.* Many editions.

J[ohn] A. Doyle, *English Colonies in America* (New York, 1882). Inscribed: "Woodrow Wilson 1883."

* Dorman B. Eaton, *Civil Service in Great Britain: A History of Abuses and Reforms, and their Bearing upon American Politics* (New York, 1880).

Encyclopaedia Britannica, 9th edn. (New York, 1878-89). Vols. I-XVI had appeared by 1883.

The English Citizen: His Rights and Responsibilities.
   H[enry] D. Traill, *Central Government* (London, 1881). Inscribed: "Woodrow Wilson 1882."
   Spencer Walpole, *The Electorate and the Legislature* (London, 1881). Inscribed: "Woodrow Wilson 1882."
   Spencer Walpole, *Foreign Relations* (London, 1882). Inscribed: "Woodrow Wilson 1883."
   Alexander J. Wilson, *The National Budget: The National Debt, Taxes and Rates* (London, 1882). Inscribed: "Woodrow Wilson 1882."
   T[homas] H. Farrer, *The State in its Relation to Trade* (London, 1883). Inscribed: "Woodrow Wilson 1883."

English Men of Letters, John Morley, ed.
   John Morley, *Burke* (New York [1879?]). Inscribed: "Woodrow Wilson 1881."
   [John Campbell] Shairp, *Robert Burns* (New York [1881 ?]). Inscribed: "Woodrow Wilson 1881."
   Adolphus W. Ward, *Chaucer* (New York 1880). Inscribed: "Woodrow Wilson 1881."
   David Masson, *De Quincey* (New York, 1882 [?]). Inscribed: "Woodrow Wilson, 1881."
   G[eorge E. B.] Saintsbury, *Dryden* (New York, 1881). Inscribed: "Woodrow Wilson 1881."
   James Cotter Morison, *Gibbon* (New York [1879]). Inscribed: "Woodrow Wilson 1883."
   Sidney Colvin, *Landor* (New York, 1881). Inscribed: "Woodrow Wilson 1881."
   Mark Pattison, *Milton* (New York, 1881). Inscribed: "Woodrow Wilson 1881."
   J[ames] Cotter Morison, *Macaulay* (New York, 1882). Inscribed: "Woodrow Wilson, 1883."
   Leslie Stephen, *Alexander Pope* (New York, 1880). Inscribed: "Woodrow Wilson 1881."
   Richard H. Hutton, *Sir Walter Scott* (New York, [1878?]). Inscribed: "Woodrow Wilson 1882."
   John Addington Symonds, *Shelley* (New York, [1879]). Inscribed: "Woodrow Wilson 1881."
   R[ichard] W. Church, *Spenser* (New York, [1879]). Inscribed: "Woodrow Wilson 1881."

* James A. Froude, *Thomas Carlyle: A History of the First Forty Years of His Life, 1795-1835* (London and New York, 1882).

* James A. Froude, *Caesar: A Sketch.* Several editions.

Oliver Goldsmith, *The Works of Oliver Goldsmith*, Peter Cunningham, ed. (4 vols., New York, 1881). Inscribed: "Woodrow Wilson 1883."

John Richard Green, *A Short History of the English People* (New York, 1877).

John Richard Green, *History of the English People* (4 vols., New York, 1878-80). Inscribed: "Thos. W. Wilson 1878" in Vols. I and II; "Thos. W. Wilson 1879" in Vol. III; and "T. Woodrow Wilson 1880" in Vol. IV.

* John Richard Green, *The Making of England* (New York, 1882).

[François Pierre Guillaume] Guizot, *Meditations on the Actual State of Christianity* (New York, [n.d.]).

Charles Knight, ed., *Half-Hours with the Best Authors* (6 vols., New York [n.d.]).

Henry Hallam, *Constitutional History of England* (3 vols., New York, 1877). Inscribed: "Thos. W. Wilson 1878."

Philip Gilbert Hamerton, *The Intellectual Life* (Boston, 1875). Inscribed: "Woodrow Wilson 1882."

S. S. Hamill, *The Science of Elocution* (New York, 1872).

Thomas Hughes, *Alfred the Great* (London and New York, 1871). Inscribed: "Thos. W. Wilson, Columbia, South Carolina."

* Thomas Hughes, *Tom Brown's School-days*. Several editions.

* Thomas Hughes, *Tom Brown at Oxford*. Several editions.

John C. Hurd, *The Theory of Our National Existence* (Boston, 1881). Inscribed: "Woodrow Wilson, 1883."

* [Alfred Williams], *The Interoceanic Canal and the Monroe Doctrine* (New York, 1880).

George Henry Jennings, *An Anecdotal History of the British Parliament* (New York, 1881). Inscribed: "T. Woodrow Wilson 1881."

* John Keats, one of many editions.

* Charles Lamb, *Poems and Essays* (London, [1879]).

Walter Savage Landor, *Imaginary Conversations* (5 vols., Boston, 1882). Inscribed: "Woodrow Wilson, 1883."

Henry Cabot Lodge, *A Short History of the English Colonies in America* (New York, 1881). Inscribed: "Woodrow Wilson 1883."

* Justin McCarthy, *A History of Our Own Times from the Accession of Queen Victoria to the Berlin Congress* (2 vols. in one, New York, [1880]).

* Justin H. McCarthy, *An Outline of Irish History, from the Earliest Times to the Present Day* (Baltimore and New York, 1883).

* James McCosh, *The Intuitions of the Mind Inductively Investigated* (London, 1860).

John Bach McMaster, *A History of the People of the United States*, Vol. 1 (New York, 1883). Inscribed: "Woodrow Wilson 1883."

Clemens Lothar Wenzel, Prince of Metternich-Winneburg, *Memoirs of Prince Metternich*, Prince Richard Metternich, ed., translated by Mrs. Alexander Napier (2 vols., New York, 1881). Inscribed: "T. Woodrow Wilson 1881."

John Stuart Mill, *Principles of Political Economy* (2 vols., Boston, 1848). Inscribed: "Thos W Wilson from his Uncle   Rome Ga. Aug 29/78."

* Hugh Miller, *First Impressions of England and Its People*. Several editions.

John Lothrop Motley, *The Life and Death of John of Barneveld* (2 vols., New York, [1874?]). Inscribed: "Woodrow Wilson, 1883."

John Lothrop Motley, *History of the United Netherlands, from the Death of William the Silent to the Twelve Years' Truce—1609* (4 vols., New York [n.d.]). Inscribed: "Woodrow Wilson 1883."

John Lothrop Motley, *Rise of the Dutch Republic* (3 vols., New York [1883?]). Inscribed: "Woodrow Wilson 1883."

Nassau Literary Magazine, Vols. XXXII and XXXIII (July 1876-May 1878). Inscribed: "Thos. W. Wilson Nov. 1878."

Henry J. Nicoll, *Landmarks of English Literature* (New York, 1883). Inscribed: "Woodrow Wilson 1883."

* Petrarch, One of many editions.

The Princetonian, Vols. I-III (June 14, 1876-May 1, 1879). Inscribed: "Thos. W. Wilson."

* Sir Henry Enfield Roscoe, *Chemistry* (New York, 1876 and 1879).

Eben G. Scott, *The Development of Constitutional Liberty in the English Colonies of America* (New York, 1882). Inscribed: "Woodrow Wilson 1883."

* Percy Bysshe Shelley, one of many editions.

* Samuel Smiles, *Self-Help*. Several editions.

George Barnett Smith, *The Life and Speeches of the Right Honourable John Bright, M. P.* (2 vols. in one, New York and London, 1881). Inscribed: "Woodrow Wilson 1882."

William Smith, *A History of Greece* (New York, 1875). Inscribed: "T. W. Wilson of the Class of '79."

* Albert Stickney, *A True Republic* (New York, 1879).

William Shakespeare, *The Works of Shakespeare*, rev. edn., Henry N. Hudson, ed. (6 vols., Boston, 1883). Inscribed: "Woodrow Wilson, 1883."

William Shakespeare, *Hamlet*, William J. Rolfe, ed. (New York, 1879). Inscribed: "Thomas W. Wilson."

William Shakespeare, *Macbeth*, William J. Rolfe, ed. (New York, 1880). Inscribed: "Woodrow Wilson 1881."

* William Shakespeare, *The Merchant of Venice*, William J. Rolfe, ed. (New York, 1883).

William Shakespeare, *Julius Caesar*, William J. Rolfe, ed. (New York, 1881).

William Shakespeare, *Othello*, William J. Rolfe, ed. (New York, 1881). Inscribed (WWhw): "Woodrow Wilson, from mother Christmas, 1881."

William Shakespeare, *King Lear*, William J. Rolfe, ed. (New York, 1880). Inscribed: "Woodrow Wilson."

H[ippolyte] A. Taine, *History of English Literature*, translated by H. van Laun (New York, 1879). Inscribed: "Woodrow Wilson."

William Makepeace Thackeray, *Complete Works* (10 vols., Boston, 1882-83). Inscribed: "Woodrow Wilson 1883."

* James H. Thornwell, *Discourses on Truth* (New York, 1855).

* Jacob da Silva Solis Cohen, *The Throat and the Voice* (Philadelphia, 1879).

Alexis de Tocqueville, *Democracy in America*, translated by Henry Reeve (2 vols., London, 1875). Vol. II inscribed "Woodrow Wilson."

Alpheus Todd, *Parliamentary Government in the British Colonies* (Boston, 1880). Inscribed: "Woodrow Wilson 1882."

* George M. Towle, *Certain Men of Mark: Studies of Living Celebrities* (Boston, 1880).

George Otto Trevelyan, *The Life and Letters of Lord Macaulay* (2 vols., New York, 1875). Inscribed: "Woodrow Wilson 1883."

* George Otto Trevelyan, *The Early History of Charles James Fox* (New York, 1880).

Anthony Trollope, *The Life of Cicero* (2 vols., New York, 1881). Inscribed: "T. Woodrow Wilson 1881."

Friedrich Ueberweg, *History of Philosophy, From Thales to the Present Time*, translated by George S. Morris and Noah Porter (New York, 1877). Inscribed: "Thomas W. Wilson 1878."

* Jules Verne, *Twenty Thousand Leagues Under the Seas*. Several editions.

H[ermann E.] von Holst, *The Constitutional and Political History of the United States*, Vols. I and II (Chicago, 1877, 1881). Inscribed: "Woodrow Wilson 1883."

* Charles G. Walpole, *A Short History of the Kingdom of Ireland* (London, 1882).

Daniel Webster, *The Great Speeches and Orations of Daniel Webster*, Edwin P. Whipple, ed. (Boston, 1879). Inscribed: "Woodrow Wilson 1881."

* David Ames Wells, *Our Merchant Marine* (New York, 1882).

Richard Grant White, *Everyday English* (Boston, 1881). Inscribed: "Woodrow Wilson, 1883."

Richard Grant White, *Words and Their Uses* (Boston, 1882). Inscribed: "Woodrow Wilson 1883."

Theodore D. Woolsey, *Political Science or the State* (2 vols., New York, 1878). Inscribed: "Thos. W. Wilson 1878."

William Wordsworth, *Poems* (2 vols., London, 1807).

* Robert Joseph Wright, *Principia; or, Basis of Social Science* (Philadelphia, 1875).

To Robert Bridges

Dear Bobby,   Columbia, South Carolina, August 10th 1883

I send you to-day, by express, the article for Jonas.[1] I've thrown it together rather hastily, and might have made it shorter, had I given myself time for pruning. It is, however, within the limits prescribed, and could scarcely be much shortened without leaving out altogether some of the links of the argument.

I send it to you because you have conducted the preliminary negotiations with Libby. If he should have any alterations to suggest, I shall be glad to make any that can be made without detriment to the piece, and will answer promptly any letter he may address to *Flat Rock, Henderson Co., North Carolina* (Care of Farmer's Hotel)

To which address I want *you* to give heed too, old fellow, and write me a letter there that will relieve the monotony of summer resort life. Flat Rock is on the uplands that rise towards the grand mountains of western North Carolina. It is said to be *in* those mountains, but is really only on their outskirts. It is one of numberless resorts which dot all the surface of that part of the State, small settlements swarming with gay holiday crowds from all the Southern country during the Summer, and during the Winter sleeping on their chill hill-sides against the return of Spring. It is in the neighborhood of Hendersonville, of Asheville, and of scores of minor "springs" and resorts, in which, at this season, one could if he chose, study to the very best advantage the sentiments which now prevail in Southern society. There you can see the pick of the best people of the Carolinas and hear Southern opinion spoken at every table and on every piazza. You have but to go from Saratoga to Asheville to appreciate the difference between Northern and Southern manners and society.

I'm not going to the mountains for my health. I'm as vigorous and as free from "complaints" as heart could desire. But I'm am [*sic*] at this present writing acting as escort to my mother and sister, as I did some seasons ago, and expect, before the summer is over, to come in for as large a share of fun as an easy conscience and a contented frame of mind can give me amidst gay society.

I read your piece on Buch.[2] with real enjoyment. It was indeed a big feat, and the literary success of it consists in its excellent style and easy movement in spite of tremendous haste and cramming.

What do you think of my "caligraph" work? My piece is copied with the type-writer I bought about a month ago. It's an immense convenience; but I prefer to write to my friends *in my own hand*. With renewed thanks for your unselfish kindness in helping me to get into print, and with much love,

Yours as ever, Woodrow Wilson.

ALS (Meyer Coll., DLC).

[1] The article, or a further re-working of it, was later published under the title, "Committee or Cabinet Government?" See the text at Jan. 1, 1884, the note which follows it, and Bridges to WW, Aug. 30, 1883.

[2] "James Buchanan," New York *Evening Post*, July 30, 1883, a lengthy unsigned review article on George Ticknor Curtis's *The Life of James Buchanan, Fifteenth President of the United States* (New York, 1883).

To Ellen Louise Axson

Columbia, S. Carolina, August 12th 1883

My dear Miss Ellie Lou,

Your last letter [of July 31] reached me just before I left home. I was very much distressed to hear of your cousin's illness, not only because I was interested in her from what I had heard of her, but also because I knew how much distress it would give you. I trust that she is again much better by this time, and that, in consequence, your vacation trip is again in near prospect

My vacation trip has already begun, you see. My mother and brother and I have been here in Columbia at my sister's house since Wednesday last. To-morrow morning we are to start for the mountains, accompanied by my sister and her three children. We shall go first to Flat Rock, near Hendersonville. I say 'first' because we do'nt intend to *settle* anywhere for a long stay, but shall move about from place to place as we are inclined, or as we may be driven by stress of poor fare or uncomfortable quarters. Flat Rock is a *neighborhood* rather than a *"place"*—a neighbourhood of noble country residences built by rich farmers and merchants of the low country of South Carolina. It is on the uplands which rise to the Blue-ridge rather than amongst the mountains themselves, but is in the midst of beautiful quiet scenery and is blessed with a delightful climate. Of course it is a "resort." In that part of North Carolina there is, it would seem, an hotel upon every available site, and every hotel is a resort. But Flat Rock is usually resorted to only by the best class of tourists, so that one is not there quite so liable to be thrown with as miscellaneous a crowd as is generally to be met with at fashionable watering places.

I am anxious to get settled for a few weeks somewhere in order that I may begin the short course of reading that I had planned for the Summer, but which has, of course, been so far postponed. It is now scarcely a month before the opening of the session at Johns Hopkins and I have, therefore, none too much time for getting my mind into working trim. I shall, probably, start for Baltimore on the 18th of next month. I love vacation leisure as much as other men do; but I have many reasons for wishing this one at an end. I am more eager than I can tell you to be at my life work, and I am, therefore, impatient of the long period of preparation which separates me from it, even though that period is to be spent in most congenial occupations. I want to do my best work while the enthusiasm and elasticity of youth last; so that the keen pleasures of the present—the companionship of those I love and health and leisure to enjoy that companionship to the top of my bent—are not worthy to be compared with the objects of the future.

I enclose the programme of my work at the University next Winter, in which I hope you will be interested. It would make me very happy, Miss Ellie Lou, to have the assurance that you are interested in my work and fortunes. To have your sympathy and good wishes would be an aid and an inspiration to me, because they would be genuine. To be *believed in* by the woman who has his highest esteem is, you know, all in all to a man, and is, I believe, more than usual to a certain respectable person.

I should have liked very much—not to change the subject too abruptly—to have been treated to a description of that wonderful Mother Hubbard dress. It is, as Jessie would say, a remarkable *coincidence* that you should have made a dress of that pattern. Amongst many things about which I have very decided tastes is the subject of dress. I am as unlearned as most men in the fashions; but I have very distinct notions as to what is and what is not becoming in the way of *cut* and *colour*—or, rather *shape* and colour —and when I was in Rome one of the many wishes in which I indulged was that I could see you in a *Mother Hubbard dress*, as I fancied that it would be specially becoming to you. You did'nt suspect me of such impudent wishes, did you? But, now that the dress is made, I may be forgiven for asking that you will preserve it, that I may some day see you wear it. I live in hopes of seeing you before the dress gets very old—for wishes are often fathers to very big hopes.

I am sincerely delighted that the "Graphic Arts" I sent you proved so enjoyable and, above all, so useful. Your pleasure in the book adds a zest to my pleasure in being able to send it to you.

Your saying that you did not acknowledge the receipt of the book at once not only because you wanted to read it first but also because "common humanity demanded that" you "should allow *some* time to elapse before proceeding to vex" me "and perplex" me "with another of" your "unspeakable scrawls," moves me to tell some of my recent thoughts on that score. I am not, allow me to assure you, given to writing long letters. Most of my correspondents regard me as a very poor stick in that business. But some*how*, some*times* I am in the humour to go on to great lengths of paper when writing to some *people*; and you must have realized already the effects of that humour in my correspondence with you. Well, then, what I have now to confess is that I have not reined in my inclination to run on in writing to you because I was not sure that you felt equally inclined to write to me, and, "says I to myself, says I," 'she can't have the heart to return a brief answer to a letter as long as I feel like writing, so I'll make it as long as I please.' In other words, I was going on the principle of debit and credit, and was relying on your answering "from a sense of duty, or one knows not what mixed motives." But your cordial letters have made me very much ashamed of having attempted to "force your hand" to correspondence; and I now contritely petition for forgiveness, begging, however, that you will permit yourself to credit the assurance that common humanity demands that you should write to me as often as you can.

For consider the merits of a certain respectable person sitting here at midnight spinning out *his* scrawl when he ought to be asleep, that he might pack his trunk early in the morning, and bemoaning the fact that the necessities of travel must command his insatiable writing propensity and send him to bed.

I hope that your father's health has improved since you wrote. Please give him my warmest regards, and remember me to Eddie.

Very sincerely Yours,   Woodrow Wilson

My address for the next two or three weeks will be: Farmer's Hotel, Flat Rock, Henderson Co., North Carolina.

ALS (WP, DLC). Enc.: printed circular captioned *Historical and Political Science. Programme for 1883-84.* See WW to ELA, Sept. 29, 1883, for a list of the courses that WW actually took.

Two Letters from Robert Bridges

Dear Tommy: New York, Aug 15 1883
  M.S. all right. Have sent it to Jonas. It will probably be some time as the *P. R* moves slowly.   Yrs in haste   Bob Bridges

APS (WP, DLC) with WWhw pencil figures on recto.

Dear Tommy: Westfield, N.J.   Aug 30 '83
  I have been writing all evening and only have a few minutes left for a note to you. I was very much surprised yesterday to receive an emissary from Jonas Libbey, bringing your M.S. and a message that it was too long by eight printed pages, and that he was not satisfied with the way in which the parts were joined together; also, that if returned and accepted, it might have to wait a good while for publication, as many articles are already in hand.
  I was very much provoked and annoyed—for he had led me to believe that he was pleased with the original essay.
  I asked the "emissary" just what he wanted—but he did not seem to know.
  I therefore return the M.S. today—and, if you are so minded, you can again boil it down. . . .

Your friend   Robert Bridges

ALS (WP, DLC) with WWhw notation on env.: "Ans. 9/12/83."

Marginal Note

J. A. Doyle, *English Colonies in America* (New York, 1882).

Transcript of WW Shorthand Comment

P. 193

[c. Aug. 31, 1883]

. . . The doctrine that each country should produce what it is best fitted for, and that the inhabitants may be trusted to discover that for themselves, is a thoroughly sound doctrine as applied to settled communities, where both capital and enterprise are abundant; but it does

The only question being as to the wisest means of guarding and nursing.

not apply to a new country where forms of industry, which may in time become profitable, or needful to the independence of the community, must often at the outset be guarded and nursed into life.

From Ellen Louise Axson

Dear Mr. Wilson,   Belvidere [Morganton, N.C.] Sept. 1/83

Your letter from Columbia, after wandering about in search of me for a week or so, finally reached me safely, here at Morganton. For somewhat to my own surprise, I am actually among the mountains, and have had my long-dreamed-of ride up the French Broad and the Swannanoa.

Ah, it was glorious, too! I never had so delightful a journey—the mountain half of it, at least. The first stages were quite the reverse, for I was, of course, in the depths of despair about leaving the baby.[1] She is a lovely child, fair-haired and brown-eyed, with the most beautiful mouth I ever saw, wonderfully bright and interesting too. I don't think I ever knew a little creature with so much individuality about her. In short, she is very sweet and very bad: and a visit to Gainsville is but a doubtful pleasure with the pain of leaving her as its necessary conclusion. The whole thing, her being there, and away from us, seems so unnatural. So on the whole, it was rather a woe-begone little mortal who started out from Gainsville, two weeks ago.

Then my route took me almost home again, to the very gate, as it were, viz, to Kingston. A circumstance which, as I had left with extreme unwillingness the week before, did not contribute to my peace of mind. I did not recover my usual spirits until I left Dalton, when the mountain fever began to rise.

There too, I met a charming young lady from Augusta on her way to Asheville to visit Lizzie Bean, an acquaintance of mine, and a first cousin of the Lizzie whom I was to visit. She also was travelling alone, and, as you may imagine, our intimacy grew apace; especially as we had before us the unknown terrors of a night by ourselves at an hotel. We had adjoining rooms and were a great comfort to each other.

After leaving Morristown where we spent the night, the rest of the journey was one long enchantment.

It was just such a day as I had dreamed of, and longed for, the sort I most love; one of those days which always seem to me to have something *human* about them, suggesting, for example, the maiden, "all kind of smiley 'round the lips an' teary 'round the lashes." A fore-ground all wet and gleaming, and on the distant mountains a solemn wonder of purple shadow, and broad shafts of tender, dewy light bursting through luminous clouds. A mountain with one hot, unbroken glare upon it, is little more than the "immense protuberance" of Dr. Johnson's definition. But how is it transfigured, when with the glory of sunlight is blended the mystery of shadow!

I was, indeed, singularly fortunate in my journey. It left little to be desired, except, perhaps, that my neighbours, a party of very "nice" young people, might have been a little less stupid. I could not avoid observing, with a somewhat disgusted amusement, their proceedings, as they *closed* their blinds, arranged their pillows, and settled themselves for a long day of piteous lamentations over the dust, the heat, the cinders, the smoke, &c. &c, interrupted only by a little novel-reading occasionally. One could almost have fancied there was no brain or soul to them, nor even any eyes, but only a quivering mass of sensation like some of the marine creatures; or that they were a sort of animated pincushion which some fury was pricking to their death. Yet to do them entire justice, the cinders were no joke, as we found to our cost when we took the observation car; an admirable contrivance, but, being of human invention, not altogether perfect. There the rain of cinders is a fact not wholly to be ignored, for when one's eyes are quite full of them, one can't see the view; and against such a trial of one's patience, no philosophy proposes to be proof. But, of course, no one imagines a railway journey to be the ideal method of getting at the heart of nature.

And though one doesn't see several hundred miles of mountains in one day and it isn't therefore so exciting, it is more entirely a "good joy" to "meditate in the field at eventide" and, looking across this quiet little valley, with it's beautiful river curves, [to] watch the shadows lengthen, and the sunset colours flush and fade on the distant peaks; or, better still, to watch from one's own window the shining curtain of mist roll softly away, to see the first rosy glow above the eastern hills, and then to watch it grow, and change, and brighten, "till one can look no more for gladness[.]" One can hardly realize sometimes, that those far-away dream-mountains are of the earth, earthy, so vividly do they suggest the "everlasting doors."

"Who shall ascend into the hill of the Lord; or who shall stand in his holy place? He that hath clean hands and a pure heart; who hath not lifted up his soul unto vanity."

Since I have been here, I seem always to hear that psalm, like a low refrain, running through my thoughts,—a perpetual solemn undertone.

I find Morganton itself a delightful little place. The people are remarkably kind and hospitable; and, in addition, they are almost without exception "cousins" of either Mr. Erwin or Beth. As for Beth herself, she is the same dear old girl she always was—has'nt changed a particle. This is a queer old home in which I find her. The house was built eighty-two years ago by Mr. Erwin's great-grandfather. But I have left myself no space in which to describe it, nor the merry party which, on these cool mornings, assembles around the great hearth in it's old hall.

Mr. Lawrence Adams, Beth's father, is here, with his lovely new wife.[2] From my earliest recollections, he has been one of my chief favourites, with his pleasant, handsome face, his beautiful courtesy of the most pronounced Southern type, and his bright appreciative talk about "books and things." With the new Mamy I have fallen completely in love—a pretty, graceful woman, with a peculiar *daintiness* about her, reminding one of a rare bit of old china, and the most exquisite manner, half merry, half tender.

Then there are Beth's only brother and sister; the former, a complete wag, from the tip of his boot to the top of his white head, plays his part to everyone's satisfaction. The latter is a very pretty young lady, whom in former days, I was wont to consider rather a bore because of her endless talk about "divine dancers" &c. But, having arrived at years of discretion, that "agony is abated," and she is quite a sweet girl. The only other member of the family beside its "united head," is the dear old "Auntie," as she is called by every one in the county. She is quite a character here, and a noble old soul too;—rather an amusing study to me because of her curious blending of homely simplicity in speech and manner with intense pride of birth, and a most extremely aristocratic "theory of the universe." But indeed that is a combination of qualities somewhat characteristic of this *very* high-toned place. As for Beth's idol, Mr. Erwin himself, he is a *man* "every inch of him"—but!!

But I perceive it is time for me to restrain "the exuberance of my verbosity." I had quite a laugh over your last letter and your evident astonishment at the length of mine. They are indeed a sad spectacle. I think they would serve admirably to point the moral of a Sunday-school talk; subject, "the iron fetters of habit, and how they are forged."

For you must know that they are not written of malice aforethought, but are the result of a long course of high crimes and misdemeanors, in which my accomplice was this same Beth. As I write I recall with much inward amusement—so hardened am I—certain of those documents, which required two envelopes and four stamps to carry them.

The consequence of such indulgences, coupled with the natural diffuseness of womankind, is that we really don't know how to write a short letter; we wander along as though time were no more, and are only beginning to get fairly warmed up and into our subject, such as it is, when we reach the third sheet. Yet it is emphatically true, that had you not kept me in countenance, I should have found a way, or made it, to break through the habit, however inveterate.

I was truly glad to hear that your mother had so far recovered as to be able to try that best of all remedies, a change; and trust that the wholesome air of Flat Rock has, ere this, quite completed her restoration. From all I have heard, you have found a charming retreat, and I hope your plans for the summer will no longer "gang agley"; but that the reading &c. are progressing entirely to your satisfaction. Though a fashionable resort is not the most favourable of places for undertakings of so serious a nature as your winter programme would seem to indicate.

I am I assure you sincerely interested in your plans—for in spite of an intense horror of "meddling," it is very natural to concern oneself about "other people's business," when the people in question chance to be one's friends. And of course I "believe in you"—there is no reason why I shouldn't! Not even a woman's reason, "I think it so because—I think it so!" Besides, if I didnt I fear I should be in a minority of one and I should not like to be "so conspicuous."

My address for the present is "Morganton, care Mr. Hamilton Erwin." I shall be here perhaps until week after next; then we will probably go to Asheville and Alexanders for a few days, after which I will be homeward bound. With best regards to your mother
            I remain your sincere friend   Ellie L. Axson.

ALS (WP, DLC)
  [1] Margaret Randolph Axson, ELA's sister, born about Nov. 4, 1881, in Rome, Ga. Her mother died when she was born. She was reared by her Aunt Louisa Brown until about 1894, when she went to live with the Woodrow Wilsons in Princeton. She married Edward Elliott, Professor of Politics at Princeton University, on Sept. 8, 1910. She died in Princeton on May 24, 1958. Author (as Margaret Axson Elliott) of the charming but date-less memoir, *My Aunt Louisa and Woodrow Wilson* (Chapel Hill, N. C., 1944).
  [2] Mamie Adams served as matron of honor at her step-daughter's wedding to Hamilton Erwin. Beth's baby, Mamie Erwin, was named for her and ELA was adopted as "little Aunt Ellie." See E.L.A. Erwin to ELA, Feb. 21, 1883, ALS (WP, DLC).

To Ellen Louise Axson

My dear Miss Ellie Lou,   Arden, N. C., Sept 1st. [1883]

I trust that your long silence has not been due to your having been unwell; but has, at worst, been occasioned by the interruptions and occupations of travel. I have sought to assuage my disappointment by trying to believe that you have written, but that the Post-masters at the offices we have left behind us have either stupidly or lazily neglected to forward your letter.

At any rate, I want to apprise you of my present address, and venture this note for that purpose, though I do'nt know *your* address and only guess that your [*sic*] are in Morganton. If I were sure of your whereabouts, I should be tempted to write more than these few lines; but I wont trust a letter to a mere chance of finding you in Morganton, and to the still slimmer chance of the Post-master's possessing sufficient sagacity to assign it to the proper "*care.*"

So, all that I will trust to this sheet is the assurance that a letter from your hand addressed to me at Arden Park Hotel, Arden P. O., Buncombe Co., North Carolina, would be very heartily welcome.

I shall be here only two weeks before starting for Baltimore.
                    Very sincerely Yours,   Woodrow Wilson

ALS (WP, DLC).

From Joseph Ruggles Wilson

My precious son—   N. Y., Sept 4, 1883.

As I wrote to the dear mother on yesterday I will be in B[altimore] on 18th if possible. I can be there more conveniently (so far as I can now see) on the Saturday previous (15th). *Where* we can meet (in the city) I may be able to say in my next. I do not wish to take you from your mother (to whom you are so great a comfort) a moment sooner than may be needful—yet you ought not to put off your advent in B. to the last day before entering the College. Arrange therefore, to be in B. on Saturday the 15th, if your dear mother and you think this to be advisable—for I am unadvised as to the very day of the College opening.

Your letters have been very interesting, and show much talent for hitting off character with one or two strokes that suggest all. I advise you to cultivate this gift, which is rare and as valuable as rare.

Tell dear mother that I am still of the opinion that she ought not to return to Wilmington until about Novbr 1,—or, until I can positively advise her after my getting home.

My life here is somewhat stupid—yet there is always something to entertain the eye and stimulate curiosity. Then, one has the quiet of one's own room to which to resort. But the daily wonder with me is that I have so little desire to bestir myself—that I am, in short, so lazy—more of an animal than an intelligence. Doing nothing I have time for nothing. Love to the precious mother & Dode & Annie & all. F.

ALS (WP, DLC).

Marginal Note

Eben G. Scott, *The Development of Constitutional Liberty in the English Colonies of America* (New York, 1882).

Transcript of WW Shorthand Comment

P. 269:

. . . Whenever absolutism once feels the ground growing firm beneath its feet, it takes upon itself the shape of a personal government, with all *those features, so odious to the Saxon mind,* of *direct action, absence of parliamentary deliberation, secrecy,* and *closet administration.* [WW's italics]

[c. Sept. 5, 1883]
Are not the last three characteristic of congressional government by committees.

From Ellen Louise Axson

Dear Mr. Wilson,   Morganton [N. C.], Sept. 7/83.

It seems the fate of our letters, always to cross one another. On Tuesday morning Mr. Erwin took into town one directed to you at Flat Rock, and brought back your note from Arden. Have concluded that perhaps it is advisable to drop you a line to that effect, in case the postmasters should be "so stupid" as not to forward.

I am now in Morganton on a short visit to the Andersons[1] and Mrs. Thornwell. They are delightful people, and I am enjoying it exceedingly.

We had expected to leave for Asheville next week, but must now postpone it until the week after, as Mr. Erwin is unfortunately obliged to serve on a jury. He thinks he will get off in a week; and as I am *wild* to stop in Asheville and climb to the top of *some* mountain, I have decided to wait on him that length of time. But, if they keep him longer, I shall be obliged to give it up, and go directly home. So as you may imagine, I am at present taking a deep interest in the proceedings at court.

But matters of importance—viz., an inviting bed, with the example of Nannie asleep on it, and a book by Emanuel Swedenborg in which I have been absorbed all day, and which is the very thing for soothing one into a sweet sleep and pleasant dreams—forbid my scribbling any more at present. So with kind regards to your mother, I remain   Your sincere friend,   Ellie L. Axson.

By the way, the process of signing my name reminds me that I had an observation to make on that subject, a-propos of something in one of your letters. "Which I wish to remark" that you are quite welcome to call me anything you please *except* Ellie *Lou*. I have a decided dislike to that name—indeed to all compound names. And it is used by none of the family except my father and one aunt, and by *very* few of my friends—though I believe that your relatives, with the exception of Mr. Bones, are among the minority.

I have quite an assortment of names among which to choose; —am called Ellen, Ellie, Nelly, Louise, Eloise, and "Alleluia"— anything but Ellie Lou; I don't answer to that. All of which is respectfully submitted.   E. L. A.

ALS (WP, DLC).
  1 The Rev. Dr. and Mrs. Robert Burton Anderson. He was pastor of the Presbyterian Church of Morganton. Mrs. Thornwell was the widow of Dr. James H. Thornwell and Mrs. Anderson's mother.

The first page of Wilson's shorthand draft of his letter to Ellen Louise Axson, Sept. 9, 1883.

Draft of a Letter to Ellen Louise Axson

[Arden, N. C.] 9/9/83

Opening:

My dear Miss Ellie Lou,

I am in great perplexity to account for this long pause in our correspondence. It has been more than a month since I had a line from you,[1] and in the meantime I am completely in the dark as to your whereabouts. I know from a letter of Marion Bones to my brother, that you left Rome some time ago, and my conclusion is that, as you did not intend remaining in Gainesville, you are now probably in Morganton; but I have very stupidly forgot the married name of your friend there, and I am therefore by no means sure that a letter addressed to you there will ever find you. I am more interested to know certainly whether you are in Morganton or not, because I expect to leave here for Baltimore at the end of this week, and Morganton lying directly on my way, I shall certainly stop over a little while if there is to be any chance of seeing you, taking it for granted that you have no objections to my doing so.

I am specially concerned at my ignorance of your whereabouts because I know that it is not your fault; for I am sure that you must have written to me (unless, indeed, there was some imperative reason why you should not) and that the letter has not been forwarded to me. I wrote a short note to you about a week ago,[2] addressing it simply "Morganton," which, I suppose is still ownerless in the postoffice there.

Our plans were altogether changed soon after I wrote my letter to you from Columbia.[3] Our first resort proved far from our taste.

I hope that you were duly impressed with the description of Flat Rock given in my last letter,[4] seeing it as the very properest place for quiet people, seeking peaceful surroundings and refreshing air rather than amusement or gay society. But that was of course an outside view of Flat Rock, colored by glorious anticipation (for I had been confiding enough to believe what was told me); and having done the place the justice (?) with that description I am now at liberty to tell you how it looks from the inside. If you have had much experience [with] summer resorts you will not be surprised to learn that, seen from within, it is as disappointing and as unenchanting as are gallant trappings of the stage when seen in the greenroom or from behind the scenes. In spite of its beautiful situation in the midst of splendid countryside, it is unattractive and undesirable, just as they are unrelated to sham and tawdry, despite the fine show they make in the eyes of those who see their best side from the pit or their rouging from the flattering distance of the galleries. In short, not to put [it] to a finer point, Flat Rock is not what it is cracked up to be.

Still there are plenty of nice gentle folks here; but have all the pretty girls quit traveling? Possibly your stronger eyes could stand the strain, but mine are sore with seeing so many plain women. There is not enough philosophy in the world to enable [one] to face these women, nor science enough to investigate them. They almost outrun in number the college men who every hour of the day congregate in this part of the country. Of course I am hard to please—as you would say to yourself while reading this—but it is not altogether answerable—is it?—to shift to something more than unsubstantial figures, architectural faults and lackluster eyes.

The company here is composed, for the most part, of people from the low country of the stuckuppest sort, though with the very slimmest funds, either generally or personally, for their stuckupness. Perhaps the most prominent figure is Miss P—'s. Miss P. is a person of vast proportions and military bearing, carrying herself with that perfect firmness and arrogantness and that air of command which mark the general in any company, without aid of uniform. She is a feminine type of Lieutenant B., for all gentlemen of the company can, I think, bear witness that she is a born commander of men, having the assurance to order that sex about, though she has not had the audacity to appropriate one of them as her own peculiar possession. She is one of those "very maiden" ladies who suppresses children with a high hand when she can, and discountenances all forms of youthful frivolity whenever opportunity offers.

Conspicuous among the gentlemen is Doctor DeS—, not because of his size, however, for he is very small, nor because of his influence, for he seems to have very little, but because of his witty playfulness of disposition and festive selfsufficiency—really a very nice, wellmeaning fellow, but he has little force in the intellectual world. Then there is Mr. Prattle, who, as his name implies, is a lawyer; numerous other men without individuality (for all Flat Rock differs from other summer resorts in having more men than ladies in number of its guests); and ladies of various marked individuality: the romantic who chafes at the dullness of the place, looks innocently into the eyes of the men, and repines at the fate which keeps her ball dresses buried at the bottom of her trunks; Celia who is beginning to manifest that peculiar interest in the origin of benevolent schemes which is one of a series of symptoms presaging oldmaidism; Amelia who is listless and languid, casting her large eyes about at nothing, and dressing in elaborate unbecoming manner; and others of every summer variety.

But I am afraid that, if I multiply these descriptions, you will think that I am misanthropic and that I like to describe my fellow-men and sistermen to their disadvantage. But that is because I think that the weak side of people is generally their most amusing side, that is all. Their good qualities are many, but are deformed and when I watch them I watch them for deformation. Folks without failings are very dull creatures.

Compared with Flat Rock, Arden Park is like paradise. Indeed its habits and comforts have done much towards reconstructing my much shaken belief in the pleasure of summering away from home. How I wish that you could see this quaint house and its charming surroundings! Everywhere I have been, of late, I have gotten many vain wishes that you too were there, but this time I wished for your sake and not selfishly, as before, for my own sake only: for of all the resorts I ever saw this, it seems to me, offers the most attractions for anyone with artistic tastes. Perhaps you have heard all about the place from someone else, but risking that I must tell you something about it. Maybe I ought to get mother or sister to write a description for me, because there is so much here that women would be better at describing than I am; or, though I cannot discover to you the secrets of the needlework and embroidery, I can give you some idea of the effects produced by clever hands of the ex-seamstresses of the place. Originally only part of a private establishment, Arden Park was made the site of a hotel by some of its owners. Having decorated every nook and corner of her own little house Mrs. Bell wanted a wider scope from the original ideas of the architect and in decoration, so she had built under her own direction this income home for summer health and other seekers. Every pretty effect of curtain or cornice or mantel, every graceful style of furniture, every pretty table cover or chair tidy, every ornamental wall pattern that she ever saw in books of design or in splendid dwelling sites[,] she has pleased herself by reproducing here in the cheapest materials. At least she has done as much towards that end as time and her own strength have permitted. The result is a house in which there is constant rest and pleasure for the eye, a constant comfort for the body in the depths of cushioned easy chairs, a house providing a homelike air and altogether a pleasant place of abode because so unlike all other resorts one ever saw. One of the parlors ("the Chestnut room") is specially admired for its handsome mantel, which, constructed under Mrs. B's direction by a common carpenter, makes as fine an appearance, with its series of oaken shelves, its turned columns, its brassbound door, and its quaint roof, as if it had been made by more skilled hands and at greater cost. If I see you on Saturday [September 15], I will show you a photograph of it.

But that is a confession that my description has broken down, isn't it? Well, of course it has broken down. One might—I do not say that *I* might—describe the beauties of natural scenery in such way that only a painter's brush could make it more vivid; but any one can describe that whose chief charm lies in upholsterer's details.

Since I last wrote you I have satisfied the dare which I expressed, as chief in possession of me at that writing: I have gotten at my books once more and have completed the course of reading I had laid out for myself, having come safely through three volumes of colonial history.[5] I feel now as if I were in some sort of trim for my winter's work. And those three books have left a good taste in my mouth. Written within the past 5 years, they are thoroughly in my own spirit and illuminated with my own methods of investigation. They give one a just sense of the distance of the times treated of, though the treatment manifests that coolness of judgment and preserves that justness of proportion which are altogether of the present. If this letter reaches you in season, please drop me a line to say that I will find you in Morganton—though if you should have planned visiting out of town for that day, do not think of foregoing it because I am to be there in search of you. I must take my chances, may they be good ones!

Transcript of WWshL (draft). (WP, DLC).

[1] WW had not yet received ELA's letters of Sept. 1 and 7, 1883. See the Editorial Note, "The Engagement."

[2] WW to ELA, Sept. 1, 1883.

[3] WW to ELA, Aug. 12, 1883.   [4] That is, WW's letter of Aug. 12.

[5] They were J. A. Doyle, *English Colonies in America: Virginia, Maryland, and the Carolinas* (New York, 1882); Henry Cabot Lodge, *A Short History of the English Colonies in America* (New York, 1881); and Eben G. Scott, *The Development of Constitutional Liberty in the English Colonies of America* (New York, 1882). WW had purchased these books while in Wilmington, just before he left for Columbia and western North Carolina. See the receipted bill dated Aug. 2, 1883, from J. B. Lippincott & Co. (WP, DLC).

To Robert Bridges

Dear Bobby,   Arden, N. C., Sept., 12/83

Your letter of August 31st., sent to Flat Rock, has been forwarded to me here at Arden, whither we have flown in supreme dissatisfaction at the accommodations of the "Farmers Hotel."

Of course I am much chagrined at Libby's cavalier conduct in regard to my piece; but I must simply swallow my disappointment; for the piece cannot be shortened without complete mutilation—unless it were to be entirely rewritten, which is now quite out of the question, as the session of the University is at hand. I am, all the same, however, deeply indebted to you for the trouble you took, and the deep interest in the matter.

I hazard addressing this note to Shippensburg, surmising that you are there by this time. I shall reach Baltimore on the 17th, D.V., and I sincerely hope that you can manage to be there about the same time. I shall be sorely disappointed if I don't get at least a glimpse of you.

In deference to the closing of the mail,

Yours in haste, and with love,   Woodrow Wilson

ALS (Meyer Coll., DLC).

From Ellen Louise Axson

[Morganton, N. C.] Sept. 12/83.

Dear Mr. Wilson,

Your letter from Arden [of September 9] was received late last night,—and by the same mail two cards from Father telling me that he is ill, and desiring my immediate return. I hope from the way he has worded them, that it is not *very* serious, but of course I am wretchedly uneasy, and will leave by the next train—the same which carries this note.

I am extremely sorry that I shall miss seeing you. It seems all the more unfortunate that it is just a miss, and no more. But "what can't be cured must be endured."

Our letters seem to have crossed each other, as usual. I suppose the one of last Friday [September 7] has reached you ere this. The other [of September 1], I rather suspect, is held at Flat Rock for postage; for, to tell the absurd truth, I knew it was a double letter, but disregarded the fact, because I knew the sight of that second stamp would be the signal for most unmerciful teasing from the gentlemen here.[1]

Hoping that you will have a pleasant journey, believe me as ever

Sincerely your friend,   Ellen L. Axson.

ALS (WP, DLC) with WWhw notation on env.: "Rec'd while on visit to Arden with the writer Sept. 15th 1883."
[1] Her fears were unfounded: the letter was forwarded.

EDITORIAL NOTE

THE ENGAGEMENT

The peculiar sequence of events that culminated in Woodrow Wilson's engagement to Ellen Axson tempts one to believe that they were later right in ascribing the result to a kind Providence.

As the letters to this point have already revealed, Wilson with his mother and brother visited Annie Wilson Howe and her family in Columbia in early August of 1883. On August 13, he, his mother, brother, and Annie and her children went to cooler Flat Rock and, a short time later, to Arden, near Asheville, North Carolina. Ellen Axson, in her letter to Woodrow from Rome of July 31, had indicated that she might visit friends in nearby Morganton, at about the same time. But there was no connection between her possible visit and the Wilsons' decision to go to Flat Rock.

Woodrow replied to Ellen's letter on August 12, while he was in Columbia, telling her that he and his family would go to Flat Rock on the following day. Receiving no reply, he wrote again from Arden on September 1 and addressed the letter to Morganton, with no street address, in the hope of finding her there. Ellen on that same day wrote a long letter to Woodrow from Morganton. This letter was mailed on September 4 to the address—Farmer's Hotel, Flat Rock—that Woodrow had given in his letter of August 12. Ellen's letter, forwarded from Flat Rock, did not arrive in Arden until after September 9. Ellen, after receiving Woodrow's note of September 1 on September 4, wrote again three days later that it seemed unlikely that she would be able to get to Asheville before the week of September 17—and Woodrow in his note had said that he had to go to Baltimore on about September 14.

Woodrow, not yet having received Ellen's letters of September 1 and 7, wrote once again on September 9, saying that he would stop at Morganton on his way to Baltimore if Ellen approved.[1] Ellen received this letter on September 11. In the same mail she received two cards from her father saying that he was ill and wanted her to come to Rome at once. Ellen replied to Woodrow on the following day that she would leave for home by the next train and miss seeing him. The notation on its envelope makes it clear that Woodrow did not see this letter until September 15.

Ellen's departure was somewhat delayed, and she went to Asheville on Friday, September 14, to take the train to Rome by way of Knoxville. She probably arrived in Asheville in the morning and, being unable to get a train to Knoxville until evening, put up at the Eagle Hotel. By sheer coincidence, not knowing that Ellen was in Asheville, Wilson went there on that same day, perhaps in the late morning. While passing the Eagle Hotel he saw Ellen in the window of her room on the second floor and recognized her vanishing figure by the arrangement of her hair.[2]

Ellen agreed, obviously in response to Woodrow's pleading, to postpone her departure until he had left for Baltimore on Sunday, Sep-

[1] The original of this letter is lost, but see the transcript of WW's shorthand draft printed at Sept. 9, 1883.
[2] WW to ELA, Oct. 30, 1883.

tember 16. They spent the next two days together in Asheville, but the paucity in their letters of accounts of their activities shields their privacy during most of these precious hours. Wilson, in his letters to Ellen of December 8 and 18, 1883, indicates that he spent Friday night in the Eagle Hotel and did not sleep much on account of his excitement, and that he and Ellen also took a short drive in the country on Friday or Saturday. Annie Wilson Howe's letter to Woodrow of September 18, 1883; Joseph R. Wilson, Jr.'s letter to Woodrow of September 19, 1883; Mrs. Wilson's letter to Woodrow of October 3, 1883; and Ellen's letter to Woodrow of Sept. 25, 1883, all make it clear that Woodrow drove Ellen out to Arden on Saturday afternoon to meet his family, that Ellen was extremely nervous, and that Woodrow packed and took Ellen back to the Eagle Hotel that night.

Meanwhile, since their meeting on Friday Woodrow had been maneuvering most cautiously, putting off his declaration of love until the last moment because he feared a negative response that would send him away from Ellen at once.[3] On Sunday, not long before he was to take the train to Baltimore, he confessed his love and asked Ellen to marry him. Ellen was dazed and tongue-tied. Woodrow, pressing hard, said that he was sure of himself and that any uncertainty about Ellen's love would interfere with his work in Baltimore. Ellen, wretched at the thought of their separation, said yes but forgot to profess her own love.[4] They sealed their engagement, in proper fashion, with their first kiss, and Wilson took what he called a "bus" for the station. Before Ellen was out of sight, he realized that he did not know the size of her ring finger. He rushed back to the hotel, borrowed a ring from her, and then returned to the "bus."[5]

[3] WW to ELA, Sept. 27, 1883.
[4] ELA to WW, Sept. 21, 1883, and WW to ELA, Sept. 18, 1883.
[5] WW to ELA, May 19, 1885, Vol. 4.

To Ellen Louise Axson

Office of Foreign Missions,
111 N. Charles Street.

My own darling,   Baltimore, Md. Sept. 18th 1883.

Don't think that I'm going into the business of converting the heathen. I am only in Dr. Leighton Wilson's office, and can't find it in me to delay writing to you until I get back to my hotel.

I wonder if you are longing for me as I am longing for you? Why, my darling, I can't tell you how completely I am yours in my every thought. I did not know myself how much I loved you until I found out that you love me; and I did not realize how happy I had been made by that sweet discovery until I was fairly away from you and on my journey. That scene at the hotel—the formal, embarrassed, almost stiff, declaration in the public hall-way, the sweet hesitating acceptance, the constraint of surroundings, and the hateful publicity—the whole scene forms a very curious memory, as well as a very dear one, dos'nt it? Were ever the advances of a lover met as mine were—by sweet, self-sacrificial doubt, by persuasions of his lady-love that maybe she was not worthy of him and could not make him happy? If you could know my heart as I know it, you would have very few doubts and fears as to the future, my pet. No love like mine can be a mistaken love, when it is returned by love like yours; and I am sure you would be supremely content if I could find language in which to tell you how happy I am. Before I left you on Sabbath [Sept. 16] I did not realize what had happened. But what could be sweeter that [sic] my feelings when I was alone in the driving, noisy train, and had time to think? Why I thought that my heart would grow too big for its tenement. The deep sense of joy and peace that came over me was like the stealing delight of soft distant music—no it was'nt. It was not like anything but itself, not like anything I ever imagined— But, why should I go on so? All that I can say is summed up in the simple truth that *I love you with all my heart.* Do you know that you did not *say* that you love me—did not say it in so many words? and now I am longing to hear you say those words.

I can't help smiling at your idea that you are *homely. My* humble opinion is that yours is the sweetest face in the world, and everybody that has ever seen you agrees in thinking it lovely both in form and in expression. I can't allow you to entertain that extremely original idea of yours any longer, but must ask you to come into the orthodox creed. You are not of that respectable class of plain women with whom we are all called upon to sympathize.

I found father here waiting for me at the station when the train came in at midnight, last night. He sends his warmest love to you, my darling, and his "sympathy." He says that he is *jealous* of you for having so much of my love, to the ousting of everything else; but he will love you as much as you can wish, and the sending of his love is no formal courtesy but the true word of his heart. I shall write again when I can write in quiet without the buzz of conversation around me; and when I get into settled quarters I shall write to your kind father. In the mean time, what would I not give to have *now* the lines of love from you that I know you have sent or are about to send? In present haste,   Your own   Woodrow.

ALS (WP, DLC).

From Annie Wilson Howe

My darling Brother,   Arden Park. Sept. 18th 1883.

It would be impossible for me to tell you how we miss you. Mother was right blue for a while, but she seems all right now. Father said in his letter yesterday that he would not see you if you got to Balt. late in the day. So I suppose you missed him altogether. He understood finally that you would *not* be there on the 15th.

The postal from Miss Ellie came yesterday. The letter is still on the way. I know you must have enjoyed your ride home Saturday evening. Miss Ellie is so lovely—and you had such a delightful horse. You must tell us all about it when you write. What you said, and what she replied &c. Don't forget. . . .

Father said he was going to hunt you up a boarding place, if possible—so I hope you will not have any trouble in that direction.

I just write this hasty note to let you know how much we all miss you, and to remind you how dearly we love you. All unite with me in warmest love to you. Jessie sends a kiss to you.

Your loving sister,   Annie—

ALS (WP, DLC) with WWhw notation on env.: "Ans Oct 8/83."

Wilson's Application for Admission to The Johns Hopkins University

[Sept. 18, 1883]

Candidates for admission are requested to answer, in their own hand-writing, the following questions. Candidates at a distance will be advised by mail, (after their replies to these questions have been received) whether they should present themselves for examination.

I. Date of application.
   Sept. 18th 1883
II. State your name in full, year and place of birth, and present post-office address.
   Woodrow Wilson, born in Staunton, Va., Dec. 28th 1856. Present address, Wilmington, N. C.
III. Name in full of your parent or guardian, and his post-office address.
   Rev. Joseph R. Wilson, D.D., Wilmington, N. C.
VI. Enclose your credentials (a diploma, certificate or letter of recommendation), and give a list of them here.
   I have a diploma from Princeton College, which I can present if necessary, and letters of recommendation which I presented last May with an application for a fellowship and which are still in the possession of the Univ. authorities
V. Name the schools or colleges in which you have been taught, and the time of your residence in each.

One year ('73-'74) at Davidson College; four years at Princeton College ('75-'79.) A.B. '79 A.M. '82 and one year and three months at University of Virginia law course ('79-'80.).

VI.   State, somewhat freely, in your own way, the purpose which you have in view in coming to this University, and the studies you wish to pursue.

My purpose in coming to the University is to qualify myself for teaching the studies I wish to pursue, namely History and Political Science, as well as to fit myself for those special studies of Constitutional history upon which I have already bestowed some attention.

VII.   State in what subjects you are prepared to be examined and indicate, by textbooks or otherwise, how far your studies have gone.

I am prepared to be examined upon the Constitutional machinery of the English government (Bagehots Eng. Constitution) upon the general course of colonial history, i.e. the history of the Eng. colonies in America (Lodge's Short History, Doyle's Virginia, Md., and the Carolinas, Scott's Constitutional Devpt.) upon the phases of the Free Trade controversy and upon other general topics of Political Economy which I have studied in Prof. Fawcett's writings and in the lectures of the late Prof. Atwater of Princeton. My preparation is one of general reading rather than of special training.

Printed form with WWhw entries (MdBJ).

To Samuel Edward Axson

                                        Mount Vernon Hotel
                                        West Monument Street.

My dear Mr Axson,   Baltimore, Sept. 19th 1883

Your daughter has no doubt prepared you for the receipt of a letter from me by telling you what passed between us in Asheville. I know that you will not be surprised, and I trust that you will not be displeased, to learn that she has won my warmest love and that I have declared my love to her and been accepted; and it is my earnest desire to obtain assurances of your sanction of our engagement. That engagement must necessarily be prolonged, because my course here will cover two years and our marriage at the end of that period must depend upon my securing a professorship. These facts made me hesitate for some time about declaring my feelings to your daughter, because I felt that I should be selfish to ask her to engage herself to me when my prospects were so indefinite. But our almost providential meeting in Asheville upset my judgment, which is of so little force in such matters, and I yielded to the consciousness of the fact that my work here this winter would suffer if I allowed myself to continue to be harassed by uncertainty as to her feelings towards me, upon which my happiness so much depends. I trust, therefore, that you will sanction the engagement.

I cannot tell you how happy I have been made by a knowledge of my possession of your daughter's love. I feel not only thankful for so pure a woman's confidence and affection but I feel honored and bettered by her love. My love for her has not run a long[,] but it has run an irresistable[,] course. From the first I was attracted by her beauty and her modesty; but it was only by degrees, though by *rapid* degrees, that I discovered in her those graces of mind and of character which changed my interest into such love as I never thought to feel—a love that has taken complete possession of me and which has won a return of love which is more precious to me than I know how to say.

But I need not tell you how lovely she is; I need only ask your forgiveness for asking your permission to take her as soon as possible from you.

I sincerely hope that your health is entirely restored by this time and that with the return of autumn weather you will experience a complete return of strength. I was very much concerned to hear of your sickness; for my esteem for Mr. Axson is part of my home training and is of much longer life than my interest in his daughter—tho'. I hope you wont tell her so—having only been strengthened by his kindness to me since I have known him for myself.

With sincere regards,
                    Yours Very Affectionately,   Woodrow Wilson

ALS (WP, DLC).

From Joseph R. Wilson, Jr.

My darling brother: Arden N. C. September 19th 1883.

We received your note, telling us of your good fortune, yesterday. And I want to congratulate you, and have the pleasure of saying—*I told you so!* You remember when you were here last Saturday, I told you that people would think you were engaged, and you said—"I wish we were"—then I told you that you could be if you chose. You see my prediction was true. I wonder what cousin Hattie will say when she hears it? *"Sister"* Ellen's letter came this morning, and I will send it right off. Please remember me to my *future sister* when you write. . . .

We are *so* glad that you are engaged to Miss Ellie Lou, because we know that it makes you happy besides setting *our* minds at rest about it, we knowing her to be such a sweet girl. . . .

As I said before, we are all well and unite in unbounded love to you.

Please write soon to your loving brother

J. R. Wilson.

P.S. I am so glad you are engaged to Miss Ellie Lou.

Josie.

ALS (WP, DLC) with WWhw notation on env.: "Ans. Oct. 14/83."

To Ellen Louise Axson

My darling,   Baltomore, Md., Sept. 21st 1883

I was about to date my letter the 20th, but it is after midnight and I must of course be strictly accurate. A quarter past twelve is not the best time for beginning a letter, but you shall have that time, since I've had none other to give you. I am not at present my own master, for I am a guest in a friend's house. An old (though young) college friend[1] has taken me in keeping since my arrival and insisted upon my staying at his house until I can find a boarding place to my taste; and I am, therefore, likely to spend some days as I have spent to-day. The whole of this morning was consumed in looking up all sorts of houses in all sorts of localities where I had learned that board and lodging were to be had if sought by single gentlemen; and dinner was scarcely over in time to admit of its digestion before it was high season to dress for the evening. For this evening Miss Woods had company here to a late tea and I must needs be dragged into making myself agreeable to young ladies and polite to young gentlemen who were utter strangers to me. I did my duty nobly (myself being the judge) but it consumed a tediously long time in the doing, it seems to me. I was all the time longing to get off to write my letter to you; but I believe I *did* succeed in contributing to the pleasure of some of the party, because I am just now, I must inform you, in splendid spirits and anything seems easy to do. Maybe I am feeling the beneficial effects of the mountain air! It must be that, if you too are feeling light-hearted and happy—for we were both in the mountains. *Is* it so with you too?

I shall have nothing to do at the University until next Wednesday (for, as, you remember, I told you, instructions are not resumed until a week after the opening of the University), so that I can make haste slowly in settling in quarters. In the meantime I am unreasonably chafing at being kept here where there is no work a-doing when I would give all the world to be with you. And the way I am being carried captive to kindness the while! Tomorrow afternoon I am to be carried out into the country to play lawn tennis with the young ladies who were here to-night, after which I know not what things lie in store for me.

I wrote to your father yesterday, my darling; and I believe I never did harder work. I wanted to say what I had to say as earnestly, simply, and respectfully as possible, and I succeeded only in being unusually awkward and stiff. But I trust he read the letter indulgently, making due allowances for the circumstances under which it was written and the peculiar difficulties of the subject.

I have heard nothing from you yet. There has scarcely been time for a letter to reach me since you got to Rome; but it has occurred to me that possibly you may have been hesitating to write before I had given you some particular address in the city. I shall, however, be sure to get anything that may come to the general post office until I have a street and number. I am very hungry for a line of love from you. I do'nt believe I can ever make you know how passionately I love you, my own darling; for no expression of word or deed can convey half of the fulness of my love for you. Good-night. I'll go to bed and dream of the kisses I cannot give you.   Yours with all my full heart,   Woodrow.

ALS (WP, DLC).
1 Hiram Woods, Jr.

From Ellen Louise Axson, with Enclosure

My dear Friend,   Rome [Ga.,] Sept. 21/83.
Your thrice welcome letter was received today, and I hasten to answer, though in some little perplexity of mind; for you know I have'nt the slightest idea as to your address? I waited to receive your letter before writing in order to learn it, but it seems you have forgotten it—or perhaps I am the crazy one, and you really gave it me in Asheville, but I have no recollec.

Sept. 24.
I enclose this fragment simply by way of demonstrating that it is not my fault that I have not written before. For just at that

juncture my physician made his appearance and in the most arbitrary fashion bundled me off to bed. In fact I had rather a hot fever, but I "was'nt a-caring." Eddie had a little touch of diphtheria before my return, seemed quite well again; yet I tried to take it from him—as I always do if there is any in the county. This time, however, my little effort was nipped in the bud, and I am now all right again, only fearfully tremulous from the effects of a bottle or so of quinine. So you must excuse this scrawl. I can do nothing with my hand—and not much with my head. I think my getting sick just then was the most selfish thing I ever heard of anyone doing. For the house was a perfect hospital, as it was. I think Papa rather stretched the truth when he reported himself "not much sick." He was not seriously ill, but was so overcome by nervous exhaustion and insomnia that the doctor had put him to bed as the shortest way out of it. And there I was shocked to find him. But he is up again now and very much better; the spell seems to be broken.

I waited until he was better to tell him my little secret, fearing it would excite him too much. Meant to intercept your letter too. But being too shy to take Stockton into my confidence, I trusted to my own watchfulness to effect it, and of course, failed. It reached him in due time and was his first information on the subject. However, he was so much better then that it made no difference.

He was very sweet and good about it, though intensely surprised. He had no idea of my doing such a thing; I had so frequently assured him that I *never* would, under any circumstances. So then Grandmother laughed at him for being so credulous, and I was very contrite. "I certainly never expected to, but then I never expected to meet you;—if I had'nt I never would have done it!"—with other equally luminous remarks! Then he said any number of nice things about you, to her, which caused me to smile all over, and concluded that it had his unqualified approval. However I will let him answer his own letters—which he will do as soon as he is able—as to "say my own say" is far more than I have time for at present.

I never felt before anything like the impatience with this tedious thraldom to pen and ink, which possesses me when I think of all I would like to ask, to hear, and to say, and which it seems to me I could never gain the courage to write.

But I knew how it would be even *then*, when I sat there all dazed and tongue-tied, feeling as though I were in some strange dream—I knew I was letting those few precious moments slip away unused, and that when they were gone I would be left mourning over lost opportunities.

Yet it is not strange that I should have been bewildered to find things had ended so differently from what I intended when you began to speak. For I was resolved that I would not let you do anything so foolish—certainly not for a long, long time, not before you had well considered. But then you should not have said —insisting all the time that you were so sure of yourself—that the uncertainty would interfere with your work, and spoil your year. I could not bear to think of that; though perhaps it was foolish in me to believe that it would make so much difference, whatever you thought or said. I only hope and pray that I hav'nt, like many other short-sighted mortals, in trying to escape from one evil prepared for you another infinitely greater.

And to think that, after all I have said, I should decide such a question without even waiting "to sleep over it"! But that was'nt my fault; it was only because there was *no* "tomorrow." You were going away,—and that is the secret of it all. Ah well, I suppose most theories are constructed only to be toppled over again, or slowly undermined, and it seems one *can* find one's self out, very completely, between the asking of a question and it's answer! I had no smallest idea how much I loved you until I found how wretched I was made at the thought of your leaving—though indeed, when I saw someone drive up before a certain door, and felt my heart give a great suffocating throb, and then a wild desire to escape until I could get myself well in hand, I was sadly afraid that something had happened.

I think my friend Beth will be delightedly triumphant, but not much surprised when she hears my little story: having treated me and my statements with such derision, when in answer to certain searching questions, I confessed that I had finally seen someone whom I *could* love, but that I did *not* love him and never meant to. But the joy of a sudden meeting and the pain of an imminent parting, turning a strong light on one's heart, will reveal things which whole months of ordinary comings and goings would not have discovered. But however the sweet lesson was taught me, one thing at least is *sure*—I *know* it now, right well. You would have me say the words? Then, dearest, I know that I *love you entirely*, now and always, "with the smiles, tears, breath of all my life, and if God choose I shall but love you better after death"; aye, and I love you too, "to the level of every day's most quiet need, in sunshine or in shade."

And I am very, very happy too. I don't know that I was at first.

I was too excited, and too lonely. But the next day! Ah that was a wonderful journey through an enchanted land![1] How I will always love the French Broad! What beautiful memories haunt each one of its fairy-like vistas! How often will I live over again that "white day," and seem once more to see the river, and its valley, running like a shining thread, a fair embroidery, across the web of my dreams, while "in the stronghold of my heart, held back, hidden reserves of measureless content kept house with happy thought."

But I am amazed and abashed at myself! Just now my cheeks were burning at the mere thought "going on so," as you express it, and now I am learning the trick unconsciously! I wonder if I am a very bold sort of person after all. I don't know anything about myself under such new and strange conditions. But I must'nt "go on" any more at present—at least not on paper. I wonder if anyone's mind ever dwelt on one thing as constantly and intently as mine has done during this past week.

This letter is really a disgrace, but I have the palsy, and can't help it. If you can't read it "dinna fash yesel" for it is all nonsense anyhow.

I don't believe I would like you to know how perfectly idiotic I have been over your last. I was so glad to know that you did not miss your father. Was very much afraid you would be disappointed. Please give him my best love, and warmest gratitude for his kind messages. I can't tell you how deeply I appreciate them.

With truest love   Your own   Ellie.

ALS (WP, DLC) with WWhw notation on env.: "Ans. Sept. 27th 1883."
[1] She refers to her trip from Asheville to Knoxville on September 17, 1883.

ENCLOSURE

From Samuel Edward Axson

My dear Woodrow   Rome [Ga.,] Sept 24, 83.

I am just out of my sick bed, where I have lain for a week and been much enfeebled. I am not able to send you such a reply to your pleasant letter as it deserves: but this I do say: I entirely sanction Ellies engagement to yourself. I cannot think that her happiness will be at all hazarded in your hands

I trust the guiding hand of a loving heavenly Father is in this matter. May his abundant blessing be upon you both.

Yrs affectionly—S. E. Axson

ALS (WP, DLC).

Two Letters to Ellen Louise Axson

My own darling,   Balto., Md., Sept. 22nd/83

See what an irrepressible tendency I have to be all the time writing to you! Next week I shall be too busy to write so often and shall have to fix upon certain days, the least occupied by University duties, on which to open my mind and heart to the precious little lady whom I love above all other created beings. It will be a hard struggle to limit myself to one long letter a week, but I shall be helped by knowing that I should not be pleasing you if I were to write oftener than the most thorough attention to my work may allow. In the meantime, however, nothing stands in the way of such self-indulgence and I can soothe my impatience at not hearing from you by telling you over again as often as I please the story of my love. I wish I could just once, by the aid of some happy inspiration, express that love in all its fulness as I feel it! Surely no other woman was ever loved as you are; and surely no other man was ever made happier by the acceptance of his love than I have been!

What should turn up at the post-office this morning but your errant letter which you sent long ago to Flat Rock! I read it with very queer sensations. Here was a letter from Miss Ellen Axson, not from *my* Ellen! Or, am I wrong? Were you consciously mine, darling, before that letter was written? You must have know[n] by that time—you may have seen long before—that I was in love with you. At any rate, that was a sweet, interesting, delightfully long letter, and I devoured it with a huge appetite against the coming of the still sweeter lines that are now on the way to me—sweeter because the hand that wrote them is pledged to me.

Enclosed with your long-lost letter came the note from dear mother which you will find in this.[1] I know that you will read it with pleasure, for you could have no richer possession than my sweet mother's love. In the same mail came a letter from Josie in which he expresses his delight at our engagement not only in the body of his letter and with a "we" which speaks for the whole family part at Arden, but also in a postscript with a capital "I." You seem to have won the hearts of all the Wilson family, my darling.

I can tell you of another person who will be delighted beyond measure at the news, and that's Jessie Bones—not to say Brower. May I tell her of it? I feel like telling everybody, but I will be silent about it in whatever quarter you wish. I would not for the world have you annoyed by having your engagement get to the itching ears of the Rome gossips; but such ears are not apt to hear of such things from my East Rome relations, and I should think it very sweet of you if you would yourself carry the glad news to Jessie.

I am still in search of a boarding house, and it begins to look as if I were not to find just such quarters as I should like to have—at least not at the rates I can afford to pay. I shall make myself comfortable sooner or later, however. I am still sanguine of better fortune when I resume the search in new directions next week.

How often do you think of me, my love? as often and as fondly as I think of you, I wonder? Give my affectionate regards to your father, please, and recommend me in my new relation to your brother Stockton. With love unbounded,   Your own   Woodrow.

1 Missing.

My own darling,   Balto., Md., Sept., 25th 1883

I am sick at heart from not hearing from you. It is now a week since you must have reached home and not a line have I had from you. I am filled with apprehensions. I have been dreaming of sickness keeping you in that horrid, yet blessed, little Asheville, of mishaps in Knoxville, of accidents by the way; I have imagined you ill; I have feared that you found your father worse; I have scared myself with all sorts of images of misfortune that might account for your silence, that has seemed to me so long. I know that there must be some reason for it, but what can it be? It cannot be that my letters from mother and Josie have been delivered all right by the carriers according to my directions and that only yours have been left at the wrong door—and yet not a word have I heard from father who reached home six days ago, and who is usually so prompt and careful about writing of his safe arrival at a journey's end. I give up guessing. I'll try to command patience enough for a few days more of waiting, before allowing my fears to get the upper hand.

Well, the tennis parties, &c. are over and I am at the threshold of my work[.] To-morrow I ought, according to the University programme, to have my first lecture. The past week has seemed to me like a month—I am astonished to find it still September—so full has the time been of searchings in all quarters of this great town for a boarding place, of meetings with strangers, of joy and hope, of weariness, and, latterly, of apprehension. See what a foolish, doting swain I am—and how much in need I am of your sweet, sunny disposition to look always on the bright side of things! It's been two days more than a week since I saw you, and because in that time I've not heard from you I'm torturing myself with all sorts of fears about your health and safety!

I find that Baltimore has as many pretty girls in it as ever—some pretty because of their grace and vigour and ruddy glow of health, some because of their symmetry of figure and of feature, some because of their radiant inteligence of expression, some because of all these combined; but not one have I seen, my darling, who was half so pretty as you are, you precious "plain" little maiden, you. Why, the first time I ever saw your face to note it, when you were an utter stranger to me and I could look at you in dispassionate criticism, I thought that face the sweetest, comeliest, most radiant I had ever seen, with its glory of colour and those wonderful liquid eyes! Will I make you vain, my love, telling you these things that force themselves out of me?

I found a ring to-day that suits me and shall send it to you at once, together with the one you lent me. I know that you will think it pretty. I have had nothing engraved in it. I preferred having that done after conferring with you and ascertaining your taste and preference in the matter. I want you to wear the ring as it is until I can come to you. Then we can have what you please put in it and I can put it on your hand with appropriate ceremonies of our own inventing, and of which I should like to have the direction!

With a heart brimful of love,   Your own,   Woodrow.

ALS (WC, NjP).

From Ellen Louise Axson

My dear Friend,   Rome [Ga.], Sept. 25/83.

As I find myself today at the most comfortable stage of convalescence, doomed to do nothing at all but enjoy myself, it occurs to me that there is no reason why I should not write a few lines to you; notwithstanding my long scrawl of yesterday. Ah, that was a white day; it brought two letters from you! They both came together, after I had written, which constitutes excuse enough for writing again today.

This is a perfect autumn day and I have been spending it in the most luxuriously lazy fashion, swinging in the hammock, and reading Shakespere and those letters by turns. (I vow to you, my love, the last were the finer of the two.) For the last hour or so, I have been chiefly engaged in dreamily watching the flickering lights on yonder garden wall, while lost "in the sessions of sweet silent thought." And now I will still further vary the programme, and, by way of fitting conclusion, send a message North-ward.

I am glad you have found such pleasant friends in Baltimore— am especially glad that you have found them at the first, when you needed them most, and when being at leisure you have most time to "show yourself friendly." Dear old Dr. [Leighton] Wilson is indeed a friend worth having. I well remember him, in Sav[annah], when I was a little child, and how kind he was to me there. You know, I always had a passion for a certain sort of old man; and he being Grandfather's friend and such an "extra Christian," was always one of those whom most especially I thus worshipped from afar.

I thank you very much for sending your dear mother's note, and *with all my heart* I thank both her and your brother for their kind words. I think they must like me because they had made up their minds before-hand that they *would*, and were determined not to be thwarted. I am not really "likeable," at least not to *well regulated* minds, under the best of circumstances; and I must have been most emphatically the reverse on that day at Arden if, as I know was the case, I looked and acted half as "queerly" as I felt. In truth, I was frightened beyond measure—no, not frightened exactly; yet that word must answer for lack of a better.

I can usually exercise a fair amount of self-control, provided always I am not taken unaware, but have time given me "to screw my courage to the sticking point.["] But as we drove through Arden Park, I certainly felt it "oozing out at the tips of my fingers"; as I took off my hat, I could see for myself that I was positively *pale* with fright—or whatever it was—and I could'nt for the world have told then, why or wherefore.

By the way, I don't know why you should abuse your letter to Father. I am sure I heard it very much praised. Was too confused myself to give a clear report but have a vague recollection of hearing the words "manly" "earnest"—"the right ring" &c., with an assortment of other complimentary adjectives.

I will certainly tell Jessie if you wish; that is if she does'nt know already, for Papa informed me last night that *he* had, under pledge of secrecy, told Mr. Bones. They are such very special friends, and on such confidential terms that he thought it no harm. Mr. Bones was pleased to say that he had heard nothing in a long time which gratified him so much. Surely your friends are all very good; and it is a most charming feature of the case to me, that they should be *my* friends too; together with Agnes, the *dearest* friends I have in Rome. Both Jessie and Marion I have loved with my whole heart since they were babies, almost, and nobody knows how I loved their mother.

I shall probably see Jessie in a few days now for I am going to East Rome on Friday. On that day we all scatter for a time. Father and my Grandparents to Gainsville, Stockton to school at Fort Mill, while Eddie and I go to sojourn with Agnes. Papa seems quite himself again now, but I am determined he shall go away for a while. It was a great mistake, his insisting upon remaining at home all summer.

But I perceive it is impossible for me to write a short letter even when I write daily. However, I too will be very busy next week and obliged to deny myself, so it makes no difference now. Though it is a shame that I am not writing to Beth, for not a line have I sent since my return home, even to report my safe arrival. But then I was taken ill very soon, and before that I was so desperately busy with the effort to evolve order out of the confusion which one's absence is sure to engender, and with the nursing—the latter beginning before I had taken off my hat,—indeed, I hadn't time to take it off for half an hour or so.

But it grows so late that I must close, whether I will or no.

I have scarcely left myself light or space to say once again that *I love you.* Ah, my darling, I have no words—will never find them—to tell how much; nor how very, very happy it makes me to hear you say—and repeat it—that you love me. Whenever I read it in your letters, were it several times on one page, it gives me a new and distinct thrill of delight. Goodnight, dear love,

Yours with all my heart.   Ellie.

ALS (WC, NjP).

From Joseph Ruggles Wilson

My dearest Woodrow   Wilmington [N. C.], Sept 25, 83.

You would have heard from me before this had I known where to direct a letter which you would be likely to receive. As it is, you do not give Woods' address—so this must go to the general P. O. Not indeed that I have anything to write that can be of special interest to you—except that I reached home all safe and in due time. ... My health is not satisfactory[.] That head-swimming continues. On Sabbath I was not able to preach, but, fortunately it was raining hard, and I had at hand a good substitute, the Rev. Mr. [Samuel H.] Chester of Maysville, Ky., who is here a-courting. I will doubtless be all right in a few days, with care. In my preparation of sermons I find no difficulty from *this* source.

I am sorry you are so bothered as to a boarding place. Better pay $8 than be troubled any longer, to the detriment of your plans of study.

What you say of your future wife is of course very pleasing to me, who must be delighted with whatsoever delights one whom I love more than I love myself. But, my son, don't let this affection for her *consume* yr thoughts, as it is natural it should. Always remember how much depends upon this year's course at Baltimore.

Believe me to be—   Yours in every sense—   Father.

ALS (WP, DLC), with faint WWsh notation on env. Enclosed in this env. is a Johns Hopkins form, dated Sept. 27, 1883, acknowledging receipt from WW of $10, "caution money, to be repaid on his withdrawal from the University, and return of this card."

Classroom Notebook

[Sept. 27, 1883-May 5, 1884]

Inscribed on inside front cover:
(WWhw) *"Woodrow Wilson 1883"*

Contents at front of notebook (on recto and verso pages):

(a) WWhw schedules of classes in history, political economy, and international relations at The John Hopkins University, first semester, 1883-84.[1]

(b) WWsh and WWhw notes and bibliographies taken in Professor Herbert Baxter Adams' course, "Sources of American Colonial History," Oct. 4, 1883-March 20, 1884. Additional notes covering lectures on April 17, May 1, May 8, and May 15, 1884, are on loose sheets in WP, DLC.

(c) "Diagram of Committee Gov't."

Contents at back of notebook (on verso pages only):

(a) WWhw note (on one page) about the Boston Public Library, the Boston Athenaeum, the Brooklyn Public Library, and the Library of Congress.

(b) WWsh and WWhw notes taken in Professor Herbert Baxter Adams' course, "The Old German Empire and the Rise of Prussia," beginning with the heading "European Constitutions," March 24-May 5, 1884.

Student notebook (WP, DLC).
[1] WW gives another such schedule in WW to ELA, Sept. 29, 1883.

To Ellen Louise Axson

My own darling,   Balto., Md., Sept. 27th 1883

Your letter reached me this morning, together with the enclosed lines from your father. I was very grateful for those few lines of his: they were so kind and so cordial and bore such a reassuring and gratifying message that I actually found my eyes filling as I read them. Your own letter, my love, I read with mixed feelings— with over-flowing joy at your sweet confessions of love, with pain and apprehension at the news of your sickness, as well as at what you said of your father's and Eddie's ill health, and with a strong desire to correct the impressions conveyed by certain words which,

[Page of shorthand notes with partial longhand annotations:]

I. Sources of European History:

II. Sources of English History:

Authorities: {
Elton's Origins of Eng. Hist.
Guest's Arch. Essays.
Rhys David's Celtic Brit.
Grant Allen's Ang. Sax. Brit.
}

Ed. III and Chaucer

III. Sources of American History:

Authorities {
Lodge's Short History of Eng. Col.
Doyle's American Colonies
American Commonwealths
}

*A page from Wilson's shorthand notes
taken in Professor Herbert Baxter Adams' course in
"Sources of American Colonial History."*

if your mouth had formed them in my presence, I should have felt compelled to kiss away. I know, my darling, and appreciate the unselfishness which prompts you to express the hope that you "hav'nt, like many other short-sighted mortals, in trying to escape from one evil, prepared for" me "another infinitely greater"; but the very existence of such a hope is abundant proof, if proof were needed, that there is not the slightest foundation for the fear it implies, and it hurts me just a little, my pet, to have you say such things. I know that you don't doubt my love; but I want you to believe that it is for *you*, and not for imaginary qualities which you may disclaim possessing. I don't think my darling perfect; but I am quite sure that I prefer her before all others, and that I am made supremely happy by the possession of her love.

So I was wise after all in putting off opening my heart to you until I was about to come away! That declaration was on my lips many times during those three days in Asheville, but it was kept back by my inability to read your heart before you had opened it. I realized that a refusal would send me at once away from you, and, wishing, under any conditions, to be with you as long as possible, I delayed the revelation, in order that, if the worst came, my heart might be preserved from breaking by being plunged at once into the distractions of travel, of a new life in a strange city, and of hard study. That study would have been a poor, half-hearted thing without your love to illuminate it and your promise to animate it; but it *might* have saved me from dispair. Since you loved me, my darling, it would have been cruel to send me away without a promise and a kiss; and I am profoundly thankful for "the joy of a sudden meeting and the pain of an imminent parting" which prevented you from making the great mistake of witholding your hand where you had given your heart.

I cannot describe to you my delight at the receipt of your letter. I had come away from the post-office with a heavy heart so often during the last few days that the revulsion of feeling was tremendous when I took your letter from the envelope this morning, and I was almost frightened at the way my heart beat. It was the sweetest letter ever written—and it seems to have been written with great rhetorical art, for it observed the laws of climax, beginning "My dear Friend" (as if I were nothing more!) and ending in confessions of love which are surely the sweetest, as well as the most modest, that ever a maiden made! May God bless "my own Ellie"!

What are the things, my love, which you would like to ask, and hear, and say, but which you cannot gain the courage to write? It need not require much courage to say to me anything you please. I do not know of anything that I would not tell you without reserve; and I cannot imagine anything in any way concerning yourself that I should not delight to hear. It is the greatest privilege of our present relation to one another that we can open our minds to each other absolutely without reserve, and I shall esteem it the best earnest of your love if you will write to me as freely as you would commune with yourself.

But this letter will not catch the next mail if I go on. Give my love to your father and brothers, and thank your father for his answer to my letter. I trust that he is quite well again by this time, and that you, my darling, are quite strong again.

You may direct your letters hereafter to 146 N. Charles St., where I will be by day after to-morrow.

With tenderest and most unbounded love,

Your own   Woodrow.

ALS (WC, NjP).

To Ellen Louise Axson, with Enclosure

146 N. Charles St.,[1]

My own darling,   Balto., Md., Sept. 29th/83

How can I sufficiently thank you for your sweet letters, so over-flowing with love and tenderness? They fill me with an indescribable delight: all the more because I know that such confessions cost you a little struggle with your natural shyness and reserve in such matters. I love you with all my heart, my darling, and it makes me unspeakably grateful to know that I have won your *first* love and won it so completely—by I know not what attractions. I am really, then, the only man you ever met that you thought you *could* love? No wonder friend "Beth" was derisively incredulous of the delightfully self-confident assertion of a certain lovely maiden, that she knew whom she *could* love but had power to will whom she *would* love!—especially if friend "Beth" suspected that said possibly-lovable man was deeply in love with said lovely maiden and that he was eagerly bent upon testing her determination not to love him by every honorable art at his command.

Are you thinking, my love, as you read this, that you were *not* the first to win *my* love? and did I guess right when I guessed that what you were hesitating to ask in ink when your first letter was under your pen was about a certain un-named lady of whom I told you once as we walked on the rail-road? Well, I wont tell you anything about her—not even her name—until you ask me; but, to make the asking easy (if you want to ask) I'll volunteer one little piece of information, which is that I never knew what love was until I knew you, and that, if it was love that I felt for the character which I supposed that lady to possess, it was a very contemptible dwarf beside the strong passion which is now at large in my heart, and which leaps with such tremendous throbs of joy at thought of your love. You need not shrink from hearing me speak of what I have heretofore taken for love: for no woman, my darling, ever had more entire love given her than I have given you. I don't know why I should have spoken of this, or why I should have made that guess; maybe I have altogether mistaken your thoughts and done you an injustice; but there can be no harm in any topic which gives me an introduction for another declaration of my love for you.

Ever since you fitted me with that description which stands opposite the date of my birth in that birth-day book I have been casting about to find a description that would serve as a moderately correct picture of yourself. I can't find any that suits me entirely; but here's one I beg you to read. Though taken from an obscure writer it is better than any other I have found: "A maiden of slight but firm and graceful figure, bearing herself with a sweet, demure grace and a charming modesty of demeanor; 'a maiden fair to see,' with the brightest of faces—a face ever and anon illuminated with the sunniest smiles and the prettiest play of vivid colour—a face fairest when she was speaking or smiling, but always beautiful because of its wide, liquid, eloquent eyes of richest brown and the chaste lines of its mouth, so inviting and often so tremulous with meaning; a maiden sweet to know not only because of her womanly accomplishments, but most of all because of her flow of glad spirits, her bright and kindly wit, and her loving, confiding disposition."[2] If this fellow never saw you, he probably saw once somebody very like you. He might have turned out a better sentence, but he could not have drawn a prettier picture.

Yesterday was the day on which you were to go to East Rome, and it occurs to me that you may have left town before the ring reached you. I sent it by express, addressed in care of your father, and the company may be perplexed what to do with it when they try to deliver it and find the house closed. Will you feel more like an engaged person when you wear the visible token of the contract?

You seem to have felt during those last moments that we were together in Asheville very much as I felt. I too was dazed and tongue-tied. I hardly realized what had happened; for I cannot say that I *expected* to succeed. Although I knew the strength of my love for you, and felt sure that you must have seen it, you had concealed from me all evidence of your true feelings towards me, you coy little actress you! and I hardly dared to hope that I had won your love on a four months' acquaintance; and when you allowed me to discover your love I was almost incredulous of my own senses. I was not sure of them until I had kissed your sweet lips, my darling. But, even if we did let those last precious moments slip without that delicious interchange of confidences which was then possible, we'll be together again some day, my love, and can then tell each other what sweet secrets we will. Oh, how I do long for the time when I may hold you close to me and *hear* you say that you love me!

Somehow I take very kindly to this new business of love-letter writing! When one's heart and mind and even his very being is full of one subject, it's marvellously easy and delightful to write about it. The ease exists because the treatment of such a subject as this consists in ringing every conceivable change upon one single declaration which one's correspondent likes to hear as well as one likes to write it.

But, by way of variety, I must tell you about my new quarters. I have secured board, after much worrying and fatiguing search, in one of the pleasantest portions of the town, within one square of the monument and within three of the University. I am just accross the street from the Peabody Institute, in whose splendid library I shall do most of my reading this winter, and my room is bright and comfortable. I moved in this morning, and already begin to feel as if I were in trim for work. Knowing that you would like to know how my time is to be employed from day to day, I enclose a schedule of my exercises at the Hopkins. The first meeting of the "Seminary" took place last night and was very interesting.[3] I will describe its meetings to you some time when I am not at the end of my letter.

My darling, I can't tell you how much distressed I was by the news of your illness. Are you quite well again? Do take care of yourself, my precious one! You know you have an additional reason now for being careful of your health; and unless I know that you are prudent I shall be miserable. You are more to me than all the world beside, and if I were to lose you my heart's light would go out, and I should care infinitely less about living myself. Without hope of your companionship, what work could I do?

Give my love to your father when you write to Gainesville and to Stockton when you write to Fort Mill. Does the latter know our secret? Where *is* Fort Mill? Is it a school of repute?

Give my regards, please, to Mr. and Mrs. Tedcastle.

Good by, my precious one. Write as often as you can to

Your own   Woodrow.

ALS (WC, NjP).

[1] The street address on WW's following letters will not be reproduced until a new address is used.

[2] Actually this was WW's own composition. See ELA to WW, Oct. 2, 1883, and WW to ELA, Oct. 9, 1883.

[3] This was the Seminary, or seminar, of Historical and Political Science, founded in 1876 by Austin Scott and conducted after about 1880 by Herbert Baxter Adams. It met first in the Maryland Historical Society, then in a base-

ment room of the Peabody Library. The Seminary moved to the Bluntschli Library in a new university building in 1883, after a group of German Americans of Baltimore presented the library of Professor Bluntschli of Heidelberg University, Adams' professor, to the University.

Adams and his assistants, Drs. Ely and Jameson, both identified below, were the faculty members of the Seminary in 1883-84. The student members were Edmund K. Alden, T. Alexis Berry, Davis R. Dewey, John A. Fisher, Edgar Goodman, Elgin R. L. Gould, William P. Holcomb, Edward Ingle, John H. Kennard, Jr., Charles H. Levermore, Stewart B. Linthicum, B. James Ramage, Daniel R. Randall, Edson P. Rich, Adoniram J. Robinson, Shosuki Sato, Walter B. Scaife, Albert Shaw, Charles Howard Shinn, Basil Sollers, William B. Steel, Bond V. Thomas, Lewis W. Wilhelm, Woodrow Wilson, Thomas K. Worthington, and Arthur Yager. Members who had a more or less special relationship to WW will be more fully identified as the relationship develops in this and future volumes.

No minutes of the Seminary were kept until Jan. 4, 1884. Adams then began keeping a systematic record through student members who served as acting secretaries. These records, preserved in the Library of The Johns Hopkins University, even in their cryptic form reveal much about Adams as a graduate teacher. WW served as secretary on Feb. 22, 1884, Feb. 27, 1885, and May 1, 1885. Extracts will be printed to reveal both WW's participation and the character of the discussion in the Seminary.

E N C L O S U R E

Schedule of Exercises at The Johns Hopkins

[c. Sept. 29, 1883]

Mondays: 12-1   International Law* (with Prof Adams)
            4-5   Advanced Political Economy (Dr. Ely[1])
Tuesdays: 12-1   International Law.
Wednesdays: 12-1   International Law.
            4-5   Advanced Political Economy.
Thursdays: Sources of American Colonial History (Dr. Adams.)
            12-1.
Fridays: 12-1   Eng. Constitutional History (Dr. Jameson[2]);
            4.-5   Advanc'd Pol. Econ.;
            8-10   Meeting of Seminary of Hist. and Pol. Science.[3]

* This is really a history of international relations.

This schedule is for only the first term, up to Christmas.[4]
[WW's note]

WWhw (WC, NjP).

[1] Richard Theodore Ely, born Ripley, N. Y., April 13, 1854. A.B., Columbia University, 1876; Ph.D., University of Heidelberg, 1879. Taught at The Johns Hopkins University, 1881-92; Professor of Political Economy, University of Wisconsin, 1892-1925; Professor of Economics, Northwestern University, 1925-33. One of the founders of the American Economic Association, which he served as secretary 1885-92 and president 1899-1901. Distinguished author and lecturer in many fields of economics. Founder and editor of The Journal of Land and Public Utility Economics.

[2] John Franklin Jameson, born near Boston, Sept. 19, 1859. A.B., Amherst College, 1879; Ph.D., The Johns Hopkins University, 1882. Fellow, Assistant, and Associate in History, The Johns Hopkins, 1881-88; Professor of History, Brown University, 1888-1901; Professor of History, University of Chicago, 1901-1905. Director, Department of Historical Research, the Carnegie Institution of

Washington, 1905-28; Chief, Manuscript Division, Library of Congress, 1928-37. Managing Editor, *American Historical Review*, 1895-1901, 1905-28; president, American Historical Association, 1906-1907. Author and editor of many works in American history. Died Sept. 28, 1937.

³ WW, in the lecture schedule that he wrote in the student notebook described at Sept. 27, 1883, noted that these classes met in Room A, 113 W. Monument St., Baltimore. WW also attended Ely's undergraduate course in political economy.

⁴ WW was mistaken. The Johns Hopkins was on the semester system.

To Ellen Louise Axson

My own darling,   Baltimore, Oct. 2nd, 1883

This is a dark, stormy day here. The rain pours dismally, and I feel lonely and homesick. With all the hardening experience of eight years absence from home, I have never grown altogether reconciled to being away from those I love. I suppose there never was a man more dependent than I am upon love and sympathy, more devoted to home and home-life; and, my darling, my heart is filled to overflowing with gratitude and gladness because of the assurance that it now has a new love to lean upon—a love which will some day be the centre of a new home and the joy of a new home-life! I shall not begin to lead a complete life, my love, until you are my wife. Who is more affected by the character of his home than a student, and who has sweeter opportunities for unselfish ministrations than a student's wife? She may be all in all to him.

> "for his gayer hours
> She has a voice of gladness, and a smile
> And eloquence of beauty, and she glides
> Into his darker musings, with a mild
> And healing sympathy, that steals away
> Their sharpness, ere he is aware."¹

Unless, indeed, he be a bear who repels love and receives sympathy with ungracious surliness! I don't think, my precious one, that I shall prove a bear. I think that I can promise that you will have no reason to regret having married me: that is, if love and tenderness can keep regret away.

I dreamed about you all last night, my darling—and that was the first time I've dreamed about you since we parted in Asheville! I've thought about you so constantly every day that my mind seems, heretofore, to have insisted upon being allowed a recess during sleep. But that was a joyous dream of last night! I woke up laughing, this morning. I had been doing in the dream what I have never done in reality; had been showing you a side of my disposition that you have never seen. I dreamt of the jolliest frolic that we had together; of gay chases through the house (*some* house); of playful caresses and stolen kisses; of mischievous intentions and coy counter-plots; and so it was that I awoke in a glee. You do'nt know what a jolly goose I can make of myself upon occasion, when I am with people of whose esteem I am sure, and who will think no less of me for my nonsense. Can you love me in my every humour? or would you prefer to think of me as always dignified? I am afraid it would kill me to have to be always thoughtful and sensible, dignified and decorous. But I'm not apprehensive as to what you may think! If you love the uninteresting man that is in me—for "I am not really 'likeable,' at least not to *well regulated minds*"—I have no fears as to what you will think of the boy that is constantly cropping out, when I'm not under the constraint of "company manners." Ah, my sweet Ellie, how I like to dwell upon your love for me! It is precious to me beyond expression! And my love for you? Why, my darling, just imagine, if you can, how much you want and then multiply that an hundredfold and you will have some measure of it.

Good-bye, my love. The clouds, the actual clouds as well as the figurative, have broken and shown signs of clearing away since I've been writing this letter, the mental clouds having passed altogether off. Consider the warmest of kisses pressed upon the sweetest centre of your lips by   Your own   Woodrow.

P.S. My love to your father and S., when you write—also love to Eddie and regards to Mr. and Mrs. T.   Your   W.

P.S. No 2: Upon reading this letter over I can't help smiling at it! Love certainly leads a man into writing as he never dreamt of writing before!   Lovingly,   W.

ALS (WC, NjP).
1 From William Cullen Bryant's "Thanatopsis."

From Ellen Louise Axson

My darling,   East Rome [Ga.,] Oct. 2/83.

This morning brought me at once, your two letters—of the 27 & 29—and therefore this has been, like the day on which, I believe, I last wrote, "high holiday." "All it's moments, lightly shaken, saw themselves in golden sands." I wonder if you would laugh, or what you would say, if you knew how perfectly daft your letters make me! But no one could be expected to receive such letters, and keep very cool. They are so like yourself, dearest, so—no, I take it all back! They are simply, very absurd, especially your *quotations.* You are a naughty person to perpetrate such a "goak," as Mr. A. Ward would say, on me. I feel victimized. You ask if I am likely to be rendered vain by *such stuff?* Perhaps it might have that effect, if I had not such a very decided mind of my own and were not so abominably hard to influence, when I once make it up. But that seems always to have been a trait of mine; and since it is so often a very bad trait, it certainly ought by way of recompense, sometimes to serve me in good stead—as for instance in keeping my head from being turned, as the result of the amiable weakness of my friends. I am reminded of one of those little reminiscences of my infancy in which the Grandmama was indulging, a few days ago. It seems she was trying the effect upon me of moral suasion, on some disputed point; and pleaded thus: "Ellie, Grandmama don't do that and Mama don't do it, and Little Auntie don't do it." Whereupon I calmly observed, "Yes, but *I* do." So in this case, I simply aver that "there is no disputing about tastes," and continue of the same opinion still. Yet, alas, for the consistancy of our poor humanity; I am made most unreasonably happy by that perverted taste of yours! I mean I am *so* glad *you* have a perverted taste! It is especially unreasonable in me, because I know you can't always be so deceived.

No, dearest, I don't mean again to "hurt" you by even seeming to doubt your love. I *do* believe that you love *me* and not some imaginary qualities. I only mean to say that you will find cause to change your mind on *certain points.* But then I hope you will continue to love me "for dear love's sake," and because I love you so very, very much, and am so entirely yours. Ah me, what would I not give to be everything that is good and lovely for your sake! Surely it is true that one may grow better and wiser, when one wills it so strongly. Yet how can I deceive myself into believing that I will become for your sake, what in all these years, I have not become for my Saviour's sake, whom I love still more.

The ring also came this afternoon. It is a *perfect beauty* in every respect. The setting is extremely chaste and the whole thing in *exquisite* taste. It is sparkling now on my hand most brilliantly, and giving me what Janie[1] would call "quite a turn." I can't tell you, my darling, how much I prize it. You are very, very good—but are you not also very extravagant? Please excuse my impertinence, but really I was startled and amazed at the unexpected apparition of a *diamond.* You know, it is not absolutely necessary that one should wear that particular sort of ring in order to "feel engaged."

Yes, perhaps I do feel more engaged with this outward symbol of it on my hand. Or perhaps it is simply that as time passes, it becomes more like my normal condition. I seem already to look back at my former self, the girl who had never loved, as at a stranger, and to recall with wonder and amusement some of the thoughts and opinions which she entertained. Yet my "theories" have been, by no means all over-turned. On the contrary, those of any consequence I have made good. As I was writing to Beth the other night, about *you*, I suddenly stopped in full career, while a great pity filled my heart as I thought of the letters which she wrote me two years ago, upon a similar occasion. The curious undertone of apology running beneath all that passionate love; the evident effort to justify herself and defend her choice. Poor Beth, she is *always* on the defensive where Mr. Erwin is concerned, and she has need to be. Whereas I could so honestly say that I had found my—yes, I must say it—my "ideal," though I am a little out of humour with that much-abused word. Now I know you will laugh at me; but it is so! Why even those lines which Beth and I selected together, years ago, as best expressing our idea, were written for you! I never saw so perfect a description of anyone. A "Jersey" jacket could'nt fit more closely! You may remember the words, for with calm audacity I quoted them to you myself, knowing that you could not read my thoughts as I did so.

> "A mouth for mastery and manful work.
> A certain brooding sweetness in the eyes.
> A brow the harbour of grave thought."[2]

But see what an inveterate scribbler I am. Two whole sheets are gone, and I feel as though I had scarcely begun. I have not even replyed to certain questions in your letters which demanded an answer. Yet I must close now, for as Mr. Tedcastle is so good as to read to us in the evenings, it was quite late when I began to write. So as I want you to know at once that the ring is safe—I will send this *short section* of a letter tomorrow, and another chapter as soon thereafter as possible!

I am very glad that your weary search for an abiding-place has ended so successfully. You must have charming quarters. Of course it is unnecessary to say that I was greatly interested in your weekly programme. I trust your work and your home will prove equally pleasant. What sort of things are "the meetings of the Seminary"—a free discussion on a given subject?

I get very encouraging reports from Father. He has slept *well* every night since he left, and of course, as that was the principal trouble, he is *much* better. Eddie and I are both entirely well again, and are having a delightful visit with Agnes. Goodnight dearest. With best love, and many, many thanks for your beautiful gift, believe me as ever   Your own   Ellie.

ALS (WC, NjP).
  ¹ Janie Porter, a girlhood friend then living in Savannah.
  ² From Jean Ingelow's "Laurance."

Classroom Notebook

[Oct. 3-Nov. 26, 1883]

Inscribed (WWhw) on inside front cover and first page:
"*Woodrow Wilson 1883*" and "Dr. Ely *Political Science*"
Contents:
  (a) WWsh and WWhw notes and bibliographies taken in Dr. Richard T. Ely's undergraduate course in political economy at The Johns Hopkins University, first semester, 1883-84. Examples printed at Oct. 29, 31, Nov. 2, 1883.
  (b) WWsh and WWhw loose pages of notes on political economy and economists, and bibliographies, which seem to have been prepared for purposes of review.

Student note book (WP, DLC).

From Janet Woodrow Wilson

My precious Son,   Hendersonville N. C. Wednesday Oct 3–83.

I was *so* glad to get yours of the 30th, last night. I hoped to write you long before this,—but there was not much satisfaction in writing you with a feeling of uncertainty as to my letter's reaching you. Now that I have your address, it is all right. I am so glad to hear that you are so pleasantly situated in the matter of boarding—from your description—as to location, and so on,—I think you are very fortunate in your choice. Tell me as much as you can about your view &c, that I may have some idea of your surroundings, in your present "home." . . .

How could you fear, my darling, that I could for one moment doubt your true affection for me! The precious love that my dear boy has invariably shown me all his life! No, dear—my heart was very sad, at seeing you drive away that second time—but it was a comfort to me that you were not alone—that you had at your side the sweet girl you loved so much—and who, I thought, I had reason to hope, loved you in return. No, sir—never imagine that your mutual love, & happiness, can ever cause *me* anything but joy & thankfulness. Tell dear Ellie that she did not show her fright—during her visit at Arden—except by the sweetest & most natural behavior. I wonder when she will be able to come & make us a visit? It is a great happiness to me to know that your heart is at rest, my precious boy—and I like to think what a comfort your correspondence with dear Ellie must be to you[.] Please give her my warmest love. I must not write more now—as I will barely have time to write my daily note to dear papa. Josie is well and happy —has made friends, as usual, with the boarders. He is quite anxious to go home, however. God bless you—

Yours, as ever,   Lovingly   Mother.

ALS (WP, DLC).

From Edward Ireland Renick

Dear Wilson,   Atlanta Octo. 3/83

I am very sorry that after having planned for an acquaintance with my very interesting Grandmother in Balto. you will not be able ever to see her in this world. The good woman, having outlived all of her early friends, died a few days since in her 85th year. . . .

This is intended to draw from you, if possible, the first of what I trust will be a long series of lengthy & valuable letters. I shall write fully in reply. We all send best wishes—Gaddy & I especially—

Yours sincerely   Renick

ALS (WP, DLC) with WWT notation on env.: "Ans. Oct. 25th., 1883"; also misc. WWhw and WWsh notations.

From Joseph Ruggles Wilson

My darling Son—   Wilmn [N. C.,] Oct. 4, 83

Your two letters were very welcome you may be sure. I am so glad that you have procured such good quarters in so pleasant a part of the city, and so convenient both to the U'y., and to the great library. More pleased, however, am I because of the fine spirits which you seem to enjoy, together with the manly studious purpose that is in you. God bless you, my noble boy, and give you abundant success. Try to let *Him* guide all yr. thoughts and plans. As to the church-going, it seems to me that you might freely use your own pleasure, seeing that you are only temporarily a resident. Were you to *connect* yourself with a Baltimore Church with a view to permanent membership, I would advise connection with either Dr. Lefevre's[1] or Dr. Murkland's[2] Ch. As it is, if you prefer "Memorial" Jones,[3] I can see no good reason for so denying yourself as to go elsewhere. I could wish, however, that sometimes you would hear Lefevre (1) because he is my personal friend (2) because he thinks. As to Murkland, he is very much of a puppy—

yet they speak of him as "eloquent." When he returns, see what you can make of him as an "orator" (save the mark![)]

Your dear mother expects to leave H[endersonville] on Saturday, (6th) & after remaining a few days in Columbia, to get home by Friday the 12th[.] Won't I be glad to see the dearest of women, (not excepting yours)!

These MSS. came to hand several days ago. I hope you can still make use of them, as they deserve.

My health is fair enough—although I am still troubled with occasional dizziness. I *must* have had a partial *sunstroke* when in N. York. There is no other theory that will account for the facts in the case. I am very lonely—yet the hope of seeing your mother & Dode so soon cheers me wonderfully.

Please give my love to Ella Lou when you next write—for I suppose you do write say once a month!!   Your affc   Father

P. S. Acknowledge receipt, please, of MSS.

ALS (WP, DLC).
[1] The Rev. Jacob A. Lefevre, pastor Franklin Square Presbyterian Church, Baltimore.
[2] The Rev. William U. Murkland, pastor Franklin Street Presbyterian Church, Baltimore.
[3] The Rev. John S. Jones, pastor Brown Memorial Presbyterian Church, Baltimore.

To Ellen Louise Axson

My precious Ellie,   Baltimore, Oct. 4th/83

It may seem very selfish or exacting of me to clamour for so many letters from you; but it is now a week since I've heard from you, and I am beginning to be tortured by the fear that maybe, after all, your apparent convalescence when you last wrote was deceptive and that it is a return of sickness that has kept you silent this long week past. If you could know how miserable that fear makes me, you might get some conception of the ardour of my love for you, my darling. I try to reassure myself by recalling your declaration that you expected to be too *busy* this week for writing; but I can't help being anxious. I have a suggestion to make about our future correspondence, my love. Suppose we each fix upon some certain day of the week for writing—not restricting ourselves to writing on that day only (for, judging from my present inclinations in the matter, I shall not, for my part, be always able to satisfy myself with the writing of only one letter a week), but writing on that day anyhow, if only a few lines: in order that we may be able to look forward with confidence to the coming of a message by a certain mail. Don't you think that that would be a

pleasant arrangement? It certainly would be to me. Now that
the secret's out; now that I may say to you just what's in my mind
and indulge in what delightful confidences I please, there'll be no
calculating with any certainty the times and seasons of my letters
—at least, not further than the limitations of the above suggestion.
Of course I am not weak enough to postpone duty in order to indulge in the pleasure of writing to you; but there are snatches of
legitimate leisure which can be utilized, and which count for a
great deal when one is on the lookout for chances for self-indulgence. When my heart has time to brood in silence, it runs so
eagerly to you, my love, and is so filled with yearning tenderness,
that its passion just *must* find vent somehow; and how else can it,
but by sending you multiplied assurances of its love? I hope that
you delight as much in my declarations of love as I delight in the
modest love passages of your letters—passages in which I can almost see the pretty blushes with which you write them. If you
do'nt, you can't enjoy my letters at all, for each one of them has
been, like this one, only one long love passage. I've read those
sweet paragraphs of your two letters so often, my darling, that I
know them by heart; and I never tire of recalling them.

Have you written yet to friend "Beth," or to that poor fellow in
Florida? I pity him from the bottom of my heart. He has lost what
it has *made* me to win, the sweetest treasure in the world, the love
of a peerless woman. His loss has been my gain, but he has lost
what he can find nowhere else.

But he is not the only one—is he?—whose hopes have been
dashed by what happened away off from them, on the French
Broad. In spite of all your shy avoidance of society, I know that
you have not been able to hide yourself from mens' eyes, and I
have some recollection of a certain persistent widower who made
me furious one night at prayer-meeting by presuming to join you
in your own pew; and of a certain young jeweller of whose attentions Jessie warned me (for Jessie shrewdly guessed my secret
long ago) and for whom I was at one time inclined to feel the
utmost antipathy. I wish I could see you and *talk* about these
things, which now you may tell me! Out upon this tedious spreading of ink, this slow pen, this featureless paper! But what shall we
not say to each other some of these days, my love, if God spare us?
Pen and ink are poor enough substitutes for loving personal intercourse, but they are better than nothing; and maybe it will be
easier for you to write about these things *first*. I have'nt forgotten
what you said about the superior facility of writing as a vehicle
for certain thoughts, and I am too impatient to hear everything

about yourself to be willing to wait till I can hear that everything from the tongue I so long to hear. So you wont mind my asking such impertinent (?) questions, will you?

I've some right funny things to tell you, my darling, about those two last visits of mine to Rome, those visits during which you stole my heart; but they are things which would be spoiled in the writing and which must really be saved for future telling. While you, according to your Morganton confessions, were concluding simply that you had seen a man with whom it might be possible for you to fall in love, I had actually fallen in love, had gotten in desperately deep, and was making a rare goose of myself in consequence. Since you've promised to love the goose, I may promise to expose him some of these days.

Well! I began this letter with the full intention of trying to make it interesting by describing my quarters, my University duties, and my professors, and here I've almost reached the bounds I've set myself and not a word of that description is penned, and I shall have to tell you about "the Hopkins" in another letter. There is little to be said about my quarters. My room is not large, but it is a cheery front room with good-looking, shapely furniture in it and lighted by a broad, generous window which looks out upon a handsome square whose fountain and plats of grass and ornamental shrubs are grateful to the eye in the midst of a great city; and across upon the brave architecture of the noble Peabody Institute, as well as upon the graceful shaft of the beautiful Washington monument. The outlook is, indeed, everything that could be desired; but within I am sometimes very lonely, for I do not yet know my fellow or sister boarders well and feel my isolation all the more because I've so recently come from the hospitable home of cordial and intimate friends. But I'm fast making pleasant acquaintances amongst the University students, and I find lots of company amongst the books of the Peabody library. My exercise is taken strolling about these busy streets, getting infinite amusement out of the curious people I see. Did I say, lately, that Baltimore was as rich as ever in beautiful women? Well, she has plenty of ugly ones too. (This must comfort "plain" persons like yourself!). There are two especially that I am forever seeing on this very Charles St. They are evidently sisters and remind me of nothing so much as *wasps*, with their exceeding small waists, their round bodies that spread without curve to the shoulders, and their narrow visages set in each upper corner with a prominent eye! I hurry by them, lest they should sting me.

But here I am at the end of my paper, and the other queer forms of the streets must wait. Good-night, my precious one. I am anxious to hear that you are well and that you are wearing the ring I sent you with a heart full of love for the sender. I can't hear that often enough. With love unspeakable,

Your own   Woodrow.

ALS (WC, NjP).

From Ellen Louise Axson

My darling,   East Rome [Ga.], Oct. 6/83

This is the fourth time I have seated myself with this tablet to write you & each time I have been interrupted before I had even begun—how is that for an Irishism! So now it is Saturday afternoon, and something will probably interfere again, yet I will at least make the attempt. What with reading in the evening, driving in the afternoon, & *talking* in the morning, I don't seem to have many moments to myself here. But I am having a charming visit. Agnes and I thoroughly enjoy being together, and she is *such* a dear old girl—and so too is Mr. Tedcastle! I am in a high good humour with him at present; partly, I suppose, because he shines so brightly by contrast with Mr. Erwin, with whom, to tell the truth, I was rather disgusted. He is certainly just as "nice" to Agnes as he can possibly be, and they seem to be insanely happy.

I too am insanely happy today; for I have received a most delightfully encouraging letter from Papa. He says "things have taken a new turn, and he believes he is going to get *entirely* well." And *I* believe that if he *thinks* so, the battle is half won; is'nt it almost literally true in these nervous and mental troubles, that "there is nothing either good or ill but thinking makes it so"? It may be merely a passing mood, but I certainly hav'nt heard him talk so for three years, and it sounds cheerful.

Your charming little letter of the second, full of dreams, and other good omens, was received yesterday. You dear delightful boy! I don't think I am very dreadfully shocked at any of the revelations it contains; and I faithfully promise to love you in your every humour. Something rather a-pro-pos to that happened last night—Mr. T. and Agnes had been frolicking about like two children, and when they stopped, to rest, he looked at her quizzically, and asked me if I ever imagined she would "turn out" like that. For you must know that Miss Beville[1] the school-mistress was a most dignified young person. I replyed that "I 'never did,' and I was shocked, grieved, and mortified." Whereupon Agnes declared that I would be a great deal worse some day, and Mr. T. inquired if I thought that possible. I had opened my lips for an indignant negative, when Agnes looked imploringly, and whispered "say yes, please"; and I suddenly remembered that it would never do to reflect on my friend's conduct in so decided a fashion. So I sagely remark that "we know what we *are*, but we know not what we shall be," and get well laughed at for my pains. But, to do Mr. Tedcastle justice, that is his first offence. He has been very good to me. When he brought me your two letters, the other day, just at dinner-time, and I had only time to read them once before going to the table with my cheeks all aglow and oh, so absurdly absent-minded, that adorable man not only made no remarks, but did'nt even smile—when I was looking. Agnes found out my secret by "the natural method," and then teased me to let her tell Mr. T. I knew, of old, that he could keep a secret, and I feared that if I stayed in the house, he, too, would discover it for himself, and, unless put upon his honnour, would reveal it; I also knew that it would torment Agnes to hide anything from him, so I consented—quite a high mark of confidence, considering that I have told no one else, not even my own Uncle.

So you wish to know what it was which I could not gain courage to ask, or to say, and if your "guess" was correct? Why, no, it was *not*, exactly. I was not alluding to any one matter, in particular. I would ask all sorts of questions on all sorts of subjects —such silly questions as these, for instance; when was that "first time you ever saw my face to note it"; and, when did you first discover that you were not regarding it with "dispassionate criticism" &c. &c? I am deeply curious to know how this strange thing came about. This is a case in which "details are *not* melancholy." I dare say Emerson did not think so himself when he was in love with Miss Ellen Louise Somebody, or Miss Lidian Somebody else.

Yet I did think of that other little matter too; and now, since you have suggested it, I will play jealous, and ply you with questions. So you will inform me Sir, if you please, who it was, and when, and where, and how, and why, and wherefore—the beginning and the end! Was the wound entirely healed before last summer, and did it leave a very deep scar? Are you very sure there isn't the *least* little rankling pain remaining? So much for No. 1 —and don't overlook any of my questions! Now for No. 2.

What are your relations with Miss Katie Mayrant, exactly? And, especially, how does she regard you? Is she your confidante?

Does she know about me? Do you correspond with her—but of course you do, since you go several hundred miles to see her. It is a queer little business, you know; such instances of disinterested friendship are so rare, that my curiosity on the subject is pardonable.

Now, honnour bright, did you not, at some stage of your acquaintance, imagine that you might, could, would or should fall in love with her; and then, upon learning to know her better, decide that it was a mistake? But that is a sufficient display of jealousy for one letter. I will "ask" no more.

As for the things which I would, and would not, like to "say," there is no need for you to concern yourself about *them*, my love. It is very evident that I *do* find the necessary courage, and I *am* saying them, with a vengeance. True, I always want to *unsay* them again immediately, I am so ashamed of myself! I did make a fresh start once. This very letter has had several narrow escapes from burning, and I really don't know how the last one ever managed to get mailed. Yet almost in the moment of repentance I repeat the offence—and so it goes. When in my calmer moments I suddenly strike, after my fashion, the spectator attitude, I cannot but laugh at the pendulum-like regularity with which I am continually passing from one conflicting mood to the other. But if my darling *likes* to hear me say whatever comes into my head, or rather whatever comes out of my heart, so I *will*, though it does make my cheeks burn. What I would like to say, dearest, is something that would make you half as happy as some of your "sayings["] have made me.

But are you very sure that you are not haunted like myself by the dark suspicion that I am a desperately brazen sort of creature?

You ask about Stockton's school. It is a Presbyterian school, not famous except among Presbyterian preachers. Dr. Buttolph, Cousin Edward Palmer and Dr. Giradeau(?) all sent their sons there, and recommended it to Father as a particularly fine training school. Fort Mill is in Yorke District and I fear a very shabby little town from Stockton's account.

The poor boy is home-sick beyond measure. I have been really distressed about him, though I suppose it is good for him now to be thrown somewhat on his own resources.

But I have reached the crossing-place and so must end. Agnes & Mr. T. send their kindest regards. With *best* love—no, I said that before and it was not true, for I love you better every day— if this thing goes on in endless progression I don't know what will become of me—with truest love believe me, now and ever, your own   Ellie.

P. S.

I open this to say that yours of the 4th has just been received[.] I am sorry, dear love, that you have been again rendered anxious by not hearing. I knew you would be, the first time, and was distressed at my inability to prevent it. I will, if you like it as well as any day, always write on Monday night, mailing my letter Tuesday morning.

Yes, I have written to Beth and received an answer today, which, perhaps, I would show you if you were here. Have not yet written to Florida. By the way, I don't know what could possibly have suggested that jeweller story. I solemnly assure you that never in my life have I had even a "bowing acquaintance" with *any* jeweller! As for the little widower, why should we waste time over him when there are so many more interesting subjects to talk about?

I have seen Jessie since I came to East Rome, but not alone; Miss Brower and a friend are visiting her. "The baby" has grown wonderfully and is lovlier than ever.   Lovingly, Ellie

ALS (WC, NjP).
¹ Tedcastle's first wife, as appears in WW to ELA, Nov. 26, 1884, Vol. 3.

From Joseph Ruggles Wilson, with Two Enclosures

My darling Son   [Wilmington, N. C., c. Oct. 9, 1883]

I enclose a couple of missives for you—and take the opportunity to say that I greatly love you; and also that it is just possible for yr Mother to be here on Thursday morning the 11th.

Good bye & God bless you   Your affc Father

P. S. If you send the draft back here payable to me or to your Mother it shall be deposited with the am't already in bank

ALS (WP, DLC), with WWhw notation on env.: "Ans Oct. 12th 1883."

ENCLOSURE I

From Melville R. Hopewell

Dear Sir   Tekamah [Neb.] 9/18/83

Yours 13. at hand inclosing note C. A. Jack $300. for col. Same will have attention   M. R. Hopewell

APS (WP, DLC).

From Melville R. Hopewell

Dear Sir   Tekamah, Neb., Oct. 5th 1883

I remit Proceeds of Chas A Jack note as follows—

Principal	300.
Int.	51.75
	$ 351.75
Chgs &c ex[tra?]	5.
Dft. enclosed =	$ 346.75

Do you wish to sell your lands at present? I have had inquiry for prices.   Truly Yours, M. R. Hopewell

ALS (WP, DLC).

Two Letters to Ellen Louise Axson

My own darling,   Baltimore, Oct. 9th 1883

I *did* laugh at the idea of my being your "ideal" (because I am such very gross stuff out of which to construct an ideal!); but my amusement was mingled with another feeling which was the predominant one—with a keen delight at the assurance that your love for me is great enough to overlook my faults and weaknesses and enthrone me in your gentle heart. God grant, my precious Ellie, that you may never have cause to regret my kingship there! Your letters afford abundant evidence of the good faith of your declaration that I am your ideal; for I suppose that ideals are above such smallness as vanity or self-conceit, and that you feel quite safe in saying all the sweet things you say to and about me because you are sure that I am not in danger of being drawn by them into undue self-complaisance. I have my serious doubts on that subject; but, for fear you might quit saying these sweet things out of consideration for my weakness, were I to express those doubts, I will pretend so far to be ideal, and will assure you that you need have no fear of spoiling me by anything you can say. I promise to remain (?) humble in spite of the triumphant pleasure of being loved and admired by the lovliest of women[.]

Meantime I am quite safe in showing you without reserve all the lovely forms you yourself take in my eyes, for, by your own showing, you are proof against all opinions but your own in such matters. In one view I am very glad that you are prone to hold so fast to your own opinions; for the habit will doubtless make you tenacious of your opinion of *me* in the face of all possible discoveries!

Speaking of discoveries, how did you come to recognize the authorship of the "quotation"? There are but two possible explanations—tho' I am afraid that you will not acknowledge either of them as the correct one—either the authorship was betrayed by the interior literary style, or the description was recognized as too minutely accurate. Apparently the former is the true explanation, for you speak of the whole passage as "such stuff." Now, dearest, listen to that poor humbled, "obscure writer" while he solemnly avers, with his best manner, that, having intended that as a portrait of yourself and having expended upon it, for love of you, his best talents, he now feels constrained, since you reject it with ridicule, to abandon forever his vocation as painter of the human face and form, and, renouncing ambition, to return with resignation to his humble inheritance, the trade of a sign-painter, in which lowly but honest calling he may win credit amongst his fellow men by diligence in painting such signs of the time as do not fall within the contracts of his fellow-craftsmen. He believes in his heart that that was a truthful picture, whatever its faults of execution; but without your patronage he cannot continue what was undertaken only for your service.

I am delighted, my love, that you approve my taste in the choice of a ring (do you also assent to my directing the ceremonies with which it shall as soon as possible be put on your finger by myself?); and I was not surprised that your first thought had been that I had been rather extravagant. Poor men ought not, I admit, to buy diamonds *under ordinary circumstances*. But that was a purchase, my darling, which a man has to make but once in a life-time. That is a token which you are to wear all your life, and I must be forgiven for indulging the desire that this ring which meant so much to me—which symbolized the happiest event of my life and which stood for the brightest promise of my life—should be in itself as beautiful as possible. I fancied that gold by itself was not of a pure enough lustre: I wanted, besides, the clear, spotless transparency of the purest of gems.

Do you know, dearest, that I am sometimes now-a-days very much embarrassed when writing to you? I do'nt mean that I am ever embarrassed in the ordinary sense, but that I am at a loss to know just how to express myself. Here's the difficulty: my inclination is to be "making love" in every sentence, to warm every turn of subject with an indearing epithet. No term of endearment could run beyond the reality of my feelings: *but one can't convey vocal tones to the written sheet*, and I have as great an aversion from "sweet talk" as from set and formal expressions of affection. That often *reads* like gush which would give only pleasure to the most refined and fastidious ear if earnestly uttered or gently whispered. There are no words which can express the sentiment of a kiss. A kiss is one of the gestures of that unspoken language which is often so much more eloquent of the deeper and subtler feelings than are any spoken words. And so it is that when I write to you I don't know *how* to write. My heart is so full of love and yearning tenderness for you, is so dominated by *feeling*, that every attempt I make to express myself seems to me at best only stiff and artificial, having nothing like the freshness and fulness of the sentiments it is meant to convey. I would tell you all my thoughts, my darling: for will it not be our joy to be wedded in mind and in heart as well as in legal form?— but I cannot with this *pen*. So I must, perforce, be content to use these formulas, "my love," "my darling," &c., instead of the much more adequate language I might use, or even invent, were I with you; begging you to believe that whenever I use them, if it be twenty times on a page, *my whole heart is in them*, and that they are never used *as* formulas.

Do you know that you have said nothing about that lecture of my father's that I left with you? Have you read it yet? or did you forget it and leave it in Asheville? or did'nt you like it? *I* liked it for its originality of idea and beauty of language; but may-be you did not?

Whenever I write to you a thousand questions suggest themselves, but I wont ask them all. I'll ask only, whether you've seen Jessie yet; and what you do with yourself all day. You know, my darling, I've never seen into your daily life at all yet, and I want so much to see into it! There's nothing about yourself that I *don't* want to hear; but most of all I want to be able to be with you in imagination as you go about your ordinary duties. Nothing that you may have to do or that you may want to do is without interest to me, you may be sure.

Which remark reminds me of my own duties and recalls a promise which, in ordinary decency, ought to be fulfilled. I promised to tell you some things about the University, and here I'm nearing late bed-time and the end of the eighth closely-written page of this epistle without having done any more than tell you, what you knew before, and what by this time might go without the saying, that I love you. Well, maybe you will forgive me for the many variations and repetitions of this declaration and will agree that the University and the "Seminary" can wait[.]

I told mother what you said about your feelings at Arden, and here's an extract from her last letter to me: "Tell dear Ellie that she did not show her fright during her visit to Arden, except by the sweetest and most natural behavior. I wonder when she will be able to come and make us a visit? It is a great happiness to me to know that your heart is at rest, my precious boy, and I like to think what a comfort your correspondence with dear Ellie must be to you. Please give her my warmest love." This is from father's last: "Please give my love to Ella Lou when you next write—for I suppose you do write—say once a month!!" Mother is in Columbia on her way home.

Give my love to your father when you write to him, commend me to Stockton (my questions about whom you have not answered) and to Eddie, and keep for yourself just as much love as you want from   Your own   Woodrow.

P.S. Regards to Mr. and Mrs. T.

My own darling,   Baltimore, Md., Oct. 11th/83

Your letter of the 6th reached me this morning and prompts me to write at once. Your letters always do have a wonderfully stimulating effect on me, and I like to answer them while the delight they give me is in its first freshness. I've got my hand full this time, though. No less than *ten* big questions, not counting subdivisions, stare me in the face, each equally imperative for an answer! Well, I brought it on myself, so I must set about my confessions with as good a grace as possible under the circumstances. I take the liberty of reversing the order of your questions and proceed, first of all, to give account concerning "No 2." It would be next to impossible for me to say just what *are* my relations with Miss Katie, tho' I know very clearly what they *were*. I corresponded with her until August last, but then she, quite mysteriously to me, stopped writing. Just before I left Wilmington for the summer she sent me an embroidered band which she had promised me for my new spring hat (the band you saw in Asheville), accompanying it with one of her pleasant letters. I could not reply at once, but did reply very soon, from Columbia, sending my most cordial thanks —and that, apparently, was the end of the correspondence. Not a word have I had from her these three months. Our relations *were* those of the closest intimacy, though I never for a moment thought that I "might, could, would, or should fall in love with her," and she knew that I did not. She was my confidante in many things and I had several times spoken to her of you; but she knew nothing about my feelings towards you. How can I tell, you darling little inquisitor you, how she regards me? I'm accounting only for my own feelings, and am no keeper of her conscience. I wish I knew, that I might tell you, but I do'nt.

Well! how do you think I'm getting on? There are five questions disposed of concisely and, I hope, to your satisfaction. I allow myself no breathing time, however, before plunging into the others. Some of them I shall answer in narrative form, for I can tell the story now with nothing but satisfaction.

When I went to the University of Virginia to take my law course Aunt Marion [Bones] was, as you may remember, living in Staunton, and I, of course, frequently went over from Charottesville to see her, being glad to get away from my books whenever I could, and being especially glad to get away to Staunton, where I was born, where, consequently, I had many friends, and where, in the school season, a fellow could see as many pretty girls as anywhere else on the continent. As it happened, however, that was just the time when it was dangerous for me to be thrown much with attractive members of the opposite sex; for I was just fresh from Princeton where for four years I had been leading what was, to all intents and purposes, a monastic life. At any rate, it had been a life spent away from all society but the society of men, and I was absolutely *hungry for a sweetheart*. I had always had a great capacity for loving the gentle sex, and had, of course, never been without a sweetheart until I went to Princeton. But just at that time the stock seemed to have run out, and for four years I was in the abnormal condition of caring no more for one damsel than for another. I went to Virginia with a deep sense of the inconvenience and discreditableness of my condition and with a definite determination to find a lady-love if possible. Seriously, I *was* in need of a sweetheart. No young man lives a complete life who is not lifted out of himself by love for some woman who stands to him for a type of what is pure and lovely. If he has no such love, a great motive power is lacking in him. Even you, my darling, do'nt know yet how intensely I can love (though you shall know it some day); and at the time I speak of I did not know you, who were to claim the utmost gifts of my love. I felt then that I had a great unexpended store of affection which some one ought to appropriate; and it was while that feeling was in possession of me that I met, at Auntie's house, the girl I came to think entitled to that store of affection. That girl was my cousin, Hattie Woodrow, whom you have met, and who was then at Miss Baldwin's with Jessie. I had not seen her since we were both children; but I had received occasional letters from her, and I had formed a very extravagant idea of her character—an estimate which was not likely to be lowered by our free and delightful intercourse that winter, nor by the fact that she was the idol and admiration of the whole school. I had about made up my mind beforehand to fall in love with her, and afterwards it seemed an easy enough thing to do. During the next winter (for she was then at home in Ohio) we corresponded quite regularly and quite voluminously; and in the summer of 1881 Jessie and I went out to Ohio to make her a visit, and it was during that visit that I completed the little drama by proposing to her and being refused.

Such is the bare outline of a story that is full of a great many interesting, and some very curious, particulars, which it is much better to keep for telling some other day. There are strange plots of dear Auntie's mixed up with the history of those two years which cannot be committed to paper; and there is an interior view of my intercourse with Hattie which cannot be reproduced in a letter. A epoch of my life seems to me to have closed at dear Auntie's death. She had been connected in a very peculiar way with that love story, and at her funeral I met Hattie, with comparative indifference, on the anniversary of the day on which I had proposed to her.

I will not say that I was mistaken in her character: perhaps I was not; but I had been mistaken in thinking that she was *capable of loving*. She has no heart to give. I know that you will not think, my love, that I say this in pique, because she had no love to give *me*. I say, knowing whereof I speak, but in all kindness towards her and without the least particle of bitter feeling, that I now know that she is heartless; and that before last summer came all traces of the wound she had given me were gone. No scar remained anywhere but on my *pride*, which winced a little at the memory of the huge mistake I had made with such wilful blindness.

So now the confessions have been made! How I wish, my precious one, that I could now hold you in my arms and seal these confessions with kisses on your sweet lips! They would be both seal and commentary.

But there is a most delightful task remaining: there are two more questions to be answered. Oh! you dear, delightful, egotistic girl! So, you want to know when I first saw your face to note it—

do you?—and when I first discovered that I did not regard it with dispassionate criticism. In other words, you want to know, from the most authentic source, when and how I fell in love with you. Well, you shall. But let me first warn you to beware how you ask such questions: you may get more than you bargain for! To have you press such interrogatories do'nt fill me with any "dark suspicion that" you are "a desperate brazen sort of creature" (on the contrary the freer you are in showing me everything that is in your heart the happier I am); but consider the license you give me by your example! I have been burning to ask similar questions myself, it being a deep mystery to me when and why you fell in love with me, and I have been restrained from asking them only out of consideration for you; but can I refrain much longer now, think you? Reflect how delightful it would be for a certain respectable person to hear what it is that you like about him.—But the questions are waiting.

The first time I saw your face to note it was in church one morning during the first of my last spring's visits to Rome—in April, was'nt it? You wore a heavy crépe veil, and I remember thinking 'what a bright, pretty face; what splendid, mischievous, laughing eyes! I'll lay a wager that this demure little lady has lots of life and fun in her!' And when, after the service (I think it had been a communion service) you spoke to Mrs. Bones, I took another good look at you, and concluded that it would be a very clever plan to inquire your name and seek an introduction. When I learned that this was Miss "Ellie Lou" Axson, of whom I had heard so often, quite a flood of light was let in on my understanding and I was conscious of having formed a small resolution. I took an early opportunity of calling on the Rev. Mr. Axson. That dear gentleman received me with unsuspecting cordiality and sat down to entertain me under the impression that I had come to see only him. I *had* gone to see him, for I love and respect him and would have gone to see him with alacrity if he had never had a daughter; but I had not gone to see him *alone*. I had not forgotten that face, and I wanted very much to see it again: so I asked rather pointedly after his daughter's health, and he, in some apparent surprise, summoned you to the parlour. Do you remember?—and do you remember the topic of conversation? how your father made me "tackle" that question that was so much too big for me, 'Why have night congregations grown so small'? What did you think of me *then*, my darling? But, though I was still delighted with that face, I still to the end of that call could regard it with dispassionate criticism. But that dispassionate state of mind did not last very long. It was not very long after that that I walked home with you from Jessie's one afternoon as you were returning from Mrs. Tedcastle's, and I remember leaving you that afternoon with a feeling that I had found a new and altogether delightful sort of companion. Passion was beginning to enter into the criticism, and had pretty nearly gotten the better of it by the time we had climbed to the top of that hill. What do *you* remember of those two walks? Oh, you naughty girl! Here you've kept me till past midnight answering your questions! How can I tell the *stages* of my falling in love with my darling? They were imperceptible; but they have culminated in a love which is now part and parcel of my very being! Good-night, my sweet Ellie; I love you "more than tongue can tell."   Your own,   Woodrow.

Regards to Mr. and Mrs. Tedcastle.

ALS (WC, NjP).

From Ellen Louise Axson

My darling,   East Rome [Ga.], Oct. 11, 1883.

Do you remember the old story of the farmer who had so many things to do, he *couldn't* decide which to do first—so, *he went a-fishing!* On the same principle, I, having any number of duty letters demanding attention, but being unable to determine which has the first claim, will quietly write to you instead! I must, however, try to write a short one, if such a thing is possible, for my friend, Mr. Thornwell,[1] has been—*entertaining* me this evening, and it is now eleven o'clock. I have already spent enough time today reading and rereading your letters, to have written quite a long one; but then I was somewhat "low in my mind" in consequence of not hearing from you, and that was the best means of consoling myself. Though if that be the proof, I need consolation for something—can it be your absence?—every day. One of my regular habits, I have been here now long enough to grow domesticated, and form them, is to linger in the piazza alone, while Agnes drives in for Mr. T., and by the slowly waning light, to assure myself that I made no mistake, when I read in those letters certain never-to-be-forgotten things.

Memories of Agnes and her home will always, I think, be interwoven with the fairest passages of my life; for it was at the close of my last visit to her, in the spring, that my first meeting of any consequence, with you "came to pass."

And one of my chief mental occupations, during the last two weeks, has been the going over and over, in endless, happy retrospect, the intervening time. I always thought that I had *not* a circumstantial memory, but it is odd how clearly I recall every little incident of that time, words even, and looks, thoughts and feelings. It is a curious and sweet revelation to myself, this looking back and learning how "silent as one that treads on new fallen snow, did love come on me, ere I was aware." Silently, yes; but very swiftly too! I can scarcely realize that I have know[n] you so short a time; only between the early and latter rains—the first winter yet to come.

Ah these beautiful, peaceful autumn days! They have been indescribably happy ones to me—

> "Thou need'st not ask of me
> What this strong music in the soul may be!
> What and wherein it doth exist;
> This light, this glory, this fair luminous mist,
> This beautiful and beauty-making power."[2]

I have always loved best of all the year, the golden October, and thought that to be in the country then was all that heart could wish. What joy to drive between the quiet fields, with this warm, mellow light over all the world, or to stand at my window, in the early morning, and look over at those violet hills, or watch the level rays break across the valley, touching here and there with sudden, transient gleams, the nearer woods and meadows!

> "Bliss was it in that dawn to be *alive*,
> But to be *young* was very heaven!"[3]

And now having already, with the aid of Wordsworth, exhausted the resources of the language, and employed the most daring of superlatives upon very ordinary occasion, what remains to be said, when, to those sources of contentment, is added the trifling circumstance of being in a frame of mind similar to that of the lark, when,

> "He sings, and he sings, and forever sings he,
> I love my love and my love loves me!"[4]

Alas, alas, what a letter! Three quotations too, on one sheet—disgraceful! I still cherish the hope that at some future time I shall be able to give these documents a slight sprinkling of sense—or what passes for sense, with me—but at present there is certainly no wandering from the subject.

However, my backward glance over the two happy weeks just past has had one good effect at least; it has made the present moment almost equally happy, which it was not before. To tell the truth, I felt seriously disposed to *cry*, this morning, when the mail came in. Nothing but pride prevented. But I don't want to be unreasonable; and if your duties forbid your writing but once a week, I will try to be—no, I *will* be content. But unless you can assure me that such self-denial is absolutely necessary, I shan't be satisfied, at all. You see, you ought, if you can, to write me more than once, whether I do or not, because my scrawls are so much longer. Though I don't write you as *often*, I have written you as *much*. As I said before, I can't write a short letter. It teases me to try; as at present, when I am really cross, because I am compelled to say "good-night."

I still hear good reports from Father. He will remain until next week, and I will be in East Rome 'till he comes. Indeed, I may decide to stay always, for Mr. Tedcastle says he is going to adopt me as his daughter! With much love to you[r] parents and all the family, when you write, and a whole heart-full for yourself, believe me, dearest,   Yours always.   Ellie.

ALS (WP, DLC).
  1 Charles Thornwell, a gently but firmly rejected suitor, and the son of the Mrs. Thornwell visited by Ellen in Morganton the previous month. He seems to have gone far away. See E.L.A. Erwin to ELA July 6, 1885, ALS (WP, DLC).
  2 From Coleridge's "Dejection: An Ode."
  3 From Wordsworth's "The Prelude."
  4 From Coleridge's "Answer to a Child's Question."

To Robert Bridges

Dear Bobby,   Baltimore, Md., Oct. 12th., 1883.

At last I can sit down to indite you a letter. Your note[1] sent to me while I was with Hiram on Eutaw place[2] came to me in due course of mail, and it should, by every rule both of friendship and of courtesy, have been answered long ago; but the rules of necessity and of the University in this case overcrew all others, and so this letter is only just now begun.

When your note reached me, and for many days before and afterwards, I was busier and more anxious than I can tell you in conducting a wide-extended search for a boarding house. It was imperative that I should find one as soon as possible in order that I might be settled and in trim for steady, uninterrupted work by the time the University exercises were to begin. As it was, I was not ready at that time, nor for some days later. I came to my present quarters only about two weeks ago; and ever since then I have been over head and ears in work—work which for the first week consisted for the most part in trying to get into harness, trying to learn the ways of the 'Varsity. My quarters are very pleasant indeed, and located at the most convenient of all places, between Peabody Institute and the University, just accross the street from the former and only three blocks from the latter. Most of my studying time is spent in the library of the Institute; for these 'Varsity men send us poor fellows on all sorts of reading excursions which we can make only in some great museum like the Peabody. As soon as I can get into college ways once more and avoid kicking over the traces, I shall, I think, like the work here thoroughly well. Certainly I shall not lack for stimulating examples or for intelligent guidance.

Just now we are hearing a very suggestive series of lectures from Dr. Von Holst.[3] We caught him on the fly as he was returning from the West and he is not, therefore, delivering written lectures, for he had no time to prepare such; but the extemporaneous talks we are having from him are, I think, possibly more stimulating and invigorating because they come from him in unsubdued fires. He is to lecture every afternoon for two weeks and in the course of that time we ought to get a good deal of juice out of him.

I need not say, old fellow, that Hiram and I were extremely sorry that we could not meet you at Pen-Mar[4] as you proposed. You may rest assured that it was only because it was absolutely out of the question for us to come. Hiram was very much mortified about the mistake concerning the telegraphing. His plan was, as he thought he had announced it to you, that he should telegraph in case we could come, but keep silence in case we could not.

I am going to write you another letter as soon as ever it is possible, but I must not close this one without telling you the great news of the season: that I am engaged to the fair damsel of whom I wrote to you not long ago. I'll tell you more of her by-and-by; for the present you must be content to know that I am the most serene of men.

With love unabated and unabatible,

Yours as ever,   Woodrow Wilson

WWTLS (Meyer Coll., DLC).

[1] Bridges to WW, Sept. 27, 1883, ALS (WP, DLC).

[2] The Woods home at 374 Eutaw Place, Baltimore.

[3] Hermann Eduard von Holst, born in Fellin, Estonia, June 19, 1841. Ph.D., University of Heidelberg, 1865. Assistant Professor of American History, University of Strassburg, 1873-74; Professor of Modern History, University of Freiburg, 1874-92; Professor of History, University of Chicago, 1892-99. Died Jan. 20, 1904. His most famous work, *Constitutional and Political History of the United States* (7 vols., Chicago, 1876-92), was a highly partisan and nationalistic account concentrating on events of the period between Jackson and Lincoln.

[4] A resort near Blue Ridge Summit on the state line east of Waynesboro, Pa.

To Ellen Louise Axson

My own sweet Ellie,   Baltimore, Oct. 14th/83

I have not forgotten that scarcely two days have elapsed since I wrote you a twelve-page letter: I am quite conscious, on the contrary, that I am carrying this matter of letter writing beyond all bounds of reason. But, then, I do'nt intend *this* to be a twelve-pager, and I feel justified in writing on this particular day because it is a sort of *mens*iversary: just four weeks ago to-day you were sweet and imprudent enough to promise to marry a certain respectable person whose life has been brightened beyond measure by that promise, and who has felt every Sabbath afternoon since that memorable 16th that he had cause for special thanksgiving that He who ordereth all things had given him the love of such a woman as could fill his life with sweet contentment and his life-work with joy. What would have become of me, darling, if you had *refused* me? That afternoon as I forced myself to tell you of my love, it was not ordinary embarrassment that made the declaration cold and awkward: I trembled with the consciousness of how much depended on your answer. I was rendered almost dumb by the terrible conflict of hope and fear within me.

You knew that I loved you before I told you; did'nt you, love? Why, I had told you often enough by plain enough signs, and even by pretty plain words. Do you remember the verses I gave you in the wagon as we rode home from the picnic? I remember the charming blush with which you read them, but did not dare to interpret it as I wished I might. Did you imagine that I had copied all those lines to give you just because I thought them pretty and hoped they would interest you from a literary point of view? Had you not noticed my manner as I asked you to correspond with me, during that delightful talk in the hammock? and did you not remember what I had told you then about how I regarded you—how near I had come to telling you *then* that I loved you? I would have done so, if I had dared—what would you have said? In one of your letters you say that you did not know how *much* you loved me until you found how wretched it made you to have me go away (from Asheville). Then you had known before that that you loved me *some*? How long had you known it? Tell me all about it, if you do'nt mind telling. And tell me something else: tell me what were those thoughts and opinions of the dear little stranger, your former self, ("the girl who had never loved") which now so amuse you and fill you with wonder? Am I asking too many questions? You need not feel bound to answer any of them, my darling. I ask them only because they seem appropriate to the day, and because it would gratify me so much to have you confess all the secret particulars of that brief but delightful courtship which has bound our hearts so close together. Such confessions cannot be unmaidenly *now*.

I shall write to you, dearest, every Tuesday evening and mail my epistles on Wednesdays. My letters will reach you, therefore, on Fridays; yours will reach me on Thursdays. What happy days Thursdays will be with me! Ah, you powerful little maiden! You've got one Woodrow Wilson entirely under your thumb: his happiness is altogether in your hands! Please treat him well and write to him as often as you can. And now, my darling, I renew my vows. May God bless us in this sweet day of hope and give us his grace in that blessed coming day when we shall be man and wife! With love unbounded,   Your own— Woodrow.

ALS (WC, NjP).

From Joseph Ruggles Wilson

My darling Son—   Wilmington [N. C.], Oct 15 83

Dode sends to-day yr. box, via Bay Line to Balt. It is directed to you at 146 N. Chas St. It ought to get to you by Wednesday or Thursday

As to Latin Dict. I cannot find your own. I therefore send mine. If *yours* should be in this box it will be a pity that you did not say so. The German Dict. also non est. You can buy one, however, for 20 or 30 cts:—you don't want a *fine* copy. The two Dict's are sent by Express.

We are all well, except myself whose head is still in a whirl more or less. To write *long* letters I feel that I cannot:—but love you I do all the same. I need hardly add that Mother and Dode are full of affection for "brother."   Your aff   Father

P. S. As you do not *say where* yr. Lat. Dicty is, I will wait until you get your box: it must be in it—if not, then I will go to the expense of sending mine. I send the French Dict. by mail

ALS (WP, DLC) with brief WWsh quotation and bibliographical references on verso of letter and WWhw notation on env.

From Marion Wilson Kennedy

My dearest brother—   Little Rock, Oct. 15th 1883

Your letter contained as pleasant a piece of news as I have often read. Indeed I am delighted, for your sake and for *ours*, as well.

These brothers are such troublesome chaps generally, they seem to make a rule to try to offend mother and sisters when they marry; but you are a happy exception, my brother. I do not know as much of our prospective sister as I hope ere long to know, but all I do know of her is as good as good can be. Isn't she too good for you? No; you know very well I am in no danger of thinking that. Can't you just see dear Mother's eyes flash if anyone were to ask her or to hint that they thought that? . . .

Ross joins me in warmest love and hearty congratulations. Give my love to *her*, if there is any corner left of any letter you write in which to squeeze it.   Lovingly your sister, Marion.

ALS (WP, DLC).

From Ellen Louise Axson

My darling,   East Rome [Ga.], Oct. 15/83.

I am not surprised that you found your hands full last Thursday evening, with my ten questions and their sub-divisions. My only surprise is that you escaped so easily! I thought I was preparing for you even greater "toil and trouble." But it takes a man thus to grapple with a subject which isnt quite to his taste, and dispose of it summarily and effectually. I have found, from *observation*, that a woman, whether she designs it or not, is disposed to talk all around a subject like that, and finally glide away from it altogether, without throwing much, save indirect, light on the matter.

Yes, I will avow myself satisfied—for the present at least. I may desire a commentary on the text when I see you.

With regard to Miss Katie, I would merely remark that it seems a pity such a beautiful example of disinterested friendship should apparently be on the point of coming to grief. Would it not be well for you to fly to its rescue? Such a rarity deserves to be tenderly cherished. I am not surprised at Miss Katie's part of it, for I know *women* can remain faithful to feelings "purely platonic"; but *you* form a notable exception to a general rule. I don't doubt, however, that you *are* an exception. For if you say so, it is *so*, if it *isn't* so!

About "No. 1," I have nothing to say at present. I havn't had time to adjust my ideas to the surprising new light thrown on the subject. How very odd that it should occur to one to fall in love with one's first cousin! Perhaps that was the trouble with her— not that she was heartless, but that you seemed too much like her brother. Such a strictly family affair I should judge rather unfortunate, for even where it ends well, there are serious objections;

and where it ends badly, it is also apt to end all pleasant, *natural*, cousinly intercourse. Yet after all you were very excusable, for she is remarkably pretty and charming. I was altogether fascinated with the little that I saw of her, and I have always heard wonders of her various gifts and graces.

But I believe that in the two letters now requiring answer, you have given *me* quite a budget of assorted questions, to which it would be well for me to give my attention. One of those questions, I am ashamed you should have had the opportunity to ask. I have intended, in every letter, to tell you how much I "enjoyed" your father's lecture; but, like the "University" and the "Seminary," that expression of opinion has somehow always managed to get itself postponed—I assure you altogether against my will! I did like it *exceedingly*. Both the thought and mode of treating it were strikingly original and beautiful. It was certainly *entertaining* in the highest degree, besides being a great deal else that is even better, and beyond that. And some things in it were extremely suggestive. I would like to talk it over with you; and in the meantime I think you might let me show it to Papa and Uncle Will.[1]

And now for some of your other questions. I must turn to the letters to see what they are, for they are the only parts of those letters which I ever forget! Oh yes, "have I seen Jessie," and "what do I do with myself all day." The first I have already answered; I have not, as yet, seen her the second time. As for the second question, let me think,—my doings are not important enough to make much impression. I have, since I have been here, made some curtains, a set of hemstiched ties, and a jacket for Agnes, and fifty dollars for myself;—is that circumstantial enough to suit you! I have also made Agnes read to *me* to my heart's content. I have a mania—a positive craze—for hearing people read aloud. No one has any peace when I am about. Mr. Tedcastle is a jewel in that respect; he is as fond of reading as I am of hearing it, so he entertains us in the evening. In the afternoon we drive. At home I am occupied in the same way, viz. with sewing and drawing, minus the driving, and plus a good deal of what Janie calls "bumming around," anglicè—housekeeping. At night I always read, except on those three evenings in the week when I have been accustomed to do penance for my sins; but "nous avons changé tout cela," or at least, I *hope* we have.

So much for the way in which I have busied myself heretofore. What I will be doing in the near future is another matter, and one quite beyond my ken. Papa has announced his determination to carry out his long-talked-of purpose, and resign his charge and leave Rome, on account of his health. But as that isn't the pleasantest thing in the world to think about, and as thinking of it will do not a particle of good at present, I will let the matter drop.

There are several questions yet remaining, but I fear they must wait until next time[.] One of them, "what I remember of a certain walk up a hill," I must be sure to answer then, because, while doing so, I will also throw a ray of light on that "dark mystery," —"what it is I saw to like about you."

But now I must say good-night, (and begin another sheet for the purpose!).

You need not be afraid, dear love, of telling me certain sweet truths too often, for, indeed I can never *hear* them too often, but read them with an ever renewed delight. If voice and eyes are necessary to their proper understanding, why, I have a vivid imagination, you know, and will endeavour to supply them so;—not so difficult a task as you may suppose, for I can see with strange distinctness certain expressions of those eyes, and hear certain tones of that voice.

By-the-way, I am sorry I should have discouraged your efforts in "high art." I certainly did not design to do so. On the contrary, I think you show great talent that way. Your picture, though not good as a portrait, was a *very* pretty fancy sketch, and there was a grace and delicacy about the execution which was charming! I *do* protest most heartily against both your explanations of your detection. One does'nt recognise an author's—or I should say an artist's—style so much by it's defects as by it's characteristic beauties.

But it is very late and I really must close. Agnes and Mr. T. send their kindest regards. I am, as you see, still here; this is the postscript to my visit. I expected Father tonight, so early this morning packed up my goods and chattels and moved back home. After flying around for an hour or so airing rooms and beds, &c. &c., I put on my hat and started for market, but at the door met Mr. Tedcastle with a telegram from Father. He had concluded to remain longer. So Mr. T. forthwith bundled me and my "things" back again, in the most summary fashion.

Please give my warmest love to your dear Mother and Father when you write; and believe me, my darling,

Yours with all my heart,   Ellie.

ALS (WP, DLC).
1 William Dearing Hoyt, M.D., proprietor of a drugstore in Rome, Ga.

Two Letters to Ellen Louise Axson

My own darling,   Baltimore, Oct. 16th/83

What a dear, affectionate little girl you are! I had no idea that you would be made so disconsolate by having to wait a few more days than usual for a letter from me. You must have written just before receiving the first eight of the twenty pages I sent you last week. I could not write sooner in the week, because I was busy then with all sorts of odd jobs, bent upon finding the depth of several new subjects sprung upon me by my professors. As I promised you in one of my recent letters, I will always write more than once during the week, if it is at all possible; and you may always be sure that if I do not I *cannot*. Writing to my far-away darling is one of the greatest pleasures I have—the greatest next to receiving letters from her; and my only difficulty is in keeping my inclination sufficiently within bounds to allow duty free play. If I were inclined to selfish, malicious mischief, I should sometimes let some time intervene between my letters in order to draw sweet, musing letters from you such as that that came yesterday morning, and in order to enable you to understand how I feel while waiting for your next letter. But I would not wilfully hurt my darling for all the world.

You say that "memories of Agnes and her home will always be interwoven with the fairest passages of" your life. I am glad, unspeakably glad, my darling, that you are so happy and that the memories of our first meetings are so sweet to you; but I have a small remark to make concerning that confident assertion of yours, which is, that I hope it wont prove true, since I intend to do all in my power to make your *married* life *the* fairest part of your mundane experience. It is a delight to *me* to think of those first days of our acquaintance (though I remember being then very much concerned about the *impression* I was making on a certain bewitching maiden), but there is a much keener delight in looking *forward* to that blessed time when that same maiden shall be *mine*, always with me, sharing my joys and my sorrows, the beloved mistress of my *home*! It is odd, is'nt it? that almost at the very time that I was writing to you, begging you to tell me the secrets of the inner history of those first meetings of ours you should have been in a measure complying. I want to know *all*, if my precious one will tell me. What did you think of me, my love, that night we went to the concert together? I remember that when we started out that night I was in my ordinary spirits; but before the entertainment was over some evil spirit seemed to have gotten hold on me—a dumb spirit. On the way home I was conscious of being insufferably dull, and after leaving you I was down in the very depths, being convinced that I had proved myself in your eyes an empty-pated, stupid fellow! Were you not really very much bored?

It seems to me as if I had been engaged for more than one month, because that month has been so full of new and joyous heart experiences, and because it seems so much more than a month since I left you; but the fact is that this is only the 16th of October. How I wish I could write you tonight such a letter as I should like to write; but it seems as if my love for you were *literally* unspeakable. How can a fellow who is not inspired pour out joy and love and contentment in *words*? Thoughts of you fill all my life. You seem to be in everything I read, in everything I do. I can't enjoy myself without wishing that you might share the enjoyment; I can't read anything that is stimulating or eloquent or instructive without wishing that I might read it to you. I involuntarily smile in sympathy with anyone who seems happy, because I am happy; I pity every one who seems down-cast, because I imagine that they are not loved by those whom they love. I am fast losing all semblance of a reputation for dignity because of the way I frolic and joke and rejoice in the manufacture of light-hearted nonsense when I am with my friends. I feel as if I should like very much to repeat poetry all the time, if I knew any to repeat. I am in a fair way to be run away with by this love that has taken possession of me. If you continue to love me and to write me such elating letters (the idea of putting "if" to such a sentiment!) I don't know what will become of this hitherto respectable person!

I am feeling very much encouraged to-night about my work at "the Hopkins." I had been somewhat downcast at finding that there was no line of study pursued here that could quite legitimately admit under it such studies as have been my chief amusement and delight during leisure hours for the past five or six years, namely, studies in comparative politics. I have looked into the administrative machinery of England and our own country enough to get a pretty good insight into them, and it was my strong desire to make a similar study of the national governments (as perhaps also of the *local* governmental machinery) of France and Germany. When I got within range of these professors here, however, I found that they wanted to set everybody under their authority to working on what they called "institutional history," to digging, that is, into the dusty records of old settlements and colonial cities, to rehabilitating in authentic form the stories, now almost mythical, of the struggles, the ups and the downs, of the first colonists here there and everywhere on this then interesting continent—and other rumaging work of a like dry kind, which seemed very tiresome in comparison with the grand excursions amongst imperial policies which I had planned for myself. But after tea this evening I went to see Dr. Adams, my chief, and made a clean breast of it: told him that I had a hobby which I had been riding for some years with great entertainment and from which I was loath to dismount. He received my confidences with sympathy, readily freed me from his "institutional" work, and bade me go on with my "constitutional" studies, promising me all the aid and encouragement he could give me, and saying that the work I proposed was just such as he wanted to see done! Do you wonder that I feel elated and encouraged?

You see, my sweet Ellie, I want to give you a share in all my thoughts and aspirations. If I loved study as much as I love you, I could soon make the world ring with admiring plaudits of my scholarship. I want to give you, in these small doses of my plans, some warning of the way I intend to inflict you some of these days when I shall have you in my power and shall make you listen to all sorts of political and historical disquisitions.

But I must stop, because it is bed time and I have to walk a mile to mail this letter, so that it may go early in the morning. I love you a thousand times more than I love myself—I love you *as much as you can wish.*

Yours entirely,   Woodrow.

Love to your father and kindest regards to Mr. and Mrs. T.

My own darling,   Baltimore, Oct. 18th/83
Your letter of the 15th made proper schedule time and reached me this morning. My dear, sensitive little woman seems to have been a good deal shocked by some of the revelations drawn out by her questions—was it because she was not prepared to receive such conclusive evidence that her "ideal" was, after all, a very weak, foolish fellow? Did you think that I had invited your questions as I did because it would be *pleasant* to answer them? Very far from it. I invited them because I wanted to have no secrets to keep from you. It would break my heart, my precious Ellie, to lose your love—I could not now live without it!—but it would break it quite as surely to have you imagine me wiser and better than I am, and afterwards discover that you had been *mistaken.* Not

that I thought that there was anything *discreditable* in what I had to tell: ever since long before Chaucer and Dryden did so, all *man*kind has been prone to fall in love with its cousins (as someone has said); but then one would like to have people think him *less* of a fool than his fellows, if he *could* conscientiously allow them to think so, without convicting himself of hypocrisy. It *was* weak and silly in me to do so "unfortunate" a thing as fall in love with my cousin; but I may say, by way of excuse, that probably even I should not have done so if she had been, before I met her in Staunton, *like* a cousin to me, if she had not been up to that time as much a stranger to me as if there had been no kinship between us.

But, happily, all that is now passed by, and is as if it had never happened. I am not a boy any longer. It was left for you to teach me the vast, the immeasurable, difference between a youth's fancy and a man's overmastering love. Why, my darling, I am sometimes absolutely frightened at the intensity of my love for you! It makes me tremble to think what might become of me if my present confidence that you will one day be altogether mine should be blotted out, if anything should come between us, if any turn of Providence should take you from me! Do you remember what I said to you as we sat in the hammock at *the* picnic [on June 29, 1883]? how I declared that you were the only woman I had ever met to whom I felt that I could open all my thoughts? I meant much more than I dared to say: I meant that I had begun to realize that you had a[n] irresistible *claim* upon *all* that I had to give, of the treasures of my heart as well as of the stores of my mind. I had never dreamed before of meeting any woman who should with no effort on her own part make herself mistress of all the forces of my nature, in the exercise of a sort of right of dominion which I could not explain but had to recognize. I am proud and wilful beyond all measure, my darling; and I used to think, like other young men I suppose, that I should never pay any but entirely voluntary homage to any woman. With an absurd pride of intellect, like Lydgate's, I thought it might be possible to get along with a wife as a leisure-moment companion, dispensing with intellectual sympathy. Not that I did not *want* such sympathy—I knew that there would be a dreary side to life without it—nor because I thought women as a rule incapable of giving it; but principally, I believe, because I thought it would be unreasonable to expect my wife to go with me, even in spirit, into all the so-esteemed dry paths into which my studies were naturally leading me. See, therefore, how valuable to me, my sweet Ellie, was that conversation about the characters in "Middlemarch," as we were returning once from "a certain walk up a hill." I had not read "Middlemarch" then, but I had the delight of hearing you expound the significance of its plot; and from that exposition I made a discovery that thrilled me: that you knew what sort of a wife *I* needed—though you were not applying the moral to my case, and did not know how directly the story came home to my experience. I don't mean to compare myself with Lydgate. I have not yet proved myself possessed of any extraordinary talents; and I cannot claim the possession until I have put away certain discursive habits and brought all the powers I have into the line of some concentrated effort. But there is a very distinct parallel between Lydgate's aspirations and my own, and between the conditions—the conditions of home-life—necessary to my ultimate success and those which might have ensured his. No man who has a heart cast for the domestic relation, no man who is'nt *merely* a student, simply a thinking machine, could wish to marry a woman such as John Stuart Mill married and doted on, who expels sentiment from life, knows as much as her husband of the matters of his special study, and furnishes him with opinions, ministering not to his love but to his logical faculty. How can Mr. Erwin respect himself with a wife so greatly his superior in mind and accomplishments? But, on the other hand, a man with any of the keen sensibilities of the student must be miserable if he have a study into which his wife cannot come as his close companion. I do'nt expect or wish my darling to go back with me into those prehistoric times in which government originated, because there was much in early society that no one would care to see except in the interests of complete knowledge; but I know that she will not frown at my abstraction in such studies. As we came down from the hill I found a little maiden who *could* give me all the intellectual sympathy I might desire, if I could but make her love me. And I *did* make her love me!—*how* I don't know—but of the blissful fact I am sure.

> "Sing, ye feathered songsters,
> Sing in full concert all your tuneful strains;
> Each richest note that melody contains,
> Each pleasant chord, each harmony sonorous
> Join ye in one ringing chorus;
> Your voices raise in sweetest praise:
> My love is won and joy fills all my days."[1]

Don't you think that you are a very matter of fact little maiden? I do. To read your circumstantial enumeration of the curtains, the set of hem-stitched ties, the "jacket for Agnes," and the "fifty dollars for your-self" which you have made, one would suppose that I had called upon you to account for yourself and prove that you were not in the habit of being idle; whereas, in fact, my wish was to know how you were in the habit of occupying yourself during the different portions of the day, in order that I might follow you in my imagination through all the round of your daily life, following you always with my loving sympathy. But I don't object to particulars. Anything that concerns you is more than interesting to me. I have a great regard for those curtains, and should be reverential in the presence of those hem-stitched ties. Do you remember that queer, winding straw trimming on the hat you wore in Asheville? Well, everytime I've met a lady on these crowded streets who happened to have similar trimming on her hat, I've felt strongly inclined to show my affection for that peculiar kind of ornamentation by lifting my hat in respectful salutation.

I was surprised beyond measure, my darling, to hear that your father's thinking seriously of leaving Rome; and I am grieved at the news, not only because of the reason assigned, but also on the church's account, and because I know that to leave her long-time home will be a sore trial to the sweet little maiden I love, and whose griefs are henceforth *my* griefs. Don't fail, dearest, to keep me informed as to his plans. I hope he will find reasons to change his mind.

Guard your own health I beg of you, my love. Your letters are *everything* to me, and I need them sorely in this big city where I am so lonely: their comings are like the visits of ministering angels; but I do'nt like to hear of your sitting up so late to write them, depriving yourself of the sleep every young person needs. It is like signing the death-warrant of my sweetest pleasure to ask you thus not to write at what seems to be your only writing time; but is there no other time?

With sincere love to your father—and to Eddie, and more for yourself than all the mails of the world could carry,

Your own,   Woodrow.

ALS (WC, NjP).

1 WW's "A Song," printed at Dec. 8, 1881.

From Joseph R. Wilson, Jr.

My darling brother: Wilmington N. C. October 22nd 1883.

I want to tell you the news, I went down to find out what Mr Gordon could let me have a 52 in. Standard Columbia bicycle for; He said he could not give me any discount this time, and then I asked him if he would let me have a gong with the machine? he said he could and that I would not have to pay the freight charges. I came on up and met pop and mom on Front St in the buggy, I told papa all about it and he said "Its getting more and more hopeless is'nt it Dode?" I said that I was afraid so. I was getting kinder discouraged you know. Well, just as papa and mamma were driving off, papa said "Well Dode, order one" I said "order what a bicycle?" he said "yes" You can guess how happy I felt, cant you? Mother said she never saw a face light up as mine did then. I ran down and told Mr Gordon to order one for me, and I am in hopes it will be here by the time you get this letter. *Hurrah*!!!! for the bicycle.

I have been waiting anxiously for my promotion to Vice Admiral, when are you going to send it?

We have all gotton to love "sister" Ellie, and to feel as if she was a relation of ours already. Father said to mama the other day You know Jeanie I am getting to look on Ellie Lou as a daughter. Please give my love to her when you write. How many times a day do you write fourteen page letters to her. You can tell Miss Ellie what I say about *her* but *please* dont send her *this* letter, because it is too badly written. Mother is not quite so well today because she took a cold yesterday. Pop is better, and I am just as rosy, and fat, and wishing my bicycle would come, as ever.

Please write *very* soon to your loving bro.   Joseph.

ALS (WP, DLC) with WWhw notation on env.: "Ans. Oct. 28th 1883."

To Ellen Louise Axson

My precious Ellie,   Balto., Oct. 23rd, 1883

If I were a disciple of the admirable Mr. Mark Tapley,[1] I should feel heartily ashamed of myself whenever I sit down to write you a letter; for, if the cheerful doing of disagreeable work is the only source of just credit, this correspondence of ours must, as far a[s] I am concerned, be a most discreditable business, there being, in my estimation, few delights comparable with the privilege of telling my far-away darling just what is in my heart with perfect freedom, and with a perfect confidence that what I write will be read, by love's interpretation, just as it was meant to be read. This out-spoken intercourse, hampered though it is by the circumscriptions of pen and ink, is to me especially refreshing in comparison with that diplomatic reserve and indirection which I felt bound to observe in the early stages of our acquaintance. I have observed that no diplomacy is very profound; all diplomats are very soon found out; and you no doubt saw through my devices long before I suspected; but I did not dare to throw them off, although they were so very burdensome and so very clumsy. How cheap and awkward a poor fellow feels when he is trying to find out something about which he cannot venture to ask a direct question! I remember walking, one afternoon in the early summer [in Rome], with a certain sweet friend of mine. We had chosen the railroad bed as our path because it led along the bank of the river, and would lead us to where we could find a seat near the water on a big jutting rock which stood with its feet in the river, commanding a view of one of the prettiest bends of the stream. Not an incident of that walk have I forgotten. It would be very strange if I had forgotten how we talked as we sat on that rock, for no man ever more enjoyed a cosey chat with a pretty woman, a free, unreserved interchange of opinions and sentiments with an intelligent woman, than I did then and there. But the point of my reminiscence is in what came after that delightful tête-à-tête. I was quite conscious that I was very much in love with my companion, and I was desperately intent upon finding out what my chances were of winning her; so I adopted a plan which was doubtless very indiscreet, but which was the best I could devise upon the moment. I made her my confidante concerning a very foolish love affair of mine, some time before exploded, and, with that preface, proceeded to discourse somewhat at length upon my needs and embarrassments as regarded her sex. I told her what sort of life I should probably lead, as a teacher; pointed out the uncertainty of my prospects and the narrowness of my means; and then, as an indirect invitation of her opinion, avowed the disinclination I felt to ask any woman such as I could love to make the sacrifice of marrying me. All this I could say in perfect earnestness and good faith, of course; but I said it with diplomatic purpose, in order to ascertain whether *she* was inclined to regard such an alliance as a very dreary and uninviting prospect for any maiden free to choose. I do'nt know yet whether or not she suspected my purpose, but her comment was very brief and non-committal, tho' not altogether uncomforting. She thought that such a marriage might, like Mrs. Carlyle's, be less burdensome than the common fate of marriageable damsels, who might expect to keep house for some hum-drum tradesman, or at best for some plodding village doctor. I was left to suppose that it was a question in no way concerning herself; but that, in her disinterested judgment, I was may-be wasting my pity on professors' wives.

That was one of many diplomatic failures: for that charming maiden, excelling the rest of her sex in so many ways, excelled them also in the art of concealing her feelings. I could'nt for the life of me tell what progress I was making in her esteem, and had, finally, to declare my love in face of my better judgment. I *then* found out that she loved me as much (if that were possible) as I loved her; and you may imagine the joy of the unexpected discovery! Somehow I always found it hard to believe that anyone could fall in love with me—not because I had a poor opinion of myself, for I have always entertained a quite high enough estimation of my own gifts; and I had always felt sure that, if some girl on the lookout for somebody to love could but discover what a big capacity for loving and for appreciating love I had, she might feel quite safe in marrying me. But I felt that the rub would be in anybody's making such a discovery; for I knew that I was not good looking enough to attract admiring attention, and I was conscious of wearing, towards all but a few intimates, a cold exterior which was no more likely than my limited conversational powers to win favour from the fair sex. I thought that, by passing me by, some body would miss the chance of getting a faithful husband, and I used to derive some whimsical amusement from regarding, in anticipation, my doleful plight—a very lovable gentleman undiscovered; unmarried because nobody could be brought to look upon him as in the market!

But now how changed are my opinions! Having learned to my profound astonishment that the lovliest woman in the world had actually fallen in love with me, and having at length come into a full realization of that stupendous fact, I am conscious that the leaven of vanity has gone fairly to work in me. I look in my mirror with some complacency, feeling sure that if, as I am assured by my dear little charmer, mine is a face about which three whole lines of poetry are true, there must be some handsome lines in it, even though I am unable to discover where they are. It must be that I do'nt get the right point of view. Then, too, I am enabled to see daily proofs of how engaging my manners are, how captivating my conversation! Why just hear the compliments that have been paid me. While I was staying with my

friend Woods, a very pretty and attractive young lady from Philadelphia, who was spending a few days at the house, declared
(though not to me), when Miss Woods admonished her of the
approach of the time at which they had an engagement, that
she had no idea of the lapse of time *while talking with me*. Not
content with repeating *this* overwhelming compliment to me,
Miss Woods also told me that the most charming of her Baltimore friends (whom I had met on several occasions) had said
that I was "splendid," and that she did not know what she might
not have felt inclined to do if she had not known that I was engaged! That rascal Woods had given my secret away (they do'nt
know what it is to keep such a secret in this part of the country), presumably—as I tell *him*—to prevent my unwittingly "cutting him out"! So you see what you have done: you've ruined my
humility. You have actually inclined me to believe such "stuff."
I could not so discredit your judgment as to continue to think
that you had chosen to love an altogether unattractive man!

Ah, my darling, if I can but make you as happy as you have
already made me by the gift of your love, you shall, one of these
days, be the happiest little woman in Christendom! I wonder,
by-the-way, whether you ever have such dreams about me as I
have about you: for I had a *second* one the other night, not at all
like the first one, about which I wrote you, but quite as delightful. I do'nt mean to describe this one. You might be scandalized
by the number of kisses and caresses to which you submitted in
that dream-meeting with your lover. But your lover was'nt scandalized, I assure you. He woke up in the happiest humour conceivable and seemed to have a new spirit of content and jollity
in him all day long. The fact is that he can't manage to love his
darling in moderation. He so constantly and so ardently longs
for her presence, that when that presence is vouchsafed him
(even in imagination) he ought to be excused for some excess of
demonstration. But here I am on the tenth page of my letter
without having advanced one step beyond the old story!

I am delighted, my love, that you enjoyed father's lecture. It *is*
full of suggestion and of inspiration. I wish that I could believe
that I had inherited that rarest gift of making great truths attractive in the telling and of inspiring with great purposes by sheer
force of eloquence or by gentle stress of persuasion. Of course
you may show the lecture to your father, dearest; by asking you
not to show it to anyone I meant only that father would prefer not
to have it commonly read. I am quite willing to trust to your discretion in the matter.

While I was over in the Peabody library this morning, having tired of wrestling with a French book that I could'nt read with-[out] constant, tedious resort to a Dictionary, I called for the *illustrated* edition of Hamerton's "Graphic Arts." How I did wish that you were there to look over it with me! The illustrations are marvellous counterfeits of the originals, not all of them pretty in themselves, but all extremely suggestive as illuminations of the text[.] Speaking of pictures, I am led to a very humiliating confession of inconsistency: I want a photograph of *you*, if you have any that is even tolerably good. Yes; I know what I said about not wanting pictures of my friends, about prefering to *remember* their choice expressions, &c. &c, and I have not given up that sentiment; but I want every possible memento of you; want it in a sort of *idolatrous* spirit. I can't set your letters on my bureau to look at. It would be a great delight to me to have even your "counterfeit presentment" to greet my eyes whenever I enter my door. It would be symbolical of your presence.

I have a dim suspicion that you are very cruel—or is it only that you want to test my ability to be jolly under adverse circumstances?—because I have already hinted how hard it is for me to keep my spirits up when you let a whole week separate your letters. You ought to have pity on a poor lonely mortal away off here by himself! I've been waiting all this time for the answers to my questions. Be sure you don't overlook any of them; I shall not let you off until all the sweet particulars are told!

Give my warmest love to your father and keep for yourself, my own darling, my peerless Ellie, the whole heart of
Your own   Woodrow.

ALS (WC, NjP).
  1 The light-hearted servant and companion of Charles Dickens' Martin Chuzzlewit, who took great pride in his ability to be jolly in the most adverse circumstances.

From Ellen Louise Axson

My darling,   Rome [Ga.], Oct. 23, 1883.
  I was'nt able to write my letter last night, having made a previous engagement with Papa, which demanded all my attention. He returned last week, much improved, we think; certainly much more hopeful, but with his old fondness for "vigorous" remedies still unabated. He has a special weakness for fly blisters, with one of which we were having a frolic last night. He thinks they are "good for the nerves"—so soothing, you know!
  I didn't get my patient settled for the night in time to write—

may be able to do so tonight, but will, for the sake of my promise, try to get a hasty line off this morning.

How shall I thank you, dearest, for your sweet letters of last week. Did not my heart burn within me as I read! Each in turn I longed exceedingly to answer when first received; but since Father's return I have had not a moment. He has been made more nervous than usual by his worry about "resigning" &c., and when in one of his "spells," he can't bear me out of his sight an instant.

We will leave Rome soon—think of going to Decatur, near Atlanta, for the winter—or at least Father will. He thinks that climate very fine.

But our plans are as yet very uncertain. He has resigned, but they have not yet accepted it, wishing I believe to make it a leave of absence instead. He thinks, and so do I, that six months rest would entirely restore him. Yet even in that case it is doubtful whether he should return to Rome, as the climate does'nt seem altogether to suit him.

But I must mail this at once, so "good-bye" for the present, dear love. With much love for your parents and the rest, and for yourself more than I can ever tell, believe me, darling,

Yours ever   Ellie

ALS (WP, DLC).

To Ellen Louise Axson

My own darling,   Balto., Oct. 25th 1883

I take back what I said in my letter of Tuesday about your being cruel in not writing to me oftener (even though I did say it only "in fun"). It is I who am unreasonable, not you who are unkind. I knew, without being told by the note that came from you this morning, that there was some good reason for your not writing: and I was afraid, too, that that reason was just what I now know it to have been, your dear father's need of your care. I cannot tell you how distressed I was to learn of the continuance of his nervous troubles, or how startled I was at learning that his resignation of his pastorate was already an accomplished fact and that the breaking up of your home in Rome is now in immediate prospect! From all that I learned and saw of the place during several short visits there to the Ansleys, while I was in Atlanta, I think that there can be no doubt that Mr. Axson is making a wise choice in fixing upon Decatur as his winter resort; but you intimate, my darling, that you will not accompany him. What are *your* plans? Will you go to Savannah? This whole move takes me so entirely by surprise that I hardly know what to think about it. If such a wish were not so grossly selfish as regards your father, I could wish, my precious one, that a certain professorship were secured and—but no! such wishing makes my heart beat too fast; and I do'nt mean to allow myself to be either selfish or impatient in this matter. Duty and necessity are both quite clear and such a blessed consummation is worth the discipline of years of waiting and work! Sometimes it does seem as if I *could'nt* wait. Though not given to nervous "spells," I think I should find it as impossible as your father does to bear your absence even for a single moment if I did not know that I *just had it to do*. Why, my darling, the longing for you that is in my heart is sometimes almost intolerable! It is only by a supreme effort of the will in keeping my thoughts from dwelling too constantly on you that I am enabled to keep my spirits up. If I were not hard at work, there's no telling what would become of me. You can understand, therefore, why it is that your letters are so essential to me. I seem to stand in absolute need of constant outpourings of your love and sympathy. Dear me! what a tyrant love is! The idea that I, who have always entertained such high ideals of self-reliance and mastery, should be so absolutely led captive by a gentle, shy little maiden who seems to have made no effort to capture me! And, strangest of all, I delight in my captivity and have no desire to assert or regain my independence! Ah, you darling little charmer you! you have'nt made a very *notable* conquest (your captive is'nt "much punkins") but you've made a marvellously complete one! You've conquered in such sly fashion that you've made the conquered think himself conqueror.

I tell you this same story of my love over and over again, my sweet Ellie, not so much because of the gratification *I* derive from the telling—for there's doubtful satisfaction in only *half* saying what I want to say, in always falling infinitely far short of the fervour and point I would give it—as because my chief end in writing is to give *you* pleasure. Since the simple truth, even imperfectly told, gives you pleasure, it is my unceasing delight to write it as best I can. Yes, there's another reason too. I could'nt help repeating that I love you, even if I would. It will out. My heart would burst if there were no ear open to it; for this love that has so taken possession of me grows day by day. Here's a heart, Miss, that you are taxing to its utmost capacity, and I give you fair warning, as your legal adviser, that you will be responsible for all damages if it suffer from wear and tear! You'll have to give it your constant personal attention.

But here I'm going to stop for to-night. It's so late that I must wait and add another chapter to-morrow, by which time I trust that I shall have received the letter promised in your sweet note of Tuesday. Good-night, my darling; I may send you a loving good-night kiss, may I not?

Oct. 26th

Well, a letter did come to me from Rome this morning, but not from my darling. It was from uncle James Bones, and you shall read the part that is not on business. He says, "Mr. Axson told me some time ago of the engagement between Miss Ellie and yourself. I congratulate you, my dear boy, on your great good fortune. You have secured one of the lovliest girls I know of anywhere. I have watched her closely for years and she is one whom anyone might be proud to have secured as a life companion. I think you are admirably suited to each other, and if nothing occurs to prevent your union, your prospects for a happy married life are very bright." And now listen to what my dear, warm-hearted brother has to say in his last: "We have all gotten to love 'sister' Ellie, and to feel as if she was a relation of ours already. Father said to mama the other day, 'Jeanie, you know I am getting to look on Ellie Lou as a daughter.' Please give my love to her when you write." To which he adds, "How many times a day do you write fourteen-page letters to her?"

Now do'nt you think that your reception into the family promises to be a very warm one? All this adds to my happiness in our engagement, my darling; but no one can know the joy that has come to me with the possession of your love. I *am* proud to have won you, my precious Ellie; and I am determined, more-over, that my success shall never be anything but a source of happiness to you

I am very anxious, my love, to learn your plans for the winter. I hate to think of your going still farther away from me. In a distance reckoned by so many leagues I do'nt suppose a hundred miles or so would really make much difference; but there is to me a great deal in local associations, and all the local associations connected with you in my mind (excepting, as sacred, the scenes connected with those two never-to-be forgotten days in the valley of the French Broad) are Roman. Memories of those bright days of our early friendship are inseparable from memories of Rome. Its streets, its rivers, all its surrounding country are dear to me because of their associations with the dear little maiden who taught me there what it was to love with a perfect, an over-mastering, love; who inspired me with a passion at once pure and all-powerful; and who there *learned to love me.*

Give my love to your father. I sincerely hope that his health may speedily be entirely restored. Remember me to Stockton when you write. Good-bye, sweet love, till next time. Though I sometimes stop writing to her I never cease thinking of my darling who has all the love of

Her own— Woodrow.

ALS (WC, NjP).

From Ellen Louise Axson

My darling,   Rome [Ga.], Oct. 26/83.

I seem to have been fated about writing for the last week or more. I am generally on duty with Father, and whenever I get him asleep, the house quiet, and myself cosily settled for a long chat with you someone is sure to call—generally some woman to weep over his departure. I shall make another attempt tonight and if it fails I will really be in despair—I can't very well fall back on postals, as I do with Papa. Mr. Tedcastle was disposed to tease me somewhat about the "six cents for Baltimore, and one cent for Gainsville"! But then Papa had himself given me the postals for that purpose; they were the daily health bulletins which were all he wished.

I had much to say anent various things in your last week's letters, but now I have gotten so in arrears that I presume I will never catch up, or even answer all the questions they contain. In the first place, I wish to remark that I am very sorry anything in my last letter should have led you to imagine that I was "shocked" by the revelations in yours. I protest, dearest, that such was not the case. On the contrary, I read the letter in question with much serenity, even smiling over it a little. My very strongest feeling was one of surprise that "the fair unknown" should prove to be not unknown, after all, but your own cousin. And I freely admit that, in view of that young lady's many attractions, and the innumerable worthy precedents of which you remind me, I had no right to be even surprised—I assure you *I* saw *nothing* either "weak" or "silly" in the whole proceeding! How could you for a moment imagine, my darling, that there was anything in the matter to affect in the slightest degree my opinion of you?

No, I don't suppose that you invited the questions because it was "pleasant," but because it was *right* and honest to do so. And I told the entire truth when I said I was satisfied. If I played at jealousy it was literally a make-believe. It is strange, indeed, that you should love me, but you have said it, and you are *true*.

> "In love, if love be love, if love be ours,
> Faith and unfaith can ne'er be equal powers:
> Unfaith in aught is want of faith in all."[1]

I believe in *you altogether*, my darling, and in the same degree do I believe in your love. Should I do otherwise I would, indeed, prove myself singularly unworthy of the large-hearted man who has given me that great treasure.

But I perceive that word "ideal" seems to rankle a little, and it is not surprising. I shouldn't like anyone to call me names after that fashion; so I herewith drop it. The trouble seems to be that the word as commonly applied is descriptive, not simply of the sort of *man* a person most admires, but of some creature of the fancy from which all the manhood, the human nature, has been carefully eliminated.

I remember some sentimental girl teasing me, long ago to describe my ideal, and my telling her that I could'nt bear "ideals," I thought them monstrosities. I was very sure that if those constructions of ours could be vivified, like Galatea, they would do their makers no credit, but would be, if such a thing were possible, more disagreeable than any of their flesh and blood fellows. One half of them would be "prigs" and the other half dare-devils. True, when my friend continued to urge me, I informed her that my ideal was "a great big man, with a great big brain, and a great big heart!" But that was only a rough sketch dashed off upon compulsion, and allowing no play to the imagination.

One would not describe our friend Lydgate as an *ideal* character! He is altogether human; and the most vividly *real*, and life-like person I ever met in a book. It is partly on that account that our sympathies are so excited on his behalf. He does'nt seem a creature of the imagination at all, but a personal friend. What a splendid fellow he was, by the way. One loves his very faults! "I have no ambition to see a goodlier man."

You must know that I too have been using Middlemarch for my own purposes—drawing parallels &c.—and though I didn't begin the business as soon as yourself, I dare say, I have carried it farther. I have been thinking for some time that the phenomenal enthusiasm which from the first I have so faithfully retained for that character was another "coincidence[.]" How Beth & I used to rave over him, two years ago! Of all the heros of fiction, he was our declared favourite.

I am delighted, indeed, to learn that things are working out so well in regard to your studies. How very fortunate that they hav'nt a cast-iron system in vogue there, and that you are enabled to follow your bent. And it seems to me that your "hobby" is not only better suited to your disposition, than the professors, but more interesting in itself, and altogether better "worth while." I am very sure that the subjects most attractive to you are, not rumaging among dry bones, but vital questions, *live* issues, the deeper relations of past and present, and the workings of great laws and principles. But you don't mean to say that you expect me to do other than "frown" on such things! I am surprised! Well, I suppose I must resign myself, and promise to be interested to the extent of my humble capacity—chiefly a capacity for "wanting to know," a great thirst for information.

I doubt not I could get up a quite respectable enthusiasm over *anything* you elected to investigate; yet I am at the same time very glad that your line of thought should be of such grand importance and absorbing interest as "the long results of time." I am glad, on the whole, that you are concerned about something of larger significance than—*beetles*, for instance, or snails, or even the brains of fishes, the subject to which a certain friend of my cousin, Clara Bliss, has dedicated *his* brains

Before leaving the subject of brains, I wish to remind you again that I am a most unmitigated simpleton. You may not believe it—but it is so; and when you do find it out, remember, "I told you so"!

"The full sum of me is sum of nothing." I could, dearest, repeat, from my heart of hearts, all the words of that "unlessoned girl," did I dare to say so much of good for myself.

But I am not making much progress in answering questions, am I? I must now save them for another time, and acknowledge the letter which came yesterday. I am extremely obliged to you for enclosing that delightful one from your sister. How *very* sweet and lovely, and altogether charming she must be! Your family does seem, like ours, to "run heavily on the preachers." Is Mr. [A. Ross] Kennedy a minister's son?

> "Of all sad words of tongue or pen,
> The saddest are these, 'it might have *be'n*.'["]²

Didn't those words occur to you when you found you were working such havock among the fair sex? I am truly sorry for you, my poor boy, but I can't help it. I warned you not to be so precipitate; and now see what you have lost by it! You might have picked and chosen among all those elegant "city girls"! But I am not to blame

—any more than the other girl is to blame for thinking you "splendid." Of course you are just splendid! I was much edified by your former ideas about yourself, but it is just as well your eyes were opened; for as Minnie[3] says "What's the use of being pretty and nice if you don't *know* it, and get some satisfaction out of it? You would be no better off than the ugly ones!"

I see that the place in Jessie's album where your photograph once was, is still vacant; so I presume she didn't tell you of the practical joke she played on me last summer. I havn't time for details now; but having involved me in much comical perplexity and embarrassment it ended, altogether against my will, in your pictures changing hands—not "*hands*" either for *mine* had nothing to do with it. She was here the other day, and demanded it from me again. But I told her I would certainly keep it now, since she had given it to me when I didn't want it. Whereupon she read me a lecture on fibbing—I should have said "when I didn't want to *take* it." Now, if you please, I should like to receive one in the orthodox way, and then I will return her this one. There is something else that I want too. Can you guess what? "A piece of you," but only the *darkest* part—not your eyes or your smile. "It is best" you know "to see the dark side of a person first, and then whatever comes after is a pleasant surprise." Do you know who said that, and when?

Yes, I will send you a photograph, with pleasure, since I have one so much better looking than myself, that if I had'nt a passably good reputation for veracity, my statements as to whom it was intended for, would be received with suspicion. I will also send a small one. Am curious to see which you like best. I have been amused at people's comments on those pictures—some like one, some the other; but whichever they like, they invariably think the other *abominable*.

But perhaps fourteen pages is a long enough letter for one who is so "dreadfully busy." And by the way I did'nt suppose I was being "called to account" for my doings, by any means; but enumerated the "curtains for Agnes" &c. &c. "just for fun" as the children say.

Papa is somewhat better today. I think he is beginning to feel the good effects of having thrown of[f] the burden of the church. His resignation goes to the people on Sunday.

He sends his love to you—though he says he is going to write and tell you he "has changed his mind." "Everyone must let me alone, and you must find another girl!"—so there is a loop-hole

of escape for you, in case you find the Baltimore girls "too splendid for anything."

Goodnight, dear love. With much love to that sweet sister of
yours and all the rest, I remain,

Yours with all my heart,   Ellie.

ALS (WP, DLC) with WWhw and WWsh notation on env.: "Received 10/30/83."
    1 From Tennyson's "The Idylls of the King: Merlin and Vivien."
    2 From Whittier's "Maud Muller."
    3 Mary Eloise ("Minnie") Hoyt, ELA's cousin in Rome, Ga., daughter of Dr.
William D. Hoyt.

Notes Taken in Dr. Ely's Minor Course in
Political Economy

X.

Physiocrats: Oct. 29th 1883

The errors of the Physiocrats were too plain to admit of systems
having a long life. Its very errors however enabled it to perform
its mission. A nicer system would hardly have answered the purpose. It was bold and rough. It enabled everyone to become a
statesman: It was full of short crisp generalities and was easily
grasped. No reason can be given for laissez faire. The physio-
cratic system appealed to the public imagination.

It was well too to emphasize the importance of agriculture. It
is not surprising that rent of land was supposed to be only *produit
net*. At the time when Q[uesnay] wrote this was the chief source
of additions to the capital of the world. The additions of profits
on capital are mere matters of origination. The profits from manufacture and industry are of *very recent* origin. So also were fortunes derived from profits of transportation. There is too an actual
difference between profits derived from land rent and those derived from other sources. Upon this difference is based George's
"Progress and Poverty"—this is its only solid basis.

But there is a surplus and profit wherever there is a saving. A
system was needed which would include manufactures and commerce. This was the more catholic political economy of Adam
Smith.

David Hume furnished Adam Smith with many ideas concerning money etc.

Josh. Tucker

Ferguson also predecessor of Adam Smith. They treated separate economic problems in the spirit afterwards taken by Adam
Smith. They come between the Physiocrats and Adam Smith.

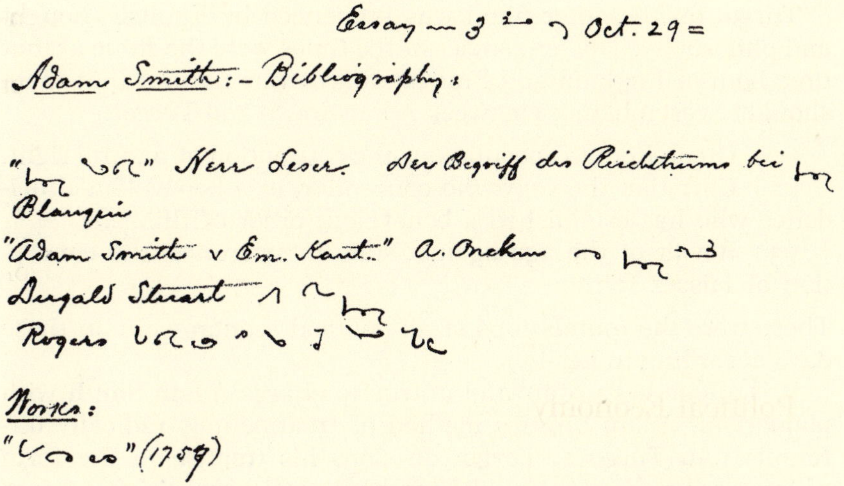

[Handwritten manuscript notes:]

Essay — 3 ᵈ ⁊ Oct. 29 =

Adam Smith : — Bibliography :

" ⌇ ⌇ " Herr Leser.   Der Begriff des Reichthums bei ⌇
Blanqui

"Adam Smith v Em. Kant." A. Oncken ⌇ ⌇ ⌇

Dugald Stuart ⌇ ⌇ ⌇

Rogers ⌇ ⌇ ⌇ ⌇ ⌇ ⌇ ⌇

Works :

" ⌇ ⌇ " (1759)

A bibliography on *Adam Smith* jotted down by *Wilson*
in Professor Richard T. Ely's undergraduate course in political economy.
The essay mentioned in the first line became
Wilson's lecture on *Adam Smith.*

Adam Smith:
  Outline of his life
  Strong similarity between Adam Smith and Turgot. Smith had
lived for some time in France and became an intimate friend of
Turgot and Ques. He had a most profound admiration for Q the
founder of the Physiocrat system. He admired also the system of
the Physiocrats regarding it as the best thing written up to that
time. Adam Smith and Physiocrats were at one in opposition to
the mercantile system and in the advocacy of freedom of trade
in grains.
  Adam Smith's views seemed to have changed because of his
visit to France as shown by difference between Theory of the
Moral Sentiment published in 1757 and his Wealth of Nations,
the visit to France having intervened. The principle of the one
book is sympathy, the principle of the latter, self-interest. Self-interest was at the core of a great deal of the French philosophy of
that day. Helvetius struck the key note of this philosophy, and
this book of H's was attracting much notice in France at the time
when Adam Smith visited it.
  The influence of the French sensationalistic philosophy of that
time was very widespread. Blackstone emphasizes the principle
of self-interest and selfish feelings more than Adam Smith (his
contemporary) did.

Turgot on the other hand was influenced by English thought and philosophy. The tendencies of the times were the same at that time both in England and France* and it was natural that there should be resemblances between Adam Smith and Turgot.

(1) Greek-Roman speculation—the conception of natural right.
(2) Christian theology—the conception of a benevolent Providence who has established a benevolent order of things.
(3) Revolt of the age against state interference—the conception of laissez faire.

These were the foundations of all political economy etc. in those days according to Leslie.

It is altogether unfair and untrue to charge Adam Smith with plagiarism. Adam Smith's method of treatment is radically different from Turgot's. Turgot develops his treatise in the form of successive proposition like mathematical propositions. Adam Smith has nothing of this method of treatment. Besides his ideas are on many points quite different. Adam Smith for instance did not confine productive energy to the production of raw material. There is a certain sort of idealism in Turgot which is missing in Adam Smith. Turgot admits exceptions to his general rules just as Adam Smith does (Navigation Act) Adam Smith did not care for any ideal but made everything utilitarian, bringing in natural right only as a convenience. Smith was no more of a plagiarist than all men are from their predecessors.

Smith maintains his general rules often without any regard to his admitted exceptions. And there must be utmost freedom for the individual. There is an important point in this connection. Was Adam Smith simply an advocate of this absolute free system and were his exceptions only by the way; or were these exceptions an essential part of his system? Historically Adam Smith was quite rightly in favor of repeal of all laws regulating relations between laborer and capitalist because those laws were then (as they are not now) all based in the interest of the capitalist. This is a very important distinction and one which occurs to no one but a student according to the historical method. And though Adam Smith may have been right does it follow that Cobden was also right? Yes.

Notice Adam Smith's comments on the *Navigation Act*.
Plagiarism See Adam Smith's Self Defense.

*"Essays on Moral and Political Economy" by Cliff. Leslie—
"The Political Economy of Adam Smith" one essay.

Transcript of WWsh notes in classroom notebook described at Oct. 3, 1883. A few
words in WWhw.

To Ellen Louise Axson

My own darling,   Balto. Md., Oct. 30th/83

Being quite sensible of the tendency of a certain very alluring topic to engross all the spaces of my letters, if I once allow myself to enter upon it, I purpose *beginning* this one with the fulfilment of a long-standing promise. I am going to tell you something about the ways and means of "the Hopkins," as far as those ways and means concern me. And I am going to do this, not because I think the subject intrinsically a very interesting one, but because I have, heretofore, been showing you only what was in my heart, and nothing of all the schemes that are in my head. I want to share everything with you, my darling; I want your sympathy in everything. You know I am naturally extremely reserved. It would be a sheer impossibility for me to confide anything concerning only myself—especially any secret of my intellect—to anyone of whose sympathy I could not be absolutely sure beforehand; but there can be no greater delight in my life, my love, than making you the keeper off [*sic*] *all* my secrets, the sharer of all my hopes, *because I am sure of your love*. I used to *try* to tell you of the objects of my ambition when I was sure only of my love for you; but I could not do it because I did not know of your love for me.

Then, too, there is something else that urges me to tell you all about myself, and that is the desire that your love should be founded upon knowledge. Of course I do'nt believe that a woman can love a man for anything but qualities of heart and traits of character. She can't *love* his *intellectual* qualities. But it is nevertheless true that those qualities enter largely into the make-up of his character. They cannot all be acquired. Some of them must be in the essential fibre, current in his blood and native to his constitution. I know that you love me altogether and that you are quite willing to take me on trust:—if I were not convinced of that, I should be miserable indeed; but in giving myself I don't want to give by halves. I want you to know just what sort of fellow you are getting.

I think that it is only very recently that I have known myself—indeed I am not altogether certain that the acquaintance is complete yet. Like everybody else I have learned chiefly by means of big mistakes. I've had to earn my own experience. It took me all my college days to learn that it was necessary and profitable to study. Having made that tardy discovery, I left college on the wrong tack. I had then, as I have still, a very earnest political creed and very pronounced political ambitions. I remember forming with Charlie Talcott (a class-mate and very intimate friend of mine) a solemn covenant that we would school all our powers and passions for the work of establishing the principles we held in common; that we would acquire knowledge that we might have power; and that we would drill ourselves in all the arts of persuasion, but especially in oratory (for he was a born orator if any man ever was), that we might have facility in leading others into our ways of thinking and enlisting them in our purposes. And we did'nt do this in merely boyish enthusiasm, though we were blinded by a very boyish assurance with regard to the future and our ability to mould the world as our hands might please. It was not so long ago but that I can still feel the glow and the pulsations of the hopes and the purposes of that moment—nay, it was not so long ago but that I still retain some of the faith that then prompted me. But a man has to know the world before he can work in it to any purpose. He has to know the forces with which he must coöperate and those with which he must contend; must know how and where he can make himself felt, not reckoning according to the conditions and possibilities of past times but according to a full knowledge of the conditions of the present and the possibilities of the immediate future. He must know the times into which he has been born: and this I did *not* know when I left college and chose my profession, as I proved by my choice. The profession I chose was politics; the profession I entered was the law. I entered the one because I thought it would lead to the other. It was once the sure road; and Congress is still full of lawyers. But this is the time of leisured classes—or, at least, that time is very near at hand —and the time of crowded professions. It is plain to see why lawyers used to be the only politicians[.] In a new country, in communities where every man had his bread to earn, they were the only men (except the minister and the physician) who stopped amidst the general hurry of life to get learning; and they were the only men, without exception, who were skilled in those arts of forensic contest that were calculated to fit men for entering the lists at political tilts, or for holding their own in legislative debate. They could hope, too, when a turn of parties might have come, or their own popularity might have waned, to return to their places at the bar to find a place still open for them, to find themselves not altogether and hopelessly crowded out; they could even, like Webster and Jeremiah Mason and many others of less genius, make law and statecraft live and thrive together, pleading causes in the courts even while holding seats in the Senate or leading parties in the House.

But those times are passing away. A man who has to earn a livlihood cannot nowadays turn aside from his trade for intervals of
office-holding and political activity. He cannot even do two things
at once. He is constrained by a minute division of labour to bend
all his energies to the one thing that is nearest at hand. Even in the
law men are becoming specialists. The whole field of legal knowledge, which former generations of American lawyers have super-
ficially worked, is too big for any one man now, and practitioners
are contenting themselves with cultivating small corners of it,
digging deep and getting large crops out of small areas. And of
course these small tenant farmers have to work much more diligently than did the great proprietors of former times. The law is
more than ever before a jealous mistress. Whoever thinks, as I
thought, that he can practice law successfully and study history
and politics at the same time is wofully mistaken. If he is to make
a living at the bar he must be a lawyer *and nothing else*. Of course
he can compass a certain sort of double-calling success by dint of
dishonesty. He can obtain, and betray, clients by pretending a
knowledge of the law which he does not possess; and he can often
gain political office by the arts of the demagogue. But he cannot
be both a learned lawyer and a profound and public-spirited statesman, if he must plunge into practice and make the law a means
of support.

In a word, my ambition could not be fulfilled at the bar; the
studies for which I was best fitted, both by nature and by acquired habit, were not legitimate in a law office, and I was compelled in very justice to myself to seek some profession in which
they would be legitimate. Evidently, however there was small latitude of choice. A professorship was the only feasible place for me,
the only place that would afford leisure for reading and for original work, the only strictly literary berth with an income attached.
True, professorships were scarce and hard to get, and professors
could not participate actively in public affairs; but even a professorship might be gotten as soon as a competence at the bar, and
the occupancy of office had never been an essential part of my
political programme. Indeed I knew very well that a man without
independent fortune must in any event content himself with becoming an *outside* force in politics, and I was well enough satisfied with the prospect of having whatever influence I might be able
to exercise make itself felt through literary and non-partisan agencies: for my predilections, ever since I had any that were definite,
have always turned very strongly towards a literary life, notwithstanding my decided taste for oratory, which is supposed to

be the peculiar province of public men. With manhood came to me an unquenchable desire to excel in two distinct and almost opposite kinds of writing: political and *imaginative*. I want to contribute to our literature what no American has ever contributed, studies in the philosophy of our institutions, not the abstract and occult, but the practical and suggestive, philosophy which is at the core of our governmental methods; their use, their meaning, "the spirit that makes them workable." I want to divest them of the theory that obscures them and present their weakness and their strength without disguise, and with such skill and such plenitude of proof that it shall be seen that I have succeeded and that I have added something to the resources of knowledge upon which statecraft must depend. But the *imaginative* writing? I do'nt mean that I want to write poetry. I am quite aware that at my birth no poet was born; but the imagination has other spheres besides the creations of a poetic fancy and can freshen and beautify the world without the aid of the musical cadences of verse. I believe that there's entirely too much moping and morbid thought amongst jaded human beings, that there's a great deal of joy and fun in the world that people miss for lack of time to look around; and I believe that there are inexhaustible sources of cheer, just as there are endless combinations of music, in our *language*[.] Now is'nt it a legitimate ambition to wish to write something (!) that will freshen the energies of tired people and make the sad laugh and take heart again: some comedy full of pure humour and peopled with characters whose livers are in order, who live up to the moral that life, even with the pleasures of vice left out, is worth living: lay sermons full of laughter and a loving God: a fiction that may be suffered to live, if only because it has real people in it and no sham enthusiasm? I could wish to be the favoured correspondent of children, as well as a counsellor of the powers of the earth.

But where does oratory come in? It does not generally come into the lectures of college professors; but it should. Oratory is not declamation, not swelling tones and an excited delivery, but the art of persuasion, the art of putting things so as to appeal irresistibly to an audience. And how can a teacher stimulate young men to study, how can he fill them with great ideas and worthy purposes, how can he draw them out of themselves and make them to become forces in the world without oratory? Perfunctory lecturing is of no service in the world. It's a nuisance. "The mind is not a prolix gut to be stuffed," as father used to tell his students, but a delicate organism to be stimulated and directed.

And so I'm brought back, by association of ideas, to the point from which I set out, the University. Its chief charm for advanced students, as well as its chief *danger* perhaps, is its freedom of method. The professors act rather as guides and counsellors than as instructors. Their lectures are intended to direct our work, to point out sources of information and suggest points of view. Each man is allowed to follow his own methods of study, which he can safely and profitably do if he have matured purposes, but which allows him full opportunity to fritter away his time if he have no fixed habits of study. The temptation in my own case is to confine myself to those paths of constitutional study which have become familiar, and therefore most attractive, to me. I have a distinct dread (partly instinctive and partly instilled by my home training) of too much reading, and I am, consequently, so much averse from *scattering* my forces that I possibly limit them to too narrow a sphere.

The sessions of the *Seminary* are occupied in the reading of papers (generally by students of longest standing in the University) upon special subjects political and social, such as the Spanish settlements in Florida and the constitution and history of such socialistic communities as Brooke farm and others more obscure; and the preparation of these papers illustrates one of the best features of University work, its *coöperative* feature. Instead of requiring all to go over the whole field in any given branch, each man is assigned a limited topic for special study upon which he is expected to make a report in class; and his knowledge of the other topics involved is gained from the papers read by his classmates.

But I must really draw this huge letter to a close. Its bulk is already alarming, and I have a dim suspicion that, after all my writing, I have told you very little that you did not know before. What I have wished to emphasize is the *object* for which I came to the University: to get a special training in historical research and an insight into the most modern literary and political thoughts and methods, in order that my ambition to become an invigorating and enlightening power in the world of political thought and a master in some of the less serious branches of literary art may be the more easy of accomplishment. To charge me with egotism and presumption in entertaining such an ambition would, I freely admit, be a just commentary on my plans; but I am conscious in my most secret heart of making not the least pretension to *genius* and of relying altogether on hard work and a capacity for being taught. I am by no means confident of reaching the heights to which I aspire, but I *am* sure of being able to climb *some* distance; and I shall never be embittered by finding myself unable to get to the top. It will be invigorating to breast the hill anyway—much more invigorating than easy walking on level ground—and all my energies are eager for the exercise. One thing at least shall not retard my influence, if I can help it, and that is a lame *style* in writing. Style is not much studied here; *ideas* are supposed to be everything—their vehicle comparatively nothing. But you and I know that there can be no greater mistake; that, both in its amount and in its length of life, an author's influence depends upon the power and the beauty of his style; upon the flawless perfection of the mirror he holds up to nature; upon his facility in catching and holding, because he pleases, the attention: and style shall be, as, under my father's guidance, it has been, one of my chief studies. A writer must be artful as well as strong.

You will doubtless smile at the character of this profuse epistle, as I have done; but its composition had done me lots of good. I've worked off any amount of stored-up steam in writing it!

Your letter of the 26th, with the photographs, came this morning and gave me infinite pleasure. You can't imagine how hard it is for me to fight off "the blues" when your letters are long delayed in coming! I conjure up all sorts of fears and get all wrong in my work—unable to think, capable only of anxiety. I am, indeed, most unreasonably susceptible to circumstances and am, consequently, constantly subject to all sorts of ups and downs of spirits. A letter from you, however, can always bring my spirits out of the cellar and treat them to the finest views from the upper windows! I need not be ashamed of being dominated by circumstances, tho', for they are big things. Consider the arrangement of a lady's hair, for instance: her habit in the matter is a trivial enough circumstance in itself; but if a certain little woman who is very dear to me had departed once from her usual way of coiling her hair about the back of her shapely head, it is more than probable that I should not have recognized a certain vanishing figure at the window of a certain hotel in Asheville—and what then? I could'nt have been very happy in Morganton.

Thank you ever so much, my darling, for the photographs. The large one is splendid, the small one "abominable." You are much prettier than either of these photos., my love, because they have not the life of expression, which is so much in your face; but the "cabinet" is an excellent likeness, and I shall never tire of looking at it. I never knew before of the joke Jessie's mischief perpetrated on you. What a girl she is! I have no copy of my likeness; but I will get one for you as soon as it's *get-able*

If this were not the nineteenth (!) page of this stupendous epistle, I should read you a lecture, my dear, sly little lady, on your evasive delay in answering my questions lately propounded[.] "I have found, from *observation*, that a woman, whether she designs it or not, is disposed to talk all around a subject like that, and finally glide away from it altogether, without throwing much, save indirect, light on the matter[.]" "Do you know who said that?"

There are many things in your letter on which I have remarks to make, but I can't make them at the tail end of *this* document. I am *very* glad and very much relieved to hear that your dear father's health is beginning to mend. Give him my love, and tell him that he is helpless now. Is it not so nominated in his own bond? That is not a revocable instrument, unless he can show utter worthlessness on the part of the *donee*. Good-bye, my darling: let me tell you a secret: *I love you beyond all else in this world.*   Your own   Woodrow.

ALS (WC, NjP).

From Ellen Louise Axson

My dearest Woodrow,   Rome [Ga.], Oct. 30/83.

I seem to be fulfilling my promise of a letter on Tuesday, rather "in the letter" than the spirit; but to anyone situated as I am, at present, it is decidedly dangerous to say "I will" do anything. My "times" are not in my own hands.

There were last evening, nine visitors here, and as one of them, Anna Harris[1] spent the night with me, I could not find the opportunity to write, even by waiting until "the wee sma' hours." However, it doesn't matter so much after Saturday's budget.

I hope that sometime in the course of human events I will again be able to keep "the even tenor of my way," but at present we are rather "stirred up." We are just on the point of going out to Mr. Tedcastle's again; they think the change of scene will do Father good and help to divert his mind. Those good friends, who have the trick of doing a kindness with the manner of persons on whom a great favour has been conferred, have been in, six or eight times during the last week, to beg Papa to come and "take care" of Agnes. Mr. T. leaves today, and "is always obliged to get someone to stay with her," and would so much rather have ["]his pastor than his clerks"! We will be there a week or so, & after that, if he regains his strength rapidly enough, we will immediately begin to prepare for leaving. I am afraid the "packing up" will drive him "raving distracted,["] so I have almost pursuaded him to go off to Marietta and leave me to my own devices. I should be extremely glad to get rid of him on all such occasions.

But I have no time to talk about plans—or anything else, now. —must send my little maid flying to the office to get this off in time. Please excuse haste. Your letter was received yesterday, my darling, and made a day, stormy without, all sunshine within. With best love, believe me   Your own Ellie.

ALS (WP, DLC) with WWhw and WWsh notation on env.
¹ ELA's classmate at the Rome Female College and one of her closest friends in Rome. See ELA to WW, Dec. 10, 1883.

Notes Taken in Dr. Ely's Minor Course in Political Economy

XI.   Oct 31st 1883

Adam Smith (continued)

Position in history of political economy:

The English speak of him as the father of political economy. In one sense this expression is not incorrect. It ought rather to be said that [political] economy originated with the Physiocrats who were the first to treat such a system as a whole. But the study did not take its first great impulse from them but from Adam Smith who gathered up all the forces that had gone before. Adam Smith entered into the labors of Hume, Tucker, Ferguson, and others who had studied certain phases of the great subject, to give a great lasting impulse as a system, as a complete study. Adam Smith is the central or pivotal point of political economy.

Classes of political economy

(1) Historical (statistics and history enter largely into this school: little a priori.[)]
(2) Socialists who differ from both a pri. and historical school.
(3) The a pri. school of England.

All, however, go back to Adam Smith. The historical school show how much Adam Smith drew from history and statistics. The a pri. school go back to him for their great leading principle: Self interest without restraint.

A more systematic division of the subject matter of political economy is found in Adam Smith than in any other. Perhaps for the first time in him was there anything like a systematic division. Previously isolated parts and factors had been treated.

5 main parts or books:

(1) The causes of improvement in productive powers of labor and order according to which these produce are distributed among the people.

(2) Capital; employment of stock as capital.

(3) Progress of opulence: increase of wealth of countries.

(4) History of political economy

(5) Finance

Even in him these matters treated all systematically but still the system is not the best. Mill also has 5 books and his system is more perfect. Röscher has a still better division.

Mill: production, distribution, exchange, national influences, finance.

Rös.: production, circulation, distribution, consumption, population.

Adam Smith is regarded as representative of the *bourgeoisie* in the history of political economy and he did represent them more than any other class. All previous schools had represented the b. also, even the American. The same is true to a certain extent of the Physiocrats. Then Adam Smith developed this bo. political economy more fully and completely and pushed the triumph of this class to its culmination.

The political economy he founded is called the industrial system. He recognized the *productive* character of all pursuits. He favored freedom of trade and commerce, between employer and employee, and in so doing he favored the bo. as opposed to the fourth estate, more than he was himself really. The classes with capital never need any defense, anything but freedom. Before the power of capital became enormous the bo. were naturally in favor of protection.

Adam Smith however did not forget other classes. He thought only of the bo. when he made some of his sweeping assertions. He recognizes the fact that state interference in favor of the laborers may be just and benevolent. It may be necessary also to protect the bo. at home against the bo. abroad.

Exceptional Cases

Favors any measure, like the Navigation Act, which is necessary for the benefit of the country.

When protection has already obtained income and has raised up a class of manufacturers dependent upon it, he would favor only a slow advance towards the freedom of trade.

Favors custom duty where there is excise duty.

Favors in certain cases retaliatory duties against foreign countries, if the foreign countries are likely to abandon their course because of this retaliation.

It is right to lay import duties on goods which are taxed at home. If that be true why not levy such duties to counterbalance any additional expense on home product? Such expense, for instance, as *higher wages. Non sequitur*

The original and imperfect system of taxation is to be found in Adam Smith: called, ever since, economy in the levy, etc., etc.

Transcript of WWsh notes in classroom notebook described at Oct. 3, 1883. A few words in WWhw.

Research Notebook

[c. Nov. 1, 1883-Jan. 1884]

First page begins (WWhw): "(12-13) 32-36 36-51."
Contents:

(a) Research notes, mainly in WWsh, from various sources and authorities, for *Congressional Government.*

(b) Loose pages of notes, mainly in WWsh, for WW's "lecture" on Adam Smith in Dr. Richard T. Ely's undergraduate course in political economy at The Johns Hopkins University, first semester, 1883-84.

Student note book with brown cover (WP, DLC).

From Edward Ireland Renick

Dear Wilson,   Atlanta Ga. Nov 1st 1883.

Your very legible and readable letter was thoroughly valued. Both Gaddy & myself have been anxious to hear from you—we talk almost every day of you. At length I wrote, determined to set at defiance the rule which imposes upon you the first letter. I am, as you must know, not only deeply interested in you, but in your pet studies. It is from you that I had my desire made strong to set sail for those coasts where you have now (if not long since) landed, and the capitals of which you will speedily subdue. . . .

Gaddy now acts as Clerk of the City Court—gets $50.00 a month, with good hopes of an increase. I am glad to say that I am doing first rate. The Perry case will be heard today, & with his consent, here. I withdrew your traverse & demurred to his answer in order to bring the whole matter before the judge. I feared the jury of his vicinity. Besides, I found a bully decision of Jeremiah Black's to the effect that an att'y who neglects or refuses to pay over money which he has collected, or to notify his client of such collection is entitled to no compensation whatever. The

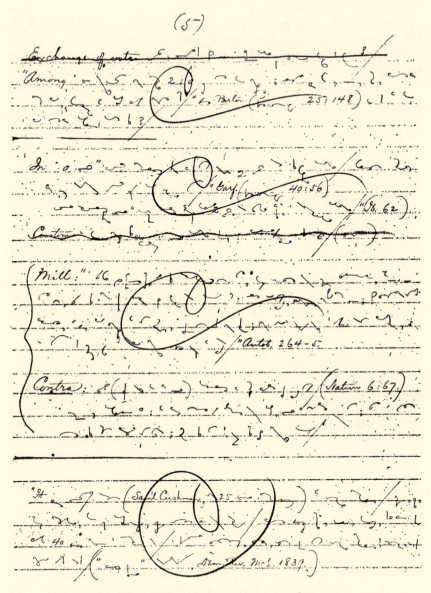

A page from Wilson's shorthand research notes
for CONGRESSIONAL GOVERNMENT.

reason of the rule is that a party must not be put to two suits to recover the same debt.

The Brower case has not yet been set. Hammond is sick, & Glenn is waiting for some interrogatories to return. . . .

Now as to your studies. I impatiently await an account of your change of view on any subject. Are not these principles true:

1st That trade between countries is by means not of sale but of exchange.

(2) That the amount of coin brought into a country is in general only as much as circulating requirements demand.

(3) That if such amt. exceeds the amt sent out—it signifies not that the country's trade is to that extent profitable, but simply that a debt has been paid, or a loan advanced?

It will gratify you to hear that the News & Courier has in a real masterly way handled the Macon Telegraph & Augusta Chronicle on the subject of Protection. The controversy has been spirited, decent, & protracted. The victory is clearly a free trade victory.

Be so kind as to suggest to me such authorities, & points of view as have been suggested to you. Tell me about your Princeton Review Article—your chance for a fellowship—your views of the Johns &c. Try to meet G. V. Yonce if he still attends the lectures of biology there.

I am studying Cooley's Principles of Constitutional Law at present—what can you recommend in that department?

Gaddy read with considerable ease your shorthand postal. Before he got his present situation he studied regularly and arduously his Graham. . . .

I write subject to many interruptions. Please let me hear from you soon.   Yours as ever   Renick

ALS (WP, DLC) with WWhw notation on env.: "Ans Nov. 15/83."

To Ellen Louise Axson

My precious Ellie,   Balto., Md., Nov. 1st, 1883

I can fancy the amusement and astonishment you will feel tomorrow morning when you get those twenty closely-written pages I sent you last Tuesday. That letter illustrates very well a rather whimsical habit of mine which you have doubtless noticed—the habit of giving a *reason* for everything, whether one is called for or not. If I remember correctly the contents of that letter, I occupied much of the first pages of it in giving an elaborate exposition of the motives which prompted me to write it. Now, those reasons were well enough in themselves, and true enough, but not at all necessary to be given, and evidently, even on the face of them, not the main reason. It is such a luxury to be loved by the dear little woman whose love is all in all to me, that to tell her of all my whims and schemes, sure as I am of her affectionate sympathy, is a mere act of self-indulgence: and that is the main reason which might have gone without the saying.

Your photograph, my darling, is a great comfort to me. I have put it in a frame and placed it where I can see it from all parts of the room; and I make all sorts of loving speeches to it—such as would make your cheeks burn if you could but hear them, but which do not make *it* change countenance in the least;—a fact which I can account for only on the ground that the picture was taken before you knew me and is, consequently, the effigy of a young lady who was not prepared to appreciate such remarks from *me*. Somehow the original of that photograph is unspeakably dear to me and I can't help making certain passionate declarations even to this which is but her "counterfeit presentment." I may have occasion to repeat similar declarations to the lady herself some of these "good days coming"—but she will then be so close to me that I can't see her blushes.

I had intended saying something about fine city girls, *a propos* a passage in your last letter; but I received a paper this morning in which it is said for me much better than I could say it, so I send you the paper. The piece is marked, and was written by Bob. Bridges, of the N. Y. *Evening Post*, a classmate of mine, and my dearest and most intimate friend.[1] Whether any part of the idea of it was suggested to the rascal by the last letter I wrote him I don't know.

I am overcrowded with work at present, having just been assigned a big piece of writing by one of my professors;[2] but, with the utmost indiscretion, I over-taxed my eyes yesterday, and am to-day suffering with a dull ache through my head and with throbbing orbs that refuse all use, even use in writing a long letter to my darling. I must indulge them with absolute rest for about twenty-four hours. But even these four pages can carry my love as well as any number can. I wonder if you will ever know how unspeakably dear you are to me! You have sweetened my ambition even; for now I strive after success for your sake. When I am tired of study, all my energies are brought back by the thought that I am working for my darling, not for myself alone. If I succeed, hers shall be the honour; if I were to fall short, hers would be the sorrow! In the things of this world, my darling, my precious

Ellie, I live for you. With love to your dear father and regards to
Mrs. T.,   Your own   Woodrow.

P.S. Your note of Tuesday came this morning. Its opening ("My
dearest Woodrow") reminded me of a note which began "My dear
Mr. Woodrow"—do you remember? I like you to use the name,
                                                    Woodrow.

ALS (WC, NjP).
¹ "A Susceptible Bachelor," *Life*, II (Nov. 1, 1883), 219. It was a poem in
which the subject goes on about gay city girls and ends by saying that they
are "but toys of the dance" and that he will marry Belle, a "bright country-
born maiden."
² It was a "lecture" on Adam Smith, which Dr. Ely asked WW to give in his
undergraduate course in political economy. See WW to ELA, Nov. 4, 20, and 27,
1883, and Jan. 16, 1884. A transcript of a fragment of the "lecture" is printed
at Nov. 20, 1883, following the Editorial Note, "Wilson's Lecture on Adam
Smith."

Notes Taken in Dr. Ely's Minor Course in Political Economy

XII.   Nov. 2nd 1883

The method of Adam Smith? Inductive or deductive?

Buckle says that it was entirely deductive—from the phenomena
of one characteristic of human nature. Rogers ranks Adam Smith
among the great inductive philosophers[.] Lowe claimed for Adam
Smith the honor of having raised political economy into a true
science—that is, a fuller system of knowledge. Price on the contrary says that Adam Smith did not intend to give even a systematic treatise of the phenomena of wealth but simply treated
of a few practical and important subjects—a few remarks upon
everyday affairs.

Explanation: Sometimes Smith uses one method at one time
and the other at another time. The deductive school is more indebted to Adam Smith than any other. The inductive school was
a protest against the tendencies of Adam Smith. He was writing
a practical treatise for practical men—wishing to correct certain
errors in practical politics. He wrote on any aspect that would be
likely to accomplish this end. His care was for the effect his work
was to have. Leslie explains how the 2 schools could take their
rise from Adam Smith.

Within a few years after its publication Adam Smith became
active and made himself felt in politics. The younger Pitt was a
declared follower of Smith and student of the Wealth of Nations.
He would have gone farther had circumstances (the French Revolution) permitted. Pitt's power rested above all upon the classes
who were still persuaded that wealth meant something. Still he

effected a considerable number of improvements in legislation. He removed numerous custom duties, by which means he raised his revenues. One of his first measures was an attempt to conciliate Ireland by removing restrictions upon customs between the 2 countries. 1785 a bill which did away with every obstacle to trade between England and Ireland. This passed the Parliament of England only to fail in the Parliament of Ireland. 1800 he accomplished his purpose by the union of England and Ireland.

The political economy of Adam Smith reached its climax in the abolition of the Corn Laws in 1846. See Morley's Cobden.

Stein was a follower of Adam Smith. Abolished serfdom, removed restrictions (internal) on commerce.

Adam Smith's work was too exclusively English to furnish a basis broad enough for the positive work of construction which he evidently required. It was good so long as the times required negative work. His political economy was individualistic or atomistic. He considers only the *consumer*.

Adam Smith's political economy was introduced into France about 1790. One of the earliest translators was Germain Garnier who wrote a little work on political economy. "Abrégé des princpes de l'Economie politique. [WWhw]" He attempted to reconcile Adam Smith with the Physiocrats. He argued for the production of useful service and for the doctrine which considers material goods as wealth. Canard "Principles of Political Economy" published in 1802. These paved the way for Say, as David Hume, Tucker, etc., paved the way for Adam Smith.

Say is greatest French exponent of Adam Smith—next to Adam Smith the greatest exponent of that school of economy. His work appeared first in 1803 and acquired a very quick and complete success. It was translated into English. The sixth edition 1834. Besides his "Traité" he wrote a "Cours d'Economie politique pratique" (1828) a separation of political economy into 2 parts: power and principle. Say occupies an important position as a French representative of Adam Smith and one who is an important instrument in spreading his principles throughout the world (especially in this country).

He carried the political economy of Adam Smith farther than anyone else in the direction of system. Divided economic phenomena into production, distribution, and consumption and divided his book into 3 corresponding books. S. was the first one to introduce *consumption* as one of the leading divisions of political economy.

The Germans divided political economy into 3 parts (taking

their cue from a man named Jacob, who wrote a political economy in 1805) (1) National economy (2) Police [Political] Science; (3) Finance. *Rau* separated economic administration from other branches. R. represents highest development of Adam Smith in Germany. (1) Divided into production, distribution, consumption, population, etc.

Say is noted for the discovery of what many consider the true theory of markets, opposed to the common belief of over production. He was the first to say that there is no such thing as over-production (a mere quibble) the wants of all human beings being not satisfied. This would be true if the people were properly distributed and there were a perfect machinery of distribution of economic goods. More is produced than under the actual condition of things can be consumed. S. made distinction between productive consumption and unproductive consumption. Unproductive unless it produced an equal value to the several things consumed.

After Adam Smith:

McCulloch
D. Stewart

*Malthus (1766) a clergyman, investigating during travels. The circumstances which led Malthus to study population of which the principle was the following of short crops (1760) after a series of abundant crops. Said that under the most favorable conditions food could increase only in arithmetic progression, while population increased in geometric progression. The natural rate of increase therefore could never become the actual rate, without runing against the limits of subsistency.

*Cencus [WWhw] reports of various countries.
"Overpopulation and Its Remedies" Thornton.
Röscher Book V.
"Moral Statistics" by Al. von Oettinger argues against the American interpretation of statistics.
Schönberg a very interesting discussion of the theory of population by important men. (Vol. I 1203-44)
Rob. von Mohl gives considerable information upon the literature of the subject (Vol. 3: 411 et seq)
Cliff Leslie "The Celibacy [WWhw] Nation"
Benj. Franklin, see, "Observations Concerning the Increase of Mankind and the Peopling of Countries" (Sparks edition) Vol 2: 311-320

Transcript of WWsh notes in classroom notebook described at Oct. 3, 1883. A few words in WWhw.

From Marion Wilson Kennedy

My dearest brother,   Little Rock, Nov. 2nd/83.

Your letters are like breaths of fresh, pure air, of late, they sound so like the brother I *used to know*. I am so glad, dear boy, that you are so happy, and with such just and satisfactory cause. If I didn't feel afraid my new sister would think me foolish, I would dearly like to thank her, *direct*, for the immense good she has done my dear brother. Do you know, I have always felt that you and I could understand each other better than anyone else understood either of us? In consequence of this peculiar sort of sympathy, I suppose it is, I feel the greatest desire to give those "dainty lips" more than one kiss, from the depths of my heart. And I *can* imagine myself as *loving her dearly, as I do now*, all the rest of my life, and yet never knowing any more of her than what she is to you. Do not infer, though, that I am not anxious to see her, for that is far from being the state of the case. What is her age? You see, if asking questions will help me, I intend to know all you do about your love before long. Have you any idea as to the probable length of your engagement? . . .

Do write very soon again. Give my love to the sister that is to be, and keep "*lots*" for yourself,   Your sister   M.

ALS (WP, DLC) with WWhw notation on env.: "Ans. Nov. 11th 1883."

To Ellen Louise Axson

My own darling,   Balto., Nov. 4th 1883

For fear you should be anxious about my eyes, because of what I reported of their condition in my last letter, I must write you a few lines this afternoon to say that they are quite well again, completely restored by the rest to which I treated them. Nothing serious was the matter with them: all work and no play had made them dull, that was all. I am just at present under such a stress of work that the temptation to overwork my eyes is very strong. A week ago one of my professors appointed me, as he had appointed others upon other subjects, to prepare, within three weeks, a "lecture" of an hour's length on Adam Smith. Now, since the professor himself has in his own lectures touched upon all the leading points of Adam Smith's life and opinions, since the preparation of my "lecture" involves the reading not only of Adam Smith's works but also of all the principal things that have been written about him, and since within these three weeks I have to prepare for an examination on a work of this same professor's, I feel as if at present I had about as much as I could do, even more than sensitive eyes can accomplish without irritation. But I like pressure of this sort. It is as bracing as walking against a strong and keen head wind. The more one has to do, the more one *can* do, and the greater the incentive to do it *well*.

How I long for your presence, my darling, on these Sabbath afternoons when my work lulls and I can stop and think about myself, about my privileges and my duties, about my relations to my fellow men and about my relations to God. It would be *such* a comfort and such a pure delight to sit in sweet communion with you at such times; to talk of the future, of how we shall sustain each other in love, of how we shall work together to do good, to make a bright spot around us in this world, to construct a perfect Christian home, from which pure influences shall go out to those around about us! Of course my longings for your presence are not confined to the Sabbath afternoons; they are constant; they almost torture me sometimes; I dare not think of what a delight it would be to have your loving ministrations to gladden my work, to have fatigue conjured away by your caresses, and discouragement or disappointment chased away by your sympathy, to have your smile go with me and your kisses greet me as I go to a[nd] fro to meet my appointments! If I allowed my mind to dwell on such things I should be paralyzed with discontent. When there's work to be done, it's folly to dream and build castles in the air. But when I reach these pauses in the week I feel justified in resigning myself to all sorts of pleasant reveries and day-dreams; and I think it quite legitimate to wish then for happy conferences with my precious Ellie, who is to be all in all to me in my life-work, my sweet help-meet and companion.

I am reminded, in this connection, of *your* wish for "a piece of me." Do you mean a lock of my hair, my darling? If so, you must wait to cut it off for yourself: for before your letter came I had had my hair trimmed so short that it will be a long time before there's any respectable lock to be had.

Tell me all about your plans, dearest. How I wish I could go down and help you pack! I'm a good hand at such work, I assure you! Love to your father and regards to Mrs. T. With love unspeakable for yourself,   Your own   Woodrow.

ALS (WC, NjP).

From Ellen Louise Axson

My dearest Woodrow,   Rome [Ga.], Nov. 5, 1883.

If I were not sure that you understand, to a small extent at least, how I am situated at present I should feel afraid that you would consider me very heartless, to so disregard those moving words in one of your recent letters, about your anxiety when mine are delayed. But I have already explained matters sufficiently, so will waste no time now in apologies. I have not written solely because I *could* not. And I was particularly anxious too, to acknowledge your Thursday's letter, and thank you for it.

It is hardly necessary, dearest, to tell you with what profound interest and pleasure I read it; or even to say how I will keep all these things and ponder them in my heart. If the most entire, loving sympathy and faith can be accepted as any small return for your confidence you may be very sure, my darling, that they are yours.

To tell the truth, I am "quite too awfully" proud of you! When I think of your various gifts and the high, pure and noble purposes to which they are dedicated, I feel a quiet little glow and thrill of admiration, tingling out to my very finger-tips. I well remember the first time you caused me to experience that particular sensation—or rather that sensation with a difference, a vast difference; for then it was "none of my business," and my admiration was, one might almost say, impersonal—bestowed upon qualities rather [than] the person who possessed them. It was as we climbed the hill together, that I had that first glimpse of your aims in life, and learned, not only how you had found it "better to fight for the good than to rail at the ill," but also with what resolute courage, what generous enthusiasm, you courted the conflict. What though "the time *is* out of joint"—"there is so much the more to be done"; all the greater need for good work, and true, brave workers; and therefore, to one who would live the best and *fullest* life, it is the *best* time. Do you remember saying anything at all resembling or suggesting that? To be an enobling, inspiring influence in the world,—that is surely a pure ambition! And it seems to me that the peculiarity of such an ambition—the ambition to do all the good you can, and for that purpose to develop and use your powers to the best advantage—is that it *cannot* end in failure. For you have great allies; your will runs in the same groove with God's will. *Fame*, perhaps, is, as some one says, but an accident; yet in the truly great life, is'nt it also but an incident, a circumstance not altering the facts of the case?

I was very sorry to learn from your Saturday's letter that your eyes have been over-taxed, and are giving you trouble. I hope to hear soon that the twenty-four hours sufficed to make all well again. I shall be obliged to read you a lecture about "sitting up late at night," and, the "amount of sleep which young people need"!

Speaking of eyes, I have gotten into a most absurd scrape today with reference to mine. It is such a good joke that I must give you the benefit of it. The beginning of it was anything but a joke, however. I heard, yesterday, that a person, whom I supposed one of Papa's best friends, had treated him very unkindly behind his back. It was rather heart-breaking to hear of such a thing from so unexpected a source—a sort of an "et tu Brute" case, you know! So I must needs lapse into an extremely lachrymose condition, in consequence. As I don't do such a thing more than once in two or three years, it never occurred to Papa that I had been crying. He thought they were "inflamed with cold," and began to propose remedies and insist upon complete rest! Started it again before breakfast this morning, and has actually made me lose more than half the day—of course I wouldn't for the world have given him the real explanation. He objected again to my writing tonight; but now he has gone, my conscience does'nt forbid! Rather a high price to pay for the luxury of tears, is it not?

That isnt the only joke either about "those weeps." It is well to get all the entertainment we can even from our tribulations; and we certainly had a ridiculous scene yesterday. Anna Harris was unfolding the tale, when I suddenly tumbled over on the bed, and went into the business, with the most charming abandon. She, alarmed at the completeness of my collapse, flew to the rescue; whereupon I sobbed out, "take care, my picture is on the bed, and you'll spoil it,"—it was a photograph of a very particular friend of mine, but I couldn't think of telling you *who*! Whereupon she, thinking a diversion had been created, and the worst was over, began to laugh; but was somewhat nonplused to find that I didnt see the fun, but continued, for an hour or so, absorbed in my woes and oblivious to ordinary matters. She has been making various satirical remarks today about "the ruling passion strong in death," &c.

The paper arrived safely on Sat., with your letter. Was much pleased with Mr. Bridges "Bachelor." Was especially impressed with one of his *rhymes*—"whom I take to the opera," "nice for a hop or a"! That is really a stroke of genius is'nt it? Is he, Mr. B., the one whose picture you showed me once. What has become of "Charlie Talcott"?

You ask about our plans. I hav'nt seen Father on the subject since tea, so I really don't know (see Judge Underwood)! He changes his mind every day, so that it hardly pays to record any plan at present. The latest is that he will spend the winter "quietly here, in his own home, where he can be most comfortable" and leave in the spring. We did not go to Agnes. He "backed out" at the last moment—did'nt feel well enough to leave home. He has been worse again since I last wrote, but seems a great deal better the last two or three days. We will probably go to Sav[annah]. as usual, for the holidays, unless he decides that there is too much malaria there for him to risk it. I am anxious for him to leave Rome as soon as possible. I think his mind will be diverted into fresh channels, and he will improve more rapidly.

But I am wanted again, so I will bring this scrawl to a hasty close. This is, I believe, about the seventeenth time I have been called off since I began to write—if I seem distraught you will be able to account for it.

With love to your mother and the rest, believe me, dearest,

Yours with all my heart,   Ellie.

I suppose you "heard that" Mr. Brown[1] gained *three* cases last week. The "Pierce case," the the [*sic*] "Bank case," and the one concerning the house next door to us. The first was non-juried (?), and on the second, the jury were out five minutes. Is'nt that good news.

ALS (WP, DLC).
[1] Edward T. Brown, a lawyer, son of Warren A. Brown and cousin of ELA. For a fuller identification, see ELA to WW, Aug. 20, 1884, n. 1, Vol. 3.

From Joseph Ruggles Wilson

My darling Son—   Wilmington [N.C.], 11/6, 1883.

Your excellent letter came to hand this morning. Please find enclosed my check for $50.00. Mr. Inglis will cash it; so he promised. As to allowance I hardly know what to say, because my stay here is becoming more and more uncertain by reason of the state of my health, mainly. But so long as I do remain, yr. allowance shall be the same as at Atlanta.

It affords me satisfaction to learn that you *love* to work. Whilst this is the case too much of it is hardly possible, provided it be not hurried but is proceeded with coolly and systematically. Happily, too, you have now reached an age when it is not needful to pore with wrinkled brow over yr books in order to understand their contents:—but when you can with unstrained mental eye peer direct into every meaning. This is a high advantage and a source of noble joy. There is only one advantage higher[,] only one joy greater (speaking intellectually)—and those are found in doing your own thinking; i.e. out of every studied book getting a book of your own make, and which no one else of course can equally secure. I am sure that rote is not your danger; but too great facility in comprehending truths may be:—for that which easily slides *into* the mind as easily slides out of it. It has to be gripped by the teeth that chew, and assorted to all uses by the digestion that gives blood, and retained by a sort of life-instinct as a constituent part of the man. No thought is *mine* until it is a portion of *me*: and when it shall have become a part of me it is as sure to be original when again expressed as that my idiosyncrasies are not another's. But a truce to all this. You know as well as I do, what study is & does when it is genuine and hard without being burdensome, and large without being thin.

Touching the probabilities of your getting a place in a large Institution as Assistant Prof., I have thought a great deal. The chances are not first-rate unless you get the signal endorsement of Johns Hopkins. Secure this, and then we shall see. My personal influence seems to be small whenever I attempt to place young men where they wish to be. I hardly know why. And in recommending my own son the drawbacks would be increased (1) because he is my son (2) because I would be compelled to water the wine of my commendation out of modesty.

Get some one or more of yr Professors interested in your desire, and they will for the sake of their own Institute, try to put you where they believe you would fit in. And the most successful method for interesting them in such a matter, is to command their admiration by imperial work.

Your dear Mother's health is improving, but she is frail: yet not so frail as to forbid the hope that care will bring her along until a fine strength is reached.

My own in'nards are peaceful. The head whirls now and then—but does not interfere with my work.

Dode is all right, enjoying his Bicycle, and alive to every thing except study which he seems to avoid as a contagion.

All send love, and plenty of it.

Your affectionate   Father

ALS (WP, DLC) with WWhw notation on env.: "Ans. Nov. 11/83."

Three Letters to Ellen Louise Axson

My own darling,   Balto., Nov. 6th, 1883

Since my whole evening will be taken up by a lecture, I must content myself with a short letter to-day, and I know that you will the more readily forgive its brevity because I have for some time past been writing to you every other day. I wish I could write my darling such a letter as she needs and would most enjoy just at this time. I know how the pressure of anxiety and of responsibility must weigh on her loving heart, and, since I cannot, for all my ardent longing to be able to do so, relieve her of any part of the care she has at present to carry, I am all the more eager to send her such assurances of my love and admiration and confidence and sympathy as will lighten her labours a little, and will make uncertainties of plan seem a little less formidable and the fatigues of packing a little less irksome. You don't know how constantly my thoughts are with you, my precious Ellie. You are such a brave, hopeful little woman that I am not sure that you feel the need of loving sympathy; maybe you do'nt think that it would be an unmixed blessing to have me to help in the packing up (and I confess that it is just possible that I should give more attention to *you* than to the work); but, however that may be, my heart makes common cause with you of its own accord, and insists upon having you know that all your cares are its cares, as far as you allow it any share in a knowledge of those cares, and that, according to its nature, it is probably even more anxious than yourself about your present duties and your future plans. You did a most dangerous thing, young lady, in capturing me. You don't realize it now, perhaps; but you will some day. Then you will know what a vital, practical, insisting, obtrusive thing my love is, not allowing you to have any private joys or griefs into which it can't enter. For the present you must make allowances for it, however, because of the disadvantages under which it laboured for a long time. I began to love you very early, you must remember, and had to love you for what seemed to me an endless period without any encouragement, haunted even up to that blessed hour in Asheville with the conviction that it would never enter into your head to love me; and I feel entitled now to a certain license of demonstration as a recompense for the pain of long suppression. You emancipated me when you made your sweet confession—emancipated me from the slavery of concealing love under the colder forms of friendship, or, at least, of *trying* to conceal it: for I believe you knew long before I told you. Now

that I am sure you know it, I am eager to be telling you again and
again that *I love you with all my heart*. Do you know how much
that means, my darling? If you do, then you know how entirely
my happiness and all that I am is in your keeping. You must have
wrought a sort of revolution in me, my love; for I have hitherto
had the reputation of being undemonstrative! Do'nt be incredulous; it's so; though I admit that *you* would be justified in disbe-
lieving it. You have a great deal to answer for. How can a fellow
in Baltimore write a lecture on Adam Smith when he's forever
thinking of a girl in Georgia?

I sincerely hope that your father is decidedly better ere this.
Give him my love, please; and give my kindest regards to Mrs.
T. I'm not going to tell you again how much love you may keep
for yourself.

Your own   Woodrow.

My precious Ellie,   Balto., Nov. 8th 1883

It is only by a hard struggle that I can keep off "the blues" to-
day, because, though this is "the day," not even a note have I
had from my darling. I know that it's all right: that she would
have written had it been possible, and that my pleasure *ought* to
be postponed to the performance of her home duties; but I can't
help thinking the day gloomy and my work irksome for a' that.
My fears suggest that my darling is sick, or that her dear father
is worse; but I try not to heed such suggestions, and am very
clear on one point: that my not hearing is no ground for my not
writing. I may even count upon lightening my own disappointment by contributing to my Ellie's happiness; and I have no idea
of letting her get again "low in her mind," or of allowing her once
more to have to force back the tears, because the mails bring her
no letter from her lover. I gravely suspect that I am spoiling her
by writing to her so often, and I am quite sure that no busy student can *legitimately* find time to write twice a week to the same
person; but there are some men who can't mix discretion with
their love, who are too doting by half, and who make the indulgence of those whom they love a matter of *self*-indulgence!

Every man may have, if he will, a sort of home manufactory
of spiritual sunlight from which to supply his *own* light at least;
but I should like to make enough to *dispense*. I should like to write
letters, for instance, that would make themselves felt as sources
of comfort and light. But my machine, my home apparatus, gets
out of order and often leaves even me in darkness; which is as
much as to say that I am constantly in need of a supplementary

source of light; and such a suplementary source I have found *in my love for you*. I used to get wofully out of sorts, discouraged, worn-out, disgusted; but now I have only to let my thoughts run to you and take a sort of foretaste to that sweet time when we shall be always together in order to banish all darkness and get out into the clear working-day again. Formerly I had to let my blues *work* off; now I can *cure* them. Witness the effect of this short letter. I sat down to it in a most despondent humour; but the simple concentration of my thoughts on you has brought back all my spirits. You are a dear little sorceress: and you can exercise your arts at long range. I should have imagined, independently of experience, that as long as I was in Baltimore and was separated by several States from my sweetheart, I could get up a little temporary interest in these city girls, as a sort of by-play and diversion; but I can't; my heart is in Georgia all the time. I used to suspect last Spring that I was coming under a new power, and since September came I've had to con[s]truct an entirely new working theory of life. I'd like to lay a wager with you that I think of you oftener than you think of me. The wager shall be a kiss: so that it won't be burdensome to either party to pay, or, in case of mistake, to refund with interest. I'm a grand goose, am I not? But, if you win that wager, you'll prove your*self* a goose; for no one could think of anyone more than I think of you without being very foolish!

With love to your dear father and regards to Mrs. T.—and for yourself just as much love as you can wish for between this time and the time of my next letter,

Your own   Woodrow.

P.S. Query: Would you rather have frequent *short* letters, or occasional *long* ones? Lovingly, W.

My darling Ellie,   Balto., Md., Nov. 11th 1883

I sometimes wonder nowadays how I used to get along without you. Thoughts of you, purposes and plans of which you are the centre, constitute now so large a part of my life that I look back upon last winter as full of a very blank existence. There is one view of my past life which may not have struck you, during my late confessions, but which has often filled my thoughts of late. Just as I was entering upon my preparation for the bar, I met and fell in love with my cousin, thus at the same time choosing a profession for which I was not suited, and which I was eventually to leave in disappointment, and being led away by an infatuation which was to issue in nothing but distress; but as soon as I had determined to leave the law and had set my face towards the right intellectual goal, *I found you*, my darling, the woman whose love was to make my life complete. These things were not accidental. Everything goes wrong with a man until he gets on the right road. Of course there are trials in store for me—for *us*—on *this* road; but they will be as tests of strength, not like burdens of chains; and, for my part, they can't hurt me as long as they come in the course of duty and I am sustained by your love.

I was half amused and half distressed by your account of those tremendous "weeps" that got you in such a scrape. Why, you energetic little woman, you! You don't mean to say that every time you cry you go into the business in such a wholesale fashion! If years of abstinence from tears result in such an *accumulation*, it would be prudent for you to cry oftener. I am proud of my darling because she *can* find fun in such experiences. If anything warrants tears, it is betrayed friendship; and it says a great deal for your disposition that you are able to shake off the effects of such trials. But who is Miss Anna Harris? You have a very refreshing way of taking it for granted that I know all your friends without so much as an introduction. Now I have no doubt that Miss Harris is a very estimable young lady—though, if I had been in her place, I should not have told you of the unkindness of your father's friend—but I never heard of her before, as far as I remember, except that in one of your recent notes she figures as having spent the night with you, and thereby cheated me out of my letter.

The only news that I have to impart is that I have been elected a member of the "University Glee Club,"[1] and shall "warble" with them every Monday evening. My "pipes" are somewhat out of singing order; but I know I can sing with a lot of fellows: it's the best fun of its kind that I know of, provided the other fellows can avoid strong-voiced discord.

I am glad that you were not altogether overwhelmed by that twenty-pager of mine; and let me tell you that I think your answer to it as sweet as possible. "If the most entire loving sympathy and faith" can be taken as any return for my confidence! Why, my love, *that* would, in my eyes, be return enough for anything. If my whole heart is return enough for your love, which makes me so unspeakably happy, why then know that you can never be the creditor of

Your own   Woodrow.

Love to your father and to Eddie.

ALS (WC, NjP).

¹ This is WW's first reference to his participation in the Johns Hopkins Glee Club, about which he and his friends will write more in future letters. Undergraduates had formed a glee club in 1879, but it became defunct at the end of that academic year. This letter makes it clear that William Bayard Hale, *Woodrow Wilson: The Story of His Life*, pp. 92-93, was probably incorrect in saying that WW was one of the two organizers of the glee club in 1883, but Hale's account is the fullest on this particular subject. WW sang first tenor.

From Ellen Louise Axson

My dearest Woodrow,   Rome [Ga.], Nov. 12, 1883.

Your three letters of last week came duly to hand, and were, indeed, more than welcome. I can't tell you how much I thank you for writing so often. I know the motive which prompts you; and with all my heart, I appreciate the thoughtful tenderness, which causes you, busy as you are, to pause and send those shafts of sunlight down to me. I assure you that they fulfil their mission entirely—they are messages of *good cheer*.

It must be a serious trouble indeed, which they cannot go far to remedy; and the "uncertainty of plan, and fatigues of packing" are not of that number. I am not in the least disturbed by those things. After all, there are very few evils wholly unmixed with good; and if a thing *has* a bright side, why not keep it resolutely turned "right-side up with care"? Papa's ill health is the only feature of the case which is'nt capable of being turned into a frolic. If he were only well, I should be the happiest girl in the world, though I were forced to pack as often as a Methodist preacher, or a circus company, and each time to go forth, like Abraham of old, "not knowing whither (!) he went."

In fact I have extracted a good deal of amusement from Father's constantly changing purposes, partly at his expense and partly at my own. You see, I am so self-willed, that when I can't have my own way I like to make myself believe that I have. I am too proud to enjoy the sensation of being coerced; so I don't believe that I ever found myself obliged to do anything, without getting myself throughly convinced, before beginning it, that it was the very thing I had always wanted to do,—that I had really been *pining* to do it all my life. I should'nt like to say how many times I have gone through with that process in the last few weeks. Just as I have become throughly persuaded that a certain scheme is "the very thing," and have found a dozen delightful circumstances connected with it, Papa topples it all over; and I forthwith begin my argument again on a new basis.

Many thanks for your kind desire to help me pack. I only wish I had the opportunity to accept your assistance. One of my old sweethearts, by the way, has made the same offer, and I am seriously inclined to avail myself of it! He is a remarkably "handy man," and "better is a friend that is near than a 'lover' that is afar off"—in a matter of "crockery"! The difficulty is that I should'nt like to receive aid under false pretences, and I fear he would'nt be so eager to lend his, if he knew what an uncommonly nice little place I discovered Asheville to be. Oh dear me! you have no idea what trials and tribulations girls are subjected to!

You can't imagine how I have been perplexed since my return, to know how best to wind up certain little affairs! Of course, there is one very simple and effectual way; but I have an intense dislike to taking them into my confidence except as a last resort. I naturally want to try every other expedient first. One of them, the little widower, has gone his way; but the other two still report themselves once or twice a week, as usual. You see they have gotten so used to "wet blankets, cold streams, slow drizzles," and every other known form of *damper*, that even my most vigorous measures fail of their effect! I see I must "come to it," and that very shortly. Indeed, it is hardly fair to them to do otherwise, for they are "old fellows" and have no time to waste over an "engaged" girl! It would hurt me very much to have them go away abusing me—saying that I had "treated them badly" &c; they have always said, "it was not my fault," and I would wish them to retain that opinion of me. For though it is an open secret that they are "poor creatures" a girl will keep a kind feeling for one who has asked her to be his wife, that is if she is a "penniless lass" and so can't suspect interested motives. I want them to think kindly of me, as well. I should'nt even like them to say I "have no heart." If I found them tempted to think such a thing of me, I would prefer to give them the simple explanation of that phenomenon, viz., that it is

> "Gone—out of my keeping!
> Lost—past recovery, right and title to it,
> And all given up! And he that's owner on't,
> Is fit to wear it; were it fifty hearts
> I'd give it to him all!"

I won't spoil the quotation by giving only half, though the last part didn't refer to the matter in hand.

I suppose I really ought to close this now, and answer some Sav[annah]. letters, received on Sat., but I dont feel at all disposed to do so. I wish that if we decide on Sav., we could go before the 20th; on that day dear old Helen Porter writes me, her marriage will "come off." By the same mail Janie, our own girl, Papa's "adopted daughter," announces her engagement to one of Col. Milton Chandler's sons of Decatur. How my friends are breaking ranks! There is nobody left but the two Annes, of Rome and Savannah.

In answer to your query I would say that, I prefer frequent short letters *and* an occasional long one! I am badly spoiled, you see—am glad you accept the fact so cheerfully. Still I am not altogether unreasonable. I don't want you to make the letters a burden, especially when you have such a weight to bear as the "Wealth of Nations." So in such emergencies I will unselfishly dispense with the long letters; and even if the short ones don't come as often as I wish, I won't grow plaintive. How does the lecture progress? I am much interested in that huge piece of work. I earnestly hope your eyes won't suffer in consequence. Was very glad to hear of their entire and speedy recovery from their recent trouble.

So you would like "to lay a wager with" me, rash youth that you are! I won't accept it, however, for I wouldn't like to overwhelm you with such confusion of countenance as would be sure to follow. What arguments did you expect to bring forward on your side? I can establish my point with the certainty of a mathematical demonstration. The proof lies in the simple fact that, while your work is mental, mine is manual. You *can't* think of me and Adam Smith at the same time; while I can "lay in," "work out," and "touch up" the whole Smith family without being disturbed in the even current of my thought. There sir! what have you to say now? I think you are effectually "done for."

That is one thing in which I have the advantage over you; there is no reason why I should not think of you just as much as I please! That is a constant and unalloyed happiness. The trouble begins when I wish to translate those thoughts into words. Ah, dear friend! you can't know how much I love you,

> "I yearn to tell you, and yet have no one
> *Great heart's-word* that will tell you."

As ever   Your own   Ellie.

ALS (WP, DLC) with WWhw and WWsh notes on env.

Two Letters to Ellen Louise Axson

My sweet Ellie,   Balto., Md., Nov. 13th/83
    There is one thing about both of the photographs you sent me

that I don't like, and that is that the eyes are turned away. My imagination is vivid enough to make a likeness hanging on my wall symbolic of the person's actual presence, spiritual if not bodily, and when the eyes seem to follow me about the room, the effect is, of course, very much heightened; but the thoughts of the person in this picture here before me seem to be ever so far away from me and from all that concerns me. Still, that face makes my bureau wonderfully bright and attractive, and it is none the less dear to me because its expression is one of far-away thought.

My landlady has her full share of woman's curiosity; and several days after your photographs came, she stopped me on the stairway, as I was coming in from a lecture, and said, "Mr Wilson, that was a suspicious looking package that came for you the other day; I think I have a right to see what was in it." She is such a kind, motherly old lady that it is impossible to treat her inquisitiveness as impertinent, so I smilingly assented to her right and showed her the picture. She made a little exclamation of pleasure upon seeing it, and, after examining it through her adjusted eye-glasses, bade me be a very good boy in order to deserve so lovely a partner—for she immediately concluded that it was not a picture of my sister. Miss Woods, too, went into exstacies over that picture; for she had made me promise to let her see a photograph of you, should I get one, and I took it to her the other night. It is, indeed, a lovely picture, but it is not as pretty as you are, my darling. Allow me to remark, however, Miss Axson, that it was not your face that captured me, but something of which that face is only an index, your unaffected grace, your loving heart, your sweet womanly ways—I should add your bright, sympathetic *intelligence*, if I were not forewarned that you would declare me deluded on that point—; and if these good ladies who admire your photograph so much could but know the original, as I know her, they would see greater beauty yet in that dear face.

Speaking of pictures, is'nt the bed a rather odd place to keep a picture? I wonder whose it could have been that happened to be in such a queer place and was threatened with destruction by Miss Harris!

I assisted last night at caramel-making, at the house of the young lady whose hasty opinion that I was "splendid" you were rash enough to endorse. We had a very jolly time, and I am afraid that I was not as dignified as I might have been. The company consisted of the young lady aforesaid, her two sisters, a young damsel from Philadelphia, Miss Woods and two of her brothers, and one or two other men besides myself. We compounded the caramels in the dining room, boiled them in the kitchen, and ate them in the parlour; but before these numerous stages had been passed I had had numerous frolics with the young lady aforesaid and had been three times locked up in the pantry, each time gaining my freedom by making demonstrations towards demolishing the larder, and once having one of the young ladies as a fellow-prisoner. I do'nt always misbehave so when I go out into company; but candy making is scarcely an occupation requiring much dignity; the other men were rather inclined to be dull; and Miss Jennie (the young lady aforesaid) moved me to emulation by her own overflowing spirits and by the sly mischief that laughs in her pretty eyes. You've never seen me make a thorough goose of myself, have you? I remember telling you once, though, in one of my first letters to you, that I was apt to do so in some companies.

I often laugh when I think of those letters I used to write you last summer. What transparent frauds they must have been—love-letters in a very ill-contrived disguise. I used to flatter myself that some passages in them were rather adroit, containing suggestions of love only between the lines; but I suspect that love crept into the lines themselves rather boldly often. Were you too unsuspecting to detect it? or did you dimly see it all the time? I need not ask you questions on these points, though; for you wont answer them, you coy little maiden, you! Serves me right, I suppose. I have tried my best to get you to make circumstantial confession of your love, begging for your first impressions of me, and for the whole history of the mystery; but you are right, maybe, in refusing to feed my vanity by complying; and I will try to be resigned and contrite.

I meet old friends every few days on the streets here—friends made during my Princeton or my University days, and who had almost passed out of my memory. It is pleasant to renew these acquaintances, especially since these refound friends are all so cordial and so kind, but I can't accept their invitations—I must be at "the Peabody" at their dinner hours. It's a queer life to lead, this life in the reading room of a great library. One sees all sorts of odd people in such a place, and feels their oddities because they are, for the time being, in a certain sense his companions. There are dainty fellows in kid gloves who come to *look* at books and who feel none of the subtle influences of the place; grimy mechanics who consult the enclyclopaedias; grave gentlemen who call for quarto tomes and get close into them with their glasses; leisure-hour visitors who look over the foreign illustrated journals; youngsters who read novels; and school-misses work-ing up their inevitable "compositions." A very miscellaneous as-semblage, but one which is perfectly quiet, under the stringent rules of the place, and which don't interfere at all with your own reading. There's something very impressive in the sight of so many people, of all ages and classes, making use of the treasures of a noble library; and one can get a sort of additional inspiration by stepping from the reading room into the vast, silent, mag-nificent chamber in which the eighty-thousand volumes of the vast collection are stored in the recesses of tier upon tier of pillared galleries. Some day, Ellie, we'll visit "the Peabody" together, and you can see for yourself the place where I worked, drawing no small inspiration, the while, from my love for a certain sweet Georgian and from her love for me—shall we not? Does it please you to think, my darling, that your love makes easy for me the most tedious passages of my reading. Ah, my precious Ellie, you could not wish to be loved more than I love you!

Give my love to your dear father and to Eddie. My home-folks send their love to you in every letter. Yours with a heart full of love,   Woodrow.

My own darling,   Balto., Md., Nov. 15th 1883

What a sweet letter you can write! It seems to me that every-thing you write steals my heart anew. I do'nt know that you intended the letter I received this morning to illustrate one of its texts; but illustrate it it did in a very instructive way. One of its texts was, you remember, that you are very self-willed and like always to take your own way without coercion; and what an exquisite illustration that very letter afforded! for you would not tell me anything about your old sweethearts when I sought, in my indiscretion, to draw out the information, but must needs take your own time and way. My inquiries were summarily dis-posed of in a postscript, and I was given full time to reflect upon the deserved rebuke to my impertinent inquiries, before you volunteered your full confidence. Not that it is quite *full* yet. You have'nt told me the *names* of "the other two"; but I know bet-ter than to *ask* what they are. I am learning the wisdom of letting you go your own way, which is the *sweetest* way, after all; for nothing gives me such pure delight, my darling, as to have you open your secrets to me of your own accord. Hereafter I shall ask as few questions as possible. It is'nt in human nature not to ask *any*; but I shall trust to the promptings of your knowledge of what will best please me to gain me that share in all your secret thoughts for which I so much long. I quite appreciate your disclination to take "the other two" into your confidence; but I am sure that whether you do so or not, they can have no reason to think you *heartless*. She only is without heart who proves herself thoroughly selfish, who gives positive encouragement to attentions whose object is avowed, either in words or in unequivocal acts.

So you think you have proved your title to the *wager*, do you? But you have not, my ingenious little maiden. You show, I admit, that you seem to have better *opportunities* for constant thought of me than I have for as constant thought of you, but you do'nt even assert, except by a very dim and indirect inference, that you *take advantage* of your exceptional opportunities. That is a very grave and notable omission in the argument; whereas I can say for myself that, for all the preoccupations of Adam Smith and his "Wealth of Nations," and despite innumerable other distractions big and little, thoughts of you run through all my waking moments—and through numberless dreams for the matter of that. Is'nt it natural that a man, even in the midst of his work, should think of the person he's working for, the person whose love animates all his undertakings? It's a strange psychological fact that since my short visit to Asheville I've been able to write with much more satisfaction to myself than formerly in all graver composition. My "lecture" is much better than I could have made it three months ago—much better in *execution*. I wish I had time, my darling, to make this a longer letter—I've many more things to say on this head and on others—but I must stop and say goodbye for this time. I love you, my sweet Ellie, *with all my heart*. With love to your dear father and to Eddie. In haste

Your own   Woodrow.

ALS (WC, NjP).

From Ellen Louise Axson

My dearest Woodrow,   Rome [Ga.], Nov. 17, 1883.

I have just been giving myself the treat of re-reading some of your letters, and now I think I will still further indulge myself by writing you a short one—if that be possible. Indeed, the former occupation is one which always creates a strong desire for the latter; for of course I carry on a sort of running commentary, as I read, and of course too, I am tempted to give you the benefit of it. But as it is, I can't even record the most vivid impressions produced by them. The impression deepest, just at present, is

wonder at what I might call the "*expressive* power of a new affection." When I think I already love you as much as is possible,
comes another of these letters revealing some new depth of tenderness or goodness, and I, in my turn, feel myself sinking a
fathom or so deeper in that gulf, which must indeed be, as Rosalind affirmed, like the bay of Portugal, which cannot be sounded.
I suppose all that is a common experience—

> "Those lines that I before have writ do lie
> Even those that said I could not love you dearer;"[1]

—still it *is* strange how rapidly liking—or disliking—can grow "in
meditation," and in that absence, which is supposed to cause *for-
getfulness*! I am amazed when I think of the difference between
my mental attitude at the time of your exit on that Friday in June,
and that which marked your next entrance on that other Friday in
Sept. And yet even on that first occasion I can now perceive that
I loved you better than I knew. At the present rate perhaps there
will be as much difference between the last meeting and the next.

I have especially been reading and pondering anew that sweet
letter of Sunday the 4th. I like to imagine you thinking of me on
these quiet Sunday afternoons, and thinking of me *so*. I sometimes fear, my darling, that my thoughts dwell *too* constantly on
you then. Yet I am sure that my love for our best Friend is not
coldest at those times, and I trust He will forgive me if I link the
human love with the Divine in a prayer that He would watch between us while absent one from another; and that He may help
us to make our lives indeed such as you describe, "part of the divine power against evil—widening the skirts of light, and making
the struggle with darkness narrower." I was very grateful for that
letter, dearest, and especially that it was put into your heart to
write it on that day—the darkest day of all the year to me, the anniversary of my first great sorrow.[2] How little I thought two years
ago, or even last year, when from the sun itself the glory seemed
to have passed away forever, that it would rise again with its old
brightness upon my life, all flowering afresh. Oh, the wonderful
loving kindness of God! Does He not give us "blessings beyond
hope or thought"! We ask for *patience* and He gives us *joy*. I asked
that I might walk with cheerful courage upon a somewhat steep
and rocky path—I could not frame a larger prayer—but, lo! He has
made the path itself to blossom as the rose. Yet never in all those
two years have I so longed, as during the last two months, for
the mother-love. I think I would give half my life to be with her,
to feel her sympathy, for one short hour.

"Wilt thou fill that place by me which is filled by dead eyes
   too tender to know change?
That's hardest! If to conquer love has tried,
To conquer grief tries more—as all things prove,
For grief indeed is love and grief beside."[3]

It actually begins to look as though we were going to leave
Rome in good earnest. The Sav. plan is in the ascendant just
now; and Father is sure that he wants to go next week. He is so
desperate here that any change seems worth trying. He has had
almost no sleep for the last four nights; and after such an experience his condition is beyond measure distressing—a sort of
"frenzy of nervousness," as he says. Insomnia is surely the most
mysterious thing in the world; the cause and the remedies seem
equally unknown. Then it is so strangely capricious in its comings and goings; he will be almost beside himself for a week,
and then it will suddenly "let him go" and for a time he will seem
entirely well,—no diminution of strength, appetite good, &c.

But he will want me in a short time, so I must close. Besides I
have already indulged myself long enough, and should be about
my business. I have been spending a gay afternoon at the *dentist's,*
and came back disposed to "take it easy." I think I need protection
from that old sinner; he has been abusing me outrageously—you
never heard such grumbling. He says I keep him worried all the
time; he "likes people to tell him when he hurts them, for sometimes it can be avoided"; but I am "one of those creatures who
would'nt make a sign if he was literally killing" me!

But I must end this. With love to your family, and "just as much
as you want" for yourself, I am yours forever

Ellie.

ALS (WP, DLC).
   [1] Shakespeare, Sonnet cxv.
   [2] A reference to the death of her mother, Margaret Hoyt Axson, on Nov. 4,
1881.
   [3] Elizabeth Barrett Browning, "Sonnets from the Portuguese," xxxv.

Two Letters to Ellen Louise Axson

My precious Ellie,   Balto., Md., Nov. 18th 1883
Sometimes when I think of our engagement I wonder if I have
not been *dreaming* the last two months; surely it is almost too
good to be true! When I recall my first feelings towards you; how
passionate love grew rapidly upon me; how all my thoughts used
to centre in plans to win you; what castles my hopes used to build
and how I used to sicken at the prospect of hope deferred; and

then how, much sooner than I had dared to hope, how by a seeming accident, we met and you gave your heart to me, it all seems so like a sweet dream that I am almost afraid to credit my memory. The impression is perhaps heightened by the fact that I left you before I had time to realize that you had pledged yourself to me. Although you had spoken those words which will always live in my memory, "I will do anything to make you happy"; although I had taken that sweet sealing kiss; and although I had been permitted to hold you for a moment in my arms, I remember calling you "Miss" Ellie to the last and being utterly unable to speak any part of the love and joy that were in my heart. I recollect thinking, as the train sped along with me that evening, that I had left you without any idea of the passionateness of my love for you; and, for the matter of that, I don't believe you know yet of what passionate love I am capable: for I can't write on the cold unsympathetic page what I could *say* to you were you near. I *have* to give vent in my letters to *some* protestations of love, because I feel as if my heart would break with its fulness if I did not; but the half is not told yet. Have you thought of what we may do together next Summer, Ellie? You'll let me take you on a visit to Wilmington, wont you? I don't know what effect your constant presence will have upon me under the circumstances, because I've never yet been tested by supreme happiness; but I can promise to preserve passable decorum *in company*. We can *read* together, for one thing. I am, unfortunately, a very poor reader; but I know that you will be an indulgent critic, and I shall try to improve in an art which contributes so much to your enjoyment. I have heeded your oft-repeated declaration of your passion for being read to, but I have hitherto refrained from promising you my untiring services in that line because I thought that it might go without the saying that I would delight in doing *anything* that would give you pleasure. Besides, though not good at it, I am very fond of reading aloud. But *you* must do some of the reading yourself, for I too love to be read to. We can begin with "As You Like It," and you can take the part of Rosalind! I have always been in love with Rosalind, and if you would read the part I could love her in proper person. I'd be willing to play the "motley fool," melancholy Jacques, and all the rest for the privilege of playing Orlando to your Rosalind!

My darling's last letter was specially enjoyable to me because she evidently wrote in high spirits and was able to write with a light heart. You have but to show your happiness, my sweet Ellie, to make me happy. One convincing proof of the fact that I think

of you *all the time* is that my spirits are *constantly* under the dominion of my love for you. Give my love to your father and to Eddie, and keep for yourself the whole heart of
Your own   Woodrow.

My own darling,   Balto., Md., Nov. 20th 1883
Your letter which delighted me by its unexpected coming this morning reveals a terrible state of things! If, as seems to be the case, we are both daily sinking deeper into love's Portugal-bay, we shall be in a desperate strait by the time we meet again, next summer. The knowledge that your love for me is ever growing makes me inexpressibly happy, my love, and keeps me steadfast in the resolve to live worthy of that love; but, if your love for me daily increases, what shall I say of my love for you! I have so much more to love than you have! It's a little odd—"quite a coincidence," indeed—that you should have quoted Rosalind in this letter, since I was myself dilating upon that charming young person at almost the same time in writing to you. Do'nt *you* think Rosalind charming? Both the art and the simplicity of her love are irresistible—especially when reënforced by her capitivating wit.

So you *did* love me a little bit on "that Friday in June" when I made my exit after the picnic?[1] The secret history I long to hear is leaking out by degrees! I loved you very passionately even then, my precious Ellie, though nothing to compare with my present love for you. Do you think that you could have found out your love then between a qu— but I forget my resolve not to ask questions!

I am reminded that answers to two of your recent questions have been crowded out of my last letters. You wanted to know whether the picture I once showed you was a photograph of the author of the "Bachelor."[2] It was. If you remember that little tin-type, you probably remember that it represented a face by no means handsome, but, on the contrary, heavy and unattractive. One cannot see the dear old Scot's *eye* in that picture, else one might guess even from that what a rare soul there is in the man. A stauncher man or a more gifted mind I don't expect to find. My only fear is that he will suffer deterioration under the influence of the *superficial* work of a daily paper. Your other inquiry concerned the fate and whereabouts of Charlie Talcott, my old chum. He is such an inveterately poor correspondent that I can't give a very coherent account of him, though I have done my best to keep within sight of him. This I know, however, that his career has been a very honourable one; that he is beginning to get a foot-hold in the law; and that since his graduation he has become, what he was not before, an active Christian—all of which constitutes a very satisfactory record. There can be no doubt that, if Charlie is but pushed enough by ambition, he will make a mark in the world. There's stuff in him for the making of a very great orator; but he's held back by indolence and lack of self-confidence. He is an exceedingly lovable man—I'm glad you never met him. Thinking of Talcott reminds me of the connection in which I mentioned him, and of my having re-found in Burke, the other day, a passage from which I must often unconsciously have been quoting. Here's the pith of it: "Public duty demands and requires, that what is right should not only be made known, but made prevalent; that what is evil should not only be detected, but defeated." That, it seems to me, is no bad motto.

It delights me to know that my letters give you comfort and relief from sorrow, my darling; and I need not tell you how much I wish that my love could take the place of all love that is lost, even though that love were a mother's. Ellie, *my* Ellie, my *darling*! Oh that I could show you my heart, that you might see how much you are loved, and how that heart is torn by the thought that there is *any* love or sympathy that you *lack*. Even my love, I know, cannot take the place of your sweet departed mother's love; perhaps a man's love can replace no *woman's* sympathy; but I know that there is for you in my heart a tenderness, a longing to shield you from all sorrow, which is *great* enough to be all-sufficient, even though it be not of that womanly *kind* that would make it suffice. I know not what love a mother feels, or what subtile quality a woman's sympathy possesses, but this I do know, that my Ellie will never open her heart to me in vain, and that I *would* be all in all to her!

God has indeed been merciful to us, in giving us each the other's perfect love. Indeed God has never had anything but blessings for *me*. It makes me almost tremble to think of the uniform good fortune that has followed me all through life. I feel often, with a sort of superstition, that I am carrying a great weight of obligation; and I have the heathen's instinctive desire to do for Providence some signal service in token of gratitude, if not by way of payment of the debt. Love has brightened all my life, *your* love crowning the wonderful dispensation. As if to fortify and prepare me against the coming of sorrows I have never tasted, the loss of dear relations, which cannot long be delayed, I have, it would seem, been given your love to be my stay and solace. I do'nt know why I should think of these things. Possibly it is because my dear mother fails to regain her strength. A postal from Josie to-day informs me that she has had malarial fever; and ever since her too-early return home she has been so far from well that she has done what she never did before, failed to write to *me*. For the past two months Josie and father have written in her stead. This explains, my love, why she has not written to *you*. She constantly sends her love to you, as they all do, but she has wanted to *write* to you, and will do so as soon as she is able. I still hope that she will finally recover her wonted strength, the regaining of strength being always painfully slow after typhoid fever. Did I not have such hope, I should be miserable indeed: for what other man was ever blessed with such a mother!

You will doubtless be gratified to know that Adam Smith and his "Wealth of Nations" are done for as far as I am concerned. The great "lecture" is completed.[3] I have'nt read it yet before the class, and there's no immediate prospect, after all the hurry, that I shall be called upon to do so; but the *mss.* are carefully stowed away, and I am over head and ears in other work. A man can't call his mind his own in this institution, and my only hope now is that I shall get on to Christmas without suffering academical shipwreck.

If you are, after all, to get off for Sav. this week, this letter may be too late to catch you, for it has already been delayed beyond the early evening mail that would take it to Rome by Thursday and must run the chance of finding you there on Friday. Give my love to your dear father and to Eddie, and keep for yourself as much as you think will last you till you hear again from

Your own   Woodrow.

ALS (WC, NjP).
  [1] The picnic on Friday, June 29, 1883.
  [2] Robert Bridges.
  [3] Fragment printed at Nov. 20, 1883, below.

EDITORIAL NOTE

WILSON'S LECTURE ON ADAM SMITH

Wilson began work in the autumn of 1883 on what was to become his first academic lecture. "A week ago," he wrote Ellen Axson on November 4, 1883, "one of my professors [Richard T. Ely] appointed me . . . to prepare, within three weeks, a 'lecture' of an hour's length on Adam Smith." He went on to note that his task was all the more difficult "since the professor himself has in his own lectures touched upon all the leading points of Adam Smith's life and opinions, since the preparation of my 'lecture' involves the reading not only of Adam Smith's works but also all of the principal things that have been written about him, and since within these three weeks I have to prepare for an examination on a work of this same professor's, I feel as if at present I had about as much as I could do, even more than sensitive eyes can accomplish without irritation."

In approximately three weeks, despite the pressures of other course work and distracting thoughts about "a girl in Georgia," Wilson was able to write his fiancée, on November 20, 1883: "You will doubtless be gratified to know that Adam Smith and his 'Wealth of Nations' are done for as far as I am concerned. The great 'lecture' is completed. I have'nt read it yet before the class, and there's no immediate prospect, after all the hurry, that I shall be called upon to do so; but the *mss.* are carefully stowed away, and I am over head and ears in other work."

Eventually he did deliver the lecture, probably during the early part of January 1884.[1] But since the manuscript of this lecture is not extant, Wilson's shorthand research notes for it assume unusual importance. Fortunately, these contain specific citations of sources that afford clues to the content of Wilson's lecture and the amount of research on which it was based. However, to speculate intelligently regarding the nature of the lecture, one also has to consider the relation of the research notes to two other items composed by Wilson: a fragmentary shorthand draft of one page with the heading "Adam Smith," and the essay, "An Old Master," published for the first time in 1888.[2] Of less importance but helpful in estimating the scope of Wilson's research for his lecture are three bibliographies on Adam Smith: the first, a brief list (in Wilson's longhand and shorthand) evidently written in Ely's undergraduate course on October 29, 1883;[3] the second, a working list (in longhand except for brief additions in shorthand) at the very beginning of the research notes; the third (in Wilson's longhand), on the verso of the page containing the "Adam Smith" shorthand draft. In these three items there is a duplication of some titles.

Wilson's research notes are on eight loose sheets of lined paper in the notebook[4] containing notes for *Congressional Government.* Apparently, these loose sheets were at one time torn and cut from this notebook; for not only are they of the same size and kind of paper as the remaining sheets, but one sheet (torn in a very irregular fashion) matches exactly one of the stubs at the back of the notebook. The notes themselves are written almost entirely in shorthand on both rectos and versos, making a total of sixteen pages. Wilson filled the recto pages almost completely but used the verso pages—some of which have only one or two notes—sometimes for brief notations and at other times, apparently, to preserve some of the ideas that occurred to him during the course of his research.

[1] Early in December 1883, WW wrote ELA that he did not expect to deliver his Adam Smith lecture for some weeks. But he wrote to her on January 16, 1884, that he had "inaugurated" the series of student lectures in Ely's class "by the reading of that remarkable essay upon Adam Smith."
[2] *Princeton Review,* VI (Sept. 1888), 210-20.
[3] This bibliography immediately precedes WW's shorthand classroom notes of Ely's first lecture on Adam Smith (Oct. 29, 1883), delivered in the undergraduate course in political economy.
[4] Described at Nov. 1, 1883.

*A page from Wilson's shorthand research notes
for his lecture on Adam Smith.*

There can be little doubt that these were the notes that Wilson took in preparation for his lecture on Adam Smith. In the bibliography preceding these notes, he wrote: "Works [of Adam Smith] 1305" and "1365 (P) Bagehot's 'Economic Studies.' " These were the call numbers of items then in the Peabody Institute Library of Baltimore, where Wilson customarily did his research during his graduate school years.[5]

In identifying the sources that Wilson actually used for his lecture, we seem justified in eliminating entirely from consideration two titles which appear only in the first bibliography: Emanuel Leser, *Der Begriff des Reichthums bei Adam Smith* (Heidelberg, 1874), and August Oncken, *Adam Smith und Immanuel Kant* (Leipzig, 1877). It is not likely that his knowledge of German was adequate to use these works; furthermore, there is no evidence in his research notes that he did so. Also, it is highly improbable that he read anything on Adam Smith written by Jérôme Adolphe Blanqui, who is represented only by his surname in the first bibliography and not at all in the research notes.

Next, there are the sources occurring at least once in the three bibliographies which Wilson possibly read but which are not represented in the research notes. These are as follows:[6]

Anonymous, "Adam Smith and Highland Laird," *Blackwood's Magazine*, III (July 1818), 419-20.

Anonymous, "Ricardo Made Easy; or What is the Radical Difference between Ricardo and Adam Smith?" *Blackwood's Magazine*, LII (Sept., Oct., Dec., 1842), 338-53, 457-69, 718-39.

Walter Bagehot, "The Postulates of Political Economy," *Economic Studies* (London, 1880).

Eric S. Robertson, "The Author of 'The Wealth of Nations,' " Dublin *University Magazine*, II (Oct. 1878), 452-68.

Thomas E. C. Leslie, *Essays in Political and Moral Philosophy* (Dublin and London, 1879), containing "The Political Economy of Adam Smith," pp. 148-66.

Preface to James E. T. Rogers, ed., *An Inquiry into the Nature of the Wealth of Nations* (2 vols., Oxford, 1880), I, v-xxxix.

Although Wilson's research on Adam Smith was fairly extensive if it included the foregoing list, his research notes indicate that he used a relatively small number of books and articles; for the only items represented in them by quotations and summaries are as follows:

Walter Bagehot, "Adam Smith as a Person," *Fortnightly Review*, XXVI (July 1876), 18-42; "Adam Smith and Our Modern Economy," *Economic Studies* (London, 1880), pp. 95-134.

Henry Thomas Buckle, *History of Civilization in England* (3 vols., London, 1878).

Adam Smith, *The Nature and Causes of the Wealth of Nations* (Book I and Book II, chapters 1-2), in *The Works of Adam Smith* (5 vols., London, 1812), II. There are no quotations from or summaries of Book

[5] *The Catalogue of the Library of the Peabody Institute* (5 vols., Baltimore, 1883-92) shows that 1305 was the call number of *Works of Adam Smith* (5 vols., London, 1812) and 1365, of Walter Bagehot, *Economic Studies* (London, 1880). WW used both these works for his research on Adam Smith.

[6] When WW did not give all information usually included in formal bibliographies, the editors have attempted to supply it. WW's citations in his research notes have furnished most of the clues to the editions he used.

ii, chapters 3-5, and Books iii-v (Volumes iii and iv of this edition) in Wilson's research notes.

Dugald Stewart, "Account of the Life and Writings of Adam Smith," Sir William Hamilton, ed., *The Collected Works of Dugald Stewart* (10 vols., Edinburgh, 1858), x, 5-98.

Travers Twiss, *View of the Progress of Political Economy in Europe since the Sixteenth Century* (London, 1847).

A close examination of this list and the research notes reveals that Wilson needed to do no more research to produce his essay, "An Old Master," in which he limited himself almost entirely to discussing Adam Smith as a man—his intellectual interests, gifts as a lecturer and conversationalist, and style as a writer. In fact, every quotation that appears in the essay can also be found in the research notes. But this, of course, does not mean that the text of the lecture is identical to that of the essay. Quite the contrary, Wilson, as the transcript of his lecture, printed following this note, shows, felt himself obligated, in speaking to Ely's class, to concentrate on Adam Smith as a political economist.

The research notes also contain a considerable number of quotations and summaries pertaining to Adam Smith's political and economic views. Extracts from *The Wealth of Nations* dealt with employment, wages, profits, components of prices, regulation of usury, and retaliation in trade. Moreover, those segments of the research notes that appear to be his first thoughts give additional evidence of what he intended to develop in his lecture. One comment in his research notes seems to foreshadow what he was to say later in the campaign of 1912 about the regulation of competition:

"It seems to me that those who favor government control of monopolies do so in the interest of the principles of Adam Smith, for monopolies are those employments in which freedom of competition is impossible and therefore the legitimate object of governmental control would be to so integrate enterprise and capital into those islands of competition which keep prices at a proper level of justice."

Another comment is of a more general nature:

"Though Adam Smith writes in the spirit of the philosopher he writes also in the spirit of the philosophic historian—and it is in the historical spirit. He is not insensible even of physical conditions and regards the limiting conditions of geographical formation—before the introduction of the more perfect methods of land transportation. He has theories for almost everything, but these theories never stand in the way of the doctrines of practical sense. Smith got the flavor and spirit of his work in actual life—he speaks of practical matters and lives in the real world. He seems to have had a very deep regard for statistics—a regard which must be a whit ancient as well as of the modern school of economists—and he so discussed practical measures—for instance in regard to regulation of the relative value of gold and silver. His illustrations always contain real life, from practical affairs. His work abounds in comparative studies of the economic conditions of peoples and nations."

The manuscript of the fragmentary shorthand draft with the heading "Adam Smith" itself gives final proof that it was a draft of the lecture and not of "An Old Master." The draft is written on rough tablet paper, a kind that Wilson seems to have used only while at The Hopkins. In fact, the editors have found only two other shorthand items written by Wilson on this kind of paper, and both of them unquestionably belong to the period when he was a graduate student.[7]

A comparison of the transcript of the fragment of the lecture with "An Old Master" will show clearly that Wilson used the lecture as the point of departure for his essay. Indeed, he used many paragraphs with only minor revision.

[7] These two items, notes on American colonial history, are dated "May 8, 1884," and "May 15, 1884," in WWhw.

Fragmentary Draft of a Lecture

[c. Nov. 20, 1883]

Adam Smith

Scotchmen have long been reputedly strong in philosophic doctrine, and Adam Smith was a Scot of the Scots. But though Scotland is now renowned for her clear philosophy, that renown is not of immemorial origin. It was not until the last century had well advanced that she began to add great speculative thinkers to her great preachers. Adam Smith, consequently, stands nearly at the opening of the greatest of intellectual eras of Scotland; and yet by none of the great Scotch names which men have learned since his day has his name been eclipsed.

It is natural to wish to know much of a man who made such a notable figure in the intellectual world, and yet of Adam Smith *as a man* we know very little; and it may, without injustice, be deplored that we owe that little to Dugald Stewart, the worst, because the most self-conscious, of biographers, whose stilted periods run a page without advancing the sense a step, and whose style both of thought and of expression is excellent to be avoided. Even from Dugald Stewart, however, we get a most pleasing picture of Adam Smith. He was not, perhaps, a *companionable* man: he was much too absent-minded to be companionable; but his was that absent-mindedness which is but an indication of *affluence* of mind—a mind stored with wonderful riches of learning and observation, and often, in familiar company, lavishing its richness upon delighted hearers—a mind of rare versatility of power, making its finest displays upon topics introduced by others, rather than upon those invented by itself.

Those who met Adam Smith in intimate intercourse are said to have been struck chiefly by the gentility and benignity of his manner—traits which would naturally strike one in a Scotchman, for men of that unbending race are not often distinguished by easiness of temper or suavity of manner, being generally both *fortiter in re et fortiter in modo.* His gentility was, probably, only one phase of that timidity which is natural in absent-minded men. When he talked his hearers marveled at the ingenuity of his reasoning, at the constructive power of his imagination, at the fertility of his resources, at the comprehensiveness of his memory; but he did not often talk; his inclination was always towards silence.

He was not, however, disinclined to public discourse, and his lectures were full not of thought only, but also of beauty. "Commonly, indeed," says Mr. Bagehot, "the silent man, whose brain is loaded with unexpressed ideas, is more likely to be a successful public speaker than the brilliant talker who daily exhausts himself in sharp sayings." Adam Smith seems to have owed his advancement in the literary world, or rather in the university world, to his gifts as a lecturer. Under the advice of Lord Kames, an eminent Scotch barrister and a man of some standing in the history of philosophy, he volunteered a course of public lectures in Edinburgh almost immediately upon his return from Oxford, and the success of this course had hardly been established before he was elected to the chair of Logic in the great University of Glasgow; and in the following year he had the honor of succeeding to the chair of Moral Philosophy, once occupied by the learned and ingenious Hutcheson. "Moral Philosophy" seems to have been the most inclusive of general terms in the university usage of Scotland at that time, and indeed for many years afterwards. It seems to have been taken as embracing all philosophy that did not immediately concern phenomena of the physical world, and accordingly, allowed its doctors very free play in their choice of subjects. Adam Smith, in Glasgow, could bring within its big family not only the science of mental phenomena and of moral precepts, but also the whole philosophical organization and history of society; just as, long afterwards, in Edinburgh, John Wilson could insist upon the adoption of something very like belles-lettres into the same generous and unconventional family circle.

Adam Smith seems to have been immediately successful in raising his new chair to a position of very high consideration in the estimation of the university world. His immediate predecessor had been one Thomas Craigie who has left behind him so slight a reputation that it is, doubtless, safe to conclude that his department was, at his death, much in need of a new infusion of life. This it received from Adam Smith. The new professor entered upon a fourfold course of lectures. First he unfolded the principles of natural theology; (2) he illustrated the principles of ethics in his series of lectures which were afterwards embodied in his published work on "The Theory of Moral Sentiments"; (3) he discoursed upon that branch of morality which relates to justice; and lastly, coming out upon that field in which we are now most interested, he examined those political regulations which are founded, not upon the principle of justice, but upon that of *expediency*, and which are calculated to increase riches, the power, and the prosperity of the state. Such was his felicity of exposition, such the attraction of his treatment, of these subjects that, as we are told by one who had sat under his teaching, "a multitude of students from a great distance" were drawn to Glasgow by the fame of his eloquence. The success of his lectures was not altogether a triumph of natural gifts, however; it was in great part a triumph of art. Adam Smith had the true instinct of an orator and teacher. He saw what everyone must see who speaks not for the patient ear of the closeted student only, but also to the great ear of the world, which must be pleased in order to be instructed, that clearness, beauty and strength of style are necessary to one who would draw men to his way of thinking, nay, to one who would induce the great mass of men to give any heed to what he is saying. He bestowed the most careful thought not only upon what he said but also upon the *way* in which he said it. Dugald Stewart speaks of the "ornaments of that flowing and apparently artless style, which he had studiously cultivated, but which, after all his experience in composition, he adjusted, with extreme difficulty, to his own taste." He had none of the outward graces of the orator; his utterance was rugged and his action angular and awkward. The charm of his discourses must have lain in the power of statement which gave them life, in the clear processes of proof which gave speed to thought, and in the vigorous imagination which lent illumination to the argument. There were no clouds about his thoughts, they could be

Transcript of WWsh draft of lecture (WP, DLC). Assigned for delivery in Professor Richard T. Ely's undergraduate course in political economy.

From Ellen Louise Axson

My dearest Woodrow,   Rome [Ga.,] Nov. 20 1883

Many thanks for the photograph of yourself, just received. It has no post-mark on it, but I presume it came direct from Atlanta, did it not? Speaking of pictures, I don't approve of your taste in that respect—I am sure that the small one of myself is much better than the "moon-faced" one as Papa calls it. Aside from the flattery in the latter, to which I perceive it is useless to call your attention, you must admit that I never presented the imposing appearance which it would indicate, nor was my face ever so large and round. In fact it is of the heroic size altogether. I said that *I* liked it because the eyes were so much too large, and I always had a weakness for "big eyes"; someone asked if I had a weakness for big mouths too, for it was just as much out of proportion.

I am in the very depth of packing at present. We have decided quite suddenly at the last to go to Sav.; will leave on Thursday; so of course I am desperately busy. Only write now to say that I can't write; two or three people are wanting me at this moment. There were visitors last night until late, which prevented my stealing the time then. Will try and write a long letter as soon as I reach Sav.; when I *will* be good and answer some of your questions to the best of my ability. But to most of them there can be no reply because I don't *know myself*.

Father is about the same as when I last wrote. I hope he will be better when this storm subsides, and we are safely in Sav.;— though he is absent in the body—I have sent him off to Uncle Rob's[1]—I fear he is present in the spirit, and that isn't so easily helped.

But I must close; excuse haste. Did you know that I am "the sister of Mark Tapley"! "Anna Harris" has just informed me that she is sure I am.

Yours with all my heart,   Ellie

You should see the costume in which I am writing—dusting cap and "high-necked" apron[.] I assure you it is "quite killing."

ALS (WP, DLC).
[1] R. T. Hoyt, druggist for his brother, W. D. Hoyt, of Rome, Ga.

To Ellen Louise Axson

My sweet Ellie,   Balto., Md., Nov. 22nd 1883

So you are actually off for Savannah to-day, and my last letter will have to follow you thither. I am glad to think that your packing is all over by this time. May God prosper you in your journey, my darling, and enable your dear father to find in change of scene speedy relief from his distressing disease! I am, as I said once before that I should be, unreasonable enough to be discontented at the move, because I've never been to Savannah and cannot imagine your surroundings there. I was familiar with the little house in Rome and could picture to myself your occupations there; but even my imagination can't conjure up distinct visions of Savannah.

I should have liked nothing better than to see you in that "killing" costume of dusting cap and high-necked apron, tho' I don't know that my desire to see you depends in any way on your costume. As for the question of the photographs, I do'nt know that the larger one *is* more like you than the one by Motes—at least than the *face* of the one by M.—but the *position* in the latter is such as to give an altogether incorrect idea of the shape of the head, besides making you look limp and round-shouldered. It is extremely inartistic, giving a fair enough idea of your features, but awkward in all its outlines. The other photo. is both a good likeness and a pretty picture.

Yes, my photo. was sent you direct from Motes. He was long in sending it: I was beginning to fear that my order had miscarried. You have never said whether you thought it a good likeness or not. I rather hope you do not. It gives me a sunken chest, dough features, and a blank expression which are by no means flattering —but which, "for a' that," may, I confess, be quite like nature. Now that Jessie is beyond the reach of your wrath, I may tell you something on her. Soon after the exit of "that Friday in June," she wrote me a letter in which this passage occurs: "Ellie Lou called on me not long after you left, and I could not refrain from a little guarded teasing, which she took with the prettiest of pretty vivid blushes. She asked while here to see my photograph albums, and evidently with one purpose, as she has looked through them before, if I mistake not. She thought your likeness splendid, and I noticed, although she did not see that I was watching her, that she turned back to the front part of the album a number of times before she got to the end." It is interesting to compare this with a passage in a letter of another correspondent, written about the same time: "I stopped there the other day (to return the pamphlet, which I persistently forgot to give you) . . . .[1] By the way, Jessie professed to be much concerned for your safety, and disturbed at not having heard from you. Perhaps I should have relieved her anxiety, and, especially, have given her the news from your mother, but—I did'nt. Very stupid, no doubt. But it is the way of the world to put very astonishing constructions on the simplest facts, and I feared they might not be any wiser in their generation than 'tout le monde.' " You are at full liberty to declare the first passage a libel; I do'nt care *now* whether Mrs. B's conclusions were just or not; I know only that they gave me immense comfort at the time, and that a recent letter contains the confession that you loved me even then "better than you knew."

I believe you are, as the *incognito* Miss Anna Harris says, related to the Taply family. What a jolly little wife you will make for a sour, tiresome, moody professor! But I mus'nt get on *that* subject—of what a delightful little lady you will be as my all-day companion and ruler—because I must bring this letter to a close before the hour of Mr. Bryce's[2] lecture. Mr. Bryce, as you may know, is a distinguished Oxford professor, a prominent M. P., and author of a work on the "Holy Roman Empire" which has given him standing amongst the greatest of living English historians. He is a great traveller, and we have caught him on his way back from the Sandwich Islands, in order to get from him a few lectures on Roman legal history, of which, as professor of the Civil Law, he is supposed to know a great deal. We have had one lecture from him, the second comes this afternoon, and we are to have three besides. If you should like to know the impression made upon your humble servant by this British celebrity, you may learn in another letter.

Give my love to your dear father and to Eddie, my kindest regards to your grandparents,[3] and, if you think you would like a little love for yourself, estimate the amount you want and draw on me for double the sum.

Your own   Woodrow

ALS (WC, NjP).
    [1] WW's elision.
    [2] James Bryce lectured on Roman law at The Johns Hopkins on Nov. 20, 22, 23, 24, and 27, 1883.
    [3] The Rev. and Mrs. Isaac Stockton Keith Axson. I. S. K. Axson was born at Charleston, S. C., Oct. 3, 1813. Married Rebecca Randolph. Was graduated from The College of Charleston, and from Columbia Theological Seminary in 1834. Ordained by the Charleston Presbytery, Oct. 1835. Pastor, Dorchester, S. C., Presbyterian Church, 1835-36; co-pastor, Midway Presbyterian Church, Liberty County, Ga., 1836-54. President, Synodical Female College (later the Rome Female College), Greensboro and Rome, Ga., 1853-57. Pastor, Independent Presbyterian Church, Savannah, Ga., 1857-91. Died March 31, 1891.

From Janet Woodrow Wilson

My precious Son,   Wilmington, N. C. Friday Nov. [23, 1883]

I cannot tell you how I have I have [*sic*] regretted my inability to write you for so long a time. I did not seem to improve in strength after you left me at Arden Park. Your companionship was everything to me, my darling. Annie is very sweet, very lovely —but you know how sensitive she is—and I had to be so careful in our intercourse, that it was not the *rest* it might have been. And dear Josie's fondness for company, made him more of an anxiety than comfort. However, the time passed as pleasantly as could have been expected. Mrs. Ripley's is a *very* comfortable house, but I doubt if you would have liked it as well as you liked Arden Park. I was very glad to get away after our stay of two weeks. After your father confessed that he was far from well, I could not rest till I got his permission to return home. So, as everybody here assured him that there could be no danger, he consented to our coming on the 13th of Oct. I am so glad that I came—for I found him very unwell—needing all the attention and comfort I could give him. He is greatly improved since our return—though still not quite well. I am going to get a bottle of the medicine you recommend, and will see that he takes [it] for I think it is just what he needs.

Not very long after my return home—two weeks ago, last Sabbath night, I think—I had a long and painful chill, and very high fever during several days and nights following. I seemed to lose all the strength I had gained during the summer. I wrote to George about it, & he pronounced it malarial fever, and prescribed for me. The amount of quinine I have taken is astonishing. As soon as I was at all able to be about, I began to prepare the house for Synod. We expected to entertain Dr. Leighton Wilson & Dr. Craig.[1] As it turned out, Dr Leighton did not come, and Dr. C. was with us only one day. We had a number of guests to dinner & tea each day, however—and, I tell you dear, I don't think I ever spent such miserable days in my life. As to my bodily feelings, I had *two chills* during the Synod, which fact I had to conceal from your father till after it was all over, for we *had* to have company, you know, or we would have been greatly misunderstood. I had two green house-servants—(the second one being recommended to me as a perfect treasure for such an occasion)—so that I had an anxious painful time. But I worked hard, in spite of my condition, and got up nice dinners & suppers—and then, as soon as they, the guests, were out of the house, I went to bed. I think I must really be very strong, or I could not endure that sort of thing. I am not feeling well yet, but have had no more chills. I have written all this about myself, dear, that you may see that it has been impossible for me to write even to you—and also to explain why I have not written to dear Ellie. I will write to her after I finish this. I have written the dear girl many a letter in imagination, when lying in bed—too sick to put my thoughts upon paper. It has been such a comfort to me to know that my darling far-away boy has had *her* sweet letters to comfort him, in the absence of those which should have gone to him from home.

Most lovingly Your own Mother

Papa & Josie send love inexpressible

ALS (WP, DLC).

[1] The Rev. Dr. John Newton Craig, recently elected as secretary of the Home Mission Committee of the southern Presbyterian Church.

Two Letters to Ellen Louise Axson

My own darling,   Balto., Md., Nov. 25th/83

The jolly Chinaman who does my washing for me is a talkative little fellow and whenever he finds me in my room insists upon having a chat with me. His first question yesterday afternoon concerned your photograph; he wanted to know if that was my *wife*; and when I replied with a simple negative, he told me that I *ought* to get a pretty wife like that! I did not tell him that there was a violent probability that I should, because I have a very decided aversion from making such matters common subjects of conversation with inferiors, or, for the matter of that, with *anybody*; but it struck me as odd that the fellow should see the significance of my having the picture in so prominent a place in my room, and I was set a-thinking again of the time to which I now so often look forward with a passionate longing and upon which I never dwell, as you know, with so free a fancy as on these quiet Sabbath afternoons, when I can almost fancy that I can feel your presence. Ah, my darling, does it make you happy to think that you will some day make me the happiest man in the world? When you are my wife, I am sure that I can do anything!

I am very impatient to learn how you fared in the moving. It would be contrary to all precedent if you were to make a journey of any length without unusual delay, so I suppose you missed connection somewhere. Or did your last delay, by bringing unspeakable joy out of what seemed a misadventure, discourage the evil genius who has hitherto presided over your travels[?] I wonder that that genius has not long ago given over his sinister schemes, because you seem *always* to have extracted more fun than annoyance out of missed connections; but his last scheme was his crowning defeat. I was about to suggest that the Asheville delay was planned by your *good* genius; but it would argue considerable cheek on my part for me to say that it was your good fortune that gave you to me. More probably the thing fell out so by the contrivance of *my* kind fairy.

But these recondite speculations are by the way. I was about to say that I shall be very miserable until I hear of your safe arrival in Savannah, and that you did not overwork yourself in packing. I hope that you were saved the trouble of dismissing "the other two" *with cause*; though it is scarcely kind to them to hope that they were left even to desperate hope.

I rec'd a letter from dear mother yesterday giving me the particulars of her sickness, which came in the midst of the session of Synod in Wilmington, and concluding thus: "I have written all this about myself, dear, that you may see that it has been impossible for me to write even to you—and also to explain why I have not written to dear Ellie. I will write to her after I finish this. I have written the dear girl many a letter in imagination, when lying in bed, too sick to put my thoughts upon paper. It has been such a comfort to me to know that my darling far-away boy has had *her* sweet letters to comfort him—in the absence of those which should have gone to him from home." Do you like to have me send you these extracts, my darling? I send you this one to show you what a sweet mother I have. She will be your mother too some day; and, if anybody can take the place of the dear mother who is gone, she can and will. She loves me most unreasonably, but she can love you with reason, and you can make up what I lack.

I sincerely hope that your father is already benefitted by the change. Give my love to him and to Eddie, and my kindest regards to your grandparents. You know how much I love you; if you don't, I can't tell you.

Your own,   Woodrow

ALS (WP, DLC).

My precious Ellie,   Balto., Md., Nov. 27th/83

This is my day for writing to you, though I have of late gotten to using so many days for that purpose that Tuesday may be said almost to have lost its exclusive privileges as a day set apart. If I were to go on very long multiplying letters at the present rate, you would soon have to begin destroying them for lack of storage room in which to keep them—would'nt you? I have made several beginnings towards writing to you to day, this being the third attempt. To tell the truth, I am not feeling at all well to-day. I have done what I thought I had gotten out of the habit of doing—I have *caught cold*, and feel, in consequence, as if my system were full of some pestilential humour, by which I am rendered very dull and "thick-headed"—*unusually* so, I mean—and very unfit for intelligent composition. My first two attempts at writing were made in "the Bluntschli Library of historical and political science," our department's new quarters at the University[.] The late Dr. J. C. Bluntschli—allow me to explain—was professor of international law in the University of Heidelburg, where he had the honour of instructing the present head of our department, Dr. H. C. [B.] Adams. Upon his death, a couple of years ago, the German citizens of Baltimore purchased his valuable private library and presented it to the Johns Hopkins. At that time there was really no place to put it, the shelves of the University library being already full; but since then additional buildings have been erected and about a month ago the Bluntschli collection was placed in a large cheerful room of its own, in which "the Seminary" now meets, and which has already come to be regarded as headquarters for our department. It is such a pleasant room that one is tempted to do much of his studying in it, even in preference to the Peabody; for each student who is in regular standing in the department has set apart for his private use a drawer in the great table around which the Seminary meets, in which he can keep his note-books and writing materials; and of course almost every book he may have occasion to consult is there at hand, for all the standard English and American authorities have been added to Dr. Bluntschli's unreadable German books, and the materials are abundant on all historical and political subjects. One of my recent letters to you was written in an alcove of that library; but to-day I was too nervous to write there: every movement of the other fellows distracted my attention and I had to give up the attempt in disgust.

I am so seldom unwell that it fills me with impatience to be deprived of the full use and command of myself by sickness—which may be proof that the discipline is needed; but it is a great comfort to me, my darling, to write to you even when I am out of sorts. Your love is none the less sweet to me because my bodily organs are "at sixes and sevens." You have taught me to love so fast that I already find it very hard to remember how I used to get along before I knew you. I am quite sure that I could'nt live *now* without your love, and I wonder how I ever did.

Professor Bryce gave his concluding lecture this afternoon. I have enjoyed the course exceedingly. There are a strength and dash and mastery about the man which are captivating. He knows both what to say and how to say it. A taste of the instruction of such a man makes me all the more conscious of the insipidity of the lectures I hear daily in the classroom. One could not desire a better place for work than this; but for such work as mine, I can reasonably wish for more intelligent guidance than I get here. I have been much disappointed to find that the department of history and politics is more weakly manned as regards its corps of instructors than any other department of the University. Of our three Ph.D.'s, one is insincere and superficial, the second a man stuffed full of information but apparently much too full to have any movement which is not an impulse from somebody else, and the third merely a satellite of the first.[1] I liked all three at first, and I don't dislike them now; but I expect very little aid or stimulation from them; and it makes one uneasy to discover, as I did in studying Adam Smith, that his instructor is inexact and prone to take his materials not from the original and authentic sources but at second hand. My work on Adam Smith was of necessity hasty and imperfect—if you could at your distance, I should like you to read my "lecture" just as a specimen of the sort of writing one is apt to do under high pressure—but even in that hurried excursion I found my honoured professor out in several very palpable errors; and the discovery was by no means reassuring. One of the wags of our class suggested that the lectures to which we are daily invited were intended for our recreation, as agreeable interruptions to our severer studies. The same odd character declared that our fate in having new topics of study constantly thrust upon us reminded him of the unhappy spirits in Dante's Inferno who rose to the surface of the burning lake only to be thrust under again by the forked weapons of the guarding demons. We get lots of fun out of the shams of our academical "betters," but, after all, it's no laughing matter, and I should be much discouraged if it were not for the compensation of splendid library facilities and of the opportunity of learning a great deal from my fellow-students. There are a great many very choice spirits gathered together here from all parts of the country, and life with young men full of ambition and courage and equipped with a fine capacity for efficient work is very stimulating.[2]

Besides, I am working for big stakes: I am working for *you*, my darling; and the better my work the sooner you shall be won! I often wonder whether any of these other fellows here are animated in their studies by as sweet a hope as mine. I am quite sure that none of them can have *such* a prize in view; but some of them may *think* that they have.

Good-night, my love; I must go mail this letter and get to bed, to sleep off, if possible, these miserable aches. Give my love to your dear father and to Eddie, and my kindest regards to Dr. and Mrs.

Axson. To yourself you know what I would send, if there were any words that could carry it:—the unspeakable love of

Your own   Woodrow

ALS (WC, NjP).
1 WW was referring to Adams, Ely, and Jameson, probably in that order.
2 See the note at Sept. 29, 1883, for a list of these fellow-students. For a delightful memoir of WW at the Johns Hopkins, see Inazo Nitobe [known in 1884 as Inazo Ota or Ohta], "Gakusei-Jidai no Uiruson [Woodrow Wilson as a Student]," *Chūō Kōron* [*Central Review*], XXXII (March 3, 1917), 86-87. Ota was in the Seminary with WW in 1884-85. Courtesy of Kimitada Miwa.

Two Letters from Ellen Louise Axson

My dearest Woodrow,   Rome [Ga.,] Nov. 27/83.

Don't you think I am a fraud and a delusion as concerns letter-writing, leaving Rome, and various other things? We are still here —were obliged to stay over to see about renting the house—but we are *positively* (?) going this afternoon. So I must again send only a "note"; I have been trying to write for some days, but it was'nt ordained. Not that I have been so busy; in those brief moments when there are no visitors, I have been chiefly occupied in wandering about, like an unquiet spirit, seeking work and finding none. But, ah me! such gathering of the clans as this old house has witnessed—such mourning and lamenting! If Anna [Harris] had not been here, through the ordeal, to make everything ridiculous, and force me to laugh in *spite* of everything with graphic pictures of me in the act of supporting buxom mourners, who insist upon weeping in my arms, I think I should have been "all broke up" in more senses than one. Papa has certainly created a sensation for once. I had no idea they would feel his leaving so much. He has been half wild with it all. As for me, I suppose I scarcely realize it yet, it is something so unprecedented in my experience to be all pulled up by the roots.

There is another caller so I will hastily close[.] Your letter was safely received on Thursday. I was *so* sorry to hear that your dear mother continued so unwell. I hoped and supposed that she had entirely recovered her strength. Excuse haste

Yours with all my heart,   Ellie.

My dearest Woodrow,   Savannah Nov. 28/83.

At last I do actually find myself "in the house where I was born,"[1] at "the little window where the sun comes peeping in at morn" (how sentimental!) We reached Sav. this morning after a pleasant—no, not *pleasant*, for I was, of course, in the depthes at leaving home and friends—but *prosperous* journey. Papa took the journey much better than I expected; dear Mr. Bones went with him as far as Atlanta, where we make the last change, so he had no trouble on that score; then, under the new management the journey is a whole day shorter than formerly—an immense relief to him. And we actually came through without adventures of any sort, we made all the connections, and lost neither ourselves nor our trunks! My evil genius *is* doubtless discouraged and disgusted by that last "crowning defeat."

I found your two letters awaiting me, and was as glad to see them as to see the rest of my friends. I must try to assist your imagination with a picture of our street, South Broad, and our neighbour the church. As the former enjoys the distinction of being one of the two prettiest streets in the town, "views" of it do greatly abound. Two of my windows look out on the street with the broad "green" down the center and its four lines of live oaks. The others give a view of the garden[,] the church yard and the old mossy wall that divides them, which, with the leafy tracery, and tangled sunbeams on the soft grey stone of the church, is a pleasant enough sight in its way. But ones external "surroundings" are of little consequence as compared with the people who share them with us. I should like to introduce you to the inmates of the old parsonage.[2] Besides the grandparents, there is Uncle Randolph and dear Aunt Ella, gentlest and lovliest of women, with her wonderful violet eyes that haunt my very dreams sometimes. I should like to paint a madonna with those eyes. Then there is a dainty little cousin of sixteen, whose womanly ways form a pretty contrast with her fairy-like proportions; she has flaxen hair and a complexion which shows all the faint, delicate, transparent tones of the most softly tinted shell. After her there are two rolicking boys, and then the two little girls, Ellen and Carrie Belle, who, with their big violet eyes and long lashes, their beautiful mouths, and the lovely baby curves of their faces, are almost as pretty and altogether as sweet as your little niece. They are my most *intimate* friends! Whenever I am here they follow me about all day like little spaniels, and are at once my tyrants and my slaves. As for my occupations, they are the same as in Rome, except that I am, in spite of myself, dragged out and made to "take exercise" a great deal more, and that too though the inducements are by no means so great—no hills nor rivers. I always *did* hate to walk in a *street*!

Nov. 29. I was interrupted yesterday and have had no time since even to close this letter. Perhaps I should have contented myself with a simple "note" then, but I begin to grow tired of that business.

I have just had a visit from Janie Porter and have laughed my-

self into a state of exhaustion over her capers: she has been ex-
ecuting a sort of wild war-dance accompanied with shrieks of
triumph over my "down-fall." She is engaged, herself, you see,
and I suppose wants all her friends to keep her in countenance.
But it is perfectly heartless, the manner in which my friends crow
over me, and fling my former professions and opinions in my face.
I have been, by the way much entertained by their various modes
of receiving the intelligence. Janie, as I said, was uproarious;
Rose,[3] too was ecstatic; she writes that she has been laughing so
constantly since hearing it, that, as she is forbidden to explain the
cause, people doubtless think she is developing rapidly in amiabil-
ity—or imbecility; Beth was, as usual, maternal and advisory,
Agnes, very sympathetic, Min [Hoyt], my little cousin in Rome
rather awe-struck;—by-the-way, I doubt if anyone except myself
outside of your family takes a deeper interest in you than that
same little girl. As for "old Anna," she was shocked, even horrified.
You should have seen her face when I made the announcement;
it expressed positive terror as she exclaimed, almost harshly, "Do
you mean to say that you have actually *committed* yourself, that
you are positively engaged *already*, and have *given yourself away*
without reserve?" I laughed, and asked her if she had ever known
me to do anything, great or small, good, bad or indifferent, in a
half-hearted way? She shrugged her shoulders and thought she
"never had." But, she said, You are perfectly crazy, why don't
you wait 'till you *know* him? you hav'nt much more than a speaking acquaintance. "Why did'nt he wait to know me?" said I, "I
think it would be very small in me to stand back in order to *watch*
him, when he has shown such entire faith in me. Just think what
risks he is willing to run! Did you ever see such splendid courage?
Don't you know the moral effect of all great deeds is to inspire
a generous rivalry!" "Besides" I added, laughing, "it's too late to
talk about finding people out, when you've 'been and gone and
done it,' viz., fallen in love, and can't help yourself. 'I know that
I love him whatever he is.' But seriously, of course I could'nt love
him if he was not 'truly noble, and worthy a woman's trust';
and I *do know that*; if he is'nt, *nobody* is. If I know him as to
essentials all the minor qualities may reveal themselves in their
own good time, since, whatever they are or are not, they are
powerless to change the great fact of love."

Oh dear me! what rigamarole is this into which I have lapsed!
I remember reading, long ago, a receipt for writing a good "love-
letter"—and I hope it was a good receipt, for I always follow it.
It was "to begin without knowing what you meant to say, and

to finish without knowing what you *had* said"! At any rate, I never even *reach* the subjects which I mean to discuss when I begin; that, and not self-will *this time*, is the "reason why" your questions have not all been answered. What a preacher I would make. I would'nt ever remember to "give out" the text, much less stick to it! I remind myself of "Widow Bedott" with the curious way in which one thing suggests another and I go wandering along to arrive at last no where in particular.

It was indeed well for Jessie that you waited until I was at a safe distance to betray her; she would have been annihilated! It *was* a most outrageous libel! I have no words to express my indignation! In the first place, I had never seen her album before except on her wedding day, when it was empty. In the second place I didn't call for it, or even suggest it; she sent for it herself to show me Miss Hattie Woodrow's picture, as she happened to be discussing her. And I wasn't even thinking of you, sir,—so there! That my statements may be more readily believed, I freely admit that I *did* turn back several times to look at your picture, and I *did* do it very slyly and did'nt suppose she saw—one can examine the eyes of a picture more coolly and critically that [*sic*] one can it's owners. I think the picture very good as photographs go, though of course not satisfactory—the defect in the figure is very apparent. By-the-way, your bureau, as a place for keeping pictures, does'nt seem to be much more free than my own from the disadvantage of provoking embarrassing questions. I am reduced to the sad necessity of keeping some of mine, not "on the bed" generally, but all about in spots wherever I happen to be myself.

I am curious to hear your impressions of Mr. Bryce. Did he prove himself a good *speaker* as well as professor, historian, statesman and traveller?

I am glad to believe from your mother's being able to write again, that she is getting well; I do *so* earnestly hope and trust that with the return of cold weather the malaria may be entirely conquered, and she may fully recover her strength. And I *more* than *like* your extracts from her letters; they make me inexpressibly happy—for *many* reasons.

But I know that long ere you reach this point in my letter you will have begun to cry for mercy. Indeed I am as much disgusted as yourself; my fingers are literally cramped with trying to *force* this ink (so-called) to make a mark—and the result is even more erratic than usual.

With best love to your dear mother and the rest and a heart full for yourself I am as ever   Your own   Ellie.

ALS (WP, DLC).

[1] The manse of the Independent Presbyterian Church at 143 S. Broad St., Savannah, Ga.

[2] The "inmates" were the grandparents, the Rev. Dr. and Mrs. I. S. K. Axson; Randolph Axson, Sr., ELA's paternal uncle, commission merchant of Savannah, and his wife, Ella Law Axson, daughter of Judge William Law of Savannah; and their children—Leila, "a dainty little cousin of sixteen," Randolph, Jr., and Benjamin Palmer Axson, the "two rolicking boys," and Ellen and Carrie Belle.

[3] Rosalie Anderson of Sewanee, Tenn., ELA's classmate at the Rome Female College and one of her dearest friends.

To Harold Godwin

My dear Pete,   Balto., Md., Nov. 29th 1883

The coming of your letter[1] did me more good than anything that has happened to me since I became engaged. We are quits on the news, and I must add to my sincere congratulations the best wish I can make: that your engagement may bring you as much happiness as mine has brought me

It did me no end of good, old fellow, to hear from you again. The Cow and I are constantly indulging in delightful reminiscences of the old gang; and it begins to seem as if, by coming a little further North, I had begun to get into the '79 circle again.

> "When we come again together, boys,
> Vigintenial to pass,
> Wives and children all included,
> Wont we be an uproarious class!"

I'm having a pretty satisfactory time here at "the Hopkins," in spite of the many shams which a near view has enabled me to discover in the arrangements of this already renowned institution —or "foundation" as Mr. President Gilman loves to call it. Plenty of hard work and all the facilities for it ought to satisfy the would-be professor, your humble servant.

Hiram sends love and congratulations.

Write again, when to [you] can, to

Your sincere friend,   Woodrow Wilson

Much love to Bobby, as goes without the saying.

ALS (WP, DLC).

[1] Harold Godwin to WW, Nov. 26, 1883, ALS (WP, DLC), with WWhw notation on env.: "Ans. Nov 29/83."

To Ellen Louise Axson

My sweet Ellie,   Balto., Md., Nov. 29th 1883

I had not intended writing to-day, because I am pressed with work preparatory to an examination; but I remember that in my last I spoke of feeling sick, so I must drop you just a line or two to relieve any anxiety you may feel on my account. I *was* full of premonitory aches and pains that night; but a long walk after writing, to the post office, and several grains of quinine, together with a sound sleep, set me all right again; and now my usual health has returned with the return of bright weather.

With love unbounded,

In haste,   Your own Woodrow

ALS (WC, NjP).

From Robert Bridges

Dear Tommy: [New York] Nov 30th 83

Pete asked me for your address a few days ago and informed me that he was going to announce a very important occurrence. It brought very forcibly to my mind the fact that I had utterly neglected to take any notice whatever of an equally important announcement from you. I believe that I would "cut a fellow dead" forever after if he neglected to congratulate me on similar happiness—but I put great faith in your superiority to me in that respect —and so risk writing now. I know if your state of mind in any way resembles the seraphic Pete's, you are utterly oblivious to all the ordinary annoyances of life. . . .

I have no doubt that you are revelling in the freedom of study by this time. I envy you the privilege and its opportunities.

And a possibly useful hint suggests itself to me. You may have noticed that Princeton is strengthening its department of History & Politics. Alexander Johnston is a notable and worthy addition. If you have seen the Cyclopaedia of Political Science you will have noticed that he contributes all the articles on American political history. His little book on Am Pols. is one of my stand-by's.[1] Well, it has occurred to me that now would be the time to attach yourself to Princeton. There might be an opening for an assistant in the department. Sloane has taken a great interest in its organization. He came to me several months ago to find out about Johnston. If you should write to him about your plans it might result in something advantageous.

But I don't wish to seem to advise—for I know not your plans. As for your engagement it cannot be other than a joy to you. . . .

Your friend   Bob Bridges

ALS (WP, DLC) with WWhw notation on env.: "Ans. Dec. 15/83."
[1] Alexander Johnston, Professor of Jurisprudence and Political Economy. Bridges was referring to his *History of American Politics* (New York, 1880).

From Janet Woodrow Wilson to Ellen Louise Axson

My dearest Ellie,   Wilmington N. C. Dec 1st 1883.

It was my purpose to write to you immediately after hearing of your engagement to our dear son. But it has been impossible for me to accomplish my desire in the matter, partly because of our moving from point to point, and partly because of my sickness since my return home. After Woodrow had parted from you at Asheville, he wrote me a few lines—while on the cars—to tell me of his great happiness. And the good news made me very glad, dear Ellie, for I knew how he had set his heart upon you. It has not been my privilege to see much of you—to know you well personally—but I know enough to make me sure that your love will be his comfort and happiness. I will not try to tell you what I think of *him*—what he is to me—the precious son who has been so much to me—who has never given me an anxious thought—who has always been a comfort to me—without any drawback—always so unselfish, so thoughtful, and tender. I will not try to tell you of what you will soon find out for yourself.

I hope it may not be long before you can come to us. I have thought that you might be persuaded to spend next summer with us. Woodrow will be at home, and I think we could make it pleasant for you. This summer climate is very healthy, and then, you know, we are so near the sea. Wilmington is quite a summer resort for the up-country people. I am very anxious to have you with us. As your father is not keeping house now, I hope it will be possible for you to come.

We have been grieved to hear of your father's failing health. My husband joins me in warmest sympathy for him. Please give him our kindest regards.

I have been very sick—with malarial fever—since my return home, but am now much better, and hoping soon to be quite strong a[s] well. I imagine that there must be some great fund of strength, somewhere in my system, to have carried me through my severe sicknesses. I like to think that God has spared me for some special work for Him! Love from us all to your dear father. Kindest regards to your grandfather & grandmother. With love[,] unbounded love[,] from each of us three, for yourself, dear Ellie.

                    Yours most lovingly   Jeanie W Wilson

Please let me hear from you.

ALS (WP, DLC).

To Ellen Louise Axson

My own darling,   Balto., Md., Dec. 2nd 1883

My heart is nearly starved for want of a letter from you, and I know not what desperate strait it may be in if one don't come very soon. I am told that Heine once said that to correspond with a pretty girl was as idiotic as to think of tasting a Strasburg pie from the distance of Paris, since she could not delight one's eyes or give one the joy of her presence through a letter, any more than a pie in Strasburg could be tasted in Paris; but Heine was absurdly wrong, unless he was thinking of some girl who had only her beauty to recommend her; for letters may carry very sweet proofs of *love*, and that's what a man cares for more than for anything else that woman can give him. *Our* letters have had a peculiar mission, because we were separated at the very moment of receiving assurance of each other's love, and all our love-making has had to be done by letter—at least, speaking for my single self, all my *open* love-making has been, to my sad vexation, limited to that means. I've been making love to you indirectly and on the sly almost ever since I knew you. What a dear timid little girl you are in your love-making! You seem almost half afraid of your own words—as if they were not all of them full of ineffable sweetness for me! I shall never forget my sensations upon opening that first letter you wrote me after our engagement. Its first words filled me with consternation: for I did not know what might not be coming after so formal an opening as "My dear Friend"; but as I read on I was more than reassured, and before I had read it all—shall I tell it?—my eyes were full of tears, for my heart was moved as it never had been before by tenderness and joy at thought of the love I had won—a love confessed so passionately and so modestly. You have a trick of telling me of your love, my darling, just as I would have you tell it, that is, just as your heart prompts you; and it is that, I suppose, which makes your letters so indispensable to my happiness, because my happiness depends upon your love.

How odd it is that, with all our confidence in each other, we should be all the time wishing to be reassured of each other's love—and reassured in the strongest terms at that: for since we can send neither tones nor caresses with our letters, we must needs bring superlatives into service in order to do our hearts any sort of justice—at least *I* must in order to do *mine* justice: for you—you dear economical little maiden!—manage to get along with very few adjectives, without being any the less affectionate.

But I shall really have to teach you to be a little more demonstrative on some points: sometimes you use superlatives *in a comparative sense*. If I thought that there could be any *other* Woodrow of your acquaintance, I should be dissatisfied with being only your "dearest Woodrow"; because, as I would have you distinctly understand, Miss, unless in your eyes I am beyond all compare, I shall be sufficiently miserable! It is so delightful to have you call me by endearing names, that I am inclined, you see, to plead for the sweetest you can bestow.

I suppose that you *are* in Sav. sure enough by this time. I wonder what you are doing with yourself this peaceful afternoon. I hope that you are *well*, my love, and content; and that your dear father begins to feel the benefit of the change. Give him my love[.] I love you more than you can believe,

Your own   Woodrow.

ALS (WC, NjP).

From Ellen Louise Axson

My dearest Woodrow,   Savannah, Dec. 3/83.

I was very sorry to learn from your letter of last Tuesday that you had been so seriously indisposed, and equally glad to know, by means of the note received on Sat.—"for which relief much thanks"—that it was of short duration. This is the season for coughs and colds and it behooves everyone to be careful;—a text on which I am very willing to *preach*. I hope your cure was a permanent one—that your curious remedy, a long walk in the night air, did really prove effectual.

I am *so* sorry, as well as surprised to hear that the "Johns Hopkins" has proved so gravely disappointing in some respects. It is certainly very unfortunate that the professors should show themselves so inefficient in aiding and directing your studies; but there is this consolation, at least,—I don't believe you are, after all, very dependent on their guidance. You know so well what you *want* and *need*, that you *will* obtain it,—though it be in spite of them,—not so easily and pleasantly perhaps, but very thoroughly. But what a reflection on the professors that the stimulus—the quickening, exhilarating influences, which, I should imagine, the chief advantage as well as charm of University life, should come altogether from contact with one's fellow-students! Of course, under any circumstances it would come *partly* from that contact; but then it should be a sort of electric chain with the professor in charge of the battery—should it not?

I am glad you had such a treat in Mr. Bryce's lectures. He must be a most remarkable man. By-the-way, when your lecture on Adam Smith has served it's purposes there, why can't you send it to me? Pray do. I should be *delighted* to read it merely to gratify a slight curiosity as to "the sort of writing one is apt to do under high pressure."

I was amusing (?) myself with the "Excursion" [by Wordsworth] just before tea, and I came across the following lines; what do you think of them?

> "Vigorous in health, of hopeful spirit undamped
> By worldly-mindedness or anxious care;
> Observant, studious, thoughtful, and refreshed
> By knowledge gathered up from day to day"—

They made me smile, because on last "Hallow'en" they were assigned to me by fate as describing the character of my lover! Minnie and several friends of hers, intent on a Hallow'en frolic, came over at dusk to seek their fortunes in an old book of mine, by way of introduction to the more mysterious rites and ceremonies of the night.

I had *such* a kind, sweet letter from your mother this morning.[1] It has made me very happy; I despair of telling her how much I thank her for her unaccountable goodness to me. I think, sir, that, like some other spoiled boys, you must have gotten your mother in such good training that she approves of everything you do, and everything you like however disagreeable to her in the abstract! I think it is a beautiful mark of unselfishness for *any* mother to say she is *glad* of such a thing; and your mother is so very fond of you—*strangely* so, being as you say, entirely "without cause[.]" She actually says that you are "thoughtful," and "tender," and "unselfish,"—really the blindness of mothers is something deplorable!

She sends an invitation for that visit to Wilmington which you have already sketched in so captivating a style. That is a great temptation—something which it is pleasant to *think* of, whatever comes of it. But of course, under the present circumstances, it is impossible for me to make plans seven weeks, not to mention seven months, ahead. When does the year close at the "Johns Hopkins," by-the-way?

I am delighted to learn that your mother is now improving rapidly; have no doubt the more bracing weather will soon restore her strength entirely. Our invalid is progressing famously—sleeps nearly all night now—is beginning to grow impatient of his idleness already; talks of accepting a call to Chester S. C. But the doctors don't wish him to. You would laugh at the solemn conclaves we hold, trying to think of something that will amuse and divert Papa! It is a very hard thing to do; he has never taken much interest in anything outside of his work—he does'nt like "sport" of any sort, and he does'nt like light literature. If he only had some little "hobby," it would be a great blessing to him now. But as it is, the time hangs very heavily on his hands—I only wish *I* had all of his that he does'nt want, and mine too!

But I have a dear old cousin from Va. sharing my room tonight, and I fear this light is disturbing her, so I must close in haste, and very unwillingly for I have scarcely *begun*.

With much love for all your family and more than I can ever express for your dear self, believe me, darling,

Yours with all my heart   Nell.

ALS (WP, DLC) with WWsh notes on env.
¹ JWW to ELA, Dec. 1, 1883.

From Janet Woodrow Wilson

My precious Son,   Wilmington [N. C.], Dec. 4th 1883.

Your sweet & most satisfactory letter of Dec. 2nd, was received this morning. Your father has not any very good hope as to the *result* of your "plot"—but, of course, he fully sympathises with you in all your feelings & indignations—as to the state of things in your University. I hope he will write to you as to it—before the week is over—he is so wise & clear-sighted. I do hope you will make a point of making Dr. Gildersleeve your friend—and consult him before taking any important step. Do make use of Leighton Wilson's friendship & influence too. He said to me in Columbia—a few weeks ago—that he did not see why you should go to the Johns Hopkins "to a set of a [sic] fellows, who did not know half as much as *you* did!"

I wrote to dear Ellie a few days ago—and directed my letter to Savannah—care of Dr Axson. . . . I begged dear Ellie to come to us next summer. Add your arguments. I think we could make her happy here.

Your father wrote a very strong letter in your behalf to Dr. Dabney¹ with reference to a position in the Texas University—also one to Dr Smoot—as a matter of *policy*. There has not been time for any reply to these letters. Dont be anxious dear. Do what is right—and trust in God—for your future. . . .

Take care of your health, dear. Dont be anxious about us here—

for I promise I will tell you everything. Love unbounded to you, dear child, from us each one. Much love too, to dear Ellie.

Most lovingly yours   Mother.

ALS (WP, DLC) with WWhw notation on env.: "Ans. 12/9/83."
    [1] The Rev. Dr. Robert Lewis Dabney, Professor of Philosophy, University of Texas.

To Ellen Louise Axson

My precious Ellie,   Balto., Md., Dec. 4th/83

I've been in examination all afternoon and am pretty well fagged out; but I know that writing to you will brighten me up, and that I shall sleep all the better for having had a talk with my darling.

Your letter came yesterday morning and made me very happy. I had not had a *letter* from you for a long time—what seemed to me a drearily long time—and I too was getting monstrously tired of that "note" business. You are a dear little fraud! The idea of your making my supposed cry for mercy the pretext for bringing your letter to a close, after having starved me for two weeks! I am quite sure that if you were to write me twenty pages a day I should think each day's epistle too short and finish its perusal with impatience at the fact that the next day's mail was so far distant. Do you really find my frequent letters too many or too tedious? Do you ever wish them shorter?

That's an exceedingly attractive picture you give of the parsonage and its inmates, my love. Whose children are the "dainty little cousin" of sixteen, the rolicking boys, and Ellen and Carrie Belle? You may tell the last two, please, that there is a gentleman away off in the North who loves children and who would like ever so much to come and play with them; that he loves you even more than they do and would give more than they can think of in a whole year to be with you all the time as they are; and that he often wishes that he could come and see what they are doing. If you could hoodwink your conscience, you might add that he's a pretty nice sort of a fellow, *to children.*

Is it after your Aunt Ella that you are named? You see I want to know all about that household. I envy you such companionship, my darling. When one has to live off by himself, as I am doing, and shut up his heart, however much he may open his mind, from all his associates, he falls into morbid states of feeling. Living with himself alone, he gets to thinking too much about himself. I get dreadfully tired of myself as a companion sometimes; and, if I were not rooted and grounded in steady habits, I don't know what temptations I should not yield to in this great city in order to work off loneliness and morbid feeling in excitement. Every time you write me a letter you help to relieve my loneliness and to render it easier for me to make present shift to do without a home; because a message of love from you is better than all things else for driving away all my restlessness and making my present solitude bearable[.] Does it frighten you to know that the city has temptations for me? It need not. I am quite sure that my religion is strong enough to make the temptations harmless; and I tell you of these things only to show you what sweet offices your love can perform for me

Now, "in the names of all the Gods at once," who is Anna, alias "old Anna," alias Anna Harris? and what good fairy prompted you to repeat to me your conversation with her on the occasion of a certain announcement? I should'nt like to tell you what exclamatory comments I made as I read that conversation: they would make you think me the most absurdly doting swain you ever heard of, and it is not politic to let you know just how sweet I think you. But this I will say, my love, that you shall never repent the trust you have so freely put in me. It do'nt make me the least bit uneasy now that you've known me so short a time—not because I think myself lovable or faultless, or anything out of the common run, but just because I know that my love for you is perfect and that perfect love can keep a man up to almost any standard. It seems incredible to me that our acquaintance has been so brief; I feel as if I had known you for years. And I *do* know you as well as I could possibly have learned to know you in years' of ordinary friendship. Girls are enigmas to men until their hearts are opened by force of being loved and told that they are loved. You used to be such a consummate little dissembler that I never should have discovered your love for me if I had not induced you to take off the mask by a direct question.

So you think that you have convicted Jessie of a libel? But you plead guilty to the essential part of her charge. What possible interest could you have in my *eyes*, if her assertion that my picture constituted the chief interest for you in her album was untrue? The eyes were not specially worthy of notice in themselves; and, if they had been, there was no reason why you should not examine them openly instead of on the sly. And how did it happen that you could not examine my eyes as "coolly and critically" as the eyes of the picture, if, as you say, you did not think of me with any special interest in those days?

I did'nt dare to look critically at *your* eyes in those days; but then there was a very distinct reason for that, of which I was all the while quite conscious. Those eyes were too much for me and if I had looked into them long at a time I might have yielded prematurely to the even then almost irresistible desire to take you in my arms and tell you how much I loved you. Would'nt you have been astonished if I had ventured upon such a proceeding! You did'nt know what a dangerous fellow you were associating with, did you? I shall never cease to wonder at my self-control in sitting so long with you in the hammock at the picnic without making a clean breast of it; and it will always be a subject of amusing speculation what I could have said in my conversations with you, seeing that I was constantly thinking of one thing and talking of others. You had the advantage of me because, even if you did love me then a little bit, you did'nt know it, and did not have to be constantly on your guard against showing it. Do you remember your foot slipping into the water that day at the picnic, as we crossed back to the rest of the party? Well, thereby hangs a tale.

No, Mr. Bryce is *not* a particularly good speaker, but he is fluent enough, and his matter is so excellent that one forgives the defects of his manner.

It's not very gracious to rejoice in your afflictions, but I *am* glad that you are "dragged" out to take exercise. You do imagine that even light spirited young persons like yourself can preserve their bloom if they hang all day long over their painting? Would that I were there to do the dragging! Would you be kind enough to show me all the streets and all the points of interest?

Give my most respectful regards to Miss Janie Porter, if you please; and tell her that I am the proudest man in the world for having been able to contribute to that triumph of hers. You need'nt prepare her for being astonished when she sees me that such a fellow should have made such a notable conquest.

With unbounded love,

Your own   Woodrow.

ALS (WC, NjP).

Draft of a Letter to William Milligan Sloane

My dear Prof. Sloane,   [Baltimore, c. Dec. 5, 1883]

I am afraid that your recollections of most of the '79 men are not very distinct, since none of us ever had the advantage of being in your classes; but you may possibly remember me as a one-time acquaintance; and I am quite sure that you will read with indulgence anything which is addressed to you concerning Princeton by a Princetonian

I left college with the intention of studying law and entering upon its practice; I will not say with the purpose of devoting myself to the law, because that would be more than the truth. My intention was to make my living by the practice of the law and my reputation by the pursuit of more congenial studies, into which I had been led before my graduation at Princeton:—and thereby hangs my tale[.] I did study law—quite thoroughly, because under a competent and inspiring instructor—and I did set out upon the practice; but my license had scarcely passed under the seal before I saw the size of the mistake I was making. It had, of course, been only self-deception—more or less conscious, if I must confess all—that had enabled me to hope to succeed at the bar without the desire of making success there my chief success; and the more business I got—for I did get *some* during the year my "shingle" was out—the more uneasy I felt at my growing distaste for the practical duties of the profession and at my growing taste for studies in politics and administration. My reading in constitutional law and history had begun to widen about a year before I left Princeton and, though my college duties crowded system out of this extra course I had set myself, I had, before graduation, obtained, with Mr. Bagegot's[1] aid, and by numerous more or less extended excursions into other writers of a like practical spirit, a pretty complete and accurate knowledge of the Eng. Constitution as it is. My appetite for the investigation was whetted by my admiration for certain Eng. statesmen and my desire to know more of the conditions of their Parl. life; but, however whetted, it was made keener by partial satisfaction and finally demanded a comparative examination of our own constitution as it exists outside of the books and stripped of "the refinements of the literary theory." So it came about that by the end of the year I had written a paper on "Cab. Govt. in the U. S." for the Int. Rev., which you may or may not remember, and which, tho' crude enough, as I now see, was the beginning of a great deal of thorough study and hard thinking which went on, even though it was sadly out of place there, in my quarters at the Univ. of Va. and in my law office in Atlanta

All of which is prefatory to saying that I finally followed my mental nose, shut up my Atlanta office, and came on to the Johns Hopkins to study legitimately and with a clear conscience history and political science, with a view to seeking a professorship in one, or, if necessary, in both, of these branches. The reason that I am troubling you with all this personal narrative is that I have presumptuously thought it possible that by the new arrangements some room might eventually be found for me at Princeton. My plans embrace these alternatives, a position in Princeton or a chair in some Southern institution. There are many solid reasons for preferring a place in the South. I am a Southerner and should wish, for the sake of influence, to grow up with the new South; and I see, besides, that there are soon to be openings there for just the work for wh. I am endeavouring to equip myself. Neither history nor political science has ever been taught with anything approaching thoroughness in any of the Southern colleges, and it is very plainly to be seen that the setting up of new chairs for these branches must begin as soon as there's money for the purpose. But then, on the other hand, I shrink, as might go without the saying, from undertaking the work of instruction in so wide a field. Both by taste and by work already done I am fitted, rather, for teaching in the narrower sphere of constitutional and administrative systems. These I should like to have leave to make my special subjects, for in them I am sure that I could attain some mastery. But, of course, only an engagement with some institution like Princeton, which can and will pay for separate instruction in special branches, would leave me free to restrict my preparatory studies within corresponding limits

The animating motive of this long letter with which I am troubling you, is, therefore, as you are now prepared to hear, to advise with you in all candour about the possibility of there being, sooner or later, an opening for me at Princeton in the new School of Philosophy.[2] If there is such a prospect, nothing could be more rational, or more satisfactory to me than to devote all my energies here to special preparatory study of the proper kind. If there is not, I know of no other Northern institution into which I should care to sue for entrance and must confine my hopes to what chances may offer in the South. I have here exceptional library facilities for such work, though I have, I must confess been much disap. in not finding such advantages of instruction as I had reason to expect. ⟨The historical department of the Univ. is manned by men of rather small calibre.⟩

I have taken the liberty of writing to you thus freely because I know that you have, through your acquaintance with my former professors and with my classmates, Magie, Bridges, and others, every means of identifying me, and because I know that you will answer me frankly, giving me your kindest advice, even if you cannot give me any encouragement.

　　With sincere regard,

　　　　　　Yours very truly　　T. Woodrow Wilson

WWhwLS (draft). (WP, DLC).
　1 Walter Bagehot.
　2 Princeton had just instituted a new departmental organization. History and political science were taught by Sloane under the rubric of the "Philosophy of History and Political Science" in the Department of Philosophy.

Classroom Notebook

　　　　　　　　　　　[c. Dec. 6, 1883-May 20, 1884]
Inscribed (WWhw) on inside front cover and first page:
　"*Woodrow Wilson 1883*" with "1883-1886" written in the blank following printed word "CLASS," and "*Political Economy* Dr. Ely"

Contents:

WWsh and WWhw notes in Richard T. Ely's advanced course in political economy at The Johns Hopkins University, academic year 1883-84. WW notations state that he copied notes for Jan. 21, 23, 25, 28, and 30 and Feb. 1, 1884, from those of T. Alexis Berry.

Student notebook (WP, DLC).

To Ellen Louise Axson

My darling "Nell,"　　　　　　Balto., Md., Dec. 8th 1883
　Do you prefer that name? I don't quite recognize "my own Nell," but you use the name yourself, and it is certainly a very sweet one. I am sure that I can love Nell as well as Ellie, indeed so well as to wish to change her *last* name also.

　So my dear mother tried to make you believe—did she—that I am "thoughtful" and "tender" and "unselfish"? Well, it was just like her! I've always wondered at her faith in that unlikely fiction, but I am, on the whole, glad that she is deceived; and I hope, Miss, that when you answered her letter you did not attempt to undeceive her! It's too late to do any good, and the attempt would only give her pain without effecting a cure.

　But if my indulgent mother is mistaken, what shall we say of the fates of Hallow-een? It must be true, after all, that fate is blind, or else a recklessly untruthful or, mayhap, ironical genius. And I am strongly inclined toward the belief that you are a very *mischievous*—though, I admit, entirely irresistible—young person; for it must be your sly and hidden intent to poke fun at me by pretending that you find my smile described in the quotation set opposite the date of my birth in your Jean Ingelow Birth-day book, and can see my likeness in three lines about "A mouth for mas-

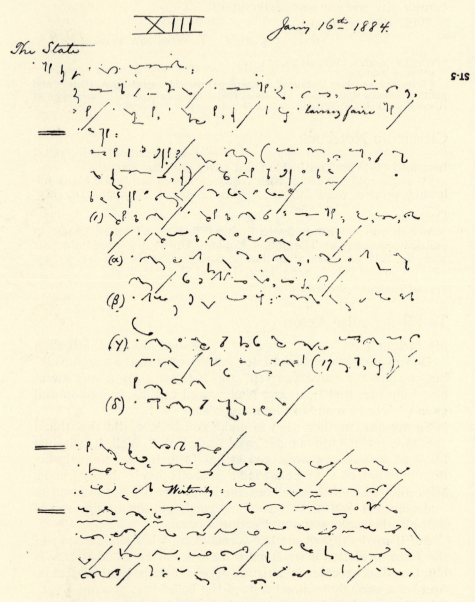

A page of Wilson's shorthand notes taken in Professor Richard T. Ely's advanced course in political economy.

tery"—&c. Pray pause in your plot and consider how unfeeling it is to put one to the blush by so artful a practical joke! Because, you know, men are very vain creatures and are anxious to believe everything complimentary that is said of them, especially when it is said by one for whose love they would barter away their lives, and the higher you lift them thus the more terrible the distance of humiliation they'll have to fall, when the truth is out. So tell me, now, ("Mr Sheriff, swear the witness.") do you really believe all these things you say about me? or do you, by a sort of blessed perversity, manage to love me in spite of the fact that you know me to be no better or more interesting than most other men? I have a sneaking hope that you *do* think me an unusually lovable fellow; nay, since I *know* that you love me, I think it extremely probable that you are possessed of some such idea; and, now that I am speaking my mind on this subject, I might as well declare the whole truth and say that you *owe* me such an opinion, by way of fair and equal exchange for I think that *you* are—no, I wont name qualities, because you would disclaim them without the least compunction: I'll say only that they are such as make it, somehow, impossible for me not to love you with all my heart, and that if I had, one year ago, been called upon to describe the woman who could be for me the dearest and most helpful of wives and make for me the brightest and happiest of homes, I should unconsciously have described a little maiden whom I was soon to meet and who was to make a certain ride by two rivers, a certain steep climb for a view, a certain chat on a jutting rock, a certain moon-lit ride in a sinking boat, a certain swing in a hammock, and a certain two days' stay in a hot and dusty North Carolina village—not to mention a rapid drive into the mountains—seem the most notable events of my life. Who will ever know—if she do'nt—how much I love that little maiden? She is the sweetest woman in the world!

Speaking of dear mother's letter to you (I *was* speaking of it!) reminds me to give you a look into her last to me.[1] "I begged dear Ellie," she says, "to come to us next summer. Add your arguments. I think we could make her happy here[.]" She did'nt know that I had already given the invitation; but I am quite ready to "add my arguments" now. The whole argument is simply this: that, although Wilmington is an exceedingly dingy, uninteresting town with no natural attraction but its splendid river, there is a very pleasant home there in which you would be more than welcome, in which you could be sure of everybody's love, and where, not to speak of the devoted services of the eldest son, you could enjoy the society of the most tender and loving and sensible of mothers, besides being as free to follow your own devices as if you were in your own home. There would, I frankly warn you, be some drawbacks to the situation. The aforesaid eldest son would probably be very persistent in his attentions and would insist in devoting his whole attention to your entertainment; he would even be very much put out if you did not appear to enjoy his company. But a woman's tact would teach you how to manage him. He is not altogether intractable, and you could easily train him to what service you chose so long as you did not assume the *air* of command. In short he is amenable to *affectionate* management, and I am sure that you would find it quite worth while to simulate affection for the laudable purpose of self-protection. I am *sure* that, in spite of him, we could make you happy; and, though of course, under the circumstances, you can give no unconditional promise, I shall consider it settled—may I not, my darling?—that you will make the visit unless some imperative necessity makes it impossible.

Why should you be interested to learn when the University term closes? However, it is an innocent enough curiosity, and I may say that the exact date is Friday, June 7th 1884. Some time before that date, though probably not before you have forgotten all about the remarkable composition which is the subject of your request, I will send you "Adam Smith." It will probably be some weeks before I am called upon to read it to the class, and in the mean time I hope to find time to put it in a little better shape, though if I do find the time it will be in the midst of examinations on other subjects, under higher pressure than ever.

Why are *you* so avaricious of time, my love? You want your father's and all of your own too! Why? That remark gives me a splendid text for a sermon about the error of too much work and too little play for young ladies who cannot boast of very robust constitutions—but I wont preach, because I feel very uncomfortable in the pulpit. I would only suggest that some people's lives are of infinitely more consequence to others than they seem to be to themselves.

I *did'nt* quite cure my cold even with the quinine and the exercise in the night air. It still lingers in the shape of a cough: but that's no matter, except as an annoyance. It will go of its own accord.

With love to your dear father—of whose improvement I am truly rejoiced to hear—and to Eddie (what news from Stockton?);

with kindest regards to the grandparents, kisses for Ellen and Carrie Belle, and for my Ellie unspeakable love, as ever

Your own   Woodrow.

ALS (WC, NjP).
¹ JWW to WW, Dec. 4, 1883.

From Joseph Ruggles Wilson

My dearest Woodrow   [Wilmington, N. C.,] Decr 8, 83

I have just received, and at once enclose, a letter from Dr. Dabney which speaks for itself. I also enclose a check for $50.00. *Please* to acknowledge the receipt of this—for I do not know to this day whether you received the first remittance! Did you get the box of law books? If not I hold the R. Road receipt and you can recover. My darling, business promptitude is not inconsistent with scholarship or study.

As to your "conspiracy" or "plot," I am not sure that I understand it; but if I do I certainly cannot approve; not because the men who are *pretending* to teach ought not to be put out, but for the reason that what is proposed can do no good, and it [is] impossible, at any rate, for it to succeed. It can assuredly do *you* no good; and whether you ought to spend time & worry in trying to benefit an *institution* until you are yourself (so to speak) an institution, I leave it for you to decide. Do not think me selfish. My mind is: never strike a blow that will not tell in the right direction, and much more never strike a blow which will never tell at all, except to your own injury.

You see, dearest one, I write in haste—but in great love—in which the other two warmly join

Your affc   Father

ALS (WP, DLC) with WWhw notation on env.: "Recd and Ans. Dec. 10/83."

From William Milligan Sloane

My dear Mr. Wilson: Princeton, Dec. 9. 1883.

Your letter of the 5th came duly to hand. You have no necessity whatever for apology in writing to me. I remember you well and most favorably, and would be glad to be of service to you in any way.

Your letter is very clear and explains your feelings and wishes most creditably. Your course is in every way commendable. At present there cannot be any opening in Princeton for reasons which you can, I am sure, appreciate. In the first place Prof. Johnston has just been elected to a chair very similar to such an one as you mark out for yourself and he and I are expected to cover the whole ground of history, social dynamics and statics, and jurisprudence for at least a few years. In the second place we cannot either of us, at present & in our untried condition, even hint at a division of labor until we show that there is enough labor to be divided. But of one thing you may rest assured—that there is a deep and kindly interest in your success in Princeton and if our new departure in philosophy, history and politics should be as successful as we hope, there is at least a chance that in a few years other instructors will be needed. It would give me great pleasure to hear from you occasionally and to remind me of your work and progress from time to time would be a help in urging your claims at the proper time.

Sincerely yours   Wm. M. Sloane.

ALS (WP, DLC).

From Ellen Louise Axson

My darling Woodrow,   Savannah Dec. 10/83

That unreasonable parent of mine has been making an invasion of my room, and after depriving me of all the luxuries of life, has ordered me, by way of penance, to "write letters"; so I proceed meekly to obey. He found me literally "enjoying poor health"— enthroned on the bed with a semi-circle of maps around me, and in for a "real good time," sore throats and head-aches to the contrary notwithstanding: and he cruelly informs me that it is very bad for the eyes to "read lying down[,]" further that maps are particularly trying on the eyes, further still—warming with his subject—that people with tremendous colds shouldnt read *at all*! And when I dolefully declare that "I don't see any fun in being sick if one can't read"; and advance my long-cherished opinion that sickness is a special provision of nature intended to give people a "chance" to read, he asks why I don't dispose of some of those numerous letters over which I had been lamenting—that would do me no harm. Whereupon I brighten up visibly, wisely refraining from any contest over that last point,—viz whether reading or writing is most injurious to eyes.

But having determined to answer a question or two in this letter, I must plunge immediately into my subject—or I will certainly lose myself before I know it in aimless wanderings. By way of beginning, I must tell you "who" Anna Harris is. In the first place, —to describe her from my individual point of view,—she is one of my best and oldest friends,—not one that I waste much "sentiment" upon, for she "does'nt go in for that sort of thing," yet she is as *true* a friend as one could well find. Indeed, I think she has a talent for friendship; she is the only person I ever knew who takes *altogether* as warm and active an interest in other people's affairs as in her own. In fact, she takes a great deal *more* interest in mine than I do myself;—she will remember and enquire about little things affecting me months, or even years, after *I* have entirely forgotten them. Of course, like all the rest of us, she has the defects of her qualities, and that little peculiarity of hers sometimes exhibits itself in an inconvenient curiosity. I never saw anyone who could ask so many questions, and for a girl with a "masculine mind" that is rather inconsistant. But after all, I believe we people who pride ourselves on never prying into what does'nt concern us are really glorying in our shame, that it is only selfishness and coldness of heart which makes us so indifferent.

But besides the distinction of being a friend of *mine*, she is in herself a very remarkable girl. She was decidedly the brightest girl in our school, and withal one of the quaintest, most original, and endlessly entertaining persons I ever saw; she has a wonderfully keen sense of the ridiculous—is, in fact, rather a dangerous friend, for she makes everything and everybody absurd, and it is impossible for her to resist sacrificing her friends, not to an epigram exactly, but to a good story. But she is a *noble* girl for all that, a very fine character—one who has learned the lesson of *self-abnegation* with a thoroughness of which few people can boast; she has had unusually good opportunities for learning it, poor girl! I would like for you to meet each other, yet it is possible that you would'nt like her, after all. I have noticed that gentlemen don't usually take to her; (and she reciprocates by having just as little use for them.) She is "such good fun" that I always thought it odd, but I have recently found the explanation—it is because she has a Roman nose!

I have been reading a paper on "noses," in which the statement was made that women with that particular form of the article were *never* attractive to men. They are, we are told, utterly devoid of *winsomeness*, of grace, of all the distinctively feminine charms, —including their *weaknesses*, which this person thinks part of their charm.

But did you *ever* see a person whose pen runs away with them like mine? I certainly didnt intend to give you a regular dissertation upon "old Anna"; but you can't deny that I have at least answered you[r] thrice repeated question, with a vengeance. But I began this letter on a large scale because I thought I had the afternoon before me and could write as much as I pleased; but my plans have been again upset, this time by a visit from Janie; and now I must think of closing.

But I will answer one more question and get it off my mind—Uncle Randolph is Papa's only brother though you "would'nt have thought it"—for they are curiously unlike; he is a handsome, "well-set-up" little gentleman, with curly brown hair, fair complexion, and beautiful blue eyes. Aunt Ella is his wife, and the five children are his also. I am not named for Aunt Ella—though we have the same initials—but for another Ellen Axson, or "Little Auntie" as I called her, Grandfather's only daughter and his idol, the darling of all our house and now it's most blessed memory. She became the wife of Mr. Legare Walker of Charlston, and died young, after a life as beautiful as a dream, for she was one of the most exquisitely lovely and lovable little creatures who ever lived. Little Ellen, "lillie Lellie Hawkes" as she used to call herself, is named for the same Aunt.

Oh dear, I suppose I *must* close though I only reconcile myself to that hard necessity by a mental promise to write again in a day or so. By-the-way you don't expect me to deign an answer to such absurd questions as that about your letters—whether they are too many or too long! You know or if you don't, you ought to know—that they are the joy of my life—nay, they *are*—my *life*. But how do I know that I would not regard them as an infliction if, like mine, they were an endless succession of hieroglyphics. Do you really manage to decypher them? If so you must have found a key which some other people—Papa for instance—don't possess. They are "too many" for him.

With best love to your dear Mother, Father, and the rest and "more than tongue can tell" for yourself. I am

Yours with all my heart.   Ellie.

What is the "tale" about my foot slipping? Pray tell.

ALS (WP, DLC).

To Ellen Louise Axson

My lovely Nell,   Balto., Md., Dec. 11th 1883

I am going to see a Georgia girl to-night—how I wish it were *my* Georgia girl! Somehow I seem to remember almost everything I ever said to you, and I recollect telling you while we were in Asheville about what a susceptible fellow my former law-partner is, and how he seemed to me to have fallen very desperately in love with a young lady who had been our neighbour in Atlanta, despite his engagement to a young lady in Va.: Do you recall anything about it? Well, it is our one-time neighbour whom I am to see to-night, Miss Sadie Wadley, a very fascinating young person, of whom her old Georgia "mammy" once said, lovingly and significantly, "Miss Sadie's *little*—but—O Lord!" She is returning home from her *Summer's* trip, and stops here for a short visit to an old friend. She has already charged several of my friends to bring me around to see her, and her friend has added *her* invitation, so of course I am going. It don't need much urging to carry me to see Miss Sadie, for she is very sweet and attractive—not, indeed, the sort of girl I should care to spend *much* time with, but a very cute, purring kitten of a girl, with pretty ways and a gentle, playful temper. She is quite a belle in Atlanta, for she has wealth in addition to her other attractions, and I used to be considered quite lacking in taste because I did not acquiesce in the common opinion that she was the most charming girl in town. I thought it sufficient praise to say that, in spite of all the attention she received, she was sweet and sincere and unaffected.

Speaking of Renick, the multiple-lover, reminds me of the wild-eyed exstasies into which I threw him by my description of *you*, after that visit to Rome during which it had happened that you were returning home "from Agnes'," when I was just beginning to know you. He declared his intention of going immediately to Rome to seek an introduction, and he has ever since been diligent in his inquiries about you. I must confess to having felt at the time a little uneasy at having divulged the secret of such a discovery to *him*; for he is an exceedingly cultivated and fascinating fellow, and I was just then forming plans and indulging hopes of my own which would have made a formidable rival exceeding unwelcome. So I did'nt offer to facilitate his meeting you and let the subject drop without ceremony. You remember the passage in Renick's letter which I showed you at the picnic, do'nt you? and my explanation that I could never keep to myself the discovery of a good thing?

By-the-way, I have made a notable discovery about *myself* recently, my love. I used to think that I had naturally a violently jealous disposition: and I could hardly have been mistaken; and yet, if I was not, I've lost it lately! I should'nt care how many Renicks went to see you now. By what sort of witchery have you conjured away my natural propensities, my darling?—I know how it has come about: by no witchery at all, but only by the power of love. I could as easily doubt my own love for you as doubt yours for me! Which reminds me that I've found a new source of self-complacency! The most passionate wish I ever formed was the wish that I were such a fellow as you could love; and the fact that that wish has been gratified—now that I have finally come to realize it—has raised me immensely in my own estimation. You can never say anything half so complimentary as that you love me.

But really I must stop this business of filling every letter with the same subject—mus'nt I?—lest you should tax me with being tiresome! The fact of the matter is that I find it very hard to avoid writing about what is uppermost in my mind, and I have'nt your art of making love the pervading colour rather than the predominant figure of the picture. Of course it is not given to everyone to paint that way; but can't you give me a few leading rules or a few guiding hints? You are under a sort of obligation to undertake my instruction because you at first encouraged me in the opposite method, allowing me to take literally your declaration that I could'nt tell you of my love too often. The implied permission suited so well with my inclinations that I have availed myself of it several times a week: and, since you have not withdrawn the permission, I'll tell you what I'm going to do: I'm going to continue this inartistic, self-indulgent practice of saying the same thing over and over again until you cry enough! So, you see, you have the remedy in your own hands, "my pretty maid"; you have but to say the word and I'll fill my letters with the most wonderful lot of stuff about professors and students and studies, about city folks and city ways and city entertainments that you ever conceived of. But I need not describe the sort of letters I should write: you know already by stern experience, unless you have forgotten those terribly long letters in which I used to spread before you most careful recitals of all the indifferent news, and descriptions of all the uninteresting people, I could think of, in my efforts to avoid letting out too soon the secret of which my head was all the while full, being, despite itself, the confidant of my heart. Do you think it unfair to coërce you with such a choice: either more love-letters pure and simple, or epistles of the formidable old style? May-be I could improve on that old style a little, because I should now be at liberty to leaven them with a little judicious (provided I could be judicious) admixture of love; but I could'nt promise that they would have leaven in quantities just sufficient to make them light.

I'm already engaged to send heavy letters to Georgia. While we were in the same office, and at the same boarding house, Renick allowed himself to become infected by my love for the study of constitutional and economical questions, and he has recently been drawing from me communications on these subjects which must have made the heart-strings of the mail bags crack. He and I together founded a "Free Trade Club" in Atlanta, which, he tells me, is flourishing, and to which I am expected to be prompted by a father's affection to write appropriate communications of encouragement and instruction(!) Don't you pity the poor fellows? I do; but I pity myself more.

Give my kindest regards to your grandparents and my love to your dear father and Eddie; kiss Ellen and Carrie Belle for me; and remember that you are owner "in fee simple" of the whole heart of   Your own   Woodrow.

ALS (WC, NjP).

From Edward Ireland Renick

Dear Wilson,   Atlanta Ga. Dec. 13, 1883
. . . Our Free Trade Club, I regret to say, has suspended. The men *cannot* be got to attend. We have private conferences, and will, when occasion offers, no doubt, have meetings, but it is to be feared, not stated ones. Faison cannot see that there is the absurdity in "Tariff for Revenue with *incidental protection*," which the Nation points out. Will you give me any new light, if you have any, on this matter? Can any more be said than this: That just to the extent that a tariff protects, it is not a tariff *for* revenue? And is not that true & the whole truth?

I have just finished a big piece of work for the City which consisted in hunting up a sufficient amount of law to support the constitutionality of assessments by frontage on adjoining lot owners for street improvements—the Constitution providing that all taxation shall be equal, uniform and ad valorem. Tell me what you think of the ruling which is very general, that the power of assessment for local improvements is not included in the word taxation as used in State Constitutions, which refers to funds raised for the support of government, whether state or municipal?

I don't, most likely, fully understand all you mean by your complaint against the stand point of Cooley et al, with reference to the construction of our Federal Const. What *is* the stand-point & who assumes it—which you approve of? You would do me a favor by sending me the address of some good young lawyer.

Tell us, without the least fear of saying too much, about the "Johns"—its lecturers—its work, its methods, it[s] students &c. By all means keep us posted about your own intellectual & social life.

I hear thro' Miss Sadie that you have met her friend, Miss Cunningham.

I have Hoke Smith's[1] wedding invitation—Dec. 19th—Miss Birdie, daughter of T. R. R. Cobb of Athens. I am at present on Bancroft's Hist of the Const.;[2] Gaddy on "The Real Lord Byron" by Jeaffreson.[3] We have both read with unusual pleasure, & can heartily recommend to you—Trollope's Autobiography. We visit no one scarcely. We continue to miss you dreadfully, & have a hundred things to recall you. Write as soon as possible—& if it suits you—to us both—& we will reply jointly.

As ever yours   E. I. R.

ALI (WP, DLC) with WWhw notation on env.: "Ans. Dec. 21/83."

  [1] Smith was a young and rapidly rising lawyer in Atlanta and later became owner and editor of the *Atlanta Journal* and prominent in politics. He was Secretary of the Interior in Cleveland's second administration and Governor of Georgia, 1907-1909 and again from July to November 1911, resigning to become United States Senator, a position he held until 1921.

  [2] George Bancroft, *History of the Formation of the Constitution of the United States of America* (2 vols., New York, 1882).

  [3] John Gordy Jeaffreson, *The Real Lord Byron: New Views of the Poet's Life* (2 vols., London and Boston, 1883).

To Ellen Louise Axson

My precious Ellie,   Balto., Md., Dec. 13th 1883

I am *so* much distressed to hear that you have been suffering from such a cold. Do be careful of yourself, my darling, for my sake as well as for your own! I sincerely trust that you will be all right again by the time this reaches you.

I really ought not to be writing—even to you—to-day, because we are just now being pressed, or rather *op*pressed, by examinations at the Hopkins. I am to go up for one on the constitutional history of England, in the first week of January, for which there yet remain some two thousand pages to be read: but then a fellow must be allowed to indulge in an occasional letter to his sweetheart, for all that

No, I *did'*nt expect you to answer my questions about whether my letters were too numerous or too long: at least I did'nt suspect that you thought them too frequent or too tedious; I was only indulging in the *argumentum ad hominem*—or rather, *ad mulierem* —for the purpose of exposing your little fraud of pretending to think that I might find *your* letters tedious. Oddsfish! my dear, I'd have you understand that I am passionately in love with you, and that whatever you may write is sure to seem to me sweeter and more interesting than anything else in the language!

"Which I wish to remark" that there seems to me to be much

poetical propriety in that fact that you are named after so attractive a person as your "little Auntie" must have been, for you
too are "one of the most exquisitely lovely and lovable little creatures who ever lived"—a truth which I have for some time been
trying to impress upon you, and which, even if you wont believe
it yourself, you must allow that it is a lover's privilege to believe—
especially after he has found it current amongst others less prejudiced than himself. I can't tell you how easily and irresistibly it
took possession of my convictions, or how violently it made my
heart beat whenever you happened to be near me. It has made
me attached to everything I ever saw you *wear* even. That simple
black gown you wore in Asheville clings to my memory as the
prettiest gown I ever saw. It *did* fit you well, and you always look
best when close-fitted, but I should have admired it even if it
had'nt been neat and pretty in itself. I could tell you, as I ventured
to say long ago, just the sort of gown which I think most becoming to you; but any costume that you might choose to don would
seem beautiful to me

I was *very* much interested in your description of "old Anna."
I think I *should* like her, if you have drawn an accurate likeness
of her—I should not have a right to lay claim to very good taste
if I did'nt.

Do you know, Ellie, it sometimes strikes me as a rather whimsical incongruity that we know so little about each other and about
each other's friends? Is'nt it odd, for instance, that I've seen only
one or two of your paintings and drawings—that I know nothing
about the work that occupies most of your time and thought? I've
often secretly longed to show you in some way how intensely
interested I am—or should like to be permitted to be—in that work,
but I'm an awkward fellow and did'nt know how, in face of the
fact that you never say anything definite about it[.] But more of
this anon: I *must* stop this and go to work. With love unspeakable,

Your own   Woodrow.

ALS (WC, NjP).

From Ellen Louise Axson

My darling Woodrow,   Savannah Dec. 14/83.

I would like for you to have witnessed a scene at which I was
present yesterday, and in which *you*, in spite of your absence,
played a prominent part. How you would have laughed! I think
you would have been flattered too,—at any rate you *ought* to have
been, for the most valuable of compliments is one from a child.

It seems the little folks were discussing sweet-hearts, and Eddie, who, under the influence of that scamp, Randolph, is rapidly developing into the "enfant terrible," informed them that he knew who sister's sweet-heart was, and if they came with him he would show them his picture; so he marches them into my room, invades my drawer and produces the picture, according to promise. Carrie Belle after surveying it gravely for a long time remarks with decision, "I like him, he shall be *my* sweet-heart—I must kiss him." Whereupon Ellen, the elder—six years old—exclaims in shocked surprise "Oh, Carrie Belle are'nt you ashamed! you *shan't* kiss it!"—taking it away—upon which Carrie comes *crying* to me to know if she "*may'nt* kiss him and if she can't have him for hers." I tell her, "certainly, she shall do both!" and she fairly beams.

She came this morning to kiss it again, and I heard her tell her mother with the "cutest" air imaginable—head tucked on one side, eyes peeping out shyly from the long lashes, that she has "a nice sweet-heart named Mr. Willie, and his picture is upstairs." So you understand, sir, that you are transfered,—if you are mine "in fee simple" I have that right! have I not? And it is an enviable lot which I have prepared for you, for she is a jewel. I must warn you, however, that this *Belle* has very fully developed the coquettish instincts of her class. You are the reigning favourite now, but I don't know how long it will last—she has quite a train of admirers here. Had it been Ellen now, you might have anticipated more peace of mind, for she, like her venerable cousin and namesake is of a constant mind. By the way, that is an unfortunate remark, coming as it does just at the time when I have to announce that I have made other arrangements for myself as well as for you. I have become engaged to my cousin, Mr. Randolph Axson, aged, nine. True, there *is* a trifling difference in our ages, but I have promised to keep at a stand-still "just as long as my friends will let me"; perhaps I can even manage to grow backward; many women have accomplished it.

I send a few views of Sav. according to promise, "to assist your imagination." The steeple in the "South Broad" picture belongs to Grandfather's church. The parsonage is just beyond it as you look down the street—the two houses occupying the square. One of the other pictures, I send, not because it was "Sherman's head-quarters," but because, besides being beautiful, it is the home of my friend, Mrs. Green, whom I visited at the Beach, you know, —and who is at present living in Baltimore.

I would indeed submit with a very good grace to being "dragged out" if you were here, and would do my little best toward showing you Sav. But don't speak of it, please, for I have already had enough to do fighting discontented and envious thoughts because Janie's "Mr. Chandler" is coming down from Atlanta for the holidays. What a pity *you* are not in Atlanta now! or at any reasonable distance. So you actually want me to add oath to oath, and "swear" that my former testimony was not a lie but an honest expression of opinion! I did'nt know you were such a doubter. I don't know that one's word is good for much when it needs to be so heavily reinforced, but I solemnly affirm that I have a good conscience and void of offence in this matter. I have never said anything about you that I did'nt *mean*. I think what I say, though I don't always say *all* that I think, that would be too large a task!—so I won't "name qualities," but the sum of the matter is that I think you "a man whom I love and *honnour* with my soul, and my heart, and my duty, and my life, and my living, and my uttermost power."

Really, I think your questions have gone from one extreme to another! Formerly they were too hard for me, now they are "too easy"—as the boy said, whom the teacher asked to name all the mountains of Mexico, "such simple questions were a reflection on his intelligence." What shall I say to such questions as those concerning your letters; do you really think they deserve an answer? However if you *do* need reassuring, I promise you that *when* I grow weary of your style in correspondence, I won't fail to let you know.

But, as I was saying, these questions at least have one merit, they admit of a clear, concise, and positive answer, whereas some of your others I have "evaded" partly because I knew that if I attempted to answer them I would lay myself open to the charge of inconsistency[.] I should probably contradict myself a dozen times; yet without "fibbing" at all, for each of my statements would have had its turn to be true. I suppose "the course of true love" in a woman is very different from a man's,—by no means so direct; and besides its windings and turnings, it is an underground stream, and of course, can't be explored—indeed its existence is hardly suspected. Or in the struggles of love with pride and shame, and various other feelings, I think it is more like the tide, which, however steadily it rises, seems to be constantly beaten back, so that we can scarcely tell whether it is rising or falling. The only thing that I can *positively* affirm as to that "secret history," is, that I would catch myself thinking of you a very great deal, and that I was intensely disgusted, indignant and angry with myself for so doing. Of course, you know, I don't mean I was thinking of you

in connection with *myself* so much! it was "you by itself you,"—
what you said, and did, and how you looked, and what you seemed
to be,—who can fathom the mystery of a girls *thoughts*, (?) that
brooding, dreamy reverie, without beginning, without end, without object[,] without results, that world of fantasy and airy nothing! You say I *must* have known in those days that you loved me;—
I assure you, sir, I knew nothing of the sort. I simply knew that
you had taken a little fancy to me, which upon further acquaintance, might, and probably would, develop into deep, sincere, and
unchangeable *indifference*;—and I don't think I would have broken
my heart *then* if such had been the end of it. I am—or used to be—
an abominably proud little wretch, and I never had the slightest
fancy for the romantic role of a "blighted being." Anna says that
mine was a serious case of "the gone-ups" before I left home last
summer, but I deny it. I am very willing to acknowledge now that
all that was the beginnings of love, but I should never have found
it out if you hadn't taught me. In fact, I had no idea what I was
about. Beth attacked me on the subject of our correspondence,
saying she thought I "had resolved never to get into any fresh
scrapes of that sort." "Yes," I said, "I did so resolve." "Then what
are you doing it for?" "I don't know," said I, "There are times
when some power beyond us seems to speak for us, while we ourselves stand by and wonder! It was a curious thing,—when he asked
me to write, I seemed *compelled* to say 'yes'; I did'nt even pause
to consider, but said it as simply and naturally as if it had been
Father and then did my *thinking afterwards*";—and a confused,
perplexed and troubled process it was. All this recalls another
unanswered question, viz., what I would have said if you had put
a certain other proposition that day—I rather think I should have
been too astonished to say anything, I dare say, I should have
thought you were joking; it would have suggested that proposal
of—whose was it?—Frere's, I believe—"A sudden thought strikes
me—let us swear an eternal friendship." You see, I was under-
estimating your native force and decision of character, your masterly power of rapidly reviewing the field and forming your conclusions!

I am sorry to hear that your cold "still lingers in the shape of a
cough"; and why is a *cough* of so little consequence? I thought it
was the worst form of a cold. I *do hope* that in your next you will
be able to report it entirely gone. I believe I mentioned in my last
that I had a cold. I am quite well again now. Your arguments in
favour of the Wilmington visit are very convincing, my darling;
I only wish I could "consider it settled"—but you don't know how

many things there are in the way; I am afraid it won't be possible; but I can only wait and see. Give my best love to your mother and the rest, and for yourself, dear friend—*I* particularly like that expression, if you *do* think it "formal"—["]keep as much as you want." Papa sends his love and so does Grandmother.

Yours with all my heart,   Ellie.

ALS (WP, DLC).

To Robert Bridges

My dear Bobby,   Balto., Md., Dec. 15th/83

Your letter reached me promptly and was enjoyed immensely. Its first result was a long letter from your humble servant to Prof. Sloane. Your advice was both kind and excellent and I was very grateful for it. Prof. Sloane replied very cordially to my letter. He sees no present prospect of a further division of labour in his new department; but he hopes to show the trustees in the course of a few years that there is work enough to be done in it to justify an additional workman or two, and promises, if I will keep him posted about my studies, their progress and results, to push my claims at the proper time: all of which is satisfactory as far as it goes. I am at least on the track there and may win something in the end. If I do, it will be your kind doing, old fellow.

I did not think at all hard of you—as I need scarcely assure you—for not answering my last letter sooner. I know just how your time is taken up, and I am rather inclined to be gratified by the occasional epistles I do get from you than irritated or offended by your delays in writing. Your congratulations on my engagement gave me very keen pleasure, my dear Bobby, because I know that they are genuine and not merely formal; but your letter as a whole gave me some concern, for I thought I detected a tone of despondency running through it. It is so unlike you to be in low spirits that there must be something serious the matter when you are. I know that it is easy for a fellow in the first months of a happy engagement to take a bright view of things and give cheery advice; but I must be permitted to remark that your talk about crawling into your bookshelves is all nonsense. If ever there was a man for whom such a course would be suicidal, that man is Bob. Bridges; and if ever there was a man fit for marrige because lovable and specially in need, by reason of a high-strung nervous temperament, of a woman's loving sympathy and companionship, that man is yourself. And I know that you will let *me* say that you are the very man who can and ought to follow Pete's and my example. I wish we could have a good old-fashioned *triangle* talk on this subject. I can say in all sincerity that I have no friend for whose happiness I care more than I do for yours; and I'm quite sure that no woman can have a happier life than you could give her. Don't think me presuming for saying these things, old fellow; I have been provoked to it by the impression created by your letter, that you are inclining to rather morbid views as to your own life.

You need not envy me my chances here. There *are* splendid opportunities for study here, in the way of fine libraries and a stimulating atmosphere, but I regret to say that the longer I stay the more deeply I am disappointed in the *instruction* given in my department. It is manned by young men altogether (Adams and Ely) who have all the faults of young men and are without some of the advantages of their age. Ely is the better man of the two, a hard, conscientious worker, but he is simply stuffed full and do'nt move except by the force of outside impulse. Adams is superficial and insincere, no worker and a selfish schemer for self-advertisement and advancement. Still, I'm given more than I can do. Just now I am overwhelmed with reading preparatory to an examination on the constitutional history of Eng. which is appointed for the first week in January and which will keep me on the stretch until then. The Cow says something about six-cent soda-water occasionally. Write as soon as you can, Bobby. With much love from Hiram and more from myself.

Your sincere friend,   Tommy.

ALS (Meyer Coll., DLC).

From Ellen Louise Axson

My darling Woodrow,   Savannah Dec 17/83

Yours of the 13th was received on Sat. It is certainly very kind of you to write when you are so busy. You must be having terrible times there now. Those reverend seniors of yours know how to pile up the work if they know nothing else; I am beginning to think your friend's illustration from Dante peculiarly apt—it is too bad that you should be so oppressed just at the holiday time. How are the eyes bearing the strain?

And what about that "trifling cough"? I feel a trifling interest in it, and want to hear the last of it. With all due respect for your friend, I am glad, on the whole, that you are not Mr. Renick—if for no other reason, because I shouldn't care to be thrown into a state of consternation whenever a "belle" appeared above your

horizon. But I can read with perfect composure of *your* being subjected to the charms of even that little enchantress, Miss Wadley.
So great is my confidence in you that I would even have liked to
throw you in the way of temptation, if there had been time. I
would have liked you to meet a friend of mine, Réné Fairbanks,
who has recently been visiting in Baltimore, with some Poulains
[Pullains]. She is one of the lovliest girls I ever knew, and one of
the prettiest—such sweet brown eyes and soft rings of fair brown
hair;—and she is such a *womanly* woman,—there is a tender tran-
quillity about her that somehow seems to *rest* one; she makes me
think of those fair young madonnas of the old German school;—
in fact I should have shown great courage in promoting your meeting, for to fall in love at first sight was the only reasonable thing
you could have done under the circumstances;—but I should have
taken care to warn you that she is supposed to be already engaged
—to Mr. Beckwith of Atlanta—the clergyman.

Yesterday I came across another unanswered question of yours,
viz. what I thought of you upon the occasion of that first meeting
of ours when you called upon Papa. I suppose I must reply, as,
owing to some remark of yours, I have suddenly grown conscientious upon that point; but would'nt it do just as well to tell you
what I *said* about you?—it is such a peculiarly graceful and modest
habit, you know, to be always acting as one's own reporter. But to
proceed, I remember one afternoon in April receiving a call from
one of the chief inquisitors; she asked me what I had been doing
all day? "Why," said I, "thus," and "so," and ["]seeing callers principally[.]" "Who called?" "Mrs. This, and Miss That, and Mr. Wilson." "Who is Mr. Wilson?" "Mrs. Bones nephew." "Ah, is he old
enough for you?" (!) Now, if there is anything that particularly
excites my contempt and disgust it is that sort of thing—the habit
of regarding every man one meets as the hero of a possible love-
story, with ones-self, of course, for the heroine; so I answered with
intense scorn—directed at *your* head, of course, "oh no, quite an
infant!"

I am here reminded, by what association of ideas I don't exactly
know, of that stroll in the dusk along the river-bank, and your
topic of conversation on the occasion—perhaps because that was
the first time you tried to elicit from me an expression of opinion
as to yourself, or rather as to professors in general. Ah, that was a
terrible moment! how often I have laughed over it since! and how
amused I was at your side of the story as related in one of your
letters! If you obtained but little satisfaction, sir, it served you
right for putting me in such a quandary. You see I could'nt forget

certain little remarks that you had made. I did'nt attach the *slightest* importance—or meaning to the remarks, but you might have *thought* that I did, if I answered in a certain way. At any rate they made me self-conscious—and it was so consummately shock-ing that there *should* be any self consciousness;—I felt disgraced in my own eyes. I could'nt say frankly and simply what I really thought,—what *any* woman with the smallest claim to the name would think—on the points proposed; yet I could'nt lie, and say that I thought your position correct, that it would be both unjust and ungenerous for you to ask any woman to share your dreary lot! What was I to do? I bethought me of an expedient!—and I assure you, I congratulated myself heartily, when I had man-aged to slip out by lugging in poor Mrs. Carlyle. I could be, as I wished, perfectly noncommittal, in repeating without comment what *someone else* thought.

Pray tell me, if you please, sir, what answer you wished made to your queries? Did you expect me to say that you had greatly over-estimated your difficulties, because love laughs at such things, or rather ignores them altogether; so that you had only to secure a woman's *love*, and the rest would take care of itself; and that you, being an extremely lovable young gentleman, would have no difficulty in achieving that little task? Moreover, that your scruples were, apart from all that, singularly superfluous, because *other people* failed to see anything so dreary and uninviting in a professor's life. Indeed, that it offered peculiar attractions to young persons whose bane in life had always been an unreason-able and unreasoning love of books; a blind instinct, foolish and barren enough—a sort of mouse-in-the-library passion for small nibblings upon them, for looking at them, for living among them.

Perhaps you would have liked me to indulge in *reminiscences,* and describe to you two little girls, who, in some far remote period of time, were wont to curl themselves, day after day, in a cosy nest high up in an old mulberry tree; and who while munching cakes and apples, occupied themselves with passing in review their small *real* world and their vast imaginary one, telling fairy-stories, of planning their future, as girls begin to do at a very early age—see "Little Ellie and the Wild Fawn's nest." One of these two would on such occasions describe a sort of "Prince Charming" out of a fairy-tale; but the other thought that sort of young gentle-man silly, and "too much like girls,"—her "not impossible he" must be "oh, awfully smart!" "What should he be—a preach-er[?]" Ah, no, not a preacher—because—well, just *because!* "Not a lawyer, for she did'nt believe they were very good." "What then."

"Well, either a *professor* or an *artist*," she hardly knew which. "Artists were *ever* so nice, but she was afraid they were not always *smart*," she rather thought he must be a professor!

But if I say much more you will begin to think that I was attracted to you chiefly by a desire to prove myself consistent; wont you? Not so, for I had long before abandoned those theories; I simply returned to my first opinion.

> "Is it so true that second thoughts are best?
> Not first, and third, which are a riper first?"[1]

Aunt Ella, who has just been in, says I must give you her love "if you are really as nice as I pretend, & as you ought to be," and as her love is very especially worth having I wont neglect her message.

Give my best love to your family, an[d] believe me, my darling, yours with all my heart,

                                        Ellie.

Three months today since I left Asheville, and three months yesterday since—the 16th of Sept. Did you remember it? It seems much longer, so full has the time been of life and love. They have been very happy months to me, in spite of many cares and troubles, and *you alone* have made them so, dear love. I was reading the other day some lines which not long ago had been especial favourites of mine—they were so *cheering* and comforting—but somehow they seemed to have lost all their meaning, so completely had the world changed for me.

ALS (WP, DLC).
[1] From Tennyson's "Sea Dreams."

Two Letters to Ellen Louise Axson

                               Balto., Md., Dec. 18th, 1883
Do you know, my sweet, peerless little woman, that you puzzle me sorely sometimes by seeming to put an entirely wrong construction on some passages of my letters? Did you really think me a "doubter" because I asked you to "add oath to oath" in confirmation of your sweet expressions of love and admiration? Why, Ellie, I should be altogether unworthy of your love if I were capable of doubting even in the least degree anything you say; and when I playfully call upon you to "swear" to your opinions you should read the words as in no way inconsistent with the most passionate love and the most confiding trust on my part, interpreting them as you would were I holding you in my arms and

begging to hear again those declarations of love and faith which fill me upon every repetition with such unspeakable joy and thankfulness. *Of course* I know that you have never said anything about me that you did'nt mean; if I had not known that, I should not have wished to hear you *add* anything; I should not have been busy to manufacture provocations to induce you to *repeat* what you had said. I could'nt love my precious Ellie if I did not *know* that she is sincere, and there could be no more abundant demonstration of my unquestioning trust in her than the fact that I love her, with a love such as I had never dreamed of until I saw and knew her, a love which seems to be the whole of my existence, which has made her all in all to me and her love for me the perpetual joy of my life!

You ought to be very contrite, Miss, for having put me to this self-defence, in view of the fact that you do'nt hesitate, when *I* express opinions about you, to pronounce them altogether without weight, sincerely held, no doubt, but quite erroneously and blindly. I am prepared to triumph over you now, however, on at least one point of those opinions. You doubtless remember that I have several times ventured to announce my belief in your *beauty*? Well, be it known to Your Royal Scepticalness that I have recently discovered convincing proof of the reasonableness of that belief. In one of the art stores here, amongst the splendid photographs of the masterpieces of the celebrated "Dresden collection" of paintings, I found one entitled "Checkmated," the work of some modern "master" with an unpronounceable name, and said to be one of the latest additions to the collection. The "situation" of the picture is easily enough read. The earnest gallant has defeated his fair opponent at chess, but he has carried his advantage beyond the board and she knows not what move to make next as she sits with averted face and downcast eyes, avoiding his eager, questioning gaze. The whole picture is beautiful, but her face is the centre and crown of its beauty. In it the artist has evidently sought to give a type of modesty and purity, and the remarkable thing about his work is, not that he has succeeded, but that, working in his far-off European studio, he has created by his imagination a face which may be found in the life in Georgia. It is not your face in every line, but in the slight particulars in which it differs it differs to its own disadvantage. It is so striking a suggestion of your face that my unexpecting eye was caught by it at once in a rapid glance through a whole case of like photographs, and a closer examination only made my heart quicken its beat very tumultuously.

During my daily walks, my "constitutionals," I frequently stop in at the stores of the better sort to see new engravings, new paintings, and the like, and not many days ago I was attracted by a card which announced, from behind the generous pane of a broad window, that a collection of Mr. Whistler's etchings and "dry points" was on exhibition within. In I went, of course; and, after being constrained by a handsome young women [sic] to buy a catalogue which I did not want, I set myself to as critical an examination of Mr. Whistler's productions as my ignorance of artistic canons would allow. Well, I must confess that, in my unenlightened soul, I was disgusted, and more than ever indifferent to the possession of the catalogue, except that it was much more interesting as a curiosity than the etchings are as pictures. Some of Mr. Whistler's critics object that his later productions, of which those I saw are specimens, are mere suggestions; I think they would have been nearer the truth in some cases if they had said that they suggest nothing—a few lines, a possible face, a conjectural group, a hazy beginning of something—one cannot tell certainly what the picture might have been, had it been completed; though here and there one does find a sketch suggestive of life and beauty. As compared with these unsatisfactory dashes of helter-skelter lines and irresponsible patches of shade, recommend me to the staring chromo with its honest ugliness!

Speaking of pictures, I am reminded of the exceedingly amusing scene with which you begin the sweet letter I received this morning—the scene in which my photograph played so prominent a part. I do feel flattered by the dear little child's liking for my effigy. She must have discovered somewhere in the face signs of that great love which its owner feels for all sweet children such as she. Give her as many kisses as you please from her sweetheart and tell her that she may call him hers as long as she pleases—quite as safe a promise as yours to "that scamp, Randolph," to wait for him "just as long as your friends will let you." You may say to Mr. Randolph Axson, jr., for me, if you please, that he'd better not let me catch him making love to my sweetheart! If he does, it will go none the less hard for him because she consents to the love-making.

I think that I have met "Janie's Mr. Chandler" (though he probably does not recollect it) in Decatur; and if he is the one I met there, I am curious to see what you will think of him when you meet him. I saw him for only a few moments; but I have a very irrational habit of forming an instantaneous opinion of the men I meet, and I am, consequently, quite ready to compare notes with you. If he is the man I'm thinking of—as, I doubt not, he is—I know several of his familiar friends, and I have never heard any but the most complimentary opinions expressed about him. He seems to be universally esteemed and admired by those who know him well: tell me just what *you* think of him. Lucky dog that he is! What would I not give to spend the holidays in Savannah! I'll hardly realize the passage of the Christmas season here, because I expect to have to study all through it; and I am rather glad of the necessity: for only imperative work can save me from the blues that would be sure to master me if I had time to think of those delights which I am compelled to forego.—But, let's change the subject! I can't trust myself yet awhile to speak of being with you. I am so grateful for the assurance of your love, which I did not think to have won, that I am ashamed to rebel against being denied those sweet joys which we might derive from each other's presence now that we know each other's hearts. I have often had to drive out the regret that we were separated just at the moment when it became possible to associate without reserve—but I *must* change the subject: let us hope that next summer will bring pleasures sufficient to compensate for its slow coming!

Do you ever see our little friend, Miss Stoddard (?) for whom I picked the thistles? She was a rare piece, and she easily saw through your humble servant (as, I suppose, did her parents also)[.] As I was restlessly waiting for you to come up from dinner, on that memorable Sabbath afternoon, my heart beating fiercely with resolve and fear, she came up to me and declared, her eyes fairly overflowing with knowing mischief, that "*she* knew who I was waiting for"; "Who?" "Miss Axson!" What a waking dream my life was during those forty-eight hours, when I happened to be away from you! The proprietor of the "Eagle Hotel" was put to very small expense for my maintenance. I could not eat anything, and my use of my room was little more than a formality. I did not sleep enough to get on good terms with the bed!

Thank you, my darling, for the passages from the "secret history" you give me in this letter of this morning. I *did* ask questions that were too hard; but you have answered them in a way that makes me very glad that I asked them. Nothing could be sweeter to me, as a revelation of the character of the dear little maiden I so tenderly love, than this natural story of how love for me took stealthy possession of her heart. It did not take me long to discover that I was conquered, for, though mine was not love at first *sight*, it *was* love on first *acquaintance*; and I was curious to learn how far you became conscious of my love for you before our correspondence began. In other words, I want to know how I "taught you" to love me.

One of your answers suggests another question: when "Beth" attacked you on the subject of our correspondence by asking if you had not once "resolved never to get into any *fresh* scrapes of that sort," what other "scrape of that sort" did she refer to?—But I know that it binds you unpleasantly in the choice of subjects when you know that you have questions to answer, so I'll not ask any, but will leave you free to "wander on" (as you express it) in your letters just as you please, because those free, artless wanderings of yours are monstrously charming to me. The only difficulty is that you can never wander far enough to satisfy me—you can never make your letters as long as I want them to be: not even if you send me two loaded envelopes at once as you used to do to favoured "Beth."

Yes, my darling, my cough is quite gone and I am *perfectly* free from all physical ailments both small and great. When I said that my cough was of little consequence I did not mean that a cough as a cough is not a serious thing, but only that that particular cough of *mine* was little more than an annoyance, proceeding as it did from a tickling irritation of the throat and not from a cold on the chest. A cold on the chest is indeed no laughing matter. I am *so* glad to know that *your* cold too is gone!

Give my love to your dear father and grandparents, and to Eddie, and for yourself take the unbounded love of
Your own   Woodrow.

My darling,   Balto., Dec. 19/83

I must drop you just a line this morning to acknowledge the receipt of the stereoscopic views. It was very sweet of you to think of sending them. They are exceedingly pretty in themselves, but their chief value in my eyes in [is] their association with you, my darling. They *do* assist my imagination very much. Two of them I *remember* very well—the one that gives a glimpse of the parsonage, and the one of the church (or, rather, of its steeple)—for you showed them to me one day in Rome: and my memory is wonderfully tenacious of everything you ever did in my presence.

With love unbounded,   In haste,   Your own   Woodrow.

ALS (WC, NjP).

From Janet Woodrow Wilson

My precious boy—   Wilmington, N. C. Dec. 21st 83

I have time to send you only a little note today. I have tried to think of something you might like, as a Christmas present—but have not been able to decide upon anything I can find here. So, dear, I enclose you five dollars—(how I wish I could make it a hundred!) which you can use in any way you like best, of course. . . .

I want you, dear, to write to Josie—and use all your influence with him to induce him to study. He will *have* to study hard the coming months—or he will be mortified when he goes to school—as he will have to do next year—to find himself so far behind hand. I have plead with him—and tried to *insist* upon his studying in earnest—and he makes fair promises—but the result is not very encouraging. Of course he labors under great disadvantages—for you know what his interruptions are. But I could protect him from all that—if his heart was in the matter. He is a dear good boy—and has not half a chance—so I dont mean to complain of him[.] I only want the help of your influence over him—which is great[.] It is *very* hard for me to stop when writing to you, dear! With warmest love to dear Ellie—and unbounded love to yourself from us all

Lovingly yours   Mother.

ALS (WP, DLC).

Two Letters to Ellen Louise Axson

My own darling,   Balto., Dec. 21/83

I must protest against your laughing at me when you see the unportable size of the present I sent you yesterday. I confess that there *is* something rather whimsical in the idea of sending to a *nomad* an article which has to be packed in order to be carried; but, after all, you wont have to lug it around with you *wherever you go*, and it will serve to remind you of the penalty attached to falling in love with a fellow who is apt to follow his fancy in some things to the ousting of his judgment. I know that you will think the picture beautiful; and I am quite sure that you will understand why I chose it, in preference to others equally handsome, but not equally attractive. I should like to write you a real Christmas letter this evening to go with the picture, but you know already what I would say: you do'nt need to be told how much love I send with it, or how I shall be constantly with you in thought during this Christmas season, which will be by far the happiest of my life.— the happiest as compared with my *past* life, but not as against those that are to come! There will come Christmas seasons which I may spend *with you*, when you will be mine, my precious wife, the joy and light of my life; when we can approach the opening of the new year with common plans for our united lives; when, in a home of our own—a home made happier than all others by constant interchange of the little services of love, which make up the great whole of life for those who are wedded in love, and rendered as holy as any by love for God and diligence in the work he gives us to do; when—but my heart is too full, when I think of the time when you shall be my constant and loving companion, to allow me to draw any coherent pictures of it. This I know, that, if love can make you happy, your life shall be full of joy and of sunlight. I have given you my whole heart without reserve, and I hope that some day you may know how much that means.

I should have liked very much to meet Miss Fairbanks, my love; but I can bear the disappointment: and I should have had very little fear of her extraordinary charms, because I have found somebody else with exquisite brown eyes, with soft brown hair, with beauty and grace and womanly ways, who may, for aught I know, fill other people with a sense of *rest*, reminding them of fair young madonnas and the like ideal personages, but who fills me with unspeakable love and with an intense desire of possession such as no German madonna ever had or could have charm enough to do. She fills all my life, and the attractions of the rest of her sex are a matter of astonishing indifference to me. I do'nt seem to be conscious of them, as I used to be. My power of loving has all been devoted, by right absolute, to another, and it has become literally impossible for me to exercise it in any other quarter.

What message shall I send to your Aunt Ella, my darling? I assure you I valued *her* message most highly; and you may tell her that I shall hope some day to win her love in my own right by proving myself worthy of you.

And now, my precious, my matchless Ellie, a merry, happy Christmas to you! May God bless my darling and all who are dear to her[.] Give my love, and the greetings of the season, to your dear father and Ed., to your grandparents, to your kind Aunt Ella,—to all and keep for yourself a heartful of love from
Your own   Woodrow.

My precious Ellie,   Balto., Dec 22nd [1883]
I confess that this is sheer self-indulgence, this daily letter-writing; but it's Christmas time and why should'nt I indulge myself, especially since by this particular sort of self-gratification I can

contribute also to your pleasure? Besides, you so constantly haunt (if *good* spirits can be said to *haunt*) my waking thoughts that writing to you is only doing formally and deliberately what I should anyhow be doing involuntarily if I were to try to read for my examination: I should, under any circumstances, be spending much of my time in holding imaginary conversations with you, telling you again and again how much I love you, and striving to picture your sweet smiles given in return; beguiling myself with dreams of the future and with visions of the Christmas doings at the parsonage on South Broad St; and otherwise wandering away from my lines of study. But the biggest part of my preparation for examination is done, and *comparative* leisure, working together with the natural influences of the season, gives me an easy conscience in these excursions of fancy. I still have plenty to keep me busy, but not enough to drive me at the top of my pace; and it has always been my habit to study by brief spurts rather than with steady and persistent speed. I like to read *much* but not *many things*—at least, not many things *at once*. I go on the principle that father used to announce in very strong English to his pupils in Columbia, namely, that "the mind is not a prolix gut to be stuffed," but a thing of life to be stimulated to the exercise of its proper functions, to be strengthened, that is, to do its own thinking. I *can't* "cram"; I must eat slowly and assimilate, during intervals of rest and diversion. My chief ground of indictment against my professors here is that they give a man infinitely more than he can digest. If I were not discreet enough to refuse many of the things set before me, my mental digestion would soon be utterly ruined. My original friend, author of the apt Danté illustration, last night said that we are here taught to swim by being thrown into unfathomable depths and left to shift for ourselves, to drown or swim. If we had'nt had some practice before hand, we should be like to drown unpitied.

What will you say when I tell you that I wrote to Miss Katie Mayrant the other day? The letter was prompted by very sad news. Renick writes me that Mrs. Mayrant (Miss Katie's mother) is at the point of death in Atlanta—ill beyond all possibility of recovery. To add to the sadness of the case is the fact that Miss Katie will be left overwhelmed with debt and in a state of entire dependence. Her mother had just begun to take boarders in Aiken and was bound not only for the rent of a large house but also for the price of a large stock of furniture which she had obtained on credit. But I wont distress you with the particulars of an extremely sad case. I felt bound to write Miss Katie assurances of my sincere sympathy. I have'nt for a long time been so moved to pity; and I shall lose in Mrs. Mayrant a friend who was untiring in her kindness to me. She was a noble, self-sacrificing woman.

My curiosity was excited by a passage in a recent letter of yours. When you were "enjoying poor health" why had you enthroned yourself amidst *maps*? What led you into so diligent a study of geography? I have been engaged in a somewhat similar pursuit. I've been following the Celtic and Saxon invasions of Britain with the aid of a "relief map" of the island—and a wonderful assistance to the imagination and the understanding it is! With the mountains and the valleys under one's eye it is easy to follow the course of conquest because it is plain what lines of advance invading hosts *must* by physical necessity have taken. It is only necessary to run one's finger over the map to feel the resistance of the uplands which the Saxon armies must have felt.

I am looking forward with a sort of grim amusement to the Christmas at 146 N. Charles St; because we are there such an awfully solemn household. We eat our meals in sober silence, and I have been so long in getting on easy terms with my fellow boarders that it has now become next to impossible. They doubtless regard me as a rare book-worm with no joy in my soul, incapable of sentiment, smileless and given over to dead lore. I have to go often to call on the Woods in order to let off steam—whereby I have made myself the regular playmate of the children of the household, being judged no long capable of dignified deportment or of sensible speech. I am at a loss how and where to assume my normal character.

I send you several Christmas cards, of which the colored ones are curiosities because they represent the few simple, tasteful, pretty cards to be found amongst the thousands of ugly ones on sale in the stores of this much-stocked but not well-stocked town, and of which the uncolored ones are curiosities because they are such clever imitations (?) of etchings. I liked the latter because they are out of the usual run, and the former because they are moderately pretty. Sometimes I wish that I could draw or paint, for I (like everybody else of any imagination, I suppose) often construct pictures in my fancy which seem to me worth keeping, if they *could* be kept—pictures wh. can't be constructed out of words, being too delicate for the rude tools of language. It's sad to think what the world has lost by my not being an artist, is'nt it? My artistic leanings must be the explanation of my falling in love with you!—must'nt they? I never thought of that explanation before—principally, I suppose, because I have been content with the simpler explanation, that you are the sweetest, most lovable little woman in the world, and I am afraid that this new theory can't face the violent probability than [*sic*] you would have stolen my heart just as easily, had you never seen a pencil, a crayon, a brush, or a palette. Still this fact remains, that I can take as much interest as you could desire in your favourite pursuits. I could, indeed, love anything that you love, simply because you love it; but in this case that may serve as an *additional* reason.

But I must not write any more to-day. I've indulged myself already to the full length of my conscience-rope.

Give my love to all—especially, however, to your father and your dear Aunt Ella. As for yourself, *I love you with all my heart*— that is the simplest and best expression I can command of the fact that in every thought of my life I am

Your own   Woodrow

ALS (WC, NjP).

From Ellen Louise Axson

My dearest Woodrow,   Savannah Dec. 22/83.

I must admit that it really is a shame for me to continue so persistantly *seeming* to put wrong constructions on your questions —giving you all the unnecessary trouble of self-defence. Though if you make your protest itself so charming, I may be tempted to betray you into another. No, I really did *not* think you a doubter at all. I was not quite so stupid as not to see through your little game of "manufacturing provocations"!—preparing *openings* for renewed expressions of my sentiments! I simply meant to avail myself of the excellent opportunity offered me. Yet I am not surprised that my letters puzzle you—it is an old trick of mine, and a very crazy one, to fly from jest to earnest and back again in a most unexpected, inconsequential fashion; so that not even the most nimble wit could be expected to follow a course so eratic. I have been trying to recall what I said—being *myself* puzzled to know how you happened to misunderstand *me*—and if I mistake not, the explanation may be found just there—I *began* to answer in the same tone as yourself, but having indulged in a flash of seriousness you naturally thought me through-out in desperate earnest. I am only surprised that you ever manage to make anything out of my nonsense without the natural interpreters of voice or smile. Ah well, letters are at best a most lame and impotent substitute for something better—yet don't imagine, dearest, that I will miss your meaning.

> "I promise by true love
> And perfect friendship, by all trust that comes
> Of understanding, that I will not fail,
> No, nor delay to find it."[1]

I wont fail to give your message to Carrie Belle—she is still deeply smitten. By the way, you would find it hard to guess what the little folks are busied about, at present. They have been all seated around their low table, here in my room, drawing *tombstones*!—tombstones of every shape and size;—shade of Tommy Traddles,[2] with all your attendant train of skeletons, arise and look! you have found worthy successors! Randolph having begun to "take lessons," and proving himself a very promising pupil, the little ones are, of course, inspired to do likewise. I presume the agony will abate in a few days, but at present I "keep school" all day with an evening supplement—there is scarcely a moment when someone is'nt calling "Cousin Ellie, do this top!" or Cousin Nell, "fix this grass," or "write this 'scription" or "Cousin Ellie, make my *grave*! I tant do it."

The old "scrape of that sort" was simply a correspondence "purely platonic" at first, but which did'nt so continue, on one side, and which accordingly ended uncomfortably. But I *must not* write longer this morning, for "Christmas is coming," and I must go to meet him!

The hat-band I enclose is *by no means* intended to displace Miss Katie's—that would indeed be a poor exchange. But that was sent to adorn "your new summer hat," and you now feel doubtless a great and imperitive need of one for your *new winter* hat!

With best wishes for a "Merry Christmas" and with a heart full of love believe me darling

Your own   Ellie.

Excuse haste.

ALS (WP, DLC).
[1] Jean Ingelow, "Friendship," in *Songs with Preludes.*
[2] A character in Dickens' *David Copperfield.*

To Ellen Louise Axson

My own darling,   Baltimore, Md., Christmas Eve., 1883

I am more and more convinced that you are the sweetest and most sensible little woman in the world! It was the truest of instincts that told you that I would value most as a gift from you something made with your own hands. What would I not have given to be able to send you something that I had made myself rather than a gift such as anybody else could have *bought*! Besides, my darling, this hat-band is exquisitely beautiful—prettier than any other I ever saw—so that it has a double value. You would have had a good laugh at me if you could have seen me, just before dinner, struggling with thread and needle, and with fingers that were all stiffer, bigger thumbs than usual, to fasten the band in my hat. Being anxious to make the delicate adjustment in the best manner possible, I of course suffered special tribulation in overcoming the many difficulties of the unaccustomed operation. I must say, however, that I had famous success after all, if the black (!) thread *did* show a little!

Your confession and repentance for having so *puzzled* me by apparent misconstructions of certain questions in my letters were very sweet, my darling. They give me occasion to explain the rather comical quandary which made my perplexity real. Just after reaching Baltimore, as you know, I wrote to my sister, Marion, in Arkansas, telling her of our engagement. In her reply she declared that my letter had delighted her because I wrote again like my old self (whom I had been writing like in the indefinite meantime, she did not say) and that she was going to write to you to thank you for having made me so happy.[1] I immediately despatched a playful protest; assuring her that in my secret heart I quite agreed with her, that you *had* done a most kind and charitable thing in accepting such a fellow, but that I *did'nt* think that to *thank* you for having done the family so signal a favour would come quite gracefully from her. Besides, was it quite politic to tell you that you deserved *credit* for this act of indulgence? I wouldn't have had her "give me away"! Imagine my astonishment when a subsequent letter from the (not usually so) matter-of-fact little lady disclosed the bewildering truth that she had taken my protest *in earnest* and was hastening to explain![2] Do you wonder that I began to distrust my own sentences and to suspect them of conveying to you, as well as to her, meanings just the opposite of those I had intended them to bear? You see, it was *myself* I was beginning to be puzzled by, rather [than by ?] my darling. I was beginning to wonder (as I wrote sister) whether I had lost the trick I once possessed of giving a joke the walk and mien and complexion of a joke and should be obliged hereafter to *label* my pleasantries. You *have* an odd trick of half-serious jesting that makes a fellow sometimes stop and think; but I don't think that I should ever have been really puzzled by it, if I had not had sufficient cause for suspecting myself of being an awkward blunderer at expressing myself and for fearing that I *had* written some sentence which had pained you by wearing a dress of meaning which it had stolen from my dull brain, not borrowed from my heart. I'm greatly relieved to find that it was not so! I should'nt like to have to guard the expressions of my pen when writing to you: so that your assurances bring me out from the embarrassment of what, I must confess, was quite a joke on myself.

Christmas morning.

My writing was interrupted last evening by a visit from a fellow student who is also a fellow-sufferer in being practically banished from home for the holidays. If the truth must be told, we both confessed to feeling very lonely last night, because Christmas is essentially a season of *family* festivities and, no matter if the town were full of one's friends, one would'nt feel at liberty to seek them out during the holidays because he would feel as if he were intruding upon family circles to whose pleasures the season is sacred. So we comforted and laughed at each other until by the time the evening was over we were ready to go to bed prepared for very pleasant dreams. It was some time before any dreams at all came to me, however, because I could'nt go to sleep for thinking of and wishing for you.

To-day I've been re-reading *all* your letters, from the very beginning, as a special Christmas feast, in order to keep off a return of my lonliness. Your first letters recall some curious reminiscences of the contents of *my* first epistles to you. I remember now that I told you long ago, long before I told you that I loved you, why you were an exceptional young lady—just such a one as I had often dreamed of and longed to meet but had despaired of finding—just the sort (though I did not tell you *this* then) to make the most helpful of wives for a peculiar mortal like myself. Do'nt you remember that you laughingly replied that there were some men almost clever enough to make something out of nothing? But I was not inventing. Every day, as it seems to me, brings fresh proof that I was right. Shall I tell you what sort of wife I am going to get? I will; giving you fair warning that if you undertake to plead "not guilty," I'll skip the passage in your letter that contains the plea. A single sentence may be made to contain the picture: A little lady of rare lovliness and grace, giving to her husband a wealth of pure love; entering into his intellectural labours with keen sympathy and appreciation; beguiling his lighter moments with "a voice of gladness and a smile and eloquence of beauty," and strengthening his graver moods by a womanly love of wisdom; turning with eager enjoyment to the music and the greater thoughts of poetry, refined by her love and mastery of art, but greatest in feminine charms and in tender, wifely affection—such shall be my wife. Do you like the picture, my darling? If you are still inclined to demur to sitting for such "fancy pictures," remember that I think you such, and that not all a life time can bring disproof to *me*. I should'nt love you if you were perfect; but I love you altogether *as you are*, and *for me* you will be a *perfect wife*!

I am looking forward to a great treat in near prospect. On Thursday evening I am to see Henry Irving and Miss Terry in *Hamlet*. Of course my curiosity is on tip-toe about this greatest of living Eng. actors. Seeing him will be my Christmas indulgence. What would I not give to have you with me! You know I am deeply interested in the drama; and am thinking seriously of arising as the American Shakspere—good plan!—do'nt you think so?

In return for that beautiful hat-band—which is more valuable in my eyes than anything else I own—imagine yourself kissed a score of—but no! do'nt do anything of the kind! I'll keep the kisses to give you when I see you. I'll not care how much in arrears I am in such payment next summer!

With much love to yr. dear father, your sweet Aunt Ella, and the rest, and "more than tongue can ever tell" for your precious self,   Your own   Woodrow.

ALS (WC, NjP).
    [1] Marion W. Kennedy to WW, Nov. 2, 1883.
    [2] Marion W. Kennedy to WW, Dec. 5, 1883, ALS (WP, DLC) with WWhw notation on env.: "Ans. Dec. 15/83."

Two Letters from Ellen Louise Axson

Savannah Dec. 25/83.

Many, *many* thanks my darling, for your *beautiful* present. I *can't tell* you how lovely I think it, or how much I appreciate it. No, I did not feel the slightest disposition to laugh at its "unportable size";—I think you showed remarkably fine taste in its selection; and, as you can well imagine, I shall prize it, all my life long, as one of my chief treasures; both for the associations, and for its own sake—for I think it really one of the most *exquisitely* beautiful things I ever saw by "a modern master." As for the wonderful "resemblance," I wont "aggravate" you by saying anything on that point—but I only wish I *was* like this girl. We had a grand excitement over the box, by the way,—I suppose you did'nt know that it was directed to "Miss *Belle* Axon 143 Broad St."! Aunt Ella told the man that there was no such person in the house, and tried to make him take it back; but he would'nt do it; and we told her

it must be meant for Carrie Belle! Then there were great speculations as to whether Mrs. Green could have sent her something—
someone in *Baltimore*! who *could* it be? very mysterious! At last,
when Uncle R. came home, they decided to open it; but having
gotten the cover half off, and perceiving it to be a handsome picture, their courage failed them again. It *could'nt* be meant for
Carrie, there must be some mistake, they would send it back to
the office. But I, in the meantime, had caught sight of two heads,
one with "averted face and downcast eyes," the other with "eager
questioning gaze," so I begged them to let us see what it was, at
least. Whereupon they, examining my face more closely, and
finding it very suspicious, exclaimed that they believed I was a
"hypocrite" and that I had known about it all along[.] "No," I said
"I hadn't; and I was'nt sure that I I [*sic*] knew now; if it was named
"Checkmated" I did, if it wasn't, I didnt"! ! "Checkmated" it proved
to be, and I laid claim to it, though until your letter came, following hard upon it yesterday, it was a disputed claim. They insisted
that I must tell *what* I knew about it, and as I refused to do that,
they declared that I had by no means demonstrated my right to
Miss Belle Axson's property.

Your delightful letters of the 21st & 22nd were both received
yesterday, also the Xmas cards; you have my *best* and most appreciative thanks for *all*; those little etchings are *charming*, and
Marcus Stone is, as ever, the prince of artists in the card-painting
line. What a curiosity the Whistler catalogue is! Does that man
ever do *anything* like anybody else! I suppose not, certainly the
man who calls his mother's portrait "an arrangement in black and
gray"! can claim originallity, if nothing else. I am surprised that
these latest achievements hav'nt tempted Mr. Ruskin to fall upon
him again; but I suppose he considers him now fallen beneath
his notice.

I was *so* sorry to hear of Miss Mayrant's trouble. It is indeed a
pitifully sad case. Is she the only child; whom will she be "dependent" upon?

I am glad that you are not obliged to study so hard for the
present;—but you must work with a rush while you are about it,
to dispose so rapidly of that mountainous task. I hope now you will
enjoy the holidays after all, with your good friends, the Woods,
and the rest. It can't be otherwise than merry with us, in this
housefull of children. I think Christmas, like every other anniversary, is apt to be a sad rather than a happy time to "grown-up"
people. It suggests too much retrospection, and makes contrasts too
vivid; but fortunately there is one unfailing remedy, viz., to look

at it through the children's eyes, and fortunately too I have always had that remedy at hand.

I too would like to write you a "Christmas letter," but that is hardly possible on Xmas day with Bedlam let loose and ranging at will in every nook and corner of the house; especially when the Bedlamites are clamouring for one to join tea-parties gotten up in honour of new arrivals in the doll community, or to take part in still wilder dissipations; and when certain savages—wild men of the woods—are making violent onslaughts on one every few minutes. To be accurate, I believe they say they are Chinamen, "Sing Lee" and "Sing Song" by name; though those soft, gentle, quiet Orientals would certainly never recognize them as belonging to their race.

But I must close or I will not get this into the usual Tuesday's mail—I was too busy dressing dolls and filling stockings to write last night—I have just received *beautiful* cards from your mother and your sister Annie, and one from your sister Marion on Sat. It was so sweet and kind in them. Please give my love to them all. You should see the remarkable "card" (?) I have just received from Mr. Thornwell, a most elaborate affair in a big box—and simply excruciating. Poor soul, he don't seem to have much confidence in his own taste, for he sends rather a pathetic note with it; "whether the card is pretty or not it's sent with the best wishes of your friend." I have also a lovely one from Marion Bones. Do you ever hear anything from them? I know nothing. Papa had a letter from Mr. Bones sometime ago, but I suppose it was "business," for when I asked him what was in it, he said, "nothing, except that he loved me as one of his own daughters."

But I really must close. I wish that yours may be a *merry* Xmas, and something *more* than merry.

> ["]Before all merriment and glee,
> Dear friend, I wish *hearts-ease* for thee,
> That *peace* which none can take away—
> Be thy rich gift, this Christmas day."

I too love you *"with all my heart,"*—and I find it is a much bigger heart than I ever imagined.

With love to you and yours, believe me darling,

Yours forever   Ellie.

My darling Woodrow   Savannah, Dec. 26/83.
    I find that there are no mails sent from Sav. on Xmas day;—the

post-office department takes holiday as well as every one else, and the boxes are not emptied at all; so that the letter which I dropped in yesterday will not reach you at the usual time—am sorry, but it can't be helped. As that letter does'nt leave until this afternoon, it is sheer "self-indulgence" to write again now; yet I *must* send you a few lines to wish you many happy returns of your natal day; following the little box which was forwarded this morning, and which I hope will duly reach you on that day.

You will perceive that it would hardly "do" for me to laugh at the "incongruity" of sending bulky articles to "nomads," when at the very moment of your box's arrival, I was at my easel preparing to do an exactly similar thing. Yet this isn't so very large, after all. I dare say it will slip into your trunk, even though, not being a woman, you probably don't boast of a "Saratoga." At any rate I *wanted* to send it, and I am beginning to protest in thought, as in *deed*, I have always sufficiently protested, against the impression with which I grew up, that it is *always* wrong to do what one *wants* to do. I only wish *protesting* would destroy the impression itself; then perhaps I would'nt torment myself as much as I do. But I digress. I was going to say that you would probably find many other things about the contents of this box more laughable than it's size;—and in case you should feel duty bound to say you *like* it, —remember I absolve you from any such obligation. They have all, except Aunt E., been making fun of it here—saying it looks "*mad*" &c.; I tell them it would sound better to say it looked "*wistful*" or to talk about "*pathos*," and the like! And now, dearest, once again I wish you many happy birthdays;—and what other wish shall I add;—

> "I wish your store of good
> May leave you poor of wishes;
> And I wish—no more.["]¹

With many loving thoughts turning to you on this day, your birthday, and *all* days, believe me, my darling,

Yours with all my heart   Ellie.

I had another birthday book given me the other day—a Shakespeare. What do you suppose was your motto in it—"Poor Tom's a-cold"! Another coincidence! I wonder what principal of selection is followed in the getting up of these books.

But the other quotation, under the same date does a little better, "So we'll live, and pray, and sing, and tell old tales."

ALS (WP, DLC) with WWhw notation on env. of ELA's letter of Dec. 26: "2 Letters: *Dec. 25 and 26*."

1 Paraphrased from Richard Crashaw's "Wishes to his (supposed) Mistresse," in *The Delights of the Muses*:

> "I wish, her store
> "Of worth, may leave her poore
> "Of wishes; And I wish—No more."

Three Letters to Ellen Louise Axson

My own darling,   Balto., Dec 28/83

You are a truly wonderful little woman, to keep a secret so well! Not a word, even in the sweet letter that came this morning, about the beautiful birthday present that surprised and delighted me by its unexpected coming just now! It is more than beautiful, my darling, because it contains, in speaking counterfeit, a face upon which it does one good to look long and often. There's real education and a very pure pleasure in dwelling on its lovely, wide-eyed childish innocence, its thoughtful, unconscious, wondering gaze. It seems a face made for gleeful laughter, to which only a momentary pause of sweet, brooding repose has come. But, above all, it is of your drawing, and *that* makes it, in my eyes, better worth having than all the works of all the "old masters." I shall show it to my friends as an exquisite piece of drawing, but shall prize it myself as *your* drawing and as a token of your love. Ah, my sweet Ellie, you can't know how precious that love is to me: but you can know that I am not sending merely formal thanks for your splendid gift when I say that I am made happier by its possession, and by the possession of a band for "my new winter hat," than by any—than I can tell.

I had my misgivings about the direction on the box containing "Checkmated," for when I went down to see if it had been shipped when and as I had ordered, I was shown the Express Company's receipt and noticed that it was for a box directed to "Miss Belle Axon." I said to the suave picture dealer that I hoped that that did not indicate a corresponding misdirection on the box, intimating that it would be inexcusable stupidity in him if it did, since I had given him the name and address in as plain characters as I could write. "Oh no! It was the hurried, careless copying of the hard-pressed Express clerk: my memorandum had been exactly followed in addressing the box!" Seeing that it reached you all right anyhow, I wont go and break his head for a mistake which caused only amusement and gave no serious trouble!

I am delighted, my love, that the picture pleases you so well: as for the resemblance between yourself and the girl who is so completely checkmated, I should like to take the testimony of other witnesses. Has *no* one else remarked it? It would be not a little curious that I should have been at once struck by a resemblance for which I was not looking, if no one else can discover any traces of it: so I shall expect you to report all testimony on the subject, that I may know whether or not my constant thoughts of you have "struck in" and affected my vision. Mayhap I need stronger glasses!

Well, I had my treat last night. I saw Irving and Miss Terry in Hamlet; and I'm sure it will be many a long day before I see such acting again. Never have I seen anything more perfect or more touching, more exquisitely natural and pitiful, than Miss Terry's simulation of madness in the fourth act. It simply and literally beggars description. As for Irving, his acting is characterized by great ups and downs. His voice, for one thing, though wonderfully fine in the expression of deep or violent emotion, is quite incapable of the lighter and easier tones. It is fair to say that his Hamlet is not so *uniformly* fine as Booth's; but, on the other hand, his acting rises, in certain scenes, to a pitch of grandeur such as Booth has never reached, such as, probably, he cannot reach. Irving was unsurpassably great, for instance, in the scene in which the mock play is enacted. It was, as far as his acting was concerned, the crowning scene of all. When the play began he was lying at Ophelia's feet away from and opposite the throne, his intense eyes fixed upon the features of the King; but as the players proceeded, and the significant plot of the play approached its climax, he slowly slid, with the movement and the glare of a serpent, towards the royal seat till he lay at the foot of the throne: whence he rose and with indescribable accents of hate hissed his explanation of the play into the King's guilt-blanched face. The King in terror calls for lights, the company breaks up in questioning consternation, and Hamlet remains standing on the steps of the throne, celebrating his triumph with maniacal laughter! I ne'er shall see the like again! Oh, that you could have seen it!

It's absurd for me to try to describe such a scene; but the fact that I have attempted it may serve to show how powerfully I was affected by it. Miss Terry, with her sweet face and wonderful acting, quite won my heart—but only my *audience*, my dramatic, heart, not the one that belongs to you!

This is a pretty serious business, this thing of growing older: is'nt it? To think that this is my *twenty-seventh* birthday! It's well it's no worse. The season of preparation has been long, and will yet last a little while; but there's still time, God willing, to do some good, honest, hard work in wh. the accumulated momentum of the time past may be made to tell. I am sometimes a little startled and out of countenance when I think how small a proportion my achievements bear to my years; but that's a very idle and unprofitable way of looking at the facts. It should be left for silly women in their dotage to live in the past. Steady resolution, slow and sure of its resources, is worth all the regrets that were ever wasted; and if I, with sound mind, strong health, backed by the devoted love and confidence of my family and of many friends, *and promised a wedding with you*, were to suffer regrets to drive out hopeful determination, I'd deserve to be kicked and deserted! Anniversaries *do* often bring sadness, as you say; and not all sadness is without benefit; but no occasion ought to be suffered to bring despondency. My conscience, therefore, is void of offence to-day, because my spirits are as light and my courage as strong as ever they were in my life. I'm in full sympathy with the day, which is glorious with sunlight. I remember suffering from rather low spirits on my twenty-sixth birthday; but not so now. I wonder what makes the difference? It must be that something has happened in the meantime wh. has altered my views of things. Doubtless my summer in the North Carolina mountains braced my constitution, and so bettered my mind! It's wonderful what good may be found in the mountains!

But I must stop for to-day and go sing with the Glee Club, as I've promised. Kiss Carrie Belle for the quaint, pretty card she sent me; give my love to your father, your grandparents, your dear Aunt Ella, and the rest; and accept for yourself once more, on this anniversary which is in some sort my own, the vows of my increasing and unfailing love.

Your own   Woodrow.

My own darling   Balto., Md., Dec. 29th/83
I must write just a note this morning in answer to yours which has just reached me. Your letter of Xmas day did come at once and by due course of mail, after all, getting here twenty-four hours ahead of the note written on the 26th[.] The P.O. authorities in Savannah must have known how anxiously my heart was expecting that letter, and made an exception in its favour

I've had a good laugh over the contents of your note: first because there is, as it suggests, a sort of poetic propriety in our keeping each other in countenance by exchanging, unwittingly, gifts of a similar character; and second because you give me leave to laugh, not at the note, but at the *picture*! I'm so glad to find that somebody besides myself lacks confidence in their own powers for doing well their own peculiar work. I only hope that you may find my careful compositions, when you come to read them, as fine as I think this drawing of yours beautiful! Then we can comfort each other: for I invariably regard my own writings as simply *execrable*. I wont *re*-estimate your picture from the new stand-point of your note, because I've already given my candid opinion about it and do'nt find it possible to see it in this new light. It is simply lovely! You must have known how I delight to study a beautiful child's face. By dwelling on such a face I seem to be able to get an inspiration of innocence and of purity of thought, to recover such a child-likeness as is a preparation for the kingdom of heaven.

"Poor Tom's a-cold!" Alas, what a coincidence! But what follows redeems it. For when my birthdays are crowned with the supreme happiness which your presence will bring, "we'll live, and pray, and sing, and tell old tales." That's not a bad programe, if the "old tales" be made to stand for unpedantic learning, the living for its *full* meaning, the praying for a true trust in God, and the singing for hope and light-hearted courage! It will be worth while to live that way

My creed, my darling, is that it's never wrong to do what one wants to do, so the "wants" be grounded in pure motives: and certainly you have—or, at any rate, I have—every reason to be glad that you did what you wanted to do in regard to my birthday gift.

Your love has made this natal day just past the happiest of my life: and that same love will make the birthdays (both yours and mine, I trust) that are to come happier still.

Yours with unspeakable love   Woodrow.

My precious Ellie,   Baltimore, Md., Dec. 30th/83
What's the use of a vacation, if a fellow can't use it to write to his sweetheart as often as he likes? He can't help thinking of her, and to think of her is to long to talk to her and tell her how much he loves her. True, when it comes to trying to tell her, he finds that he can't, that his heart is immensely bigger than his vocabulary; but there's much satisfaction in trying, and the results of a great many endeavours may *sum up* to something near the whole truth. Then, too, letters are exceedingly "lame and impotent" substitutes for "something better," as we've both found out; but they are so much better than nothing (especially when they are like your letters) that they are a delightful resource, after all. Sometimes, when I take the "spectator attitude" (as I too am in the habit of doing), I am moved to reason with myself, as thus:

Alter Ego: Now, Woodrow, look here! It seems to me that you ought to be ashamed of yourself for being so unceasingly and outrageously impatient to see your sweetheart. I know that she is the sweetest and most lovable little woman in the world, and I would'nt blame any man for being half wild to see her, especially if he were sure of a loving reception from her; but you ought to be reasonable about it. Why, you go on as if it were a great grievance that the Johns Hopkins is not in Savannah; as if you did'nt already have a great deal more than you deserve, in the possession of her love and the promise of her hand. I make all due allowance for the fact that, even if you have a cold and solomn visage, you have ardent passions; but you ought not to let them get the better of you. I say it is'nt *reasonable*; you don't show a proper thankfulness and submission.

Woodrow: Well, that's all very sensible; but it's too sublime! Just reflect upon the circumstances of the case! Don't you remember that I had to hurry off to this delectable institution within ten minutes after hearing her first confession of love, before my dazed senses had come out of the tumult of those first confused emotions and allowed me to realize what had happened; that I had to leave her at the very moment that I was admitted to the privileges of an accepted lover? Oddsfish! man! I should'nt be human if I did'nt chafe against having to wait six months for "something better" than present circumstances permit! A fellow can't help listening to his heart; and when I listen to mine, I'm quite sure that I would give more for one hour of her presence, for a single opportunity to hear her sweet voice and see the lovelight in her eyes, for but one touch of her lips, than for all the knowledge stored in all the books!

Alter Ego: All right! go your own way: I see it's no use arguing with you. I don't blame you, old man! but you're liable to make a considerable goose of yourself, if you don't moderate your pace a little! If she do'nt keep you in countenance, you'll cut rather an awkward figure, I fear. Fortunately, she is the only witness, besides myself, of your carryings-on, and if you can gain her indulgence, I wont give you away.   [*Exeunt severally*

I did'nt tell you of my little adventure of a week ago, did I? There hung above my fire-place, until just seven days ago, a long, old-fashioned, time-stained mirror—an heir-loom in the Turnbull family, and therefore valued in spite of its ugliness—which, as I sat opposite it writing some Christmas letters to the dear sisters and home-folks, was moved, either by excitement at the approach of Christmas or by the rotting of the cord by which it hung, first to settle suddenly down on the ledge above the fire-place (for there is no mantel-piece) and then to bow its tall head over towards your humble servant—in short to fall and be shivered to fragments. I saw it coming in time to save myself and my writing table from annihilation, but not in season to save it from its fall. As you may imagine, my nerves were almost as much shattered, for the time being, as the glass itself by the sudden and startling catastrophe, and it was some time before I added my intercepted signature to my just-finished letter. I miss the old mirror: it filled so much wall space; but its fall was opportune, for there was no other place in my little den that would have accommodated the picture you sent me.

If my delight in it is sufficient reward, you are fully repaid, my darling, for the labour spent on that picture. The more I look at it the better I like it. It seems to grow more beautiful every day. I would give anything for the companionship of a child the living counterpart of this one in the picture. The drawing is *exquisitely* done, my love! Though I'm no connoisseur, I'm quite sure that I know fine drawing when I see it; thus presenting a sort of parallel to the case of a certain remarkable man in the West. It is credibly reported that a man has been found in Arizona who can tell the truth: He was'nt found telling it, but can tell it when he hears it.

Having spoken of mirrors, I am reminded of the chief service of mirrors to men—to reflect their lathered faces when they are in the agonies of shaving—and that one of your letters came near being the occasion of my cutting my throat. I was just about half through shaving when the servant brought up the just-delivered letter, and I was so eager to get through and read what my love had to say that the marks of hasty shaving have scarcely left my throat yet, for all the week that has passed! I must take care not to shave again at the hour at which the postman is due!

But there's a question I should answer—about Miss Katie Mayrant. She is not the only child. She has a younger brother who is smart and means well, but has very little genius for success, and who will, with his sister be left dependent on their aunt, Mrs. Boylston, with whom I boarded in Atlanta. It is indeed a sad, sad case. I remember, in this connection, that you some time ago fell into an historical error in saying that I had gone several hundred miles to see Miss Katie. Aiken lay only eight or ten miles off my most direct route from Atlanta to Wilmington.

You asked me another (*post-scriptural*) question concerning the tale connected with the slip of your foot in crossing the stream at the pic-nic grounds; but I must beg permission to post-pone the answer until next Summer; because the tale is too long for a letter—and too thin.

Much love to all, a kiss for Carrie Belle (I'll repay, with interest, the kisses you expend for me) and for yourself the unbounded love of

Your own   Woodrow.

ALS (WC, NjP).

From Ellen Louise Axson

My darling Woodrow,   Savannah Dec. 31/83.

Alas, alas, what has become of this evening—it has certainly passed by, but I don't know whither it went;—here is Papa already making remarks about "bed-time," and my letter not begun,—and I shan't have a moment tomorrow morning either. But I have taken no note of time, so greatly perturbed have I been over a most unwelcome holiday present just received; and I have managed to waste most of the evening examining it and lamenting over it, vowing that I would send it back, being convinced by my counsellor in chief, Aunt Ella, that it "would never do," and finally writing my most hypocritical and unthankful note of thanks. I am a perfect fraud, and I feel as mean as possible. It is Dorés Dante—the "Purgatory," and "Paridise"; he sent me the "Inferno" last Xmas, and I hadn't any such terrible compunctions then. But this is receiving presents under false pretences, decidedly.

Your letters of the 28 & 29 were both received this morning;— am very glad and a good deal surprised to hear that you liked the little picture so much, for they did abuse it outrageously here. Grandmother really did'nt like it because it was an Italian, was named "Piccola," and "looked so foreign." But the others are terrible teases, and it is possible were merely practising their arts on me. You should see how Uncle Randolph treats me at the table; I continually threaten to desert him and seek protection between the babies at the other end;—he thinks it a standing shame—a perfect outrage—that I neglect the beef as I do, seeing it comes from "Baltimore";—*that*, as a small specimen of his style of conversation!

But I am surprised to find that "somebody beside myself" is in the habit of finding everything they do "simply execrable"! The riddle is to know whence comes the delight in work, which urges one on, in spite of that supreme disgust, and in spite of the knowledge that the result *must* be "but the pitifullest infinitesimal fraction of a product."

Before I leave the subject of pictures I must answer your question as to that "resemblance." Not a single member of the family observed it, oh thou gifted being, with the grand imagination! I must admit however that the only outsider who has seen it,—for I assure you I was'nt generous enough to leave it down stairs for the benefit of the public,—Mrs. Hammond, startled me with the information that "the girl in your picture is strikingly like yourself." After that the family discussed the matter, and some were of the opinion that there *was* a certain resemblance, while others thought the idea "absurd."

I am in a state of the greatest excitement at present,—hot and cold by turns, as the scales dip one way or another,—over the possible arrival of another girl that looks like me—presumably,—my oldest and most tenderly-loved girl friend, Rosalie Anderson. Her two sisters are living here now, and the three of us together hope to prove a magnet strong enough to draw her away from "Mac." But I fear it is "too good to come true." I have been with Janie for a day or so past attempting the impossible, and I fear somewhat thankless task of consoling her for the departure of Mr. Chandler.

By-the-way, you have excited my curiosity to know what you do think of that individual. What meaneth that carefully reserved opinion, and those second-hand compliments? I hope you don't intend to "damn with faint praise." I won't express any opinion either, for it would hardly be fair when I scarcely heard him open his lips. I don't know what was the trouble. He did'nt impress me as being shy; indeed I fancied he could go to the other extreme upon occasion, and I also fancy he has an excellent opinion of himself; but some dumb spirit had seized him that day; he volunteered only one—no, *two* remarks—simply sat there, and looked handsome. By-the way, which one did you meet? Murphy—a lawyer—very ugly? or *Sam*—rail-road man—rather handsome? this is "Sam."

We are all very much interested in a wedding which is about to take place in the Chandler family. The groom is an uncle of this Mr. C.,—the young lawyer who, as you may remember, was so terribly mutilated by falling from the train, last spring. He was engaged at the time of the accident to a girl in Fla.,—had only known her seven weeks by-the-way,—had been engaged four of them. What a queer old world this is! how curiously yet inextricably, the terrible, the ludicrous, the pathetic are sometimes intermingled—it *is* a joke, though a strangely ghastly one, that this poor young fellow, who it seems was sensitive about his size, should have had himself made several inches taller than before, and his *new* feet made smaller than the old ones!

How splendid Irving and Miss Terry must have been! Am so glad you saw them. "Oh that I could have been them" indeed; but perhaps it is just as well, for I might have lost my senses. 'Tis odd that I should have so little desire to see most plays, yet should be so perfectly *wild* to see some of Shakspere's.

But I really must not chatter any longer, on this solemn occasion

> "Toll ye the church bell sad and slow
> And tread softly, and speak low,
> For the old year lies a-dying"!

I wont stay to be one of the watchers, but will say "good-night" at once to you and this dear old friend; for he *has* been very kind to me,—

> "He gave me a friend and a true true love."

By-the-way, that is an unlucky quotation! is it not? You remember what follows? In good truth, my darling, small fear have I of what is to follow; you have inspired me with a great trust in yourself, and in the years.

> "I love you with the passion put to use in my old griefs,
> and with my *childhood's faith*."

Much love to all your family. Papa and the rest send love. Wishing you once again, many happy New Years, believe me, dearest,
>   Yours with all my heart,   Ellie.

No sir, *decidedly* I *won't*, because I *can't*, imagine "a score of kisses"! Who ever heard of such a thing! Really this is the most impudent youth I ever encountered! There is a[n] old saying about "inches" and "ells" which just fits him. I wonder if he thinks I've no principles because when people are going away, "it may be for years, & it may be forever," they—he—I mean she thought— that is, she did'nt—oh dear, we'll change the subject—Good-night.

ALS (WP, DLC).

A Political Essay

>   [c. Jan. 1, 1884]

Committee or Cabinet Government?

"The only conceivable basis for government in the New World is the national will; and the political problem of the New World is how to build a strong, stable, enlightened, and impartial government on that foundation."—Goldwin Smith.

"A humorist of our own day has laughed at Parliaments as 'talking shops,' and the laugh has been echoed by some who have taken humour for argument. But talk is persuasion, and persuasion is force; and the one force which can sway free men to deeds such as those which have made England what she is."
—J. R. Green.

The House of Representatives is a superlatively noisy assembly. Other legislative bodies are noisy, but not with the noise of the House of Representatives. We are told that the slightest cause of excitement will set the French National Assembly frantically agog; that the English House of Commons is often loud voiced in its disorderly demonstrations; and that even our stolid cousins, the Germans, do not always refrain from guttural clamor when in Reichstag assembled. Our own House of Representatives, however, indulges in a confusion peculiar to itself. Probably the representatives themselves soon become accustomed to the turmoil in which they are daily constrained to live, and are seldom heedful of the extreme disorder which prevails about them; but a visitor to the House of Representatives experiences upon entering its galleries for the first time sensations which it is not easy to define or to describe.

The hall of the House is large beyond the expectation of the visitor. For each of the three hundred and twenty-five Representatives there is provided a roomy desk, and an easy, revolving chair —a chair about which there is space ample enough for the stretching of tired legislative legs in any position of restful extension that may suit the comfort of the moment. The desks and seats stand around the Speaker's chair in a great semi-circle, ranged in rows which radiate from that seat of authority as a center. Here and there a broad aisle runs between two rows of seats, from the circumference of the semi-circle to the roomy spaces about the Clerk's and Speaker's desks. Outside the seats, and beyond the bar which surrounds them, are other broad, soft-carpeted spaces; and still there is room, beyond these again, for deep galleries to extend on every side their tiers of benches, before the limiting walls of the vast hall are reached. Overhead, framed by the polished beams which support them, are great squares of ground glass, through which a strong light falls on the voting and vociferating magnates below.

One would suppose that it would require a great deal of noise to fill that great room. Filled it is, though, during the sittings of the House. It is not the noises of debate, but the incessant and full-volumed hum of conversation, and the sharp clapping of hands that strikes the ear. The clapping of hands is not sustained and concerted, but desultory, like a dropping fire of musketry; for these gentlemen in their easy chairs are not applauding any one—they are only striking their palms together as a signal-call to the young pages who act as messengers and errand-boys, and who add the confusion of movement to the confusion of sound, as they run hither and thither about the hall. Members, too, stroll about, making friendly visits to the desks of acquaintances, or holding informal consultations with friends and colleagues. When in their seats, they seem engrossed in assorting documents, in writing letters, or in reading newspapers, whose stiff rattle adds variety to the prevailing disorder.

Some business is evidently going on the while; though the on-looker in the gallery must needs give his closest attention in order to ascertain just what is being done. Now and again a member rises and addresses the chair, but his loudest tones scarcely reach the galleries in the form of articulate speech; and the responsive rulings of the speaker are not so distinctly audible as are the ineffectual rappings of his restless gavel. Naturally, therefore, very few members try to speak. They do not covet an opportunity to do so, in a hall which none but the clearest and strongest voice could fill, even if the silence of attention were vouchsafed. However frequent one's visits to the capitol, he will seldom find the House engaged in debate. When some member, more daring, more determined, more hardy, or more confident than the rest, does essay to address the House, he generally finds that it will not listen, and that he must content himself with such audience as is given him by those in his immediate neighborhood, who are so near him that they cannot easily escape listening. His most strenuous efforts will not avail to make members in distant seats conscious that he is on the floor. They are either indifferent to what he is saying, or prefer to read it in the "Record" tomorrow.

This, then, is seemingly a most singular assembly. It seldom engages in lengthy debate, being apparently content to leave that dignified and generally unexciting exercise to the Senate; whose hall is, because of its smaller size, better suited for such employments, and where greater decorum prevails. It would be a mistake, however, to conclude that the careless manners of the House betoken idleness. Its sessions are, on the contrary, generally quite busy. It has been known to pass thirty-seven pensions bills at one sitting. The chief end of its rules is expedition in business, and such wholesale legislation is, accordingly, not only possible but usual; for, be it remembered, the House does not have to digest its schemes of legislation. It has Standing Committees which do its digesting for it. It deliberates in fragments, through small sections of its membership, and when it comes together as a whole, votes upon the bills laid before it by these authoritative Committees, with scant measure of talk.

It is this plan of entrusting itself to the guidance of various small bodies of its members that distinguishes our House of Representatives from the other great legislative bodies of the world. It is not peculiar in being omnipotent in all national affairs; the Commons of England and the Assembly of France are equally omnipotent; but it is peculiar in being awkward at exercising its omnipotence. Though, as a matter of fact, above the Executive in undisputed supremacy; though the President and his Cabinet are its servants; though they must collect and expend the public revenues as it directs; must observe its will in all dealings with foreign States, are dependent upon it for means to support both army and navy—nay, even for means to maintain the departments themselves; though they are led by it in all the main paths of their policies, and must obey its biddings even in many of the minor concerns of every-day business; though whenever it chooses to interfere, it is powerful to command: it is altogether dissociated from the Executive in its organization, and is often mightily embarrassed in wielding its all-embracing authority. It directs the departments; but it stands outside of them, and can know nothing clearly of their operation.

Its immediate agents in its guidance of executive affairs are its Standing Committees. Constrained to provide for itself leaders of some sort or other, Congress has found them in certain small and select bodies of men, to whom it has entrusted the preparation of legislation. It could not undertake to consider separately each of the numberless bills which might be brought in by its members. If it were to undertake to do so, its docket would become crowded beyond all hope of clearance, and its business fall appallingly into arrears. It must facilitate its business by an apportionment of labor, and by dividing make possible the task of digesting this various matter.

Accordingly, it has set up numerous Standing Committees, whose duty it is to prepare legislation and to act as its immediate agents in all its dealings with the executive departments. The Secretary of the Treasury must heed the commands of the Finance Committee of the Senate and the Ways and Means Committee of the House; the Secretary of State must in all things regard the will of the Foreign Affairs Committees of both Houses; the Secretary of the Interior must suffer himself to be bidden, now by the Committees on Indian Affairs, now by those on the Public Lands, and again by those on Patents. The Secretary of War must assiduously do service to the Committees on Military Affairs; to still other committees the Postmaster-General must render homage; the Secretary of the Navy must wear the livery of the Committees on Naval Affairs; and the Attorney-General must not forget that one or more of these eyes of the Houses are upon him. There are Committees on Appropriations, Committees on the Judiciary, Committees on Banking and Currency, Committees on Manufactures, Committees on Railways and Canals, Committees on Pensions and on Claims, Committees on Expenditures in the several Departments, and on the Expenditures on Public Buildings, committees on this and committees on that, committees on every conceivable subject of legislation.

And these Standing Committees are very selfish. Congress, by spoiling them with petting, has made them exacting. It indulges their every whim; for the rules of the House of Representatives provide for the expedition of business by securing beyond a peradventure the supremacy of its committees. Full of puzzling intricacies and complicated checks as these rules seem, this is their very simple purpose. There must be the utmost possible limitation of debate. Every session, of course, a great many bills, sometimes several thousand, are introduced by individual members, and there is not time to discuss or even to vote upon them all. Accordingly, the right of individual representatives to have their proposals separately considered must be sacrificed to the common convenience. The bills which are sent by scores to the clerk's desk every week when the roll of States is called are, therefore, all sent to the Standing Committees. Scarcely a topic can be touched which does not fall within the province of one or another of these committees, and so no bill escapes commitment.

But a bill committed is a bill doomed. Suppose, for example, that the Appropriations Committee has fifty or a hundred bills referred to it—and that would doubtless be much fewer than usual—how can there be a separate report upon each? Time would not serve for such an undertaking. The committee must simply reject utterly most of the bills, and, having from the remainder culled the provisions they like, frame for submission to the House a comprehensive scheme of their own.

As a rule, therefore, the debates of the House of Representatives are confined to the reports of the committees, and even upon these reports the House does not care to spend much time. Consequently, its debates upon their contents can seldom with strict accuracy be called debates of the House. They are in the House, but not of it. The period of debate and the number of speakers are usually limited by rule. So long a time, and so long only, is devoted to each discussion, and during that time the members of the reporting committee are accorded right of precedence for the presentation of their views upon the subject in hand, other members gaining the floor only when committeemen are courteous enough to give way to them.

The House makes its nearest approach to business debate when in Committee of the Whole. Then something like free and effective discussion takes place. Even then, however, members are not given unlimited scope. They must not talk longer than five minutes at a time. Though the House is no longer the House, and has put on the free habits of committee work, it still retains its predilections, and still binds itself by rules which are stingy of time to those who would speak. Five-minute speeches, moreover, gain little more attention than is vouchsafed to the one-hour speeches of committeemen during a regular session; for the Committee of the Whole is no better listener than its other self, the House. Members are almost quite as noisy and inattentive as when the Speaker is in his chair.

The conclusion of the whole matter, then, is that legislation is altogether in the hands of the Standing Committees. In matters of finance, the Committee of Ways and Means is, to all intents and purposes, the whole House; on questions affecting the national judiciary the Judiciary Committee practically dictates the decision of the whole House; and so on, from the beginning to the end of proval of the Appropriations Committee, they have virtually received the sanction of the whole House; the recommendations of the Committee on Naval Affairs are as a matter of course the will of the whole House; and so on, from the beginning to the end of every chapter of legislation. All the House's work is done in the committee rooms. When measures issue thence, only the formality of a vote in regular session—a vote often given without debate— is needed to erect them into bills, acts of the House of Representatives.

By whom, then, it becomes interesting to inquire, are these masterful committees named? And what is the rule of their organization? The privilege and duty of their appointment are vested in the Speaker, and by such investiture Mr. Speaker is constituted the most powerful functionary in the government of the United States. For what can he not accomplish through this high prerogative? He may, of course, discharge his exalted trust with honor and integrity: but consider the temptations which must overcome him if he be not made of the staunchest moral stuff. Is the public treasury full, and is he bent by conviction or by personal interest toward certain great schemes of public expenditure? With how strong a hand must he restrain his inclinations if he would deny himself the privilege, which he can enjoy without authoritative contradiction from any one, of constituting men of like mind with himself a controlling majority of the Appropriations Committee? Has he determined opinions upon questions of revenue and taxation which he has reason to fear will not be the opinions which are likely to prevail in the House? Who, if he do not prevent himself, will prevent him from naming those of the same opinion a ruling number on the Committee of Ways and Means? Has he friends whose influence was potential in bringing about his elevation to the chair? Who will be surprised if he give those friends the most coveted chairmanships? Does one of these friends feel a special interest in building up the navy? That friend will consider Mr. Speaker a shameless ingrate if his gratitude do not move him to the bestowal of a place of highest authority on both Naval and Appropriations Committees.

As a matter of fact—unless many outrageous calumnies are allowed to run abroad unchallenged—very few Speakers forbid their own personal preferences and predilections a voice in the appointment of committees. Many Speakers are men of strong individuality and resolute purpose, who have won their position by dominant force of will; and such men are sure to make themselves seen and felt in the composition of the committees. They are acknowledged autocrats. Other Speakers, on the other hand, are mere puppets—obscure men who have been raised to the chair by accidents, such as sometimes foist third-rate politicians into the Presidency—men whom caucuses have hit upon simply because they could not agree on anybody else. Such men appoint committees as others suggest. They go as they are led. In their appointments only those are favored who have established a claim upon their gratitude, or an influence over their irresponsible wills, or those who are nominated to their favor by an irresistible custom of the House.

But, turning from Mr. Speaker to his nominees, it is proper to ask: How and where are the proceedings of the committees conducted? With a simple organization of chairman and clerk, each committee sits in a room apart in comparative privacy, no one who is not on its roll being expected to be present uninvited. To assist it in its determinations, it may invite the presence of any executive officer of the government—though it does not appear that it has power to compel his attendance—and it often allows the advocates of special measures to present their arguments at length before it. But any committee that pleases may shut its doors against all comers and sit in absolute secrecy. On what grounds a committee acted is seldom clearly made known to the public. Why this or that bill, which was introduced by some member and referred without debate to the committee, was rejected by it no one can easily tell. The minutes of the committee, if any were kept, are not accessible, and all that appears from the journals of the House is that the committee, when it reported, said nothing of the bill in question. The public, in short, can know little or nothing about the motives or the methods of the Standing Committees: and yet all legislation may be said to originate with them, and to pass through all its stages under their direction.

The feature, therefore, which distinguishes our national legislation from that of other nations is, that it is the fruit of this unique system of Committee government, which we may claim the credit of having invented. In our Federal relations, we are directed by laws issuing from the privacy of irresponsible committees, and promulgated without debate. These committees are the wheels of the American system: but it is not in them that its motive power resides. We have not seen the whole of our machinery of government until we have visited that caucus where all the fires of legislative action are kindled.

There are caucuses and caucuses, separating themselves into two principal kinds, nominating and legislative. Of the first sort are those small bodies, too often bands of schemers and office-holders, of idlers and small "bosses," which meet in every election district, however little, to nominate candidates for local officers; those larger bodies, which generally work themselves into a heat of vexation and intrigue in naming insignificant men for State offices; and those great stormy conventions whose frenzy gives birth to a "ticket" for President and Vice-President of the Union. All office-holders, from town-clerks through Congressmen to Presidents, are children of caucuses of this pattern. But these are not the caucuses with which we are now most concerned; these are not the caucuses which immediately dominate legislation. Of such authority is the caucus legislative, the deliberative party committee. Representatives of the same party, when assembled in Congress or in State Legislature, feel bound to do whatever they do in the most inviolate concert: so they whip themselves together into deliberative caucus. If any doubt at any time arise as to the proper course to be taken in regard to any pending measure, there must be secret consultations in supreme party caucus, in order that each partisan's conscience may be relieved of all suspicion of individual responsibility, and the forces of the party concentrated against the time for actual voting. The Congressional caucus rooms are the central chambers of our Constitution.

The caucus was a natural and legitimate, if not healthy offspring of our peculiar institutions. Legislative caucuses and even nominating caucuses were necessitated by the complete separation of the legislative and executive departments of our government. By reason of that separation Congress is made supreme within the sphere of the Federal authority. There is none to compete with it. To it belongs the hand of power—the power of the purse and of the law—and it has naturally stretched forth that hand to brush away all obstacles to the free exercise of its sovereignty. But, although always master, it was at first, as has been said, embarrassed to find efficient means of exercising its mastery. It was, from the beginning, a rather numerous body, and in order to rule with vigor it was necessary that it should itself be ruled. It was, however, so organized, and so isolated from the other branches of the Federal system, as to render any authoritative personal leadership impracticable. There could scarcely be in either House any man or body of men able from sheer supremacy of genius or influence of will to guide its actions and command its deliberations. Some man of brilliant argumentative gifts and conspicuous sagacity might gain temporary sway by reason of his eloquence or a transient authority by virtue of his wisdom; but, however transcendent his talents, however indisputable his fitness for the post, he could never constitute himself the *official* leader of the Legislature; nor could his fellow members ever invest him with the rights of command. Manifestly, however, the House must have leadership of some kind. If no one man could receive the office of command, it must be given to sub-committees—to bodies small enough to be efficient, and yet so numerous that predominant power would be within the reach of no one of them. In such bodies, accordingly, it was vested; and so birth was given to that government by committees which now flourishes in such luxuriant vigor.

But that very feature of Committee government which makes it seem to many persons the best conceivable legislative mechanism, is the principal cause of its clumsiness, and is that which makes the Congressional caucus an absolute necessity. It is because the committees are too numerous to combine for purposes of rule; because they cannot act in concert; because there is and can be no coöperation amongst them; because, instead of acting together, they must frequently work at cross-purposes; because there can be no unity or consistency in their policy; because they are disintegrate particles of an inharmonious whole, that the deliberative party caucus exists and is all-powerful. If either of the national parties is to follow any distinct line of action, it must make its determinations independently of its representatives on the committees, who cannot act with that oneness of purpose which is made possible only by prevised combination. The party itself must come together in committee whenever, in critical seasons of doubt, it is necessary to assure itself of its own unity of purpose. It does so come together, and its deliberations are known as the sittings of a caucus. Such, therefore, was the natural and inevitable generation of the caucus legislative.

How the caucus legislative grew strong and bold, and how finally it has usurped the highest seats of government, or how the nominating caucus had its birth and growth, it is not in this place needful to relate. Suffice it to say that, as everybody knows, it has at length come to pass, by reason of the power of caucuses, that we are governed by a narrow oligarchy of party managers, that we have no great harmonious party majorities, that factions are supreme; factions manipulating caucuses and managing conventions; factions sneaking in committee rooms and pulling the wires that move Mr. Speaker; factions in the President's closet and at governors' ears; that cliques scheme and "bosses" manage.

None can doubt, therefore, that we are fallen upon times of grave crisis in our national affairs, and none can wonder that disgust for our present system speaks from the lips of citizens respectable both for numbers and for talents. Every day we hear men speak with bitter despondency of the decadence of our institutions, of the incompetence of our legislators, of the corruption of our public officials, even of the insecurity of our liberties. Nor are these the notes of a tocsin which peals in the ears of only a few panic-struck brains. The whole nation seems at times to be vaguely and inarticulately alarmed, restlessly apprehensive of some impending calamity. Not many years ago it required considerable courage to question publicly the principles of the Constitution; now, whenever the veriest scribbler shoots his small shafts at that great charter, many wise heads are wagged in acquiescent approval. It is too late to laugh at these things. When grave, thoughtful, perspicacious and trusted men all around us agree in deriding those "Fourth of July sentiments" which were once thought to hallow the lips of our greatest orators and to approve the patriotism of our greatest statesmen, it will not do for us, personifying the American eagle, to flap wing and scream out incoherent disapproval. If we are to hold to the old faith, we must be ready with stout reasons wherewith to withstand its assailants. It will not suffice to say, "These are the glorious works of our revered ancestors; let not profane voices be lifted up against them, nor profane hands seek to compass their destruction." Men whose patriotism is as undoubted and as indubitable as our own are lightly and freely flinging their taunts at these sacred institutions of ours, and it must be that they represent a large body of our countrymen who believe that corruption and personal ambition are converting the public service into a money-making trade.

Already discussion of the evils that beset and distress us is assuming definite shape and uttering a determined voice. Incoherent grumblings and passionate appeals are giving place to calm suggestions of remedy and distinct plans of reform. Echoes of such discussion have been heard even beyond the sea, so loud and bold have they grown, and foreigners are pricking up their ears to hear what it is that we are about to do. They realize that great changes are a-making.

Of all the suggestions that have been ventured, the one which we can best afford to ignore is that one which is most frequently made, that by some ingenious nineteenth-century device political parties be altogether ousted from our system. This is much too weak a pill against the earthquake. It is sadly true—let it be admitted—that in this country party government has of late years sunk into a degradation at once pitiable and disastrous. But party government is inseparable from representative government. Representative government is, indeed, only another name for government by partisan majorities. When the people govern, they must govern by majorities. Majorities rule in municipal, in State, and in national affairs alike. Representative government is government by majorities, and government by majorities is party government, which up to the present date is the only known means of self-government. It is the embodiment of that habit of popular rule which is the peculiar glory of our race, which is surrounded by so great traditions, and hallowed by so glorious memories.

In political action, as in all other action, men must join hand and purpose. "Burke admitted that when he saw a man acting a desultory and disconnected part in public life with detriment to his fortune, he was ready to believe such a man to be in earnest though not ready to believe him to be in the right. In any case he lamented to see rare and valuable qualities squandered away without any public utility. He admitted, moreover, on the other hand, that people frequently acquired in party confederacies a narrow, bigoted, and proscriptive spirit. But where duty renders a critical situation a necessary one, it is our business to keep free from the evils attendant upon it, and not to fly from the situation itself. It is surely no very rational account of a man that he has always acted right, but has taken special care to act in such a manner that his endeavors could not possibly be productive of any consequence. . . . When men are not acquainted with each other's principles, nor experienced in each other's talents, nor at all practiced in their mutual habitudes and dispositions by joint efforts of business; no personal confidence, no friendship, no common interest subsisting among them; it is evidently impossible that they can act a public part with uniformity, perseverance, and efficacy." "He pointed out to emulation the Whig junto who held so close together in the reign of Anne—Sunderland, Godolphin, Somers and Marlborough—who believed 'that no men could act with effect who did not act in concert; that no men could act in concert who did not act with confidence; that no men could act with confidence who were not bound together by common opinions, common affections, and common interests.' "*

What we stand in need of, therefore, is party responsibility, and not the abolition of parties. Provided with parties in abundance, and entertained with many nice professions of political principle, we lack party responsibility. American parties are seldom called to account for any breach of their engagements, how solemnly soever those engagements may have been entered into. They thrive as well on dead issues as on living principles. Are not campaigns still yearly won with the voice of war-cries which represent only bygone feuds, and which all true men wish were as silent as the lips that first gave them utterance? "Platforms" are built only for conventions to sit on, and fall into decay as of course when conventions adjourn. Such parties as we have, parties with worn-out principles and without definite policies, are unmitigated nuisances. They are savory with decay, and rank with rottenness. They are ready for no service, but to be served. Their natural vocation is to debauch the public morals, to corrupt and use the people; and the people's only remedy is a stern and prompt exercise of their sovereign right. These parties must be roughly shaken out of their insolence, and made to realize that they are only serv-

* Morley's Burke (Eng. Men of Letters Series), pp. 52, 53. [WW's note]

ants, and, being servants, will be expected and required to act with trustworthiness, with all honesty and all fidelity.

But how? There is much talk afloat about the duty of good citizens to go to the "primaries" and withstand in force the iniquities of the mercenaries of machine government. Many voices are uttering very manly calls upon public opinion to assert itself and make exercise of its sovereignty; but they do not advise this multitudinous monarch—the people—how it is to act. Everybody admires outspoken denunciations of wrong, and applauds exhortations to turn again to virtue and to rectitude; but very few care to go into an undiscovered country unless they be guided. The reform of government is not an everyday business, and one would like to be taught the out-of-the-way trade. We are enjoined to the work, but no one will lead or direct. One would suppose that it must be, after all, that the means of reform are so obvious that its advocates do not deem it necessary to point them out. The people must make imperative demand to be better governed, that is all.

But there's the rub, the trouble, and the puzzle. This very demand seems to be daily a-making. There is every reason to believe that the public mind is already quite made up. So stiffly does the breeze of opinion set towards reform, that nearly all the political papers of the country have long since gotten well before it; even the one-time open pirates of the spoils system busily trimming their sails, and none so bold as to beat up directly against it. Besides, those who are striving with all their breath to blow this wind into still fiercer blasts, complaisantly tell us that all who are still assaying to weather it are fast losing heart. Or, the metaphor changed, it may be said that the people has declared its will; that the land is full of heralds whose loud voices proclaim its decree. The winds seem to be bringing to each community from every quarter of the land the news that upon this great question the whole country is agreed. The nation is of one mind. What then? Has the blow been struck? Do the rulers hear the voice of their over-lord, and is reform already inaugurated, or do we still wait for its coming? "If it were done when 'tis done, then 'twere well it were done quickly."

The fact is, that in this matter, as in so many others, public opinion seems to be in danger of being disappointed of its omnipotence. Those who enjoy the spoils system love the caucus, and do not readily bend the knee to the people; and those who hope some day to come in for the favors of that system, themselves equally in love with the caucus, cautiously draw rein, and will not lead the hunters who would pursue it to its destruction. Public opinion, meanwhile, is left to hum and haw in distressing embarrassment over the question, What is to be done? How is the popular will to enforce its authority? What advantage is there in being unanimous?

It is only by making parties responsible for what they do and advise that they can be made safe and reliable servants. It is plain to see that this caucus on which our present party system rides is a very ugly beast, and a very unmanageable one. He cannot be driven with a chirp, nor commanded with a word. He will obey only the strong hand, and heed only the whip. To rail at him is of no good. He must be taken sternly in hand, and be harnessed, whether he will or no, in our service. Our search must be for the bit that will curb and subdue him.

In seeking an escape from the perplexity, manifestly the safest course is to content ourselves with traveling ways already trodden, and look to the precedents of our own race for guidance. Let, therefore, the leaders of parties be made responsible. Let there be set apart from the party in power certain representatives who, leading their party, and representing its policy, may be made to suffer a punishment which shall be at once personal and vicarious, when their party goes astray, or their policy either misleads or miscarries. This can be done by making the leaders of the dominant party in Congress the executive officers of the legislative will; by making them also members of the President's Cabinet, and thus at once the executive chiefs of the departments of State and the leaders of their party on the floor of Congress; in a word, by having done with the Standing Committees, and constituting the Cabinet advisers both of the President and of Congress. This would be Cabinet government.

Cabinet government is government by means of an executive ministry chosen by the chief magistrate of the nation from the ranks of the legislative majority—a ministry sitting in the legislature and acting as its executive committee; directing its business and leading its debates; representing the same party and the same principles; "bound together by a sense of responsibility and loyalty to the party to which it belongs," and subject to removal whenever it forfeits the confidence and loses the support of the body it represents. Its establishment in the United States would involve, of course, several considerable changes in our present system. It would necessitate, in the first place, one or two alterations in the Constitution. The second clause of Section Six, Article I, of the Constitution runs thus: "No Senator or Representative shall, during the term for which he was elected, be appointed to any civil office under the authority of the United States which shall have been created, or the emoluments whereof shall have been increased, during such time; and no person holding any office under the United States shall be a member of either House during his continuance in office." Let the latter part of this clause read: "And no person holding any other than a Cabinet office under the United States shall be a member of either House during his continuance in office," and the addition of four words will have removed the chief constitutional obstacle to the erection of Cabinet government in this country. The way will have been cleared, in great part at least, for the development of a constitutional practice, which, founded upon the great charter we already possess, might grow into a governmental system at once strong, stable, and flexible. Those four words being added to the Constitution, the President might be authorized and directed to choose for his Cabinet the leaders of the ruling majority in Congress; that Cabinet might, on condition of acknowledging its tenure of office dependent on the favor of the Houses, be allowed to assume those privileges of initiative in legislation and leadership in debate which are now given, by an almost equal distribution, to the Standing Committees; and Cabinet government would have been instituted.

To insure the efficiency of the new system, however, additional amendments of the Constitution would doubtless be necessary. Unless the President's tenure of office were made more permanent than it now is, he could not fairly be expected to exercise that impartiality in the choice of ministers, his legislative advisers and executive colleagues, which would be indispensable to good government under such a system; and no executive Cabinet which was dependent on the will of a body subject to biennial change—and which, because it is elected for only two years, is the more apt to be ruled by the spirit of faction and caught by every cunningly-devised fable—could have that sense of security without which there can be neither steadiness of policy nor strength of statesmanship. It must become necessary to lengthen both Presidential and Congressional terms. If the President must expect his authority to end within the short space of four years, he must be excused for caprice in the choice of his Secretaries. If no faithfulness and diligence of his can extend the period of his official authority by even so much as a single week, it cannot be reasonable to expect him to sacrifice his will to the will of others, or to subordinate his wishes to the public good during the short season of that brief authority's secure enjoyment. And, if Cabinets be vouchsafed but two years in which to mature the policies they may undertake, they cannot justly be blamed for haste and improvidence. They could not safely be appointed, or safely trusted to rule after appointment, under a system of quadrennial presidencies and biennial legislatures. Unless both Presidential and Congressional terms were extended, government would be both capricious and unstable. And they could be the more easily extended, because to lengthen them would be to change no *principle* of the Constitution. The admission of members of Congress to seats in the Cabinet would be the only change of principle called for by the new order of things.

Cabinet government has in it everything to recommend it. Especially to Americans should it commend itself. It is, first of all, the simplest and most straightforward system of party government. It gives explicit authority to that party majority which in any event will exercise its implicit powers to the top of its bent; which will snatch control if control be not given it. It is a simple legalization of fact; for, as every one knows, we are not free to choose between party government and no-party government. Our choice must be between a party that rules by authority and a party that, where it has not a grant of the right to rule, will make itself supreme by stratagem. It is not parties in open and legitimate organization that are to be feared, but those that are secretly banded together, begetters of hidden schemes and ugly stratagems.

Cabinet government would, moreover, put the necessary bit in the mouth of beast caucus, and reduce him to his proper service; for it would secure open-doored government. It would not suffer legislation to skulk in committee closets and caucus conferences. Light is the only thing that can sweeten our political atmosphere— light thrown upon every detail of administration in the departments; light diffused through every passage of policy; light blazed full upon every feature of legislation; light that can penetrate every recess or corner in which any intrigue might hide; light that will open to view the innermost chambers of government, drive away all darkness from the treasury vaults, illuminate foreign correspondence, explore national dockyards, search out the obscurities of Indian affairs, display the workings of justice, exhibit the management of the army, play upon the sails of the navy, and follow distribution of the mails—and of such light Cabinet government would be a constant and plentiful source. For, consider the conditions of its existence. Debate would be the breath of its nostrils: for the ministers' tenure of office would be dependent on vindication of their policy. No member of a Cabinet who had identified himself with any pending measure could with self-respect continue in office after the majority, whose representative he would be, had rejected that measure by a formal and deliberate vote. If, under such circumstances, he did not at once resign, he would forfeit all claim to manly independence. For him to remain in office would be to consent to aid in administering a policy of which he was known to disapprove, and thus to lose the respect of all honorable opponents and the support of all conscientious friends. It would be sacrificing principle to an unworthy love of office; prefering mere place to integrity; openly professing willingness to do the bidding of opponents rather than forego the empty honors of conspicuous station held without conspicuous worth. A man who held an office thus would soon be shamed into retirement; or, were no place left for shame, would be driven from his authority by a scorn-laden vote.

Moreover, the members of the Cabinet would always be *united* in their responsibility. They would stand or fall together in the event of the acceptance or rejection of any measure to which they had given their joint support. Otherwise, they would be no better leaders than the present Standing Committees; the differences, the disputes, and the antagonisms of the council-board would be renewed and reheated in the debates on the floor of Congress; the country would be scandalized at seeing ministers cross swords in open contention; personal spites would flame out in public between uncongenial ministers; there would be unseemly contests for the leadership. An ununited Cabinet could offer neither effectual guidance to the Houses nor intelligible advice to the Executive. United responsibility is indispensable in Cabinet government, because, without it, such government lacks its most admirable and valuable, its quintessential feature: namely, responsible leadership. Every deliberative body should have an accepted and responsible leader, and a legislative body without such a leader must dissipate its power like an unbanked stream. And a Cabinet that leads must be itself led, and act as if with one mind; else legislation will drift as helplessly and as carelessly as it does now, under the Committees, for want of some one influence to guide it.

A ministry united in action and in responsibility for their acts, must, manifestly, rule by debate. Their power and success would depend on the ascendency of their policy, and the ascendency of their policy would depend on the suffrages of the Houses. That policy must be vindicated in the eyes of Representatives and people alike. Defeat on a measure of importance would bring the necessity of resignation, and resignation would mean the incoming of the opposition leaders to power and authority. Debate would, therefore, of course be sought by Ministry and Opposition alike—by the one, that the triumph of their party might be approved a righteous triumph; by the other, that that triumph might be changed into defeat, and they themselves snatch victory and command. What greater earnest of sincerity and fidelity could there be than such a system as this? No minister could afford to ignore his party's pledges. Abandoned party platforms would furnish fine material for stout party coffins, and the ranks of the opposition would supply hosts of eager undertakers. How could a Cabinet face the ordeal of debate, after ignoring its promises and violating its engagements? And yet, how could it escape that trial when the Opposition were demanding debate, and to decline it would be of all confessions the most craven? Always eager to assail the ministers, the champions of the Opposition would have an unquenchable zeal for the fight, and no Ministry could afford to refuse them battle.

It becomes every citizen to bethink himself how essential a thing to the preservation of liberty in the republic is free and unrestricted debate in the representative body. It requires the fire of the universal criticism of the press not only, but the intenser flame of expert criticism as well, to test the quality and burn away the crudities of measures which have been devised in the seclusion of the study, or evolved from the compromises of disagreeing committeemen. The press is irresponsible, and often—too often—venally partisan. But representatives must criticise legislation in their own proper persons, and in the presence of the knowledge that constituencies have ears, and that by any blunder of judgment, or meanness of sentiment, the fairest reputation may be stained and the safest prospects blasted. It is good for these things to be done in the glare of publicity. When legislation consists in the giving of a silent judgment upon the suggestions of committees, or of caucuses which meet and conclude in privacy, lawmaking may easily become a fraud. A great self-governing people should as soon think of entrusting their sovereign powers to a secret council, as to a representative assembly which refuses to make debate its principal business. It is only when the whole nation is audience to their deliberations that legislators will give heed to their ways.

Very much good might be done by insisting upon debates upon the reports of the Standing Committees under our present system. But there is no use insisting. No one would care much for such debates. They would mean very little. The rejection of a report would have no other result than to give its subject-matter back to the defeated Committee for reconsideration, or, possibly, to postpone the question indefinitely. The Committee would not even feel the rebuff. No one committeeman would feel responsible for the result. Neither party would feel rebuked, for each Committee is made up of members from both sides of the House. It is because of these inconveniences and these feelings, that Committees generally have their own way. It is most convenient to let them guide, and little can be gained by opposing them.

There is much object and rare sport, on the other hand, in assailing a responsible Ministry. They will die game at least. They will not tamely suffer themselves to be ousted of their authority. Then, too, they do represent a party: they represent the very pick and flower of their party. In their defeat or victory, the whole army of their co-partisans suffer rout or enjoy success. Between the majority whom they represent, and the minority to whom they are opposed, every debate must become a contest for ascendency, and the introduction of each measure must open up long series of eager and anxious combat.

Here, then, is surely everything that could be desired in the way of a bit for ugly beast caucus. Party interests would constrain the nominating caucus to make choice of men fitted for the work of legislation. In a body whose chief function is debate, neither the supporters nor the opponents of a responsible Cabinet can afford to have many weaklings; still less can they afford to have spokesmen whose integrity is under a cloud of suspicion. Thorough debate can unmask the most plausible pretender. The leaders of a great legislative assembly must daily show of what mettle they are. Besides meeting many watchful adversaries in debate, they must prove themselves "able to guide the House in the management of its business, to gain its ear in every emergency, to rule it in its hours of excitement." Rhetorical adroitness, dialectic dexterity, even passionate declamation, cannot shield them from the scrutiny to which their movements will be subjected at every turn of the daily proceedings. The air is too open for either stupidity or indirection to thrive. Charlatans cannot long play statesmen successfully when the whole country is sitting as critic. And in Congress itself a single quick and pointed and well-directed question from a keen antagonist may utterly betray any minister who has aught to conceal. Even business routine will tear away any thin covering of plausibility from the shams of dishonest policy.

There is nothing so wholesome as having public servants always on public trial.

Since, then, victory must generally rest with those who are vigorous in debate and strong in political principle, it would be imperatively necessary for each party to keep on the floor of Congress the ablest men they could draw into their ranks. To stand the tests of discussion they must needs have champions strong of intellect, pure of reputation, exalted in character, and cogent in speech: and to this imperious necessity beast caucus must yield himself subject. Nominating conventions would hardly dare, under such circumstances, to send to Congress scheming wire-pullers or incompetent and double-faced tricksters, who would damn their party by displays of folly and suspicions of corruption. How could such men lead a minority against a powerful ministry, or face the bitter taunts of opponents and the scornful distrust of fellow-partisans?

But more than this: a new caucus-master would be raised up in the elevation and instruction of public opinion. Free and prolonged Congressional debates, conducted on the one side by men eager and able in attack, and on the other by men equally quick and strong in defense, would do more towards informing and instructing public opinion than the press unaided can ever do. Men do not often read newspapers which profess political doctrines or acknowledge party connections different from their own. They read altogether on one side and they read in colors. No staunch Republican paper will often venture to exhibit the flaws in Republican principles; and the paper which is not stalwartly partisan will surely have a small subscription list. Democratic papers must hold up Democratic dogmas in the lights most favorable to them, and in such lights only, else good Democrats will not patronize them. So it is that men read in colors—some in Democratic tints, some in Republican tints, a select few in neutral tints, and none at all in the clear, dry, uncolored light of truth. It must, however, be different were all political interest to center in the debates of the legislature. Still men would read their party papers as before—perhaps even more assiduously and loyally than ever—but into whatever paper they might look there must have crept therein at least a skeleton of the great debates at the capital, and the whole text of the speeches of the party leaders; and these would, of course, be carefully scanned by every reader who had any thought for the government—as diligently read on the one side as on the other. It would be understood by all that on these debates hung all the issues of national policy, and that unless these tournaments were watched one could not forecast anything concerning the political morrow, or think anything definitely concerning the next campaign.

How much more information regarding the questions of the day can be gained from such debates than from the editorials and correspondence of the press! For such debates are led by men whose chief business it is to study the subjects on which they speak; whose chief desire it is to exhibit each topic of discussion in every phase that it can possibly assume; whose personal authority as men of understanding or of reputation depends on the mastery of principle and of detail they display in these legislative contests; whose fame as orators depends on the clearness of statement, the cogency of reason, the elevation of sentiment, and the ardor of patriotism with which they present their cause and enforce their principles; and whose success as men of affairs, whose dearest ambition as public men, must be achieved or blasted according as they acquit themselves well or ill in the eyes of the nation. Responsible government would transform Congress into a grand national inquisition; for under such a system the ministers are always present to be taxed with questions, and no detail of administration can be kept back when anyone in either House chooses to ask about it, and insists upon particular information. Are the navy estimates before the House? Yonder sits a watchful member who has a pigeon-hole in his memory—or, at least, in his desk—for all the items of every appropriation bill that has been passed during the last ten years; and he is on his feet every half hour with several pointed queries to put to the head of the department. "What, Mr. Secretary, does this item mean? Is not this a much larger amount than we gave you last year for the same purpose? Does the Administration mean to put the navy on a war footing, that it asks so much? Why do you come to us again for money to complete those new frigates? How did it happen that your original estimates fell so far short? Has there been a sudden rise in provisions, that you ask more for victualing the fleet this year than you did a year ago? What is the idea of the Department in buying less ammunition this year than heretofore, notwithstanding the fact that you are putting more vessels than ever into service?" What patience of spirit and diligence in business must Mr. Secretary exhibit to reply to all these vexing interrogations with satisfactory fullness, and at the same time with unruffled equanimity!

Public opinion, informed by such proceedings, could easily control, as supreme "boss," the "bosses" of the caucus. Whilst the nominating caucus would be brought into servitude by such a government, the legislative caucus would be killed. Its occupation would be gone. How could there be any necessity for a party often to confer in secret, and constantly to marshal itself for the contests of policy, when under the recognized leadership of a Ministry whose principles are well known and whose course is easily forecast, or even when united and organized in well-understood opposition? The occasion for caucus conferences would no longer exist. Parties could act in concert without them. They could follow distinct lines of policy without resorting to this clumsy and artificial method of manufacturing unanimity. They would have capable and trustworthy leaders under whom to act, and definite, well-recognized principles to advance. They would represent ideas; and would not be bent upon being supreme for mere supremacy's sake.

Of course, no interest is felt now in the debates which take place at Washington, because nothing depends upon them, and the administration of the government is not in the least perceptible degree affected by them. No newspaper cares to print even the chief speeches of a session, because there are no leaders who speak with authority. Seeing this, an observant Englishman—Mr. Dale, of Birmingham—has acutely remarked, that "the Americans care very little about politics, but a great deal about politicians." There are under our system no ordinary means by which the national parties can be united on grounds of distinct and consistent policy, so that there is of course nothing in our political contests to excite any lasting interest in the principles involved. How can any one be interested in parties that have no complexion; which are one thing to-day, another to-morrow, taking their color from the times? Lookers-on can understand, however, the aspirations of this or that politician for office, and they are interested in the contest. The rivalry is entertaining. The race is diverting and exciting. Now and then, it is true, great questions do engage the public attention. At some crisis, when some overshadowing issue has aroused the sentiment of the constituencies and forces itself forward at the election, candidates are asked with interest and emphasis what their position is with regard to it. But generally politicians need no creed, and can safely rely for success on their personal popularity, or on an indefinite thing called their "record."

But Cabinet government would not only instruct public opinion and elevate Congress into a great deliberative body; it would also set up a higher standard of effectiveness in the executive departments. The ministers, being also the chief officers of the departments, must be able to discern much more readily and clearly than could the most diligent and inquisitive Standing Committees, the lines of administration which are practicable, and means of management which are available. They know the daily perplexities of departmental business, and can appreciate the complexity of the executive machinery. They are in a position to weigh the thousand minor considerations which must sway the determination of administrative officers in the conduct of their official business, and have every means of ascertaining those necessities of the departments which it is the province of legislation to supply. They are not outsiders, as the Committees are, and have, therefore, the incalculable advantage of knowing both the needs of the departments, and the temper of the assembly they are leading; being thus enabled to conform legislation at once to the requirements of government, and to the sentiments of the public; to be both prompt and prudent, both liberal and economical.

Nor would such a union of legislative and executive functions in a single Cabinet-committee either jeopardize the independence of the Executive, or derogate from the privileges of the Legislature. As chiefs of the executive bureau, the ministers would have a personal interest in preserving the prerogatives of the Executive; and as official leaders of their party in Congress, they would be zealous to protect the rights and vindicate the authority of the Houses. They *would* not infringe the powers of the Executive, and they *could* not coerce Congress if they would. They would be simply the intelligent counsellors of the latter, not its masters; its accountable guides and servants, not its autocrats.

Even the imperfect view of the conditions of Cabinet government that I have been able to give here in these limited magazine spaces is sufficient to make it clear why the establishment of such a system in this country would necessitate a lengthening of the legislative term. Biennial elections to the lower House serve well enough under our present form of government. Even the oft-repeated contests for the Speakership, and the frequent reconstructions of the Committees which are attendant upon the reorganizations of the House; even the insecurity of tenure which makes the representative office a station less of usefulness than of profit, and the derangements of business which are incident upon quick recurring elections, do not altogether condemn the system. It is well enough that representatives should have a continuing sense of constant dependence on the approving judgments of their constituents. If there is to be no other feature of responsibility than this in our government, by all means let this be retained. But with

Cabinet government, biennial elections would prove a source of too great instability. Each election would decide an issue between parties; would determine which should have power and enjoy ascendency; and no Ministry would care to inaugurate a policy which might be broken down at the end of two years. A Cabinet coming into office at a crisis, or bringing with them many promises of great things to be accomplished, might be ousted at the end of two brief years, before their schemes had fairly matured, by a wave of opposition raised by the natural and transient disappointment of the country, that everything promised had not *already* been done. Ministers would not plan for so short a future. They would not have the nerve. They would legislate from hand to mouth. "A mind free from the sense of insecurity is as necessary for great works of statesmanship as for great works of poetry." Biennial elections would be too much like biennial convulsions. Their quick recurrence would keep the country in a fever of political excitement, which would either warm into riot or waste into exhaustion and indifference.

With the responsible chiefs of administration always under the public eye, the permanence and success of civil service reform ought to be assured. They could be cited for every violation of its principles, and for every deviation from its proper practices. Their own mastery would depend upon the efficiency of the administration, and the efficiency of the administration would depend upon the maintenance of true business principles in the manning of the departments; or, in other words, upon the rigid observance of the doctrines of civil service reform.

The uncertainty of their own tenure of office would offer no contradiction to these doctrines. Beyond question, the greater part of the affairs of the departments is altogether outside of politics. The collection and ordinary disbursements of the revenue, the general superintendence of the army and navy, the regulation of the mail service, the administration of justice—all the usual and daily functions of the executive departments—what concern have they with party questions? In these things business capacity and honest diligence are all that are wanted. Political belief does not affect an officer's efficiency any more than his religious belief might. This is the oft-established principle which lies at the source of the great movement towards civil service reform, in which all the currents of public opinion are now united, in a tide before which the stoutest dykes of party custom and party interest have gone down. It is now universally seen and acknowledged that the public service to be efficient should be non-partisan; and that so far as the nation at large is concerned, it can make no possible difference whether the rank and file of its servants entertain this, that, or the other political creed. Not in one office out of five thousand can opinion affect a man's value as a business agent of the government. But there are executive offices which are political. Those ministers who direct the general policy of the government—if any such there be—must represent the party dominant in the State, just as the Standing Committees which now stand in the place of such ministers are, properly and as a matter of course, representatives of the ruling majority.

Much might be made of the objection that ministers acting thus as both executive officers and legislative leaders, absorbed as they would be in the business of the Houses and in the marshalling of their party forces in the daily tilt of debate, could not have the leisure to master properly their duties as heads of the departments, and would inevitably fall short of fulfilling their official trusts. This objection is an evident and a weighty one. It must, however, be remembered at every turn in the endeavor to solve this tremendous and perplexing problem of government, that we are commanded by the inexorable necessity of compromise. We must take the least imperfect thing we can get; and surely it is far better to have the business of the executive departments directed by men who know something of their interests, rather than by men who know nothing of those interests: by men who are in constant, intimate, and authoritative communication with subordinates who spend their lives in close and exclusive attention to departmental affairs, rather than by men who can command no such means of information; by men whose personal interests, nay, whose very ambition, must unite them in behalf of good administration; and who are able, therefore, and willing to agree upon a definite, uniform, and consistent policy, rather than by several scores of men divided into numerous, disconnected, and inharmonious committees who cannot coöperate, and who are only too often indifferent as to the results of measures they ignorantly recommend.

So long as we have representative government, so long will the Legislature remain the imperial and all-overshadowing power of the State: and so long as it does remain such a power, it will be impossible to check its encroachments and curb its arrogance, and at the same time preserve the independence of the Executive, without joining these two great branches of government by some link, some bond of connection, which, whilst not consolidating them, will at least neutralize their antagonisms, and, possibly, harmonize their interests. A Cabinet-committee would constitute such a bond; for it would, as we have seen, be a body which, from its very nature and offices, would be at once jealous of the pretensions of the Houses and responsible for the usurpations of the Executive; interested, and therefore determined, to yield not a jot of their lawful executive authority, and yet bound to admit every just claim of power on the part of their legislative colleagues.

That must be a policy of wisdom and prudence which puts the executive and legislative departments of government into intimate sympathy, and binds them together in close coöperation. The system which embodies such a policy in its greatest perfection must be admired of all statesmen and coveted of all misgoverned peoples. The object of wise legislation is the establishment of equal rights and liberties amongst the citizens of the State, and its chief business, the best administration of government. Legislatures have it constantly in charge, and specially in charge, to facilitate administration: and that charge can be best fulfilled, of course, when those who make and those who administer the laws are in closest harmony. The executive agents of government should stand at the ear of the Legislature with respectful suggestions of the needs of the administration, and the Legislature should give heed to them, requiring of them, the while, obedience and diligence in the execution of its designs. An Executive honored with the confidence of the Legislature, and a Legislature confiding itself with all fullness of trust, yet with all vigilance, to the guidance of an Executive acknowledging full responsibility to the representatives of the people for all its acts and all its counsels: this is a picture good to look upon—a type of effective and beneficent self-government. The changes in our form of government which the establishment of such a system would involve are surely worth making, if they necessitate no sacrifice of principle.

It cannot be too often repeated, that while Congress remains the supreme power of the State, it is idle to talk of steadying or cleansing our politics without in some way linking together the interests of the Executive and the Legislature. So long as these two great branches are isolated, they must be ineffective just to the extent of the isolation. Congress will always be master, and will always enforce its commands on the administration. The only wise plan, therefore, is to facilitate its direction of the government, and to make it at the same time responsible, in the persons of its leaders, for its acts of control, and for the manner in which its plans and commands are executed. The only hope of wrecking the present clumsy misrule of Congress lies in the establishment of responsible Cabinet government. Let the interests of the Legislature be indissolubly linked with the interests of the Executive. Let those who have authority to direct the course of legislation be those who have a deep personal concern in building up the executive departments in effectiveness, in strengthening law, and in unifying policies; men whose personal reputation depends upon successful administration, whose public station originates in the triumph of principles, and whose dearest ambition it is to be able to vindicate their wisdom and maintain their integrity.

Committee government is too clumsy and too clandestine a system to last. Other methods of government must sooner or later be sought, and a different economy established. First or last, Congress must be organized in conformity with what is now the prevailing legislative practice of the world. English precedent and the world's fashion must be followed in the institution of Cabinet Government in the United States.

Woodrow Wilson.

Printed in *Overland Monthly*, 2nd Ser., III (Jan. 1884), 17-33. A comparison of the text of this article with that of "Government by Debate," printed at Dec. 4, 1882, will show how WW excerpted the latter and bridged the excerpts with new transitional sentences to form the text of "Committee or Cabinet Government?" About 40 per cent of the article was taken from the first chapter of "Government by Debate" and about 60 per cent from the third. The manuscript of WW's second draft of "Government by Debate," in WP, DLC, bears the evidence of WW's markings and additions, often written on the verso pages, before he copied out "Committee or Cabinet Government?"

As Robert Bridges to WW, July 30 and Aug. 15 and 30, 1883, and WW to Bridges, Aug. 10 and Sept. 12, 1883, indicate, WW prepared the copy of "Committee or Cabinet Government?" in response to the request of Jonas Libbey, editor of the *Princeton Review*, and was chagrined when Libbey rejected the article because it was badly put together and too long. The documents are silent concerning WW's disposition of the article. However, he undoubtedly put it aside once he went to the Johns Hopkins. He probably showed it to Charles H. Shinn (identified at Jan. 21, 1884, note 1), a fellow-graduate student and brother of Milicent W. Shinn, then managing editor of the *Overland Monthly* of San Francisco. Shinn in turn must have suggested that WW send the manuscript to his sister.

WW's copy of "Committee or Cabinet Government?," which was typed on his Caligraph, has not survived.

From Joseph Ruggles Wilson

My precious son—   Wilmington [N.C.], January 1, 1884

Please find enclosed my check for $50.00.

You may be sure that we all felt badly because of our inability to send you a fitting Christmas & birth-day gift. But, with a slow church treasury and the many demands upon my sinking bank balance, we did not feel that it would be best to launch into an expense, whose launching would not have afforded you more than a momentary satisfaction, and the non-launching of which you, in your love for us, would so readily understand the necessity for. In truth, my darling, so long as we have a steadfast and an unquestioning love to interchange, we need not care for much else on the one side or the other. And that you have our unqualified and imperishable affection, I again assure you on this opening day of a new *year* but not of a new *yearning* towards our beloved one. Our hearts are wholly yours now or in any event. It is true we are anxious as to your future—just as you yourself are—but, as you do, we will let hope brighten it until it shall come to put on a lustre of its own.

Dode received yours, this morning, and was greatly pleased therewith. I dare say he will take yr. advices—or, at any rate, resolve to do so. He is, as yet, however—although the sweetest of sons—an undetermined problem, causing his dear mother & me much thought.

Please present me most affectionately to that enchanting one who is, and who ought to be, more to you than all else including parents.

With love from us all who are happy in yr. love, I am as always,

Your affectionate Father.

ALS (WP, DLC).

Two Letters to Ellen Louise Axson

My own darling,   Baltimore, Md., New Years Day, 1884

If you should, in the course of this letter, notice any very marked degeneracy in the hand-writing, pray attribute it, not to carelessness, but to the fact that I have been writing all day long and that my hand begins to threaten to rebel against its hard usage. I've opened the new year by a day of diligent work on my favourite constitutional studies. I've planned a set of four or five essays on "The Government of the Union," in which it is my purpose to show, as well as I can, our constitutional system as it looks in operation.[1] My desire and ambition are to treat the American constitution as Mr. Bagehot (do you remember Mr. Bagehot, about whom I talked to you one night on the veranda at Asheville?—) has treated the English Constitution. His book has inspired my whole study of our government. He brings to the work a fresh and original method which has made the British system much more intelligible to ordinary men than it ever was before, and which, if it could be successfully applied to the exposition of our federal constitution, would result in something like a revelation to those who are still reading the Federalist as an authoritative constitutional manual. An immense literature has already accumulated upon this subject; but I venture to think that the greater part of it is either irrelevant or already antiquated. "An observer who looks at the living reality will wonder at the contrast to the paper description. He will see in the life much which is not in the books; and he will not find in the rough practice many refinements of the literary theory." (B.)

Of course I am not vain enough to expect to produce anything so brilliant or so valuable as Bagehot's book; but, by following him afar off, I hope to write something that will be at least worth reading, if I should ever publish it, and which will, in any event, serve as material for college lectures which will put old topics in a somewhat novel light. Does this big programme make you wonder what I've been writing to-day? Something very ordinary. Only an historical sketch of the modifications which have been wrought in the federal system and which have resulted in making Congress the omnipotent power in the government, to the overthrow of the checks and balances to be found in the "literary theory." This is to serve as an introduction to essays upon Congress itself, in which I wish to examine at length the relations of Congress to the Executive, and that legislative machinery which contains all the springs of federal action— But what sort of New Year's letter is this I'm writing! I've been so absorbed in my pet subject all day that I forget myself: I can't easily think of anything else. Fortunately for me, you've promised not to "frown" on these severe pursuits of mine. Some day I'll appall you by reading this introductory essay, or one of its successors, to you, just to show you how dull I can be upon occasion. I seldom talk with my chief professor [H. B. Adams] nowadays on these subjects which most interest me, and upon which I feel most competent to talk; because I have found him possessed of a very quick faculty of *acquisition* and prone to use as his own any original material which one may inadvertently lay before him. He has nothing of that mean prejudice, now so common, against plagiarism! But the fellow's not to blame: his stock of ideas is small and needs replenishing!

I have never been inclined to regard the opening of a new year with any special reverence. Of course the passage of time is a solemn thing, and it does a man good to reckon with his past and by its results plan his future. But that's a rather silly, spasmodic sort of virtue which indulges in "good resolutions" at this special season[.] Such resolutions, to be satisfactory to the resolver, must have such a definite shape that they are for that very reason unserviceable. It may be an excellent plan to read a scene from Shakspere every day, for instance, or to refrain from all harsh speech, and yet it is easy to imagine circumstances unnumbered under which very harsh words and total abstinence from Shakspere might very properly and virtuously be permitted. For my part, I am interested in the turn of the season because it seems to bring me in sight of certain indescribably delightful prospects. I've been through college terms enough to have noticed that the time runs much more rapidly away after Christmas than before it: and I can anticipate the rapid approach of summer with the greatest equanimity. Indeed, I am conscious of being quite careless how fast that season draws near. I should'nt mind if several months were skipped in the head-long progress: for, besides its other attractions, this is to be the summer of *leap* year, and I shall confidently expect you to do all the courting, when we are together, to tell me and to show me that you love me as often and as demonstratively as I should tell and show you, were this the year of man's privilege! I should be delighted if you would begin practice now by writing me leap year letters. If arguments are needed to induce you to do so, I would suggest that you could thereby do yourself a good turn by writing me such letters as you would have me write you, and thus putting me in the way of pleasing you most hereafter by an altogether improved method in correspondence! The only draw back to the plan would be that I could'nt play *my* part successfully: I could'nt write such sweet letters in response as you now write to me

I received a letter the other day which had had a curious history.[2] It was from an old University of Virginia friend who is studying in Germany. It had been written last July and sent to Atlanta; not finding me there, it was returned to Germany whence it had been sent out again, to Wilmington. When it reached me it had three envelopes about it: the original one, much scored and way-worn, the one in which it had undertaken its second trip to America, and the one in which dear mother enclosed it in forwarding it to me: so that, as I opened it, it dwindled rapidly in size from its first promise. I found the original envelope thus endorsed: "Dear Tommy: This remarkable looking epistle has crossed the ocean twice, and I shall now send it on a third voyage—hoping that it may find you this time. What its contents are I have by this time forgotten." Its contents proved very enjoyable and not at all stale, for Dabney is no ordinary fellow, and his friendship is of the hearty, genuine type.

I need not tell you, my darling, how often I have thought of you in connection with this opening year. All my future is to be linked with yours; and the happiest office of my life is to be to make your life bright and full of love. May God bless and keep you, my peerless little sweetheart!

Forgive this stupid letter, please; I find that I'm *excessively* tired and have written all my sense out in that essay that has occupied me all day. I did'nt know how hard I had been working until I found how jaded my faculties are.

With a heart full of tenderest love,
Happy New Year to all.   Your own   Woodrow.

1 WW refers here to what would become his first and most famous book, *Congressional Government*. An Editorial Note on the development of the idea of the text will appear in Vol. 3.
2 It was R. H. Dabney to WW, July 22, 1883.

"Bluntschli Library"
My own darling,   J.H. University, Balto., Jan'y 4, 1884

I think that this snug little alcove in which I have written more than one of my letters to you, and in wh. I am again writing this morning, will always seem to me one of the brightest and best-worth-visiting spots in Baltimore because of its association with you. Saving the time spent in reading your letters, my happiest hours are those which I give to writing to you. It is an unmixed delight to me to have leave to tell my secret thoughts without reserve to one whom I love more than my own life and who, I can be sure, will interpret all I say with a whole-hearted sympathy and with a love as great as my own! I wish I could tell you, *just once* (if I might be so inspired) how much I love you. If I could, you would wonder, as I often do, how I managed to stay in Baltimore, and not go, in spite of the dictates of long-sighted wisdom, on the next Southward-bound train[.] My own explanation is that a thin purse can restrain the most impetuous disposition, under circumstances which would disarm all other powers.

I am beginning to think that I made a mistake in working all through the vacation without allowing myself any respite at all. I kept to my books (when I was not writing to you, or my Xmas letters to the home folks) almost all the time, and did not go near any of my friends. I am, as you have no doubt found out for yourself, an excessively proud and sensitive creature (or "wretch," as you would say of yourself), and, since I look upon the Xmas season as one specially sacred to *family* reunions and festivities, I did not choose to call upon any of the families of my acquaintance lest I *might*, by some possibility, interfere in some way with the freedom of their holiday arrangements. So, in order to escape intolerable lonliness, I went in self-defence to my studies. As a natural consequence, I overdid the business—a discovery which I made on New Year's day, when, after the hardest day's work I ever did, I tried to write to my darling. I was both exhausted and intensely nervous, and I am just now beginning to feel like myself again. The last day or two I have been restlessly wandering about trying to bridge over a sort of enforced idleness, the most interesting results of my half-crazy condition having been three successive, all-night dreams of *you*. The first visions were delightful: for in them you were always with me, soothing me with sweet, inimitable ministrations of love: but in the last, from which I awoke only a few hours ago, and wh. still haunts me, I suffered unutterably. *I dreamt that you were dead*—you, without whom I would not care to live, nay, whose loss would make me wish to die. But why should I distress you so by telling you of all this! I am ashamed of my weakness! It need not distress you, for it's all past now, and I promise you that, as I was never in such a condition before, so I will never let myself fall into such a condition again. I am not often subject to the dominion of my nerves, and it requires only a very little prudence to enable me to maintain that mastery over myself and that free spirit of courageous, lighthearted work in which I pride myself. Interpreted by the accepted canons of superstitious exposition, besides, even that terrible dream of last night brings a delightful prophecy of *marriage*, which ought to remove one of my chief causes of anxiety—indeed the *only* thing that stands in the way of my complete happiness— namely, the uncertainty of my prospects. When nobody else's future depended on my own, I used to be wonderfully, sublimely, free from this particular sort of anxiety. I always felt a sort of calm, uncalculating assurance of my ability to make successful shift to support myself; but now that the time for the realization of my sweetest hopes depends on my securing a good position, I begin to feel very keenly the uncertainty of the prospect. I know what you would say, my darling: I have a perfect assurance of your love and of your willingness to abide the chances of my fortune; but I am none the less eager to make our engagement as short as possible. I would give a great deal to see your face as you read this! You will say to yourself, with heightened colour, "why this impudent youth talks as if *his* were the supreme will in this matter, as if he had but to say 'come along' and I'd be glad to go! Oh, *wont* I give it to him when I write! I'd have him understand that *I'm* the chief disposer of that matter! The dear, self-sufficient

monster! *He* 'make our engagement as short as possible' indeed!"
Yes, little lady, I confess that that was a very impertinent thing to
say; and I'm very contrite. But you do'nt mean to say that, when
I get an appointment to teach and a home of my own, you'll be so
cruel as to send me off to occupy it by myself, condemning me to
a continuance of this dreary, lonly bachelorhood! As I was counting, not on my own rights, but on your kindness, when I made
that venturesome remark, you ought to forgive it. The fact of the
matter is that I feel entitled ("if I do say it meself, as should'nt") to
a great deal of credit for being as patient (?) as I am. Why, on our
wedding day, Ellie, will be fulfilled the dreams of a whole life-time.
If a man reasoned about such things, I should probably have
been slower about falling in love with you: for it's manifestly impossible to read all sides of a character and be sure of your ground
in two weeks: and yet I had'nt known you two weeks—it was not
two weeks after our walk "from Agnes' "—before I was in love with
you. I *knew*—by what means I do'nt know; but with a certainty that
made it impossible to treat your objections in Asheville with any
degree of allowance—I *knew* then as I know now, that you were
the woman whom I had been dreaming about and looking for ever
since I had been able to form any rational ideas about the sort of
wife I wanted to make my life complete in usefulness and in happiness. I had, hitherto, allowed myself to be attracted by beauty
and brilliant gifts, by vivacity and dash, in other women because
I had given up all hope of finding you. Lydgate was a fool for
marrying Rosalind; but he did'nt know any better: he had never
met Dorathea! I do'nt mean to compare myself to Lydgate, nor
you to Dorathea, who was not, for all her noble, lovable qualities, the sort of woman I should wish to marry; but the case is in
point, because Dorathea would have been the making of Lydgate.
So you should make allowances for a fellow who is in such desperate straits of love as I am; who feels that he shall begin to live
only when his life is supplemented by yours. You *can't* be vexed
with him for wishing to hasten the coming of the best day of his
life! Besides, I've made a vow in the performance of which I shall,
I fear, have frequent occasion to deprecate your indignation. I
have resolved not to torment myself, as I have heretofore always
done, by locking up in my heart all the thoughts which concerned
only myself. I remember confessing to you, as we returned from
our climb up the hill (I remember the very spot—it was on a long
stretch of straight road as we neared the rail-road crossing), the
principle upon which I had always acted in my intercourse with
others—a principle which I had found to be based on my ignorance

of women and on my experience of the selfishness of men—namely, never to trouble anyone with confessions of my private thoughts and motives, and to be self-sufficient in all my own, individual concerns. Now, as it is only with reference to you that I make the "new departure," you will see to what dangers I expose myself: for when I add to tedious unfoldings of my literary and other ambitions confessions of my selfish (?) schemes about yourself (as above) I am like to get into hot water—as witness my unguarded message about the kisses! Why should I have given myself away so, but for the unsettling influence of this new vow which has broken into my old stubborn reserve? I'm glad that you had'nt the heart or the words to finish that last sentence of your letter, because it would have destroyed my belief that you could'nt be so hard-hearted as to deny to a lover who can see you for only one short season in the twelve-month your sweetest favours, fairly starving him, and giving him leave only when he should be at the point of leaving for a long, long absence, and when all joy was swallowed up in the great grief of separation. Such favours are for the holiday seasons of the soul: and you must reflect that, during a short vacation, it is perfectly legitimate to regard each other as *always* "about to go away"! Moreover,—But I'd better not say any more, for fear of drawing down upon my head an answer of completed sentences! All I ask for is a suspension of judgment until the plaintiff may be heard in person. He can't do himself justice—nor get justice from the court—when pleading thus "by brief."

What a dear *secretive* little being you are! All that about the present of Dante's works is very interesting indeed, and I thoroughly sympathize with you under the exceedingly embarrassing circumstances—but who *is* "he"? I think that both you and "Aunt Ella" were right: you in your desire to send the books back, and she in her conviction that "it would never do" to bring yourself under the necessity of making very awkward—nay, quite impossible—explanations by yielding to your desire: but none of this throws any light on the question, who is "he"?

So Mrs. Hammond *did* see the resemblance, did she? and not only saw but pronounced it "striking"? Hurrah for Mrs Hammond! And she was the only one outside the family who saw it: so that it follows, "as the night the day," that Mrs. H., too, is a "gifted being, with a grand imagination"? As for the testimony of the family, it is—with all due deference to them—quite without weight, for families are notoriously incapable of judging of such things. I shall not need a new pair of spectacles!

I don't want to close this letter even here, but this is "Seminary" night and I must attend: so good-night, my darling. Forget the first part of this letter and think of me as I am now, well and jolly, and too much in love with you to think of anybody else

In closing his last letter, father says, "Please present me most affectionately to that enchanting one who is, and who ought to be, more to you than all else."

That little card you sent in your letter is beautiful, and the quotation more than beautiful. Love to all, and uns[p]eakable love for yourself, from

Your own   Woodrow

ALS (WC, NjP).

From the Minutes of the Seminary of Historical and Political Science

Johns Hopkins University.
Bluntschli Library, Jan. 4, 1884.

The Seminary was called to order at 8 p.m. There were present Drs. H. B. Adams, R. T. Ely and J. F. Jameson and Messrs. Berry, Dewey, Levermore, Steele, Ramage, Yager, Wilson, Worthington, Shaw, Scaife, Ingle, Fisher, Shinn, Goodman, Linthicum, Robinson and Thomas. The chair was occupied by Dr. H. B. Adams.

The Chair outlined plans for the preservation of records of the proceedings of The Seminary, and appointed a Secretary for the evening.

The Secretary read abstracts of a paper by Dr. Charles Gross on "*Gilda Mercatoria*," which had been read in full Nov. 23, 1883, and of a paper by the Rev. S. W. Dike on "The Family as a Practical Question in American Politics" which had been presented by Mr. Dike, Dec. 1883. It was announced that this paper would shortly appear in "The Princeton Review."[1]

Mr. Ingle called attention to the reproduction of Merchant Guilds, or similar institutions, in the laws of Virginia; and showed the development of the same into the later town government.

Mr. Shinn presented a review of "The American Magazine" of History for December, 1883. The eclectic character of the book reviews was adversely criticised.

Dr. Adams called attention to recently acquired files of "The Historical Magazine and Notes and Queries."

Mr. Wilson presented a review of "The Banker's Magazine" for December, 1883.

Mr. Scaife read a paper on "The Study of Roman Law and History," of which an abstract prepared by Mr. Scaife here follows:—[2]

Dr. Adams supplemented the paper by remarks upon the growing interest in the study of Roman Law and the dearth of competent instructors.

Mr. Yager presented a review of the *"Revue Historique"* for November and December, 1883, giving especial attention to an article on Mirabeau.

Mr. Shaw presented a review of the *"Preussische Jahrbücher"* for November, 1883, giving especial attention to an article on the Tractarian Movement in the Church of England and to a published oration on Luther.

Dr. Jameson called attention to "The Academy" for December 8, 1883, as containing a review of new Luther material from the Vatican collection.

Dr. Adams laid upon the Seminary table the complete proof-sheets of the Rev. Dr. E. D. Neill's "Maryland in the Beginning,"[3] a brief submitted to the Seminary by Dr. Neill [in] 1883.

Classified collections of newspaper clippings were assigned to members of the Seminary for examination and for sifting preparatory to filing them for preservation.

Attention was called to a bust of Francis Lieber recently presented to the Seminary by his widow; and mention was made of a rare book—a copy of the original edition of "Province Laws of Massachusetts in the Time of William and Mary"—lately given to the Library by Mr. Ramage. Attention was called to bound copies of Vol. 1 of the "Historical and Political Science Studies" of the Seminary.[4]

Adjourned.

J. A. Fisher, Secretary.

Bound ledger book (MdBJ).

[1] Samuel W. Dike, "Some Aspects of the Divorce Question," *Princeton Review*, XIII (March 1884), 169-90.

[2] This paper was not copied into the Minutes.

[3] Edward D. Neill, *Maryland in the Beginning* (Baltimore, 1884).

[4] *The Johns Hopkins University Studies in Historical and Political Science* (Baltimore, 1882–). The lead monograph in the first volume was Edward A. Freeman, *An Introduction to American Institutional History*.

From Ellen Louise Axson

My darling Woodrow,   Savannah Jan. 7/84.

Your delightful letter of the 4th was received this morning; many thanks for it, as also for the other one received since I last wrote—the one of Tuesday. You were especially good, almost *too* good, I fear, in writing the latter, after that tremendous day's work. I think I should have rebelled against so much as "making my mark" under the circumstances. I appreciated it in proportion to the effort it must have cost; and I assure you, you never made a greater mistake, than in saying you had "written away all your sense." I was *intensely* interested in it all. So you have actually gotten fairly into your great subject—have made a very deep plunge, indeed!

I wish you all joy in it. Though in view of the immediate consequences of this first plunge, I am glad you recognize the fact that you "overdid" it; and that your New Year's day is to serve as a pattern only in modified form for the other days of the year. My experience has given me a most profound respect for "nerves," especially the nerves of students. Perhaps I should'nt use the word "experience," for I certainly know nothing of nervousness in my own person, and Papa says no one can understand it at all without feeling it, but I am sure that all we have gone through together with his nerves entitles me to speak on the subject with a more vivid and profound knowledge than that which comes from mere *observation*. I was truly glad and relieved to read as the summing up of today's letter, that you had recovered from your exhaustion, and are again "well and jolly"; and I trust you will not be further tormented even in dreams. What an uncomfortable time those ancients must have had who felt called upon to believe or to interpret all the visions of the night! Surely they could not have dreamed as much as we, or they would have been, like ourselves, amused rather than impressed. I remember once dreaming myself that I was dead and being highly entertained by it.

Rather oddly, I was all this morning thinking, off and on, of dreams, by reason of a singularly vivid and complicated one which I had last night, and the origin of which I was puzzling my brains, in vain, to discover. Certainly I never saw anything like the "lordly pleasure house," "so royal rich and wide" in which I found myself last night, and which I seemed to know in all its details of quaint carving, of rare hangings of violet and gold, of deep, glowing colour. Gleaming here and there among the dusky purple shadows were marble statues, beautiful beyond description; and by-and-bye when it was night, I and another girl hiding in the darkness saw these statues gliding about the halls & whispering to each other,—and one of them—"oh, a most delicate fiend!"—sang,—ah, *how* she sang! I seemed to know her then, and all day long I have been trying to recall what beautiful enchantress she represented. However, we knew her last night, and my friend addressed her by name; and in so doing broke a spell, or wove one, I don't know which, and fell into her power. "Then in a moment presto, pass!" everything had vanished, and instead of the fairy mansion, there were savage mountains, an airy bridge over a vast chasm, and passing over it, in their ascent of the mountain, all the goblins and witches I ever read of, and many more beside; among them my friend in the clutches of "la belle dame sans mercie"–in short an orthodox Walpurgis night. But enough of this nonsense,–I must leave my friend where my dream left her, in the middle of the bridge,–for after the tantalizing fashion of dreams I woke just then. So you think I am tantalizing, or worse still "secretive," in neglecting to mention the only important fact about my Dante? viz. who "he"–Dante?–is! Of course, there is'nt the slightest objection to telling you *that*[.] It came from a gentleman, who as I supposed, made a decidedly puzzled, somewhat disgusted, but certainly *final* exit some three months ago. So I was surprised, as well as otherwise disturbed, by the affair[.] It came from–but stay,–you, too, read short-hand, so I will write it as "he" has written it in the book, [shorthand outlines which, when transcribed, read: "Jim Wright Tallulah Georgia"]. No, in things which concern "only myself," I am, with my chosen few, not at all secretive; but in these matters I am conscious of a curious little struggle between conflicting feelings. On the one side is the dislike to having secrets, even insignificant ones, from you; and I have no doubt that if you were present in person, that feeling would conquer, and you would readily learn all you chose to ask or to hear. Because we really *ought not* to have secrets from each other! But on the other side there is my long time rule of action, and the strong feeling that it is a point of honour not to talk about one gentleman to another–nor indeed to *anyone*, with the usual feminine exception of one's "confidante" or advisor!–because these things are the gentlemens secret no less than ones own. And at a distance from you that motive seems to be the stronger,–to say the least I don't *enjoy writing* of such things; it gives me a mean sense of betrayal to sit down in cold blood and commit to paper "such stuff"–such irrelevant stuff too!

By the way, I think that vow of yours an extremely wise and proper one. I hope you will always live up to it; and as I think you should be encouraged therein, I promise that, for the present at least, you shan't have occasion to "deprecate my indignation"; and I therefore carefully abstain from expressing the least disapproval of any "impertinence" into which it may have inadvertently betrayed you in the present letter! But I am sorry to confess that as a general thing I don't strike much terror into beholders, and I fear you would'nt consider my indignation worth deprecating if you knew what a small affair it was—at least when its only object is really "such a darling!"

But I would beg leave merely to recommend, as one of your sincere friends and well-wishers, that you permit that little sweetheart of yours to remain as long as possible at safe distance, while you *dream* about her. I would mildly suggest that you rest as contented as human nature will permit with the present state of affairs, lest you find yourself, some day, in the deplorable condition of those people, who are ever lamenting, "that," or the other, ["]was the happiest part of my life, if I had *only known* it."

What would you? with youth, and health, and congenial work, great and inspiring thoughts, high hopes and worthy ambitions, well-founded, *and* "the woman of your dreams"? Forsooth!—I am glad that you properly appreciate that dream-maiden while she is yours, for she won't last long!—ere you are aware she will have vanished away, as is the fashion in dream-land.

I am afraid you had a rather dreary Xmas in your voluntary banishment from all your friends. Am glad there was at least Irving and Miss Terry to create a diversion. I really felt sick at heart to think of our poor boy, Stockton, spending his holidays in that dismal village, all the boys gone save one; but I fancied you would be having a "good time" in *Baltimore*, even though you were away from home. What are the elements constituting that staid household at 146? and how did they spend Xmas? Do any of the other "fellows" from the Hopkins board there? Are there any girls?

But the bottom of the page warns me that I must close. Love to all your family[.] I had a sweet letter from your sister Marion the other day.[1] Will answer it very soon. Hoping you will continue well and jolly believe me dearest

Yours with all my heart   Ellie

ALS (WP, DLC).
   [1] Marion W. Kennedy to ELA, Dec. 28, 1883, ALS (WP, DLC).

Six Letters to Ellen Louise Axson

My bonny Nell,   Balto., Jan'y 7th/84
   I have time for only a few lines this morning to tell you of my *change of address*. Cold weather and superior inducements elsewhere have driven me out of my too polar quarters at 146—or will

have driven me out before another week has passed—so that after this you will direct your letters, so please you, to No. 8 McCulloh St. Particulars anon.

In haste, but with unbounded love,

Your own—Woodrow.

My precious little enchantress,   Balto., Md., Jan'y 8th 1884

Have I told you of my conversion, since the beginning of my acquaintance with you, to a belief in witchcraft? I believe I have, but not of the latest confirmations of my belief. I am not conscious of having changed in my appearance or demeanor since April last, and yet my friends here declare that I'm very different from the fellow I used to be. You may be sure that I do'nt volunteer confidences upon certain subjects, or even allow myself to be betrayed into them, and yet one of my recently-acquired lady acquaintances confidently assures a common friend that "Mr. Wilson is awfully in love." How did she know *that*? It could not have been because my eye kindled and my words grew enthusiastic as I replied to her question as to what sort of woman I most admired; nor because I'm lighter hearted than I used to be: for *she* don't know what I used to be, and, besides, I never was anything else but light-hearted for any considerable periods together. I *do, for some reason or other*, feel merrier and happier than I ever did before; but this inward contentment is not likely, I suppose, to encamp very conspicuously on my grave visage, or to ride out very ostentatiously in my society conversation upon trivial, everyman's topics. I know very well—no one knows better!—what a revolution you've worked in my poor, unoffending heart, that never did you any harm; but, as far as my mirror tells, there's been no corresponding change in my outward person. It must be that you've bewitched me, and that I unconsciously do things that "give away" my irresponsible condition!

But the evidence is'nt exhausted yet. Do they not say that bewitched persons are dominated by *dreams*, in which they are supposed to be under the power of the witch herself? Well, so am I! I used to be able to let my dreams pass unheeded, but now I must needs go all the day laughing and compelling other people to laugh because I've seen my bonny lassie over night in my dreams, have whispered to her certain things that she smiled to hear, and have heard her say, with the brightest and prettiest of blushes, what it made my heart leap to hear. Ah! that was a wonderful, incoherent, vivid, uncircumstantial dream! I was in Savannah, I suppose, for I saw the church—the gray stone and the ivy that are said to be visible from my lady's window—and I was looking through the house for you; but, what was best of all, I found you, and found you alone, and—oh no! not that! I'm not a youth to go an ell because once allowed an inch! But you were very glad to see me and were very kind to me, not making me keep at a very great distance from you. You were even surprised into a very sweet, affectionate demonstration of your joy at seeing me: for you had not expected me, you know; and you had to forgive me for the one or two offences against decorum and "principles" into which I was betrayed by my delight at being with you: for no one else was present and—and the dream was soon to end. I dare not tell you the particulars of our interview, for fear you should say that I am getting more and more impudent: but it cannot be impudent to say that even the keen disappointment of waking up in *Baltimore* did not prevent my being made uncommonly happy by even that imaginary visit to my darling.

You propounded a puzzling question in your last letter (by-the-way, I've had but one letter from you *this year*!). If sensitive folks like ourselves find everything they themselves do "simply execrable," "whence comes the delight in work, which urges one on, in spite of that supreme disgust, and in spite of the knowledge that the result *must* be but the pitifullest infinitesimal fraction of a product'?" That *is* a "riddle," and I can think of no solution, except that there is always satisfaction in hard, conscientious work, in the earnest pursuit of a clearly-seen, however distant, ideal, and in the consciousness that one's hand are *acquiring* a skill and *learning* a cunning which may enable them some day to turn out forms of beauty such as will delight even our own eyes. We admire and strive after virtue none the less because we know we *have* it not.

As for your work, my winsome lassie, you are very unreasonable to be dissatisfied with *it*. I can find in it nothing but beauty—and I am not blinded *altogether* by love of the fair hand that worked in those faultless shadings. If you like my writing as well, and with as good reason, I shall be more than content! If I could tell you what I *would* do, you could appreciate my intense disgust for what I *have* done, when you came to see that latter. I know that my careful compositions of to-day are vastly better than I could have written five, or even three, years ago—and that's very encouraging—but what is my style to what it should be! I have imagined a style clear, bold, fresh, and facile; a style flexible but always strong, capable of light touches or of heavy blows; a style that could be driven at high speed—a brilliant, dashing, coursing speed—or constrained to the slow and stately progress of grave argument, as the case required; a style full of life, of colour and vivacity, of soul and energy, of inexhaustible power—of a thousand qualities of beauty and grace and strength that would make it immortal.—is it any wonder that I am disgusted with the stiff, dry, mechanical, monotonous sentences in which my meagre thoughts are compelled to masquerade, as in garments which are too mean even for *them*!

Whew! What a tempest in a teapot! But this tragic affair has a ludicrous side to it, as what tragedy has not (for a man cannot mend himself after the damage of a fall from a rail-way car without the most laughable display of vanity!)? Suppose you had to draw or paint your letters to me! If you did have to do so, you could appreciate my comical embarrassment at having to write poor letters to a young lady who knows that my chief study is the art of writing. Is it not rather an odd fix to be in, this of being compelled to furnish constant proof of one's inability to do that which one professes to be able to do better than anything else? That my letters give you so much delight is only proof of how perverse some people can be!

I hope, my darling, (to come back to talking sense once more) that the terribly cold wave that sent the thermometer down below zero in Atlanta did not strike Savannah as it did Charleston and make my dear little sweetheart as miserable as it made us here! By-the-way, I have'nt explained yet why I'm about to change my quarters, have I?[1] Well, that must be reserved for next time, for I *must* close now, whether I will or no—and it is possible that I may not be able to write again this week, for the long-expected examination is at the doors and immediately after it must come the moving to No. 8—but you'll be patient, I know, and you may be sure that I'm thinking of you all the time. Love to all the family and a whole heart-full for your precious self, from

Your own   Woodrow.

[1] WW was still at 146 North Charles Street.

My bonny lassie,   Balto., Md., Jany 10th/84

I *must* snatch just a minute or two for writing a few lines to accompany the pamphlet I send you. The article marked is a fine example of the disadvantages of magazine contribution, being so much compressed, from a mass of materials large enough to fill such a number of the "Overland" twice over, as to have little life left in it. It, of course, does not represent my constitutional studies; but is merely controversial. Judge it with love, and tell me candidly what you think of it.

Hastily and lovingly,

Your own   Woodrow

My own darling,   Balto., Md., Jan'y 11th 1884

I've just come out of examination, but those three hours of hard, ceaseless writing have not tired my hand so much that it cannot pen a few lines to *you*. Having done what it rebels against doing, it wont refuse to do what it takes to with exceeding kindliness. By-the-way, I wish to remark, in regard to this matter of correspondence, my dear Miss, that there is no proof that you are as fond of writing to me as I am of writing to you. I remember hearing that a certain lovely little maiden once felt very much like crying because a whole week went by without bringing a letter from her lover: but that lover, not knowing how to comfort himself with tears, has to make the best of his lonliness by what devices he can command when seven days run away without bringing him any word from the little lassie of whom he is always thinking and whose words of love are more precious to him than his life itself. He never before knew how long, how wearily long, a time a week was. From Thursday to Thursday *must* be more than seven days![1]

What a wonderful dream that one of yours was, to be sure! It beats mine "all hollow," though, if I had my choice, I'd rather see *you* in my dreams than that lordly palace with its animate marbles and that weird procession of elves and witches.

Yes, my sweet little quizzer, I am resting "as contented as human nature will permit with the present state of affairs," and do "appreciate that dream-maiden" as highly as dream-maidens are appreciable; but I am shocked and grieved, Miss, that it should be *your* wish that I "permit that little sweet-heart of mine to remain as long as possible at a safe distance"! For my part, I am satisfying myself with dreaming of her *because I must*, and notwithstanding the fact that her dream-self is an infinitely poor substitute for her real self. Nothing delights me more than the prospect that this maiden of my dreams will soon vanish away, as you predict, and give place to the lady of my love. Permit me to say that you betray your ignorance of the true character of this "chap," your most humble servant, and pay him a very doubtful compliment, when you picture him as in love with an ideal lass, made of such stuff as dreams are made of, and not with a con-

crete lassie quite as real as himself. I refuse, even at your suggestion, to love anybody but yourself: and will even venture, in face
of your recommendation to the contrary, to declare my determination to leave my lady-love "at a safe distance," not as long
but as short a time as possible!

My darling, I appreciate your feelings about speaking by name
of the men who have addressed you, and I ought to beg your pardon for having asked you to *write* of such things; but I wish that
you could look upon telling *me* anything as telling it to only *your
other self*. The revealing of such secrets results only in making
me have a profound respect and great liking for the men concerned, and I pry into them, not from curiosity, but because of an
intense longing to be identified with you in everything! But you
may take your own sweet way and choose your own time for telling me what you are willing that I should know. I'll ask no more.

Love to all, and for yourself, my darling, the perfect, yet ever-
increasing love of

Your own   Woodrow.

1 WW is complaining about the long interval between receipt of ELA's letters
of Dec. 31, 1883, and Jan. 7, 1884. He received the first on Thursday, Jan. 3, and
the second on Jan. 10, 1884.

Balto, Md. Jan'y 15/84

Will my precious little sweet-heart patiently wait until tomorrow for the "regular" letter of the week (it's quite a joke for a fellow who writes every two or three days to have a "regular" day for
writing, is'nt it?)? I have just finished moving, and neither I nor
my room is quite in trim for letter-writing. Besides it will be more
propitious and inspiring to write on the *16th*!

With love unbounded,

Your own   Woodrow

No 8 McCulloh St.,[1]

My lovely Nell,   Balto., Md., Jan'y 16th 1884

At last the tribulations of moving are overpast and I am en-
sconced in my new quarters, with somewhat orderly surroundings,
so that I now have leisure to tell you *why* I am in new quarters at
all. When I said that my little room on Charles St. was delightful
it was mild Autumn weather, you remember: and a change of
weather brings about wonderful changes in a great many other
things, notably in the comfort of some rooms. The room did not
grow any less cheerful than it was when I moved into it: the square
in front of the window is just as pretty powdered with snow as it

was when bathed in warm sunlight; but the winter draughts were terrible, and there was simply no regulating the temperature of the room. It was heated scarcely at all by the furnace, and when there was a fire in the diminutive grate I used to feel that I was like to be roasted, that the side of me which was next to the blazing coals must be "done to a turn," for the room was so small that there was no getting away from the fireplace.

But there was other coldness besides the "winter's flaw" to drive me away from 146: I was lonely there beyond measure, for I was the only Hopkins man in the house, and amongst all the twenty boarders there was not one who took the least interest (except a *gossipping* interest) in me, or in whom I could find any attraction. One or two of the young ladies there showed a very evident willingness to become better acquainted, making all the advances that lady-likeness would permit—and they were very nice girls, well-bred and sweet-looking—but they talked with typical society soullessness, and I had neither the time nor the inclination, even if I had had the power, to feign an interest in them which I did not feel.

Here I am much better off, established, as I am, in a larger and warmer room and surrounded by what I may, I think, call "picked specimens" of the University men, fellows of various characters, of course, but of equal enthusia[s]m in intellectual pursuits, sensible, well-informed, jolly, and unaffected[.] It's a much more healthful atmosphere for me than that which I have left, because it do'nt do for me to live for long periods together beyond the reach of congenial companionship. I do'nt fall into exactly *morbid* moods when I keep to myself, but I do find my thoughts under such circumstances running in ruts which are very tiresome and wearing. At least I get to thinking too much upon that most unprofitable of all subjects, *myself*. I shall try to describe my companions here, for your amusement, in some future letter, when I have come to know them more intimately: for they are all well worth knowing, and each one seems to have a strong individuality which will make a descriptive introduction of him comparatively easy.

I am sure that you will be glad to hear, my darling, that the Western papers have praised my article in the "Overland" very highly and that it has met with a most favourable reception at the University. The men there whose opinions I value most have expressed their almost unqualified admiration of both the matter and the style of the piece. That they should commend the *style* is a ground of genuine surprise to me, for it is in my judgment much too *staccato*. There are too many short, incisive sentences, and, in the effort at condensation, I have left the *transitions* of the argument much too awkward and abrupt. Trying to manage a six-horse team where there was scarcely room enough to do justice to the paces of a single steed has resulted in making the bad driving unnecessarily conspicuous. But, nevertheless, it's the *style* of the article which has come in for the most unanimous plaudits. "Wilson," said one critic, "you've picked up a capital literary style somewhere" ("Picked up," indeed! Has'nt my dear father been drilling me in style these ten years past?) ["]Upon whose style did you form it? Did you come by it naturally, or have you consciously modelled after Macaulay?" (Poor Macaulay!) Another friend, who has to follow me in the course of "lectures" inaugurated by the reading of that remarkable essay upon Adam Smith, cooly asks whether I would be willing to take his materials and "put them into literary form"! I'm sure I have pain enough in putting my own materials into literary form without going through the like labours for other people.

I am immensely pleased that the *style* of "Cabinet or Committee Government?" should have been considered good, because I'm sure that I can write much better prose than that—nay, that I am writing better upon the subject I opened up on New Year's day; though, if I had to characterize either, I should consider it more accurate to say that what I am writing now is expressed, not with greater force and felicity, but with less roughness and awkwardness, not quite so stiffly or so coldly—because I am giving myself room and can drive with a freer rein.—But a truce to all this! I've already told you of the infinite trouble I have with my style, and I have nothing different to add now.

I write to you freely and at large about such things because I can imagine that I see in yours [sic] sweet eyes, the while, unbounded sympathy and love; whereas I know that when I talk to my companions here about my literary difficulties they suspect me of slyly doing that smallest and most contemptible of all kindred things, *fishing for a compliment*. Why can't we all of us be honest and straightforward? Why should a fellow, when he asks to have the faults of his writing pointed out, that he may correct them, be suspected as of course of seeking flattery?

My success in literary effort has recently become much surer than it once was or promised to be, because until within a few months I lacked the true source of inspiration: I was then writing

for myself, but now I am writing for *you*! This is no mere sentiment, my bonny lassie. The addition of power is very real and
very appreciable—and, besides, it was to have been expected. No
man is complete until he has learned what perfect love for another is. His nature don't expand and get free play until it has
been bound up with the life of another. I'm speaking the truest
philosophy when I say that this 16th day of the month com-
memorates the date upon which I first became fully myself: for
my love was not, and could not be, perfect, until I knew that it
was returned and thereby sanctioned. You are in all the work that
I do, my love; and, if you were not in it, it would'nt by [be] half
so good as it is. My heart seems to have been growing bigger and
bigger ever since the 16th of September, and with its growth my
whole nature, my mind included, seems to have expanded.

Have'nt you found your drawing easier than it used to be?

But I must say good-night, darling, for I must write a letter to
the dear folks at home before I take my walk to the P.O. With love
to all,

Yours with all the powers of my heart and all the thoughts of
my mind,

Woodrow.

ALS (WC, NjP).

¹ The street address on WW's following letters will not be reproduced until a
new address is used. The boardinghouse at No. 8 McCulloh Street was run by
Mary Jane Ashton. It was a favorite among graduate students for many years,
and Wilson returned to it when he lectured at the Johns Hopkins in the late
eighties and the 1890's.

From the Minutes of the Seminary of Historical and Political Science

Johns Hopkins University.
Bluntschli Library Jan. 18, 1884.

The Seminary was called to order at 8 P.M., by Dr. Adams in
the Chair. There were present Drs. H. B. Adams, R. T. Ely, and
J. F. Jameson, and the members of the Seminary with the exception of Mr. Gould. Mr. E. P. Allinson of Philadelphia¹ was also
present. Mr. Dewey having read the minutes of the previous meeting, and the same having been accepted; the Chair appointed Mr.
Berry secretary for the evening. Dr. Adams briefly referred to a
plan for preserving in a permanent form the transactions of the
Seminary. After speaking of the great advantages to be derived
from a comity of relations with other historical societies, centres
of education, &c., Dr. Adams introduced Mr. E. P. Allinson, a
member of the University Club of Philadelphia. Mr. Allinson read

a paper—Reviewing Von Holst's Theory of the Constitution—as set forth in his Constitutional History of the United States. Mr. Allinson claimed, that although Von Holst as a foreigner was unable to comprehend the theory on which our government rests, *viz*— the coexistence of national and state rights, still his Constitutional History is the best which has yet appeared. Mr. Allinson's views in regard to the proper interpretation of the sentence, in the preamble of the Constitution, "We the People of the United States," &c. provoked an animated debate. The debate was participated in by Dr. Adams, Messrs Wilson, Ingle, Kennard, Shaw, and others. . . . The Chair announced the appointments for the review of Magazine literature for the ensuing meeting. At 10.05 P.M. the Seminary was adjourned.

T. Alexis Berry, Secretary.

1 Edward P. Allinson, an authority on the history and government of Philadelphia and collaborator of Boies Penrose.

Two Letters from Charles Howard Shinn[1]

Dear Friend—   [Baltimore] Monday [Jan. 21, 1884]

I have to write in haste, because it is time to go to the "Vas[.]"[2] You have been steadily in my thoughts all this time—you speeding south,[3] on the wings of fire, I northward,—and the thread of sympathy and affection unbroken between us,—as it would unbroken remain though we put a hemisphere's vast mound between. . . .

I want you to give my most cordial regards, as your friend, to the dear girl who is to become your wife, some time, when these troubles have melted from your world, as glaciers long ago melted from earth's garden-spot valleys. You will have a love-lit, holy cottage-home, somewhere, blossoms around it, the stars keeping guard above, the peace-mark of angels invisibly on the portal—and I'll come and see you—and be your bachelor-friend, and buy a silver cup for your eldest boy and a Madonna picture for your eldest daughter. I think you and she are irretrievably part of my closest, nearest circle of "freundschaft." Blessings be upon you. I said "bachelor" a minute ago. Thank God, I have not lived without that in my life that makes the love you have for your sweet princess-maiden, fairly and fully comprehended by me. But the shadow of a life-long sorrow has now for more than a year fallen across my world. I've been pulling myself together & keeping a stiff upper lip, and doing all I could to forget. But why I write this is just that you shall see that my full heart throbs and thrills with every pulse of yours, that the little I could do was just a straw—just a mite of what I should like to do.

"Adios." Dinna forget me—   Charles H. Shinn

ALS (WC, NjP).
[1] Charles Howard Shinn, born William County, Tex., April 29, 1852. Attended University of California, Berkeley, and The Johns Hopkins University. Managing Editor, *Overland Monthly*, 1884-89. Forester with University of California and United States Department of Agriculture, 1890-1923. Author, among other works, of *Land Laws of Mining Districts* (Baltimore, 1884). Died Dec. 2, 1924.
[2] The "Varsity," or University.
[3] WW had just left for Savannah, where he visited the Axson household until January 27, 1884. He was growing desperately eager to see Ellen, and this was certainly one reason for his visit. But the most important reason was the fact that Ellen's father had been committed to the Georgia state mental hospital in Milledgeville on about January 10, apparently after becoming violent. See Anna Harris to ELA, Jan. 14, 1884, ALS (WP, DLC). ELA's letter or letters to WW telling about this sad event are missing. She must have poured out her grief to Woodrow and he must have decided on the spur of the moment to go to Savannah and informed her of his decision by telegram. WW stopped for a visit with his parents on his way northward.

Dear old fellow—   [Baltimore] Tuesday [Jan. 22, 1884]

All the boys are anxiously awaiting your return[.] I've said you was called off by sudden business demands, and everybody says: "How can we survive a week without our dear Wilson?" Glee Club met last night. Corson[1] lectured to as vast a crowd as that square Peabody hall w'd hold. He "padded" awfully, used half of one of his last year lectures over, & read a ten minute quotation from Aurora Leigh & another from Bacon. "They all do it[.]" When you're Prof. in Harvard, "Don't Pad[.]" Sift out the bran. . . .

                                Adiosa,   C. H. Shinn.

ALS (WP, DLC).
[1] Hiram Corson, Professor of Literature, Cornell University, author of many books on English literature.

From Jessie Bones Brower

Dear Cousin Woodrow,   East Rome. Ga. 28 Jan'y 1884.

I think you are certainly the most forgiving person I ever knew. You dear old fellow, after waiting and waiting for ages for a reply to your letter you write again & never once upbraided me for my neglect, and then when that fails to bring an answer you send me a postal letting me know of your new address. . . .

My dear Cousin, you don't know how deeply I sympathize with poor Ellie Lou. I declare it seems as though that poor girl had more than her share of sorrow in this world. Oh I am *so* glad that she has promised herself to you, & that she has the comfort of your love in her great trouble. How much better that you should be engaged, even though you have to wait a long time, & be sure of each others love, than to go on for a year or more torturing yourself by every conceivable conjecture, as you would have done. It did really seem like a meeting specially arranged by Providence, didn't it, & a man certainly would have been a fool to have let it pass. Dear girl, she seemed so happy & so dreadfully embarrassed when she told me about your engagement. And her poor father was *so* glad, & I think it gave him a great deal of comfort in all his sickness to know that his daughter would not be left alone should he be taken from her. . . .

We still carry on the busy life that we did when you were with us, only now-a-days Abe & I have no more milking to do. . . . Abe has not heard from the Burford case, & so presumes that as Mr. Hammond had to go to Washington he had the case continued by consent. If you should at any time run down to Washington while Congress is in session Abe would like it if you saw Hammond & learned from him what he still thinks of the prospects of the case. . . .

Your aff. cousin, Jessie B. Brower.

ALS (WP, DLC) with WWhw notation on env.: "Ans. 2/17/84."

To Ellen Louise Axson

My own darling,   Wilmington, N.C., Jan'y 28th 1884
I reached here this morning not much the worse for wear. My heart is still sore from the wrench of parting from my precious Ellie, after our sweet week's intercourse; but that sorrow is almost eclipsed by the joy of feeling so much nearer to her, so much more her companion and stay in this time of dire affliction.

I made the journey without much inconvenience and am feeling almost well this morning. I find the dear parents here not in perfect health, but much better than they have been. They are most tenderly and lovingly interested in everything that concerns you and your dear father, my darling. Father wrote to your grandfather last week, expressing for himself his and mother's sympathy and solicitude.

I did not know how—so awkward was I—to express my gratitude to your dear grandparents and to your uncle and aunt for their hospitable and considerate treatment of me. I hope that they found in me as much to love and admire as I found in them.

I find my incorrigible father inclined to regard my sickness of Saturday night in the same way that Mrs. Duncan did, as a sickness of *heart* at having to leave you. Mother, however, has taken seriously to the administration of medicine—the vilest, I protest, that I ever had to swallow—and I am likely to be quite on good terms with my physical parts by the time night comes and the train goes.

Give my love to all, and remember that you are "a' the world" to
Your own   Woodrow.

ALS (WC, NjP).

From Ellen Louise Axson

My darling Woodrow,   Savannah Jan. 28/84.

I mean to make an *attempt* at writing tonight, though I am afraid my patience will soon be exhausted; the effort seems doubly unsatisfactory and tantalizing, just now; by contrast with yesterday. Yet my thoughts have, as you may well imagine, been with you so constantly all day, that I feel as though they *must* find some expression;—even the feeble resource of writing is better than nothing. How I wish I had the gift of second-sight to aid my fancy, and tell me where you are now, what you are doing and *how* you are, *especially*! I hope for a card at least, tomorrow, relieving my mind on that last point. Have been *so* anxious about that head-ache all day. But I hope your mother charmed it away as completely as Grandmother seemed to think she would. The dear old lady, most tender-hearted of mortals, seems to keep the deepest place in her sympathies for babies committed to the mercy of nurses, and for young men away from their mothers; she can cry over either at a moment's notice. She has just been giving me some very characteristic comfort; "it would be *very* selfish in me not to be *glad* (!) you were gone to your mother! You must have been *so* miserable to be away from her when you were unwell;—she was, oh, *so* sorry for you; for much as she wished to, she of course could'nt take her place, as regards your feelings, or give you the sense of being cared for, and watched over.["] Her long experience seems to have resulted in the firm conviction that men were made to be taken care of, and that they are not one whit less helpless than the afore-mentioned babies!

She worries about health almost as much as dear Papa; is distressing herself about *me* now,—is afraid I have been "too excited" (!) for the last week, and that now I will "get sick"! Is'nt that a novel idea? I told her I did'nt propose to do anything of the sort; nothing could induce me to; I thought it would be the depth of ingratitude. I have been fighting the blues most vigorously all day, and have been fairly successful, considering! Tried the best of all remedies, hard work;—after finishing that inevitable picture, I spent my time at the machine;—there is a certain rattle and dash about that occupation, which is sometimes of service in relieving unfavourable symptoms. In the afternoon I went to Janie's.

I am anxious to learn the condition of your right *ear*. I have been afraid it would be reduced to ashes, there have been so many nice things said about you today. Grandmother says she is prepared to fully endorse Papa's opinion, and she is eagerly seconded on all sides. As to the nature of that opinion, I have given you only a very faint idea.

The children are all lamenting, especially the little ones. Ellen says she didnt want to tell you "good-bye." She can't bear to say that to those she likes! She thinks you are "so awful nice"! And indeed, I think so too! and even those strong and expressive words don't convey *quite* all I think. Why *can't* I find that "great hearts-word that will tell you"? I am disgusted with the English language, and indeed with all speech. Oh my darling, you don't know how much I love you! I did'nt know, myself,—or rather, I did'nt know there was room in my heart for the love to grow as it has done. I thought I already loved you as much as was possible. When Helen wrote me that I probably *thought* I knew something about love, but I did'nt—I had only made a *beginning*; I laughed at the idea; I thought *she* did'nt know what she was talking about. Yet comparatively speaking, she was right, because I had only *begun* to know *you,* my great-hearted friend—tender and true! There are many noble uses of adversity, and among them is the power, which, beyond all else, it has, of knitting soul to soul. Thank God that while this remains a world of sin, it is also a world of sorrow! Without it, I believe it would gradually become a "howling wilderness," with selfishness, heartlessness, cruelty, reigning supreme. But sorrow keeps us human,—nay, does it not develop qualities that are *divine*, revealing the almost effaced likeness to the God, after whose image we were made?

You know you wove your spells so cleverly, last week, and changed my mood so strangely, that now I am almost ready to accuse *myself* of heartlessness, for being as happy as I was. Of course, one ought to be as bright as possible in time of trouble— to appear cheerful. How often I have struggled to wear "a face of joy," and found smiles the most convenient of masks! But last week there was no *seeming*; for much of the time I was strangely, deeply happy, with a new kind of happiness, far greater than that which belonged to many a time, which seemed all mirth and gladness.

That philosopher's pendulum, which, according to the story, marks at once the degrees of both joy and sorrow, has been, with me, describing a great semicircle, of late.

Do you remember that theory?—that pain and pleasure—with the *capacity* for feeling them,—are always accurately balanced;—so that if the pendulum of life vibrates but feebly, one learns little of either, but remains at a low level of experience, a dully quiescent state. Old bachelors, (!) adds our philosopher, furnish the best example of that condition! But if one chooses, the pendulum may have a sweep, large, full, and free. Yet if we grasp at great happiness we pay the penalty, for there is an exactly corresponding point on the other side, which it must always reach,—Mr. Thornwell's doctrine of compensations, you see, reduced to a system. But the end of the page warns me that I must close.

Goodbye, my darling. Take care of yourself. Give my love to all your family. All here send love. My kindest regards to *Mr. Shin*, and believe me, dear love,

Yours always and altogether   Ellie.

ALS (WP, DLC).

From Annie Wilson Howe

My darling Brother,   Columbia. Jan 29th/84

. . . I cannot tell you how shocked and grieved I was to hear of Mr. Axson's illness. How does Ellie bear it? Poor child, it is about the most terrible affliction that could come upon her. I have wanted to write to her, but was afraid to worry her. Please give her my warm love. I am afraid *you* suffer almost as much as she does. I never imagined any such trouble in connection with Mr. Axson—he was so gentle, mild and quiet in manner—I do trust it is only temporary. . . .

George joins me in *warmest* love to our dear Brother.

Your devoted sister, Annie.

P.S. omitted. ALS (WP, DLC) with WWhw notation on env.: "Ans. 2/17/84."

Three Letters to Ellen Louise Axson

My own darling,   Wilmington, N. C. Jan'y 29th 1884

I am still in Wilmington, you see, detained to be nursed. I was feeling scarcely equal to travelling last night and was, therefore, easily persuaded to delay my departure for twenty-four hours. It was fortunate that I did, for I was quite unwell again this morning; but my sweet Ellie need not feel at all uneasy, for I understand my present ailment very thoroughly and know that the fact that I am feeling perfectly comfortable now is proof that the malady, which was not alarming at its worst, has run its course, and that I can without risk or inconvenience resume my journey to-night.

I wish, my precious little sweet-heart, that I could give you some idea of the estimation in which you are held in this household. It is no formal compliment given for *my* sake when they send you their love. They love you and sympathize with you as sincerely and as wholeheartedly as if you were already their daughter. They give me leave to talk about you all day long.

I send you the "class" picture of which I spoke, and which you expressed a desire to see. You'll hardly recognize your "Mr. Wilson" all "shaven and shorn"; but you may get from the photograph an idea of how I looked when I was a "Princeton man," for it is an excellent likeness, not one whit uglier than I was when it was taken.

Good-bye, my darling; don't be anxious about me, for I'm getting on famously, and will write as soon as I get to Baltimore. Give my love to all, and keep for yourself the love of my brother and dear parents, and the unspeakable love of

Your own   Woodrow.

My own darling,   Balto., Md., Jan'y 30th/84

Here I am at last, safe and sound in my own room, not *quite* well—it will take a good night's rest to bring about that "consummation devoutly to be wished"—but as well as could be expected. I find that I have lost nothing by my absence. The work has by no means run away from me—though, for the matter of that, no loss would have been comparable with the gain of my trip.

I will write again to-morrow, at more satisfactory length. May God bless my darling. With love unspeakable,

Your own   Woodrow.

My own darling,   Balto., Md., Jan'y 31st/84

Your sweet letter of Monday came this morning and gave me great comfort because of the evidence it afforded that you continue in a calm and comparatively happy frame of mind. Why, Ellie, there can be nothing "heartless" in your being happy now. It is not the happiness of self-indulgence or of carelessness, but that holiest and purest and most elevating of all happiness, the happiness of *sorrow*, of being sustained in the greatest grief of your life by your trust in a loving God and by the love given you by friends who would make all your sorrows their own. It is *right* to be happy, if you can. You were given a sunny, hopeful disposition, as it seems to me, in order that you might be just what you have been, an aid and comfort and joy to those about you; and certainly there is no reason why you should deny your nature now. This is a terrible trial that has overtaken us, but hope is not denied. As for myself, I am *very* hopeful as to your dear father's future. From what I know of the history of the case, there seems to me to be no reason for regarding his present condition as anything but the culmination of his nervous disease, the temporary breakdown of his system; and every reason for believing that with the restoration of his health will come the permanent restitution of his mind. Don't think too much, my darling, of how you feel: don't be a "spectator" of yourself any longer; but be as happy and as hopeful as you can, remembering that I love you beyond expression.

I have been staying in the house to-day, taking care of myself, being in that comfortable stage of convalescence at which quiet and rest, and consequently ease and self-indulgence, are the best medicines. I think that I should have been still in Wilmington, under the nursing my dear mother began and was so anxious to continue, if it had not been for the fact that I had bought a limited ticket and did not think myself sick enough to justify me in forfeiting it. I am getting along all right here, however, for I have not been *lonely* even, having had visitors more than enough—so many as to interrupt this letter many times and almost to prevent its composition altogether. I must close now in order to get Shinn to mail it before the last collection from the letter boxes. Give my warm love to all. I love you, my peerless darling, with all my heart. I'll write again tomorrow if I'm not *quite well*.

Your own   Woodrow

ALS (WC, NjP).

INDEX

NOTE ON THE INDEX

THE reader is referred to the Note on the Index to Volume 1 for a statement of general principles and practices for this series, including the treatment of Wilson's Marginal Notes. The alphabetically arranged analytical table of contents eliminates duplication in both contents and index, of references to certain documents, like letters. Letters are listed in the contents alphabetically by name and chronologically for each name, by page. The subject matter of all letters is, of course, indexed. The Editorial Notes and Wilson's writings are listed in the contents chronologically by page. In addition, the subject matter of both categories is indexed. The index in general covers significant references to books and articles in text or notes, but does not furnish bibliographical information or cover routine documentation. Footnotes and descriptive-location notes are indexed. Page references to footnotes which place a comma between the page number and "n" cite both text and footnote, thus: "624,n3." On the other hand, absence of the comma indicates reference to the footnote only, thus: "55n2," where the page number indicates where the footnote appears. The letter "n" without a following digit signifies an un-numbered descriptive-location note.

An asterisk before an index reference designates identification or other particular information. Re-identification and repetitive annotation have been minimized to encourage use of these starred references. Where the identification appears in an earlier volume, it is indicated thus: "*1:212,n3." Thus a page reference standing without a preceding volume number, is invariably a reference to the present volume. The index will usually supply the fullest known forms of names of persons of more than casual interest, and, for the Wilson and Axson families, relationships as far down as cousins. Persons referred to in the text by nicknames or shortened forms of names, can be identified by reference to entries for these forms of the names.

A sampling of the opinions and comments of Wilson and Ellen Axson covers their more personal views, while broad, general headings in the main body of the index cover impersonal subjects like the South, Congress, the Negro. Occasionally opinions expressed by a correspondent are indexed where these appear to supplement or to reflect views expressed by Wilson or by Ellen Axson in documents which are missing.

INDEX

Adams, Elizabeth L., *see* Erwin, Elizabeth Adams

Adams, Herbert Baxter, *391,n1, 442, 447n3, 480, 551, 552,n1, 586, 642

Adams, Herbert C., *391,n1

Adams, Lawrence, *416

Adams, Mamie, *416,n2

"Agnes," *see* Tedcastle, Agnes V.

agriculture, cotton and rice crops in postwar South, 20-21

American Whig Society, *1:75,n1; 10

Anderson, Dr. and Mrs. Robert Burton, *419,n1

Anderson, Rosalie ("Rose"), *555,n3, 613

"Anna," "Old Anna," *see* Harris, Anna

Anti-Corn-Law League, 38

"Anti-Sham," 97, 99, 113; 108-109; 154; origin of pen name, *98n

Ashton, Mary Jane, *660n1

Atlanta Constitution, 30, 53, 66, 68, 106, *125n, 132n2, 143n1, 144

Atwater, Lyman Hotchkiss ("Dad"), *1:132,n1; 5n, 343, 357; WW asks reference from, 337; death of, 340

Augusta Female Seminary, *1:486,n1; 13,n2, 45

"Aunt Ella," *see* Axson, Ella Law

Axson, Benjamin Palmer, first cousin of ELA, *557n2

Axson, Carrie Belle, first cousin of ELA, 554, *557n2, 564

Axson, Edward Stockton, nephew of ELA, *372n2

Axson, Edward William ("Eddie"), brother of ELA, *372,n2, 383, 434, 441

Axson, Ella Law, paternal aunt-in-law of ELA, 554, *557n2, 564, 595

Axson, Ellen, *see* Walker, Ellen Axson

Axson, Ellen, first cousin of ELA, 554, *557n2, 564

Axson, Ellen Louise, fiancée of WW, *334,n2, 367; birthplace of, at Savannah, *553,n1; named for Ellen A. Walker, 576; her "first great sorrow," 532,n1; her family at Savannah, *554,n2, 555; leaving Rome, Ga., 476-77, 553; the move to Savannah, 545, 549-50; her hatband for WW's Christmas, 602; her drawing for WW's birthday, 606, 611, 612

AS SEEN BY

WW's family, 429, 484, 491; JWW, 365, 369, 370-71, 548-49, 571-72; WW, to Bridges, 393, 472; Bridges' replies, 395, 558; WW, to her father, 430

HEALTH

434, 439, 574; her lack of nerves, 650; dreams, 650-51

OPINIONS AND COMMENTS

art, 400, 603; "Checkmated," 602-603; disposing of suitors, 471n1, 526, 604, 647, 651; her name, 420, 569, 576; WW and Katie Mayrant, 383, 459-60, 475, 599; WW's replies, 398, 465-66; WW and Hattie Woodrow, 475-76, 492; WW's replies, 466-67, 480; JRW's lecture, 476; reading aloud, 476; WW's studies, 494

READING

a sampling of authors read and alluded to:

E. B. Browning, 533
Coleridge, 470
Crashaw, 605,n1
Dickens, 599
George Eliot, 493
Emerson, 459
Jean Ingelow, 452, 569, 599
Dr. Johnson, 415
Shakespeare, 384, 439, 532, 605
Sterne, 372
Swedenborg, 420
Tennyson, 493, 589
Artemus Ward, 451
Whittier, 494
Wordsworth, 470, 562

Axson, Florence Leach, sister-in-law of ELA, *372n2

Axson, Isaac Stockton Keith, paternal grandfather of ELA, *334n2, *547n2, *557n2

Axson, [Isaac] Stockton [Keith] II, *see* Axson, Stockton

Axson, Leila, first cousin of ELA, 554, *557n2

Axson, Margaret Jane Hoyt, mother of ELA, *334n2,3; death of, 533n2

Axson, Margaret Randolph, *see* Elliott, Margaret Axson

Axson, Randolph, Jr., first cousin of ELA, *554n2, 591

Axson, Randolph, Sr., paternal uncle of ELA, 554, *557n2; his family described by ELA, 576

Axson, Rebecca Law Randolph, paternal grandmother of ELA, *334n3, *547n3

Axson, Samuel Edward, father of ELA, *334,n3, 372; WW asks consent of, 430, 433; consent given, 436, 442; health of, 425, 431, 434, 441, 452, 458, 471, 488, 525, 533, 545; decision to leave Rome for Savannah,